A Companion to
Medical Anthropology

The *Blackwell Companions to Anthropology* offers a series of comprehensive syntheses of the traditional subdisciplines, primary subjects, and geographical areas of inquiry for the field. Taken together, the series represents both a contemporary survey of anthropology and a cutting edge guide to the emerging research and intellectual trends in the field as a whole.

1. *A Companion to Linguistic Anthropology* edited by Alessandro Duranti
2. *A Companion to the Anthropology of Politics* edited by David Nugent and Joan Vincent
3. *A Companion to the Anthropology of American Indians* edited by Thomas Biolsi
4. *A Companion to Psychological Anthropology* edited by Cornerly Casey and Robert B. Edgerton
5. *A Companion to the Anthropology of Japan* edited by Jennifer Robertson
6. *A Companion to Latin American Anthropology* edited by Deborah Poole
7. *A Companion to Biological Anthropology* edited by Clark Spencer Larsen
8. *A Companion to Medical Anthropology* edited by Merrill Singer and Pamela I. Erickson

Forthcoming

A Companion to Cognitive Anthropology edited by David B. Kronenfeld, Giovanni Bennardo, Victor de Munck, and Michael D. Fischer

A Companion to Medical Anthropology

Edited by
Merrill Singer and
Pamela I. Erickson

WILEY-BLACKWELL

A John Wiley & Sons, Ltd., Publication

This edition first published 2011
© 2011 Blackwell Publishing Ltd.

Blackwell Publishing was acquired by John Wiley & Sons in February 2007. Blackwell's
publishing program has been merged with Wiley's global Scientific, Technical, and Medical
business to form Wiley-Blackwell.

Registered Office
John Wiley & Sons Ltd, The Atrium, Southern Gate, Chichester, West Sussex, PO19 8SQ,
United Kingdom

Editorial Offices
350 Main Street, Malden, MA 02148-5020, USA
9600 Garsington Road, Oxford, OX4 2DQ, UK
The Atrium, Southern Gate, Chichester, West Sussex, PO19 8SQ, UK

For details of our global editorial offices, for customer services, and for information about
how to apply for permission to reuse the copyright material in this book please see our
website at www.wiley.com/wiley-blackwell.

Library of Congress Cataloging-in-Publication Data is available for this book.
Hardback 9781405190022

A catalogue record for this book is available from the British Library.

This book is published in the following electronic formats: ePDFs 9781444395280;
Wiley Online Library 9781444395303; ePub 9781444395297

Set in 10/12.5pt Galliard by SPi Publisher Services Ltd, Pondicherry, India
Printed and bound in Singapore by Markono Print Media Pte Ltd

Contents

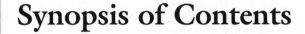

Synopsis of Contents

By setting the development of medical anthropology over the last 60 years in historic
context, this chapter focuses on ongoing struggles to define the field. During the
1960s and 1970s, debate and organizational efforts in medical anthropology centered
on issues of applied versus theoretical approaches and whether a specialized focus on
application would fragment the field. Also of importance were the alternative visions
of biological and cultural orientations within medical anthnropolgy, an issue of continued importance. In the aftermath of these discussions, the issue of culture took
center state, with strong input from critical perspectives and multidisciplinary thinking. The relationship of the field to biomedicine remains a troubled issue. Expressing
concern that an unthoughtout embrace of biomedicine's factorial model, which disa-
gregates health-related contexts and experiences into discrete units or factors to be
counted, gives undue attention to the parts rather than the whole while treating culture like just another variable in a researcher-imposed equation. Instead, an argument
is made for retaining a holistic, systems-oriented, comparative approach within medical anthropology.

It is the argument of this chapter that in response to the highly reductive biological
orientation of the dominant biomedical system's explanations of health and illness,
over the course of its history medical anthropology increasingly became focused on
socio-cultural and political aspects of health. The turn away from the biology and

evolution while understandable, is none the less unfortunate. Biocultural approaches can provide a fuller understanding of how large scale political–economic processes "get under the skin." In this light, this chapter stresses the importance of biocultural approaches which have emerged over the past two decades that are designed to enhance the interface between biology and critical understandings of health. The goal is not to reduce health and illness to biological terms and mechanisms; rather, it is to see human biology and health as inherently social and cultural.

3. Applied Medical Anthropology: Praxis, Pragmatics, Politics, and Promises
    Robert T. Trotter, II

This chapter examines the eclectic nature of applied medical anthropology application and theory by reviewing several important contributions of application to medical anthropology in particular and anthropology as a whole. These contributions include the mobilization of theory in an applied setting and how this theory is challenged by other theoretical viewpoints from other disciplines, the numerous contributions that medical anthropology has made in the development of highly useful research methods while also expanding the methodological tool kits of the other social and biomedical sciences and humanities, clarification of the relationship between midrange theory and applied medical anthropology methods, and recognition of the fundamental importance of ethics in anthropology. These points are illustrated using examples drawn from the applied arenas of HIV/AIDS and drug use and health organization evaluation research but the primary issues of concern crosscut specific health-related issues that are addressed in medical anthropology.

4. Research Design and Methods in Medical Anthropology
    Clarence C. Gravlee

While medical anthropology's holistic and integrative approach to the human experience enriches our understanding of sickness and health, it also raises a challenge regarding the configuration of research methods that are relevant to the field. Drawing on the whole toolkits of all of the social sciences, as well as methods from public health, biomedicine, and the life sciences, the question is raised about how to best match methods to the kinds of research questions raised by medical anthropologists. Medical anthropologists embrace a wide range of theoretical perspectives, including positivist, critical, constructivist, interpretive, evolutionary, and ecological orientations and no method can lay unique claim to possession of any method. Consequently, this chapter shows why fluency in a broad range of methods is essential for developing successful collaborations within medical anthropology and across disciplinary lines, and for designing research that matters. Taking advantage of methodological developments throughout the social sciences contributes to the continued intellectual and practical relevance of medical anthropology.

5. Medical Anthropology and the Policy Process
    Merrill Eisenberg

This chapter is directed at students and practitioners of medical anthropology who work in communities and want their work to contribute to the development of a more humane and just world through social policy development and implementation. I attempt to integrate the disciplines of policy studies, public health, and medical anthropology to approach policy issues in applied medical anthropology. I first address the centrality of policy to the human social experience, provide definitions of policy, public policy and public policy mechanisms, and describe how policy both creates and addresses health concerns. Next, I review the anthropological study of policy from both narrative and critical perspectives. The remainder of the chapter focuses on using medical anthropology research to inform the development of public policy through advocacy and empowerment activities that medical anthropologists can undertake. The importance of understanding the policy making endeavor ethnographically is emphasized as a tool to guide participation in the policy process. Models that can be used as a lens for understanding the public policy making process are presented, and a typology of participation is proposed. The examples in this chapter are based on the US public policy experience, assuming government that is elected and responsive, to some degree, to citizen input and may not apply to other political contexts. Many of the concepts can also be applied in private policy making settings, such as the policies of non-governmental health-related organizations, health care provider institutions, and public health programs.

PART II   CONTEXTS AND CONDITIONS

6. Culture and the Stress Process
William W. Dressler

The risk of illness increases when individuals are subject to stressful experiences in the social environment and are unable to cope with or resist those experiences. Culture shapes the stress process. This chapter reviews anthropological research on this topic. There have been three general approaches to the study of culture and the stress process. First, primarily in the 1960s and 1970s, research focused on the stressful effects of migration and culture change, especially what was referred to as "modernization." Second, beginning in the 1970s and continuing today, anthropologists have adapted social-psychological models of the stress process to settings outside North America and Europe, showing how the definitions of stressful circumstances and coping resources change in different cultural settings, and how the interactions among these elements are modified by culture. Third, and most recently, research has focused more precisely on how individuals incorporate cultural models into their own beliefs and behaviors – referred to as "cultural consonance" – and how low cultural consonance can be a stressful experience. Research on the stress process in medical anthropology has been fruitful both for increasing our understanding of the causes of poor health and for the insight into the dynamics of culture it has afforded.

7. Global Health
Craig R. Janes and Kitty K. Corbett

In this chapter we assess the engagement of medical anthropology with the rapidly growing field of global health. Our discussion is presented in six parts. We first develop a definition of global health, drawing on current thinking on globalization and its intersection with public health and anthropology. We then present what we consider to be the four principal contributions of anthropology to global health: (1) grounded and/or contextually situated analyses of health inequities and their political and economic determinants; (2) assessments of the impact on local social worlds of global science and technology; (3) interrogation and critique of global public health programs and policies; (4) analysis of the consequences to health of the reconfiguration of the social institutions responsible for international health development. We conclude by calling on anthropologists to be more interdisciplinary and collaborative, to attend more closely to the literature generated externally to anthropology, and to engage more directly and deliberately in proposing and participating in solutions.

8. Syndemics in Global Health
Merrill Singer, D. Ann Herring, Judith Littleton and Melanie Rock

Building on the work of all four authors and other researches, this chapter examines existing and emerging applications of the syndemics model in global health research, past and present. The syndemics approach to understanding disease is rooted in medical anthropology, especially the theoretical framework known as critical medical anthropology. Syndemics theory recognizes the fundamental biosocial nature of health and that constellations of diseases and other health conditions can interact synergistically, in consequential ways. This interaction involves multiple biological and psychosocial channels and mechanisms, including biochemical changes in the immune system, damage to cellular repair processes, and psychopathological effects on behavior. Further, the syndemics orientation emphasizes the ways that social conditions shape disease processes, often through broader environmental mediation. Consequently, the syndemics approach examines both the emergence and nature of "disease concentrations" (i.e., multiple coterminous diseases and disorders affecting individuals and groups) and "disease interactions" (i.e., the ways in which the presence of one disease or disorder enhances the health consequences of other diseases and disorders).

9. The Ecology of Disease and Health
Patricia K. Townsend

An ecological-evolutionary theoretical framework characterized much of the classic work in medical anthropology by the 1960s and 1970s, before being eclipsed by diverse theoretical perspectives. A series of developments outside of anthropology during the 1990s energized a new wave of interest in ecological approaches in medical anthropology, this time with a more sophisticated integration of the political economy of health. The first of these developments was the increasing attention to threats to biodiversity accelerating the loss of species. The second was the introduction and popularization of the concept of emerging infectious diseases. The third was the increasing recognition of the seriousness of global climate change. All three converged to suggest that anthropogenic changes in the global environment affecting human health are far more extensive than formerly thought.

10. The Medical Anthropology of Water
     Linda M. Whiteford and Cecilia Vindrola Padros

Anthropologists have studied water in many forms – as it relates to the distribution of power, to the spread of agriculture, to the development of sedentary communities, to religious rituals, and to peoples' worldviews. However, fewer anthropologists have explicitly focused on water and related health outcomes as measurable variables, thus failing to track how access to a clean and reliable water supply changes the patterns of preventable diseases. Understanding the multiple layers and kinds of connecting points between water, human health, structural violence, and disease is a quintessentially interdisciplinary enterprise. In this chapter we review some of the anthropological research on water, and discuss the innovative contributions medical anthropology can make when teamed with, for instance, engineering and epidemiology. We try to connect the worldwide water crisis and its global health consequences with the role that anthropological research and analysis can make. The chapter includes examples from our own water-based research and interdisciplinary collaborations, and concludes with suggestions for future transdisciplinary training of students, and the effective design and implementation of health policies.

11. Political Violence, War and Medical Anthropology
     Barbara Rylko-Bauer and Merrill Singer

This chapter examines the ways in which medical anthropologists have engaged with the topic of political violence and war, by focusing on four areas where significant contributions have been made, but challenges still exist. These include: (1) denaturalizing violence by making ethnographically informed additions to the growing compendium of studies that challenge the notion of war and political violence as inevitable, biologically-determined features of human life; (2) using critical ethnographic methods to "revisualize" – make visible – the causes, embodied realities, and consequences of political violence and war; (3) reconceptualizing these phenomena as biosocial disease that takes a great toll on the well being and health of individuals, families, societies, and the world order, while also recognizing the role of health care and public health in peace building; (4) building on medical anthropology's applied tradition of engaged involvement that combines theory and praxis so as to increase the likelihood that our witness and analysis contributes to diminishing the incidence and the human costs of political violence and war.

Part III   Health and Behavior

12. Humans in a World of Microbes: The Anthropology of Infectious Disease
     Peter J. Brown, George J. Armelagos and Kenneth C. Maes

All humans harbor infections of pathogenic organisms and suffer the consequences at some time in their lives. Yet the particular diseases that afflict people – as well as the way in which symptoms are interpreted and acted upon – vary greatly across different societies. We have three goals in this chapter. First, we describe how the application of specific medical anthropological concepts can provide a nuanced and full understanding of the biocultural etiology, epidemiology, and ecology of infectious disease. Second, we use epidemiological transition theory to demonstrate the importance of social and historical contexts for explaining changes in the prevalence of infectious diseases. Finally, we use the example of the HIV/AIDS pandemic in Africa to illustrate how interactions between biology, behavior, political economy and culture must all be included in an anthropological model of infectious disease ecology. Jonathan Mann distinguished between three separate epidemics of HIV/AIDS – the invisible virus, followed by AIDS, and the public response. The HIV/AIDS pandemic and the drama of our response to it have highlighted seemingly dualistically opposed human capacities for marginalization and compassionate care. While fear and stigma can spread like an epidemic, so can positive human responses to AIDS. A key challenge to medical anthropologists is to understand these interacting microbial and cultural epidemics by paying attention to human behavior, culture, and political economy in addition to infectious pathogen and host biology.

13. Sexuality, Medical Anthropology, and Public Health
     Pamela I. Erickson

Based on a review of the evolution of relevant research, this chapter argues for the expansion of human sexuality as a topic within medical anthropology and public health. Noting that sexuality and sexual behavior were long overlooked topics, and that even the resurgence of interest in human sexuality in the 1970s, sex continued to be largely eschewed by anthropologists as well as other social science disciplines for another ten years or more. In particular, this chapter argues, anthropology was disinclined to legitimate scholars who engaged the topic of human sexuality as a serious and worthy topic of anthropological inquiry. Further, this chapter argues that the anthropological literature on sexuality and reproduction has much relevance for sexual and reproductive health. At the macro level, it calls attention to the diversity of social arrangements for sexual expression, the existence of sexual subcultures that may have different health risks from the other groups, and the extent to which political-economic factors affect the ability of people situated in different contexts to exercise their sexual and reproductive rights and desires. At the micro level, it provides a rich description of the ways that sex, love, and reproduction play out in people's lives. There is a deep need for a meaning-centered understanding of sexuality in the health field in order to develop interventions that speak to the real needs and concerns that people have about protecting their health.

14. Situating Birth in the Anthropology of Reproduction
     Carolyn Sargent and Lauren Gulbas

This chapter examines the anthropological study of childbirth in the context of a large and sophisticated body of research on reproduction. We review central and enduring topics that have characterized ethnographic research on childbirth from the 1970s to the present, including birth as a cultural production, comparative explorations of authoritative knowledge, birthing systems across the technological spectrum (ranging from diverse local, low-tech birthing systems to high-tech biomedical systems), and ethical and moral issues surrounding reproductive technologies. In particular, we highlight how grounded, theoretically informed ethnographies enable anthropologists to apprehend the complexities of childbirth meanings and practices in personal, local, state, and global contexts. We also propose "potential frontiers" in future studies of childbirth, and we point to the continuing importance of ethnography as a means for carrying out nuanced and fine-textured analysis of these issues.

15.   Nutrition and Health
      David A. Himmelgreen, Nancy Romero Daza and Charlotte A. Noble

The interplay between food and nutrition, on the one hand, and culture and biology, on the other, has been of central interest to anthropologists throughout most of the discipline's history. While anthropologists of all subdisciplines have contributed to the extensive literature on this topic, this chapter focuses exclusively on the work of cultural and biological anthropologies during the last decade. Three major themes are examined. First, the influence of globalization on food choices and nutritional health, including issues of migration and immigration in relation to dietary acculturation and nutritional status. Second, issues of gender, emphasizing gender inequalities, economic insecurity, and cultural beliefs as factors in nutritional health. Finally, topics examined through biocultural approaches, such as the fetal or developmental origins of life history and the reconsideration of the origins of Type 2 diabetes. This chapter concludes by discussing the way in which this anthropological knowledge can be applied to address nutritional health in present day populations.

16.   Anthropologies of Cancer and Risk, Uncertainty and Disruption
      Lenore Manderson

Screening, early diagnosis and improved therapeutic approaches have reduced the high mortality rate associated with many cancers. But despite this, the diagnosis of any cancer provokes anxiety and fear, contributing to a cultural silence around different cancer diseases and adding to the reluctance of many people to participate in screening programs or to present for care. In this chapter, I draw primarily on examples of breast and cervical cancer, for which most anthropological research has been undertaken. I illustrate cultural and social perceptions of risk and cause, the pervasiveness of fear, and the difficulties that people face in relation to prevention, screening, diagnosis, treatment, and prognosis. In settings where resources are limited, I note too how household and local economics affect decision-making and outcome, while in particular cultural settings, I describe the reluctance of doctors to tell patients that they have cancer, and for patients who know their diagnosis, for them to tell it to others. In conclusion, I point to the gaps in the anthropological research on concern, and the importance for us to place disease in context, attending to how people are exposed to toxins and pathogens, the action or inaction in face of risk, the cultural underpinnings of prevention and screening programs, and the politics of access to care.

17.   Generation RX: Anthropological Research on Pharmaceutical Enhancement, Lifestyle Regulation, Self-Medication and Recreational Use
      Gilbert Quintero and Mark Nichter

This chapter describes an anthropological research agenda focused on the use of prescription psychoactive drugs for personal enhancement, lifestyle regulation, self-medication and recreational purposes. Anthropological investigations of prescription drug use can add to our understandings of a number of socio-cultural practices, including the use of substances to manage, increase, and improve aspects of work, leisure and self. Other topics warranting interest include the interrelationships between legitimate medical and non-medical use of prescription drugs, as well as consideration of recreational pharmaceutical use as a form of voluntary risk-taking. We suggest an expansion of analyses that more fully considers standard public health models and narrow, problem-focused, sensationalist representations of prescription drug use in the popular media. This will be accomplished by directing greater critical attention to the limitations of current survey-based drug use surveillance systems, through more careful assessment of commonly accepted drug-related risk constructs, and by providing broader evaluations of the impacts of prevention programs and media representations of drug use problems. Overall, we underscore the continued importance of understanding the social, symbolic, economic, and political contexts framing prescription drug consumption in order to comprehend emerging drug use trends.

18. Anthropology and the Study of Illicit Drug Use
    J. Bryan Page

Although some anthropological research had produced literature on non-Western patterns of drug use before the formal founding of the Society for Medical Anthropology (SMA), that founding coincided historically with worldwide trends in which consequences and meanings of drug use became important topics in medicine, civil society, and inevitably, politics. Castaneda and Dobkin de Rios published their works on psychedelic drugs and their acute effects about the time when the founders of SMA were working on that organization's statement of purpose. For the rest of the 20th century, funding agencies in the United States realized the potential of ethnographic study to further knowledge of drug use, especially illicit drug use. This trend led to studies of cannabis in three foreign sites, funding of ethnographies of opioid use in the United States, and ultimately, employment of ethnographers in efforts to characterize and prevent risk in the era of AIDS. Key ethnographically facilitated findings on consequences and meanings of drug use include Cannabis' subtle, sub-clinical effect on its users' cognitive function, the importance of social environment in the spread of HIV, and the positive impact of harm reduction strategies in not only preventing HIV spread, but linking drug users to health service resources.

PART IV HEALTHWORK: CARE, TREATMENT, AND COMMUNICATION

19. Ethnomedicine
    Marsha B. Quinlan

Ethnomedicine examines and translates health-related knowledge and theories that people inherit and learn by living in a culture. Each society has a particular medical culture or "ethnomedicine," which forms the culture's medical common sense, or logic. An ethnomedical system has interrelated notions about the body, the causes and prevention of illnesses, diagnosis and treatment, such that ethnophysiology, ethnopsychiatry, practitioner-seeking behavior, and ethnopharmacology are all ethnomedical topics.

20. Medical Pluralism: An Evolving and Contested Concept in Medical Anthropology
     Hans A. Baer

This chapter provides an overview of the concept of medical pluralism which recognizes that complex societies are characterized by a conflation of medical subsystems which generally compete with each other but sometimes may cooperate or collaborative with each other. It discusses the theoretical underpinnings of the concept, particularly in the work of Charles Leslie, and cultural interpretive, biocultural, and critical perspectives of it. Finally, this chapter examines the stance of various national socio-cultural systems toward medical pluralism and efforts to improve on the concept of medical pluralism, particularly by recognizing the phenomena of medical syncretism and the transnationalization and globalization of medical systems.

21. Biotechnologies of Care
     Julie Park and Ruth Fitzgerald

Anthropological studies of technologies that intervene in life (biotechnologies) and anthropological studies of care in health and medical settings are often undertaken separately. This chapter, however, explores their complex intersections and in doing so discusses some of the community, hospital, individual, and discursive public contexts of biotechnologies and care. These intersections have prompted us to consider the "low-tech/high touch" aspects of biotechnologies as well as the more usual "high-tech/low touch" contexts, and we have directed our attention to the kinds of care backroom technicians demonstrate in their work, as well as to studies of interpersonal interactions. Early anthropological studies of care have proved useful in our consideration of the broader and often unintended consequences of biotechnologies. The authors, who are based in New Zealand, have drawn largely on studies from outside the United States and United Kingdom and argue that much can be learned from studies of everyday carers and taken-for-granted biotechnologies in a diverse array of global settings.

22. Social Interaction and Technology: Cultural Competency and the Universality of Good Manners
     Kathryn Coe, Gail Barker and Craig Palmer

The increasing diversity of populations has directed attention toward promoting cultural competency in all arenas that involve social interaction, but particularly in the health care arena as interactions are often enduring and intense. Driving this interest is the assumption that a more culturally competent workforce will help reduce health disparities. In this paper, we take a close look at cultural competency trainings and attempt to identify what elements are missing that might be of critical importance, particularly in a world in which social interactions are increasingly technologically mediated. We argue that manners are a key issue in the management of successful social interactions and that even through there are culturally unique aspects to manners, there is considerable cross-cultural agreement on what constitutes good manners. Not only does a concept of manners exist in all cultures, but there are also certain aspects of social interactions (i.e., good manners) encouraged in all cultures, while others (i.e., bad manners) are discouraged. We describe some of these universal aspects of manners and argue that the recognition of their existence makes an important contribution to the concept of cultural competency and has practical implications for improving interactions via new technologies (e.g., Internet, cellular devices, video conferencing).

23. Biocommunicability
    Charles L. Briggs

This chapter bridges linguistic and medical anthropology by drawing on critical perspectives in both areas in an attempt to forge cross-fertilization. It draws on the perspective of biocommunicability, which examines how cultural models project the production, circulation, and reception of knowledge about health, disease, and the body. I argue that even as medical anthropologists have attended to models and practices used in making biomedical statistics, technologies, practices, and epistemologies and making them seem autonomous and objective, they often reproduce the commonsense cultural models of language and communication that play a key role in this process. I discuss research on illness narratives, suggesting that in viewing stories as revelations of the experiences and explanatory models of narrators, medical anthropologists become inattentive to the social lives of narratives, to their materiality, and the inequalities that shape their production, circulation, and reception. In a world in which epidemics reach us first (and often only) through media and Internet representations, new biomedical objects are biomedical and communicative hybrids, shaped by cultural models and practices that span both biomedical and media institutions – which are increasingly fused. This chapter thus provides a framework for analyzing the spatial and temporal features, forms of subjectivity, notions of scale, projections of materiality and objectivity, and the affective and ethical states that are deemed to be imminent dimensions of biomedical objects and epistemologies by revealing the implicit models of "communication" and the discursive practices that play a crucial role in their construction – and are often taken for granted both by medical anthropologists and their interlocutors.

24. Anthropology at the End of Life
    Ron Barrett

This chapter explores several important themes for anthropological inquiry at the end of life. These themes include the challenges and possibilities of conducting an experience-near ethnography of bereavement and the dying process along different trajectories. Further examination of death trajectories reveals important disjunctures and intersections between the ideals and realities of dying a "good death" in different cultural contexts and historical periods. This chapter suggests that particular notions of good death are closely linked to broader definitions of health that, in turn, serve as reference points for critical analyses of hospital-based biomedical practices at the end of life. Lastly, this chapter will examine the social history of the death with dignity movement and the ways that hospice and palliative care, and the way in which these have been translated in different societies.

PART V THE ROAD AHEAD

25. Operationalizing a Right to Health: Theorizing a National Health System as a "Commons"
Sandy Smith-Nonini and Beverly Bell

Advocates for equity in health care, including many medical anthropologists, have asserted the importance of health as a human right. To date, globally, health rights are a concept more often evoked in the breach, than universally honored, as evidenced by the spread of neoliberal policies like privatization, cuts in social services, and polarizing debates over health reform in the United States. This chapter draws on insights from critical medical anthropology, ecology and comparative systems analysis of national health systems to address the problem of operationalizing health rights. The notion of health rights presupposes a humanitarian body politic in which global citizens share goals of creating an inclusive moral order, and for this reason the argument applies the concept of a "commons" or common property regime to national health systems. An embedded case study of the French health system helps to illustrate both the possibilities and political complications in considering health as a commons. This chapter argues that insights from ecology and systems theory can strengthen anthropological analysis of health care systems.

26. As the Future Explodes into the Present: Emergent Issues and the Tomorrow of Medical Anthropology
Merrill Singer and Pamela I. Erickson

This concluding chapter envisions the future of medical anthropology in light of a number of key *ecobiosocial* factors to which the medical anthropologists of tomorrow must respond. The chapter argues that the changing ecobiosocial face of our world is being shaped by: (1) increased crowding; (2) populations migrations and mixing; (3) global urbanization; (4) polluted and resource depletion; (5) growing social inequality and felt deprivation; (6) growing cultural juxtaposition. This listing of changes suggests that in addition to many current areas of focus the medical anthropology of tomorrow will be increasingly concerned with: (1) the health effects of globalism; (2) human impact on our physical environment; (3) new and renewed and resistant diseases; (4) the commercialization of the body; (5) the impact of war and violence; (6) the struggle for human rights and the magnification of inhuman wrongs; (7) a demand relevance and application.

List of Figures

List of Tables

Notes on Contributors

George J. Armelagos is a biological anthropologist at Emory University in Atlanta Georgia. His research involves diet and disease in prehistory. He is the co-author of *Consuming Passions: The Anthropology of Eating* (with Peter Farb) and co-editor of *Paleopathology at the Origins of Agriculture* (with Mark N. Cohen) and *Diseases in Populations in Transition* (with Alan C. Swedlund). He received the Franz Boas Award for Exemplary Service from the American Anthropological Association in 2008 and the Charles Darwin Award for Lifetime Achievement from the American Association of Physical Anthropology in 2009. He was awarded the Viking Fund Medal from the Wener–Gren Foundation in 2005.

Hans A. Baer is a Senior Lecturer in the Development Studies Program, School of Philosophy, Anthropology, and Social Inquiry, and the Centre of Health and Society at the University of Melbourne. He has been a visiting professor at Humboldt University in Berlin, the University of California, Berkeley, Arizona State University, George Washington University, and the Australian National University. Baer has conducted research on the Hutterites in South Dakota, the Levites (a Mormon sect), African American Spiritual churches, complementary and alternative medicine in the United States, UK, and Australia, socio-political and religious life in East Germany, and conventional and complementary HIV clinics in a Western USA city. He has published 11 books, and published some 130 book chapters and journal articles. Some of his books include *Critical Medical Anthropology* (with Merrill Singer), *Medical Anthropology and the World System: A Critical Perspective* (with Merrill Singer and Ida Susser), *Biomedicine and Alternative Healing Systems in America: Issues of Class, Race, Ethnicity, and Gender, Toward an Integrative Medicine*, and *Introducing Medical Anthropology* (with Merrill Singer). He received the Rudolf Virchow Prize awarded by the Society for Medical Anthropology in 1994.

Gail Barker, MBA, PhD is the Associate Head for the Department of Pathology and the Associate Director of Finance for the Arizona Telemedicine Program at the University of Arizona. Her PhD is in Health Administration. Prior to moving to the

University of Arizona, she was the Chief Financial Officer for the Medical School at the University of California, Irvine. She has won awards as the 1992 outstanding Health Sciences Academic Business Officer of the Year at the University of California, Irvine, and the Vision 2000 Award for the Commission on the Status of Women at the University of Arizona. Most of Gail Barker's publications are in the area of Telemedicine Business.

Ron Barrett is Assistant Professor of Anthropology at Macalester College and a registered nurse with clinical experience in hospice, neuro-intensive care, and brain injury rehabilitation. His work on the religious healing of leprosy in the pilgrimage city of Banaras, India is the topic of his book, *Aghor Medicine: Pollution, Death, and Healing in Northern India* (University of California) which was awarded the 2008 Wellcome Medal by the Royal Anthropological Institute. His research has focused on health-related stigma, the social dynamics of infectious diseases, medical pluralism, and caregiving at the end of life. He is also co-editor with Peter Brown of *Understanding and Applying Medical Anthropology* (2nd Edition). Barrett is presently conducting NSF-sponsored research on health seeking for influenza-like illnesses in a western Indian slum community.

Beverly Bell has worked for three decades as a writer and advocate in collaboration with social movements in Latin America, the Caribbean, Africa, and the USA. Her focus areas are just economies, democratic participation, and rights for indigenous peoples. Bell won the PEN-New Mexico Award for the Literature of Social Justice for her book *Walking on Fire*. She is Coordinator of Other Worlds and Associate Fellow of the Institute for Policy Studies.

Charles L. Briggs is the Alan Dundes Distinguished Professor in the Department of Anthropology of the University of California, Berkeley. He received his PhD in Anthropology from the University of Chicago, and is the author of eight books, including *Stories in the Time of Cholera: Racial Profiling during a Medical Nightmare* (with Clara Mantini-Briggs, University of California Press, 2003, translated as *Las historias en los tiempos de cólera* by Nueva Sociedad in Caracas, 2004) and *Poéticas de vida en espacios de muerte: Género, poder y el estado en la cotidianeidad Warao* (Abya-Yala, 2008). In addition to research conducted in the United States, he has worked in Venezuela on public health, violence, the news media, and the relationship between indigenous communities and the State. He is currently conducting research on media, citizenship, and health in Cuba, Ecuador, Venezuela, and the United States. His awards include the James Mooney Book Prize in Anthropology, the Polgar Prize and the Rudolf Virchow Award from the Society for Medical Anthropology, the Bryce Wood Award of the Latin American Studies Association, the J. I. Staley Prize of the School of Advanced Research (with Clara Mantini-Briggs), and the Edward Sapir Award of the Society for Linguistic Anthropology (with Richard Bauman).

Peter J. Brown is a Professor in Anthropology in Emory College of Arts and Sciences and a professor in Global Health at the Rollins School of Public Health, both at Emory University. He is the editor of three textbooks in Anthropology, including the commonly used reader in Medical Anthropology (*Understanding and Applying Medical Anthropology*). He has a long-standing research interest in culture and disease ecology, with particular interest in malaria; he has also co-edited *The Anthropology of*

Infectious Diseases: International Health Perspectives and *Emerging Illnesses and Society: Negotiating the Public Health Agenda.* His research primarily deals with sociocultural aspects of malaria and its control, and he serves on a malaria-related Scientific Advisory Committee for the World Health Organization. He has an additional research interest on cultural issues in obesity and its related chronic diseases, especially in men. For a decade, he served as Editor-in-Chief of the journal *Medical Anthropology;* he was also president of the General Division of the American Anthropological Association. Winner of several teaching awards, he is a director of the undergraduate minor program "Global Health, Culture and Society" at Emory College.

Kathryn Coe is an Associate Professor of Public Health at the Mel and Enid Zuckerman College of the Public Health University of Arizona. She earned a PhD in Anthropology and Evolutionary Biology from Arizona State University in 1995, and has over 30 years experience conducting research and developing and evaluating health promotion programs in the United States, Mexico, Spain, and Ecuador. She has served as Principal Investigator for numerous research grants, including the Southwest American Indian Collaborative Network grant housed at the Inter Tribal Council of Arizona. She has published a book, *The Ancestress Hypothesis* (Rutgers University Press, 2003) and numerous articles on culture and health.

Kitty K. Corbett is a medical anthropologist and Professor in the Faculty of Health Sciences at Simon Fraser University, Burnaby (Vancouver), British Columbia, Canada. She has contributed expertise in change theories, multi-method strategies, social marketing, health communication, and advocacy to address public health problems including tobacco use, HIV and STIs, and antibiotic resistance. She has had leadership roles on multi-site and large scale projects including the Community Intervention Trial for Smoking Cessation (COMMIT) in the USA and Canada, the US CDC's National Network for STD/HIV Prevention Training Centers, and projects related to the use of pharmaceuticals in the USA, Mongolia, and Mexico. Her current research includes work with Mexico's National Institute of Public Health addressing antibiotic use, and the development of projects on oral cancer prevention in Canada and south Asia. She has twice been a Fulbright Scholar, in Mexico and Taiwan.

William W. Dressler is Professor of Anthropology at The University of Alabama. His research interests focus on culture theory, research methods, and especially the relationship between culture and human biology. Dressler and colleagues have examined these factors in settings as diverse as urban Great Britain, the Southeast USA, the West Indies, Mexico, and Brazil. His recent work emphasizes concepts and methods for examining the health effects of individual efforts to achieve culturally defined goals and aspirations. His research has been funded by both the National Institutes of Health and the National Science Foundation.

Merrill Eisenberg is an Assistant Professor at the Mel and Enid Zuckerman College of Public Health, at the University of Arizona. Before joining the faculty in 2005, Dr Eisenberg worked as a community-based researcher in Connecticut and Arizona. As an applied medical anthropologist, her research has addressed topics including maternal and child health, disabilities, sexual behaviors, and tobacco use. Her work has included a strong focus on policy issues and policy development. Most recently,

Dr Eisenberg has turned her attention to obesity, working with a community-based coalition, Activate Tucson, and winning a Communities Putting Prevention to Work grant from the CDC to create policy, systems, and environmental change to support healthy eating and active living in Pima County, Arizona. Dr Eisenberg has served on the editorial board of *Medical Anthropology Quarterly* and the Governing Board of the Society for Applied Anthropology, and is currently the President of the Society for Applied Anthropology.

Pamela Irene Erickson holds doctoral degrees in both anthropology and public health and is Professor of Anthropology and Community Medicine at the University of Connecticut. A former editor of *Medical Anthropology Quarterly*, much of her own research has focused on reproductive health among inner city populations. She is the author of two books, *Latina Adolescent Childbearing in East Los Angeles* (1998) and *Ethnomedicine* (2008) and co-editor (with Merrill Singer) of the book series *Advances in Critical Medical Anthropology* with Left Coast Press. In addition to her domestic field work in East Los Angeles, CA and Hartford, CT, Erickson has done fieldwork in Nepal, the Philippines, India, and Ecuador. She has served on the Governing Council of the Family and Reproductive Health Section of the American Public Health Association. Her current research focuses on barrier contraceptive use among minority young adults and college students, marriage and reproduction among the Waorani Indians of Ecuador, and the medicalization of social problems.

Ruth Fitzgerald is a Senior Lecturer in Social Anthropology at the University of Otago, New Zealand. Her research interests include ideologies of health care, innovative medical technologies, and the embodiment of health. She conducts fieldwork in Aotearoa/New Zealand and also in Utah in the USA. She is the General Editor of *Sites*, a journal of social anthropology and cultural studies in the Pacific and the Pacific Rim.

Alan H. Goodman is the Vice President for Academic Affairs, Dean of Faculty and Professor of Biological Anthropology at Hampshire College in Amherst, Massachusetts. He teaches and writes on the health and nutritional consequences of political-economic processes including poverty, inequality, and racism. Goodman is the editor or author of seven books including *Building a New Biocultural Synthesis: Political-Economic Perspectives on Human Biology* (with Thomas Leatherman) and *Genetic Nature/Culture* (with Susan Lindee and Deborah Heath). He received his PhD in anthropology from the University of Massachusetts and was a postdoctoral fellow in International Nutrition at the University of Connecticut and a research fellow in stress physiology at the Karolinska Institute, Stockholm. He is the former Dean of Natural Sciences at Hampshire College and the immediate past President of the American Anthropological Association.

Clarence C. Gravlee is Assistant Professor in the Department of Anthropology at the University of Florida, where he also holds affiliate appointments in the College of Public Health and Health Professions, the African American Studies Program, and the Center for Latin American Studies. Gravlee received his PhD from the University of Florida in 2002 and completed a postdoctoral fellowship as a W.K. Kellogg Community Health Scholar at the University of Michigan School of Public Health. The central goal of his research is to identify and address the social and cultural causes of racial inequities in health. His current work examines the health effects of racism among African Americans in Tallahassee, Florida. He has done related research among people of African descent in Puerto Rico and in Detroit. Gravlee recently joined the Tsimane' Amazonian Panel Study (TAPS) research team to examine the health consequences of globalization and culture change among indigenous peoples in the Bolivian Amazon. He is also co-founder and coordinator of the Health Equity Alliance of Tallahassee (HEAT), a community–academic partnership for action-oriented research on social inequities in health.

Lauren E. Gulbas is a Visiting Assistant Professor at the Southern Methodist University. She received her PhD in anthropology at the SMU in 2008. As a medical anthropologist interested in the intersections of gender and mental health, her research has explored topics that include eating disorders, cosmetic surgery, and suicide attempts.

D. Ann Herring is a biological anthropologist and Professor in the Department of Anthropology, McMaster University. Her areas of research interest include the anthropology of infectious disease, anthropology of health, demography, history and anthropology, and the health of Aboriginal communities in Canada. Her books include *Aboriginal Health in Canada: Historical, Cultural, and Epidemiological Perspectives* (with J. B. Waldram, and T. Kue Young), *Human Biologists in the Archives: Demography, Health, Nutrition and Genetics in Historical Populations* (edited with Alan Swedlund), *Grave Reflections: Portraying the Past Through Cemetery Studies* (edited with S. R. Saunders), and *Strength in Diversity: A Reader in Physical Anthropology* (edited with L. Chan).

David A. Himmelgreen has a PhD in anthropology from SUNY Buffalo and was a Research Scientist and Associate Director of Research at the Hispanic Health Council in Hartford, Connecticut from 1994 to 1998. He is currently an Associate Professor of Anthropology at the University of South Florida, and served as the Graduate Director from 2005 to 2007. Himmelgreen's interests include maternal and child health, nutritional assessment, food security, obesity, nutrition education, and HIV/AIDS prevention. He has conducted research in India, Lesotho, Costa Rica, and the United States. He is the Principal Investigator in an NSF-funded project examining the impact of a changing economy on nutritional health among Costa Rican rural dwellers (Romero-Daza is the Co-PI). In 2007, Himmelgreen and colleagues completed a preliminary study on perceptions of food insecurity among rural households and agricultural and public health experts in Lesotho. In addition to being a Fulbright Scholar, he has received grants from the National Science Foundation, the US Department of Agriculture, UNICEF, USF, the Patel Center for Global Solutions, and from various state and local agencies in Florida. He was awarded a Presidential Young Faculty Award in 2003 and an Outstanding Undergraduate Teaching Award in 2005.

Craig R. Janes is Professor and Director of the Global Health Program for the Faculty of Health Sciences at Simon Fraser University, Burnaby (Vancouver), British Columbia, Canada. He is interested in globalization and health, in particular the impact of liberal strategies of economic and cultural development on maternal and child health, reproductive health, and access to health care. He has worked on the problem of the globalization of market-based health reform policy since the early 1990s, first in southwestern China (Tibet), and most recently in Mongolia. His current work examines the impact of Mongolia's socioeconomic and political transition, in the context of increasing environmental hazards linked to climate change, on rural households. Janes is also the Mongolia team-leader for the Canadian Coalition for the Global Health Research project to strengthen national health systems, and is working with the Health Sciences University of Mongolia to increase research and evidence-based policymaking in the field of environmental health.

Tom Leatherman is Professor of Anthropology at the University of South Carolina, Columbia. His research has focused primarily on structural violence, social inequalities, and health among rural communities in Latin America. This work has ranged from the causes and consequences of illness on farming production and household economies in Peru to the effects of tourism on food commoditization and dietary change in the Yucatan. He co-edited *Building a New Biocultural Synthesis: Political–Economic Perspectives on Human Biology* with Alan Goodman, and *Medical Pluralism in the Andes* with Joan Koss-Chioino and Christine Greenway. Current and future research focuses on the health and nutritional impacts of armed conflict, and specifically on the effects of civil war, neoliberal economic policies, and shifts in land tenure on food security, nutrition and health in highland Peru.

Judith Littleton is Associate Professor of Biological Anthropology in the Department of Anthropology, University of Auckland, New Zealand. Her areas of interest include biological anthropology, human osteology, and health. She has conducted fieldwork in the Middle East, Australia, and New Zealand. Her recent publications, from a total of 50, include Footprints in the Sand: Appraising the Archaeology of the Willandra Lakes, Western New South Wales, *Australian Antiquity* (with Allen H. Holdaway and P. Fanning), Migrants and Tuberculosis: Analyzing Epidemiogical Data with Ethnography", *Australian and New Zealand Journal of Public Health* (with Julie Park, C. Thornley, A. Anderson, and J. Lawrence), and Memory and Time: Historic accounts of Aboriginal Burial in Southeastern Australia, *Aboriginal History*.

Kenneth C. Maes is currently a postdoctoral research fellow at Brown University's Population Studies and Training Center. He conducts anthropological research focusing on links among altruistic caregiving, key resource insecurity, and psychosocial wellbeing; as well as on the reproductive health and motivations of paid and unpaid community health workers in low-income settings, primarily in Ethiopia. He received his PhD in Anthropology from Emory University in 2010.

Lenore Manderson is a Research Professor in the School of Psychology, Psychiatry and Psychological Medicine, Faculty of Medicine, Nursing and Health Sciences, and the School of Political and Social Inquiry, Faculty of Arts, at Monash University, Melbourne, Australia. From 2002 to 2007, she held an inaugural Australia Research Council Federation Fellowship, and conducted research on chronic illness and disability in Australia and a number of Southeast Asian settings. She has published extensively in this area, on infectious disease, and on gender and sexuality. She is a Fellow of the Academy of the Social Sciences in Australia and of the World Academy of Art and Science.

Mark Nichter is the Regents Professor of Anthropology at the University of Arizona, holding joint appointments in the departments of Family Medicine and the Mel and Enid Zuckerman College of Public Health. He coordinates the University of Arizona's graduate program in medical anthropology and is actively involved in research in both the USA and in South and Southeast Asia. Relevant to his essay in this volume, Professor Nichter has carried out over three decades of research on multiple aspects of pharmaceutical practice, tobacco use, and drug-food popularity. His research interests are broad and engage contemporary social problems and global health challenges.

Charlotte A. Noble (MA Anthropology/MPH Global Health, 2010) is a doctoral student in applied anthropology at the University of South Florida. Her research interests include nutrition, HIV/AIDS, and the use of smallholder gardens to address food insecurity. She has conducted research in Haiti, Costa Rica and Lesotho.

Cecilia Vindrola Padros originally obtained her BA in Cultural Anthropology from the Universidad de las Americas, Puebla in Mexico. She is currently carrying out a PhD in Biocultural Medical Anthropology at the University of South Florida, thanks to the financial support provided by the Fulbright–Garcia Robles Grant, AAUW International Fellowship, CONACYT Complementary Doctoral Scholarship, and USF. Her previous research has focused on different health related issues (HIV/AIDS, cancer treatment, health impacts of domestic violence) with particular interest on the services provided to children within public healthcare facilities in Latin America. For her PhD dissertation, Cecilia will analyze the strategies used by pediatric oncology patients and their parents to overcome the delays and obstacles in the diagnosis and treatment of cancer within the public health system in Argentina.

J. Bryan Page is Professor and Chair of the Department of Anthropology at the University of Miami, with secondary appointments in Psychiatry and Behavioral Sciences and Sociology. Dr Page began his career as a researcher on patterns of drug use in 1973 as part of a transdisciplinary team charged with investigating the effects of long-term Cannabis use in Costa Rica. He has conducted studies in Costa Rica, Spain and perhaps the most culturally diverse of territories, Miami/Dade County, Florida. His research activity has included studies of poly-drug use among Seminoles and Miami/Dade Cubans, impact of HIV among injecting drug users (IDUs), progression of HIV and other retroviral infections among IDUs, Haitian youth, gangs, and drugs, risk behavior among youth in Miami/Dade, needle use and risk in Miami and Valencia, Spain, and prescription drug use among women. All of this work received funding from the National Institutes of Health. It has led to the publication of articles in journals ranging from *Medical Anthropology Quarterly* to *The Lancet*. His total published works including book chapters and other materials number more than 120. Dr Page has participated in the NIH's extramural system of application review for 20 years. He is also a member of the steering committee of the NIDA's National Hispanic Science Network. He is co-author with Merrill Singer of *Comprehending Drug Use: Ethnographic Research of the Social Margins.*

Craig Palmer is an Associate Professor and Director of Graduate Studies in the Department of Anthropology at the University of Missouri. He earned a PhD in anthropology from Arizona State University in 1988. His areas of specialization include cultural anthropology, human behavioral ecology, human evolution and behavior, human sexuality, and religion He has published widely on the incorporation of cultural traditions into evolutionary explanations of human behavior. He has conducted research in the North Atlantic maritimes and elsewhere in Canada and the USA.

Julie Park is Associate Professor of Social Anthropology at the University of Auckland, New Zealand. Her areas of interest are social anthropology, anthropology of Aotearoa and settler societies, health, gender, sustainability, and research methods. Her current research focuses on implications of new technologies for people with haemophilia, the political ecology of tuberculosis in New Zealand, and public discourses of new reproductive technologies. She is editor of the book *Ladies a Plate: Change and Continuity in the Lives of New Zealand Women* and has published over 50 articles in professional journals.

Marsha B. Quinlan is an Assistant Professor of Anthropology at Washington State University. She is an ecological medical anthropologist with research experience in the Caribbean and North and South America. She examines local ethnomedicine to inform her research on pathologies, family health behavior, botanical knowledge, maternal and child health, and personality.

Gilbert Quintero is an Associate Professor in Anthropology at the University of Montana. He has been active in establishing an applied medical anthropology graduate program and has conducted research on a wide variety of drugs, including alcohol, tobacco, and pharmaceuticals, with a number of different Hispanic, Native American, and college social groups. His recent research incorporates attention to drug use patterns in the life course. His most recent publications include Rx for a Party: Recreational Pharmaceutical Use in a Collegiate Setting (2009, with the *Journal of American College Health*) and Controlled Release: A Cultural Analysis of Collegiate Poly-drug Use (in press with the *Journal of Psychoactive Drugs*).

Melanie Rock joined the University of Calgary faculty in 2003, following doctoral studies in medical anthropology (at McGill University) and postdoctoral studies focused on health promotion in the context of social inequalities (at the Université de Montréal). Her primary appointment is with the Department of Community Health Sciences. Additional affiliations at the University of Calgary include the Faculty of Social Work and the Department of Anthropology at the University of Calgary, as well as the Groupe de recherche interdisciplinaire en santé at the Université de Montréal. Her area specializations are medical anthropology, science and technology studies, health promotion, diabetes, and animal–human studies. Her recent publications include People, other animals and health knowledges: Towards a research agenda, *Social Sciences & Medicine* 2007 (with Eric Mykhalovskiy and Thomas Schlich), and Animal–human connections, one health, and the syndemic approach to prevention, *Social Science & Medicine* 2009 (with B. Buntain, J. Hatfield and B. Hallgrímsson).

Nancy Romero-Daza is an Associate Professor in the Department of Anthropology at the University of South Florida. She is a medical anthropologist with specialization in HIV/AIDS research and intervention. Romero-Daza has conducted research on the impact of labor migration on the spread of HIV/AIDS in Lesotho, has studied HIV risk among injection drug users, crack users, and sex workers in the USA, and has evaluated HIV/AIDS interventions such as Needle Exchange Programs and methadone maintenance programs. In addition, Romero-Daza has expertise in the creation and coordination of HIV/AIDS prevention and education services and has administrative experience overseeing the provision of case management and counseling for women who are addicted to drugs and for Latino men who have sex with men. Romero-Daza has conducted research and training on cultural competence in the provision of HIV services in Florida, and has conducted research on the impact of tourism on the spread of HIV and other STIs in rural Costa Rica. She has also worked with rural Costa Rican women in the design and production of culturally appropriate HIV awareness materials. Romero-Daza has collaborated with David Himmelgreen on research on food security in Monteverde, Costa Rica. She has received funding from the NSF, the Fulbright foundation, the Ryan White Foundation, and the USF Patel Center for Global Solutions, and has worked as consultant for various agencies, including Family Health International.

Barbara Rylko-Bauer is an Adjunct Associate Professor in the Department of Anthropology at Michigan State University. She earned a PhD in anthropology from the University of Kentucky in 1985. Her current research interests focus on health inequities and human rights, the intersection of violence and health, medicine in the Holocaust, and applied anthropology. She is a past Book Review Editor for *Medical Anthropology Quarterly*, and recipient of the Rudolph Virchow Prize (with Paul Farmer) in 2003). Her recent publications include *Global Health in Times of Violence* (co-edited with Linda Whiteford and Paul Farmer, School of Advanced Research Press, 2009), Community Participation in New Mexico's Behavioral Health Care Reform (with Miria Kano and Cathleen Willging, *Medical Anthropology Quarterly*, 2009), Out of the Shadows of History and Memory: Personal Family Narratives in Ethnographies of Rediscovery (with Alisse Waterston, *American Ethnologist*, 2006), and Reclaiming Applied Anthropology: Its Past, Present, and Future (with Merrill Singer and John van Willigen, *American Anthropologist*, 2006).

Carolyn Sargent is Professor of Sociocultural Anthropology at Washington University in St. Louis. Her research and teaching focuses on the domain of gender and health, with a particular emphasis on reproduction, medical decision making, and the management of women's health in low-income populations. She has worked in West Africa (Benin, Mali), Jamaica, and France. Most recently, her writing has focused on how colonial and postcolonial relations between France and its former West African colonies in the context of the global economy have shaped the policies and politics of state institutions responsible for managing immigrant populations. Sargent is the current President of the American Anthropological Association. Her most recent books include *Globalization, Reproduction, and the State* (with Carole Browner) and *Gender in Cross-Cultural Perspective,* 5th edition (with Caroline Brettell).

Merrill Singer is the past Director of the Center for Community Health Research at the Hispanic Health Council. Currently, he is a Senior Research Scientist at the Center of Health, Intervention and Prevention and a Professor in the Department of Anthropology, University of Connecticut. He is also a research affiliate of the Center for Interdisciplinary Research on AIDS (CIRA) at Yale University. Dr Singer has published over 200 articles and chapters in health and social science journals and books and has authored or edited 21 books, including *The Political Economy of AIDS* (edited), *Medical Anthropology and the World System* (with Hans Baer and Ida Susser),

Introducing Medical Anthropology (with Hans Baer), *Unhealthy Health Policy: A Critical Anthropological Examination* (edited with Arachu Castro), *Something Dangerous: Emergent and Changing Illicit Drug Use and Community Health, Drugging the Poor: Legal and Illegal Drug Industries and the Structuring of Social Inequality, Drugs and Development, Global Warming and the Political Economy of Health* (with Hans Baer), and *Introduction to Syndemics.* He is the recipient of the Rudolph Virchow Prize, the AIDS and Anthropology Paper Prize, the George Foster Memorial Award for Practicing Anthropology from the Society for Medical Anthropology and the Prize for Distinguished Achievement in the Critical Study of North America from the Society for the Anthropology of North America. Dr Singer was awarded the 2010 Solon T. Kimball Award for Public and Applied Anthropology from the American Anthropological Association.

Elisa ("EJ") Sobo, Professor of Anthropology at San Diego State University, is a sociocultural anthropologist who has worked both in academia and in health care, most recently for the Veterans Health Administration. Her most recent work concerns organizational culture and quality improvement in biomedicine while previous projects have addressed pediatric health, HIV/AIDS, and rural Jamaican health traditions. A recognized expert, Dr Sobo has served as an elected member of the board for the Society for Medical Anthropology in addition to having served on the Royal Anthropological Institute's Medical Committee in the United Kingdom. She is on various journal editorial boards, including *Anthropology & Medicine* and *Medical Anthropology* and she is the Book Reviews Editor for *Medical Anthropology Quarterly.* Many of her numerous publications directly address the practice of medical anthropology in and of healthcare; her latest book is *Culture and Meaning in Health Services Research: A Practical Field Guide* (2009).

Sandy Smith-Nonini is Research Assistant Professor of Anthropology at the University of North Carolina, Chapel Hill, and former Assistant Professor of Anthropology at Elon University (2000–2005). She is the author of *Healing the Body Politic: El Salvador's Popular Struggle for Health Rights – From Civil War to Neoliberal Peace*, Rutgers University Press, 2010. Dr Smith-Nonini was awarded a Richard Carley Hunt Fellowship from the Wenner Gren Foundation in 2006, and two Mellon–Sawyer postdoctoral awards in 1999 and 2000. She received the Peter K. New Prize from the Society for Applied Anthropology in 1995. She has authored numerous journal articles and book chapters on the politics of community health, drug-resistant tuberculosis epidemics, and occupational risks of immigrant labor. She is currently doing research at the intersection of systems theory, political economy, and ecological sustainability.

Patricia K. Townsend is a Research Associate Professor at the University at Buffalo, SUNY. Her long-term anthropological field work was in Papua New Guinea. More recently, she has worked on the issues of environmental justice, mining, and toxic wastes. She is author of the widely used textbooks *Environmental Anthropology: From Pigs to Policies* (2nd Edition, 2009) and *Medical Anthropology in Ecological Perspective* (co-authored with Ann McElroy, 5th Edition, 2009).

Robert T. Trotter, II is a Regents' Professor, and Chair, Department of Anthropology, Northern Arizona University, Flagstaff, AZ. His research and applied anthropology interests include the confluences among cross-cultural health care delivery systems, traditional healing, organizational research, ethnographic methods, social network analysis, ethics, alcohol and drug abuse, evaluation research, community based participatory research, rapid ethnographic assessment, HIV/AIDS prevention, culturally competent interventions, and cultural models research. He has more than 130 publications, and his most recent books are *Ethics in Anthropological Research and Practice* (2008) (with Linda Whiteford) and *Partnering for Performance: Collaboration and Culture from the Inside Out.* (2008) (with Elizabeth K. Briody).

Linda M. Whiteford PhD, MPH is a Professor of Anthropology at the University of South Florida where she is currently holds two positions as Associate Vice President for Global Strategies, Office of the President, and Associate Vice President for Academic Affairs and Strategic Initiatives, Office of the Provost. She is a Past President of the Society for Applied Anthropology. Her research focuses on translating anthropological research into global health policies and practices, particularly concerning infectious and contagious water-related diseases. Her current National Science Foundation funded research (with Co-PIs Graham Tobin, Arthur Murphy, and Eric Jones) centers on social networks and recovery from chronic hazards such as active volcanoes. In 2008 she co-authored two books: *Primary Health Care in Cuba: The Other Revolution*, with Laurence Branch, Rowman and Littlefield Press, Lanham, Maryland, and *Anthropological Ethics for Research and Practice*, with Robert T. Trotter, II, Waveland Press. Long Grove, Illinois. In addition, in 2005 she co-edited *Globalization, Water and Health: Resources in Times of Scarcity*, with Scott Whiteford, published by the School of Advanced Research Press, *Global Health in Times of Violence* with Barbara Rylko-Bauer and Paul Farmer, published by School for Advanced Research Press, Santa Fe, New Mexico.

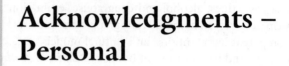

Acknowledgments – Personal

It has been said that time is that quality of nature which keeps events from happening all at once. As we all know from personal experience, lately it doesn't seem to be working. Thus, we extend a well deserved thanks to all of our contributors, who agreed, despite in most cases having already overwhelming schedules and responsibilities, to find the time, energy, and impressive insight to craft their respective chapters. Also, we warmly acknowledge the help, forbearance and gentle patience of our editors, Julia Kirk and Rosalie Robertson at Wiley-Blackwell.

Acknowledgments – Sources

Introduction

Merrill Singer
and Pamela I. Erickson

Medical Anthropology is a "baby boomer" of sorts. It came into being alongside the unprecedented interest in the health and well being of Third World peoples in the aftermath of WW II when the world was full of the hope and possibility that science, in this case biomedicine, could alleviate human suffering due to infectious disease and malnutrition, and then help eliminate or control many of the world's major health problems. Many anthropologists of that era worked with the international health community (WHO, USAID, UNICEF, etc.) to bring biomedicine to the world. The presumption guiding this effort was that shown the effectiveness of biomedicine and modern public health methods (e.g., the health value of boiling water before drinking it), while addressing contextual and cultural barriers to change, people would readily adopt new ways and the threat of many diseases would begin to diminish. Six decades later, a large proportion of the morbidity and mortality in our world is still due to the same tenacious problems of malnutrition and infectious disease (although some of the diseases, like HIV/AIDS, are new, and one old disease but only one, smallpox, has been eliminated), which have been exacerbated by escalating levels of poverty, war, genocide, and greed. The political economic systems that have resulted from unconstrained capitalism and global free market policies married to a scientific positivism whose advocates thought they would save the world have become systems of structural violence (Galtung 1969) that are especially damaging to the poor and marginalized peoples of the planet.

As Farmer (2003:1) indicates, structural violence refers to "a host of offenses against human dignity [including]: extreme and relative poverty, social inequalities ranging from racism to gender inequality, and the more spectacular forms of violence that are uncontested human rights abuses…" While experienced individually, structural violence targets classes of people and subjects them to common forms of lived oppression. Hence, the experience of structural violence and the pain it produces has been called "social suffering" (Kleinman et al. 1997). As Langer (1996:53) asserts, "We need a special kind of portraiture [and a special language] to sketch the anguish of people who have no agency in their fate because their enemy is not a discernible antagonist, but a ruthless racial ideology, an uncontrollable virus, or, more recently, a shell from a distant hillside exploding amid unsuspecting victims in a hospital or market square."

If this were not enough, we have added a whole new set of health problems due to chronic diseases (as a result of the epidemiologic transition), globalization, global warming, and environmental restructuring and degradation, all of which interact with each other to effect syndemics (Singer 2009a), ecosyndemics (Singer 2009b), and pluralea ("many threats") interactions among multiple ecocrises (Singer 2009c; Singer 2010). Indeed, in 2009, the health outlook for many people on planet Earth is bleak. As the World Health Organization (2008:5) states, "Globalization is putting the social cohesion of many countries under stress, and health systems, as key constituents of the architecture of contemporary societies, are clearly not performing as well as they could and as they should." Moreover, almost half the world's population, 2.1 billion people live on less than $2 a day. Of these, 880 million live on less than $1 a day (World Development Report 2007). It is estimated 2.8 million people died from AIDS in 2005, most of them in developing countries. Over 3 million more died from tuberculosis and malaria. Infectious disease accounts for about 29% of under-age-five child deaths in developing countries, and malnutrition plays a role in about half of these deaths (WHO 2005). When these diseases interact – HIV, for example, interacts adversely with tuberculosis, malaria, and malnutrition (Abu-Raddad et al. 2006; Gandy and Zumla 2003; Gillespie and Kadiyala 2005; Herrero et al. 2007) – the consequences are multiplied exponentially. Moreover, maternal mortality takes one in 74 women each year away from their families (World Health Organization 2004). Syndemic infection during pregnancy adds a significant additional level of risk to what is already a risky situation for most women in the Third World (Ayisi et al. 2003). Other less attended to and "neglected diseases" kill millions more people each year (Global Health Initiative 2008). Sometimes called tropical diseases, they are, as Nichter (2008:151) stresses, "diseases of poverty, development, and political ecology – not climatic happenstance." Notably, they, too, tend to occur in overlapping geographic zones and to involve polyparasitism or other comorbidities and harmful disease interactions (Hotez et al. 2006).

As Nichter's comment suggests, our world is one of great health disparities and inequalities in health status, access, and treatment that closely mirror social disparities and prevailing structures of non-egalitarian social relationship. Because health is the foundation of civil society, it has tremendous impact on political stability. The heightened anxiety surrounding the 2003 SARS and 2009 "swine flu" (H1N1 influenza) scares represented global expressions of a fragile perceived susceptibility in our new and dangerous 21st century world. While certainly there are areas in which health has improved, such as access to clean water in some locales, improvements in sanitation in many places, and progress in antenatal care, all of which are reflected in declining rates of child mortality, as the World Health Organization (2008:6) observes, the progress that has been made in health in recent years has been deeply unequal, with convergence towards improved health in a large part of the world, but at the same time, with a considerable number of countries increasingly lagging behind or losing ground. Furthermore, there is now ample documentation of considerable and often growing health inequalities within countries.

From its beginning medical anthropology was defined as "...the cross-cultural study of medical systems and ... the bioecological and sociocultural factors that influence the incidence of health and disease now and throughout human history" (Foster and Anderson 1978:1). Thus, it has long had a broad mandate to understand and interpret human beings – their behavior, their diseases and illnesses, their medical systems and the place of each of these in the encompassing sociocultural system (Erickson 2003). Medical anthropology was professionalized as a subfield within the discipline in the 1960s. Its core organization in the United States is now the second largest section in the AAA after the general cultural anthropology section. At 60 years of age it has a history of both venerated founders (George Foster, Cecil Helman, Arthur Kleinman, Charles Leslie, Hazel Weidman, Charles Hughes, Benjamin Paul, Pertti and Gretel Pelto, Arthur Rubel, among many others) and contested theoretical paradigms that have followed broader theoretical shifts in the discipline.

Academic medical anthropology in the 21st century encompasses the domains of individual experience, discourse, knowledge, practice, and meaning; the social, political, and economic relations of health and illness; the nature of interactions between biology and culture; the ecology of health and illness; the cross-cultural study of ethnomedical systems and healing practices, and the interpretation of human suffering and health concerns in space and time (Baer et al. 2003; Erickson 2008; Joralemon 1999; Lock and Scheper-Hughes 1996; McElroy and Townsend 2009; Nichter 1992; Sargent and Johnson 1996; Scheper-Hughes and Lock 1987; Singer and Baer 2007). Applied medical anthropology takes on the responsibility of making research useful for clinical or health educational applications, for influencing health policy, or for effecting social justice (Erickson 2003; Rylko-Bauer et al. 2006; Singer and Baer 2007), continuing the founding theme of bettering the public health. Despite our different interests, "our great strength is our diversity of theory and method, our holistic approach, our willingness to cross disciplinary boundaries, and our insistence on social justice" (Erickson 2003:4).

Companion to Medical Anthropology is meant not to serve as a full history of the subdiscipline (although many components of the field's history are discussed), or as an encyclopedia (although essays on many key topics are included), nor as an annual review of medical anthropology. Rather, we have identified scholars who we believe have something important to say about some of the major topics and themes in medical anthropology. We asked these authors to write about the current issues, controversies, and state of the field for their particular area of expertise from their own perspectives, and to hypothesize about the future trends and directions in their areas of expertise: where we are, what the major and emerging issues currently appear to be, and what might lie ahead. These predictions are taken up in a more comprehensive way in the final chapter as we look at the emergent forces likely to play a significant role in shaping medical anthropology in the future.

The book is designed to address students, scholars, and practitioners alike. Unavoidably, there are many more thematic and topical areas than could be included in this volume. Thus, *Companion* is not exhaustive and was not meant to be. We believe, however, that what you find in these pages will engage your interest, passion, and commitment to ensure that medical anthropology continues to matter in a world of enormous health challenges.

REFERENCES

Abu-Raddad, Laith, A., Padmaja Patnaik, and James G. Kublin, 2006 Dual Infection with HIV and Malaria Fuels the Spread of Both Diseases in Sub-Saharan Africa. Science Magazine 314:1603–1606.

Ayisi, John, Anna van Eijk, Feiko ter Kuile, Margarette Kolczak, Juliana Otieno, Ambrose Misore, Piet Kager, Richard Steketee, and Bernard Nahlen, 2003 The Effect of Dual Infection with HIV and Malaria on Pregnancy Outcome in Western Kenya. AIDS 17:585–594.

Baer, Hans A., Merrill Singer, and Ida Susser, 2003 Medical Anthropology and the World System. A Critical Perspective. New York: Praeger.

Erickson, Pamela I., 2003 Medical Anthropology and Global Health. Medical Anthropology Quarterly 17:3–4.

Erickson, Pamela I., 2008 Ethnomedicine. Long Grove, IL: Waveland Press.

Farmer, Paul, 2003 Pathologies of Power: Health, Human Rights and the New War on the Poor. North American Dialogue 6:1–4.

Foster, George M., and Barbara G. Anderson, 1978 Medical Anthropology. New York: John Wiley & Sons, Inc.

Galtung, John, 1969 Violence, Peace, and Peace Research. Journal of Peace Research 6(3):167–191.

Gandy, M., and A. Zumla, A., eds., 2003 Return of the White Plague: Global Poverty and the "New" Tuberculosis. New York: Verso.

Gillespie, Stuart, and Suneetha Kadiyala, 2005 HIV/AIDS and Food and Nutrition Security: From Evidence to Action. Washington, DC: International Food Policy Research Institute.

Global Health Initiative, 2008 In Brief: The Global Impact of Infectious Diseases. Electronic Document. http://www.familiesusa.org/issues/global-health/tool-kit/pdfs/3-in-brief.pdf.

Herrero, Maria, Pablo Rivas, Norma Rallón, Germán Ramírez-Olivencia, and Sabino Puente, 2007 HIV and Malaria. AIDS Reviews 9:88–98.

Hotez, P. J., D. H. Molyneux, A. Fenwick, E. Ottesen, S. E. Sachs, and J. D. Sach, 2006 Incorporating a Rapid-Impact Package for Neglected Tropical Diseases with Programs for HIV/AIDS, Tuberculosis, and Malaria. PLoS Med 3(5):e102. DOI: 10.1371/journal.pmed.0030102.

Joralemon, Donald, 1999 Exploring Medical Anthropology, 2nd edition. Boston: Allyn and Bacon.

Kleinman, Arthur, Veena Das, and Margaret Lock, eds., 1997 Social Suffering. Berkeley: University of California Press.

Langer, Lawrence, 1996 The Alarmed Vision: Social Suffering and Holocaust Atrocity. Dædalus: Journal of the American Academy of Arts and Sciences 125:47–65.

Lock, Margaret, and Nancy Scheper-Hughes, 1996 A Critical-Interpretive Approach in Medical Anthropology: Rituals and Routines of Discipline and Dissent. In Medical Anthropology. Carolyn F. Sargent and Thomas M. Johnson, eds. pp. 41–70. Westport, CT: Praeger.

McElroy, Ann, and Patricia Townsend, 2009 Medical Anthropology in Ecological Perspective, 5th edition. Boulder, CO: Westview Press.

Nichter, Mark, ed., 1992 Anthropological Approaches to the Study of Ethnomedicine. New York: Gordon and Breach Science Publishers.

Nichter, Mark, 2008 Global Health. Tucson, AZ: University of Arizona Press.

Rylko-Bauer, Barbara, Merrill Singer, and John Van Willigen, 2006 Reclaiming Applied Anthropology: Its Past, Present, and Future. American Anthropologist 108:178–190.

Sargent, Carolyn F., and Thomas M. Johnson, eds., 1996 Medical Anthropology: Contemporary Theory and Method. Westport CT: Praeger.

Scheper-Hughes, Nancy, and Margaret M. Lock, 1987 The Mindful Body: A Prolegomenon to Future Work in Medical Anthropology. Medical Anthropology Quarterly 1:6–41.

Singer, Merrill, 2009a Introduction to Syndemics: A Systems Approach to Public and Community Health. San Francisco, CA: Jossey-Bass.

Singer, Merrill, 2009b Ecosyndemis: Global Warming and the Coming Plagues of the 21st Century. *In* Plagues, Epidemics and Ideas, Alan Swedlund, and Ann Herring, eds, pp. 21–37. London: Berg.

Singer, Merrill, 2009c Beyond Global Warming: Interacting Ecocrises and the Critical Anthropology of Health. Anthropological_Quarterly 82: 795–820.

OK Singer, Merrill, 2010 Atmospheric and Marine Pluralea Interactions and Species Extinction Risks. Journal of Cosmology 8:1832–1837.

Singer, Merrill, and Hans A. Baer, 2007 Introducing Medical Anthropology: A Discipline in Action. Walnut Creek, CA: AltaMira Press.

World Development Report, 2007 Agriculture for Development. Washington, DC: The World Bank.

World Health Organization, 2004 Maternal Mortality in 2000: Estimates Developed by WHO, UNICEF and UNFPA. Department of Reproductive Health and Research, Geneva: World Health Organization Press.

World Health Organization, 2005 World Health Report 2005. Make Every Mother and Child Count. Geneva: World Health Organization Press.

World Health Organization, 2008 The World Health Report 2008: Introduction and Overview. Electronic Document. http://www.who.int/whr/2008/08_overview_en.pdf.

PART I Theories, Applications, and Methods

Medical Anthropology in Disciplinary Context: Definitional Struggles and Key Debates (or Answering the Cri Du Coeur)

Elisa J. Sobo

INTRODUCTION

As Scotch noted back in 1963, "Medical scholars have literally for centuries been aware of the social dimensions of health and illness and have, in their research, focused on a variety of social and cultural variables, while anthropology has only lately indulged in similar research" (p.30). Many working outside of anthropology advocated early on for socio-culturally informed approaches, and called for changes in social structure, occupational expectations, and urban environments to defeat certain epidemics (e.g., Bernadine Ramazzini, Benjamin McCrady, Lous-René Villermé, Emil Chadwick, Lemuel Shattuck, Rudolph Virchow, Henry E. Sigerist, and Erwin H. Ackerknecht (Scotch 1963:30–31). If we consider the work of these forebears as well as varied anatomists, physiologists, geographers, etc., who shared early anthropologist's scholarly interest in the human condition, it becomes clear that medical anthropology exists as the outcome of many lines of intertwined inquiry into humankind, some of which emerged in different fields independently – and some of which provoked further interest in health in anthropology proper.

A Companion to Medical Anthropology, First Edition. Edited by Merrill Singer and Pamela I. Erickson.

A crucial example of this came with the end of World War II, when medical anthropology received impetus and support from foundation- and government-funded applied work in the arena of international and public health. Data collected by anthropologists in earlier times for simple descriptive purposes proved invaluable; anthropologists helped ensure that social and cultural aspects of health and healing were taken into account in ways that promoted program success. As Foster puts it, this marked a turnaround in which the increased value of ethnological data was driven not by changes on the inside of anthropology but rather by outside interests – those of the international and public health markets (Foster 1974). Anthropology or, more specifically, ethnology, now had direct "technical" (Scotch 1963) relevance.

Indeed, the first review of the field emphasized its practical utility. It was titled, "Applied Anthropology in Medicine" (Caudill 1953). In 1959, an article by James Roney carried the shorter phrase, "Medical Anthropology," in its title (Roney 1959; see also Weidman 1986:116). But what did this label describe? What tensions did it encompass?

Building on previous historical reviews (including Browner 1997; Claudill 1953; Colson and Selby 1974; Fabrega 1971; Foster 1974; Foster and Anderson 1978; Good 1994; Hasan 1975; Lock and Nichter 2002; McElroy 1986; Polgar 1962; Scotch 1963; Sobo 2004; Todd and Ruffini 1979; Weidman 1986), this chapter examines the historical context of the struggle to define the field. In the 1960s and 1970s, debate centered on then-prominent applied-theoretical and generalist-specialist divides. The contrast between physical (later, biological) and cultural perspectives also made its mark. Later developments related to the evolving definition of culture, the influence of critical (and later synthetic) thinking on the subdiscipline, and the role of extra-disciplinary interaction.

MEDICAL ANTHROPOLOGY TAKES SHAPE

Application or theory?

Good refers to medical anthropology in the 1960s as a "practice discipline" (1994:4), dedicated to the service of improving public health of societies in economically poor nations. Indeed, initial efforts at organizing a medical anthropology interest group – diligently fostered by Hazel Weidman – resulted in an invitation from the Society for Applied Anthropology or SfAA to affiliate in 1968. A full account of this and subsequent developments is offered in Weidman's important historical review (Weidman 1986).

Although the invitation was accepted by the fledgling medical anthropology community (then called the Group for Medical Anthropology or GMA) as a practical solution to the challenges of maintaining cohesion, the endorsement of and by applied anthropology was "something of an embarrassment" to many (Good 1994:4). Even George Foster, a key founding figure, had to work through ambivalences here. "We were trained to despise applied anthropology," he once said; recalling that he did not join the SfAA until 1950; until then "I would have nothing of it" (Foster 2000, quoted in Kemper 2006).

As Scotch reported in 1963, there were those who felt that because of its practical bent, "the quality of literature in this area is not always impressive... It is superficial, impressionistic, and nontheoretical" (Scotch 1963:32). Some felt that those who elected to engage in medical anthropology were "less rigorous than their more traditional-minded contemporaries" (p.33); they were denigrated as mere "technicians" (p.42).

Generalists or specialists?   Apprehension also ran high over whether formally organizing as *medical* anthropologists would reinforce an "artificial area of study"; in support of this claim some pointed to "the lack of systematic growth and the failure to produce a body of theory" (Scotch 1963). Some feared that formal organizing might "prove detrimental to the development of theory in anthropology" as it would force the fragmentation of the field (Browner 1997:62).

The American Anthropological Association (AAA) was at that time experiencing growing pains. Its Committee on Organization described "financial and organizational disarray" in 1968 (*Anthropology Newsletter* 9(7)) and noted that while anthropologists in general desired to "retain an integrated professional identity" the profession also faced strong "fissiparous tendencies" (as cited in Weidman 1986:116). Some medical anthropologists felt, accordingly, that focusing on developing the group's then-nascent newsletter (*Medical Anthropology Newsletter*, or MAN) would be better than assembling as if a faction. This might be termed the "function but no structure" constituency (Weidman 1986:119).

It is helpful here to recall that the AAA did not, at the time, have "sections" as we know them today. Many members believed that research should contribute to anthropology in general, not just some special subgroup. Arthur Rubel, for instance, until his death "would not be pigeonholed as a medical anthropologist... for he always saw health/medical phenomena as human behavior to be understood as anthropologists understood other forms of human behavior" (Cancian et al. 2001).

An uneasy resolution

Partially due to the fear that affiliating with the SfAA, which was independent of the AAA, might distance medical anthropologists from the parent discipline unduly, and because to incorporate independently in another form would be financially costly (Browner 1997), the GMA continued to push the AAA to create a mechanism for organizing as an AAA subgroup. Eventually, largely due to the GMA's own organizing efforts, this came to pass (see Weidman 1986:121,124) and the SMA received formal status as an AAA affiliate in 1972 (Society for Medical Anthropology 1975).

This move firmly anchored the group within academic anthropology. It also allowed the AAA some control over the shape that medical anthropology took, due to imposed bureaucratic imperatives. However, in part because those *not* interested in direct involvement in the application of their work tended purposefully *not* to identify with the group (cf. Good 1994:4), the influence of applied perspectives remained strong.

Many members retained an affiliation with the SfAA and *Human Organization* (the SfAA's journal) was a popular publication outlet for medical anthropology. So was *Social Science and Medicine*, founded in 1967. Many SMA members were employed in schools of medicine, nursing, or public health. Others worked directly in the international and public health fields. From the viewpoint of those seeking practical solutions to specific health problems, theory seemed abstract, obstructive, and

sometimes even irrelevant. The authority of biomedical clinical culture, where curative work and saving lives takes precedence, was manifest (Singer 1992a).

What's in a name?   There are still those anthropologists who prefer to self-identify
as anthropologists interested in health rather than as "medical" anthropologists. In
some cases they cling to the old-fashioned academic belief that applied work is *infra
dig*. In others, their concern relates to the desire, noted above, to advance the larger
discipline or, to paraphrase George Stocking, to guard the sacred bundle (1988).
A statement issued by the SMA in 1981 defining medical anthropology addressed
this, asserting unambiguously: "Medical anthropology is not a discipline separate
from anthropology" (p.8).

But this did not offset objections related to the narrow technical or Western definition of the term *medical*, noted for instance at the GMA's 1968 organizational meeting. Madeline Leininger suggested the alternate "health anthropology" (which some
prefer today as well); "lively discussion followed" (Weidman 1986:119). It is not just
that *medical* leaves out nurses and members of the allied health professions. Narrowly
defined, it refers only to *bio*medicine. The appellation "medical anthropology" thus
has been seen by some as suggesting a biomedical gold standard against which to
measure all other healing or curing practices. Other concerns have been the implied
focus on pathology and the implicit devaluation of interpretive ethnographic methods
and of studies of non-"medical" healing.

Nonetheless, many self-identified medical anthropologists' work has nothing to do
with "medicine" as it is technically defined. For them, and even for many anthropologists working in biomedical settings, the term *medicine* is generic. It is understood to
refer to *any* system of curing or healing, no matter what specific techniques are
involved.

CULTURAL INTERESTS ASSUME THE LEAD

For better or worse, the subfield moved forward as "medical anthropology." The
SMA's incorporation in the early 1970s seemed to spur a number of "What is Medical
Anthropology?" essays. As Howard Stein noted in 1980, "I have heard the *cri du
coeur*, 'What is medical anthropology?' (MA) as a recurrent, quasi-ritualized annual
event" (p.18). While in its initial phase, generalist-specialist and applied-theoretical
tensions had prominence, in this phase the tension between cultural and biological
priorities took precedence.

A felt need
Despite physical (now 'biological') anthropology's contribution to the subfield's
growth, beginning with studies of hominid paleontology, anthropometry, and the
geographic distribution of certain traits, and later with studies of a more ecological
and adaptationist perspective, medical anthropology's official emergence was largely
fostered by culturally oriented scholars, mobilized by their new-found role in international and public health (see Paul 1963; Polgar 1962). This included those
affiliated with the "culture and personality" school (e.g., Caudill, who wrote the

aforementioned 1953 review). Thus, Colson and Selby's (Colson and Selby 1974) "annual review" of the field's progress (1974) gives much space over to work on "social pathologies" (p.253), such as drug and alcohol use or addiction, and issues relevant to "ethnopsychiatry" (p.248). A similar pattern infused the earlier review by Fabrega (Fabrega 1971), who noted "the affinity that 'medical anthropology' has always had with psychiatry" (p.186). Even Scotch's 1963 review, organized around the theory–application question, reveals the psychological influence, for instance discussing work relating "modal personality" to certain forms of mental illness (p.43). This distinct focus on "nurture" over "nature" reflects the strength of cultural determinism in early 20th century US anthropology.

The strong presence of cultural anthropologists had a sizeable impact on early efforts to organize the medical subfield. For one thing, while the seven goals drafted by the initial steering committee of the emerging medical anthropology network did refer to "social and cultural aspects of health, illness, and systems of medical care" (Weidman 1986:118), biological aspects received no mention. Further, all of the goals stressed communication (Browner 1997). While physical anthropologists had been working and publishing in and with medicine since anthropology's inception, cultural anthropologists as a whole were still at that time rather new to it and seemed uncomfortable in that milieu. In comparison to their physical/biological counterparts, they generally lacked easy access to it anyhow and could claim little authority within it. Cultural scholars' desire for increased intellectual discourse provided great organizing momentum.

Biological voices   In a 1975 "What is Medical Anthropology" commentary published in the SMA's newsletter, MAN, Khwaja A. Hasan, who (along with several others) actually used the phrase "medical anthropology" in print prior to those generally credited for inventing it, took the emerging subfield in general and, more specifically, George Foster himself, to task for neglecting the biological side of the anthropological equation (Hasan 1975). Foster made this omission in a 1974 commentary (also published in MAN) contrasting medical anthropology and sociology (Foster 1974).

Hasan argued that, rather than focusing on the culture–society distinction, which Foster did (as others have: e.g., Paul 1963), Foster should have depicted anthropology as the study of "man" (sic). "Man" is the major focus of medicine, too, wrote Hasan; this, he said, gives anthropology and medicine much more in common than anthropology and sociology. Example after example of the role that biologists and "medical men" played in anthropology's development are followed by more examples of physical/biological anthropologists at work within medicine.

It probably did not hurt Hasan's case that physical anthropology had by this time become more biologically oriented, not only in terms of data types accessed but also in terms of questions asked. In any event, Foster was quite responsive to Hasan's argument: When Foster revised the offending 1974 commentary for use in the first medical anthropology textbook, published in 1978, he and his co-author Barbara Anderson took a more biologically informed position. They included also a reference to Hasan (Foster and Anderson 1978).

Others, too, provided correctives. A key teaching text also first published in 1978 specifically highlighted biological and ecological perspectives (McElroy and Townsend 2004); a 1980 textbook that took a biocultural approach proclaimed in its subtitle to be "expanding views of medical anthropology" (Moore et al. 1980).

Concurrently, while both the introductory undergraduate and graduate "model courses" prepared by Arthur Rubel and published in the newsletter MAN in 1977 and again as part of a "model course" collection (Todd and Ruffini 1979) to aid curricular development for the subfield were short on biology, it did gain representation in Model Course VIII, "Biomedical Anthropology." This course, prepared by Frederick Dunn, also laments the "limited attention" paid to biological concerns (p.95). Model Course IV, "Nutritional Anthropology" (by Cheryl Ritenbaugh) is quite biological. Having said that, nutritionally oriented anthropologists, who had a very active SMA special interest group from the start, did break away to establish their own AAA section in 1974.

Medical anthropology's initial culturalism was not so much, then, a prejudice against biological anthropology as it was a simple artifact of the professional activities of many of medical anthropology's organizationally active founders. And yet, despite the corrective directions taken in the mid-to-late 1970s, science itself had by that time come under scrutiny. The scientific method – the paradigm that biological anthropologists most often worked within – was increasingly seen by those who dominated the field not only as an "establishment" tool. Worse, evolutionary biology was maligned by some because of its potential use by racists (D'Andrade 2000:223).

Finding itself on the "wrong" side of the culture–biology divide that had been thrown up, and upstaged by vocal and morally accusatory opponents of positivism, biological anthropology received less than its fair share of recognition from some corners. This is not to say that biological medical anthropology did not take place; indeed it did, and continues to do, in ways that have contributed greatly to advancing our biocultural understanding regarding, for example, high altitude adaptations, lactose tolerance, breastfeeding, and HIV/AIDS as well as to building a more theory-driven epidemiology. However, such efforts were often rewarded more richly outside of medical anthropology than in it.

'Function not Structure' Redux   Such goings on notwithstanding, others remained unconvinced of the merit of demarcation efforts. Indeed, Christie Kiefer's contribution to the definitional debate (Kiefer 1975) bemoans the "irritating question" to begin with (p.1). After outlining a typology of medical anthropologists ("the craftsman, who asks to be spared for his accuracy and thoughtfulness"; "the reformer, guided by a utopian vision"; and "the artist, who would rather be interesting than correct"), Kiefer worries that in trying to delimit the subfield we may cause it to wither on the vine. The quality that makes the field helpful and interesting, he says, is its very disorderliness (1975:1). This only makes us "seasick" he says because "medicine thrives on orthodoxy" (p.1); the quest to define medical anthropology reflects, he suggests, an infection with medicine's quest for "exactitude" (p.2). Contrasting "certainty on the one hand and meaningfulness on the other," Kiefer suggests we "stoutly insist" on keeping medical anthropology undefined and indefinite.

Medical anthropology: the official version

Despite this plea, the SMA itself tried to define the subfield with some exactitude in 1975 and again in 1981. The original SMA "What is Medical Anthropology?" statement essentially takes three paragraphs, starting with the bold proclamation, "As the holistic science of Man, anthropology has since its beginnings pursued the study of both human biology and the behavior of human groups" (Society for Medical Anthropology 1975).

The revision, three times as long, gives notably less attention to the biological arena. In it, we learn that most medical anthropologists "started as cultural anthropologists" (Society for Medical Anthropology 1981:8). The key questions of medical anthropologists, copied in below, do start out with the word *biological* but in the end are culturally oriented:

> How are biological processes mediated and modified by the culture? What are the dynamics of maintenance and change common to all curing systems? How are people recruited as practitioners and patients in curing systems, and how are roles learned, carried out and changed? What is the relationship between health beliefs and health behavior? How does the curing system relate to other systems in a culture? What is the relationship between the pattern of life and the pattern of disease?" (p.7).

The essay further states that although the concept of adaptation is incorporated, "the time frame is shorter than that used by physical anthropologists, who are more concerned with evolutionary processes" (p.8).

WHAT IS CULTURE?

From health to sickness

Most early medical anthropologists defined "health" as most still do now: it is a broad construct, consisting of physical, psychological, and social well being, including role functionality. What was new in the 1970s, however, was a distinction increasingly drawn between "disease" – biomedically measurable lesions or anatomical or physiological irregularities – and "illness" – the culturally structured, personal experience of being unwell, which entails the experience of suffering.

The effort to hash out such distinctions was underwritten by the increase in anthropologists taking a meaning-centered focus and the growing use of the emic-etic framework, absorbed through linguistics. "Etic" constructs (such as the temperature represented on a thermometer) are meant to be universally applicable; they are imposed from the outside onto the cultures in question. The problematic assumption of one true empirical reality notwithstanding, etic constructs are opposed to "emic" ideas: ideas (and note the implication there) that cultural insiders have about themselves and their worlds. "Disease" is an etic, a universally applicable and measureable entity. "Illness" (the emic perception) is not. As such, it can refer to a variety of conditions cross-culturally, some of which (it has been argued) do not exist in other cultural worlds.

Thinkers of the day soon realized that, however helpful, the disease–illness dichotomy recapitulates the mind–body dichotomy that biomedicine was, even then, being criticized for "trafficking in." This view took fuel in part from the bourgeoning rift between positivist-minded and interpretive or hermeneutic scholars – a rift often termed the "two cultures" or science–humanities split, a la C. P. Snow (1993 [1959]). In any case, the problem here was that while "disease," as the dichotomy defines it, is anchored in the body, "illness" is conversely anchored in the mind: disease is thus attributed (whether it has it or not) a real, concrete, scientific factuality or objectivity that illness, as a subjective category, may be denied (see Hahn 1984).

A second criticism of the dichotomy hinged on the fact that both disease and illness were being located by theorists in the individual. The term *illness* referred, as it still often does, to an individual's social relations, but generally it did and does so only insofar as these were the cause of the illness (e.g., when an offended party places a hex) or as the illness leaves the individual unable to fulfill social or role obligations. Some scholars working in the 1970s wanted to link suffering more palpably to the social order by examining how macro-social forces, processes and events (such as capitalist trade arrangements) could culminate in public health problems and poorly functioning health systems (again, see Hahn 1984). Some recommended using the term *sickness* when larger social processes are being highlighted (see Frankenberg and Leeson 1976).

Studying medical systems

The ultimately helpful work on definitional questions occurred hand-in-hand with efforts that dissembled then-prevalent understandings regarding the nature of cultural systems per se. For instance, a late 1970s contribution to the "What is Medical Anthropology?" conundrum was titled "What Kind of Model for the Anthropology of Medical Systems?" (Kleinman 1978).

In the essay in question, Arthur Kleinman accuses his predecessors of a kind of reductionism. He denigrates the era of "sweeping comparative generalizations" and "ideal-type categorization," which he paints as "superficial" and as couched at "too abstract a level to be relevant" (pp.661–662), arguing instead for a medical anthropology that can "examine health and sickness beliefs as they are *used* in the usually exigent context of social action" (p.661; emphasis in original). While the essay never says so explicitly, it in effect provides early support for the adoption of a process-based theory of culture. It also gives voice to then-emergent concerns about imputing too much systematicity to cultural systems; it questions, quite strongly, "the tacit assumption… that medical systems are more or less homogenous, unchanging, and single" (p.662).

More immediately, however, pointing to the importance of "microquestions" and effectively adopting an anti-universalizing stance, the essay applauds the use made by newer medical anthropologists of the distinction between emic and etic perspectives. Despite the issues raised above, Kleinman and others working in the 1970s found the distinction quite stimulating. Kleinman argued it fostered the growth of promising research in semantic network analysis; at the time of his essay's publication a spurt of medical anthropology work took place in this area.

Referring particularly to the semantic network studies of his institutional colleague Byron Good, Kleinman noted:

> Here particular sicknesses are studied, in contrast to their biomedical signification, as culturally constituted networks that link symbolic meanings to physiological and psychological processes and the personal experience of sickness, on the one side, and to social situations, relationships, and stressors on the other.… The upshot is something akin to an ethnomedical epidemiology of *illness* and a sociosomatics of *disease*; a systematic critique is offered of the biological language of medicine and psychiatry and a new

language is proposed for examining the relationships among biology, experience, and meaning in the social construction of sickness as a phenomenon of everyday world (p.663; italics in original).

In short, argues Kleinman, it was time to enter a new era – one in which "complex ethnographic findings... make a shambles of established dichotomies" (p.664). Rather than simply cataloging classifying cultural practices, artifacts, and ideas (part of the archival tradition which did have its merits in anthropology's early days), much work in this decade was devoted to identifying and understanding the various forces within a given cultural milieu that shape heath and health-related experiences, ideas, and actions.

And it wasn't just semantic analyses that prospered. So did the meaning-centered approach to symbolic analysis, or what was to become known as the Geertzian tradition of interpretive anthropology. Also, a good deal of inquiry (including Kleinman's own) took place through the study of illness narratives. Theory and methods stemming from discourse analysis supported a good portion of narrative-centered work. Phenomenological ideas, such as those of Maurice Merleau-Ponty and then Pierre Bourdieu were later incorporated by some who emerged from the milieu now sometimes termed "the Harvard School."

Anthropologists at this time had also come to understand more fully that medical culture was not solely the province of "primitives." Largely under the leadership of Charles Leslie, now even highly elaborated medical traditions such as Ayurvedic, Unani, and Chinese medicine were subjected to anthropological scrutiny as dynamic cultural systems – and as locally and globally interacting ones too. The role of nationalism in keeping these "great traditions" vibrant also was theorized (see Leslie 1980). The general focus on how health-related experiences are shaped and expressed or given meaning locally was thus now complemented by efforts to examine how forces from without culture did the same.

Working under conditions of explicit change, first under the post-war rubric of "development" and later as part of an acknowledged post-colonial transformation (see Marcus 2005), anthropologists increasingly studied, and created comparative frameworks for making sense of, health seeking, medical pluralism, and medical syncretism. Epistemological questions regarding evidentiary standards and modes of logic in medical decision-making, both emic and etic, were now raised more vociferously; theorists became concerned with the tendency to favor scientific or biomedical standards and the questions of legitimacy this can raise (Lock and Nichter 2002:4–5). Scholars also probed assumptions regarding systematicity itself, arguing that the apparent orderliness of some non-biomedical traditions may be an artifact of modernization, which demands an emphasis on rationality. In this intellectual context, new ideas about culture – and about neocolonial development – were given room to grow.

CRITICAL APPROACHES

Self-criticism

As the 1980s "ticked" into place, anthropology – particularly cultural anthropology – began to respond to changes in global and domestic power relations as well as to feel the heat of other disciplines' critiques of traditional ethnographic methods: "The subjects of ethnography could no longer be constituted in as objective terms as previously" (Marcus 2005:680). Definitions of culture, already in flux in the 1970s, grew increasingly "non-essentialist, fragmented, and [came to be] penetrated by complex world historical processes mediating the global and the local" (p.681). They would become more so in the 1990s and early 2000s as so-called postmodernity transmuted into globalization, but the stage was set by the 1980s for the emergence of a critical form of medical anthropology – one that took the lessons of political economy to heart.

Social criticism

Even in the 1970s and earlier, some anthropologists had taken seriously the lessons of historical materialism encapsulated in the works of Karl Marx s and Friedrich Engels. Although in the USA an anti-communist bent put dampers on academic excursions into this arena, Eric Wolf's emigration from Europe during World War II and subsequent changes in the political climate supported the eventual uptake of this line of thinking in US circles. More attention was paid, then, to the works of Ronnie Frankenberg and, through him and others, Italian revolutionary Antonio Gramsci. In this way too, the focus on conflict and reconciliation and the tensions extant between (individual) agency and (social) structure, promoted by the Max Gluckman's Manchester School, gained new ground on US shores.

As a result, a newly "critical" perspective burgeoned. Proponents denounced past ignorance of social and, more to the point, political economic factors in medical anthropology's thinking. Systems thinking, most obviously in the form of world systems theory (as per Immanuel Wallerstein) and dependency theory (as per Andre Gunder Frank), were brought into play. Building on work done in the 1970s with regard to "great traditions" and the ways in which they do and do not respond to incursions from what some by then called "capitalist" or "cosmopolitan" medicine, medical anthropology now confronted head-on the impact of hierarchical social relations on people's health status, knowledge, and action (see, for example, Baer et al. 1986; Singer 1986).

While interpretive or meaning-centered medical anthropology focused on local symbolic significances and networks of meaning, taking ideas as key, critical medical anthropology (CMA) advocates took a materialist approach – one that prioritized the examination of power structures that underlay dominant cultural constructions, and questioned the ways in which power (including the power to frame "reality") was deployed. In doing so, CMA sought (as it still does today) not only to expose local power dynamics but also to reveal how outside interests, whether regional, national, or global, affect local conditions. Further, CMA argued (as it continues to do) that health ideas and practices reinforce social inequality as well as expressing it.

ANTHROPOLOGY OF MEDICINE, IN POLITICAL AND THEORETICAL CONTEXT

Medical anthropology grew dramatically in the last few decades of the 20th century, partly due to increased opportunities for applied medical anthropologists. But perhaps more importantly, non-applied anthropologists interested in health saw that they, too, had something to gain by identifying themselves as "medical" anthropologists. The field's relevance to theories regarding culture had grown more obvious. Further, those who affiliated gained somewhat increased credibility in biomedicine and public health, and easier access to work within such organizations.

The cultural construction of biomedicine and public health itself came under increasing scrutiny now, making manifest the important distinction between anthropology *in* medicine, which many early applied efforts represented, and anthropology *of* medicine (Foster 1974 [after Strauss 1957]:2). Investigations into the medicalization of pregnancy and birth were central to real growth in this area (see Browner and Sargent 2007).

Anthropology of medicine was in part made possible through the growth of employment options in academia, which had begun after World War II. But in the post-Vietnam War era the right (and even obligation) to question authority had become an important aspect of US cultural discourse. Many in certain areas of academia endorsed it gladly. Academic anthropology, in particular, had begun a swing to the "intellectual Left" (D'Andrade 2000:219). Employment within the ivory tower thus supported medical anthropology's close questioning of biomedicine's and public health's established agendas by providing a safe space for – and indeed, a cultural climate encouraging of – contemplations not often safely brought into the workplace. Protected from the need to bring in their own contracts and grants, and invigorated by post-Vietnam "anti-establishment" sentiment, many university-employed anthropologists proclaimed participation in government or corporate sponsored foreign or domestic aid work as retrogressive – as standing in the way of real social progress.

To some extent, the progressive climate fostered within numerous anthropology departments attracted newcomers to the field; some saw medical anthropology itself as a potential "social movement" (Stein 1980:19). Plus, while many went about their work systematically and with rigor, for others science was seen as "part of the military industrial complex" (D'Andrade 2000:221) and therefore needed quashing; "theoretically relevant description" gave way, in some circles, to "moral critique" (p.222). Put off by this tendency where it arose, some scholars more committed to systematic and rigorous research inquiry than hortatory essay writing switched their allegiance to other disciplines, such as epidemiology, genetics, biology, and even sociology.

Associated with cultural anthropology's general anti-science tendency at the time, a "bias in favor of alternative, heterodox, of non-Western forms of medicine" was noted by Melvin Konnor (Konner 1991:80). In his opinion, "Criticism of medicine has become a major academic and publishing industry" (p.81). Admitting that "there is a lot that is wrong with medicine," he argued that the negative tone taken by some medical anthropologists toward biomedicine was counterproductive: "Modern medicine is not a conspiracy against humanitarianism," he wrote; "Least of all is it a capitalist plot" (p.81). The "high-minded criticism with no evidence of sympathy for the doctor's plight" (p.81) that he observed did do some damage to medical anthropology's reputation in biomedicine – but not much, because generally such critiques were not published in media that many biomedically affiliated professionals read.

Further, many critically oriented scholars still prioritized careful research. Moreover, some made common cause with biomedical insiders who also would critique the industry and its impacts in an effort to improve healthcare. These scholars bridge the divide between an anthropology overfull with hypercritical rhetoric and an anthropology that is so in tune with the biomedical point of view that it actually had been, itself, medicalized.

As Carole Browner (1999) has explained, medicalized anthropology has lost touch with the discipline's principles; its practitioners "go native" when working within the health services (p.135). Browner respects the anthropologist's need to find a common language with which to communicate with in the healthcare colleagues and to adopt some of medicine's cultural practices to gain credibility in that world. She understands the likelihood that many anthropologists will already to some extent have internalized biomedicine's categories because of their own reliance, at times, on the system. But, Browner warns, one of the grave dangers of being medicalized is the sacrifice of our "critical distance" (p.137).

Complementing a politically motivated objection to work supporting the dominative medical system's imposition was a scholarly one, then: developments in post-modern and feminist theory that led many to question the authority of truth claims in bio-medicine and biology on epistemological bases (cf. D'Andrade 2000; Marcus 2005).

Biological influences

Despite the scorn for science promulgated by some in the later 20th century, bio-logical medical anthropologists continued to attract students and quietly made sub-stantial progress. They could afford to be quiet: many journals outside of anthropology gladly accept their work. Importantly, in terms of tenure and promotion, many of the extra-anthropological journals that welcome biological anthropology have higher impact factors than those of the home discipline. They also can "count" more when applications for grants are reviewed, thereby helping assure a steadier source of fund-ing for often-rather-expensive biological research.

In the 1970s, the term *biomedical* had been applied to biologically oriented work with fairly immediate clinical applications or relevance for investigations of universal (albeit perhaps locally expressed) biological or disease processes. As time wore on, political ecology, which acknowledges that power relations affect the ways that human groups handle their natural environments (e.g., water, soil), and documents the health ramifications thereof, was increasingly popular. While its treatment of culture was still rudimentary, the political ecology approach did offer an alternative to the narrower adaptationist perspective.

By the 1990s, some biological anthropologists who had followed developments in critical theory acknowledged the reductionist tendencies fostered even in political ecology and called for a deeper appreciation of the dialectical relationship between culture and biology (see Singer 1996). A more sophisticated biocultural synthesis emerged – one highlighting the complexly interactive roles that social structures and the local and global political economies that support them play in biological out-comes (see Goodman and Leatherman 1998). Some areas of inquiry that have ben-efitted from this approach are global malnutrition, tourism's impact on host population health, the situational emergence of syndemic clusters of disease or affliction, and even how socio-culturally fostered ecological crises related to pollu-tion, deforestation, soil degradation, and global warming have affected human health. Those on the more cultural end of the biocultural continuum have begun to examine how such "anthropogenic" hazards (including those tied to declared and undeclared wars) can converge, each having a multiplier effect on the other, and thereby on human well being.

Biocultural explorations have grown in other areas as well. For instance, investigations in regard to culture's role in creating and sustaining the placebo effect led to advances in theory regarding how healing works (e.g., Moerman 2002). Questions regarding the mechanisms whereby culture is embodied enhanced our understanding of "stress" while promoting a more cognitively oriented definition of culture (e.g., Dressler 2005).

MEDICAL ANTHROPOLOGY IN RECENT YEARS

Theory to the center

As the 20th century drew to a close, theoretical and methodological advances made within medical anthropology began to truly inform and inspire the larger discipline. General debates concerning culture, power, representation, social structure, and other issues increasingly reflect advances stemming from medical anthropology. Some examples are seen in recent work on narrative or storytelling in relation to health and healing, identity creation and maintenance, and subjectivity and temporality (especially in relation to stigmatized physical and mental conditions): the role and impact of audit and surveillance systems and authoritative knowledge; healthcare consumerism, pluralism, and syncretism; local and global health inequities, and so on. Much of this work itself, it must be said (and see below), has been influenced by scholars outside of anthropology, such as: Michel Foucault's regarding "governmentality" and "biopower" (e.g., (Foucault 1998 [1976]); Anthony Giddens's and Ulrich Beck's regarding "risk" (Beck 1992; Giddens 1984); and, more recently, Johan Galtung's regarding "structural violence" (Galtung 1969; but see also Virchow 1985 [1848]).

The hope for generating generally relevant anthropological theories and concepts always has been there: as noted, some opposed the formation of the SMA because of a fear that structural factioning might contribute unduly to the fragmentation of the field as well as to falsely fence in the subdiscipline, limiting its ability to speak to pan-anthropological concerns. Yet, despite the persistent argument for medical anthropology's broader relevance – a 1974 review of the subdiscipline noted its importance to "issues of interest to the discipline [as a whole, such as] culture contact, the acceptance of innovations, the organization of professional subcultures, and aspects of role theory among many others" (Colson and Selby 1974:254) – and despite exceptions to the rule, much of the medical anthropology conducted through the 1980s drew theory from anthropology's core rather than generating new anthropological theory itself. It was not really until the late 1980s and 1990s that medical anthropology's broader relevance was strongly seen. The reverse in the flow of ideas marks medical anthropology's emergence from the margin into the mainstream of the field (Johnson and Sargent 1990; see also Singer 1992a).

Reinventing wheels?

Medical anthropology has grown to be the largest specialist section membership in the AAA. Degree programs and textbooks are proliferating. However, and perhaps partly as a result of this, much present scholarship is in some ways redundant. There are at least two reasons for this. For one thing, concepts and new bits of jargon delineated in popular publications are applied or repeated ad nauseum as others seeking to advance follow fashion. Another reason for redundant scholarship in medical anthropology today lies in our apparent abandonment of – or anyhow decrease in – interest in lengthy and thorough literature reviews. The literature is no doubt denser today than it was a generation ago, making total command quite a challenge. Further, submission length limits are shrinking as publishers try to economize (as well as to accommodate shrinking page-length tolerances among many readers). However, scholars today seem increasingly ignorant of important foundational work. Some areas of current medical anthropological interest, despite certain scholars' insistence that they are brand new, have actually been scrutinized by many scholars previously.

Take, for example, hospital ethnography, the focus in 2008 of a special issue of *Anthropology & Medicine* (vol. 15, no. 2) as well as of a special section of *Social Science & Medicine* in 2004 (vol. 59, no. 10). While those involved in these publications stake the claim that anthropologists are only now discovering the benefits of active researchers in hospital settings, Foster and Anderson (who devoted an entire chapter to hospitals in their 1978 textbook and included also a separate chapter on doctors and another on nurses) stated as many years ago that "some of the most important studies of hospitals have been done by anthropologists" (p.164). They went on to note that one of the earliest behavioral science studies of nursing was done by an anthropologist (in 1936) – adding that nurses themselves have done a good deal to advance medical anthropology. A review of medical anthropology published just a few years earlier (Colson and Selby 1974), provides a number of examples of this genre.

This is not to say that aims and approaches have not changed. It is also not to deny that subtle differences can mean the world in terms of what an article or special issue contributes to the field. The heavy institutional pressures on scholars to stake claims of novel research are also not in question (see Sobo et al. 2008). Yet it remains the case that a better grasp of the history of scholarship in a given topical area can support more efficient and effective theoretical advancement. Even this is not a new observation: it was in fact the point of many who, in the 1960s, took medical anthropology to task because "it has not been cumulative" (Scotch 1963:39). Adding to the challenge today are medical anthropology's diverse national traditions (see Sailant and Genest 2007). Scholars may not be aware of, or may be dissuaded for a variety of reasons from reading, the works of those publishing in other countries or tongues. Again, this in itself is not a new problem, but its significance has no doubt broadened as the field has grown.

The periphery's significance?
At the same time, medical anthropology continues to be positioned well to contribute to general anthropology: Its focus, health (etc.), intrinsically lends itself to intradisciplinary collaboration. It has inherent interdisciplinary ramifications, too. This has been seen in work undertaken toward such goals as: improving care for people with HIV/AIDS and other diseases, increasing our understanding of (and ability to address) health inequities, fostering the implementation of cultural changes within healthcare organizations, etc.

George Marcus has in fact highlighted medical anthropology's "interdisciplinary constituencies" while calling it "one of the most energetic and successful of the established subfields" (Marcus 2005:681). He argues that, today in anthropology, "newer topical arenas and theoretical concerns are developed through interdisciplinary discussions… not through studied debates and discussions around products of anthropological research among the community of anthropologists itself" (p.675). Marcus further contends that medical anthropology enjoys "derived prestige in anthropology by dint of this [interdisciplinary] participation" (p.681).

Some of this prestige relates to the push from within the academy to secure more grants and contracts. Financial awards from biomedical research and public health funders are generally "heftier". In addition, they have more cachet outside of anthropology than do awards from within the field. This can be important to scholars seeking career advancement: there does exist a political economy of research (see Singer 1992b; Sobo 2009). But Marcus's argument is not directly concerned with that. Rather, he worries that most "career making research projects" today are, he claims, defined "in terms of social and cultural theory produced elsewhere than in anthropology" (p.676).

Marcus reinforces his overall argument that anthropology has been "cut from its moorings" (2005:673) with a claim that the relationship between its center and periphery has "collapsed" (p.676). With no prevailing "disciplinary metadiscourse" or even simple central tendencies – even the old claim of culture as anthropology's special purview has been challenged, for instance by "cultural studies" – prestige in anthropology must come now from the margins, not the core: "Anthropologists in general tend to be most impressed with their own research initiatives that most impress others" (p.681) – work that garners recognition in extramural "authoritative knowledge creating spheres" (p.687).

This emphasis on work undertaken at the periphery or even within other arenas and then returned to the anthropological fold occurs also in the theme selected for the inaugural SMA-only (versus joint) meeting (held in 2009). The meeting theme, "Medical Anthropology at the Intersections" highlights work in twelve areas: global public health, mental health, medical history, feminism and technoscience, science and technology studies, genetics/genomics, bioethics, public policy, occupational science, disability studies, gender/sexuality studies, international and area studies. These areas build upon those identified in the 2006 SMA presidential statement, in which much like Marcus, Marcia Inhorn notes that "the cutting edges of our field are now found 'at the intersections' of many other disciplines (Inhorn 2007:249). Whether the conference subtitle, "Celebrating 50 Years of Interdisciplinarity," somewhat silences the contributions of those working squarely within anthropology – or at least of those who took an anthropology-first position in the days prior to the 1980s when the core, according to Marcus (2005), imploded – remains an open question.

Authority, passion, practice

Also open to supposition is whether and how interdisciplinarity includes the public at large. Of late, some have sought to carve out an arena termed "public anthropology," which seeks to break free of academic "intellectual isolation," engaging in a straightforward manner with issues and audiences beyond the discipline's self-imposed boundaries (Borofsky 2000). The University of California Press publishes the California Series in Public Anthropology in support of this mission.

Books in the series to date deal with numerous topics, but many speak directly to issues of concern in medical anthropology, including HIV/AIDS, organ transplantation, sexual health, genocide, war-related trauma, reproductive strategies, and the link between poverty and ill health. Many authors in the series are self-identified medical anthropologists. The prestige of being published in a series with so many important authors and whose books have won so many awards no doubt has attracted more and more medical anthropologists to submit manuscripts for consideration, supporting an efflorescence in this genre – much as the SMA's Eileen Basker Memorial Prize, given yearly since 1988, supported growth of scholarship in the area it addressed: gender and health research. (The New Millennium Book Award was specifically created in 2005 to stimulate growth in more general medical anthropology writing.)

The public anthropology book series no doubt exists to disseminate knowledge and understanding. But it also exists to make money. It unselfconsciously seeks (as per its website description) to compete directly with the success that journalists and scholars from other disciplines have had at repackaging and selling – often at quite a profit – anthropological insights. Notwithstanding, Marcus (2005) specifically sees the call for "public anthropology" as a quest for recognition from the media, which has become "the most prestigious realm" of authoritative knowledge. Marcus attributes this need to the fact, as he sees it, that anthropology is currently paradigm-poor and therefore authority-weak. In this light, public anthropology serves as "a place-holder, an attractive surrogate" and "a source of solidarity" much needed (p.687).

Public anthropology might indeed be a strategy to increase intellectual as well as financial capital. It also reflects – but at present, with its focus more on the expression of passion than praxis or pragmatic engagement (Rylko-Bauer et al. 2006), does not promise to answer – a desire, felt quite strong in today's medical anthropology circles: to have an impact on the world around us. This desire is reflected also in the SMA's "takes a stand" project, initiated in 2002 under president Mark Nichter. It has led the SMA to generate policy statements regarding current pressing issues, beginning in 2006. It is a valiant effort (and one that I should disclose having been part of). However, a thin line separates taking a stand based on careful study, and activism masquerading as academics. Marcus's warning about the need to "rearticulate" anthropology (2005:694) may be overstated but we must certainly avoid further disarticulation by demanding of ourselves – and rewarding – more original, pragmatically engaged, theory-generating scholarship.

The central fact that what Marcus calls a "strong wave of critical thought" (2005:679) ran through the humanities and then into anthropology in the 1980s cannot be denied. It also is the case that many more recent developments in medical anthropology have been greatly influenced by ideas from without the anthropological field. Whether anthropology in general and medical anthropology in particular can claim future kudos as a key generative discipline and subdiscipline rather than accepting relegation to a merely recipient field and subfield remains to be seen. But it does seem that much of today's theory-relevant activity in anthropology is indeed enacted by, and channeled to the parent discipline through, the subfield of medical anthropology.

Methodological developments

Methodologically relevant scholarship, too, is widespread in the medical subfield. I mentioned earlier a concern with medical anthropology's medicalization (Browner 1999). Dissatisfaction with this has increased in the new Millennium; calls for rearticulation here have been vociferous (for fuller accounting, see Sobo 2009). Many condemn the unthinking acceptance of biomedicine's factorial model, which separates health-related situations or experiences into discrete, static units or factors to be counted. Such research pulls experience to bits; it focuses attention on parts rather than the whole and often treats culture as just another factor or variable in a researcher-imposed equation. Instead, a holistic, systems-oriented, comparative approach should be promoted. Researchers should be free to question initial research assumptions, redefine research questions and methods as needed as research moves along, and make sure that various stakeholders standpoints are represented.

It is true today that institutional and structural forces, such as funding streams and the clinical research model so favored in biomedicine, have exerted pressure on the shape of the subdiscipline. However, the above critiques and others like them are gaining an audience not only within medical anthropology but also extramurally, in biomedicine and public health, where experts increasingly recognize the failure of clinical trials-type research to answer all questions and solve all ills. Thus, in addition to contributing various specific data collection and analysis techniques to the general field, medical anthropology has contributed greatly to the nascent growth of a new methodological openness in health research circles.

Persistent Debases?

Medical anthropology has been around, as a named subfield, for sixty years now. While debates persist within the subfield, as they should if scholarly progress is to be made, the somewhat spurious oppositions we began with (field–specialist, theoretical–applied, and biological–cultural) have proven bridgeable. The divide between university-affiliated medical anthropologists and those working outside of academia, however, has not been so easily shaken, in part due to organizational factors. A look at the awards offered by the SMA demonstrates this. Practicing anthropologists (as well as academics working in non-PhD granting institutions, where practitioners often prepare) are not well reflected in SMA awards. For instance, there is a doctoral dissertation award, but nothing for a master's thesis. The George Foster Practicing Anthropology Award was instituted in 2004, but all other awards (there are nine in total) concern academic accomplishments. None reward service to the profession, such as Hazel Weidman's history-making organizational work. Not even past presidents of SMA (let alone past board members, etc.) receive present kudos: a list of all former presidents of the society nowhere exists.

How this balance will shift and what, in the bigger scheme of things, any shift may mean for the future of medical anthropology I dare not attempt here to predict. Neither has my research for this chapter prepared me to propose which new tensions will emerge in coming years. I can, however, offer this summary observation: a subdiscipline more attuned to past arguments and achievements might be better equipped for positive future growth.

ACKNOWLEDGMENTS

Numerous individuals supported this effort; this includes particularly our colleagues who previously have written on medical anthropology's history and development and early *Medical Anthropology Newsletter* op-ed contributors (see "References"). I also thank (in alphabetical if no other order) Gene Anderson, Kim Baker, Peter Brown, Carole Browner, Alan Harwood, Tom Leatherman, Robert LeVine, Ryan Mowat, Mark Nichter, Gretel Pelto, Marsha Quinlan, Sharon Stein, and Richard Thomas for specific helpful insights regarding the history of medical anthropology, relevant journals, and the Society for Medical Anthropology. Pamela Erickson and Merrill Singer provided thoughtful editorial guidance, and Mary Bicker helped with the literature review. While the bulk of what I have to say tracks back to others' earlier reports on the state of medical anthropology and of anthropology in general, I alone am culpable for the synthesis herein.

REFERENCES

Baer, Hans A., Merrill Singer, and John H. Johnson, 1986 Toward a Critical Medical Anthropology. Social Science and Medicine 23(2):95–98.
Beck, U., 1992 Risk Society: Towards a New Modernity. London: Sage.
Borofsky, Robert, 2000 Public Anthropology: Where to? What next? Anthropology News 41(5):9–10.
Browner, C. H., 1997 Commentary: Looking Backward at the Creation of the SMA. Anthropology News 38(6):62–63.
Browner, C. H., 1999. On the Medicalization of Medical Anthropology. Medical Anthropology Quarterly 13(2):135–140.
Browner, Carole H., and Carolyn Sargent, 2007 Engendering Medical Anthropology. *In* Medical Anthropology: Regional Perspectives and Shared Concerns. F. Sailant and S. Genest, eds. pp. 233–251. Malden, MA: Blackwell.
Cancian, Frank, Johanna Shapiro, and Jerome Tobis, 2001 Arthur J. Rubel, PhD, Family Medicine and Anthropology: Irvine. *In* 2001, University of California: In Memoriam (Metacollection: University of California History Digital Archives). University of California (System) Academic Senate, ed. Vol. 2008. Berkeley, CA: University of California Regents.
Caudill, William, 1953 Applied Anthropology in Medicine. *In* Anthropology Today. A. L. Kroeber, ed. pp. 771–806. Chicago: University of Chicago Press.
Colson, Anthony C., and Karen E. Selby, 1974 Medical Anthropology. Annual Review of Anthropology 3:245–262.
D'Andrade, Roy, 2000 The Sad Story of Anthropology 1950–1999. Cross-Cultural Research 34(3):219–232.
Dressler, William W., 2005 What's Cultural about Biocultural Research? Ethos 33(1):20–45.
Fabrega, Horacio, 1971 Medical Anthropology. *In* Biennial Review of Anthropology. J. Siegel, ed. pp. 167–229. Stanford, CA: Stanford University Press.
Foster, George M., 1974 Medical Anthropology: Some Contrasts with Medical Sociology. Medical Anthropology Newsletter 6(1):1–6.
Foster, George M., and Barbara Gallatin Anderson, 1978 Medical Anthropology. New York: Alfred A. Knopf.
Foucault, Michel, 1998 [1976] The History of Sexuality Vol.1: The Will to Knowledge. London: Penguin.
Frankenberg, R., and J. Leeson, 1976 Disease, Illness and Sickness: Social Aspects of the Choice of Healer in a Lusaka Suburb. *In* Social Anthropology and Medicine. J. B. Loudon, ed. pp. 223–258, Vol. 13. New York: Academic Press.

Galtung, Johan, 1969 Violence, Peace, and Peace Research. Journal of Peace Research 6(3):167–191.

Giddens, Anthony, 1984 The Constitution of Society: Outline of the Theory of Structuration. Los Angeles: University of California Press.

Good, Byron J., 1994 Medicine, Rationality, and Experience: an Anthropological Perspective. Cambridge UK: Cambridge University Press.

Goodman, Alan H., and Thomas L. Leatherman, eds. 1998 Building a New Biocultural Synthesis: Political Economic Perspectives on Human Biology. Ann Arbor: University of Michigan Press.

Hahn, Robert, 1984 Rethinking 'Disease' and 'Illness'. Contributions to Asian Studies: Special Volume on South Asian Systems of Healing 18:1–23.

Hasan, Khwaja A., 1975 What Is Medical Anthropology? Medical Anthropology Newsletter 6(3):7–10.

Inhorn, Marcia, 2007 Medical Anthropology at the Intersections. Medical Anthropology Quarterly 21(3):249–255.

Johnson, Thomas M., and Carolyn F. Sargent, eds. 1990 Medical Anthropology: Contemporary Theory and Method Westport, CT: Greenwood Publishing Group.

Kemper, Robert V., 2006 Foster, George McClelland, Jr (1913–2006) (Obituary). Newsletter: Society for Applied Anthropology 17(4):3–15.

Kiefer, Christie, 1975 The Official Medical Anthropology. Medical Anthropology Newsletter 6(4):1–2.

Kleinman, Arthur, 1978 What Kind of Model for the Anthropology of Medical Systems? American Anthropologist 80(3):661–665.

Konner, Melvin, 1991 The Promise of Medical Anthropology: An Invited Commentary. Medical Anthropology Quarterly 5(1):78–82.

Leslie, Charles, 1980 Medical Pluralism in World Perspective. Social Science & Medicine 14B(4):190–196.

Lock, Margaret, and Mark Nichter, 2002 Introduction: From Documenting Medical Pluralism to Critical Interpretations of Globalized Health Knowledge, Policies, and Practices. In New Horizons in Medical Anthropology: Essays in Honor of Charles Leslie. M. Nichter and M. Lock, eds. pp. 1–34. New York: Routledge.

Marcus, George E., 2005 The Passion of Anthropology in the US, Circa 2004. Anthropological Quarterly 78(3):673–695.

McElroy, Ann, 1986 MA.N and MAQ in Retrospect: 1968–1986. Medical Anthropology Quarterly 17(5):115 +125–127.

McElroy, Ann, and Patricia K. Townsend, 2004 Medical Anthropology in Ecological Perspective. Boulder, CO: Westview Press.

Moerman, Daniel, 2002 Meaning, Medicine, and the 'Placebo Effect'. Cambridge UK: University of Cambridge Press.

Moore, Lorna G., Peter W. VanArsdale, and JoAnn E. Glittenberg, 1980 The Biocultural Basis of Health: Expanding Views of Medical Anthropology. Boulder, CO: Waveland Press.

Paul, Benjamin, 1963 Anthropological Perspectives on Medicine and Public Health. Annals of the American Academy of Political and Social Science 346(Medicine and Society):34–43.

Polgar, Steven, 1962 Health and Human Behavior: Areas of Interest Common to the Social and Medical Sciences. Current Anthropology 3(2):159–205.

Roney, James, 1959 Medical Anthropology: A Synthetic Discipline. The New Physician 8:32–33.

Rylko-Bauer, Barbara, Merrill Singer, and John Van Willigen, 2006 Reclaiming Applied Anthropology: Its Past, Present, and Future. American Anthropologist 108(1):178–190.

Sailant, Francine, and Serge Genest, eds. 2007 Medical Anthropology: Regional Perspectives and Shared Concerns. Malden, MA: Blackwell.

Scotch, Norman A., 1963 Medical Anthropology. Biennial Review of Anthropology 3:30–68.

Singer, Merrill, 1986 Developing a Critical Perspective in Medical Anthropology. Medical Anthropology 17(5):128–129.

Singer, Merrill, 1992a The Application of Theory in Medical Anthropology. Medical Anthropology (Special Issue: The Application of Theory in Medical Anthropology, M. Singer, ed.) 14(1):1–8.

Singer, Merrill, 1992b Biomedicine and the Political Economy of Science. Medical Anthropology Quarterly 6(4):400–403.

Singer, Merrill, 1996 Farewell to Adaptionism: Unnatural Selection and the Politics of Biology. Medical Anthropology Quarterly 10(4):496–515.

Snow, C. P., 1993 [1959]. The Two Cultures. Cambridge UK: Cambridge University Press.

Sobo, Elisa J., 2004 Theoretical and Applied Issues in Cross-Cultural Health Research. *In* Encyclopedia of Medical Anthropology: Health and Illness in the World's Cultures (Vol. 1). C. Ember and M. Ember, eds. pp. 3–11. New York: Kluwer Academic Publishers.

Sobo, Elisa J., 2009 Culture and Meaning in Health Services Research: A Practical Field Guide. Walnut Creek, CA: Left Coast Press.

Sobo, Elisa J., Candice Bowman, and Allen L. Gifford, 2008 Behind the Scenes in Healthcare Improvement: The Complex Structures and Emergent Strategies of Implementation Science. Social Science and Medicine 67(10):1530–1540.

Society for Medical Anthropology, 1975 What Is Medical Anthropology? Medical Anthropology Newsletter 6(4).

Society for Medical Anthropology, 1981 What Is Medical Anthropology? Medical Anthropology Newsletter 12(4):7–8.

Stein, Howard F., 1980 Clinical Anthropology and Medical Anthropology. Medical Anthropology Newsletter 12(1):18–19.

Todd, H. F., and J. L. Ruffini, 1979 Teaching Medical Anthropology: Model Courses for Graduate and Undergraduate Instruction (Society for Medical Anthropology Special Publication No. 1). Washington DC: Society for Medical Anthropology.

Virchow, Rudolf Ludwig Karl, 1985 [1848] The charity physician. *In* Collected Essays on Publich Health and Epidemiology. L. J. Rather, ed. pp. 33–36, Vol. 1. Canton, MA: Science History Publications.

Weidman, Hazel H., 1986 On the Origins of the SMA. Medical Anthropology Quarterly 17(5):115–124.

CHAPTER 2

Critical Biocultural Approaches in Medical Anthropology

Tom Leatherman
and Alan H. Goodman

INTRODUCTION

Human health and well being is biocultural. Thus, it might be expected that biocultural perspectives on health, ones that consider the many imbrications, linkages, and intersections between biology and culture, would occupy a central place in medical anthropology. Indeed, the notion that human health and illness are interwoven biocultural processes, best understood through a variety of humanistic and scientific perspectives, has status as a foundational principle. However, as dominant biomedical perspectives illuminated reductive biological mechanisms and explanations, medical anthropology increasingly became more focused on the often ignored and in our view equally important, socio-cultural and political aspects of health. The turn away from the biological is understandable, but also unfortunate.

In our current era of global capitalism, growing inequalities and poverty, and unacceptably high levels of strife, hunger, malnutrition, and disease, there is a need for research that links human biology and health to social, cultural and political–economic dynamics. Biocultural approaches in medical anthropology can potentially provide a fuller understanding of how large scale political–economic processes "get under the skin." This chapter addresses biocultural approaches that have emerged over the past two decades that aim to enhance the focus on biology in critical medical anthropology. The goal of these efforts is not to reduce health and illness to biological terms and mechanisms; rather, it is to see human biology and health as inherently social and

A Companion to Medical Anthropology, First Edition. Edited by Merrill Singer and Pamela I. Erickson.

cultural. The question is not whether health is more biological or more cultural, but how health processes emerge and intersect as part of the "biocultural dance."

Most studies in the emerging arena of critical biocultural anthropology address the biological consequences of poverty and inequality. These approaches, in one way or the other, attempt to merge critical and political–economic perspectives with ecological and human adaptability perspectives, the later having long dominated biocultural anthropology. Efforts to build such a synthetic bridge have taken several labels, including the "Biology of Poverty" (Thomas 1998), "Critical and Humanistic Biology" (Blakey 1998), "Political Ecology of Biology and Health" (Baer 1996; Leatherman 2005), and "Critical Biocultural Medical Anthropology" (Singer 1998, 1999; Goodman and Leatherman 1998; Leatherman 1996). We use the term "critical biocultural" to locate this work at the intersection of critical medical and biocultural health studies.

Many biocultural studies do not fully consider political–economic processes and relations of power and inequality (i.e., the critical side of critical biocultural). However, most all acknowledge the importance of these processes in shaping human biology and health. Thus while the goal of this chapter is to outline the history and debates and highlight a few contributions of a "critical biocultural" approach to medical anthropology, we cast our net broadly around a range of important contributions to medical anthropology emerging from biocultural studies. The following review is biased toward contributions from biological anthropologists, since they have historically been the champions of a biocultural perspective and since their contributions have been less noted within medical anthropology (Sobo 2011, this volume). We first outline the emergence of critical biocultural approaches within anthropological studies of health and then discuss their place in medical anthropology and public health. We then review key areas of current research, and potential new directions for critical biocultural approaches.

EMERGENCE OF A CRITICAL BIOCULTURAL APPROACH

Sobo (this volume) notes that medical anthropology has been dominated historically by two broad perspectives: the symbolic/interpretive and the materialist (ecological and political economic). In the 1970s, as medical anthropology was growing as a defined subdiscipline of anthropology, bioculturally oriented medical anthropologists employed an ecological model of disease. This model initially was derived from epidemiology and framed as the interaction of host, pathogen and environment (Armelagos et al. 1992). It was used to examine specific human–environment interactions where disease or other biological indicators of stress were evident (ranging from malaria to nutritional deficiency to psychosocial stress). It also served as a framework for examining the evolution of disease and disease processes in contemporary human populations, often in terms of epidemiological transitions (Armelagos et al. 2005). In the ecological model, the host could be an individual or a group, the environment was composed of social and cultural as well as climatic and bio-geographic conditions, and pathogens were broadened from micro-parasites to a wider category of insults such as physical violence, psychosocial stressors, and anthropogenic toxins and pollutants.

The promise of such an integrative model in medical anthropology, and similarly holistic ecological models, led many to believe that anthropology had achieved a theoretically coherent integration of biological, ecological, and cultural domains (for a longer analysis see Goodman and Leatherman 1998). Yet, although medical ecological perspectives gained considerable acceptance, they only gained a "broad tacit consensus" (Landy 1983:187), and subsequently, such perspectives were found to be limited. Ecological models were critiqued for their closed systems, overly functionalist and homeostatic orientations, and explicit reliance on the biomedical models of disease. Singer (1989:223) sums up the critique from the critical medical perspective, stating "The flaws in medical ecology...arise ultimately from the failure to consider fully or accurately the role of social relations in the origin of health and illness."

At the same time that ecological models and the concept of adaptation were being reevaluated within cultural anthropology, critiques and reformulations were emerging from within evolutionary biology (Levins and Lewontin 1985) and biological anthropology (Armelagos et al. 1992; Goodman et al. 1988; Leatherman 1996; Thomas 1998). In the 1960s and early 1970s, human biologists were largely concerned with understanding adaptations to physical and biotic extremes. The initial assumption was that under stable, extreme conditions, human genetic adaptations would emerge and be identified by investigators. However, two decades of research showed that human populations exhibited many more developmental or ontogenetic responses than genetic responses to environmental stressors (Smith 1993). Thus, human adaptability and biological plasticity were recognized as the keys to understanding the adaptive process. It also became clear that groups living in challenging physical environments were often also living in social environments with limited access to means of production, wage work, political power, health care, and education. The resulting stressors with origins in relations of power, such as food insecurity and malnutrition, invariably had a greater impact on biology and health than did physical stressors such as high altitude and cold temperatures (e.g., Greksa 1986).

In the 1980s, the "small but healthy" debate brought into stark relief the theoretical and applied significance of how bodies were "read" and in particular the routine interpretation of small bodies as "adaptations" to low energy availability (Pelto and Pelto 1989:11). Developed by economist David Seklar (1981), the "small but healthy hypothesis asserts that individuals that are short due to mild to moderate malnutrition (MMM) are nonetheless healthy and well-adapted, particularly to the circumstances of marginal food availability" (Pelto and Pelto, 1989:11). Hence, economic and food resources need not be directed at them but rather, focused on the few who are suffering from more severe forms of malnutrition. In response, Raynaldo Martorell (1989) argued that while smaller people require fewer calories, their "smallness" entailed substantial social, behavioral and biological costs and Pelto and Pelto (1989:14) conclude, "...the concept of a 'no-cost' adaptation makes virtually no sense." The "small but healthy" debate was key to many anthropologists' re-examination of the adaptation concept, and alerted many to the political implications of their science, in this specific case, whether or not millions of MMM Indian children would receive food aid.

The small but healthy debate is linked to a broader critique of the "adaptationist programme" (Levins and Lewontin 1985; also Singer 1989; Leatherman 1996). The program is characterized by circular reasoning, a tendency to see all responses either adaptive or maladaptive, failure to specify contexts and appropriate units of adaptive response, as well as a tendency to quit early by failing to follow adaptive response across multiple dimensions including costs of responses. Perhaps the greatest problem, however, is the alienation of the human organism and environment, a vision of people passively responding to autonomous external environmental forces rather than recognizing their role in constructing the environments in which they operate (Lewontin 1995; Leatherman and Goodman 2005a).

Biocultural research in the 1990s increasingly became oriented toward documenting biological compromise or dysfunction in impoverished environments (as opposed to adaptations) and the biological impacts of social and economic change (Thomas 1998). Social environments took precedence over physical environments and measures of stressors expanded to include psychosocial stressors and their impact on health conditions such as hypertension and immune suppression (e.g., Blakey 1994; Dressler and Bindon 2000; Goodman et al. 1988; McDade 2002).

Yet, while it became relatively common to associate biological variation with some aspect of socio-economic variation, it was rare that the context or roots of the socio-economic variation were addressed. Similarly, research on "modernizing" populations documented how devastating such changes can be on human biology and health, but provided little or no information about processes of modernization (Bindon 1997). The socio-economic conditions, workloads, and environmental exposures that contribute to diminished health were conceptualized as *natural and even inevitable* aspects of changing environments, rather than contingent on history and social and economic relations.

Themes in a critical biocultural perspective

Beginning in the late 1980s, many biological and biocultural anthropologists turned from critiques of ecology and adaptation to working out models that could link social inequalities and human biology. These models lead to the emergence of critical biocultural medical anthropology, which we suggests offers new possibilities for anthropology generally and medical anthropology specifically. The following are some of the most salient themes (see also Goodman and Leatherman 1998). All but perhaps the last are clearly shared with critical medical anthropology. The last theme explicitly expands studies into the biological body.

Expanding geographic and historical scope   In alignment with anthropological political economy and critical medical anthropology, the first fundamental theme of critical-biocultural approach is to *expand the geographic and historical scope of analysis* to examine how nations, communities, populations, and even viral pathways (Garrett 1994) are inextricably inter-connected at regional, national, and global levels. By paying attention to this theme, we come to see the role of historical processes in shaping local environments, social relations, and hence human–environment relationships and health. For example, the poor health of Haitian workers on Bateys associated with sugar cane estates in the Dominican Republic is clearly linked to conditions of abject poverty, limited occupational opportunities, unhygienic environments, and limited access to health care (Simmons 2002). These conditions are not just unfortunate realities but products of a history of colonialism in the 18th century Caribbean, conflicts between Haiti and the Dominican Republic during the 19th century, and more recent human rights and migration policies that deny equal rights and access to resources to Haitian workers (Mintz 1985; Martinez 1995; Simmons 2002). Here, we wish to expand Wolf's (1983) effort to connect larger political economic processes from the cultures of "people without history" to their biologies as well. Understanding the roots of inequalities is a necessary first step toward posing solutions.

Relations of power and structural inequalities   A second theme is a focus not just on wealth and poverty but also *on the power relations that structure inequalities in society.* Absolute poverty is clearly related to poor health outcomes, but perceived inequalities are equally significant (Wilkinson 1996; Sen 1992). African–American males have life expectancies on par with individuals living in parts of rural India and China (Sen 1992) and infant mortality rates in the USA are well above those of other wealthy nations. Structured inequalities along the socio-political axes of race, class and, gender shape living conditions, exposure to pathogens, access to health care and other resources – and hence differentials in health (Schultz and Mullings 2006). To understand why black babies in the USA are twice as likely to die in their first year as white babies one needs to consider the intersections of gender, race, and class, and what this means for housing, employment, work stress, psychosocial stress, diet, and health care. The idea here is to move beyond identifying health disparities to a clear understanding of the inequalities that shape inequalities and these can take many forms.

Critical reflections on knowledge production   In addition to structuring lived experiences, power relations structure the production of knowledge. The third theme focuses on *critical reflections on science,* including the questions we ask, the methods and analyses we employ, the results we reach, how research is funded, and how it impacts peoples lives. If the social contexts of science and research are left unquestioned, then our subjectivities and assumptions are left unexamined. Often this has led to interpretations of inequality as inevitable and natural. A critical biocultural approach recognizes the inherent political dimensions of all research, whether explicit or implicit (e.g., political ramifications of the "small but healthy hypothesis"). Taking a critical perspective on scientific knowledge production, rather than being anti-scientific, as it is often portrayed, is a step towards a more reflective science.

Human agency   A fourth theme is a greater attention to human agency in constructing environments and actively and creatively coping with problems and uncertainties, and thus shaping the contexts of their own lived experiences. The goal here is a focus on the interplay between "structure and agency," how social relations are constructed through human actions and simultaneously serve to structure those actions. To say that peoples' actions contribute to the social and environmental contexts of their everyday lives in no way seeks to focus blame on their lifestyle choices as the cause of their health problems. Rather, the idea is to understand how inequalities constrain agency and thus create contexts where the costs inherent in social and behavioral responses to stress are likely to be amplified. Humans experience, perceive, and respond to conditions of vulnerability in different ways, shaped by their social and cultural position. It is always appropriate to ask 'adaptive for whom' and in 'what context'; who gains and who loses. As Krieger (2001:674) comments, it is important to think "critically and systematically about intimate and integral connections between our social and biological existence – and, especially in the case of social production of disease and ecosocial theory, to name explicitly who benefits from and is accountable for social inequalities in health."

Cultures create biologies   A final theme, elaborated below, is that critical biocultural approaches argue that in analyses seeking to capture the everyday realities of anthropological subjects, an *understanding of human biology and biological processes* can add a layer of information and viewpoint that is too often missed. Such analyses can reach below the skin to show how daily events, linked to political–economic processes, affect skinfold thicknesses, blood pressures, stress hormones, rates of parasitism and anemia, and cumulative fertility and mortality rates (see Dressler, this volume). Demonstrating these relationships often requires direct measures of biological status, and examinations of the biological processes linking local level experiences to biological outcomes. One arena in which we can see the focus on biology as illuminating processes of inequality is through enhanced understandings of the biological pathways involved in syndemics, the synergistic interaction of multiple diseases (or stressors) that amplify negative health consequences (Singer et al., this volume; Singer 2009; Singer and Clair 2003). The diseases that make up syndemics are often linked through pathways that connect in underlying conditions of poverty and structural inequalities.

CRITICAL BIOCULTURAL APPROACHES IN STUDIES OF HUMAN HEALTH

Points of articulation with medical anthropology and public health

Emphases on inequalities, power relations, and a critical examination of scientific inquiry align critical biocultural studies with critical medical anthropology. Tracing health inequalities upstream to the origins of inequalities is an essential starting point. However, critical biocultural approaches also broaden medical anthropology by seeking to consider evolutionary and ecological dynamics, prehistoric and historic as well as contemporary contexts, direct measures of human biology (often using biomarkers), and efforts to explicitly link the social and political to the biological; the specific mechanisms and processes through which inequalities get "under the skin" (Goodman 2006).

Interestingly, critical biocultural approaches in medical anthropology have much in common with developments in other disciplines, most notably the development of social epidemiological perspectives in public health as well as with critical perspectives in medical sociology and health geography (Cutchin 2007). They particularly share many features with Krieger's (2001) "ecosocial" approach in social epidemiology. Krieger (2001) argues for a social epidemiology that focuses upstream toward those structured inequalities that shape health disparities, but also sees the need to develop rigorous methods for making direct links between inequalities, biology, and health.

Points of distinction

As noted in the previous discussion, biocultural approaches distinguish themselves from critical medical approaches by their emphasis on biological processes (sometimes but not always including evolution) and rigorous (often standardized) methodologies. In earlier publications we argued that biological anthropologists have been reluctant to embrace new theoretical directions, and we linked this to an adherence to ecological and evolutionary models (Goodman and Leatherman 1998; Leatherman and Goodman 2005a). We did not suggest a change in paradigms as evolution is particularly important to some biocultural studies. What we did advocate for is the creation of a greater space for alternative perspectives that have much to add to our understandings of the biological impacts of poverty and inequality. Armelagos and co-workers (2005), for example, have recently articulated an evolutionary perspective on health and disease framed within epidemiological transitions that includes attention to political–economic processes and health inequalities. Indeed many insights in critical biocultural approaches were derived from evolutionary biologists (Levins and Lewontin 1985).

New work is extending many of Lewontin's (1995) earlier observations on the organism's role in constructing niches (Oddling-Smee et al. 2003), and in advancing understandings of phenotypic plasticity as a lifelong interaction of the triple helix of genes, organism, and environments, and in some cases, how this triple helix contributes to health inequalities. We have long known about the ways environmental stress affects early growth and how diminished adult stature is associated with impaired function, morbidity, and life expectancy (e.g., Martorell 1989). Recent research has extended these understanding to include the entire life course beginning with fetal development (e.g., Leidy 1996; Worthman and Kohrt 2005; Hales and Barker 2001) and to the intersections of disease processes. Wrting on syndemics, Singer (2009:55) states "Alterations of the emotions and mental health (owing to trauma or posttraumatic stress, for example), no less than physical diseases, can pave the way for other diseases to develop because our bodies *biologize emotional experience* (that is, transform it into bodily reactions and responses)." Attention to phenotypic plasticity and the developmental process through which individuals biologically internalize environmental experiences over their lives provides a means to begin specifying biological processes that link biology to life experience.

Biocultural anthropologists have used a diverse methodological tool kit which allows us to connect biology to cultural processes. Borrowing heavily from other fields, such measures include epidemiological, demographic, and nutritional assessment techniques, human energetics, and blood pressure, to more recent field assays of tissue levels of stress hormones, and immune function. What is particularly exciting is the growing ability to detect biological distress on the ground and early in the process.

Whether or not to "quantify" culture in similar ways is less clear and less developed, especially given the elusiveness of culture as an analytical category. Nevertheless, there are useful efforts at measuring components of shared culture and relating it to biology. Dressler (in this volume; 2005), for example, has developed measures of cultural consonance (degree to which individual's behavior approximate cultural prototypes). He and others have then related cultural consonance to health outcomes (using biomarkers) in a variety of projects such as on status inconsistency in Samoa (McDade 2002), on racial identity in Puerto Rico (Gravlee et al. 2005), and on culture and health in an African–American community in the southern USA (Dressler and Bindon 2000). Yet, while there are benefits to making dimensions of culture explicit, it is not necessary to quantify culture to make it central to biocultural analyses. What is important is to take culture seriously as it structures and is structured by human action, and to elicit the voices and perceptions of individuals with whom we work (Goodman 2006). Moreover, while standardized methodologies are common in biocultural studies, and of course in epidemiology as well, they can draw attention away from local contexts and appropriateness of measures. Roseberry (1998), for example, argues that households and other common units of analysis may not be stable across cultures or over time. In short, among all the methods biocultural anthropologists employ, there is no escaping the basic work of doing ethnography.

Themes in critical biocultural research

Biocultural anthropologists have increasingly focused on the biomedical consequences of social and ecological vulnerability. Here we briefly discuss four themes in critical biocultural research: social inequalities and health; populations in transition; bio-psychological stress and response; the biological consequences of race and racism. These themes are neither the only ones we could choose nor are they mutually exclusive. Rather we, present them because they are illustrative of studies that go beyond standard measures of socio-economic status to study vulnerabilities along multiple axes that include race, gender, income, occupation, and access to health care.

Social inequalities, nutrition and health   It is now well accepted that social inequalities underlay health disparities in a variety of contexts. It is also becoming clearer that inequalities are growing in contexts of globalization and present a major challenge to public health (Feachem 2000; Wilkinson 1996; Farmer 1999; Sen 1992; Kim et al. 2000; Janes and Korbett in this volume). Biocultural anthropologists have contributed to these observations over the past two decades through grounded research on the dialectical interactions among social inequalities, livelihoods, food security, nutrition, and illness.

In highland Peru, where much had been written on the biological impacts of high altitude environments (Baker and Little 1976), a research team in the early to mid-1980s investigated multiple dimensions of poverty, inequalities and health among small-scale farmers and herders (Thomas et al. 1988). This work illustrated how profound poverty and political marginalization resulting from centuries of exploitation, a failed agrarian reform, and the penetration of capitalist markets, were linked to diets, nutrition, health, coping capacity, and household production (Leatherman 1996, 2005). In short, social environments played a greater role than physical environments in human health. Poorer households with less secure access to land and few economic resources experienced worse nutrition and health and greater impacts of poor health on production and household livelihood. In this context, broad historical processes clearly shape social and economic vulnerabilities that lead to illness. As well, in conditions of constrained agency, illness furthers local conditions of vulnerability.

The FAO (2002) recently estimated that 840 million people in the world are undernourished and six million children under the age of five die each year from hunger. Thus, an important focus in critical biocultural studies has been to explore links between economic vulnerability, food security, diets and nutrition (see Himmelgreen and Romero-Daza, this volume). In an example from the global south, Panter-Brick and colleagues (2008b) recently examined multiple aspects of household livelihood and intra-familial malnutrition in Niger. They show how a host of structural and behavioral factors conspire to lead some children, but not others in the same family, to spiral down from mild to moderate to severe malnutrition. Families suffer from food insecurity especially when fathers migrated in search of work. Foods they could afford were of poor nutritional quality, families spent relatively large sums on malaria treatments, and children were weaned early due to a high premium on fertility or perceived inadequacy of breast milk. Their work shows both the necessity to consider many dimensions of class and culture to understand intra-household nutrition and also that development efforts must do more than provide basic access to food.

Links between poverty, hunger, and nutrition are also strongly implicated in the global obesity pandemic. Crooks' (1998) investigation of the relationships between poverty, diet, and obesity among poor families in Appalachia provide an example of the dynamics of these biocultural webs. Part of how poverty, diet and nutrition in Appalachia are linked is the consumption at home and in schools of caloric rich but nutrient poor foods. Home environments are linked to structures of parental work, perceptions about providing for the wants of their children, and child activity patterns. School environments offer the ready availability of calorie rich and nutrient poor snack foods because snack food concessions were one of the only sources of income for school-based extra-curricular activities in these impoverished counties. Thus, structures of poverty severely limit options for meeting personal, social, parental, and dietary goals and needs, and the result is the now global association between poverty and obesity.

Populations in transition   A deeper appreciation of history makes clear that humans are invariably in transition – from prehistoric shifts in foraging to food production to conquest and colonization, integration into capitalist economies, and tourism. Armelagos and colleagues (2005) frame the health consequences in terms of epidemiological transitions in disease patterns resulting from evolutionary, historical, and political–economic processes associated with social change. The first important social context of the epidemiological transition denotes shifts from foraging to food production, and entails substantial ecological impacts, reduced dietary diversity, and impaired nutrition and health. Goodman (1998) argues that political hierarchies and resource extraction from the peripheries to the center of precapitalist social formations played a key role in declining health in rural areas.

Colonization has had obvious health impacts through transmission of new diseases into previously unexposed populations, and the exploitation of environmental resources and labor. A well known case in point is the decimation of native populations in the Americas. Using historic records and modern epidemiological health surveys, Santos and Coimbra (1998) have researched the health effects of colonization on indigenous populations in Brazil through a series of historical events from initial contacts, to various economic booms and busts (rubber and timber), to more recent migrations of settlers into the Amazon. Their research and the extensive literature examining the biology of populations drawn into western ideologies and capitalist relations of production and consumption, for the most part, point to the damaging health effects of these transitions often glossed as "modernization." Yet, it is clear that transitions to market based economies can have negative, positive, and uneven effects on health (Leatherman 1994; Kennedy 1994; Dewey 1989; Pelto and Pelto 1983). This unevenness in the effects of markets on health and well being provides the rationale of a recent and extensive multidisciplinary biocultural investigation in medical anthropology: the Tsimane' Amazonian Panel Study (Leonard and Godoy 2008).

Tourism is a relatively new but increasingly common form of economic development. Like other forms of capitalist development, tourism can have uneven impacts on the economics, culture, nutrition and health of local groups. Recent research in the Yucatan of Mexico (Pi-Sunyer and Thomas 1997; Leatherman and Goodman 2005b) has demonstrated the impacts of tourism on the social life, economy, identity, and diets of Mayan communities drawn into the tourist economy. One aspect of this research has focused on dietary change commensurate with the commoditization of food systems and increased consumption of processed foods and 'junk' foods (Leatherman and Goodman 2005). Mexico is a leader in per-capita consumption of soft drinks, and poor children in Mayan communities may take in 20% of their calories through soft drinks and snack foods. Micro-nutrient deficiencies are evident in the diets of individuals with uneven access to secure jobs or sufficient land and labor to meet food needs through agricultural production. A pattern of undernourished and stunted children and overweight adults is emerging in these communities, which fits the pattern of emergent obesity and diabetes found in more urbanized areas of the Yucatan and elsewhere in the developing world.

Bio-psychological responses to stress   Since the early 1980s, biocultural anthropologists have focused on psychosocial stress as a pathway to link lived experiences to biology (Goodman et al. 1988). The stress perspective can be traced to the pioneering work of Hans Selye (1956) on the activation of adrenal cortical and medullary stress hormone pathway. Stressors can include an excess or dearth of stimuli, and range from noise, to hunger, to traumatic events, to frustrations and concerns over a host of lived experiences. Also, perception of stress is critical to physiological response. As well, the physiological pathways between stressful stimuli and biological responses are linked to a wide variety of health conditions, and studying these pathways can contribute to broad preventative efforts. Thus the stress perspective links culture, psychology, and political economy to a broad range of health conditions through specific physiological pathways and biological processes.

Biocultural anthropologists are now developing new methods for measuring stress responses in the field. Research has included a focus on stressful life events, social supports, and cultural consonance (Dressler 2005), status inconsistency (McDade 2002), war-related trauma (Panter-Brick et al. 2008a), and food insecurity (Hadley et al. 2008). Psychosocial stressors are then related to a series of biological outcomes such as child growth, blood pressure, cardiovascular disease, and more recently directly to stress hormones (e.g., salivary steroids) and immune function (e.g., EBV antibody level). A recent volume, *Measuring Stress in Humans*, by Ice and James (2007) provides an excellent overview of a wide range of uses in measuring stress, via catecholamines, cortisol, blood pressure, and immune function measurements. The "anthropological trick" is to not only bring these methods to the field but to connect these specific mechanisms to the larger ideological and political systems in which we live. For example, in the next section we note that racist acts (as stress events) are specific and content dependent, but are also connected in meaning and structure to broader historical and social system.

Panter-Brick and colleagues have conducted research on stress in contexts where these larger political, economic, and ideological systems are starkly evident, including among street children in Nepal (Panter-Brick 2002) and in war-torn Afghanistan

(Panter-Brick et al. 2008a). Their work in Afghanistan illustrates the sort of findings emerging from many settings of conflict, where stressors are often unevenly felt and in not entirely predictable ways. In contexts of war, political insecurity, and household and family vulnerability, they found that mental distress, prevalence of psychiatric disorders and biomarkers of stress (blood pressure and Epstein–Barr virus) were most prevalent among women and girls (i.e., significant gender differences were evident), but mapped more closely onto familial contexts and cultural prescriptions in Afghan society than to economic distress or exposure to war-related stressful events.

Critical perspectives on race and racism   Biological anthropologists have been at the forefront of questioning the naturalization of the idea of race (Blakey 1998). It is now widely accepted that race is not in our genes but rather, race becomes biological through discourses and practices. A key aspect of this work is a critical evaluation of how race is used in medical practice, specifically a systemic critique of the explanation of health differences by race as due to racial differences in genetics (Goodman 2000). As many have noted, "blaming" race-based health inequalities on genetics might work to maintain these inequalities by shifting attention away from structures of inequality and their effects on health. For example, the rise in diabetes among some Native Americans groups is often thought to be due to a genetic predisposition (Weiss et al. 1984). However, the contemporary variation in diabetes rates among Native North American groups is great, the rise in diabetes rates is a relatively recent phenomenon (Young 1994), and other groups experiencing similar shifts in diet and physical activity have experienced similar increases in the diabetes and related diseases. The diabetes pandemic provides an example of how large scale political economic change impacts local culture and ecology, in particular changing diets, activity patterns and sense of culture, and these then reach under the skin to increased insulin resistance, obesity, and diabetes.

Racism is both a powerful psychosocial stress and a structural inequality. Social epidemiologists have recently developed a number of interview and questionnaires that assess recent acts and perceptions of racism, racial discrimination, and racial harassment (Karlsen and Nazoo (2008) provide an excellent summary of this literature). In general, epidemiologists attempt to develop methods that work in a wide variety of contexts, but the context of gestures and actions is extremely important. As well, most measures of racism focus on interpersonal issues and miss connections to the historic and structural features of the political-economy of racism. Recently, medical anthropologists working with critical biocultural perspectives have begun to address some of the inadequacies in these approaches in exploring how the lived experience of race and racism might lead to health differences. For example, Dressler and Bindon (2000) have linked the realities of being African–American in the southern USA to cultural consonance, or the ability of individuals to approximate in their own behavior the shared cultural models of their society. Lack of consonance was associated with elevated blood pressure. In the end, they note that the inability to achieve the perceived goals associated with local cultural models might be anticipated for African–Americans in racist societies where frequent unemployment, low wages, and poor living conditions are part of the lived experience for many. Gravlee and co-workers (2005) begin with an ethnographic understanding of the meaning of skin color in

Puerto Rico, and demonstrate how those local meanings mediated experiences of racism and stress in specific local contexts; connecting social categories of race/color with socioeconomic status incongruities and blood pressure. These analyses offer a social, cultural, and environmentally based explanation for the racial variation in blood pressure found in much medical and public health research.

NEW DIRECTIONS

As critical biocultural anthropologists increasingly integrate anthropological political–economic perspectives into their research, they may continue to develop by drawing upon new theoretical developments. As a start, notions of structural violence (Farmer 2004; see also Briggs and Briggs 2003; Briggs, this volume) and biological citizenship (Petryna 2005) might be useful. These two concepts are gaining wide currency in medical anthropology, but are as of yet underutilized in biocultural approaches.

Structural violence

The work of the physician–anthropologist Paul Farmer stands out as an exemplary model for a critical biocultural medical anthropology in that his work combines rich history, political economy, and assessments of health while also putting people's experiences, stories, and words in the foreground. In *AIDS and Accusation* (1992), Farmer links the epidemiology of HIV/AIDS and stories of personal suffering to local level conditions of extreme vulnerability, framed within the political–economic history of Haiti and in USA discourses on Haiti as the source for HIV/AIDS.

His framing of dimensions of vulnerability using the concept of structural violence (Farmer 2004) has resonated widely in medical anthropology, and might be particularly useful for biocultural anthropologists. Structural violence attempts to capture the extremes of poverty and social and political marginalization, often expressed along axes of race, class, and gender, and how these deny access to resources, constrain agency, and limit human potential. Structural violence is embedded in ubiquitous social structures and normalized by stable institutions and regular experience. This *normalization* and *regularization* often renders it invisible and silent, part of the social machinery of oppression (Farmer 2004:307).

Within a critical biocultural approach to health, structural violence denotes the ways inequalities promote malnutrition and disease, and increase the vulnerabilities to their effects. It can manifest as chronic hunger and poverty, pollution and environmental degradation, military and police brutality, and unequal and inadequate housing, education, and health care. Farmer (2004) specifies that an analysis of structural violence and health must combine history, political economy, and biology. Too often, one or more of these key features is erased or ignored; and this limits our ability to explain the causes of malnutrition, disease, and other *biological outcomes of social processes*. For biological anthropologists working with a biocultural perspective and used to measuring biology and local environments, this approach suggests further the need to pay more attention to history and political economy.

Biocultural studies of conflict and violence   Given that structural violence shapes the ways inequalities promote malnutrition and disease, and increase the vulnerabilities to their effects, it is also often a precursor to direct violence; as political violence of the state or interpersonal violence of everyday life (Bourgois 2001). Thus, it can be particularly useful in thinking about the health costs of armed conflict and other forms of violence. The anthropology of violence is a growing theme in socio-cultural anthropology but relative new and unexplored within critical biocultural approaches. Nevertheless, biocultural anthropologists are beginning to study the social, psychosocial, and biological consequences of conflict and violence. The work of Panter-Brick and colleagues (2008a) has already been mentioned. In studies of historic and prehistoric groups, Michael Blakey (2001) and Debra Martin (2008) show how biological signatures of structural violence made be read from skeletons. In Martin's (2008) case study from the La Plata River (AD 200–1300) in northwest New Mexico, she documents the effects of forced captivity especially among women and children, and situates this analysis within a broad biocultural framework to examine the political–economic factors that maintain and perpetuate violence.

Leatherman and Thomas (2008) have used structural violence as a framing concept to examine the real and potential impacts of the 20 year civil war between *Sendero Luminoso* and the Peruvian state on the lives and livelihood of Andean communities in southern Peru. The roots of armed conflicts and violence are found in the inequalities born of structural violence, and the consequences on health and health systems have both immediate and long-term consequences. Thus, one goal of ongoing work on the costs of conflict in the Andes (Leatherman and Thomas 2008) was to identify the conditions of structural violence that led to the political violence of civil war, and how the impacts of conflict might serve to reinforce and transform patterns of structural violence currently affecting highland populations. Precursors to revolution included severe poverty, political marginalization, racism, and poor health, all of which are rooted in a history of conquest and colonization, in post-colonial exploitation of rural producers by the landed oligarchy, and the intense frustration of a failed agrarian reform, topped off in the 1980s by a catastrophic economic crisis. The impacts included severe food insecurity, fear, psychosocial trauma, mistrust, and disrupted social relations that persist today and will likely continue to affect future livelihood strategies that were historically based in part on patterns of social cooperation and reciprocity. Yet these large scale changes were uneven in how they got under the skin: some individuals showed great resilience and others heightened vulnerability. The civil war also influenced major – and uneven – shifts in land tenure and political power, which in some ways have served to benefit local indigenous peoples. Thus, these impacts have subtly shifted the very nature of inequality, marginality, and vulnerability in the region.

Biological citizenship

The notion of biological citizenship is even less developed in biocultural studies but has obvious points of articulation with critical biocultural anthropologies. Rose and Novas (2005) describe biological citizenship as encompassing all citizenship projects that link conceptions of citizens to beliefs about their biology. In other words, it refers to the way biological presuppositions explicitly or implicitly structure the discourses and practices of individuals and authorities. The examples are many, and there are obvious ways these ideas resonate with critical perspectives on racialized biologies. However, current uses of the concept tend go beyond racialization and include myriad ways that groups may shape their own identity based on biology and use this identity to advocate for rights, resources, and even research (in the case of genetic disorders).

One example of biological citizenship is provided by the work of Adriana Petryna (2005) on the aftermath of the 1986 disaster at the Chernobyl power plant. She describes how in the Ukraine, where democratization (following the dissolution of the USSR) was linked to a harsh market transitions, that the injured biology of a population became the basis for social membership and staking claims to citizenship. The individuals who suffered the ill consequences of radiation exposure, or who believed that they suffered from exposure, asserted their rights to health services and social support from the state in the "name of their damaged biological bodies." Because of ambiguities in the science of exposure and categorization of suffering, whole new dynamics of science and politics emerged with very real effects on population welfare.

On a broader level, advocacy around specific diseases based on biological citizenship is increasingly common and is part of the terrain of scientific research. The collective advocacy around HIV/AIDS provides one of the best examples. We might also think about future collectives – war veterans returning with brain damage from Iraq, or groups organizing around threats to their biology from environmental contamination. Such acts of biological citizenship would seem to provide particularly rich avenues for critical biocultural research; research that demands a thorough knowledge and integration of biology and culture.

Today, individuals and whole populations are valued for their genes, ranging from people afflicted with a recognized genetic disorder, to those considered more isolated or "native", to Icelanders who sold rights to their genomes. They use their positions to advocate for research, to become partners in research, and in the case of the Human Genome Diversity Project, to assert property rights over their own genetic material and deny scientists access to their genome. As new reproductive technologies allow ever early detection of many genetic variations and personal genomes become more affordable, an age of "flexible eugenics" (Taussig et al. 1998) is emerging. We can expect new debates over what is genetically normal, over reproductive rights, and over the use of biotechnology to modify bodies. These are issues to which critical biocultural approaches are aptly suited and ones likely to draw some critical biocultural anthropologists into new collaborations.

Conclusions

Biocultural approaches in medical anthropology have at times occupied center stage and at times have sat on the intellectual periphery. In the later half of the 20th century a "chasm" developed between biological and culture perspectives in anthropology and this was nowhere more evident than in medical anthropology. Yet, there is no escaping that human health – the focus of medical anthropology – is quintessentially a biocultural phenomenon. The question ought not to be whether to engage with biology, rather, it ought to focus us on how biocultural approaches might best enhance our understanding of biology and health in social and cultural contexts. We argue here for approaches we have termed critical biocultural that lie at the intersection of critical medical and biocultural studies of health. Like Farmer's (2004) anthropology of structural violence, or Baer and Singer's (2009) examination of the political ecology of global warming, critical biocultural approaches link human biology and health to social inequalities by drawing together large scale political–economy processes, culture, and biology. They begin with an explicit recognition that health disparities emerge from social inequalities, and that efforts to specify the source and nature of those inequalities is a critical task of medical anthropology. The sources of inequalities, whether they link to political oppression, poor access to markets, structured barriers to land ownership, or failed education and health care systems, are not trivial. The root causes of poverty or inequality shape the forms they take, discourses and practices, efforts to alleviate the problem, and these are all key to a more complete and "critical" biocultural approach in medical anthropology.

We are optimistic that such critical approaches can help bridge the divide between biology and culture in medical anthropology. Indeed, steps toward rapprochement between biocultural and critical medical anthropologies are well underway (see Baer 1996; Morsy 1996; also Singer 1998, 1999). The emergence of political ecology as a cross-disciplinary effort (e.g., in geography, anthropology, history, feminist theory, sociology, etc.) toward a "novel reformulation of the relationship between society and nature, humans and environment, biology and history" (Hvalkof and Escobar 1998:425) has helped make a "political–ecology of health" central in medical anthropology; a political ecology of biology and health is yet another way of framing critical biocultural approaches (Leatherman 2005).

The global health problems we face now and in the future are endless, but as Richard Feachem (2000) stated in the first issues of the *Bulletin of the World Health Organization* for the 21st century, addressing the health consequences of social inequalities is the most important global health task for the 21st century. We need a full range of anthropological perspectives to meet this task, and biocultural perspectives are particularly important for specifying the biological as well as social dimensions linking inequalities and health. Addressing these issues will call on us to expand our perspectives in new directions and build new collaboration across disciplines. Two examples of ways to extend biocultural perspectives into discussions of structural violence and biological citizenship were offered here. These are but two of many potential directions critical biocultural research could take. The key is how to apply these and other perspectives in new ways that enhance understandings and promote improvements in human health. Indeed, "integrating biological and socio-cultural perspectives in concrete and project oriented situations" (Hvalkof and Escobar 1998:443) may be the best means of achieving a biocultural synthesis.

REFERENCES

Armelagos, George, Tom Leatherman, Mary Ryan, and Lynn Sibley, 1992 Biocultural Synthesis in Medical Anthropology. Medical Anthropology 14:35–52.

Armelagos, George, Peter Brown, and Bethany Turner, 2005 Evolutionary, Historical and Political Economic Perspectives on Health and Disease. Social Science and Medicine 61:755–765.

Baker, Paul T., and Michael A. Little, eds., 1976 Man in the Andes: A Multidisciplinary Study of High-Altitude Quechua. Stoudsburg PA: Dowden, Hutchinson and Ross.

Baer, Hans, 1996 Toward a Political Ecology of Health in Medical Anthropology. Medical Anthropology Quarterly 10(4):451–454.

Baer, Hans, and Merrill Singer, 2009 Global Warming and the Political Ecology of Health: Emerging Crises and Systemic Solutions. Walnut Creek CA: Left Coast Press.

Bindon, James, 1997 Coming of Age of Human Adaptability Studies in Samoa. *In* Human Adaptability Past, Present and Future. Stanley J. Ulijasek and Rebecca Huss-Ashmore, eds. pp. 126–156. Oxford: Oxford University Press.

Blakey, Michael L., 1994 Psychophysiological Stress and Disorders of Industrial Society: A Critical Theoretical Formulation for Biocultural Research. *In* Diagnosing America: Anthropology and Public Engagement. Shepard Forman, ed. pp. 149–192. Ann Arbor: University of Michigan Press.

Blakey. Michael L., 1998 Beyond European Enlightenment: Toward a Critical and Humanistic Human Biology. *In* Building a New Biocultural Synthesis: Political Economic Perspectives in Biological Anthropology. Alan Goodman and Thomas Leatherman, eds. pp. 379–405. Ann Arbor: University of Michigan Press.

Blakely, Michael L., 2001 Bioarcheology of the African Diaspora in the Americas: Its Origin and Scope. Annual Reviews of Anthropology 30:387–422.

Bourgois, Phillipe, 2001 The Power of Violence in War and Peace. Post Cold-War Lessons from el Salvador. Ethnography 2(1):5–34.

Briggs, Charles, and Clara Mantini-Briggs, 2003 Stories in the Time of Cholera: Racial Profiling during a Medical Nightmare. Berkeley: University of California Press.

Crooks, Deborah, 1998 Poverty and Nutrition in Eastern Kentucky: the Political Economy of Childhood Growth. *In* Building a New Biocultural Synthesis: Political Economic Perspectives in Biological Anthropology. Alan Goodman and Thomas Leatherman, eds. pp. 339–358. Ann Arbor: University of Michigan Press.

Cutchin, Malcom, 2007 The Need for the "New Health Geography" in Epidemiologic Studies of Environment and Health. Health and Place 13:735–742.

Dewey, Katherine, 1989 Nutrition and the Commoditization of Food Systems in Latin America. Social Science and Medicine 28:415–424.

Dressler, William, 2005 What's Cultural about Bio*cultural* Research? Ethos 33(1):20–45.

Dressler, William, and James Bindon, 2000 The Health Consequences of Cultural Consonance: Cultural Dimensions of Lifestyle, Social Support, and Arterial Blood Pressure in an African American Community. American Anthropologist 102(2):244–260.

FAO, 2002 The State of Food Insecurity in the World, 2002. Rome: Food and Agricultural Organization.

Farmer, Paul, 1992 Aids and Accusation: The Geography of Blame. Berkeley: University of California Press.

Farmer, Paul, 1999 Infections and Inequalities: the Modern Plagues. Berkeley: University of California Press.

Farmer, Paul, 2004 An Anthropology of Structural Violence. Current Anthropology 45(3):305–325.

Feachem, R. G. A., 2000 Editorial: Poverty and Inequity: a Proper Focus for the New Century. Bulletin of the World Health Organization78(1):1–2.

Garrett, Laurie, 1994 The Coming Plague: Newly Emerging Diseases in a World Out of Balance. New York: Farrar, Straus & Giroux.

Goodman, Alan, 1998 The Biological Consequences of Inequality in Antiquity. *In* Building a New Biocultural Synthesis: Political Economic Perspectives in Biological Anthropology. Alan Goodman and Thomas Leatherman, eds. pp. 147–169. Ann Arbor: University of Michigan Press.

Goodman, Alan, 2000 Why Genes Don't Count (for Racial Differences in Health). American Journal of Public Health. 90(11):1699–1702.

Goodman, Alan, 2006 Seeing Culture in Biology. *In* The Nature of Difference: Science, Society and Human Biology. G. Ellison and Alan Goodman, eds. pp. 225–241. London: Taylor and Francis.

Goodman, Alan, and Thomas Leatherman, 1998 Traversing the Chasm Between Biology and Culture: An Introduction. *In* Building a New Biocultural Synthesis: Political Economic Perspectives in Biological Anthropology. Alan Goodman and Thomas Leatherman, eds. pp. 3–43. Ann Arbor: University of Michigan Press.

Goodman, Alan, R. Brooke Thomas, Alan Swedlund, and George J. Armelagos 1988 Biocultural Perspectives on Stress in Prehistoric, Historical and Contemporary Population Research. Yearbook of Physical Anthropology 31:169–202.

Gravlee, Clarence, William Dressler, and Russell Bernard, 2005 Skin Color Social Classification, and Blood Pressure in Southeastern Puerto Rico. American Journal of Public Health 95(12):2191–2197.

Greksa, Lawrence, 1986 Growth Patterns of 9–20 Year Old European and Aymara High Altitude Natives. Current Anthropology 27(1):72–74.

Hadley, C., A. Tegegn, F. Tessema, J. A. Cowan, M. Asefa, and S. Galea 2008 Food Insecurity, Stressful Life Events and Symptoms of Anxiety and Depression in East Africa: Evidence from the Gilgel Gibe Growth and Development Study. Journal of Epidemilogy and Community Health 62:980–986.

Hales, C. N., and D. J. P Barker, 2001 The Thrifty Phenotype Hypothesis. British Medical Bulletin 60:5–20.

Hvalkof, S., and A. Escobar, 1998 Nature, Political Ecology, and Social Practice: Toward an Academic and Political Agenda. *In* Building a New Biocultural Synthesis: Political Economic Perspectives in Biological Anthropology. Alan Goodman and Thomas Leatherman, eds. pp. 425–450. Ann Arbor: University of Michigan Press.

Ice, Gillian, and Gary James, eds., 2007 Measuring Stress in Humans: A Practical Guide for the Field. New York: Cambridge University Press.

Karlsen, Saffron, and James Y. Nazroo, 2008 Measuring and Analyzing "Race," Racism, and Racial Discrimination. *In* Methods in Social Epidemiology 86–111.

Kennedy, Eileen, 1994 Health and Nutrition Effects of Commercialization of Agriculture. *In* Agricultural Commercialization, Economic Development, and Nutrition. Joachim Braun and Eileen Kennedy, eds. pp. 79–99. Baltimore: The Johns Hopkins University Press.

Kim, Jim Yong, Joyce Millen, Alec Irwin, and John Gersham, 2000 Dying for Growth: Global Inequality and the Health of the Poor. Monroe, Maine: Common Courage Press.

Kreiger, Nancy, 2001 Theories for Social Epidemiology in the 21st Century: an Eco-social Perspective. International Journal of Epidemiology 30:668–677.

Landy, David, 1983 Medical Anthropology: A Critical Appraisal. *In* Advances in Medical Sciences. J. Ruffini, ed. 1:185–314.

Leatherman, Thomas, 1994 Health Implications of Changing Agrarian Economies in the Southern Andes. Human Organization 53(4):371–380.

Leatherman, Thomas, 1996 A Biocultural Perspective on Health and Household Economy in Southern Peru. Medical Anthropology Quarterly 10(4):476–495.

Leatherman, Thomas, 2005 A Space of Vulnerability in Poverty and Health: Political Ecology and Biocultural Analyses. Ethos 33(1):46–70.

Leatherman, Thomas, and Alan Goodman, 2005a Context and Complexity in Human Biological Research. *In* Complexities: Beyond Nature and Nurture. S. Mckinnon and S. Silverman, eds. pp. 179–195. Chicago: University of Chicago Press.

Leatherman, Thomas, and Alan Goodman, 2005b Coca-colonization of Diets in the Yucatan. Social Science and Medicine 61(4):833–846.

Leatherman, Thomas, and R. Brooke Thomas, 2008 Structural Violence, Political Violence and the Health Costs of Civil Conflict: a Case Study from Peru. *In* Anthropology and Public Health: Bridging Differences in Culture and Society, 2nd edition. Robert A. Hahn and Marcia C. Inhorn, eds. pp. 196–220. Oxford: Oxford University Press.

Leidy, Lynette, 1996 Lifespan Approaches to the Study of Human Biology: An Introductory Overview. American Journal of Human Biology 8:699–702.

Leonard, William, and Ricardo Godoy, 2008 Tsimane' Amazonian Panel Study. Economics and Human Biology 6(2):299–301.

Levins, Richard, and Richard Lewontin, 1985 The Dialectical Biologist. Cambridge: Harvard University Press.

Lewontin, Richard, 1995 Genes, Environment, and Organisms. In Hidden Histories of Science, Robert Silver, ed. New York: A New York Review Book.

Martin, Debra L., 2008 Ripped Flesh and Torn Souls: Evidence for Slavery in the Prehistoric Southwest, AD 800–1500. In Invisible Citizens: Captives and Their Consequences. C. Cameron, ed. pp. 159–180. Salt Lake City: University of Utah Press.

Martinez, Samuel, 1995 Peripheral Migrants: Haitians and Dominican Republic Sugar Plantations. Knoxville: University of Tennessee Press.

Martorell, Reynaldo, 1989 Body Size, Adaptation and Function. Human Organization 48:15–20.

McDade, Thom, 2002 Status Incongruity in Samoan Youth: a Biocultural Analysis of Culture Change, Stress and Immune Function. Medical Anthropology Quarterly 16:123–150.

Mintz, Sydney, 1985 Sweetness and Power: The Place of Sugar in Modern History. New York: Viking Press.

Morsy, Soheir, 1996 More than Dialogue: Contributions to the Recapturing of Anthropology. Medical Anthropology Quarterly 10(4):516–518.

Oddling-Smee, F. John, Kevin M. Laland, and Marcus W. Feldman, 2003 Niche Construction: The Neglected Process in Evolution. Monographs in Population Biology 37. Princeton: Princeton University Press.

Panter-Brick, Catherine, 2002 Street Children, Human Rights and Public Health: A Critique and Future Directions. Annual Review of Anthropology 31:147–171.

Panter-Brick, Catherine, Mark Eggerman, Aman Mojadidi, and Thomas McDade, 2008a Social Stressors, Mental Health and Physiological Stress in an Urban Elite of Young Afghans in Kabul. American Journal of Human Biology. 20:627–641.

Panter-Brick, Catherine, K. Kilpatrick, and K. Casiday, 2008b Saving Lives, Preserving Livelihoods: Understanding Risk, Decision Making, and Child Health in a Food Crisis. Social Science and Medicine 68(4):758–765.

Pelto, Gretel H., and Pertti J. Pelto, 1983 Diet and Delocalization: Dietary Changes since 1750. Journal of Interdisciplinary History 14:507–528.

Pelto, Gretel H., and Pertti J. Pelto, 1989 Small But Healthy? An Anthropological Perspective. Human Organization 48(1):11–15.

Petryna, Adriana, 2005 Life Exposed: Biological Citizens After Chernobyl. Princeton: Princeton University Press.

Pi-Sunyer, Oriole, and R. Brooke Thomas, 1997 Tourism, Environmentalism and Cultural Survival in Quintana Roo, Mexico. In Life and Death Matters: Human Rights and the Environment at the End of the Millenium. Barbara Johnston, ed. pp. 187–212. Walnut Creek, CA: AltaMira Press.

Rose, Nikolas, and Carlos Novas, 2005 Biological Citizenship. In Global Assemblages: Technology, Politics and Ethics as Anthropological Problems. Aihwa Ong and Stephen Collier, eds., pp. 439–463. Oxford: Blackwell.

Roseberry, William, 1998 Political Economy and Social Fields. In Building a New Biocultural Synthesis: Political–Economic Perspectives in Biological Anthropology. Alan H. Goodman and Thomas L. Leatherman, eds. pp.75–91. Ann Arbor: University of Michigan Press.

Santos, Ricardo, and Carlos Coimbra, 1998 On the (Un)natural History of the Tupi-Monde Indians: Bioanthropology and Change in the Brazilian Amazon. In Building a New Biocultural Synthesis: Political Economic Perspectives in Biological Anthropology. Alan Goodman and Thomas Leatherman, eds. pp. 269–294. Ann Arbor: University of Michigan Press.

Schultz, Amy J., and Leith Mullings, eds., 2006 Gender, Race, Class and Health: Intersectional Approaches. San Francisco: Jossey-Bass.

Sekler, David, 1981 Small but Healthy: A Basic Hypothesis in the Theory, Measurement and Policy of Malnutrition. *In* Newer Concepts in Nutrition and their Implications for Policy. P. V. Sukharme, ed. pp. 127–137. Pune, India: Maharashtra Association for the Cultivation of Science Research Institute.

Selye, Hans, 1956 The Stress of Life. McGraw-Hill: New York.

Sen, Amartya, 1992 Inequality Re-examined: Cambridge, MA: Harvard University Press.

Simmons, David, 2002 Walk of Death on a Dominican Batey. Anthropology News, 43(1).

Singer, Merrill, 1989 The Limitations of Medical Ecology: The Concept of Adaptation in the Context of Social Stratification and Social Transformation. Medical Anthropology 10(4):218–229.

Singer, Merrill, 1998 The Development of Critical Medical Anthropology: Implications for Biological Anthropology. *In* Building a New Biocultural Synthesis: Political Economic Perspectives in Biological Anthropology. Alan Goodman and Thomas Leatherman, eds., pp. 93–123. Ann Arbor: University of Michigan Press.

Singer, Merrill, 1999 Toward a Critical Biocultural Model of Drug Use and Health Risk. *In* Integrating Cultural, Observational, and Epidemiological Approaches in the Prevention of Drug Abuse and HIV/AIDS. Patricia Marshall, Merrill Singer, and Michael Clatts, eds., pp. 26–49. Bethesda: US Department of Health and Health Services, National Institutes of Health.

Singer, Merrill, 2009 Introduction to Syndemics: A Systems Approach to Public and Community Health. San Francisco: Jossey-Bass.

Singer, Merrill, and Scott Clair, 2003 Syndemics and Public Health: Reconceptualizing Disease in Bio-Social Context. Medical Anthropology Quarterly 17(4):423–441.

Smith, M. O., 1993 Physical Anthropology. *In* The Development of Southeastern Archaeology. J. K. Johnson, ed., pp. 53–77. Tuscaloosa AL: University of Alabama Press.

Taussig, Karen-Sue, Rayna Rap, and Deborah Heath, 1998 Flexible Eugenics: Technologies of the Self in the Age of Genetics. *In* Genetic Nature/Culture: Anthropology and Science Beyond the Two-Culture Divide. Alan Goodman, Deborah Heath, and Susan Linde, eds., pp. 58–76. Berkeley: University of California Press.

Thomas, Brooke, 1998 The Biology of Poverty. *In* Building a New Biocultural Synthesis: Political Economic Perspectives in Biological Anthropology. Alan Goodman and Thomas Leatherman, eds., pp. 43–74. Ann Arbor: University of Michigan Press.

Thomas, Brooke, Tom Leatherman, James Carey, and Jere D. Haas, 1988 Biosocial Consequences of Illness Among Small Scale Farmers: A Research Design. *In* Capacity for Work in the Tropics. K. J. Collins and D. E. Roberts, eds., pp. 249–276. New York: Cambridge University Press.

Weiss, Kenneth, R. Ferrell, and C. L. Hanis, 1984 A New World Syndrome of Metabolic Diseases with a Genetic and Evolutionary Basis. Yearbook of Physical Anthropology 27:153–178.

Wilkinson, R. G., 1996 Unhealthy Societies: the Afflictions of Inequality. London: Routledge.

Worthman, Carol M., and Brandon Kohrt, 2005 Receding Horizons of Health: Biocultural Approaches to Public Health Paradoxes. Social Science and Medicine 61(4): 861–878.

Young, T. Kue, 1994. The Health of Native Americans: Toward a Biocultural Epidemiology. New York: Oxford University Press.

CHAPTER 3

Applied Medical Anthropology: Praxis, Pragmatics, Politics, and Promises

Robert T. Trotter, II

INTRODUCTION

Applied medical anthropology is a natural extension of basic anthropology theory and methods into a practical exploration of the relationships between culture, society, health, healing, and the definition of distress and disease, with the ultimate goal of deliberately improving health, healing, medicine, and the overall well being of individuals, communities, cultures, and societies.

Modern applied medical anthropology has its roots in the earliest exploration of cultural differences in the common everyday experiences that shape peoples' lives (Rylko-Bauer et al. 2006). While some areas of anthropological research draw heavily on a relatively narrow range of theory and methods, applied medical anthropology tends to draw from all of the primary and secondary areas of anthropological theory. This empirical and eclectic approach often produces crucial new links between different theoretical perspectives and viewpoints within anthropology. It also challenges, supports, expands, and even defeats theoretical paradigms from psychology, economics, political science, public health, epidemiology, and other parts of the biomedical and health research spectrum.

One of the virtually unique conditions that applies to medical anthropology in general, and applied medical anthropology in particular, is the confluence between the very American cultural ideal of a synthesis of the theory and methods embodied in a four field approach to anthropology (socio-cultural anthropology, linguistic anthropology, biological anthropology, and archeology or prehistoric anthropology). Many US anthropology programs have stubbornly clung to the

A Companion to Medical Anthropology, First Edition. Edited by Merrill Singer and Pamela I. Erickson.

desire to maintain all four fields in their undergraduate and graduate programs, in the face of both intellectual challenges and the tendency to fragment into competing departments or programs as is common in Europe. Medical anthropology has benefited from this stubbornness by producing individuals who are both comfortable and competent in multidisciplinary, multi-theory, multi-foci projects and programs.

Applied medical anthropology has also been strongly impacted by external theoretical and methodological pressures, as well as discipline specific values, theories, and dialogs from the biomedical sciences and from the other social sciences. In many ways, that impact has clearly moved and modified anthropological theory in both directions. There are numerous instances where other disciplines, theoretical approaches, and values have been significantly influenced by medical anthropology. However, the reverse is equally true. One of the reasons for the growth of applied medical anthropology is the size of resources that are devoted to medicine and the health care industries in the United States and the success that medical anthropologists have had in competing for those resources because of a partial change that has occurred in the biomedical paradigm. Also at work here is the expertise of medical anthropologists in culture theory and qualitative (exploratory, formative, comparative) methods and the demonstrated value of these in the health domain.

Applied medical anthropology is full of interesting dualities, competitions, and correspondences. Two of the most commonly addressed paradigms are the biomedical model, which embodies a strong orientation towards positivism and modernism (logic, evolutionary change, and progress through scientific research), and American individualism, which embodies the ideals of self determinism and free will (resulting in a focus on psychosocial dynamics such as self efficacy, individual responsibility, and competence). A good deal of applied medical anthropology hinges on a dynamic balance between universalism (from the search for biomedical certainties to international classifications of diseases, syndromes, and conditions), and particularism or cultural (and individual) relativism in which everyone participates in a unique life experience and constantly constructs and reconstructs their perception of reality, and of themselves, through a post-modern lens.

This chapter explores the eclectic nature of applied medical anthropology theory, applications, and opportunities. The following sections address or exemplify several important issues, approaches, and challenges that applied medical anthropology has contributed to medical anthropology in general and anthropology as a whole. These include the role of theory in applied medical anthropology as it is has been impacted by various theoretical viewpoints from other disciplines; the numerous contributions that medical anthropology has made in the development of highly useful research methods while also expanding the methodological tool kits of the other social and biomedical sciences and humanities, examples of the relationship between midrange theory and applied medical anthropology methods, and the central place of ethics in applied medical anthropology. Given the history of my own research, many of the examples I draw on come from the applied arenas of HIV/AIDS and drug use or health organization evaluation research but the relevance of the issues under discussion crosscut the specific health-related concerns addressed in applied medical anthropology.

THEORY IN APPLIED MEDICAL ANTHROPOLOGY

There is nothing so practical as a good theory.

Historical or "grand" theory in anthropology

There are a number of very solid contemporary books on anthropological theory, mostly presented as a historical progression of both positivist and humanistic dialogs and developments. That approach provides students with an interesting view of the anthropological theoretical debate as a dialectic process of point, counterpoint and synthesis, leading to new (often labeled "neo") iterations of the basic theories and counter theories. These theoretical paradigms are sometimes labeled "grand theory" and, for some anthropologists, function more as foundational philosophies for understanding culture and human behavior than hypothesis-generating "testable theory." In contrast, the other social sciences predominantly consider testable theory as the "gold standard." The distinction between adherence to "grand theory," as opposed to a practical focus on testable midrange theory is one of the common distinctions between applied and non-applied medical anthropology.

The primary theoretical threads in anthropology can be cataloged as one of five cultural themes, with associated subthemes that accommodate competing definitions and explications of the basic theories. The five themes include: (1) evolutionary theories that focus on creating an understanding of individual, social and cultural "change through time"; (2) cognitive or cultural domain theories that explore the relationships between what and how people think, and what and how they behave – these theories explore the shared mental processes that exist primarily within human minds (e.g., thought processes, beliefs, emotions, knowledge, etc.) and how those processes link to the observable behaviors that those same individuals exhibit (behaviors, actions, etc.); (3) theories about the structures that humans create and the organization of human behavior beyond the individual level (within kinship, social networks, associations); (4) theories of human manipulations of symbols (the domains of linguistic anthropology, symbolic anthropology, communication theories, etc.); and (5) the theories that explore integrated cultural–ecological relationships (biology and behavior interactions at multiple levels), including relationships of humans to the biological and physical environments within and surrounding them.

To theorize or not to theorize; When to theorize without putting the cart before the horse (or Descartes before De Horst)

Anthropology is unique amongst the social sciences in having three different but defensible theoretical frames that are determined by the nature of the ethnographic research process. One justifiable research configuration in applied medical anthropology is conducting "atheoretical" research. In this form, no explicit explanatory or exploratory theory is adopted or expected to emerge. This approach is used predominantly in descriptive projects with the intent of presenting an "insider" view of a culture and adopting a culturally relativistic stance that avoids critique or cultural shaping from alternative viewpoints. If theory emerges from this approach, it does so because of the use of cross-cultural comparison and analogy, rather than systematic interpretation from another viewpoint. A second approach is to use an anthropological version of "Grounded Theory," sometimes described as an emergent theory approach where theory is derived from the data themselves. In this process, the data shape the theory rather than the theory shaping the data collection. The result of the emergent theory approach is the development of new theory or the modification of existing theory; but the end product is still a theoretical framing for the research (from an inductive rather than deductive stance). The third approach involves conducting theory based or theory framed research (the more classic inductive stance in research where causality is a key feature to be explored). All three approaches can be framed from a humanistic (hermeneutical, phenomenological) approach where theory allows for an interpretation of the anthropological data, or they can be framed from a positivist approach where data are analyzed (rather than interpreted) and theory is tested against that systematic analysis. The most common approach in applied medical anthropology, which normally has to be justified or even "sold" to both communities and sponsors, is to lean toward the positivist, empiricist, and even modernist end of the theoretical spectrum.

Inquiry in mid-level theory

Applied medical anthropology contributions to the study of substance abuse, for example, have followed two general approaches: (a) "atheoretical" (descriptive–comparative) approaches, and (2) approaches that develop and/or apply mid-level anthropological theory. Midrange theory, in anthropology, is the testable portion of one or a combination of the grand theory themes described above. Both of these approaches have been incorporated in single disciplinary research (where only anthropology theory and methods are used to explore the nature of health and healing), and in multidisciplinary approaches where both theory and research methods are drawn from multiple disciplines (such as psychology, epidemiology, sociology, geography, biology, public health, etc.). The latter approach is much more challenging, and is often much more productive of change in a health care system.

Most applied medical anthropology exists in a complex multidisciplinary space where each of the scientific specializations has a strong and defensible history of both theory development, and the development of associated methods that support those theories and allow them to be used to frame critical applied research questions. Disciplinary specialization has commonly led to intensive elaborations of highly specific methods to extract information in minute detail from closely defined phenomena. In some ways, anthropology is in competition with these trends and has to accommodate the assumptions and the biases behind the operative paradigms. Much of the research conducted in medical schools, research institutes, and corporate research and development laboratories works within well defined boundaries of established disciplines. In the context of both multidisciplinary (multiple disciplines individually focused on a problem at the same time) and transdisciplinary (approaches that synthesize across disciplines) research highly developed but narrow fields of study can form synergistic relationships that reunify results from the laboratory to the everyday human condition. In this context, the anthropological approach is often described as inductive research which attempts to build (or find, or identify) theory during the data gathering process. In this case, atheoretical or emergent theory studies conducted by sociologists (cf. Strauss and Corbin 1990) or anthropologists (cf. Agar 1980; Spradley 1980) start out with very few assumptions about how the phenomena to be studied fit together in terms of an explanatory schema. This lack of assumptions (an attempt at neutrality, if not objectivity) allows the investigator to collect information and examples of the studied phenomena wherever and in whatever condition they may be found, without making a priori assumptions about what should be, or must be, or ought to be found. For example, in a study of needle use among injecting drug users, it became clear through participant observation that needle "sharing" was inadequate as a descriptive term for use of contaminated injection paraphernalia (Page 1990) because the term *sharing* suggested an exchange or mutual use of the injection equipment. By not accepting the "sharing" gloss which had general acceptance among health researchers (cf. Magura et al. 1989) before going into the field, it was possible for the investigator to identify more accurately the actual kinds of risky behavior that took place among injecting drug users (IDUs). These behaviors included use of "pooled" syringes (Page et al. 1990), transfer of drugs from syringe to syringe (Inciardi and Page 1991), use of common water containers (Page et al. 1990), and drug cookers, and cotton filters. In fact, sharing in the sense of passing a used needle from one person to another did not occur in any of the observational settings reported in these articles. Subsequent investigations by Koester (1994) and Jose et al. (1993) have supported the development of a theoretical concept of "indirect contamination" by these and other means. On a practical level, when drug users were told to "not share needles," they could reply that they were not sharing, yet they were still becoming infected because of the sharing of other equipment or the sharing of liquefied drugs (now called "indirect sharing"). Prevention campaigns that resulted from this applied approach were modified to fit the reality of the risks, so eventually people were cautioned to not share directly or indirectly, with considerably more success than the old messages that were not effectively changing behavior.

Using Theory and Applying Methods: The Marriage of Midrange Theory and Theoretically Driven Methods to Accomplish Change

There is a crucial relationship between theory and methods in all of the social sciences. In applied medical anthropology, the theory–methods connection is primarily associated with testable midrange theory, rather than with the broader grand anthropological theory discussed above. Applied ethnographic methods are the primary levers by which medical anthropologists justify moving the world a little closer to where it ought to be (in terms of human health and well-being). The theory provides a framework for understanding and praxis, while the methods provide a transparent and defensible process for linking theory with reality. This linkage also helps address the question of whose vision of "ought to be" is one that is finally implemented, ranging from top down research on public health issues to fully implemented community based participatory designs. With the possible exception of the "constant comparative method" most applied medical anthropology methods are direct decedents of focused ethnographic midrange theories with links back to grand theory.

THE IMPORTANCE OF BEING ABLE TO TELL PEOPLE HOW YOU ARE GOING TO DO SOMETHING: METHODS IN APPLIED MEDICAL ANTHROPOLOGY

Once a decision is made to conduct an applied medical anthropology project based on either an emergent theory or a testable theory approach, it becomes necessary to clearly describe the basic "who, what, when, where, why and how" of applied anthropological research. These elements are the core methodological components of applied medical anthropology. Theory frames the research and provides the overall direction that focuses the process. Methods become the active connection between theory and culture. The "who" element is the sampling process. It is the systematic process for selecting the individuals and groups that are going to tell their important cultural stories and provide the basic findings that can result in some type of problem solving applied action. The "what" dimension is the cultural domain (area of everyday life) that people are describing. The "where and when" elements of anthropological methods are the physical and temporal contexts that surround the individuals and their actions. The anthropological "how" of applied anthropology methods is a complex mix of interviewing, observations, participation, explanation, validation and cultural learning that allows the anthropologist to match what people say and do, when they say and do it, and where these activities occur with the theory that will explain it. Finally, the "why" dimension of ethnographic methods is the opportunity for all of the participants (researchers and researched) to explain, interpret, and clarify what is happening from each stakeholders' point of view.

There is a vast literature on human field research design, site entry, methodology, informant relationships, and the personal effects of field studies on the researcher. Older references tend to contain practical advice that is slowly being lost for new generations of more theoretically driven ethnographers. Newer works tend to assume knowledge of these classics, and expend their efforts refining theory, describing advanced methods, or defending the descriptive nature of ethnographic techniques in an increasingly quantified world. One of the earliest works describing the practical art and the science of ethnographic field studies includes Kroeber's seminal text, *Anthropology Today* (Kroeber 1953) which defined such seminal concepts as role and status. However, the time period circa 1970 is clearly the bench mark era for systematic methods development. This time period also coincides with the rapid emergence and impact of applied medical anthropology in the United States. The link between foundational methods training and successful application is clear. Classic works from that time describe the ethnographic research process, its effects on the researcher, and the practical conditions one could expect to encounter in the field. Examples are Epstein's *Craft of Social Anthropology* (Epstein 1967), the Glazer and Strauss (1967) text, *The Discovery of Grounded Theory*, and Spradley and McCurdy's (1972) *The Cultural Experience: Ethnography in Complex Theory*. These works mark the initial formalization of ethnographic studies. Other "circa '70" books provide behind the scenes details about field research; a necessary complement to works which describe theory and methodology, but leave out the human factor. One edited volume, *Marginal Natives: Anthropologists at Work* (Freilich 1977), contains a detailed history of field work theory and research designs. Other classics of this period include works with practical advice for field work survival by Rosalie Wax (1971) *Doing Fieldwork: Warnings and Advice* and Beteille and

Maden, *Encounter and Experience, Personal Accounts of Fieldwork* (Beteille and Maden 1975), which contain advice about overcoming the problems of doing research in foreign countries. In a more generic vein, a seminal text which links ethnographic research with larger theoretical concerns during this time period is Pelto and Pelto's (1978) *Anthropological Research: The Structure of Inquiry.* Revisions in formal approaches to ethnographic research methods, training, and theory then begin to appear on about a ten year cycle. Jumping forward to the present, the most commonly used ethnographic methodological texts are Bernard's (2005) *Research Methods in Anthropology: Qualitative and Quantitative Approaches* and Schensul and Le Compte's (1999) *Ethnographer's Toolkit,* which is a seven book multi-authored resource set for designing and conducting ethnographic research, including essential ethnographic methods. Specific theory and methods combinations are also extensively explored in the *Journal of Field Methods,* which provides up to date discussions of both midrange (testable) anthropological theory and methods.[1] Another specific resource, in that it focuses on one methodological issue in one topical area in applied medical anthropology is J. Bryan Page and Merrill Singer's *Comprehending Drug Use*: *Ethnographic Research at the Social Margins* (2010). These works have provided applied medical anthropologists with a substantial literature that is currently used in successful grant writing and the development of high impact applied projects.

Examples of eclectic midrange theory: ethnographic research at the social margins

Many applied medical anthropology projects deliberately and appropriately utilize a diverse set of midrange anthropological theories which allow them to: (1) describe the cultural models of health and illness which provide a framework for understanding individual and group knowledge and beliefs; (2) monitor both the stability and the change in behavior; (3) identify the key social contexts in which cultural beliefs and values are turned into action; (4) establish the intervening conditions that either allow for change (protective forces) or prevent change (barriers); (5) understand the cultural–environmental and the political economy of health; (6) provide a theoretical framework for determining the decision making and sustainable actions of the group and identify the conditions that are necessary for sustained maintenance of behavioral change for individuals; (7) identify the symbolic and communication conditions imposed by cultural systems that relate to health behavior and behavioral change; and (8) either initiate or restructure culturally competent and effective interventions at the individual and group level. The following sections provide some examples of these approaches and their link to larger theoretical models.

Connections between the internal and the external (cognitive and psychological approaches)

The research on aspects of the internal–external connections between thought and behavior has developed predominantly within psychological anthropology and cognitive anthropology, although other approaches have also played a part in this area of midrange theory development. The midrange theories that appear to be in the most common use include Cultural Models, Cultural Beliefs Systematic Comparison, and

Cultural Cognition (domain analysis). Some specific examples of the use of cultural models or cultural health beliefs models include research on building culturally congruent prevention systems which are more than models; they are actual structural programs that test the models and their gender sensitivity for use in intervention programs (Weeks et al 1996).

Cultural Domain Analysis provides an arena within which midrange theories have been successfully applied to both research questions and the development of HIV and drug interventions among other applied efforts. These approaches can provide excellent models for providing culturally competent, and locally motivated information prevention information, as in the case of a Puerto Rican study of what individuals wanted to know about substance abuse and AIDS education from risk reduction programs (Finlinson et al. 1996). They can also provide key information for qualitative–quantitative bridges to find predictors of risk perception, as seen in the work of Singer (1996) among women drug users.

Systematic explorations of mental health and other illness domains have been pursued through the use of three interlocked cognitive anthropology methods. These are techniques for: (1) exploring the content and limit of cultural domains (e.g., free-listing, sentence frame completion, contrast sets); (2) techniques for establishing the structural and cognitive relationships among the elements of cultural domains (e.g., pile sorts, dyad and triad tests, Q sorting, matrix profile analysis); (3) techniques for establishing the cultural consensual framework for these systems of knowledge and belief (Trotter 1991, 1995). These techniques are amenable to being used in a standard pre-test/post-test design to analyze changes in cultural models or cognition over time as a result of intervention or culture change. Many of these techniques provide a format for systematic ethnographic rapid assessment. They also provide a methodological basis for bridging between ethnographic and standard survey or experimental (quantitative) research designs, since they are typically analyzed using both qualitative (description of meaning) and quantitative (cluster analysis, multidimensional scaling, correspondence analysis) algorithms. As an example, Trotter and Potter (1993) conducted an HIV risk pile sort with Navajo teenagers, using a list of risks that had been generated in focus groups and ethnographic interviews with Navajo cultural consultants. The project was offered as a service component of the Flagstaff Multicultural AIDS Prevention Program, and it explored the ways that the teenagers related the risks in their lives (including alcohol, drug, and HIV related risks) to other risks (violence, school problems, sexuality). The results of the project demonstrated that the students were linking risks within bounded risk areas (e.g., drug risks, school risks, violence risks, etc.), and that the linkages between those areas were weakly associated. The models of risk for the teenagers were then valuable in constructing HIV and other risk prevention programs which improved the students understanding of the need to link risks in order to prevent negative outcomes, and the need to strengthen boundaries between risks to avoid them.

Social organization and structure: cultural contexts research

The bulk of health related research in other disciplines has either focused on individuals and their attributes, or on population samples collected through probabilistic sampling procedures. While this approach has a number of strengths, its weaknesses are twofold. First, the cultural context of health problems is all too often ignored by individually centered approaches. Second, people spend a significant portion of their lives within small interactive groups, where their behavior may be impacted as much or more strongly by the group than by any individual characteristic that they bring to the group. Anthropological midrange theory has been highly productive in establishing the importance of cultural contexts and the organization and structure of human systems. These approaches derive from theories of kinship and social network analysis and the impact of cultural structures on human behavior.

Ethnographic network mapping allows applied anthropologists to describe the participants, the behaviors, the kinship and friendship ties, and the consequences of small "bounded groups" in a community. It is accomplished through extensive qualitative interviewing at the community level. In the drug field, the composite ethnographic characteristics of the networks have subsequently been used to create a "drug network" typology or classification system that describes the individual and group context of drug use (such as crack houses, local manufacturing and distribution, etc.). Trotter et al. (1995), and Williams and Johnson (1993) have demonstrated that this type of data is extremely useful for targeting intervention and education activities for the highest risk groups, based on multiple risk criteria. The data can also provide important information about the sub-epidemics that are likely to be part of drug use in network groups (Trotter et al. 1995; Williams and Johnson 1993). In HIV and drug risk prevention, several projects have tested very useful midrange theory to identify network structural elements. These findings provide public health measures of HIV and drug risk conditions (Trotter et al. 1995; Weeks et al. 2001, 2006) as well as epidemiological comparisons of HIV risks within their personal network context in cities around the United States (Williams et al. 1995).

Cultural ecology, critical medical anthropology, and cultural epidemiology theories

The midrange theories related to cultural ecology, critical anthropology, and cultural ecology that have been successfully tested include Barriers to Change research (Environmental Factors Research), Cultural Congruency Models (Conflicts in Belief and Process), Human–Biological Interactions Research, Comparative Cultural Models Research, Deconstructionist Models, Critical Theory approaches, and studies of the political economy of health and illness (cf. Hill 1991; Singer and Baer 1995). These theories have provided a wide range of evidence for the effectiveness of midrange critical theory, cultural ecology, and HIV risk reduction. These range from more theoretical constructions to models for application of the theories (Singer 1995a, 2006), and the politics of HIV research (Singer 1994b).

In addition, the direct observation of behaviors to determine the impact of the environment on behavior constitutes a primary methodology for health ecological studies. Some of these studies have targeted the results of prevention or behavioral change programs and culturally competent interventions in risk-taking behavior. A linked series of studies of needle sharing and needle hygiene practices supported by the National Institute on Drug Abuse exemplifies midrange theory combined with observational methods in a cultural ecological context. The component studies of this project focus on context specific uses of injection equipment among drug users in the

United States, as part of HIV risk reduction efforts for drug injectors. Descriptive observations in this realm (Page et al. 1990; Page 1990; Koester 1994) explore both the meaning and the processes of injection drug use, needle sharing, and the public health consequences of drug paraphernalia laws (laws that restrict the possession of syringes that might be used for drug abuse). Later studies (Singer et al. 1995; Clatts et al. 1996) explore the micro-environmental consequences of needle hygiene and needle sharing in-depth. One example of the latter approach is the Needle Hygiene Project, conducted by the National Institutes on Drug abuse Cooperative Agreement Program (Needle et al.; Koester 1994). These studies have led to changes in the recommended messages and training processes for HIV risk reduction among injection drug users.

Cross Cultural Applicability Midrange Theory and Methods

One of the most obvious and most practical midrange theories in medical anthropology is the theory of cultural relativity. It is also one of the most miss-applied and politically misused theories in anthropology. This theory is an expression of the empirical findings of anthropologists and other social scientists that groups tend to share consensual world views within the group, and differentiate those world views from others outside the group. Finding examples, from folk medicine to health care prevention programs, is easy, but the findings also frequently result in highly complex actions and recommendations (from calls for cultural competency, to representations that only members of the same culture, or social strata, or language group, or gender, or lifestyle orientation, etc. can understand X culture and therefore can be sufficiently culturally competent to deal with the health and medically related problems of that culture). These forms of cultural particularism tend to reinforce difference at the expense of the possibility for cross-cultural understanding and action. At the same time, the "one size fits all" universalism found in some health interventions is based on a view that constantly stumbles over social and cultural difference, to the detriment of understanding the actual confluence of culture, health, healing, and medicine in peoples' everyday lives.

One example of a successful applied medical anthropology project in this arena of work is the revision of an international classification of disabilities, the ICIDH CAR[2] study. The study had to satisfy 12 data needs in relation to both the ICIDH revision process: (1) identify linguistic equivalencies for conceptual transfer of elements of the classification into local languages and back to English; (2) explore the cultural contexts, practices, and values concerning disablements in the local culture; (3) investigate whether the proposed structure of the classification has good cross-cultural stability; (4) conduct an item-by-item evaluation of the cross-cultural applicability of each facet of the classification; (5) explore alternative models for the classification; (6) collect data on the parity or lack of parity in accommodation and level of stigma between mental health and physical disablements; (7) collect data on the boundaries between the three levels of the classification system; (8) establish information on the thresholds that apply to disablements (when someone is considered disabled and when are they not shows significant cultural variability); (9) investigate information on stigma attached to various types of disablements; (10) produce a description of the current programs and need for programs that serve populations with disabilities; (11) compare the relative importance of different types of disabling conditions in different cultures; and (12) create a general description of the place and meaning of disabilities and disability programs in local cultures. The practical aspects of the design required conducting the research at a number of different centers around the world that have varying levels of experience with qualitative and quantitative research methods. The methods had to be easy to use, inexpensive, comprehensive, and capable of producing defensible results. The ICIDH CAR model was designed to address a consistent issue for multisite cross-cultural applied research. The research requires a standardized sampling framework that does not place an extreme burden on the various centers. A qualitative sampling procedure was used for the bulk of the CAR study, except in those cases where statistical power needs dictated a quantitative sampling approach. The ethnographic sampling framework was comprised of selected individuals who were especially knowledgeable about their culture, rather than randomly selected individuals who might not be able to contribute substantively to the study (cf. Trotter and Schensul 1998; Johnson 1990a,b). The process appropriately differs from probabilistic (forms of random) sampling due to the goals of the study, especially the need to interview individuals who are cultural experts and who have substantive knowledge in the area of disablement. The final results of the study and application was a consensual, multi-national, revision of the old disabilities classification system into a new system for assessing functioning in cultural context, which is a significant paradigm shift for both WHO and the disabilities communities. (Ustun et al. 2001).

RAPID ASSESSMENT AS A METHODOLOGICAL FRAMEWORK: COMBINING EMERGENT THEORY WITH MIDRANGE THEORY AND ETHNOGRAPHIC METHODS

One of the highest impact methodological innovations in applied medical anthropology is the development of systematic rapid ethnographic methods and techniques targeted at emerging public health problems. This approach has been used to respond to problems such as malaria, diarrheal disease, dengue, breast and bottle feeding, and now drug abuse, AIDS, and disaster relief. Rapid assessment was first formally described in the mid-1980s (Scrimshaw et al. 1987; Bentley et al. 1988; Scrimshaw et al. 1991) along with other rapid assessment and evaluation models developed about the same time. Rapid ethnographic assessment fits into the general model of rapid assessment paradigms, including those used for rapid environmental appraisal (Oliver and Beattie 1996; Stohlgren et al. 1997), rapid epidemiology (Anker 1991; Smith 1989), rapid disaster assessment (Malilay et al. 1997), and rapid assessment of biomedical conditions (Lee and Price 1995). Rapid ethnographic assessment has a well-documented history of success in both international and domestic contexts (e.g., Vlassoff and Tanner 1992; Dale et al. 1996). It has been used in developing countries as a substitute for survey and other quantitative data-collection processes and as a compliment to existing data sets and surveillance systems. Examples include research about malaria in the Philippines (Miguel et al. 1999), HIV among young people in Cambodia (Tarr and Aggleton 1999), family planning in Burkina Faso (Askew et al.

1993), preschool children exposed to pesticides in Mexico (Guillette et al. 1998), sexually transmitted disease and HIV prevention in Turkey (Aral and Fransen 1995), and injection drug use in Vietnam (Power 1996). Rapid assessment is also used as a complimentary data collection process in developed countries. In this role, it is seen as valuable in targeting conditions and contexts that are more highly concentrated than those identified by normal surveillance and epidemiological efforts. It provides information for spotting emerging conditions that are not yet visible in other data sets and allows for the development of interventions successfully configured for local contexts, especially where local cultural conditions and values differ from the dominant cultural system. Examples of these types of rapid assessment projects include information on the health problems of homeless youth in Baltimore (Ensign and Gittelsohn 1998), identification of priority health issues for health care management policy review in France (Lerer 1999), assessment of home-based care for people with AIDS in the United States (McDonnell et al. 1994), and the RARE project (Trotter et al. 2001) which provides an integrated framework to help assure that rapid assessment will be conducted within the context of strong scientific methodological standards within a community controlled context. The RARE program includes the creation of a guide for community leaders and advisory committees, a methods work book, the use of existing data sets (epidemiology, surveillance, and research), oversight by individuals with experience in the method, methodological training for local field teams, direct involvement of community leaders and health providers, accommodation of the methodological concerns raised in various critiques of the process, and an evaluation component to assess intervention implementation. This has lead to a sustained use of the RARE based approach in the areas of intervention development and intervention evaluation (Trotter and Singer 2005; Needle et al. 2008; Bates et al. 2007; Conviser et al. 2007). In addition, there has been an continuing technological transfer of the rapid assessment approach within applied medical anthropology to encompass evaluation research targeted at both institutional reform and program improvement (Sobo et al. 2008; Stimson et al. 2005; Rugg et al. 2004), disaster relief and ancillary health issues (Low et al. 2005), and current health disparities research within a participatory action framework in public health (Hernandez et al. 2008). This broad diffusion of innovation demonstrates that scientifically sound rapid assessment contains an important set of tools (ethnographic theory, methods, and community orientation) that are of significant use to applied medical anthropologists.

ETHICS AND APPLIED MEDICAL ANTHROPOLOGY: A COMFORTABLE FIT[3]

Applied medical anthropology has (and needs) a strong ethics core that anchors medical anthropological praxis to appropriate standards of conduct. The complexities of ethnic and cultural nationalism, combined with the excesses and outright abuses of power during both colonial and post-colonial globalization periods have had a powerful impact on anthropologists' ability to do applied medical anthropology.

Applied medical anthropologists face two complex, interwoven, yet frequently dichotomized ethical challenges that must be negotiated, addressed, and jointly accommodated. These two challenges are the ethics of professional praxis and the ethics of conducting cross-cultural research on health, healing, and medicine within a global multicultural context. The first challenge is to construct and conduct research in an ethical manner by successfully anticipating, addressing, and appropriately applying the numerous, often vague (sometimes culture bound), contradictory, and challenging disciplinary, national, and international ethical rules, and guidelines and treaty obligations surrounding the conduct of science and research. The history of human research is unfortunately littered with the cultural debris of harmful actions on the part of the researchers and their sponsors. Following the principles, guidelines and laws that protect people from unethical research is a critical requirement for protecting humans from harm at the hands of researchers. An equally important complementary ethical challenge for anthropologists is to conduct their professional activities (teaching, applied practice, and knowledge dissemination) ethically within and across competing social and cultural boundaries. Anthropologists must be particularly ethically vigilant when they are using anthropological theory, knowledge or praxis that might be a direct (and sometimes even indirect) cause of harm for vulnerable people. People's lives can be impacted by what anthropologists say and what anthropologists do in their personal and professional capacity.

Anthropologists have been intimately involved in the public debates and explorations of the ethics of research ever since the emergence of the disciple in the late 1800s, when much of the ethical elements of the debate revolved around the meaning of evolution, the relationship of science to theology, and the nature of "civilization" to other forms of social complexity, as opposed to other cultural conditions. Since that time, the discussion of ethics in anthropology has consistently paralleled the concerns, explorations, and debates focused on science in general, on the impact of changing technology and globalization for all cultures around the world, on war and conflict, and on the emerging ethical concerns in the other social sciences (such as deception or sociobiology). One of the first public explorations of ethics in anthropological research is the American Anthropological Association's participation in the drafting of the Universal Declaration of Human Rights (United Nations 1948).

> The Board collaborated in preparing the Declaration on Human Rights, which appeared in the October 1947 *American Anthropologist*, Vol. 49, No. 4. The original draft was written by Melville J. Herskovits. Contacts concerning this statement have been made, either in person or by mail, with various State Department and United Nations commissions. (*American Anthropologist* 1948:380)

One of the key anthropological contributions to the Declaration was the establishment of the principle of cultural relativism (Herskovits 1958). The first formal code of ethics for anthropologists was published by the Society for Applied Anthropology, in 1949, which indicates the ongoing concern among applied anthropologists for the ethical conduct of their research and praxis, since it preceded the development of a code of ethics for the general discipline by several years, even though it was essentially the same individuals who were involved in all of the primary anthropological associations of that time (i.e., it was a very small world). Those professional guidelines for ethical research have been subsequently reviewed and revised to take into account more recent changes in the standards and practices that are the core of anthropological research (American Anthropological Association 2005). The following statements (shown in Table 3.1) are excerpts from the American Anthropological Association

Table 3.1 Key excerpts from the American Anthropological Association Statement on Ethics.

In a field of such complex involvements, misunderstandings, conflicts, and the necessity to make choices among conflicting values are bound to arise and to generate ethical dilemmas... Where these conditions cannot be met, the anthropologist would be well-advised not to pursue the particular piece of research.

1. Relations with those studied
In research, anthropologists' paramount responsibility is to those they study. When there is a conflict of interest, these individuals must come first. Anthropologists must do everything in their power to protect the physical, social, and psychological welfare and to honor the dignity and privacy of those studied.

2. Responsibility to the public
Anthropologists are also responsible to the public – all presumed consumers of their professional efforts.

3. Responsibility to the discipline
Anthropologists bear responsibility for the good reputation of the discipline and its practitioners.

4. Responsibility to students
In relations with students, anthropologists should be candid, fair, non-exploitative, and committed to the student's welfare and progress.

5. Responsibility to sponsors
In relations with sponsors of research, anthropologists should be honest about their qualifications, capabilities, and aims. ... Anthropologists should be especially careful not to promise or imply acceptance of conditions contrary to their professional ethics or competing commitments. ... Anthropologists must retain the right to make all ethical decisions in their research.

6. Responsibilities to one's own government and to host governments
In relation with their own government and with host governments, research anthropologists should ... demand assurance that they will not be required to compromise their professional responsibilities and ethics as a condition of their permission to pursue research.

statement of professional responsibilities which identify the basic ethical issues that have been discussed and debated on virtually an annual basis as a part of the overall ethical dialog within the discipline. Table 3.1 provides key excerpts from the American Anthropological Association Statements on Ethics and shows where anthropology in general fits in present and future trends for addressing cross-cultural and global ethical concerns.

Epilogue

When anthropologists, by their actions, jeopardize peoples studied, professional colleagues, students, or others, or if they otherwise betray their professional commitments, their colleagues may legitimately inquire into the propriety of those actions, and take such measures as lie within the legitimate powers of their Association as the membership of the Association deems appropriate.

These principles are generally accepted by anthropologists, but not without debate, discussion, challenges, and recommendations for revision to make these guidelines more (or less) compatible with both national and international formal ethical principles and guidelines. One of the critical trends in the debate is the ongoing tension in applied medical anthropology between science and humanism, between positivism and other more interpretive paradigms, and between modernism (especially the concept of progress and the concept of universalism) and post-modernism (especially the concepts of cultural particularism, cultural relativism, and constant cultural constructions). A large number of the current ethical problems medical anthropologists face result from the unanticipated consequences of multidisciplinary research designs that may have competing ethical frameworks from disparate disciplines. Others result from the unfortunate clash of two positive ethical principles. These are labeled as ethical dilemmas; a situation where two or more of the basic ethical principles are in conflict, and where adherence to one of the principles may violate another (see Singer et al. 1999). For example, medical anthropology researchers promise confidentiality to each and every person they interview, and promise to protect any information they provide (such as their health status). But they also promise to limit any harm that might result from participation in the research, to every participant (Fisher et al. 2008). As a consequence, they are faced with the dilemma of what to do if a married couple is enrolled in an AIDS project, and they find out one partner is HIV positive and is having unprotected sex with their uninfected partner, but is not telling the other that they are living with an infected person. There is a clear conflict between the two principles of confidentiality and do no harm for the project. In this kind of situation, the researcher may have to decide if they have a greater obligation to protect confidentiality, or to prevent harm to the uninfected person. Preventing harm may help the one individual, but breaking confidentiality may harm the entire project, since anyone who heard about the breach would either quit the project or would not participate. There are times when the researcher is forced to decide which of two ethical principles takes precedence in a particular research situation, and the choice of one principle causes the other principle to be violated in some minor or major way. Applied medical anthropologists have an obligation to both challenge and to contribute to the advancement of research and practice ethics, based on evolving cultural theory and practice.

Conclusions

In many ways, the distinction between applied medical anthropology and any other form of medical anthropology is a false dichotomy, or an unnecessary distinction. All forms of medical anthropology are framed by the same theoretical paradigms and are exploring strong theoretical positions within the same cultural contexts. The methods that are used to create, assess, expand, challenge, or demolish existing theories are identical. Both approaches are susceptible to external debates and challenges of anthropology's cross-cultural paradigms, and are susceptible to anthropology's internal critiques, debates, and synthetic movements. Perhaps the single difference that is important to applied medical anthropologists, and to the communities they work with, and the sponsors for their projects, is the fact that applied projects are deliberately targeted at solving problems, rather than simply producing cultural changes as a result of serendipitous or accidental or unintended consequences. This level of intentionality is important to many of the stakeholders that are engaged in improving the human health conditions on a local or global level.

NOTES

1 One of the key reasons that this section presents a general history of the development of ethnographic methods is because the current works do an excellent job of discussing theory and methods, but are missing most of the practical and pragmatic advice for rapport building, survival, and data management processes that are present in the earlier works. It is worth a little historical "diving" to find that advice. The earlier works are more student-oriented, and the later works more professionally oriented.
2 This study, conducted by the World Health Organization, was designed to make the International Classification of Impairments, Disciplines, and Handicaps cross-culturally applicable and to increase the utilization of the classification system for international health research.
3 Excerpts in this section, and expansion of the ideas presented, can be found in Linda Whiteford and Robert T. Trotter, II (2008), Ethics in Anthropological Research and Practice, Boston MA, Wadsworth.

REFERENCES

Agar, M., 1980 Professional Strangers: An Informational Introduction to Ethnography. New York: Academic Press.

American Anthropological Association, 2005 Code of Ethics (first published in June 1998). Arlington VA: The American Anthropological Association.

American Anthropologist, 1948 Report of the Secretary, January–May 1947 – Proceedings of the American Anthropological Association for the Year ending December 1947. American Anthropologist 50(2):375–404.

Anker, Martha, 1991 Epidemiological and Statistical Methods for Rapid Health Assessment. World Health Statistics Annual (WHO) 44(3):94–101.

Aral, S. O., and L. Fransen, 1995 STD/HIV Prevention in Turkey: Planning a Sequence of Interventions. AIDS Education and Prevention 7(6):544–553.

Askew, I., P. Tapsoba, Y. Ouedraogo, C. Viadro, D. Bakouan, and P. Sebgo, 1993 Quality of Care in Family Planning Programs: A Rapid Assessment in Burkina Faso. Health Policy and Planning 8(I):19–32.

Bates, Christopher, Merrill Singer, and Robert Trotter, 2007 The RARE Model of Rapid HIV Risk Assessment. Journal of Health Care for the Poor and Underserved 18(3 Supplement):16–34.

Bentley, M., G. Pelto, W. Straus, D. Schumann, C. Adegboda, and E. de la Pena, 1988 Rapid Ethnographic Assessment: Applications in a Diarrhea Management Program. Social Science and Medicine 27(1):107–116.

Bernard, H. Russell, 2005 Research Methods in Anthropology: Qualitative and Quantitative Approaches, 4th edition. Walnut Creek CA: AltaMira Press.

Beteille, Andre, and T. N. Maden, eds., 1975 Encounter and Experience, Personal Accounts of Fieldwork. Honolulu: University of Hawaii Press.

Clatts, M., W. R. Davis, S. Deren, D. Goldsmith, and S. Tortu, 1996 Risk Behaviors among Injection Drug Users in New York City: Critical Gaps in Prevention Policy. *In* Global AIDS Policy. Douglas A. Feldman, ed. Westport CT: Bergen and Garvey.

Conviser, Richard, Merrill Singer, and Moses Pounds, 2007 Adapting RARE to Assess Barriers to Service Receipt among People Out of Care. Journal of Health Care for the Poor and Underserved 18(3 Supplement):52–68.

Dale, J., C. Shipman, L. Lacock, and M. Davies, 1996 Creating a Shared Vision of Out of Hours Care: Using Rapid Appraisal Methods to Create an Interagency, Community Oriented, Approach to Service Development. British Medical Journal 312:1206.

Ensign, B. J., and J. Gittelsohn, 1998 Health and Access to Care: Perspectives of Homeless Youth in Baltimore City, USA. Social Science and Medicine 47(12):2087–2099.

Epstein, A. L., ed., 1967 The Craft of Social Anthropology. London: Tavistock.

Finlinson, H. A., B. Guberti, R. R. Robles, and H. M. Colon, 1996 What We Want to Know About HIV/AIDS: An Analysis of Questions Asked by Substance Abuse Clients Attending AIDS Education Classes in Puerto Rico. Human Organization 55:370–378.

Celia Fisher, Matthew Oransky, Meena Mahadevan, Merill Singer, Greg Mirhej, and G. Derrick Hodge, 2008 Marginalized Populations and Drug Addiction Research: Realism, Mistrust, and Misconception. IRB Journal 30(3):1–9.

Freilich, Morris, ed., 1977 Marginal Natives at Work: Anthropologists in the Field. New York: Schenkman Publishing Company.

Glazer, Barney G., and Anselm L. Strauss, 1967 The Discovery of Grounded Theory. Chicago: Aldine.

Guillette, E. A., M. M. Mercedes, A. M. Guadalupe, A. D. Soto, and G. I. Enedina, 1998 An Anthropological Approach to the Evaluation of Preschool Children Exposed to Pesticides in Mexico. Environmental Health Perspectives 106(6):347–353.

Hernandez, Agueda, Gilbert Saint-Jean, Sian Evans, Ida Tafari, Luther G. Brewster, Michel J. Celestin, Carlos Gamez-Estefan, Fernando Regalado, Siri Akal, Barry Nierenberg, Elaine D. Kauschinger, Robert Schwartz, J. Bryan Page, and David Richard Brown, 2008 A Participatory Action Research Pilot Study of Urban Health Disparities Using Rapid Assessment Response and Evaluation. American Journal of Public Health 98(1):28–38.

Herskovits, Melville J, 1958 Some Further Comments on Cultural Relativism. American Anthropologist 60(2):266–273.

Hill, C. E., ed., 1991 Training Manual in Applied Medical Anthropology. American Anthropological Association Special Publications No. 27, Washington DC: American Anthropological Association.

Inciardi, J. A., and J. B. Page, 1991 Drug Sharing among Intravenous Drug Users. AIDS 5(6):772–773.

Johnson, J. C., 1990a Selecting Ethnographic Informants. Qualitative Research Methods, vol. 22. Beverly Hills and London: Sage Publications.

Johnson, J. C., 1990b Selecting Ethnographic Informants. Newbury Park CA: Sage Publications.

Jose, B., S. R. Friedman, A. Neaigus, R. Curtis, J.-P. C. Grund, M. P. Goldstein, T. P. Ward, and D. C. Des Jarlais, 1993 Syringe-Mediated Drug Sharing (Backloading): A New Risk Factor for HIV among Injecting Drug Users. AIDS 7:1653–1660.

Koester, S. K., 1994 Copping, Running, and Paraphernalia Laws: Context and High Risk Behavior. Human Organization 53(3):278–295.

Kroeber, Alfred L., 1953 Anthropology Today. Chicago: University of Chicago Press.

Lee, T., and M. Price, 1995 Indicators and Research Methods for Rapid Assessment of a Tuberculosis Control Program: Case Study of a Rural Area in South Africa. Tubercle Lung Diseases 76(5):441–449.

Lerer, L. B., 1999 Health Impact Assessment. Health Policy and Planning 14(2):198–203.

Low, Setha M., Dana H. Taplin, Mike Lamb, and Setha M. Low, 2005 BATTERY PARK CITY. An Ethnographic Field Study of the Community Impact of 9/11. Urban Affairs Review 40(5):655–682.

Maguara, S., J. I. Grossman, D. S. Lipton, K. R. Amann, J. Kroger, and K. Gehan, 1989 Correlates of Participation in AIDS Education and HIV Antibody Testing by Methadone Patients. Public Health Reports 104(3):231–240.

Malilay, J., W. D. Flanders, and D. A. Brogan, 1997 Metodo Modificado de Muestreo por Conglomerados para la Evaluacion Rapida de Necesidades Despues de un Desastre (Modified Cluster Sampling Method for the Rapid Assessment of Needs after a Disaster). Revista Pana-mericana de Salud Publica/Pan-American Journal of Public Health 2(1):7–12.

McDonnell, S., M. Brennan, G. Burnham, and D. Tarantola, 1994. Assessing and Planning Home-Based Care for Persons with AIDS. Health Policy and Planning 9(4):429–437.

Miguel, C. A., V. L. Tallo, L. Manderson, and M. A. Lansang, 1999 Local Knowledge and Treatment of Malaria in Agusan del Sur, the Philippines. Social Science and Medicine 48(5):607–618.

Needle, R. H., S. L. Coyle, H. Cesari, R. T. Trotter II, S. Koester, M. Clatts, L. Price, E. McEllen, A. Finlinson, R. Bluthenthal, T. Pierce, J. Johnson, T. S. Jones, and M. Williams (no date) HIV Risk in Drug Injector Networks: Multiperson Use of Drug Preparation/Injection Equipment. National Institute of Drug Abuse (NIH). Unpublished working paper.

Needle, Richard, Karen Kroeger, Hrishikesh Belani, Angeli Achrekar, Charles D. Parry, and Sarah Dewing, 2008 Sex, Drugs, and HIV: Rapid Assessment of HIV Risk Behaviors among Street-Based Drug Using Sex Workers in Durban, South Africa. Social Science and Medicine 67(9):1447–1455.

Oliver, I., and A. J. Beattie, 1996 Designing a Cost-Effective Invertebrate Survey: A Test of Methods for Rapid Assessment of Biodiversity. Ecology Applied 6(2):594–607.

Page, J. Bryan, 1990 Shooting Scenarios and Risk of HIV-1 Infection. American Behavioral Scientist 33(4):478–490.

Page, J. Bryan, and Merrill Singer, 2010 Comprehending Drug Use: Ethnographic Research at the Social Margins. Princeton NJ: Rutgers University Press.

Page, J. Bryan., P. C. Smith, and N. Kane, 1990 Shooting Galleries, their Proprietors, and Implications for Prevention of AIDS. Drugs and Society 3(1):69–85.

Pelto, P. J., and G. H. Pelto, 1978 Anthropological Research: The Structure or Inquiry. 2nd edition. Cambridge: Cambridge University Press.

Power, R, 1996 Rapid Assessment of Drug-Injecting Situations at Hanoi and Ho Chi Minh City, Viet Nam. Bulletin on Narcotics 48:35–52.

Rugg, Deborah, Michel Carael, Jan Ties Boerma, and John Novak, 2004 Global Advances in Monitoring and Evaluation of HIV/AIDS: From AIDS Case Reporting to Program Improvement. New Directions for Evaluation Autumn (Fall) 2004(103):33–48.

Rylko-Bauer, B., Merrill Singer, and J. Van Willigen, 2006 Reclaiming Applied Anthropology: Its Past, Present, and Future. American Anthropologist 108(1):178–190.

Schensul, J. J., and M. D. LeCompte, 1999 Ethnographer's Toolkit. Walnut Creek CA: AltaMira Press.

Schrimshaw, S., M. Carballo, and E. Hurtado, 1987 Rapid Assessment Procedures for Nutrition and Primary Health Care. UCLA Latin American Center References Series, 11. Westwood CA: UCLA.

Schrimshaw, S., M. Carballo, L. Ramos, and B. Blair, 1991 The AIDS Rapid Anthropological Assessment Procedures: A Tool for Health Education Planning and Evaluation. Health Edu-cation Quarterly 18:111–123.

Singer, Merrill, 1994a Community-Centered Praxis: Toward an Alternative Non-Dominative Applied Anthropology. Human Organization 53(4):336–344.

Singer, Merrill, 1994b The Politics of AIDS. Social Science Medicine. 38(10):1321–1324.

Singer, Merrill, 1996 The Evolution of AIDS Work in a Puerto Rican Community Organization. Human Organization 55(1):67–75.

Singer, Merrill and Hans Baer, 1995 Critical Medical Anthropology. Amityville, NY: Baywood Publishing Company.

Singer, Merril, Patricia Loomis Marshall, Robert T. Trotter, II, Jean J. Schensul, Margaret R. Weeks, Janie E. Simmons, and Kim E. Radda 1999 Ethics, Ethnography, Drug Use and AIDS: Dilemmas and Standards in Federally Funded Research. *In* Integrating Cultural, Observational, and Epidemiological Approaches in the Prevention of Drug Abuse and

HIV/AIDS. Patricia Loomis Marshall, Merrill Singer and Michael C. Clatts, eds. pp. 198–222. USDHHS/National Institute on Drug Abuse, NIH Publication No. 99–4565. Bethesda MD: NIH.

Singer, Merrill, Greg Mirhej, Claudia Santelices, Erica Hastings, Juhem Navarro, and Jim Vivian, 2006 Tomorrow is Already Here, or Is It? Steps in Preventing a Local Methamphetamine Outbreak. Human Organization 65(2):203–217.

Smith, G. S., 1989 Development of Rapid Epidemiologic Assessment Methods to Evaluate Health Status and Delivery of Health Services. International Journal of Epidemiology 18:S2–15.

Sobo, Elisa J., Candice Bowman, and Allen L. Gifford, 2008 Behind the Scenes in Health Care Improvement: The Complex Structures and Emergent Strategies of Implementation Science Social Science and Medicine 67(10):1530–1540.

Spradley, James P., 1980 Participant Observation. New York: Holt, Rinehart and Winston.

Spradley, James P., and David W. McCurdy, 1972 The Cultural Experience: Ethnography in Complex Society. Chicago: Science Research Associates.

Stimson, Gerry V., Matthew Hickman, Tim Rhodes, Francisco Bastos, and Tobi Saidel, 2005 Methods for Assessing HIV and HIV Risk among IDUs and for Evaluating Interventions. International Journal of Drug Policy 16:S7–S20.

Stohlgren, T. J., G. W. Chong, M. A. Kalkhan, and L. D. Schell, 1997 Rapid Assessment of Plant Diversity Patterns: A Methodology for Landscapes. Environmental Monitoring and Assessment 48(I): 25–43.

Strauss A. L., and J. Cobin, 1990 Basics of Qualitative Research. Grounded Theory Procedures and Techniques. Thousand Oaks CA: Sage Publications.

Tarr, C. M., and P. Aggleton, 1999 Young People and HIV in Cambodia: Meanings, Contexts and Sexual Cultures. AIDS Care: Psychological and Socio-Medical Aspects of AIDS II(3):375–384.

Trotter, Robert T. II, 1991 Ethnographic Research Methods for Applied Medical Anthropology. In Training Manual in Applied Medical Anthropology. Carole E. Hill, ed. pp. 180–212. American Anthropological Association Special Publications No. 27. Washington DC: American Anthropological Association.

Trotter, Robert T. II, 1995 Drug Use, AIDS, and Ethnography: Advanced Ethnographic Research Methods Exploring the HIV Epidemic. In Qualitative Methods in Drug Abuse and HIV Research. E. Y. Lambert, R. S. Ashery, and R. H. Needle, eds. pp. 38–65. NIDA Research Monograph 157. Rockville MD: USDHHS, National Institute on Drug Abuse.

Trotter, Robert T. II, and Potter, J. M., 1993 Pile Sorts, a Cognitive Anthropological Model of Drug and AIDS Risks for Navajo Teenagers: Assessment of a New Evaluation Tool. Drugs and Society 7(3/4):23–39.

Trotter, Robert T. II, and J. J. Schensul, 1998 Methods in Applied Anthropology. In Handbook of Methods in Cultural Anthropology. H. R. Bernard, ed. pp. 691–736. Walnut Creek CA: Altimira.

Trotter, Robert T. II, and Merrill Singer, 2005 Rapid Assessment Strategies for Public Health: Promise and Problems. In Community Intervention and AIDS. Edison Trickett and Willo Pequeqnat, eds. pp. 130–152. Oxford: Oxford University Press.

Trotter, Robert T. II, A. M. Bowen, and J. M. Potter, J.M., 1995 Network Models for HIV Outreach and Prevention Programs of Drug Users. In Social Networks, Drug Abuse, and HIV Transmission. Richard H. Needle, S. L. Coyle, S. G. Genser, and Robert T. Trotter II, eds. pp.144–180. NIDA Research Monograph 151. Rockville, MD: USDHHS, National Institute on Drug Abuse.

Trotter, Robert T. II, Richard H. Needle, Eric Goosby, Christopher Bates, and Merrill Singer 2001 A Methodological Model for Rapid Assessment, Response, and Evaluation: The RARE Program in Public Health. Field Methods 13(2): 137–159.

United Nations, 1948 Universal Declaration of Human Rights (December 10th). New York: United Nations.

Ustun, T. Bedirhan, Somnath Chatterji, Jerome E. Bickenbach, Robert T. Trotter II, Robin Room, Jurgen Rehm, and Shekhar Saxena, eds., 2001 Disability and Culture: Universalism and Diversity. ICIDH-2 Series. Seattle: Hogrefe and Huber Publishers.

Vlassoff, C., and M. Tanner., 1992 The Relevance of Rapid Assessment to Health Research and Interventions. Health Policy and Planning 7(I):1–9.

Wax, Rosalie H., 1971 Doing Fieldwork: Warnings and Advice. Chicago: University of Chicago Press.

Weeks, M., J. Schensul, S. Williams, M. Singer, and M. Grier, 1996 AIDS Prevention for African American and Latina Women: Building Culturally and Gender-Appropriate Intervention. AIDS Education and Prevention 7(3):251–263.

Weeks, M., S. Clair, M. Singer, K. Radda, J. Schensul J., and D. Wilson, 2001 High-Risk Drug Use Sites, Meaning and Practice. Journal of Drug Issues 31:781–808.

Weeks, M., J. Dickson-Gomez, K. Mosack, and S. Clair, 2006 The Risk Avoidance Partnership: Training Active Drug Users as Peer Health Advocates. Journal of Drug Issues 36(3):541–570.

Williams, M. L., and J. Johnson, 1993 Social Network Structures: An Ethnographic Analysis of Intravenous Drug Use in Houston, Texas. *In* AIDS and Community-Based Drug Intervention Programs: Evaluation and Outreach. D. G. Fisher and R. Needle, eds. pp. 65–90. Binghamton NY: The Haworth Press, Inc.

Williams, M. L., Robert T. Trotter II, Z. Zhuo, H. A. Siegal, R. R. Robles, and A. Jones, 1995 An Investigation of the HIV Risk Behaviors of Drug Use Networks. Connections 18:58–72.

CHAPTER 4

Research Design and Methods in Medical Anthropology

Clarence C. Gravlee

Medical anthropology is the study of health and healing in cross-cultural and evolutionary perspective. This expansive definition matches the scope of the field: it is at once a humanistic and scientific enterprise that crosses both disciplinary and sub-disciplinary boundaries and values both applied and basic research. Medical anthropology's holistic and integrative approach to human experience enriches our understanding of sickness and health, but it also poses a challenge in attempting to delineate the range of research methods relevant to the field: medical anthropologists draw on the whole toolkit of social science, and many researchers also integrate methods from public health, biomedicine, and the life sciences.

My goal in this chapter is to review the basic elements of research design and provide a framework for matching methods to questions across different research traditions. Medical anthropologists come from a wonderful array of paradigms – positivist, critical, constructivist, interpretive, evolutionary, ecological, and more. It's true that certain methods may be associated more often with one tradition or another, but no one tradition can lay claim to any particular method (Pelto and Pelto 1996:294). As Bernard (2006:2) puts it, "Methods belong to all of us." Indeed, fluency in a broad range of methods is essential for developing successful collaborations and for designing research that matters.

RESEARCH DESIGN

Research design is about posing good questions and finding empirical answers. The hallmark of well-designed research is that it justifies the claim that *your* particular answer is better than the alternatives. The goal is not to claim perfect knowledge – that goal is unattainable – but rather to generate systematic evidence that minimizes

A Companion to Medical Anthropology, First Edition. Edited by Merrill Singer and Pamela I. Erickson.

the errors of everyday reasoning and casual observation. Good research design thus requires researchers to be explicit about the methods and logic we use to connect theory and data, so that others can evaluate the validity of our claims.

Whole books have been written about research design, and several extended treatments discuss applications to anthropology in particular (Bernard 2006; Brim and Spain 1974; Johnson 1998; LeCompte and Schensul 1999; Pelto and Pelto 1996). This work is essential reading for medical anthropologists. Here I outline some basic ideas for connecting data and theory through research design.

Qualitative, quantitative

Medical anthropology, like the social sciences generally, is often described in terms of a dichotomy between "qualitative" and "quantitative" methods of social research. However, a growing number of methodologists across the social sciences advocate "taking the 'Q' out of research" (Onwuegbuzie and Leech 2005; Sobo 2009).

There are at least two reasons why the qualitative–quantitative distinction is usually counterproductive. First, the collection and analysis of both qualitative and quantitative data are compatible with the same logic of inquiry (King et al. 1994; Teddlie and Tashakkori 2009). From this perspective, researchers should use whichever methods work best for a particular research question. Second, the qualitative–quantitative distinction conflates data collection and data analysis. Bernard (1996) identified this problem by noting the ambiguity of the phrase "qualitative data analysis." From the syntax alone, we cannot tell whether the phrase means the analysis of *qualitative data* or the *qualitative analysis* of data. We can avoid this ambiguity by using "qualitative" and "quantitative" to modify specific types of data and types of analysis – not types of research.

Figure 4.1 illustrates the point (Bernard 1996). The stereotypes of qualitative and quantitative research are depicted in cells A and D, respectively. Cell A captures interpretive approaches to text, including traditions such as grounded theory (Charmaz 2006) and discourse analysis (Farnell and Graham 1998). Cell D captures the statistical analysis of numerical data, such as from closed-ended survey research. But these combinations don't exhaust the possibilities. In cell B, the qualitative analysis of quantitative data refers to the act of extracting meaning from the results of statistical analysis or mathematical processing. In fact, all so-called quantitative research involves this interpretive act; without it, there would be little point in running a regression model or producing a scatterplot. Last, methods in cell C generally involve turning words – or images or photos or artifacts – into numbers to look for patterns. That's the essence of classic content analysis (Krippendorff 2004). We can also place methods for cultural domain analysis like free listing and pile sorting in this cell (Weller and Romney 1988).

The point is that medical anthropologists, like all social scientists, have access to many tools for data collection and analysis, and we ought to use the right ones for a given research question. Dividing the toolkit of social science into qualitative and quantitative methods tends to obscure that point.

Exploratory–confirmatory questions

A better starting point for thinking about research design is to recognize a continuum of research objectives, ranging from exploratory to confirmatory research questions. Exploratory questions seek to understand how and why things work as they

Types of Data

	Qualitative	Quantitative
Qualitative	**A** Interpretation of text; hermeneutics; grounded theory	**B** Search for meaning in results of quantitative processing
Quantitative	**C** Turning words into numbers; classic content analysis; cultural domain analysis	**D** Statistical and mathematical analysis of numeric data

Types of Analysis (vertical axis label)

Figure 4.1 Qualitative and quantitative data and analysis. Adapted by courtesy of Sage Publications from Bernard, H. R., 1996, Qualitative Data, Quantitative Analysis. *Cultural Anthropology Methods Journal* 8(1) [http://www.analytictech.com/borgatti/qualqua.htm].

Questions

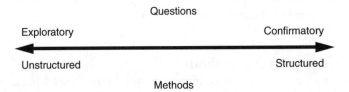

Exploratory   Confirmatory

Unstructured   Structured

Methods

Figure 4.2 A continuum of research questions and methods of data collection and analysis. Figure by Clarence C. Gravlee.

do; confirmatory questions seek to test hypotheses based on new or existing theory. These different types of questions imply different types of methods along a parallel continuum of relatively unstructured to structured methods of data collection and analysis (Figure 4.2). This framework is useful because it helps to ensure that decisions about research design flow from the research questions.

Exploratory research questions are common in medical anthropology. For example, Chavez et al. (1995) studied beliefs about breast and cervical cancer in Orange County, California. They asked: "'Do Latinas, Anglo women, and physicians have cultural models of breast and cervical cancer risk factors? If so, how similar or different are their models?' Another way of asking this question is, 'Do they agree on the relative importance of risk factors?'" (p. 42). Here researchers began with limited expectations about what they would find and sought to detect patterns that would help to generate theory. This approach is appropriate whenever there is insufficient existing theory or evidence to establish expectations.

When prior theory and evidence warrant specific expectations, confirmatory research questions are more appropriate. One distinctive feature of confirmatory research in medical anthropology is that it often builds on an exploratory phase in the same study. For example, in their exploratory work, Chavez et al. (1995) found that Latinas' beliefs about cervical and breast cancer differed from biomedical models more than Anglo women's beliefs did. "We were left wondering," they later wrote (Chavez et al. 2001:1114), "to what extent these patterns of belief were associated with behavior, specifically the use of Pap exams, a screening test for cervical cancer. In other words, to what degree do cultural beliefs matter in the use of medical services?" Chavez et al. (2001) used ethnographic interviews and survey research to address this question and found that, under certain circumstances, beliefs matter a lot.

Dressler's (2005) research on culture, stress, and health also illustrates progression from exploratory to confirmatory research questions. The central thread of Dressler's work is to identify how culturally meaningful aspects of social status shape the distribution of stress-related health outcomes. This objective entails (a) a set of exploratory research questions about how social status is culturally constructed in specific times and places, and (b) confirmatory research questions about the relationship between locally meaningful aspects of social status and health. This example illustrates the interdependence of exploratory and confirmatory questions in medical anthropology. Dressler drew on existing theory to anticipate an association between social status and health. This theory – and substantial empirical evidence – justified confirmatory, hypothesis-testing research, but Dressler first adapted the general theory to specific ethnographic contexts through exploratory research. Dressler refers to this strategy, which depends on working across the exploratory–confirmatory continuum, as "the ethnographic critique of theory" (Dressler 1995:45).

Unstructured–structured methods

The continuum of exploratory to confirmatory questions is useful because it informs the choice of methods for data collection and analysis. One approach is to strive for a fit between exploratory–confirmatory questions and unstructured–structured methods (Figure 4.2). By "structure," I mean the amount of control researchers impose on data collection. The difference between a structured and unstructured interview, for example, is the likelihood that all participants respond to the same questions in the same order. The basic principle for matching methods and questions is that *the less we know about any given phenomenon, the less structure we ought to impose*, so that we remain open to discovery. As we learn more and begin to develop hunches about what's going on, we often want to impose more structure to test our ideas (Weller 1998).

Note that "structure" does not mean "qualitative" or "quantitative"; qualitative and quantitative data and analysis cut across the continuum. For example, informal interviews conducted during participant observation generate qualitative data and fall at the unstructured end of the continuum. But we could also obtain qualitative data from more structured methods, such as an open-ended survey that poses the same questions to each respondent in the same way. The choice between these methods depends on the balance between exploratory and confirmatory objectives. Informal interviews would remain open to discovery, whereas an open-ended survey would permit systematic comparisons between respondents.

We can also place both qualitative and quantitative methods of data analysis along the entire spectrum. Both grounded theory (Charmaz 2006) and semantic network analysis (Doerfel 1998) could be described as unstructured methods, in the sense that researchers try not to impose a prior theoretical framework about the concepts and relations in a given corpus of text. Both approaches are appropriate for exploratory aims. Yet grounded theory relies only on words, whereas semantic network analysis relies on turning words into numbers and on mathematical processing.

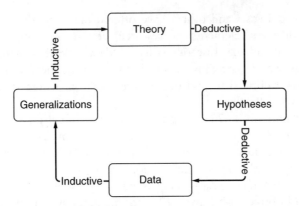

Figure 4.3 Inductive and deductive modes of reasoning in the cycle of research. Figure by Clarence C. Gravlee.

You may have noticed that the exploratory–confirmatory and unstructured–structured framework mirrors another important continuum in research design: that between inductive and deductive logic. Inductive reasoning starts with empirical observations – data – and works toward empirical generalizations to develop theory. Deductive reasoning begins with theory and works toward specifying expectations, or hypotheses, that can be checked against empirical observation. As Figure 4.3 suggests, these modes of reasoning are inextricably linked in the logic of social research, which seeks to generate (inductive) and verify (deductive) theory about how the world works. Regardless of their epistemological perspective, most researchers engage in both types of reasoning at one point or another. Decisions about which methods to use at any point in time should be informed by consideration of where researchers are in the research cycle.

Elements of research design

Good research design consists of an explicit, logical plan for connecting data and theory. In all types of research – participant observation, surveys, experiments – the major components of this plan are the same:

- Formulating research questions (and hypotheses, if appropriate).
- Selecting a research site where the research questions can be addressed.
- Developing a sampling strategy for selecting observations required to answer the research questions or test hypothese.
- Choosing methods to collect data needed to answer research questions.
- Creating a plan for managing, documenting, and archiving data.
- Selecting methods for analyzing data to answer specific research questions and test hypotheses.

This list makes clear how research questions ideally permeate all major components of research design – sampling, data collection, and data analysis. Well-designed studies (and grant proposals) make these links explicit.

Medical anthropologists and others have offered practical advice to enhance the links between different elements of research design. LeCompte and Schensul (1999:138) recommend that researchers use a "data collection matrix" to fit questions to methods. Their matrix involves listing what researchers want to know, what types of data they will need to find out, where and from whom they can find such data, and how they will collect it.

Carey and Gelaude (2008:237) emphasize the logic of design in the development of interview materials. They recommend creating an "intents list" to make explicit the rationale for each question in an interview. In a study of HIV risk, Carey's team duplicated the semistructured interview guide and, below each question, added a one-line description of why the question was being asked. They also created a spreadsheet with three columns: (1) project objectives, (2) specific interview questions, and (3) citations related to the rationale or design of each question. These tools ensured that the design of interview materials was tightly integrated with the research questions and also proved useful in interviewer training and data monitoring. Carey and Gelaude (2008:244–52) also recommend applying this logic to data management and analysis plans before the project begins.

Having an explicit, logical plan to connect data and theory enhances the validity of all types of research. DeWalt and DeWalt (2002) discuss how to design research with participant observation. Spradley's (1979; 1980) Developmental Research Sequence is a model for designing ethnographic research with progressively more focused methods of data collection and analysis. Bernard (2006) shows how the logic of experimental design helps researchers avoid common threats to validity – even if you never run an experiment. Johnson (1998) discusses research design in systematic anthropological research, and LeCompte and Schensul (1999) show how the logic of research design cuts across specific methods of data collection and analysis. Each of these sources provides many examples from research in medical anthropology.

Basic research designs

True (1996) noted that research design plays different roles in the training of medical anthropologists and epidemiologists. In epidemiology and allied fields, researchers recognize a set of basic research designs that have different strengths and weaknesses for answering particular types of questions. Medical anthropologists are generally not trained to think in these terms. However, familiarity with the range of research designs commonly used in other social and health sciences can enhance the validity of research in medical anthropology and increase our impact on neighboring disciplines and policy-makers.

Figure 4.4 illustrates a typology of basic research designs. The first major distinction is between observational and experimental designs.

Experimental designs   Experimental designs are distinguished by two features: random allocation and manipulation of the key causal variables. In classic experiments, researchers randomly assign participants to either an intervention or control group and measure one or more dependent (outcome) variables in both groups. Participants in the intervention group are then exposed to a treatment designed to test the causal effect of an independent (explanatory) variable, and both groups are measured again on the dependent variable. Random allocation, when done well, makes groups comparable with respect to

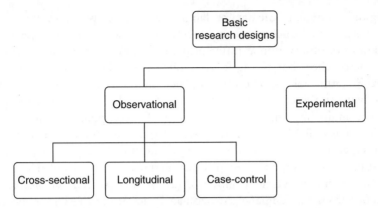

Figure 4.4   Basic research design options in medical anthropology and neighboring disciplines. Figure by Clarence C. Gravlee.

unmeasured variables, such that whatever differences emerge between groups after the intervention are likely to reflect the true causal effect of the intervention.

Experimental designs are not common in medical anthropology, but there are successful examples. Shain et al. (1999) combined ethnography and a randomized trial to test the effect of culture- and gender-specific interventions to prevent sexually transmitted infections in African–American and Mexican–American women in San Antonio, TX. They first collected ethnographic data (observations, 25 focus-group discussions, 102 in-depth interviews) on the cultural context of sexual behavior, perceptions of risk, and motivations for behavior change. They used this information to design culturally appropriate messages about recognizing risk, committing to change, and communicating about sex. Then, 424 Mexican–American and 193 African–American women were randomly assigned to receive either the culturally appropriate messages (intervention group) or standard counseling (control group). One year later, Shain et al. found that women in the intervention group were 49 percent less likely to have a sexually transmitted infection than were the controls.

Observational designs   Most research in medical anthropology, as in other health-related social sciences, is observational. Observational studies lack the defining features of experiments – random assignment to comparison groups and control over independent variables – and so are not well suited to demonstrate causal effects. But they are preferable to experiments for exploratory questions and have other advantages in confirmatory research, including higher external validity (generalizability), greater feasibility, and often fewer ethical objections.

We can distinguish three broad classes of observational designs: cross-sectional, longitudinal, and case-control studies (Figure 4.4). These three types of studies are recognized as the basic design options in epidemiology and biomedical sciences, but they are also used to varying degrees in medical anthropology. Cross-sectional studies, in which data are collected during one point in time, are the most common type. Although data collection often lasts for months or years, the study is still considered cross-sectional if the data are taken to represent one point in time. Thus, even long-term ethnographic research is usually cross-sectional in design (Gravlee et al. 2009).

In longitudinal designs, the data pertain to two or more points in time. In the last 50 years, longitudinal studies that incorporate panel data – repeated measures from the same units of observation at different points in time – have become increasingly important across the social, medical, and public-health sciences, but they remain relatively rare in anthropology. The lack of panel studies in anthropology represents a mismatch between theory and method, because panel data are particularly apt for the study of continuity and change – central areas of anthropological inquiry (Gravlee et al. 2009). For example, there is long-standing debate about the consequences of market integration and culture change for the health of indigenous peoples. Most relevant studies, however, use cross-sectional designs, which cannot track the effects of market integration over time. Godoy et al. (2009) used panel data collected annually (2002–2006) from the Tsimane' Amazonian Panel Study (TAPS) to fill this gap. Results suggest a general improvement in well being over time, with the highest rate of change in villages closest to the market town. This longitudinal study provides a better test of theory than would a cross-sectional design.

Case-control studies (Figure 4.4) are relatively rare in anthropology, although they are among the most common designs in epidemiology. The classic example in medical anthropology is Rubel and colleagues' (1984) study of *susto*, a folk illness reported in many parts of Latin America. Based on ethnographic accounts, Rubel et al. developed specific hypotheses about the sociocultural factors that shape susceptibility to *susto*. To test these hypotheses, they compared a sample of people who suffered from *susto* (cases) with people who did not (controls) in three communities with different histories, language, and cultures in the Oaxaca Valley of Mexico (Zapotec, Chinantec, and Mestizo).

Cases and controls were matched to form pairs of people who differed in whether they reported *susto* but were similar in other respects: age, gender, community, and complaints of being sick. Rubel and colleagues then tested cases and controls for differences social stress, psychiatric symptoms, and physical health problems. There were no significant associations between psychiatric symptoms and *susto*, but people suffering from *susto* did experience more social stress, including perceived difficulty in performing important social roles – a pattern Rubel et al. expected from ethnography. And this difference really made a difference: seven years later, 17 percent of people who complained of *susto* had died, but all the controls were still alive.

Rubel and colleagues' study also teaches a valuable lesson about research design in general. It is a model of good design, but it wasn't perfect – things happen in the field. Rubel et al. are honest about this fact and acknowledge their uncertainty. They realized, for example, that the gendered stigma of *susto* may have resulted in fewer Chinantecs being willing to label themselves with the illness. This pattern would have biased the researchers' conclusions about gender differences in the experience of *susto*. One of the hallmarks of well-designed research is that it makes such problems public.

SAMPLING

Some researchers collect data on an entire population, but most medical anthropologists work with samples, or subsets of the population in which they are interested. Thus, one of the key tasks of research design is to select an appropriate sampling strategy.

There are three steps in developing a sampling strategy: (1) defining the population, (2) identifying the unit of analysis (e.g., individual, household, clinic), and (3) selecting units of analysis for inclusion in the sample. The goal is to be able to say something about the units of analysis that were *not* selected for the sample. To meet this goal, it helps to be clear about what you'd like to say about your units of analysis. Do you want to estimate the average age in a population? Or, do you want to describe *what it means to get older* in that population? Medical anthropologists are likely to ask both types of questions, and they imply different types of sampling strategies.

Handwerker (2002) describes this distinction in terms of "life experience" versus "cultural" data. Life experience, or attribute, data refer to the characteristics of people (or other units of analysis) in a sample (e.g., age, income, blood pressure). Researchers in most health-related social sciences collect primarily attribute data of this type. Medical anthropologists collect attribute data, too, but many are also interested in questions such as "What does it mean to get older around here?" or "How important is income to a person's status in this community?" or "How do you know if you have high blood pressure, and how is it distinct from other illnesses?" These questions elicit cultural data, because they capture shared and socially transmitted systems of meaning that organize how people make sense of the world.

Attribute data generally require probability samples; cultural data do not, because the shared and socially constructed nature of cultural phenomena violates the assumption of case independence in classical sampling theory (Handwerker 2005). This assumption is often warranted with attribute data – your age is unrelated to mine. But if we participate in the same culture, your understanding of what it means to get old and mine are bound together, because people acquire cultural knowledge through social interaction. Thus, efficient ethnographic samples should select units of analysis to represent the range of variability in life experiences and social contexts related to the transmission of culture (Handwerker 2005; Johnson 1990). Probability samples are not necessary for achieving this aim: Handwerker and Wozniak (1997) demonstrated empirically that probability and nonprobability samples yield identical conclusions about cultural data.

Probability and nonprobability sampling

There are many options for probability and nonprobability sampling designs. Miles and Huberman (1994:28) list 16 types of nonprobability sampling. Onwuegbuzie and Leech (2007) identify 24 sampling designs, and Teddlie and Tashakkori (2009:170) delineate 26, including a mix of probability and nonprobability methods. These complex typologies build on a small set of basic sampling designs summarized in Table 4.1. For details about probability and nonprobability sampling in anthropology, see Bernard (2006), Handwerker (2005), Johnson (Johnson 1990), and Schensul et al. (1999).

One of the most common nonprobability sampling designs is quota sampling. Quota sampling involves identifying relevant subgroups in a population and sampling fixed proportions from each subgroup. Schoenberg et al. (2005) used quota sampling to explore differences and similarities in lay knowledge about diabetes between African–Americans, Mexican–Americans, Great Lakes Indians, and rural Whites. They set a quota of 20 participants from each group. This design balanced a desire for larger

Table 4.1 Basic probability and nonprobability sampling designs.

Method	Purposes	Procedures
Probability methods		
Simple random sampling	Generate representative sample when adequate sampling frame is available	List all members of population (sampling frame); select subset at random
Systematic random sampling	Generate representative sample; may not need to enumerate entire sampling frame	Select random starting point in sampling frame; select every Nth case
Stratified random sampling	Ensure that key subpopulations are represented; maximize between-group variation to increase precision	Divide population into subgroups; select random sample from each subgroup
Cluster sampling	Generate representative sample when no convenient sampling frame exists; sample dispersed populations efficiently	Divide population into clusters (e.g., neighborhoods, clinics); select random sample of clusters; sample within clusters
Nonprobability methods		
Purposive sampling	Sample theoretically important dimensions of variation	Identify important theoretical criteria; select cases to satisfy criteria; multiple criteria-based methods are available
Quota sampling	Generate sample with fixed proportions of key subpopulations	Divide population into subgroups; purposively select cases to fill quotas
Chain referral (snowball, respondent-driven sampling (RDS))	Construct sample of hard-to-find or hard-to-study populations	Snowball: ask seed informants to recommend others who might participate RDS: Use structured incentives to reduce bias in selection
Convenience (haphazard) sampling	Recruit participants when no other methods are feasible	Select groups or individuals that happen to be available and willing to participate

subsample sizes against practical constraints on the number of time-intensive, in-depth interviews researchers could complete. Within each group, Schoenberg et al. selected respondents whose age, ethnicity, and residential area increased the likelihood of experiencing diabetes. This strategy reflects the theoretical purpose of sampling cultural knowledge rather than estimating individual attributes.

Many medical anthropologists also use purposive sampling techniques. The goal of purposive sampling is to represent important dimensions of variation relevant to the aims of research. There are many approaches to purposive sampling, including selection of extreme, typical, unique, or politically important cases, selection to maximize homogeneity or heterogeneity of the sample, and identification of critical cases who have specialized knowledge or experiences relevant to the subject of interest (Onwuegbuzie and Leech 2007; LeCompte and Schensul 1999:113). In ethnographic research, the selection of key informants is an example of critical-case sampling.

Medical anthropologists often combine the building blocks in Table 4.1 to construct complex, multistage sampling designs. Baer et al. (2003) used a two-stage sampling design in their study of cross-cultural differences and similarities in the meaning of the folk illness *nervios* in Mexico, Guatemala, and the United States. In each of four sites, they purposively selected clusters – "a village, neighborhood, or census tract" (p. 319) – based on differences in social class, ethnicity, and other factors. Then they randomly selected roughly 40 households from each site, for a total sample size of 158.

The combination of probability and nonprobability sampling methods in multistage designs can be particularly useful for testing hypotheses about socio-cultural influences on health. For example, my colleagues and I used a variant of cluster sampling that combines probability and nonprobability techniques in our work on skin color, social classification, and blood pressure in Puerto Rico (Gravlee et al. 2005). We identified clusters purposively to maximize contrasts in key explanatory variables – social class and skin color – and sampled randomly within clusters. This strategy, like all decisions in research design, involved trade-offs: identifying clusters using nonprobability methods limited generalizability but probably made it more efficient to detect socio-cultural processes related to class and color. Given limited resources, that's a trade-off we were willing to make.

Sample size

Sample size, Bernard (2006:166–168) notes, is a function of four things: (1) how much variation exists in the population, (2) the number of subgroups you want to compare, (3) how big the differences are between subgroups, and (4) how precise your estimates need to be. These principles apply to studies large and small and are relevant to collecting either individual attribute or cultural data.

Procedures for estimating sample size in confirmatory survey or experimental research are well established (Cohen 1992). In exploratory research, however, the theoretical and empirical basis for evaluating sample size is less developed (Onwuegbuzie and Leech 2007). Morse (1994) proposes sample sizes of 5–50 informants, depending on the purpose of the study. Creswell (2007:126–128) recommends one or two participants in narrative research, 3–10 in phenomenological research, 20–30 in grounded theory research, 4–5 cases in case study research, and "numerous artifacts, observations, and interviews…until the workings of the cultural-group are clear" in ethnography (p. 128).

As Creswell's advice for ethnographers suggests, a common rule of thumb is the principle of theoretical saturation: your sample is large enough when you stop getting new information. In practice, however, there are few empirical guidelines for determining how large a sample is needed to reach saturation. Guest et al. (2006) addressed this issue in a study of HIV prevention in Ghana and Nigeria. They interviewed a total of 60 female sex workers. After every six interviews, they tracked which new themes appeared, how frequently each theme occurred, and how much codebook definitions changed. By these measures, Guest et al. reached saturation after only 12 interviews. This finding is consistent with rule-of-thumb guidelines and with predictions from cultural consensus theory (Romney et al. 1986). But Guest et al. note two important caveats. First, the semistructured interview guide was narrowly focused, and all women answered the same questions. In fully unstructured interviews, it would be harder to

Table 4.2   Stratified quota sampling design for semistructured interviews on experiences of racism among African–Americans in Tallahassee, FL.

	Age 25–34		Age 35–54		Age 55–65		
	Dark	Light	Dark	Light	Dark	Light	Total
Men							
Low SES	2	2	2	2	2	2	12
High SES	2	2	2	2	2	2	12
Women							
Low SES	2	2	2	2	2	2	12
High SES	2	2	2	2	2	2	12
Total	8	8	8	8	8	8	48

reach saturation, because new themes would appear as researchers introduced new questions over time. Second, the sample included only one, relatively homogenous subgroup: young, urban, female sex workers. Because sample size is a function of heterogeneity in the phenomenon of interest, adding other subgroups likely would have increased the sample size necessary to reach saturation.

Cultural consensus theory (Romney et al. 1986) formalizes the relationship between heterogeneity and sample size. The theory draws on a cognitive view of culture as shared and socially transmitted knowledge; it then provides a formal model for measuring the extent to which knowledge is shared or contested. The implication for sample size is that the higher the sharing, the smaller the sample necessary to detect consensual beliefs. If we wanted to know how Americans "carve up" the calendar into days of the week, a handful of informants would do, because this cultural knowledge is widely shared. But if we wanted to understand how days of the week relate to more complex domains – eating, drinking, family life, or sources of stress – we would need a larger sample to capture the variation. Consensus theory formalizes this intuition, and Weller (2007) provides tables for calculating necessary sample sizes to achieve desired levels of accuracy and validity, given varying levels of agreement among informants.

Baer et al. (2003) used this approach to calculate subsample sizes in their cross-cultural study of *nervios*. They anticipated a moderate level of consensus (0.50) and used stringent criteria for accuracy (0.95) and level of confidence (0.999). Using these conservative assumptions, the tables in Weller (2007) show that at least 29 informants were necessary in each research site. Baer et al. went a bit beyond the minimum and set subsample sizes at 40 per site "to be sure that we had sufficient individuals for comparative purposes within samples" (p. 323).

Table 4.2 shows how Christopher McCarty and I incorporated consensus theory and recommendations from Guest et al. (2006) into a quota sampling design for semistructured interviews with African–Americans in Tallahassee, FL. The goal of this ongoing study is to identify how the experience of racism and other social stressors shapes the risk of high blood pressure among African–Americans. The exploratory phase includes a round of semistructured interviews with a projected sample size of 48. We arrived at this sample size by identifying four individual attributes related to the experience of racism among African–Americans: gender, age, skin tone, and socio-economic status (SES). We then set quotas for all possible combinations of these attributes, treating them simplistically as dichotomous variables. The resulting sample size allows for comparisons between groups of 8–12 informants with different attributes relevant to experiences of racism. Based on cultural consensus theory, it should also yield confidence in our ability to detect shared beliefs and describe intra-cultural variation.

DATA COLLECTION AND ANALYSIS

The breadth of medical anthropology makes it impractical to discuss the full range of relevant methods of data collection and analysis. Instead, Table 4.3 summarizes the most commonly used methods of data collection and points to key literature for detail about specific techniques. The table briefly describes each method and the purposes for which it is appropriate. The column labeled E——C suggests the types of research questions along the exploratory–confirmatory continuum for which the method is useful. This suggestion is only a rough guide; some methods (e.g., spatial analysis, social network analysis) can be used with varying levels of structure and adapted to a wide range of exploratory or confirmatory questions.

Data collection

Methods of data collection in medical anthropology fall into three broad categories: participant observation, systematic observation, and interview methods. Participant observation is the bedrock of data collection in medical anthropology, as it is in the parent discipline. DeWalt and DeWalt (2002:2) define participant observation as "a way to collect data in naturalistic settings by ethnographers who observe and/or take part in the common and uncommon activities of the people being studied." The key task of participant observation is to create a systematic record of everyday life by writing field notes about informal observations, interactions, and conversations.

There is variation in how researchers balance the roles of participant and observer in ethnographic research (Spradley 1980). Bourgois (2003) participated intimately in the lives of crack dealers and users in East Harlem, but he remained on the periphery by virtue of his class and ethnic background – and by not using drugs himself. Bourgois also reminded informants of his role as an observer by openly tape-recording everyday conversations. In health services research, Sobo (2009:211) is more often a participating observer than an observing participant, but she emphasizes a sentiment all participant observers would embrace: "There is no substitute for being there." Barrett (2008) distinguishes between two major kinds of participant observation in his ethnography of Aghor medicine. The first is "the classic form of 'active participation' in which the ethnographer increasingly engages in the distinctive behaviors of his or her informants in order to better understand those behaviors in their appropriate cultural context" (p. 14). The second drew on Barrett's previous clinical experience as a registered nurse and volunteer at clinics in his field site. Barrett wasn't engaged in these roles during his research, as is typical in active participant observation; rather he used participation in relevant contexts as a framework for making sense of ethnographic observations.

Table 4.3 Commonly used methods of data collection in medical anthropology.

Method	Purposes	Procedures	E——C	Further reading
Participant observation	Understand everyday life from insider's perspective; generate hypotheses; enhance quality of data collection and analysis	Engage in day-to-day life; make systematic record of informal interactions, observations, and conversations	⊢	Bernard 2006:Ch. 13–14; DeWalt and DeWalt 2002; Spradley 1980
Systematic observation	Learn what people do, not just what they say; understand behavior in relation to cultural context	Define variables to be measured; develop sampling strategy; develop systematic rules about what to observe; record behavior	⊣	Bernard 2006:Ch. 15; Johnson and Sackett 1998; Borgerhoff Mulder and Caro 1985; Gross 1984
Interviewing				Bernard 2006:Ch. 9–11; Spradley 1979; Gorden 1992; Schensul 1999; Weller 1998
Unstructured	Understand lived experience from informants' perspective; build rapport; identify salient issues; discover appropriate language	Develop general interview questions; plan probes to explore for detail; listen actively; keep interview on topic, but encourage informant to lead	⊢	
Semistructured	Balance flexibility and structure; enhance comparisons across informants; best for one-time interviews; develop preliminary hypotheses	Develop interview guide; ensure all topics are covered, but allow flexibility in order and pace of the interview	⊣	
Structured	Test relationships among items in a cultural domain; test distribution of cultural knowledge; test relations between variables	Develop interview schedule or other stimuli; expose informants to the stimuli that are as identical as possible (e.g., cultural domain analysis, surveys)	⊣	
Elicitation methods				Ryan et al. 2000; Schensul 1999; Weller and Romney 1988

Method	Purpose	Procedure		Reference
Free lists	Identify contents and boundaries of a cultural domain; learn which concepts and categories are meaningful; learn how to ask questions	Conceptualize cultural domain (e.g., illnesses); ask informants to name all items in the domain	—│—	
Pile sorts, triad tests triad tests	Understand how participants perceive relationships among items in a cultural domain; examine semantic structure; describe inter- and intracultural variation	Ask informants to sort stimuli into piles that belong together; stimuli could be index cards with names of concepts or physical objects (e.g., photos, artifacts)	—│—	
Successive free lists	Explore relations between items in two domains (e.g., illnesses and symptoms); explore boundaries between categories and level of agreement among informants	Elicit free lists for initial domain (e.g., illnesses); for each item in first domain, elicit free list for other domains (e.g., symptoms, treatments)	—│—	
Frame substitution, yes–no	Test hypotheses about relations between items in two domains (e.g., illnesses and causes); describe inter- and intracultural variation	Construct frames of the form, "Can _____ come from _____?" Substitute items from related domains (e.g., illness and causes); record answers as yes–no	—│—	
Rankings, ratings, paired comparisons	Evaluate participants' perception of items along one or more dimensions; test hypotheses about semantic structure; describe inter- and intracultural variation	Ask informants to rank or rate items along some dimension; for paired comparisons, present informants with pairs of items and ask, "Which one is more _____?"	—│—	
Focus groups	Use group interaction to elicit data that would be harder to collect in individual interviews; explore perceptions of a topic or steps in a process; interpret results of survey or other more structured methods	Recruit participants (usually 6–12); decide on group composition; prepare interview guide; train moderator and note-taker; decide on level of transcription required; sample size is equal to number of groups	—│—	Schensul 1999; Morgan and Krueger 1998; Sobo 2009: Ch. 10

(cont'd)

Table 4.3 (cont'd)

Method	Purposes	Procedures	E——C	Further reading
Visual ethnography	Document behavior and cultural practices; elicit participants' perspectives; encourage collaboration and co-learning	Construct visual record (photographs or video) using degree of structure suitable for research objectives	-|-	Guindi 2004; Wang and Burris 1997
Social network analysis	Explore or test the pattern of social relations in a predefined group (socio-centric or whole network analysis) or in the web of social relations around focal individual (ego-centric or personal network analysis)	Reconstruct social ties through archival materials, record with direct observation, or elicit through interview methods	-|-|	Schensul et al. 1999; Scott 2000
Spatial mapping	Explore or test the spatial distribution of phenomena; study nested relations at multiple levels of analysis; elicit participants' understanding of space and place	Construct geographic information system using administrative (e.g., census) data or collect primary data; ask participants to make and interpret maps	-|-|	Schensul et al. 1999; Steinberg and Steinberg 2006

Note: E——C refers to continuum of exploratory to confirmatory research questions (see Figure 4.2). Hash marks suggest approximately where along this continuum each method of data collection would be appropriate. Some methods (e.g., social network analysis) are well suited to questions along the exploratory–confirmatory continuum; these methods are marked with two hash marks.

Systematic observation differs from participant observation because it imposes more structure on sampling and measurement (Johnson and Sackett 1998). For that reason, methods of systematic observation – including continuous monitoring, spot sampling, and time allocation – are best suited to confirmatory research questions. Systematic observation deserves wider use in medical anthropology, because many research questions concern what people *do*, not just what they *say*. And there is ample evidence that what people *say* is seldom a good proxy for what they *do* (Bernard et al. 1984).

Vitzthum (1994) studied concordance between maternal recall and systematic observation of breastfeeding in the Peruvian Andes. She interviewed 30 Nuñoa women with children under three years of age and asked each woman to estimate how often and how long her child breastfed each day. Vitzthum then monitored a subset of 10 women over a total of 86 hours and recorded the frequency and duration of breastfeeding to the nearest second. She found little association between observational and recall data: women generally "under-reported" frequency and "over-reported" duration of breastfeeding, but not in a consistent pattern. Thus, if we rely only on maternal recall – as epidemiologic studies of breastfeeding often do – we are likely to make mistakes.

Most of the methods shown in Table 4.3 involve collecting data through interviews. The unstructured–structured continuum is a useful way to organize the diversity of interview methods. Bernard (2006) identifies three types of interviews: unstructured, semistructured, and structured. Each type of interview, in turn, includes a diverse array of techniques. Structured interviews, for example, are used in survey research, in the collection of social network data, and in tandem with formal elicitation techniques such as freelisting and pile-sorting. Semistructured interviews and focus group discussions are likewise similar in level of structure and purpose.

Many medical anthropologists recognize the complementary value of different methods and often combine them in a single study. For example, Singer et al. (2006) designed a five-year study on the prevention of sexually transmitted infections and unwanted pregnancies among low-income, inner-city African–American and Puerto Rican youth in Philadelphia and Hartford. They used a wide range of methods: focus groups, formal elicitation (e.g., freelisting), in-depth individual sexual and romantic life histories, sexual behavior diaries, and structured interviews. This strategy paid off, because different methods yielded different insights. Focus groups helped to identify the range of relevant sexual behaviors and relationship types that people recognized, while in-depth individual interviews revealed the personal, emotional meaning of particular experiences. These complementary findings illustrate the benefit of creating redundancy, or triangulation, by using different types of methods (LeCompte and Schensul 1999:131).

Data analysis

Some of the methods shown in Table 4.3 generate text or images; others generate numerical data. There is a wide range of qualitative and quantitative methods for analyzing both types of data. The suggestions for further reading in Table 4.3 provide guidance on appropriate analytic methods for specific types of data. For a comprehensive approach to the analysis of qualitative data, see Bernard and Ryan (2010). For the analysis of quantitative data, see Handwerker and Borgatti (1998).

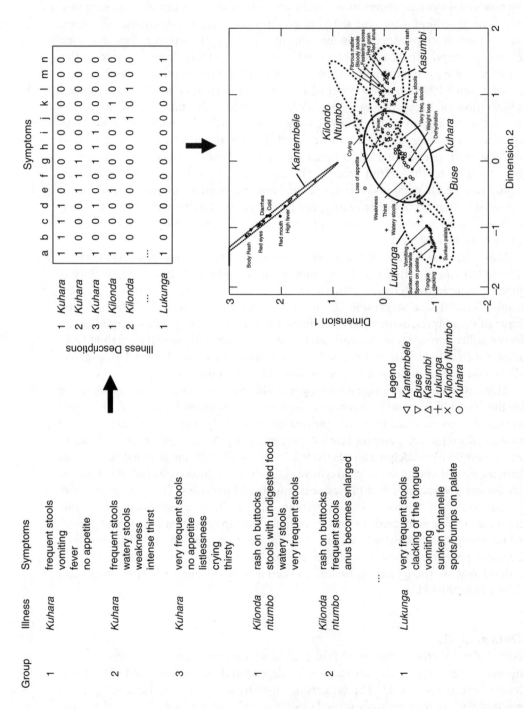

Figure 4.5 Successive free lists: analysis of relations between illnesses and symptoms. Adapted by courtesy of Sage Publications from Ryan, G. W., J. M. Nolan, and P. S. Yoder, 2000, Successive Free Listing: Using Multiple Free Lists to Generate Explanatory Models, *Field Methods* 12(2):83–107.

One example will illustrate the value of having a flexible toolkit of analytic methods. Yoder (1995) explored how mothers of small children in Lubumbashi, Zaire, diagnosed and treated childhood diarrheal diseases. The data he collected were typical of what many medical anthropologists collect. He began with unstructured, open-ended interviews with small groups of mothers, initially attempting to get as complete a list as possible of all the childhood illnesses mothers knew. Later, he probed for detail about symptoms and treatments and eventually identified six illnesses related to the biomedical category of diarrhea: *kuhara, kilonda ntumbo, lukunga, kasumbi, buse,* and *kantembele.* Last, he asked new groups of mothers specifically about symptoms, causes, and treatments associated with these six illnesses. Based on qualitative analysis of mothers' descriptions, Yoder (1995) concluded that mothers' diagnoses were based on the perception of symptoms and that ethnomedical classification shaped treatment decisions.

Because Yoder published tables of raw data from the mothers' descriptions, he and collaborators were later able to extend the analysis using other methods. Ryan et al. (2000) conceptualized Yoder's data as a series of linked lists. Yoder had collected 106 descriptions of the six illnesses. In each description, women discussed the symptoms, causes, and treatments associated with the illness. Ryan et al. converted women's descriptions into a set of matrices that indicated whether a particular symptom, cause, or treatment was mentioned in each illness description.

Figure 4.5 illustrates the steps in analyzing the relationship between illness and symptoms. The list on the left indicates which symptoms were associated with each description. For example, the women in the first group said that *kuhara* was associated with frequent stools, vomiting, fever, and no appetite. The matrix on the upper right converts the textual data into a series of ones (if a symptom was mentioned) and zeros (if it was not). This matrix contains all the information in women's original descriptions about which symptoms go with which illnesses – although the table of ones and zeros hardly clarifies anything on its own. The trick is that, once the data are in this format, Ryan et al. could use correspondence analysis (Weller and Romney 1990) to visualize the relationships between illness descriptions and symptoms.

In the graph in Figure 4.5, each solid circle represents a symptom; the other symbols represent individual illness descriptions by groups of women. The closer any two points appear together, the more strongly they are associated with each other. Thus, sunken palate and tongue clacking were often mentioned together, and both were associated with descriptions of *lukunga*. "Frequent stools" are associated with *kilondo ntumbo* and *kasumbi*, but women were more likely to mention "very frequent stools" in descriptions of *kuhara* and *buse*. The large ovals are 95% confidence intervals that reflect how much the groups of women agreed with one another about which symptoms go with which illnesses.

This analysis is no substitute for Yoder's original ethnography, of course. But is does add new insight about the level of intracultural variation, the coherence and boundaries of illness categories, and the amount of overlap in symptoms associated with different illnesses. Sibley et al. (2007) recently used the same approach to analyze women's descriptions of postpartum health problems in Bangladesh. In both cases, the transformation of words into numbers, numbers into pictures, and pictures back into words reminds us of how counterproductive it is to "divvy" research methods into either qualitative or quantitative.

CONCLUSION: LOOKING AHEAD

Medical anthropologists draw on methods from across the social and health sciences, but they are not only consumers; many are also at the leading edge of *developing* new methods relevant to interdisciplinary research on health. Some of the most important advances in the last decade include:

- A new measurement model that explicitly incorporates cultural meaning into survey measurement (Dressler et al. 2005).
- New tools for analyzing the structure and composition of personal networks (McCarty 2002).
- New methods for field-based collection of biomarkers (McDade et al. 2007).
- New approaches to the study of inter- and intracultural variation in knowledge, beliefs, and practices (Handwerker 2002; Hruschka et al. 2008).
- New tools for computer-assisted data collection in the field (Gravlee 2002; Ice 2004).
- New work on the systematic analysis of qualitative data (Bernard and Ryan 2010).

Meanwhile, medical anthropologists are likely to benefit from methodological developments in neighboring disciplines. Some trends, including the rise of participatory research (Cargo and Mercer 2008), heighten the relevance of medical anthropology to interdisciplinary research. Others, including advances in spatial and multilevel analysis (Glass and McAtee 2006), provide new tools for addressing problems of long-standing interest to medical anthropologists. Taking advantage of these developments will be key to the continued intellectual and practical relevance of medical anthropology.

REFERENCES

Baer, R. D., S. C. Weller, J. G. de Alba Garcia, M. Glazer, R. Trotter, L. Pachter, and R. E. Klein, 2003 A Cross-Cultural Approach to the Study of the Folk Illness Nervios. Culture, Medicine and Psychiatry 27(3):315–337.

Barrett, R., 2008 Aghor Medicine. Berkeley: University of California Press.

Bernard, H. R., 1996 Qualitative Data, Quantitative Analysis. Cultural Anthropology Methods Journal 8(1). Electronic document. http://www.analytictech.com/borgatti/qualqua.htm/.

Bernard, H. R., 2006 Research Methods in Anthropology. 4th edition. Walnut Creek, CA: AltaMira Press.

Bernard, H. R., and G. W. Ryan, 2010 Analyzing Qualitative Data: Systematic Approaches. Thousand Oaks CA: Sage Publications.

Bernard, H. R., P. Killworth, D. Kronenfeld, and L. Sailer, 1984 The Problem of Informant Accuracy: the Validity of Retrospective Data. Annual Review of Anthropology 13:495–517.

Borgerhoff Mulder, M., and T. M. Caro, 1985 The Use of Quantitative Observational Techniques in Anthropology. Current Anthropology 26(3):323–335.

Bourgois, P., 2003 In Search of Respect: Selling Crack in El Barrio. New York: Cambridge University Press.

Brim, J. A., and D. H. Spain, 1974 Research Design in Anthropology: Paradigms and Pragmatics in the Testing of Hypotheses. New York: Holt, Rinehart and Winston.

Carey, J. W., and D. Gelaude, 2008 Systematic Methods for Collecting and Analyzing Multidisciplinary Team-Based Qualitative Data. *In* Handbook for Team-Based Qualitative Research. G. Guest and K. MacQueen, eds. pp. 227–274. New York: AltaMira Press.

Cargo, M., and S. L. Mercer, 2008. The Value and Challenges of Participatory Research: Strengthening Its Practice. Annual Review of Public Health 29(1):325–350.

Charmaz, K., 2006 Constructing Grounded Theory: A Practical Guide Through Qualitative Analysis. Thousand Oaks CA: Sage Publications.

Chavez, L. R., F. A. Hubbell, J. M. McMullin, R. G. Martinez, and S. I. Mishra, 1995 Structure and Meaning in Models of Breast and Cervical Cancer Risk Factors: A Comparison of Perceptions Among Latinas, Anglo Women, and Physicians. Medical Anthropology Quarterly 9(1):40–47.

Chavez, L. R., J. M. McMullin, S. I. Mishra, and F. A. Hubbell, 2001 Beliefs Matter: Cultural Beliefs and the Use of Cervical Cancer-Screening Tests. American Anthropologist 103(4):1114–1129.

Cohen, J., 1992 A Power Primer. Psychological Bulletin 112(1):155–159.

Creswell, J. W., 2007 Qualitative Inquiry and Research Design: Choosing Among Five Approaches. 2nd edition. Thousand Oaks CA: Sage Publications, Inc.

DeWalt, K. M., and B. R. DeWalt, 2002 Participant Observation: A Guide for Fieldworkers. Walnut Creek CA: AltaMira Press.

Doerfel, M. L., 1998 What Constitutes Semantic Network Analysis? A Comparison of Research and Methdologies. Connections 21(2):16–26.

Dressler, W. W., 1995 Modeling Biocultural Interactions: Examples From Studies of Stress and Cardiovascular Disease. Yearbook of Physical Anthropology 38:27–56.

Dressler, W. W., 2005 What's Cultural About Biocultural Research? Ethos 33(1):20–45.

Dressler, William W., Borges, Camila D., Balieiro, Mauro C., and J. E. Dos Santos, 2005 Measuring Cultural Consonance: Examples With Special Reference to Measurement Theory in Anthropology. Field Methods 17(4):331–355.

Farnell, B., and L. A. Graham, 1998 Discourse-Centered Methods. In Handbook of Methods in Cultural Anthropology. H. R. Bernard, ed. pp. 411–458. Walnut Creek, CA: AltaMira Press.

Glass, T. A., and M. J. McAtee, 2006 Behavioral Science at the Crossroads in Public Health: Extending Horizons, Envisioning the Future. Social Science and Medicine 62(7):1650–1671.

Godoy, R., V. Reyes-Garcia, C. C. Gravlee, O. Heffetz, T. Huanca, W. R. Leonard, T. W. McDade, S. Tanner, and TAPS Bolivia Study Team, In press 2009 Trends in Adult Well-Being: 2002–2006 Panel Evidence From a Native Amazonian Society in Bolivia. Current Anthropology.

Gorden, R. L., 1992 Basic Interviewing Skills. Long Grove IL: Waveland Press.

Gravlee, C. C., 2002 Mobile Computer-Assisted Personal Interviewing (Mcapi) With Handheld Computers: The Entryware System V3.0. Field Methods 14(3):322–336.

Gravlee, C. C., W. W. Dressler, and H. R. Bernard, 2005 Skin Color, Social Classification, and Blood Pressure in Southeastern Puerto Rico. American Journal of Public Health 95(12):2191–2197.

Gravlee, C. C., D. P. Kennedy, R. Godoy, and W. R. Leonard, In press 2009 Methods for Collecting Panel Data: What Can Cultural Anthropology Learn From Other Disciplines? Journal of Anthropological Research 65.

Gross, D. R., 1984 Time Allocation: A Tool for the Study of Cultural Behavior. Annual Review of Anthropology 13(1):519–558.

Guest, G., A. Bunce, and L. Johnson, 2006 How Many Interviews Are Enough?: An Experiment With Data Saturation and Variability. Field Methods 18(1):59–82.

Guindi, F. E., 2004 Visual Anthropology: Essential Method and Theory. Walnut Creek CA: AltaMira Press.

Handwerker, W. P., 2002 The Construct Validity of Cultures: Cultural Diversity, Culture Theory, and a Method for Ethnography. American Anthropologist 104(1):106–122.

Handwerker, W. P., 2005 Sample Design. In Encyclopedia of Social Measurement. K. Kempf-Leonard, ed. pp. 428–436. San Diego CA: Academic Press.

Handwerker, W. P., and S. P. Borgatti, 1998 Reasoning With Numbers. In Handbook of Methods in Cultural Anthropology, H. R. Bernard, ed. pp. 549–594. Walnut Creek CA: AltaMira Press.

Handwerker, W. P., and D. F. Wozniak, 1997 Sampling Strategies for the Collection of Cultural Data: An Extension of Boas's Answer to Galton's Problem. Current Anthropology 38(5):869–875.

Hruschka, D. J., L. M. Sibley, N. Kalim, and J. K. Edmonds, 2008 When There is More Than One Answer Key: Cultural Theories of Postpartum Hemorrhage in Matlab, Bangladesh. Field Methods 20(4):315.

Ice, G. H., 2004 Technological Advances in Observational Data Collection: The Advantages and Limitations of Computer-Assisted Data Collection. Field Methods 16(3):352–375.

Johnson, J. C., 1990 Selecting Ethnographic Informants. Newbury Park CA: Sage Publications.

Johnson, J. C., 1998 Research Design and Research Strategies. In Handbook of Methods in Cultural Anthropology. H. R. Bernard, ed. pp. 131–172. Walnut Creek CA: AltaMira Ptess.

Johnson, A., and R. Sackett, 1998 Direct Systematic Observation of Behavior. In Handbook of Methods in Cultural Anthropology. H. R. Bernard, ed. pp. 301–332. Walnut Creek CA: AltaMira Press.

King, G., R. O. Keohane, and S. Verba, 1994 Designing Social Inquiry: Scientific Inference in Qualitative Research. Princeton: Princeton University Press.

Krippendorff, K, 2004 Content Analysis: An Introduction to Its Methodology. Second edition. Thousand Oaks CA: Sage Publications.

LeCompte, M. D., and J. J. Schensul, 1999 Designing and Conducting Ethnographic Research, vol. 1. Walnut Creek CA: AltaMira Press.

McCarty, C., 2002 Structure in Personal Networks. Journal of Social Structure 3(1). Electronic document. http://www.cmu.edu/joss/content/articles/volume3/McCarty.html/.

McDade, T. W., S. R. Williams, and J. J. Snodgrass, 2007 What a Drop Can Do: Dried Blood Spots as a Minimally Invasive Method for Integrating Biomarkers Into Population-Based Research. Demography 44(4):899–925.

Miles, M. B., and A. M. Huberman, 1994 Qualitative Data Analysis: an Expanded Sourcebook. 2nd edition. Thousand Oaks CA: Sage Publications.

Morgan, D. L., and R. A. Krueger, 1998 The Focus Group Kit. vols. 1–6. Thousand Oaks CA: Sage Publications.

Morse, J. M., 1994 Designing Qualitative Research. In Handbook of Qualitative Inquiry. N. K. Denzin and Y. S. Lincoln, eds. pp. 224–225. Thousand Oaks, CA: Sage Publications.

Onwuegbuzie, A. J., and N. L. Leech, 2005 Taking the "Q" Out of Research: Teaching Research Methodology Courses Without the Divide Between Quantitative and Qualitative Paradigms. Quality and Quantity 39(3):267–295.

Onwuegbuzie, A., and N. Leech, 2007 A Call for Qualitative Power Analyses. Quality and Quantity 41(1):105–121.

Pelto, P. J., and G. H. Pelto, 1996 Research Designs in Medical Anthropology. In Medical Anthropology: Contemporary Theory and Method. C. F. Sargent, and T. M. Johnson, eds. pp. 293–324. Westport CT: Praeger Publishers.

Romney, A. K., S. C. Weller, and W. H. Batchelder, 1986 Culture as Consensus: A Theory of Culture and Informant Accuracy. American Anthropologist 88:313–339.

Rubel, A. J., C. W. O'Nell, and R. Collado-Ardsn, 1984 Susto, a Folk Illness. Berkeley: University of California Press.

Ryan, G. W., J. M. Nolan, and P. S. Yoder, 2000 Successive Free Listing: Using Multiple Free Lists to Generate Explanatory Models. Field Methods 12(2):83–107.

Schensul, J. J., 1999 Enhanced Ethnographic Methods: Audiovisual Techniques, Focused Group Interviews, and Elicitation Techniques, vol. 3. Walnut Creek CA: AltaMira Press.

Schensul, J. J., M. D. LeCompte, R. T. Trotter II, M. Singer, and E. K. Cromley, 1999 Mapping Social Networks, Spatial Data, and Hidden Populations, vol. 4. Walnut Creek CA: AltaMira Press.

Schensul, S. L., 1999 Essential Ethnographic Methods: Observations, Interviews, and Questionnaires: Observations, Interviews, and Questionnaires, vol. 2. Walnut Creek CA: AltaMira Press.

Schoenberg, N. E., E. M. Drew, E. P. Stoller, and C. S. Kart, 2005 Situating Stress: Lessons From Lay Discourses on Diabetes. Medical Anthropology Quarterly 19(2):171–193.

Scott, J., 2000 Social Network Analysis: A Handbook. London: Sage Publications.

Shain, R. N., J. M. Piper, E. R. Newton, S. T. Perdue, E. Ramos, J. D. Champion, and F. A. Guerra, 1999 A Randomized, Controlled Trial of a Behavioral Intervention to Prevent Sexually Transmitted Disease Among Minority Women. New England Journal of Medicine 340(2):93–100.

Sibley, L., L. Blum, N. Kalim, D. J. Hruschka, J. Edmonds, and M. Koblinsky, 2007 Women's Descriptions of Postpartum Health Problems: Preliminary Findings From Matlab, Bangladesh. Journal of Midwifery and Women's Health 52(4): 351–360.

Singer, M. C., P. I. Erickson, L. Badiane, R. Diaz, D. Ortiz, T. Abraham, and A. M. Nicolaysen, 2006 Syndemics, Sex and the City: Understanding Sexually Transmitted Diseases in Social and Cultural Context. Social Science and Medicine 63(8):2010–2021.

Sobo, E. J., 2009 Culture and Meaning in Health Services Research: A Practical Guide. Walnut Creek CA: Left Coast Press.

Spradley, J. P., 1979 The Ethnographic Interview. Orlando FL: Harcourt Brace Jovanovich.

Spradley, J. P., 1980 Participant Observation. New York: Holt, Rinehart & Winston.

Steinberg, S. J., and S. L. Steinberg, 2006 Geographic Information Systems for the Social Sciences: Investigating Space and Place. Thousand Oaks CA: Sage Publications.

Teddlie, C., and A. Tashakkori, 2009 Foundations of Mixed Methods Research: Integrating Quantitative and Qualitative Approaches in the Social and Behavioral Sciences. Thousand Oaks CA: Sage Publications.

True, W. R., 1996 Epidemiology and Medical Anthropology. In Medical Anthropology: Contemporary Theory and Method. C. F. Sargent and T. M. Johnson, ed. pp. 325–346. Westport CT: Praeger Publishers.

Vitzthum, V. J., 1994 Suckling Patterns: Lack of Concordance Between Maternal Recall and Observational Data. American Journal of Human Biology 6(5):551–562.

Wang, C., and M. A. Burris, 1997 Photovoice: Concept, Methodology, and Use for Participatory Needs Assessment. Health Education and Behavior 24(3):369–387.

Weller, S. C., 1998 Structured Interviewing and Questionnaire Construction. In Handbook of Methods in Cultural Anthropology. H. R. Bernard, ed. pp. 365–410 Walnut Creek CA: AltaMira Press.

Weller, S. C., 2007 Cultural Consensus Theory: Applications and Frequently Asked Questions. Field Methods 19:339–368.

Weller, S. C., and A. K. Romney, 1988 Systematic Data Collection. Newbury Park CA: Sage Publications.

Weller, S. C., and A. K. Romney, 1990 Metric Scaling: Correspondence Analysis. Newbury Park CA: Sage Publications.

Yoder, P. S., 1995 Examining Ethnomedical Diagnoses and Treatment Choices for Diarrheal Disorders in Lubumbashi Swahili. Medical Anthropology 16 (3): 211–247.

CHAPTER 5

Medical Anthropology and Public Policy

Merrill Eisenberg

INTRODUCTION

From its inception, the discipline of Anthropology has focused on issues that are relevant to public policy. In the era of Franz Boas, discriminatory and prejudicial policy was justified by theories of cultural and physical evolution that identified some societies and peoples as superior to others based on Darwinian concepts of adaptive change over time and survival of the fittest. As an alternative, Boas' concept of cultural relativism, which is described by some as reflecting a "political agenda" (Greenfield 2001:37), proposed that culture is learned and malleable. Cultural relativism justified a more liberal approach to public policy and informed policies and programs in the post World War II era (Greenfield 2001:38). In the next generation of anthropologists, both Margaret Mead and Ruth Benedict were outspoken critics of US social and foreign policy. Since then many anthropologists have been involved in work of relevance to policy from a variety of vantage points. Whether through the lens of development, health, education, agriculture, or the myriad other topics explored by anthropologists, issues related to policy have been prominent in anthropological research, and most especially in applied anthropology (Okongwu and Mencher 2000).

Over the years, there have been many calls for a more focused study of policy and the policy making process within the discipline of anthropology (see, for example Belshaw 1976; Foster 1976; Sanday 1976; Cochrane 1980; Gruenbaum 1981; Weaver 1985a, 1985b; Anglin 1997; Durrenberger 1996; Shore and Wright 1997; Hackenberg and Hackenberg 1999; Wedel et al. 2005; Singer 2010). Other social sciences, particularly the discipline of political science and its subdiscipline of policy studies, have historically had a more focused relationship with policy and have developed frameworks

A Companion to Medical Anthropology, First Edition. Edited by Merrill Singer and Pamela I. Erickson.

and theories to describe policy processes. Notably, Smith and Larimer (2009:5–6) describe policy studies as having three general areas of inquiry: policy evaluation (the *ex post* study of policy outcomes), policy analysis (the *ex ante* identification of policy content), and the policy process (how and why policies are adopted), a framework that is useful in assessing work done in the anthropology of health policy This chapter is directed at students and practitioners of medical anthropology who work in communities and who want their work to contribute to the development of a more humane and just world through social policy development and implementation. As a practicing applied anthropologist in the health arena, I believe that medical anthropology would benefit from an examination of what the policy studies field has already done that we can use to help us understand and inform an anthropology of policy for medical anthropologists. Additionally, the public health literature is rich with accounts of how policy impacts health, as well as accounts of how policy can be used to address health problems and health disparities. In this chapter I attempt to integrate these disciplines into a medical anthropological approach to policy issues.

This chapter will first address the centrality of policy to the human social experience, provide definitions of policy, public policy and public policy mechanisms, and describe how policy both creates and addresses health concerns. Next, the anthropological study of policy is briefly reviewed, and some examples of anthropological treatments of health policy issues from both a narrative and critical perspective are provided. The remainder of the chapter is written from the perspective of applied anthropology, with a focus on using medical anthropology research to inform the development of public policy through advocacy and empowerment activities that medical anthropologists (and the people they study) can undertake. The importance of understanding the policy making endeavor ethnographically is emphasized as a tool to guide participation in the policy process. Models that can be used as a "lens" for understanding the public policy making process are presented, and a typology of participation is proposed.

Most of the research and theory described in this chapter is based on the US public policy experience. It assumes a government that is elected and is therefore responsive, to some degree, to citizen input. Some of the theoretical models of the policy process that are used in this chapter have been applied in other contexts, but the degree to which models of the US experience inform policy development in other nations depends on the political structure of the particular state of concern. Many of the concepts can also be applied in private policy making settings, such as the policies of nongovernmental health-related organizations, health care provider institutions, and public health programs.

While policy is made in many arenas in the US, both public and private, much of this chapter focuses on the creation of public policy in law and rule making contexts. It also emphasizes processes that occur at the state and local level rather than federal or transnational policy making. Policy making that has national, bi- or multinational, or global relevance has an impact that is broad and can be devastating to health, but few anthropologists have access to policy making at those levels (some of the work of Jim Yong Kim and Paul Farmer on access to antiretroviral drugs in resource poor settings, however, is an exception to this pattern). Much policy making that impacts health in the USA occurs at the state and local levels, where the process and the "actors" are accessible, where the power of corporate interests is somewhat diluted, and where local input is more likely to make a difference. I do not discount the importance of higher level policy making in creating disparity and hardship, but my goal is to enable and amplify the voice of medical anthropology in the policy conversation where we work best, from the ground up.

THE POLICY ENDEAVOR: REGULATING HUMAN BEHAVIOR

Throughout human evolution every human group has been concerned with defining acceptable behavior for the health and welfare of the group. With regard to health, every culture has rules or expectations about how resources are obtained and distributed, what we eat and how it is prepared, how the environment is kept clean, how we work, what we do to keep ourselves safe, how we care for the young, the old, and the otherwise vulnerable, how we conceptualize and respond to illness, how healers are identified, prepared, monitored and reimbursed, and how conflicts are resolved. In pre-state societies that were the traditional target of anthropological research, these things are regulated by social structure, systems of obligation, religious pre- and proscriptions, traditions, and taboos. In some cases the rules are formally codified, in others they are enforced through social norms. In complex societies today, we address these same concerns primarily through policy.

Policy is defined by Webster as "prudence or wisdom in the management of affairs" (Webster http://www.merriam-webster.com/dictionary/policy), although experience tells us that much social policy is hardly prudent or wise. At the individual level, people create personal policies – behavioral resolutions – that impact their own health. Pronouncements such as "I'm going to walk two miles three times a week" or "I'm going to stop eating junk food" or "I will rely on natural remedies when I am sick," are personal policies that guide individuals' lives. Personal level policies are shaped and constrained by policies made at higher levels of social organization, through the social institutions in which we participate as members of society.

Policy is everywhere, and it can facilitate or constrain individual behavioral intentions. While my personal policy may be to avoid junk food, at work, the vending machines contain nothing but chips, soda, and candy bars. Alas, the policy my employer made with regard to what food is available in the work site "trumps" my personal policy when I am hungry and have no time (because of my employer's work load and break policy) to walk to the cafeteria. I eat the candy. My personal policy may be to walk two miles three times a week, but my neighborhood was constructed without sidewalks or street lights, making it dangerous and scary to walk after dark when I typically have the time. Alas, the policy my city made about how the built environment is constructed overwhelms my personal policy to get regular exercise. I watch TV instead (prompted in part by my employer's policies about my workload and its effects on my personal stamina). My personal policy may be to use natural remedies when I am sick, but my health insurance policy (provided as a policy of my employer) does not recognize the services of herbalists and only covers the services of MDs. Since I can't afford to pay out of pocket to see an herbalist (as a result of the salary policy of my employer), I end up at the Internist's office. Thus, policy created at higher levels of organization – in my workplace, in my community, in my insurance company, by the state – shapes my behavior and defines how I live, whatever my personal policy and my intentions may be. Moreover, people in subordinate and marginalized groups have far less ability than do I to realize their personal policies because of structural barriers.

Of primary concern to this chapter are public policies that impact the lives of many people. There are many definitions of *public* policy in the political science literature. Public policy can be defined as "whatever governments chose to do or not to do," or "the actions of government and the intentions that determine those actions," or "the outcome of the struggle in government over who gets what" (Birkland 2005:18). Policy is made in the "public's" name, and is interpreted and implemented by public and private actors (Birkland 2005:17). For example, government laws and regulations can (and many do) require that all private health insurance policies provide coverage for specific types of services, e.g., mental health, or family planning, or some other type of coverage (though I know of no state law that requires coverage for herbalists), but this is often interpreted and implemented in different ways by different insurance providers. Sometimes, implementation is so "creative" that the original intent of the policy may not be apparent to the user (e.g., covering only one month of mental health services or levying high co-pays on contraceptive care).

One way to categorize public policy is in terms of how it serves the public good. Policies can provide benefit to the general population (distributive policies), they can provide a benefit to one segment of the population at cost to another segment (re-distributive policies), or they can place limits on how individuals, groups, and corporate entities operate (regulatory policies) (Birkland 2005:141–143). Another way is to categorize how policy works. Policies can be "carrots" that provide subsidies and incentives, "sticks" that regulate the behavior of individuals and other social actors, or "sermons" that sanction messages and provide information meant to influence behavior like the annual release of the food pyramid recommendations by the Department of Agriculture, which is meant to teach us how to eat healthier (Bemelmas-Videc et al. 2006).

Law sets the framework for public policy, but public policy is far broader than formally codified law. Public policy is also found in rules and regulations that define specifically how laws are implemented and enforced. In the USA, while the legislative branch of government makes laws, it is the bureaucrats in the executive branch that create the rules and regulations for implementing those laws. A state law may, for example, require that restaurants be smoke-free, but it is the regulations associated with that law, that are developed by the state health department, that define specifically how the law will be implemented. Rules and regulations determine whether or not smoking is permitted on restaurant patios, how far from the door smokers need to go to light up legally, or who is responsible for applying and enforcing sanctions when restaurants do not comply.

In addition, implementing agencies of the government have policies about how to apply the rules and regulations. A state law and associated regulations may provide the framework for ensuring clean indoor air in restaurants, but local health department policy may determine how frequently restaurants are inspected or whether a warning will be given before a sanction is applied for non-compliance with the law. Finally, the judicial system is responsible for ensuring that policy is written and applied in accordance with existing constitutional provisions and state and federal laws and for settling disputes related to personal harm. For example, a restaurant that does not want to become smoke-free can sue the jurisdiction that created the smoke-free law, claiming that the law impinges on the property rights, defined in law, of the business owner. Contesting policy in the legal system offers a route that citizens can take to achieve policy modification.

Public policy is ostensibly meant to address the public good. However, there are many "publics" that sometimes have opposing and competing interests. Policies that serve one public are frequently harmful to another. The anthropological literature has many examples of how policy hurts people. For example, critical medical anthropologists have documented how policies that serve capitalistic interests can have devastating impacts on people at the bottom end of the economic continuum (Castro and Singer 2004; Singer and Baer 2008). Policies can also have good intentions but unintended and unforeseen consequences. Whether it is by reinforcing structural violence or as a result of the inability to anticipate results, policies can cause harm. It is policy that:

- puts people at risk (e.g., policies that govern war, international development, immigration, offshore drilling, environmental exposures, global warming);
- creates disparities (e.g., policies that affect poverty, access to education and health care);
- creates built environments that undermine healthy living (e.g., policies that create urban sprawl, inner city conditions, limit access to open;
- allows harmful products to enter the market (e.g., policies that address tobacco, guns, lead based paint, tainted foods and other products).

In comparison with medical anthropology's largely critical approach to policy, the field of public health has taken a more prescriptive stance. Policy is one of the three core functions of public health (Institute of Medicine 1988). It has been characterized as a "tool" for public health promotion (Gostin, 2000; Mensah et al. 2004). The public health literature provides many examples of how specific public policies can be used to create interventions that address health issues. Policy "prescriptions" are proposed to address, for example, obesity (Stanton and Acs 2005), chronic diseases (Mensah et al. 2004), teen sexual activity and pregnancy (Brindis 2006), and other adolescent risky behavior (Bishai et al. 2004), and tobacco use (Brownson et al. 1995).

Policy, Anthropology, and Medical Anthropology Research

The study of policy is inherently anthropological. Shore and Wright (1997:7) point out that policies "encapsulate the entire history and culture of the society that generated them" and they function in a way that is similar to Malinowski's notion of how myths operate – they serve as a guide to behavior, a "charter for action" (quoting Malinowski, 1926). The rules for behavior, laid down in either myth or policy, both reflect and produce social norms. Therefore, making policy is making culture.

One way of thinking about how policy reflects and produces culture is to think about policy making within a systems framework. First proposed by Easton (1965), a systems view of policy making places the policy endeavor within an overall environmental context that includes government structure, social, political, economic conditions, national mood, and existing policies that govern behavior Within this context,

---

Environmental Context

Inputs
- Media coverage, public opinion, research findings, other information, decision maker personal experiences, opinions of decision maker friends and family, election issues, stakeholder positions, degree of controversy, and voter interest

"Black Box"
- The political system: relative importance of the issue, overall political agenda, political trade-offs, pressure from leadership, time constraints, and schedule

Outputs
- Laws, regulations, rules, policies, and other decisions
- Structure of the government, economic, social, and political environment

---

Figure 5.1   A systems model of policy process. By courtesy of M. E. Sharp from Birkland, Thomas A., 2005, *An Introduction to the Policy Process*, p. 202.

the inputs of the policy system include media, public opinion, election results, information provided to policy makers, and communication with policy makers. The outputs of the system are laws, regulations, and court decisions. Between the inputs and the outputs is the "black box" where the policy making process occurs. In policy making circles, the process that occurs in the black box is sometimes referred to as "sausage making" – it's messy, and the ingredients are frequently of questionable quality (Figure 5.1).

The nexus between anthropological research and public policy has been clear from the earliest days of the discipline in, for example, "anthropological historical" overviews of how anthropology has contributed to policy over time, as provided by Stull and Moos (2005) and Okongwu and Mencher (2000).

Although many early anthropologists were involved in health related research, medical anthropology did not emerge as a distinct sub-discipline until the 1970s; the Medical Anthropology Newsletter (MAN) was first published in 1972. Early discussions of the boundaries of the field that appear in MAN include no mention of policy as a research focus or as a byproduct of medical anthropology research (Foster 1976; Olesen 1974; Hasan 1975; Kiefer 1975). As the sub-discipline developed, the connection between medical anthropology and policy became more prominent and the relevance of studying policy makers and policy process soon began to be articulated. Foster's (1976:15) earliest article on medical anthropology and international health planning advised medical anthropologists to "...study administrators, planners, and professional specialists as individuals and as members of professions and bureaucracies, in the same ways and for the same reasons that we study traditional societies or any other client group." The relevance of medical anthropology to health planning, in both national and international contexts, received considerable attention in the mid 1970s, but it was never central to the field (Hughes 1976; Colson 1976; Low and Schreiber 1977; Schreiber and Low 1977).

In 1981, Gruenbaum observed that much of the research in medical anthropology was focused on cultural factors in health, illness, and curing, and the acceptance of

Western medicine, and she described this focus as "limited" because it did not include the consideration of policy (Gruenbaum 1981:47). Gruenbaum attributed this situation, in part, to medical anthropologists ceding the policy terrain to economists, historians, and political scientists, and she encouraged medical anthropologists to be more directly involved in policy development by "devis(ing) and propos(ing) policies which can affect the actual health conditions of the population and challenge the legitimacy of policies which only further the interests of a privileged minority" (Gruenbaum 1981:61).

Over the past 30 years, many medical anthropologists have addressed policy issues in their work. A few examples among many include Pillsbury's examination of the bureaucratic and sociological reasons for resistance to incorporating traditional healers into national health care systems (1982), Osterweis and colleagues' 1987 work on pain and disability, which was conducted specifically to inform the US Social Security Administration's eligibility requirements (Osterweis et al. 1987), and Ginsburg and Rapp's 1995 collection of papers on the politics of reproduction that addresses the "...impact of global processes on everyday reproductive experiences" (Ginsberg and Rapp 1995:1). Hansen (1997) explored the discourses of power in the hospital setting, and showed how the study of policy is central to understanding issues of power. Heller (2001) demonstrated how language used in the public policy discourse influenced French policy on genetically modified foods. Joralemon (1995) reports on how disputed concepts of the meaning of the body and its parts (based on the competing ideologies of gifts and property rights) and the contested definition of "death" lead to conflict in policy making targeting organ procurement for transplantation. Wilson et al.'s (1999) work in Cote d'Ivoire, which was conducted to collect information to inform the development of family planning services, takes into account the perceptions of policy makers in assessing maternal policy issues. Thus, most medical anthropologists engage with the idea of policy, but not with its formation or implementation.

The critical medical anthropology approach involves an examination of how power structures impact health and health care systems and an assessment of the role of power and unequal access in the making and enforcement of policy. In this context, policy is frequently conceptualized broadly, e.g., capitalist policy, and is viewed as the instrument that is used to create, exercise, and preserve power relationships for the enrichment of the capitalist class to the detriment of lower class, marginalized, and disenfranchised populations. For example, Singer et al. (1992) show how history, global economics, and labor policy promote alcoholism in the Puerto Rican community. The economic and political constraints that shape the use of health care among low-income immigrants are examined by Chavez et al. (1992). Farmer and Castro (2004) describe how policies that define health in economic terms have amplified the AIDS pandemic in Haiti. Lamphere (2005) describes how state policy that eliminated the "fee-for-service model" in New Mexico's Medicaid program and replaced it with a managed care system of reimbursement led to the severe deterioration of services provided to the poor. Erickson (1998) addresses how teen pregnancy prevention policy focusing on the individual ignores broader socio-cultural patterns in immigrant (primarily Mexican) Latino populations that make it normative, expected, and often welcomed in East Los Angeles. Freudenberg et al. (2006) demonstrate how policy decisions that dismantled the health, public safety, and social service infrastructure led to deteriorated living conditions for vulnerable populations, which was directly related to a rise in tuberculosis, H IV, and homicide in New York City.

The critical perspective points out how disparity and injustice are created by policy and challenges us to think about how our own work, which is frequently situated at the local level, can inform policy at the societal level in a positive way. For medical anthropologists who want to go beyond criticizing and documenting the ill effects of policy, a logical next step is to actively engage in seeing that our data and insights are considered in policy deliberations so that more just and humane policy decisions can be made.

RESEARCH TO ACTION

Recent calls for an anthropology of policy propose academic boundaries for the field that specifically exclude policy advocacy (Wedel et al. 2005:31). This is in keeping with the longstanding debate about the role of advocacy in the practice of anthropology. While Wedel and co-workers see an anthropology of policy as being restricted to "research into policy issues and processes and the critical analysis of those processes" (Wedel et al. 2005:31), many other anthropologists, particularly medical anthropologists, have been engaged in advocacy activities both as individual researchers and as part of a broader community effort (see Rylko-Bauer et al. 2006). Informing policy development is one of the aims of applied anthropology, as expressed in the purpose and vision of the professional organization for applied anthropologists, the Society for Applied Anthropology:

> The Society for Applied Anthropology aspires to promote the integration of anthropological perspectives and methods in solving human problems throughout the world: *to advocate for fair and just public policy* based upon sound research; to promote public recognition of anthropology as a profession; and to support the continuing professionalization of the field. (Society for Applied Anthropology n.d.) (*emphasis added*).

For medical anthropologists working in local communities, promoting public policy that is informed by research can mean working in policy environments that are close to the field – looking to city, county, or state jurisdictions. It is at these levels that many health related assessments are conducted to identify needs for the purpose of prioritization and attracting programmatic funding, that policies are made and enforced, that programs and eligibility requirements are designed and implemented, and that health providers and facilities are regulated. State and local policy processes are also more accessible to medical anthropologists working at the community level compared with the federal process which largely occurs inside the Washington DC beltway. Further, policy actors at the state and local level are more accessible and responsive to local citizens than are policy actors at the federal level. In my experience, most of us are "very little fish in a very big pond" at the federal level, but we can be "big fish in a smaller pond" when we work locally – and the probability of success is much higher.

Whiteford and Bennett argue that all medical anthropology is *applied* anthropology because medical anthropology research findings have "direct or indirect applications to human health and medicine" (Whiteford and Bennett 2005:121). Contributing ideas to policy development can be a byproduct of anthropological research. For example, Spradley's ethnographic work with homeless men who were repeatedly arrested for public drunkenness (Spradley 1970) was widely read outside of anthropology and is thought to have influenced criminal justice system policy, resulting in a turn to a more humane treatment of homeless men (Singer 2000). However, Spradley's capturing of the public and policy-making imagination has been more of an exception than the rule.

Many anthropologists lament the lack of success in their attempts to influence policy makers. In his plenary address to the Society of Medical Anthropology in 2000, Singer sums up the problem succinctly: "...the relationship of anthropologists and their colleagues in allied disciplines with policy makers historically has been conflicted, a thing of starts and stops, and at times a merry-go-round" (Singer, 2010). By way of explanation, Singer's address goes on to state:

> Many anthropologists who have ventured into this domain [policy making] soon realized that their findings, gained through endless hours of work under, at times, the most difficult of on-the-ground conditions, may be ignored and that their research-informed recommendations fall on deaf ears. The reason, as we well know, is that the complex "truths" our research produces are often out of harmony with the official and usually simplistic truths formulated by the few who have tended to control the health, environmental, educational, and social policy arenas and who do so overtly or implicitly in the interests of the capitalist class (Singer 2010:10).

It is certainly true that policy makers have not rushed to embrace anthropological knowledge in their policy deliberations and that the capitalist class is quite successful in commanding the attention of policy makers, but in addition to making this point, we need to assess our own competency in the culture and social context of policy making as an alternative explanation for our unsatisfying level of influence. A more phenomenological approach to policy making, developing an understanding of the policy process and actors, and an appreciation of the lived experience of policy making, would provide us with a more complete assessment of the complexity of policy maker truths. This, in turn, would help us to become more competent social actors able to communicate with policy makers in a culturally appropriate way so that our ideas can be heard and understood by those whom we want to influence. As Nader suggested (1972) and as reinforced by Foster (1976), medical anthropologists who want to inform policy need to "study up" (Nader 1972:284). Studying up can give us crucial cultural information we need to become more effective in the policy process as well as an understanding of how policy makers view particular issues; both can help us frame the information we contribute to the process (Backstrom and Robins 1995; Eisenberg et al. 2000; Montini and Bero 2001).

The ethnography of policy making is one of the research foci identified in Wedel et al.'s call for a greater focus on policy within the field of anthropology (Wedel et. al. 2005) and it is also one of the three main foci in policy studies, a subdiscipline of political science (Smith and Larimer 2009). From a research point of view, policy ethnography can answer questions like "...how should we conceptualize policy processes that tend to create particular 'policy communities?'"; "...what role do policies play in fashioning of modern subjects and subjectives?"; "...how useful is it to view policy as a 'political technology?'"; or "viewing policy through a state's administrative rules, laws, and judicial rulings?" (Wedel et al. 2005:34–35). From an applied anthropology point of view, I propose that policy ethnography can answer questions like "how can medical anthropological findings make their way into the policy conversation?" and "what can we do to change the balance of power in the health policy environment?" These are critical to influencing policy making.

ETHNOGRAPHY, FRAMEWORKS, MODELS, AND THEORIES OF POLICY MAKING

One way to conceptualize policy making is to view it as taking place in a policy "community." In his call for medical anthropologists to turn their attention to entities with power, Foster noted that "[a] bureaucracy, in its structural and dynamic aspects, is very much like a 'natural' community such as, for example a peasant village, in that it is a real society with a real culture..."(Foster 1976:15). From an anthropological perspective, policy communities are "contested political spaces...[in which]...the questions addressed are 'Whose voices prevail?' and 'How are their discourses made authoritative?'" (Shore and Wright 1997:15). As in developing cultural competency in any field, for those who seek to influence policy, whether it is in the bureaucracy or in legislative contexts, expertise in policy making requires an understanding of the community in which policy is made.

Inspired by Weatherford's (1985) classic ethnography of the US Congress, and through my own research and the peculiarities of my personal life experience in state and local government contexts, I have come to view legislatures as small societies, with an economy based on the production of laws. These societies have a hierarchical social structure that contains moieties (political parties) and "crosscutting" clans (defined by issues, structured around committees, including elected officials and lobbyists) in which kinship (real and fictive) plays an important role in communication and power distribution. For example, ancestors are revered and invoked and have authority in the discourse of policy options ("as Harry Truman used to say..."). There are also important rituals and ceremonies, both formal and informal, that occur throughout the lawmaking process, some of which promote cohesion (opening day/ end of session "sine die" activities, annual lobbyist vs. legislator baseball game) and others that are rites of passage for policy ideas (first read, second read, public hearings). There is a rhythm to the policy process in which time and timelines play a unique role (scheduling of legislative sessions, trajectory of bills from being proposed to the Governor's desk, time limits for speakers in public hearings). A special vocabulary and stylized communication patterns (rules and traditions of floor debate) and textual products ("intro sets," "fiscal notes," policy statements, fact sheets) are used in policy development. More importantly, the people directly involved in legislative policy making, including elected officials, legislative staff, executive branch bureaucrats, lobbyists, and advocacy groups, see themselves as operating within an "insider world" that is separate from the "real" world and that is not well understood by "outsiders" (Eisenberg 1996).

The policy science literature tells us that policy communities form around issue domains. While there is a general culture of policy making in Congress, state legislatures, and city councils, the actual process of developing policy content takes place in smaller communities of experts, based on substantive areas of policy interest, such as health, insurance, housing, taxes, etc. (Birkland 2005). One approach to studying policy communities is to describe them as networks. Wedel et al. (2005) identify network analysis as an important methodology for the anthropological study of policy making. Network analysis is also used in the discipline of policy studies, where these networks are recognized as a "new form of governance" (Adam and Kriesi 2008:131) that removes the process of public policy making from being strictly a governmental function. As the boundaries between the public and private spheres are blurred in the policy process, there is opportunity for anthropologists (and anybody else) to participate.

A descriptive account of policy making that may be of interest for medical anthropologists is provided in John E. McDounough's book *Experiencing Politics, A Legislator's Stories of Government and Health Care* (2000), which focuses on health policy making at the state level. Brief descriptive accounts of health policy making can also be found in the public health literature. For example, Greathouse et al. (2005) provide a case study of how a smoke-free law was passed in a Kentucky municipality, and Wilson-Clay et al. (2005) describe how lactation experts influenced breastfeeding policy in the state of Texas. While these accounts describe specific policy making efforts at particular points in time, they point out many aspects of the process that can have meaning in other policy making contexts. However, they are not a substitute for understanding those specific local contexts in which medical anthropologists may find themselves. To be effective in policy formation, we need to identify the policy community that is relevant to our work and understand the social structure and process of that community. We also need to identify points of access, allies, and key informants that can aid our efforts.

The field of policy studies offers several theories, heuristics, and frameworks for the policy process (Sabatier 2007a,b) that can help applied medical anthropologists discover and understand policy communities and how to best participate. For a detailed review of policy process theory as it relates to health policy, see Oliver (2006). Here I discuss just a few of the concepts from policy science that I have found helpful in thinking about how policy is made and how people from all walks of life can participate.

The social organization of policy making: policy communities

Policy makers have full agendas. The range of issues that they must address is vast. No matter how important you think your issue is, it is just one of many that compete for policy making attention. Getting policy makers to pay attention to your issue – that is getting on the policy agenda – is one of the first tasks for having influence in policy development. The Multiple Streams framework (Kingdon 2003) provides a helpful model for understanding how we can influence agenda setting. Kingdon's model proposes that there are three streams of situations and actors that must converge to bring an issue to the attention of policy makers. Table 5.1 provides a summary of these and shows what they bring to the policy making table, the general types of concerns they

Table 5.1   The three streams in policy communities: who are they, what are they, what concerns them, and what they do to promote public policy.

	Actors	*Concerns*
Problem Stream: with knowledge of the lived experience Main contribution: documentation	• People impacted by policy and those with a concern • People providing services to people impacted by the policy • Researchers who have information that can inform policy development	• How does this policy affect me/ the people I care about/the people I provide service to? • What do we know about this problem that can inform a more humane policy? • How can we get the policy makers to create the policy we want?
Policy Stream: with knowledge of policy issues and processes Main contribution: solutions	• Lobbyists and advocacy groups representing problem stream actors • Coalitions of organizations that have similar interests and concerns • Governmental bureaucrats that are engaged in the policy issue • Gadflies, recognized experts who participate in policy development	• Is this a good time to raise the issue? • Is there consensus about what to do about the issue? • How will the policy impact people who experience the problem? • How can we address the arguments of the opposition? • How can we address policy maker concerns?
Political Stream: with the power to enact policy Main contribution: decisions	• Officials who have the power to enact a policy • Staff members of officials who enact policy • Public opinion/voting patterns	• How does this proposal jibe with our overall policy agenda? • Who does it help? Who does it hurt? • What does it cost? Who will pay? • What do my colleagues want me to do? • What will be the impact of my vote on my political future?

have, and the activities that they engage in. In any particular policy context, the relative importance of concerns and activities will vary.

The problem stream is where the policy issue becomes a "lived experience." Actors in the problem stream include the people who experience a problem and others who are close to the problem and interested in seeing it get resolved. These might include friends and relatives, service providers, churches and other community based organizations, and researchers. These people have information and they have an advocacy position. Medical anthropologists in the field often find themselves in the problem stream. It is in the problem stream that researchers can partner with community members and participate in community-based coalitions to advocate for the interests of those who experience the results of the policy. Although Kingdon sees the problem stream as an essential component of policy making, unlike the policy and politics streams, problem stream actors are outsiders to everyday policy making.

The policy stream consists of the "primeval soup" (Kingdon 2003:116) of ideas about a particular issue and a policy "community" (Kingdon 2003:117) of experts who support particular policy ideas and who are routinely involved in policy discussion. Policy stream actors can be elected officials, legislative staffers, interest group analysts, lobbyists, researchers and academics, planners and evaluators, and other recognized experts who participate in the policy conversation over long periods of time. The organizations they represent have been involved in the policy conversation for many years. The individuals involved have worked together, sometimes in alliances, sometimes in opposition. Indeed, it is an axiom in the policy field that today's opponents are tomorrow's allies, and vice versa, as new issues arise, contexts change, and old issues are redefined. An important aspect of understanding policy making is to understand the relationships among the actors in the policy stream at any point in time. Anthropologists in the field can develop relationships with policy stream actors (whom, given anthropological jargon, we might designate as "key information recipients") and contribute their policy ideas through these individuals, or they can become policy stream actors themselves.

Finally, the political stream includes the general political climate and public opinion, and the actors are elected officials and political operatives who have the authority to make policy. It is in the political stream that policy makers are pressured by party politics to support or oppose a particular point of view for political gain rather than address an issue rationally, or where policy makers may trade votes on issues, agreeing to vote "yea" or "nay" in exchange for a vote on another frequently unrelated issue. In considering any policy issue, the three streams bring different concerns and resources to the table.

In general, problem stream actors are concerned with how the policy impacts the people who are affected by it and how to convince policy makers to create the policy they want. Policy stream actors are concerned with the merits of one particular policy idea over another strategy for promoting policies in the policy making context, including addressing opposition positions, issues of timing, negotiating and compromise in writing policy language, and organizing a lobbying effort. Political stream actors are concerned with how the issue articulates with an overall policy agenda, the balancing of interests, and political issues such as the position of leadership and fellow lawmakers, and how the voters will perceive their support or opposition.

While Kingdon's model was developed to describe Federal level policy making in the USA, it has been applied to health policy making at the state level as well. Some examples from the public health literature include Greathouse et al.'s (2005) use of the *Multiple Streams* framework to explain the decision-making process that led to the enactment of a smoke-free law in Lexington, Kentucky, a state with a strong pro-tobacco constituency, and O'Sullivan and Lussier-Duynstee's (2006) use of the framework as a prescription for action to address policy related to the health of homeless adolescents. The framework has also been applied to health policy development processes in other nations. For example, see Elson's (2004) discussion of voluntary sector policy shifts in Canada and the UK, Hoeijmakers et al.'s (2007) description of health policy development at the local level in the Netherlands, and Kwon and Reich's (2005) analysis of health policy development in Korea.

Another model of the policy making process that may be helpful to medical anthropologists is the Advocacy Coalition Framework (ACF). The ACF focuses on various interest groups within the policy community (Sabatier and Weible 2007). While the community as a whole forms around topics, these coalitions form around shared values and beliefs, and compete with each other to influence policy development. Research based on ACF "...focuses on the interaction of advocacy coalitions – each consisting of actors from a variety of institutions who share a set of policy beliefs – within a policy subsystem. Policy change is a function of both competition within the subsystem and events outside the subsystem" (Sabatier 2007:9–10). An application of ACF to health related issues is provided by Gagnon et al. (2007), who use it to describe a conceptual cognitive framework for the development of healthy public policy. Also of note is Heaney's (2006) analysis of the how competing interest-group coalitions brokered the development of the Medicare Prescription Drug Improvement and Modernization Act (PL 108–173). Heaney sees policy coalitions as a "standard part of interest groups' strategic repertoires" and he shows how "multiple sources of brokerage in policy networks contribute to interest group influence over health policy. Brokerage depends on informal communication networks, formal coalitions of interest groups, and political parties" (Heaney 2006:889).

Is policy making rational? The role of information in policy making

Many medical anthropologists see their role in the policy process as providing information. Information is one of several clearly defined "inputs" in Easton's systems model, but is only one of the inputs in the complicated ecology of policy making, so it is no wonder that providing information alone has little impact. The expectation that information will drive the policy process is based on what political and policy science refer to as "rational actor" decision making (Birkland 2005). The rational actor model posits that when policy makers are confronted with a problem, they should conduct a comprehensive analysis, which includes a clarification of values and objectives and a means/end analysis. This requires consideration of theoretical issues and the gathering of large amounts of information. Once the information is analyzed, all potential solutions and their consequences will be considered, and policy makers will choose the one that maximizes their original objective. The rational actor model underlies the field of "policy analysis" that was first proposed by Lasswell in early 1936. Lasswell envisioned a policy "science" that could be "...an applied social science that would act as a mediator between academics, government decision-makers, and ordinary citizens by providing objective solutions to the problems that would narrow or minimize, if not eliminate, the need for unproductive political debate on the pressing policy issues of the day" (Fischer 2003:3).

While appealing to social scientists, the rational actor model is an ideal, and it does not reflect the reality of policy making. The reality is that there is rarely consensus about the problem, let alone the goal. Further, there is too much information that has bearing on any policy problem, and gathering information is too time consuming to fit into the policy making cycle, as seen in the following example.

In a roundtable discussion on translating research into policy (Folz 2005), one state legislator told the story of a bill to increase drunk driving fines in Arizona. The bill was introduced in the health committee, the locus for discussion and gatekeeper for health issues in the state legislature. The legislator reasonably wondered what the impact of raising fines would have on drunk driving and the morbidity and mortality related to drunk driving. He asked researchers at a nearby university to look into the question. By the time the researchers got back to him to say that there is no evidence of an impact, the bill had been voted upon in committee and passed. The legislator remarked "I am not sure I could have made a great argument against the fine... because it seemed to be a reasonable way for the legislature to increase state revenue." This vignette illustrates some of the limitations of the rational model. First, the goal of the policy that was passed was not clear. Although the issue was raised in the health committee context, the legislator understood that the goal was not to save lives but to raise money for the general fund. Second, information to inform the decision could not be produced within the policy-making timeframe. In academic time, a week, even a few weeks, is an appropriate amount of time to produce a comprehensive literature review, but in legislative time, the information can be needed within a few hours. The end result was that the decision to raise fines for drunk driving was made without any evidence about the policy's impact on motor vehicle crashes and associated morbidity and mortality.

Even when evidence is available, the nature of science can undermine its utility in the policy process. From a policy maker's perspective, research-based information is difficult to interpret. There are always conflicting studies that support alternative policy decisions. For example, the legislator who was frustrated by the lack of evidence on the drunk driving bill mentioned above went on to describe a bill to create all-day kindergarten, a concept that was supported by a great deal of research showing positive impacts on children's overall academic achievement. However, opponents of the idea offered alternative studies that showed no impact or negative impact on future achievement. While the studies supporting all-day kindergarten were stronger methodologically and represented a consensus among scholars, some legislators chose to pay attention to the alternative view. The bill failed and the legislator commented that "what takes place in the state legislature really is values masquerading as data...if my value is 'kids ought to be home with their parents,' which is a big argument, then I can always use a select few studies and ignore the preponderance [of the evidence]" (Folz 2005:341).

From a policy maker's perspective, the values that are pervasive among the voters in their district translate into support or rejection of the policy maker in the voting booth. Thus, it is easy to see why research evidence alone might be secondary in a policy maker's mind. Even when a policy maker sees and understands the value of research-based evidence, the "structural violence" of the political system steers policy makers to support policies that have no rational basis (or refuse to support policies that have a strong rational basis) because supporting the alternative can mean political death.

Anthropological work that examines the assumptions that underlie policy discourses, such as the works of Hansen (1997), Heller (2001), and Joralemon (1995), contributes to the understanding of how information is constructed and used in the policy process. The public health literature is also a rich source for discussion of the construction and role of information in health policy debates (Wallack and Dorman 1996; Dorman et al. 2005; Glasgow and Emmons 2007; McDonough 2001; Choi 2005; Bero et al. 2001; Montini and Bero 2001; Rosenstock and Lee 2002). Discourse framing has also received a good deal of attention in the popular literature (Lakoff 2004). From a practical standpoint, resources are also available about the acquisition of the skills needed for using information in policy contexts (Wallack et al. 1999).

Additionally, the FrameWorks Institute is a non-profit organization that seeks to "advance the nonprofit sector's communications capacity by identifying, translating and modeling relevant scholarly research for framing the public discourse about social problems" (FrameWorks Institute n.d.) and is an excellent source for research and training opportunities for medical anthropologists interested in applying public discourse theory to practice.

COMMUNITY EMPOWERMENT

Understanding the social organization of policy making and how information is used in the policy process is important information for medical anthropologists seeking to inform the policy process. It sheds light on how to communicate research findings and the potential communication channels and messages we can use. Medical anthropologists may want to become policy stream actors, sitting at the table where policy is debated, acting as culture brokers, and relaying the experiences of the community to those who make policy. They may even want to become political stream actors by running for public office, although not many have chosen this option. But what about those actors in the problem stream, the people whose health and welfare our research describes? How can they directly participate in policy making?

Critical medical anthropology tells us that the power differential between those who *make* policy and those who *live* it contributes significantly to disparity and suffering. Addressing the power differential, some anthropologists see community empowerment as the essence of applied anthropological work, relegating research to a "necessary but insufficient step for fostering empowerment and adaptive policy choices" (Preister 2010:25). The promise of community empowerment in medical anthropology is perhaps best expressed in relation to the AIDS epidemic and a description of how gay activists came to influence the NIH research agenda (Epstein 1996).

Bringing the people who *live* policy into the social organization of those who *make* policy is one of the aims of participatory action research and action anthropology. These types of anthropology are "methods of research and social action that occur when individuals of a community join together with a professional researcher to study and transform their community in ways that they mutually value" (vanWilligen 2002:77). For example, Singer and his colleagues involved drug users in Connecticut in the HIV prevention and drug treatment related policy processes at the state and local levels (Buchman et al. 2004). In the language of policy studies, action anthropology raises the voice of the problem stream, coupling the problem stream with the policy and politics streams and allowing problem stream actors to compete in the arena of policy ideas.

Empowerment can be accomplished through several processes. Researchers who utilize community based participatory action research methods can mobilize communities not only to plan, conduct, and interpret research, but also to go a step further and organize for community change. By partnering with community organizers and other locally situated stakeholders, medical anthropologists and their community-based research teams can use their research to inform natural community leaders about issues and work collaboratively with them to seek policy change (Singer 2010).

Community organizing can influence the policy process by raising the salience of the issue through activities that attract press attention, express public opinion, and demonstrate political strength. Referring to the systems model of the policy process, these types of activities can be viewed as "inputs" that can change the social and political environmental context of the policy process, and influence what is happening in the "black box." This approach has been used successfully in Hartford, Connecticut, where the Institute for Community Research partners with other service and advocacy organizations to conduct community-based participatory research on a variety of health issues, involving community members not only in the research process but also in the negotiation of policy change (Schensul 2005). Anthropologists and other social scientists contribute research skills while other organizations take the lead on community organizing for political action. Medical anthropologists Robert Rubenstein and Sandy Lane have also utilized this approach to impact policy in Syracuse, New York. Working in collaboration with the Syracuse Model Neighborhood Facility, the Center for Community Alternatives, and other higher education institutions in the area to address health disparity issues due to racism, structural violence, and environmental injustice, they train students and engage community members to conduct research that is utilized in the policy making process (Rubinstein and Lane 2010).

Another approach to community empowerment can be through the legally established participatory processes. For example, public hearings and other opportunities for public comment are common avenues for citizens to express their opinion on policy issues. Grassroots and policy stream organizers usually ensure that community members show up for these occasions and sometimes orchestrate demonstrations and testimony. However, these opportunities for citizen input typically come at the end of the policy making process, when the competing arguments have already been heard, decisions have already been made, and there is a specific policy under consideration. At this point, all the community can do is speak in support or opposition to the idea being considered.

More influential involvement of citizens in policy deliberation can occur through participation on advisory or governing panels. Many public programs now require this type of citizen participation. For example, Federally Qualified Community Health Centers are required by law to be governed by a Board of Directors. At least 51% of Board members must be active, registered clients that represent the population served. These community members are in a position to make policy about how the organization operates and by virtue of their position, they are members of the policy stream who, when armed with research results, are in a position to translate research findings into policy.

The Practice of a Policy-Oriented Medical Anthropology

While many medical anthropologists want their work to inform the policy debate, the level of desired involvement in the policy process will vary among us. Some may just want to get their research findings into the hands of a powerful policy actor, while others may want to sit at the table and participate in policy negotiations. Still others may want to engage in community organizing, while others may want to "go native" and run for public office. I propose a continuum of engagement in the policy process that is multi-factorial, based on how the medical anthropologist interacts with the policy actors in Kingdon's three streams and three levels of engagement. The first level is "educating." Those who educate in the policy process merely provide information without taking a stand one way or the other about a policy issue. As an example from my own work on policy related to obesity prevention, educating would include talking with members of each of the three streams about how the built environment is related to obesity, how the built environment is particularly problematic in certain "high risk" (or from a structural perspective, "highly vulnerable") communities locally, and how other jurisdictions have addressed the problem successfully through policy interventions.

According to the Center for Lobbying in the Public Interest, "advocating" is going one step further, using your research to support a particular position or negate another position (Center for Lobbying in the Public Interest n.d. (a)). Continuing my obesity example, advocating includes educating plus endorsement of policy approaches that are known to prevent obesity, such as promoting the idea of mixed use development, or fast food menu labeling, or the development of walking trails and bike boulevards in high risk areas. These activities become "lobbying" when a specific law or policy is addressed – when we encourage policy makers to support or oppose a particular bill, ordinance, or rule. There are two types of lobbying. Direct lobbying is communicating with policy makers in support or opposition of a particular piece of legislation, while grassroots lobbying is encouraging others to contact policy makers in support or opposition to a particular piece of legislation.

Figure 5.2 shows a three dimensional continuum of engagement for medical anthropologists and gives examples of the types of activities that can occur along the continuum from "not engaged" to "fully immersed."

In addition to our own personal preferences and interests, where we operate along the continuum can also be dictated by the nature of our employment. The Hatch Act (5 USC § § 7321–7326) is a federal law that restricts the political activity for those working in government at any level or in programs funded with federal taxpayer dollars. Employees of educational or research institutions are exempt from the Hatch Act. The Hatch Act does not prohibit all political activity. For example, covered individuals may attend and be active at political rallies and meetings, and campaign for or against referendum questions or candidates in partisan elections. However, public employees may not use their official authority of governmental resources to influence an election or solicit support for a political purpose in the workplace. The regulations related to the Hatch Act are complicated. The US Office of Special Counsel provides detailed guidance on who is permitted to do what at their website (US Office of Special Counsel n.d.). State and local laws may further restrict the political activities of public employees. The National Council of State Legislatures provides a summary of state laws defining lobbying and lobbyists (National Council of State Legislatures n.d.)

Employees of private, tax-exempt non-profit organizations also have restrictions on lobbying and political activity that are imposed by the Internal Revenue Service. Non-profit organizations designated by the IRS as 501c(3) may elect a 501(h) designation that allows them to spend up to 20% of the first $500,000 of their annual expenditures and 15% of the next $500,000 on lobbying. They may not, however, support or oppose any candidate running for office, though they may organize

	Not engaged (Academic)	Engaged		Immersed (Gone native)	
		Educate	Advocate	Lobby	
Relationship with the problem stream	Share research findings	Engage in discussions of policy implications of findings;	Culture Broker: demystifying the policy process; link community members to the policy stream	Collaborate with grassroots advocacy groups to lobby policy makers	Become a community organizer
Relationship with the policy stream	No contact	Culture Broker: explain the community experience	Create information products tailored to the needs of the policy community	Long-term participation in an advocacy coalition; participate in framing and negotiating policy content	
Relationship with the political stream	No contact	Meet with politicians to discuss the issues	Conduct studies that address policy maker concerns about a particular policy approach;	Lobby policy makers; work on political campaigns of like-minded candidates	Become a policy maker

Figure 5.2   What's a medical anthropologist to do? A continuum of engagement in the policy process. Figure by Merrill Eisenberg.

candidate forums and voter registration activities. Many 501c(3) organizations have created "sister 501c(4) organizations, which are non-profit organizations that have no limitations on lobbying or political activity. However, 501c(4) organizations are prohibited from receiving federal grant funds. Monetary contributions to 501c(3)s are tax deductible; contributions to 501c(4)s are not (Center for Lobbying in the Public Interest n.d. (b)).

There are many avenues available for medical anthropologists to engage in research-informed social change. Regardless of a medical anthropologist's locus of employment and preferences for personal involvement, knowing the contours of the policy community that addresses the issues that our research informs can be a crucial first step to seeing our work utilized in the policy process. At the very least, medical anthropologists in the field can identify the specific policies that are related to our research, the jurisdictions in which they can be made or amended, and the actors in the three streams (organizations as well as individuals) that address the issue. A deeper exploration of the social structure of the policy community, the history of policy development within that community, the narrative thread of the relevant policy discussion over time, and the identification of potential points of leverage can serve to propel our research work into real and effective social change. By cultivating a deeper understanding of policy communities and the policy making process, we can develop a more nuanced understanding of why things are as they are, and what can be done by us, and more importantly, by the communities we study, to foster change in a meaningful way.

NOTE

1   In addition to growing up in a politically-engaged household, I was married to a Congressional staffer who later became a State Representative, and have participated as an "insider" in many aspects of political life at the state and local levels in both Connecticut and Arizona.

REFERENCES

Adam, Silke, and Hanspeter Kriesi, 2007 The Network Approach. *In* Theories of the Policy Process. Paul A. Sabatier, ed. pp. 129–154. Boulder: Westview Press.

Anglin, Mary K., 1997 Policy, Praxis, and Medical Anthropology. Social Science and Medicine 44(9):1467–1369.

Backstrom, Charles, and Leonard Robins, 1995 State AIDS Policy Making: Perspectives of Legislative Health Committee Chairs. AIDS and Public Policy Journal 10(4):238–248.

Belshaw, Cyril S., 1976 The Sorcerer's Apprentice, An Anthropology of Public Policy. New York: Pergamon Press.

Bermelmans-Videx, Marie-Louise, Ray C. Rist, and Evert Vedung, 2006 Carrots, Sticks and Sermons. New Brunswick: Transaction Publishers.

Bero, Lisa A., Theresa Montini, Katherine Bryan-Jones, and Christina Mangurian, 2001 Science in Regulatory Policy Making: Case Studies in the Development of Workplace Smoking Restrictions. Tobacco Control 10:329–336.

Birkland, Thomas, 2005 An Introduction to the Policy Process. Armonk NY: M.E. Sharp.

Bishai, David M., Dan Mercer, and Athena Tapales, 2004 Can Government Policies Help Adolescents Avoid Risky Behavior? Preventive Medicine 40:197–202.

Brindis, Claire D., 2006 A Public Health Success: Understanding Policy Changes Related to Teen Sexual Activity and Pregnancy. Annual Review of Public Health 27:277–295.

Brownson, Ross C., Dyann Matson Koffman, Thomas E. Novotny, Robert G. Hughes, and Michael P. Eriksen, 1995 Environmental and Policy Interventions to Control Tobacco Use and Prevent Cardiovascular Disease. Health Education Quarterly 22(4):478–498.

Buchanan, David, Merrill Singer, Susan Shaw, Wei Teng, Tom Stopka, Kaveh Khoshnood, and Robert Heimer, 2004 Syringe Access, HIV Risk, and AIDS in Massachusetts and Connecticut: The Health Implications of Public Policy. *In* Unhealthy Health Policy: A Critical Anthropological Examination, Arachu Castro and Merrill Singer, eds. pp. 275–286. Walnut Creek CA: AltaMira Press.

Castro, Arachu, and Merrill Singer, 2004 Unhealthy Health Policy. Walnut Creek CA: AltaMira Press.

Center for Lobbying in the Public Interest, n.d. (a) Advocacy Tactics. Electronic document. http://www.clpi.org/nuts-a-bolts/advocacy-tactics/.

Center for Lobbying in the Public Interest, n.d. (b) The Law. Electronic document. http://www.clpi.org/the-law/irs-rules/.

Chavez, Leo R, Estevan T. Flores, and Marta Lopez-Garza, 1992 Undocumented Latin American Immigrants and US Health Services: An Approach to a Political Economy of Utilization. Medical Anthropology Quarterly 6(1):6–26.

Choi, Bernard C. K., 2005 Twelve Essentials of Science-based Policy. Preventing Chronic Disease 2(4):1–11.

Cochrane, Glynn, 1980 Policy Studies and Anthropology. Current Anthropology 21(4):445–458.

Colson, Anthony C., 1976 A Model for a Comprehensive Low Cost Health Program in Rural Malaysia. Medical Anthropology Quarterly (OS) 7(4):13–18.

Dorfman, Lori, Lawrence Wallack, and Katie Woodruff, 2005 More Than a Message: Framing Public Health Advocacy to Change Corporate Practices. Health Education and Behavior 32(3): 320–336.

Durrenberger, E. Paul, 1996 Gulf Coast Soundings: People and Policy in the Mississippi Shrimp Industry. Lawrence KS: University Press of Kansas.

Easton, David, 1965, A Systems Analysis of Political Life 1965. Chicago: University of Chicago Press.

Eisenberg, Merrill, 1996 Capitol Culture. Paper presented at the Annual Meeting of the Society for Applied Anthropology, Baltimore, March.

Eisenberg, Merrill, Kirsten Elliott, Kristie Taylor, and Robert Woodward, 2000 Understanding Tobacco Policy Making From a Local Policy Makers' Point of View: A Study of Elected Arizona Policy Makers at the City and County Levels. Arizona Department of Health Services. Electronic document. http://azmemory.lib.az.us/cdm4/item_viewer.php?CISOROOT=/statepubs&CISOPTR=694&CISOBOX=1&REC=6/.

Elson, Peter R., 2004 Advocacy and Third Way Politics: Canada and the United Kingdom. The Philanthropist 18(3):215–224.

Epstein, Steven, 1996 Impure Science: AIDS, Activism, and the Politics of Knowledge. Berkeley: University of California Press.

Erickson, Pamela, 1998 Latina Adolescent Childbearing in East Los Angeles. Austin: University of Texas Press.

Farmer, Paul, and Aruchu Castro, 2004 Pearls of the Antilles? Public Health in Haiti and Cuba. In Unhealthy Health Policy. Aruchu Castro and Merrill Singer, eds. pp. 3–28. Walnut Creek CA: AltaMira Press.

Fischer, Frank, 2003 Reframing Public Policy. Oxford: Oxford University Press.

Folz, Christina E., 2005 Health Policy Roundtable – View from the State Legislature: Translating Research Into Policy. Health Services Research 40(2)337–346.

Foster, George M., 1976 Medical Anthropology and International Health Planning. Medical Anthropology Quarterly (OS) 7(3):12–18.

FrameWorks Institute, n.d. Mission of the FrameWorks Institute. Electronic document. http://www.frameworksinstitute.org/mission.html/.

Freudenberg Nicholas, Marianne Fahs, Sandra Galea, and Andrew Greenberg, 2006 The impact o New York City's 1975 Fiscal Crisis on the Tuberculosis, HIV, and Homicide Syndemic. American Journal of Public Health 96(3):424–434.

Gagnon, France, Jean Turgeon, and Clemence Dallaire, 2007 Healthy Public Policy, A Conceptual Cognitive Framework. Health Policy 81:42–55.

Ginsberg, Faye D., and Rayna Rapp, 1995 Conceiving the New World Order: The Global Politics of Reproduction. Berkeley: University of California Press.

Glasgow, Russell E., and Karen M. Emmons, 2007 How Can We Increase Translation of Research into Practice? Types of Evidence Needed. Annual Review of Public Health 28:413–433.

Gostin, Lawrence O., 2000 Law as a Tool to Advance the Community's Health. Journal of the American Medical Association 283(21):2837–2841.

Greathouse, Lisa W., Ellen J. Hahn, T. C. Chizimuzo, Todd A. Okoli, and Carol A. Warnick, 2005 Passing a Smoke-Free Law in a Pro-Tobacco Culture: A Multiple Steams Approach. Policy, Politics and Nursing Practice 6(3):211–220.

Greenfield, Sidney M., 2001 Nature/Nurture and the Anthropology of Franz Boas and Margaret Mead as an Agenda for Revolutionary Politics. Horizontes Antropologicos 7(16):35–52.

Gruenbaum, Ellen, 1981 Medical Anthropology, Health Policy and the State: A Case Study of Sudan. Policy Studies Review 1(1):47–65.

Hackenberg, Robert A., and Beverly H. Hackenberg, 1999 You CAN Do Something! Forming Policy From Applied Projects, Then and Now. Human Organization 58(1):1–125.

Hansen, Helle Ploug, 1997 Patients' Bodies and Discourses of Power. In Anthropology of Policy. Cris Shore and Susan Wright, eds. London: Routledge.

Hasan, Khwaja A., 1975 What is Medical Anthropology? Medical Anthropology Quarterly 6(3):7–10.

Heaney, Michael T., 2006 Brokering Health Policy: Coalitions, Parties, and Interest Group Influence. Journal of Health Politics, Policy and Law 31(5):887–944.

Heller, Chaia., 2001 From Risk to Globalization: Discursive Shifts in the French Debate about GMOs. Medical Anthropology Quarterly 15(1):25–28.

Hoeijmakers, M., E. De Leeuw, P. Kennis, and N.K. De Vries, 2007 Local Health Policy Development Processes in the Netherlands: An Expanded Toolbox for Health Promotion. Health Promotion International 22(2):112–121.

Hughes, Charles C., 1976 Culture and Health Planning or the Yoruba of Western Nigeria. Medical Anthropology Quarterly (OS) 8(1):14–19.

Institute of Medicine, 1988 The Future of Public Health. Washington DC: National Academy Press.

Joralemon, Donald, 1995 Organ Wars: The Battle for Body Parts. Medical Anthropology Quarterly 9(3):335–356.

Kiefer, Christie W., 1975 The Official Medical Anthropology. Medical Anthropology Quarterly (OS) 6(4):1–2.

Kingdon, John W., 2003 Agendas, Alternatives and Public Policies. New York: Longman.

Kwon, Sooman, and Michael R. Reich, 2005 The Changing Process and Politics of Health Policy in Korea. Journal of Health Politics, Policy and Law 30(6):1003–1026.

Lakofff, George, 2004 Don't Think of an Elephant! Know Your Values and Frame the Debate. White River Junction VT: Chelsea Green Publishing.

Lamphere, Louise, 2005 Providers and Staff Respond to Medicaid Managed Care: The Unintended Consequences of Reform in New Mexico. Medical Anthropology Quarterly 19(1):3–25.

Lasswell, Harold D., 1936 Politics – Who Gets What, When, How. New York: McGraw Hill.

Low, Setha M., and Janet Schreiber, 1977 Health Planning and Policy. Medical Anthropology Quarterly (OS) 8(2):14.

McDonough, John E., 2000 Experiencing Politics. Berkeley: University of California Press.

McDonough, John E., 2001 Using and Misusing Anecdote in Policy Making. Health Affairs 20(1):207–212.

Mensah, George A., Richard A. Goodman, Stephanie Zaza, Anthony D. Moulton, Paula L. Kocher, William H. Dietz, Terry F. Pechacek, and James S. Marks, 2004 Law As a Tool for Preventing Chronic Diseases: Expanding the Spectrum of Effective Public Health Strategies. Preventing Chronic Disease 1(1):1–8.

Montini, Theresa, and Lisa A. Bero, 2001 Policy Makers' Perspectives on Tobacco Control Advocates' Roles in Regulation Development. Tobacco Control 10:218–224.

Nader, Laura, 1972 Up the Anthropologist – Perspectives Gained from Studying Up. In Reinventing Anthropology. Dell H. Hymes, ed. pp. 284–311. New York: Pantheon Books.

National Council of State Legislatures n.d. Electronic document. http://www.ncsl.org/legislatureselections/ethics/ethicshowstatesdefinelobbyingandlobbyist/tabid/15344/default.aspx/.

Okongwu, Anne Francis, and Joan P. Mencher, 2000 The Anthropology of Public Policy: Shifting Terrains. Annual Review of Anthropology 29:107–124.

Olesen, Virginia L., 1974 Convergences and Divergences: Anthropology and Sociology in Health Care. Medical Anthropology Quarterly 6(1):6–10.

Oliver, Thomas R., 2006 The Politics of Public Health Policy. Annual Review of Public Health. 27:195–233.

O'Sullivan, Joanne, and Patricia Lussier-Duynstee, 2006 Adolescent Homelessness, Nursing, and Public Health Policy. Policy, Politics and Nursing Practice. 7(1):73–77.

Osterweis, Marian, Arthur Kleinman, and David Mechanic, 1987 Pain and Disability, Clinical, Behavioral and Public Policy Perspectives. Washington DC: National Academy Press.

Pillsbury, Barbara L. K., 1982 Policy and Evaluation Perspectives on Traditional Health Practitioners in National Health Care Systems. Social Science and Medicine 16:1824–1834.

Preister, Kevin, 2010 Public Policy as Empowerment Through Anthropological Practice: Beyond the Research Paradigm. SfAA News 21(1):24–28.

Rosenstock Linda, and Lore Jackson Lee, 2002 Attacks on Science: The Risks to Evidence-Based Policy. American Journal of Public Health 92(1):14–18.

Rubenstein, Robert A., and Sandra D. Lane, 2010 Training Students for Anthropologically-oriented Policy Research. SfAA News 21(2):37–40.

Rylko-Bauer, B., M. Singer, and John vanWilligen, 2006 Reclaiming Applied Anthropology: Its Past, Present and Future. American Anthropologist. 108(1):178–190.

Sabatier, Paul A., 2007a Theories of the Policy Process. Boulder: Westview Press.

Sabatier, Paul A., 2007b The Need for better Theories. *In* Theories of the Policy Process. Paul Sabatier, ed. pp. 3–17. Boulder: Westview Press.

Sabatier, Paul A., and Christopher M. Weible, 2007 The Advocacy Coalition Framework. *In* Theories of the Policy Process. Paul Sebatier, ed. pp. 189–222. Boulder: Westview Press.

Sanday, Peggy Reeves, 1976 Anthropology and the Public Interest. New York: Academic Press.

Schensul, Jean J., 2005 Strengthening Communities through Research Partnerships for Social Change, Perspectives from the Institute for Community Research. *In* Community Building in the Twenty-First Century. Stanley E. Hyland, ed. Santa Fe: School of American Research Press.

Schreiber, Janet M., and Setha Low, 1977 Health Planning and Policy. Medical Anthropology Quarterly (OS) 8(3):5–6.

Shore, Cris, and Susan Wright, 1997 Anthropology of Policy. London: Routledge.

Singer, Merrill, 2000 You Owe Yourself a Drunk: James P. Spradley's Enduring Perspective. *In* You Owe Yourself a Drunk, James Spradley. pp. xiii–xxviii. Prospect Heights IL: Waveland Press.

Singer, Merrill, In press, 2010 Medical Anthropology and Public Policy: Using Research to Change the World from What It Is to What We Believe It Should Be. *In* Medical Anthropology at the Intersections. Marcia Inhorn and Emily A. Wentzell, eds. Durham NC: Duke University Press.

Singer, Merrill, and Hans Baer, 2008 Killer Commodities: Public Health and the Corporate Production of Harm. Walnut Creek CA: AltaMira Press.

Singer, Merrill, Freddie Valentin, Hans Baer, and Jia Zhongke, 1992 Why Does Juan Garcia Have a Drinking Problem? The Perspective of Critical Medical Anthropology. Medical Anthropology 9(14):77–108.

Smith, Kevin B., and Christopher W. Larimer, 2009 The Public Policy Theory Primer. Boulder: Westview Press.

Society for Applied Anthropology, n.d. Vision, Mission, Values and Goals. Electronic document. http://www.sfaa.net/sfaagoal.html/.

Spradley, James, 1970 You Owe Yourself a Drunk, An Ethnography of Urban Nomads. Boston: Little Brown.

Stanton, Kenneth R., and Zoltan J. Acs, 2005 The Infrastructure of Obesity and the Obesity Epidemic: Implications for Public Policy. Applied Economics and Health Policy 4(3):139–146.

Stull, Donald D., and Felix Moos, 2005 A Brief Overview of the Role of Anthropology in Public Policy. Review of Policy Research 1(1):19–27.

US Office of Special Counsel, n.d. Electronic document. http://www.osc.gov/hatchact. htm/.

vanWilligan, J., 2002 Applied Anthropology, An Introduction. 3rd edition. Westport CT: Bergin and Garvey.

Wallack, Lawrence, and Lori Dorfman. 1996 Media Advocacy: A Strategy for Advancing Policy and Promoting Health. Health Education Quarterly. 23(3):293–317.

Wallack, Lawrence, Katie Woodruff, Lori Dorfman, and Iris Diaz, 1999 News for a Change, An Advocate's Guide to Working with the Media. Thousand Oaks CA: Sage Publications.

Weatherford, J. McIver, 1985 Tribes on the Hill. New York: Bergin & Garvey.

Weaver, Thomas, 1985a Anthropology as a Policy Science: Part I, A Critique. Human organization 44(2):97–105.

Weaver, Thomas, 1985b Anthropology as a Policy Science: Part II, Development and Training. Human Organization. 44(3):197–205.

Wedel, Janine R, Cris Shore, Gregory Feldman, and Stacy Lathrop 2005 Toward an Anthropology of Public Policy. Annals of the American Academy of Political and Social Science 600(1):30–51.

Whiteford, Linda M., and Linda A. Bennett, 2005 Applied Anthropology and Health and Medicine. *In* Applied Anthropology, Domains of Application. Satish Kedia and John vanWilligen, eds. pp. 119–148. Westport CT: Praeger Publishers.

Wilson, Ruth P., Carolyn F. Sargent, Shegou Darret and Kale Kouame, 1999 Prospects for Family Planning in Cote d'Ivoire: Ethnographic Contributions to the Development of Culturally Appropriate Policy. *In* Anthropology In Public Health: Bridging Differences in Culture and Society. R. A. Hahn, ed. pp. 257–278. New York: Oxford Press.

Wilson-Clay, Barbara, Janet Wier Rourke, Marianne Baker Boldue, Julie D. Stagg, Gretchen Flatau, and Beverly Vaugh, 2005 Learning to Lobby for Pro-breastfeeding Legislation: The Story of a Texas Bill to Create a Breastfeeding-Friendly Physician Designation. Journal of Human Lactation. 21(2):191–198.

PART II Contexts and Conditions

Culture and the Stress Process

William W. Dressler

In 1929 William Donnison, a physician who had worked for many years in Kenya, published an article in *The Lancet* based on data on blood pressure he had collected. He compared average blood pressures and their distribution by age among Africans with published data on Europeans. He was the first to document the lower average blood pressures of people living in non-Western settings compared to Europeans, as well as a smaller increase of blood pressure in relationship to age in non-Western communities. He did not attribute these differences to genetic or dietary factors, but rather to the stresses associated with rapid culture change in Europe, compared to the relative stability of traditional social structure and culture in the African setting (although he failed to take note of the disruptive impact of the colonial powers). He argued, in essence, that under conditions of rapid culture change, individuals were forced into a continuous process of adaptation which, in the long run, was deleterious to health (Donnison 1929).

Donnison presaged what was to become an important research focus in biocultural medical anthropology: the health effects of culture change. While a variety of factors associated with culture change, including shifts in diet, physical activity and access to medical care, have been investigated as explanations for findings like Donnison's, the hypothesis that the social stresses associated with culture change are an important cause of changes in disease patterns has received consistent support. Furthermore, work in biocultural medical anthropology suggests that the effects of culture change observed in these studies are actually a specific instantiation of general cultural processes that affect human biology. Processes of so-called "modernization" and migration create situations in which some individuals are at the margins of the social space defined by general, salient cultural models. This position of marginality in a social field can, in turn, be a stressful experience associated with increased risk of disease. And this is a process that is not observed exclusively in circumstances of acculturation

A Companion to Medical Anthropology, First Edition. Edited by Merrill Singer and Pamela I. Erickson.

and assimilation, but rather is a process that can occur in any community. Thus, research that began by examining the health effects of culture change in relatively isolated communities in the world has helped to reveal fundamental social and cultural processes that occur in all communities, with important implications for human biology. My aim in this chapter is to review this research and to highlight its importance for research in medical anthropology.

RESEARCH ON CULTURE CHANGE AND HEALTH

Early studies of culture and the risk of disease emphasized the effect of culture change on health. Conceived and conducted in the 1960s and 1970s, these studies were organized around a theoretical framework emphasizing the health effects of "modernization," or the transition of societies from predominantly agrarian and non-industrial to urban and industrial. Much of this work was facilitated by taking arterial blood pressure as an outcome variable. Social and psychological factors had long been suspected as significant causes of elevated arterial blood pressure, and while the technical difficulties of obtaining a valid blood pressure reading should not be minimized, blood pressure did provide an outcome that could be measured non-invasively in the field with minimal equipment. Furthermore, chronically elevated blood pressure was well known as a major risk factor for circulatory diseases in general and for overall mortality. Plus, it was not confounded by the problems associated with symptom self-reports or the semantic issues of the cross-cultural translation of symptoms. In part for these reasons, a number of important cross-cultural studies of blood pressure appeared (Baker et al. 1986; Labarthe et al. 1973; Scotch 1963; see Dressler (1999) for a comprehensive review of studies of modernization and disease).

The basic design of these studies is quite similar. Three or more communities are identified along a continuum of modernization from more "traditional" to more "modern" communities. A traditional community is usually defined as one in which there is an emphasis on subsistence production in the economy, little formal education, an emphasis on corporate unilineal descent groups in social relationships, and little recent change in religion or belief systems. In a modernized community economic production shifts from subsistence to wage-labor, formal educational systems are introduced, emphasis on social relationships contracts from corporate kin groups to the nuclear family, the household and networks of extended kin, and one (or more) of the global religious systems is introduced, usually by missionaries.

There is an increase in disease risk along this continuum of modernization. For example, McGarvey and Baker (1979) found a nearly 15 mmHg (millimeters of mercury, the metric for blood pressure) difference in mean systolic blood pressure between the most traditional and most modernized communities in Samoa for persons age 50 and over, with a nearly 20% increase in the prevalence of hypertension (blood pressure elevated in excess of 140/90; blood pressure differences this large double the risk of a heart attack). One of the interesting findings in research on modernization and disease risk is that the effect of modernization is what would be termed in epidemiology an "ecological" effect. That is, samples from communities differing in modernization also differ in mean blood pressure; however, *individuals* who are more characteristically "modern" in their lifestyle (i.e., who engage in wage labor, have a formal education, etc.) do not differ from individuals who are less "modern" in terms of blood pressure. Put differently, living in a modernized community increases one's risk of higher blood pressure; being a 'modern person' in a community of whatever level of modernization does not necessarily increase one's risk (Dressler 1999).

The question then becomes, what contributes to this risk? One of the problems in interpreting such findings is that there are so many changes, including economic, social, political, ideological, and dietary that are included under the definition of modernization, it is difficult to isolate what is causal. For example, the rise of blood pressure with modernization has been variously attributed to increasing obesity (as a result of increased caloric intake and decreased physical activity), increasing sodium consumption, and the psychological and social stresses that accompany culture change (Dressler 1999). These of course are not mutually exclusive explanations; however, adjusting community differences in blood pressure for differences in the intake of sodium and in the body mass index results in a relatively small reduction of the differences in blood pressure. This, coupled with findings on the psychological effects of modernization, led to a focus in theory and research on the stressful effects of culture change. (Just what is meant by the term "stress" or "stressful" will be discussed below.)

One of the most innovative hypotheses in this area was proposed by the social epidemiologist John Cassel and his colleagues (Cassel et al. 1960; Henry and Cassel 1969). Although it applies equally well to situations of culture change in situ, this hypothesis is best explained in relation to migration. Cassel and colleagues argued that a migrant to a novel cultural and social setting is faced with a whole new set of cultural expectations. He/she has been socialized in a particular cultural milieu and has learned the models that govern daily behavior. But, he/she is thrust into situations where he/she does not know the appropriate patterns of behavior and must, at the very least, learn them. It is a process of adaptation in which he/she experiments with his/her behavior, trying to determine what will or will not be considered appropriate in mundane social interaction. Cassel and colleagues argued that this process of adaptation would itself be demanding and potentially stressful in that it would be fraught with uncertainty; what would be most stressful would be repeated failures to achieve socially appropriate behaviors, resulting in what would now be termed "allostatic load" (see below). In the long run, these kinds of experience could lead to sustained disease.

One classic study from this period consistent with Cassel's argument is the paper by Scotch (1963). Scotch focused on two specific communities of the Zulu ethnic group in South Africa. One was in a rural area, while the other formed an enclave in an urban center. Within each community, Scotch collected data on a variety of social and cultural characteristics of individuals, finding a different pattern of associations between these characteristics and blood pressure within each community. For example, adherents to traditional religion tended to have higher blood pressure in the urban setting, while converts to Christianity tended to have higher blood pressure in the rural setting. Similarly, women who had reached menopause in the rural community tended to have higher blood pressure, while menopausal women in the urban enclave tended to have lower blood pressure. Scotch argued that this pattern of findings could be accounted for by the "fit" or congruence of the behaviors with the overall culture of the community. So, for example, in the rural community where traditional religion was practiced more widely, converts to Christianity did not match the prevailing ethos well; Christian converts would tend to fit the urban community more closely in belief and behavior. Similarly, women in rural areas gain status from their role in reproduction and as mothers; menopause, signaling the loss of this high status role, would then be stressful for them. In the urban enclave, on the other hand, having children is less status-enhancing and more problematic from an economic standpoint; menopause, in this context, removes the risk of having another mouth to feed. Overall, then, what is stressful or demanding is a lack of congruence between the cultural milieu and the beliefs or behaviors of individuals.

Studies of modernization and disease initiated a fertile program of research in biocultural medical anthropology. It was somewhat limited, however, by the concept of modernization itself. At an ecological level, community modernization is a potent predictor of disease risk; at the level of the individual, it is not. Furthermore, the term *modernization* always implied a linear process along a well defined trajectory that often failed to accurately describe local communities. Cassel's hypotheses about the stresses associated with migration and cultural change incorporated much of the best of theory in cultural anthropology at the time; with the exception of a few studies, however, these insights were not incorporated into research, and, given methodological limitations, these insights could principally be incorporated only into the interpretation of data, but not in the operational specification of research models that would provide a true test of the hypothesis.

At the same time that studies of modernization and disease were being carried out, parallel developments in sociology and psychology were occurring, principally in the development of a theory of the stress process. In that social stress was considered to be a primary cause of increased disease risk associated with modernization, a logical step in research was to incorporate these models of the stress process into studies of modernization and disease.

CULTURE AND MODELS OF THE STRESS PROCESS

Early descriptive studies in social epidemiology set the stage for social scientific studies of the stress process. Beginning with sociological studies of mental disorder, and continuing with analyses of mortality based on existing data, two patterns began to emerge: (a) individuals in lower social class groups were at a higher risk of disease; (b) individuals with more links to others through marriage and other indicators of social affiliation (e.g., church membership) were at a lower risk of disease (Anderson and Armstead 1995; Berkman 1995). The associations of these factors with health outcomes were interpreted as resulting from the stress of lower social class existence and the stress of social isolation (or, put otherwise, as the benefit of social support). Stress became the intermediate variable linking the external circumstances to health outcomes; it described a very general but plausible pattern of psychophysiologic responses that could link experience and the body.

At the outset (and perhaps continuing today), the stress hypothesis was treated with a good deal of skepticism, notably because there was perceived to be a circularity in the reasoning (e.g., "Lower social class existence is associated with an increased risk of disease because it is stressful. How do we know it is stressful? Because it is associated with an increased risk of disease"). This caricature of a circular argument has become much more difficult to maintain as the field of stress research has progressed. Most importantly, the development of a body of theory, created at the intersection of basic social theory and accumulating research results, has helped to better identify the kinds of social and psychological variables that combine to create the risk of disease, thus leading to more specific hypotheses and less ad hoc theorizing. In psychology, Richard S. Lazarus (1966) developed an influential perspective called cognitive-mediational theory. In sociology, beginning with the work of Levine and Scotch (1970) and continuing through Leonard Pearlin's syntheses (Pearlin et al. 1981), social factors in the stress process also have been clarified. Two seminal papers by social epidemiologists, both appearing in 1976, were important as well in defining the direction research was to take in subsequent years (Cassel 1976; Cobb 1976).

Briefly (a longer discussion of the stress model can be found in Dressler 2007a), elements of the stress process must be divided into two broad categories: (a) social events and circumstances that increase the risk of disease; (b) social and psychological factors that decrease the risk of disease. The first can be referred to as "social stressors," of which there are two types. The first are acute stressors, sudden and often unexpected events that alter the social fabric for an individual and lead to a readjustment or renegotiation of social relationships. These are represented especially by stressful life events such as death of a spouse or other close family member, divorce or marital separation, and unemployment. Oftentimes centered on social loss, these are events that virtually force an individual into a new set of social circumstances to which he or she must adjust, a process that can be demanding or taxing of personal resources. The second category of social stressors are chronic social stressors, ongoing problems associated with major social roles such as worker, spouse, parent, and community member. These are social roles that are central to an individual's personal and social identity, and ongoing difficulties achieving emotionally satisfactory states in these roles can be threatening to one's sense of self. The occurrence of these acute and chronic stressors place either sudden or ongoing demands on individuals, demands to which they must adjust.

Balancing these kinds of acute and chronic social stressors are the "resistance resources" that support individuals' efforts to adapt to the demands placed on them. These resources can be both personal and social. Personal resources consist of emotion-focused and instrumental psychological strategies that individuals develop as characteristic patterns of coping. An individual might have a strong sense of his or her own self-efficacy that leads to a direct confrontation of stressors to change them. Alternately, where stressors cannot truly be changed, cognitive strategies may be employed to alter the meaning of a stressor and hence its impact. Social resources can be varied, but the emphasis in research has been on social support available within an ego-centered social network. Social support also may be either emotional or instrumental. Emotional support may take the form of reassurance and expressions of caring that lessen the sense of isolation an individual might feel under stress. Instrumental support can take the form of direct and tangible help (such as loans of money or practical advice on coping) that can assist an individual in changing the stressful circumstance.

Stressors and resistance resources interact in a buffering process. The impact of a stressor on an individual's psychological or physical health is virtually impossible to estimate without information on the resources that an individual employs in adjusting to the demands imposed by the stressor. A substantial body of research has emerged demonstrating that, when an individual has social or personal resources to respond to a stressor, the impact of that stressor is reduced; when an individual lacks the social or personal resources to respond, the impact of that stressor is enhanced.

Increased understanding of the psychophysiologic intervening mechanisms involved in the stress process has also advanced research on stress and disease considerably. A great deal of laboratory-based physiologic research, especially on physiologic reactivity and the hypothalamic–pituitary–adrenal axis (a thorough discussion of which is beyond the scope of this review but see Ice and James (2007) for a review) has shown how, in the face of demands and in the absence of resources to cope with those demands, there are a number of neuroendocrine responses that "ready" the organism for action, including preparing for system repair in the case that adaptive responses fail (McEwan and Stellar 1993). In earlier incarnations of the stress model, it was thought that the aim of adaptive responses was a return to homeostasis. More recently, however, the terms *allostasis* and *allostatic load* have entered the lexicon of stress research. The term *homeostasis* refers to maintaining parameters, such as body temperature and oxygen levels in the tissues, within a fairly narrow range that insures the continued survival of the organism. Allostasis implies a similar process, except that it refers to parameters that can vary in a much wider range (e.g., blood pressure, blood glucose), and that can achieve differing "set points." For example, when blood pressure increases rapidly in response to a sudden and threatening event (such as narrowly avoiding a traffic accident), it should return to pre-event levels fairly quickly. However, when that same sudden increase occurs repeatedly (as in a treacherous daily commute in urban traffic), blood pressure may never fall to its previous level and becomes reset at a higher level. Over time, this kind of allostatic load on the body can lead to sustained disease (McEwan 2000).

What is probably most important in understanding the psychophysiology of stress, however, is the potency of symbolic stimuli or meaning in initiating allostatic processes. The effects of symbolic stimuli were simply and elegantly demonstrated by James Lynch (1985) and his associates in their studies of speaking. Blood pressure rises when an individual is actively communicating (including signing among deaf persons). In a series of experiments, Lynch and colleagues had students read passages from textbooks under two conditions. In the first, the experimental confederate was dressed as a student like themselves. In the other, an older male was dressed in a laboratory coat with the title "Dr" embroidered on it. In both conditions, blood pressure rose while the students were reading. Under the condition of reading in front of an older authority figure, however, blood pressure rose significantly more. When the social relations in the experimental condition were altered, the meaning of the interaction changed, with a concomitant change in physiologic reactivity. Meaning matters for human biology.

While work in the area of stress research has progressed substantially both in terms of social theory and in terms of our understanding of the biology of stress, a continuing challenge of this research involves adapting models of the stress process to diverse cultural contexts. There is no reason to suppose, and, indeed, every reason to doubt, that measures of stressors or resistance resources developed for use in North American, predominantly middle-class samples would be valid in societies in the Pacific, Africa or

South America undergoing culture change. Therefore, models of the stress process developed for North American and European samples were used for inspiration in studies in different cultural contexts, but at the same time were subjected to a rigorous ethnographic critique, to modify these models in ways appropriate for different societies (Dressler 1995). For example, Dressler argued that a fundamental change occurring in modernizing societies is the exposure of local populations to non-local lifestyles, specifically in the sense of material goods for domestic consumption (e.g., cars, stereo systems, televisions) and leisure time activities (such as going to movies or restaurants). The ability to accumulate consumer goods and adopt these leisure time activities become incorporated into local systems of social status, at least complimenting traditional forms of social status or, in some cases, supplanting them. The problem in developing societies, however, is that the acceptance within a community of lifestyle as a gauge of social status can quickly outstrip the growth in the economy supplying the jobs and other economic resources required to achieve that lifestyle. The likelihood is high that some individuals will attempt to achieve and maintain a modern, high-status lifestyle, but in the context of meager economic resources in low-status jobs. This is likely to be a stressful experience. This process could then be linked directly to more general theories of status inconsistency as a stressor (Dressler 2004). In research in the West Indies and Latin America, Dressler found higher blood pressure associated with this kind of status inconsistency (Dressler 1999).

This illustrates what was meant by the notion of the "ethnographic critique" of theory. The theory of status inconsistency dates back to the 1940s in sociology, when some theorists noted that it was possible to occupy unequal ranks on various dimensions of social status, as these were traditionally measured in sociology (e.g., having a very high educational level, but with a meager income). It was hypothesized that simultaneously occupying these unequal ranks led to uncertainty and frustration in social interaction (i.e., should this person be treated with deference to her high education, or indifference due to her low income?), which in turn could have effects on health. The example given here illustrates how social theory developed in studies of the North American middle class can be reinterpreted in the light of ethnographic realities in other societies (see Dressler 2004).

The application of this model to Samoan immigrants to northern California by Janes (1990), and to Samoans in Samoa by McDade (2002), further illustrates the importance of the appropriate ethnographic specification of variables. Traditionally, Samoans lived in a redistributive economy in which all economic production flowed to leaders (called *matai*) of large corporate kin groups; production was then redistributed within the kin group by the *matai*. Other *matai* had specialized political functions, and, of course, all *matai* were of high status. With modernization and migration, the *matai* status has persisted, albeit with different functions. Janes (1990) found that Samoan migrants to northern California with *matai* status who had lower socio-economic status in American society (in terms of education and occupation) had higher blood pressure. Apparently, having achieved status along a traditional dimension made it difficult for individuals to deal with the lack of confirmation of their status in the wider American society where *matai* status was unknown and not valued. This failure to receive status confirmation would be stressful.

McDade (2002) examined a similar kind of status inconsistency in Samoa. There is of course higher status accorded households that have a member with *matai* status.

At the same time, higher social status is also achieved if a household accumulates Western consumer goods and if members of the household can travel out of Samoa. McDade found that adolescents in Samoa living in households with a *matai* status, but that had lower status in terms of lifestyle, had lower immune function, as measured by cell-mediated immunity (the production of antibodies in response to immune system challenge). Again, this research points both to the chronically stressful nature of this status inconsistency, and to the importance of specifying models of the stress process in terms of local cultural contexts.

The importance of specifying variable measurement in terms of local cultural context is illustrated as well by the examination of buffers against stressful circumstances, especially social support. While modernization usually entails a contraction of the range of kin in an individual's social network, kin frequently retain a special status as providers of social support. For example, among Samoan migrants to northern California, Janes (1990) found that the large descent groups forming the foundation of traditional Samoan social organization were still present in the urban setting, but that these groups had lost much of their meaning for people. Instead, social support systems were built from networks among households of adult siblings who, traditionally, share a close affective relationship in Samoa. These kin-based networks provided a buffer against status inconsistency in this setting.

Dressler and his associates (1986) examined the cultural specification of social support in several settings. For example, in rural Mexico, they found that the most potent source of social support, as measured by the association of support with blood pressure, was the number of *compadre* relationships a man had through which he could seek help. For women, the most important source of social support was from family, and that was mainly evident for older (> 40 years of age) women. Each of these measures is sensitive to the salient social relationships that structure access to resources for men and women in traditional Mexican village social organization.

In a series of studies in the African–American community in the rural Southern United States, Dressler (1991a,b) found a clear distinction in the salience of social support received from kin versus non-kin. In studies of blood pressure and depressive symptoms, support from kin was more important in buffering the effects of stressors for older respondents, while support from non-kin was more important in buffering effects for younger respondents. These investigators argued that the extended family was the traditional support system in the black community, developed through the long period of slavery and segregation. With the advent of the Civil Rights Movement, however, the social settings in which African–Americans participated expanded dramatically to include those (such as educational and occupational settings) in which non-kin might prove more important than kin as supporters.

The effects of social context on the buffering effects of social support in the black community in the South were also observed in the effects of social stressors. Dressler (1991a) argued that the intersection of the Civil Rights Movement and economic mobility had synergistic social centripetal effects, such that younger and older (as a result of their differential exposure to the historical epoch of the Movement) and lower and higher socioeconomic status individuals would be affected by differing profiles of acute and chronic stressors, as well as differing sources of social support. In general, the results supported this argument, indicating again the need for the careful ethnographic grounding of studies of the stress process.

These studies of the stress process in specific cultural settings have proven to be fruitful for extending our understanding of biocultural processes in health generally. At the same time, the focus of studies of the stress process remains fixed on a relatively narrow set of factors to describe culture and human biology. More recent work has begun to examine biocultural processes more comprehensively, and this will be examined in the next section.

Cultural Consensus, Cultural Consonance and Health

Anthropological contributions to the study of stress and disease rest on a meta-theoretical assumption common in anthropology. To understand what a stressor or a resistance resource is in a community, an ethnographer must have an understanding of what events and circumstances, or social relationships, mean within that community. More specifically, what is the symbolic significance of different circumstances or relationships? Is the occurrence of an event or circumstance, or having a particular kind of relationship, a matter of great concern to people, or a matter of relative indifference? Furthermore, this emic understanding of stressors and resources is focused not on individual idiosyncrasies, but rather on what is *collectively* regarded as important.

The aim of examining these shared understandings is to determine what impact the occurrence of culturally-relevant stressors, or access to culturally relevant resistance resources, has on health outcomes. This requires a systematic attempt to observe the manifestation of distinctly collective concerns at the level of the individual, and then, in turn, to relate those to human biology.

These insights led Dressler (2005, 2007b) to propose a comprehensive cultural theory for biocultural research that he terms a theory of "cultural consonance." Cultural consonance is the degree to which individuals approximate, in their own beliefs and behaviors, the shared cultural models that encode prototypes for belief and behavior in given cultural domains. The concept of cultural consonance is embedded in a larger cognitive theory of culture. In cognitive culture theory, culture is that which individuals must know in order to participate in any given social setting. This knowledge is cognitively stored and structured in terms of schematic cultural models of specific cultural domains (D'Andrade 1995).

A cultural domain is any organized sphere of discourse within a society. So, eating lunch at your local university, or playing cricket, or being married, would be examples of cultural domains of varying degrees of abstraction and of varying degrees of importance. A cultural model consists of the elements that comprise a cultural domain and the basic processes that link those elements. So, for example, in the contemporary United States, when people talk about marriage, it is (usually) taken for granted that marriage is defined as a relationship between one man and one woman (at a time), that is given special legal protection and (often) sacred recognition, that includes neolocal residence in an independent household, that includes legal recognition for and the raising of children in common, that involves a stated commitment to a life-long relationship cemented by an emotional bond, and that involves the pooling of economic resources. Prototypically, marriage begins with the discovery of that emotional bond between the participants, with a sequential unfolding of a number of events that culminates in the establishment of an independent household. Now, it does not matter that external social structural events (such as contracting middle-class household incomes) are altering this prototypical trajectory for some people (e.g., young marrieds living with their parents). Nor that changing sexual mores have altered the sequence (e.g., reproduction often precedes legally-sanctioned cohabitation). Nor that there are underway efforts to change the basic definition of marriage (e.g., to include same-sex partners). These are all interesting social and cultural processes that impact how marriage is realized in practice, but they do not change the fact that when someone says the word "marriage" in the USA, there is a representation that comes to mind that does not include polygamy or arranged marriages or the transfer of "brideprice" or any number of variations of this institution cross-culturally. The prototypical American marriage is the benchmark from which all discussion flows. It is the cultural model.

It is, of course, possible to isolate certain kinds of social enclaves within the USA in which a quite different cultural model could be identified. The continued practice of polygamy in certain parts of the western USA, or the transfer of "brideprice" in the form of cash payments rather than herd animals in some urban ethnic community, could probably be described. But this only underscores the importance of defining the social boundaries within which cultural models are negotiated and shared. When the contours of social space are defined, the degree to which cultural models are shared, and the ways in which they are distributed, can be described.

What imparts a considerable causal force to cultural models, many of which (if not most) are completely arbitrary, is the consensus within a society that this is, indeed, what "we" mean by this term. Furthermore, this removes the criticism that is often aimed at cognitive theories of culture: that they amount to "reducing" culture to individual beliefs and values. In the first place, "knowing" what is meant by the term marriage in our society is very different from what you believe about it, or what parts (if any) of the institution you value. In the second place, in many (if not most) cultural models, the meanings encoded will not be exhausted by what any given individual knows. Rather, individual knowledge, and hence individual models, are likely to be partial and incomplete. Culture resides in part in individual minds, but it is also importantly distributed across individual minds. Culture is a term the referents of which are both individuals and social aggregates (D'Andrade 1995; Dressler 2007b).

A cultural model is just that – a blueprint, or schematic – and how it is realized in practice will depend on the conditions under which individuals try to implement the cultural models distributed in their society. Cultural consonance captures the sense in which cultural models are realized in practice. Individuals may, in their own beliefs and behaviors, diverge from cultural prototypes for a variety of reasons, not the least of which is that in many instances the economic resources to put cultural motives into action may be lacking. In other instances, individuals may, upon conscious reflection, choose a different course of action. Whatever the cause, in many cases, there may be a considerable gap between what a cultural model describes and what individuals are actually doing.

Given that cultural models describe what is widely expected with respect to behavior and belief, when individuals fail to correspond in their own beliefs and behaviors to these expectations (low cultural consonance) there may be confusion, misunderstanding, and negative social sanction in mundane social interaction. Individuals may fail to receive the positive social feedback in social interaction that reassures them that they are an accepted and valued member of society. Repeated unsatisfying social interactions of this kind could, in the long run, result in increased allostatic load, since it has been well-demonstrated that a lack of confirmation in social interaction leads to physiologic reactivity and mobilization of the HPA system. The end result could, of course, be sustained disease.

It is worth noting that this model can incorporate a number of earlier ideas in the anthropological study of stress and disease. For example, Cassel's (Cassel et al. 1960) hypotheses about migration, modernization and health can be completely subsumed under a theory of cultural consonance. Principally, Cassel lacked the theoretical and methodological tools of a cognitive theory of culture to operationalize his hypotheses (and hence he ultimately re-cast his ideas in terms of a conventional stress model, see Cassel (1976)). Similarly, a theory of cultural consonance can subsume many earlier hypotheses in anthropological studies of stress. For example, in the study of social support and its effects on health, the critical first issue is identifying a configuration of social relationships that is culturally regarded as appropriate for seeking certain kinds of help or assistance. Then, health outcomes vary in relation to individuals' match to that configuration in their own lives. The notion of "social support" as a specific category of social relationships can thus be subsumed under more general culture theory. Social support is sought according to a cultural model of appropriate social relationships that can provide such assistance.

More importantly, however, cultural consonance has proven to be a potent predictor of health status in a variety of studies. In the earliest exploration of its effects, Dressler and associates examined cultural consonance and blood pressure in urban Brazil (Dressler and Santos 2000), and in the African–American community in a small city in the Southern USA (Dressler and Bindon 2000). Lifestyle and social support were chosen as the cultural domains to be examined, based on previous research in each community. Lifestyle and social support represent, at the level of the individual, the lived experience of social class and social integration, factors (as noted above) that have been repeatedly shown to be associated with health in large epidemiologic surveys. In both sets of studies, these investigators first examined the degree to which there were shared models of a valued lifestyle and a preferred pattern of resort for social support. To do so involved first testing for cultural consensus using the model developed by Romney et al. (1986). Relatively small groups of informants (30–40) were asked to rate the importance of lifestyle items and behaviors in contributing to a good life, and to rate the importance of particular kinds of potential supporters in relation to specific problems. In each setting, cultural consensus analysis indicated that informants shared an understanding of each domain, and the cultural consensus model could be used to assign a consensus weight to the importance of each item in each domain.

Subsequently, in an epidemiologic survey, respondents' actual ownership of lifestyle items, adoption of lifestyle behaviors, and reported access to social supports were ascertained. Measures of cultural consonance in each domain were calculated as the degree to which an individual's reported behaviors corresponded to the consensus models derived in the prior step. In both studies, higher cultural consonance in each domain was associated with lower arterial blood pressure. Furthermore, in the Brazilian studies, higher cultural consonance in each domain was also found to be associated with lower reported depressive symptoms and lower perceived stress.

A more recent study has refined these results in a number of ways. First, the two-stage method for developing measures of cultural consonance has been improved by carrying out a more complete cultural domain analysis for each cultural domain selected for study. Cultural domain analysis refers to a set of techniques for eliciting the terms that individuals use to talk about a particular domain and then exploring in more detail the dimensions of meaning that individuals use to distinguish among those terms. These steps provide a more nuanced understanding of how persons in a particular cultural context organize and structure their understanding of a domain. A stronger foundation for testing for cultural consensus is provided through this approach, since the elements of each domain are demonstratively derived directly from everyday speech acts. Second, the measurement of cultural consonance has been improved by using more specific information from the results of cultural consensus analysis in the construction of those measures. Third, an expanded set of cultural domains has been examined (Dressler et al. 2005b).

This research was again carried out in urban Brazil. Using these expanded methods, cultural consensus within the domains of lifestyle and social support was replicated, and the association of cultural consonance in these domains with arterial blood pressure was also replicated. Cultural consensus in the domains of the family, national identity and food was also examined. Associations were found between low cultural consonance in all of these domains and various measures of psychological distress (including depressive symptoms, locus of control, and perceived stress). The association of cultural consonance and body composition has also been examined. Higher cultural consonance in multiple domains was associated with lower abdominal circumference and a lower body mass index, primarily for women (Dressler et al. 2005a, 2007a, 2008).

A longitudinal component was added to this study. Respondents were followed up after two years to examine change over time in cultural consonance and its association with changes in depressive symptoms. In the initial cross-sectional study, higher cultural consonance in all cultural domains was associated with psychological distress. In the longitudinal study, it was hypothesized that higher cultural consonance in the domain that was most highly shared (i.e., for which there was highest cultural consensus) would be most strongly associated with changes in depressive symptoms over time. The cultural model of family life was most highly shared, and, as predicted, cultural consonance in family life had the greatest effect on changes in depressive symptoms over time (Dressler et al. 2007b).

A further dimension in biocultural research was added in this study. With the mapping of the human genome, a number of genetic polymorphisms have been identified that have been linked to health outcomes, including depression. Dressler et al. (2008) hypothesized that there would be an interaction effect between genetic background and cultural consonance, such that in the presence of a particular genetic variant, the effect of cultural consonance in family life on depressive symptoms might be altered. This hypothesis was confirmed. They examined the interaction between cultural consonance and a single nucleotide polymorphism for a receptor in the brain for serotonin, a neurotransmitter that is intimately associated with the regulation of emotion. Overall, higher cultural consonance in family life was associated with lower depressive symptoms; however, this effect was enhanced in the presence of a single variant of the serotonin receptor gene.

A number of other investigators have used this same general approach to examine culture, stress and disease, without necessarily using the precise measurement model for cultural consonance. For example, Decker et al. (2003) studied individual variation in the level of the stress hormone cortisol among men in a small town in Dominica, in the West Indies. One's reputation as an honest, agreeable, and trustworthy individual is central to one's social status in this community. These investigators had each man in a sample rate every other man in the sample along these dimensions. Men who were collectively scored as high on these dimensions of sociality also had lower levels of circulating cortisol. Decker and associates conclude that this "cultural congruity" between how the notion of a "good man" is culturally constructed and an individual man's reputation contributes to lower overall stress.

Gravlee et al. (2005) used this general approach to examine the association of skin color and blood pressure in Puerto Rico. Epidemiologic studies have repeatedly shown that persons of African descent in the Western Hemisphere have higher blood pressures than persons of European descent. Two hypotheses have been suggested to account for these findings. The first is a generalized racial–genetic hypothesis, that "African" genetic background predisposes individuals to higher blood pressure. The second hypothesis suggests that darker skin color is assigned lower social status in mundane social interactions, leading to greater physiologic reactivity and sustained higher blood pressure. Gravlee (2005), using techniques of cultural domain analysis, elicited the cultural model of skin color in Puerto Rico and used observer ratings to assign individuals to emic skin color categories (that, unlike the mainland USA, include a third category for skin color) in an epidemiologic survey. Gravlee et al. (2005) found that darker skin color, as defined by the emic model of skin color, and socio-economic status interact in relation to blood pressure, and that objective skin color measured by skin reflectometry is unrelated to blood pressure. In other words, blood pressure is most closely associated with culturally defined skin color, regardless of actual skin color.

DeCaro and Worthman (2008) used a similar approach in their studies of young children's physiologic adaptation to the novel environment of school. They first examined cultural models of the family environment for young children, finding that parents emphasized the importance of stability and predictability for children; however, when actual family behavior diverged from that ideal environment, and especially when parents had fewer resources to smooth that unpredictability, children in turn had a more difficult time self-regulating physiologic reactivity to novel stimuli. This suggests that, in the long term, they may develop a pattern of over-reactivity to meaningful events and circumstances in their environments, resulting in greater allostatic load.

Sweet (2008) used this approach to examine cultural consonance with culturally constructed models of stress among African–American youth in the urban USA. Using cultural domain analysis, she elicited culturally relevant stressors for youth and determined their collective importance from cultural consensus analysis. Then, persons who experienced more of these culturally defined stressful experiences had higher blood pressure, anxiety and depression. Similarly, Kostick (2008) examined culturally constructed models of being a success in life in a multi-ethnic sample in Mauritius. Individuals who were culturally consonant with that model reported greater subjective well being, controlling for several other psychological variables thought to influence mood.

Overall, then, it appears that an individual's ability to realize in his or her own life the collective goals encoded in cultural models has important implications for well being, measured physiologically and psychologically. On the face of it, this does not seem like a remarkable statement. But asserting a proposition in this way, and being able to demonstrate it empirically, are two different things. What is important about the theory of cultural consonance is that, along with being a plausible theory linking culture and biology, there is an explicit measurement of the construct that has strong emic validity. The effects of cultural consonance can then be contrasted empirically with other factors thought to be important, and it can be examined in interaction with other factors. These studies represent significant demonstrations of the importance of culture – construed as collective meaning that is then realized in individual's lives – for human biology.

CONCLUSION

The influence of cultural factors on disease outcomes has been a productive area of research in medical anthropology for over half a century. The initial focus in this research was on the major dislocating effects on local populations of colonialism and post-colonialism, and especially the penetration of local communities by markets, political influence, and information from distant centers of power. The consistent association of variation in exposure to these "modernizing" influences with health outcomes led to a new set of hypotheses regarding how stressful events and circumstances were mediators of these effects. Further elaboration of the stress model in non-Western settings led, in turn, to a closer examination of how social relationships were re-shaped in these contexts and the implications of this transformation of the social fabric for health.

Studies of stress and disease in medical anthropology have more recently returned to a focus on basic social and cultural processes, and their implications for human biology. This is appropriate because, at many levels, human biology is inseparable from culture. We are who we are as a species because biological and cultural evolution have been a single, linked, biocultural process for millennia. We are, as individuals, suspended in "webs of significance" – of meaning – and our bodies are shaped by, and shape, that significance.

REFERENCES

Anderson, Norman B., and Cheryl A. Armstead, 1995 Toward Understanding the Association of Socio-economic Status and Health: A New Challenge for the Biopsychosocial Approach. Psychosomatic Medicine 57:213–225.

Baker, Paul T., Joel M. Hanna, and Thelma S. Baker, eds., 1986 The Changing Samoans: Behavior and Health in Transition. New York: Oxford University Press.

Berkman, Lisa F., 1995 The Role of Social Relations in Health Promotion. Psychosomatic Medicine 57:245–254.

Cassel, John C., 1976 The Contribution of the Social Environment to Host Resistance. American Journal of Epidemiology 104:107–123.

Cassel, John C., Ralph S. Patrick, and C. David Jenkins, 1960 Epidemiologic Analysis of the Health Implications of Culture Change. Annals of the New York Academy of Sciences 84:938–949.

Cobb, Sidney, 1976 Social Support as a Moderator of Life Stress. Psychosomatic Medicine 38: 300–314.

D'Andrade, Roy G., 1995 The Development of Cognitive Anthropology. Cambridge: Cambridge University Press.

DeCaro, Jason A., and Carol M. Worthman, 2008 Culture and the Childhood Socialization of Cardiovascular Regulation at School Entry in the US American Journal of Human Biology 22(5):572–583.

Decker, Seamus, Mark Flinn, Barry G. England, and Carol M. Worthman, 2003 Cultural Congruity and the Cortisol Stress Response among Dominican Men. In Social and Cultural Lives of Immune Systems. James M. Wilce, Jr, ed. pp. 147–169. London and New York: Routledge.

Donnison, C. P., 1929 Blood Pressure in the African Native. The Lancet 1:6–7.

Dressler, William W., 1991a Stress and Adaptation in the Context of Culture: Depression in a Southern Black Community. Albany NY: State University of New York Press.

Dressler, William W., 1991b Social Support, Lifestyle Incongruity, and Arterial Blood Pressure in a Southern Black Community. Psychosomatic Medicine 53:608–620.

Dressler, William W., 1995 Modeling Biocultural Interactions in Anthropological Research: an Example from Research on Stress and Cardiovascular Disease. Yearbook of Physical Anthropology 38:27–56.

Dressler, William W., 1999 Modernization, Stress and Blood Pressure: New Directions in Research. Human Biology 71:583–605.

Dressler, William W., 2004 Social or Status Incongruence. In The Encyclopedia of Health and Behavior. Norman B. Anderson, ed. pp. 764–767. Thousand Oaks CA: Sage Publications.

Dressler, William W., 2005 What's Cultural about Biocultural Research? Ethos 33:20–45.

Dressler, William W., 2007a Cultural Dimensions of the Stress Process: Measurement Issues in Fieldwork. In Measuring Stress in Humans. Gillian Ice and Gary D. James, eds. pp. 27–59. Cambridge: Cambridge University Press.

Dressler, William W., 2007b Cultural Consonance. In Textbook of Cultural Psychiatry. Dinesh Bhugra and Kameldeep Bhui, eds, pp. 179–190. Cambridge: Cambridge University Press.

Dressler, William W., and James R. Bindon, 2000 The Health Consequences of Cultural Consonance: Cultural Dimensions of Lifestyle, Social Support and Arterial Blood Pressure in an African–American Community. American Anthropologist 102:244–260.

Dressler, William W., and José Ernesto dos Santos, 2000 Social and Cultural Dimensions of Hypertension in Brazil: A Review. Cadernos de Saúde Pública 16:303–315.

Dressler, William W., Alfonso Mata, Adolfo Chavez, Fernando E. Viteri, and Phillip Gallagher, 1986 Social Support and Arterial Pressure in a Central Mexican Community. Psychosomatic Medicine 48:338–350.

Dressler, William W., Mauro C. Balieiro, Rosane P. Ribeiro, and José Ernesto Dos Santos, 2005a Cultural Consonance and Arterial Blood Pressure in Urban Brazil. Social Science and Medicine 61:527–540.

Dressler, William W., Camila D. Borges, Mauro C. Balieiro, and José Ernesto Dos Santos, 2005b Measuring Cultural Consonance: Examples with Special Reference to Measurement Theory in Anthropology. Field Methods 17:331–355.

Dressler, William W., Mauro C. Balieiro, Rosane P. Ribeiro, and José Ernesto Dos Santos, 2007a Cultural Consonance and Psychological Distress: Examining the Associations in Multiple Cultural Domains. Culture, Medicine and Psychiatry 31:195–224.

Dressler, William W., Mauro C. Balieiro, Rosane P. Ribeiro, and José Ernesto dos Santos, 2007b A Prospective Study of Cultural Consonance and Depressive Symptoms in Urban Brazil. Social Science and Medicine 65:2058–2069.

Dressler, William W., Kathryn S. Oths, Rosane P. Ribeiro, Mauro C. Balieiro, and José Ernesto dos Santos, 2008 Cultural Consonance and Adult Body Composition in Urban Brazil. American Journal of Human Biology 20:15–22.

Dressler, William W., Mauro C. Balieiro, Rosane P. Ribeiro, and José Ernesto dos Santos, 2009 Cultural Consonance, a 5HT2A Receptor Polymorphism, and Depressive Symptoms:

A Longitudinal Study of Gene x Culture Interaction in Urban Brazil. American Journal of Human Biology 21:91–97.

Gravlee, Clarence C., 2005 Ethnic Classification in Southeastern Puerto Rico: The Cultural Model of "Color." Social Forces 83:949–970.

Gravlee, Clarence C., William W. Dressler, and H. Russell Bernard, 2005 Skin Color, Social Classification, and Blood Pressure in Southeastern Puerto Rico. American Journal of Public Health 95:2191–2197.

Henry, James P., and John C. Cassel, 1969 Psychosocial Factors in Essential Hypertension. American Journal of Epidemiology 90:171–200.

Ice, Gillian H., and Gary D. James, eds., 2007 Measuring Stress in Humans. Cambridge: Cambridge University Press.

Janes, Craig R., 1990 Migration, Social Change, and Health: A Samoan Community in Urban California. Stanford CA: Stanford University Press.

Kostick, Kristin M., 2008 Buying into Culture: Do Personal, Social or Evolutionary Factors Explain Why People Internalize Cultural Norms? Paper presented at the Annual Meeting of the Society for Applied Anthropology, Memphis, March 26–30.

LaBarthe, D., D. Reed, J. Brody, and R. Stallones, 1973 Health Effects of Modernization in Palau. American Journal of Epidemiology 98:161–174.

Lazarus, Richard S., 1966 Psychological Stress and the Coping Process. New York: McGraw-Hill.

Levine, Sol, and Norman A. Scotch, 1970 Social Stress. Chicago: Aldine.

Lynch, James J., 1985 The Language of the Heart. New York: Basic Books.

McDade, Thomas W., 2002 Status Incongruity in Samoan Youth: A Biocultural Analysis of Culture Change, Stress and Immune Function. Medical Anthropology Quarterly 16: 123–150.

McEwan, Bruce S., 2000 Allostasis and Allostatic Load. In Encyclopedia of Stress. George Fink, ed. pp. 145–149. San Diego: Academic Press.

McEwan, Bruce S., and E. Stellar., 1993 Stress and the Individual: Mechanisms Leading to Disease. Archives of Internal Medicine 153:2093–2101.

McGarvey, Stephan T., and Paul T. Baker, 1979 The Effects of Moderniztion and Migration on Samoan Blood Pressures. Human Biology 51:467–479.

Pearlin, L. I., M. A. Lieberman, E. G. Menaghan, and J. T. Mullen, 1981 The Stress Process. Journal of Health and Social Behavior 22:337–356.

Romney, A. Kimball, Susan C. Weller, and William H. Batchelder, 1986 Culture as Consensus: a Theory of Culture and Informant Accuracy. American Anthropologist 88:313–338.

Scotch, Norman A., 1963 Sociocultural Factors in the Epidemiology of Zulu Hypertension. American Journal of Public Health 53:1205–1213.

Sweet, Elizabeth, 2008 Culture, Stress and Mental Health: Everyday Lives of Urban African American Youth. Paper presented at the Annual Meeting of the Society for Applied Anthropology, Memphis, March 26–30.

CHAPTER 7

Global Health

Craig R. Janes
and Kitty K. Corbett

DEFINING GLOBAL HEALTH

Global health has emerged as a major field of research and practice, producing a growing number of academic programs, departments, conferences, and professional organizations. Yet despite its current popularity, global health is rarely defined, or if it is defined, it is not often done with the consistency and conceptual clarity that would differentiate it from its historical forebears, international public health and tropical medicine (Koplan et al. 2009). The Institute of Medicine defines global health simply as an endeavour that focuses on "health problems, issues, and concerns that transcend national boundaries, and may best be addressed by cooperative actions" (1997:1) with a "*goal of improving health for all people by reducing avoidable disease, disabilities, and deaths*" (2009:5; emphasis in original). In a recent article in *The Lancet*, members of the Consortium of Universities for Global Health argue that global health, international health, and public health share a number of concerns, including: "priority on a population-based and preventive focus, concentration on poorer, vulnerable, and underserved populations; multidisciplinary and interdisciplinary approaches; emphasis on health as a public good and the importance of systems and structures; and the participation of several stakeholders" (Koplan et al. 2009:1993–1994).

What distinguishes global health from these other fields? The political scientist Kelley Lee suggests that international health becomes global health when the causes or consequences of ill-health "circumvent, undermine, or are oblivious to the territorial boundaries of states, and thus beyond the capacity of states to address effectively through state institutions alone... Global health is also concerned with factors that contribute to changes in the capacity of states to deal with the determinants of health (Lee et al. 2002:5)." Lee and others argue that globalization, emerging forms of governance, and needs for new kinds of trans-state cooperative institutions are central

A Companion to Medical Anthropology, First Edition. Edited by Merrill Singer and Pamela I. Erickson.

components of global health. Although in this sense global health can be taken as a field that transcends older distinctions between health work in high-income developed countries versus low-to-middle income countries, in reality, the majority of scholars in the field continue to be oriented to public health research and practice in low-to-middle income countries, with the justification that these are areas where health inequities and health needs are the greatest (Macfarlane et al. 2008; Kaplan et al. 2009).

We prefer to view global health as encompassing but expanding international health research and practice through an increased sensitivity to transnational social, ideological, political, environmental, and economic processes (Janes and Corbett 2009). Global health represents an effort to bring health into the domain of international relations and world systems discourses, where the study of health is integrated with the examination of power relationships not only between nations, but including intergovernmental institutions such as the World Bank and World Trade Organization, major international non-governmental organizations, corporations, and philanthropies (Lee 2003b). Thus a distinguishing feature of global health is the appreciation of the impact of multiple *globalization processes* on health.

Globalization as a construct is also characterized by a mushrooming, multidisciplinary literature; Tsing refers to the "charisma of social science globalisms" (Tsing 2000:330) and "the thrall of globalization" (p. 353). Current literature suggests four dimensions of globalization that are relevant to health outcomes. First, globalization describes the integration of economies and societies that is driven by new technologies and economic relationships, particularly by the expansion of and intensification of political–economic activities within the capitalist world system (Baer et al. 2003; Gutierrez and Kendall 2000; Kawachi and Wamala 2007). These activities contribute to further integration by "reducing the cost of distance" (Kawachi and Wamala 2007; Lee 2003b). There are clear winners and losers in the expansion and integration of the global economic system: global economic integration has resulted in increasing levels of inequality worldwide (Commission on the Social Determinants of Health 2008). Second, globalization is often described as being constituted by flows – of people, ideas, capital, technologies, pathogens, psychotropic drugs, and other proximal disease causes (e.g., toxins), and commodities. These flows refigure or create new social relationships and institutions through linking localities that were formerly distinct, erasing or blurring older social boundaries, and reconfiguring local social relations (Appadurai 1996; Kearney 1995; Lee 2003b; Ong and Collier 2005; Robbins 2007). Local patterns of disease risk, through exposure to new pathogens, drugs, technology, and social change, are similarly transformed (Gutierrez and Kendall 2000). Third, globalization has policy and institutional dimensions that together tend to reinforce integration and some degree of homogenization, typically promulgated through monetary policies, trade agreements, international standards, and international institutions (Kawachi and Wamala 2007; Kickbusch 2000; McMichael and Beaglehole 2003). These processes are not new: the modern wave of globalization has deep historical roots in colonialism and the development of global trade from the 16th century onwards. However, most scholars agree that in recent times the quantity and velocity of changes have resulted in a qualitatively distinct and linked set of economic and social forces that have had a profound effect on local life and health (Gutierrez and Kendall 2000). Fourth, globalization is a complex and uneven process, involving heterogeneous elements, that produce different consequences and pose unique risks for individuals, communities, and populations depending on their social position (Lee 2003a; Ong and Collier 2005).

These many, diverse, and complex aspects of globalization have given rise to many perspectives and frameworks within the larger context of global health research, practice, and policy. Stuckler and McKee (2008), for example, refer to five dominant metaphors within the field: global health as foreign policy; global health as health security; global health as charity; global health as investment; and global health as public health. Each of these frameworks has a different policy goal and is promulgated by different groups of institutions and organizations. Policies linked to foreign affairs or health security, for example, tend to focus on trade agreements and alliances, bio-terrorism, and protection from emerging infectious diseases, and are promulgated primarily by national political institutions. Charity frameworks place global health in the context of the fight against global poverty, and are the main orienting metaphors of the newly emergent philanthropies such as the Bill and Melinda Gates Foundation. Investment perspectives tend to focus on health as a prerequisite for rapid economic development. This perspective underlies the rationale for the World Bank and International Monetary Fund's participation in global public health. Public health frameworks focus in reducing the burden of disease, with a focus on priority diseases that make up the majority of this burden. Global public health is pursued primarily by the World Health Organization, bilateral aid organizations, and large and growing number of non-governmental organizations. Stuckler and McKee (2008) argue that these frameworks are often mixed and implicit, resulting in policies that are neither coherent nor focus on clear and specific outcomes.

How do these different frameworks relate to the theory and practice of global health within medical anthropology? For most anthropologists, the challenge is to link or "ground" these frameworks and processes of globalization to health and health-related behaviors (e.g. health movements, treatment practices, health knowledge) in local contexts. Yet what constitutes the "local" in the context of globalization? Increasingly what counts as local society or culture can no longer be bounded neatly by common space or place (Ong and Collier 2005). Here we use the definition developed by Ginsburg and Rapp (1995a:8): "the local is not defined by geographical boundaries but is understood as any small-scale arena in which social meanings are informed and adjusted."

In the context of medical anthropology, then, global health is a field of research and practice that examines how factors of global, national, and subnational origins converge on a health issue, problem, policy, or outcome in an identified local social arena. This includes work that focuses on health inequities; the distribution of resources intended to produce health and well being, including science and technology; social identities related to health and biology; the development and local consequences of global health policy promulgated by national and international institutions; the organization of health services; and the relationship of anthropogenic transformations of the biosphere to health. We argue that the ultimate goal of much anthropological work in global health is to reduce global health inequities and contribute to the development of sustainable and salutogenic socio-cultural, political, and economic systems. Although global health conceptually includes all peoples regardless of social, economic, and political contexts, its ethical and moral commitment is to the most vulnerable (Janes and Corbett 2009).

In the remainder of this chapter we consider some of the current work in medical anthropology that illuminates how global forces affect health in local settings, and, in some cases, how medical anthropology has informed effective intervention. We organize this review into four overlapping categories of contribution: (1) analysis of the social determinants of health; (2) the globalization of health sciences and technology; (3) analysis and critique of international health programs and policies; (4) the emerging social relations of international health development.

THE SOCIAL DETERMINANTS OF HEALTH

Recently the World Health Organization commissioned a study of the "social determinants of health" (Commission on the Social Determinants of Health 2008). The Commission marshalled global evidence documenting the social gradient within and between countries. They conclude that the "unequal distribution of power, income, goods and services... the consequent unfairness in the ... circumstances of people's lives... and their chances of leading a flourishing life" (p. 1) are the primary causes of the poor health of the poor. While this is hardly news to health social scientists, who generally accept the early foundational work on this subject by Virchow, Engels and others (e.g., Waitzkin 2004), formal international acceptance of the social origins of illness has important policy ramifications. The WHO calls for global action to address the social determinants of health across the lifespan. In terms of research and scholarship, the Commission argues for moving health research beyond the disease-specific biomedical focus that characterizes the vast bulk of it, in favour of a broad focus on the social and economic conditions that constitute peoples lives. Specifically in the context of assessing the impact of interventions, they argue for a multidisciplinary approach that gives equal value to multiple methodological traditions.

Evaluations of social determinants of health interventions require rich qualitative data in order to understand the ways in which context affects the intervention and the reasons for its success or failure. What counts as legitimate evidence should be determined on the basis of 'fitness for purpose' rather than on a single hierarchy of evidence (which traditionally puts randomized controlled trials and laboratory experiments at the top).

In their dedication to documenting the life worlds of the most vulnerable, medical anthropologists have contributed significantly to understanding social determinants of health and are well-positioned to contribute to the Commission's call for global action. To date this contribution has primarily been to "ground globalization" (Burawoy 2000) through exposing the processes by and through which people are constrained, victimized, or resist external forces in the context of local social arenas. There are different perspectives and styles evident in how this research is presented, mainly in the depth of engagement with local materials, the care by which the local is nested within higher level social structures (e.g., social class, urban/rural, region, state), and the degree to which the analysis is used as a platform for public health advocacy. However, this work has a common, critical theoretical perspective that focuses on explicating or grounding health inequities in reference to upstream constellations of international political economy, regional history, and development ideology. As such, it is closely linked with "critical medical anthropology," a research tradition that seeks to identify the social origins of distress and disease, recognizing that these origins are ultimately located within the processes and contradictions inherent in the capitalist world system (Baer et al. 2003; Baer and Singer 2009; Singer and Baer 1995).

Farmer (2003) invokes the idea of "structural violence" to explain the impact of political-economic regimes of oppression on the health of the poor. He writes:

> Social inequalities are at the heart of structural violence. Racism of one form or another, gender inequality, and above all brute poverty in the face of affluence are linked to social plans and programs ranging from slavery to the current quest for unbridled growth....
> ... Structural violence is the natural expression of a political and economic order that seems as old as slavery. This social web of exploitation, in its many differing historical forms, has long been global, or almost so, in its reach (p. 317).

The work of Farmer and others has contributed to redefining the concept of risk in epidemiology by redirecting attention away from "risky behaviors" attributed to individual decision-making or to cultural "tradition", (i.e., agency) to those factors in the social, cultural, and natural environment that constrain or determine such behaviour (i.e., structure). For example, early reports on the epidemiology of HIV/AIDS tended to focus on individual behaviors rather than the impact of poverty and marginality that differentially affect men and women within particular populations and communities (Farmer 1999; Farmer 2003; Farmer et al. 1996; Simmons et al. 1996; Singer 1997). Pointing to the tendency of some public health researchers to conflate poverty and cultural difference, Farmer and colleagues argue against "immodest claims of causality" that focus overly much on references to the cultural determinants of behaviour, and for a focus on, and mitigation of, the structural violence that produces ill-being on a massive scale among the poor. In similar fashion, anthropological contributions to research on infectious diseases, particularly HIV/AIDS, TB, and cholera have contributed significantly to moving global public health away from a narrow focus on risk groups (Baer et al. 2003; Trostle 2005). This work has also generated considerable methodological and conceptual innovation within medical anthropology, and has informed advances in primary, secondary, and tertiary prevention (Baer et al. 2003; Farmer 2001; Parker et al. 2004; Parker and Ehrhardt 2001).

Biehl's (2006, 2007) research in Brazil provides a good example of how careful ethnographic research, conducted at multiple levels, illuminates the development and consequences of AIDS policy for the most vulnerable and explains patterns of health inequity. He describes how Brazil shifted to an "activist state," universalizing access to free antiretroviral drugs, with a host of repercussions for pharmaceutical policy, both within Brazil and globally. At the same time, he also shows how this single-minded focus on drug treatment moved Brazilian AIDS policy firmly away from a broader public health focus on prevention to a focus principally on the distribution of pharmaceuticals, resulting of the deployment of a new kind of "governance." The Brazilian state, although offering free pharmaceuticals, distributed these only to those deemed eligible by virtue of aspects of their behaviour (ability to be compliant, etc.). In so doing, the state effectively refused treatment to many of the most poor and vulnerable. Although Biehl's claims that this pharmaceuticalized approach to HIV has not curtailed the epidemic have been challenged by Brazilian researchers (Clair et al. 2009), his multi-sited, multi-vocal research approach to public health policy is exemplary. What is notable about this study is Biehl's ability to move in his analysis back and forth from victims of the disease unable to comply with the state program, to state and international policymakers, and representatives of civil society. Fassin's (2007) study of the HIV epidemic in South Africa is a similarly-contextualized ethnographic account. Fassin demonstrates how the epidemic and responses to it, especially former President Mbeki's controversial actions and statements, can only be understood by reference to the social and political history of the country.

The social origins of infection with HIV are often bound up with or linked to a number of other threats to health and well being, and, in turn, the coexistence of two or more diseases may synergistically interact to produce a higher degree of pathogenesis (an example would be HIV and TB co-infection). Termed "syndemics," these synergistic processes suggest a biosocial model of disease (Nichter 2008; Singer and Clair 2003; Singer 2009) that conceives "of disease both in terms of its interrelationships with noxious social conditions and social relationships, and as one form of expression of social suffering... it would make us more alert, as well, to the likelihood of multiple, interacting deleterious conditions among populations produced by the structural violence of social inequality" (Singer and Clair 2003:434).

Whether or not explicitly identified as critical medical anthropology, a substantial body of scholarly work in anthropology seeks to link wider social, economic, and political forces to local experiences of sickness and suffering. In addition to the works described above, a few examples include studies of: the global circulation of tobacco and its impacts (Nichter and Cartwright 1991; Stebbins 1991); parasitic and infectious diseases (Briggs and Mantini-Briggs 2003; Farmer 1999; Feldman 2008; Ferguson 2005; Inhorn and Brown 1997; Kendall 2005; Manderson and Huang 2005; Whiteford and Hill 2005); reproductive health, fertility, and infertility (Inhorn 2003; Janes and Chuluundorj 2004; Maternowska 2006; Morsy 1995); mental ill-health (Desjarlais et al. 1995; Kleinman 1988); alcohol and drug use (Singer 2008); lifestyle transitions and non-communicable diseases (Dressler and Bindon 2000; Evans et al. 2001).

Although the ethnographic work on health inequities provides us with a close and detailed understanding of how poverty and social location influence health at the level of small groups and communities, it is also the case that anthropologists have often struggled to provide the same depth of analysis to forces operating at different social levels. There is a tension in much of this work between a close rendering of the local, especially local subjectivities, and effective engagement with global structures and processes. The challenge is simply how to extend ethnographic work to reference globalization while at the same time portraying faithfully the rich human stories that bring voice to the poor and suffering, without flattening, simplifying, or objectifying one or the other (Butt 2002). Farmer and his colleagues often juxtapose stories of individual suffering with political-economic givens, with sometimes thin analysis of intervening processes and structures. Some have observed that the concept of structural violence is a "black box," rarely unpacked (e.g., Bourgois and Scheper-Hughes 2004; Nichter 2008; Wacquant 2004).

These critiques reflect a tension in anthropology (and in social science in general) between "constructivist" and "structuralist" approaches to social life. The critical approach in medical anthropology, and to a large extent the approach taken by the

WHO Commission on the Social Determinants of Health, tends to articulate a structuralist approach to health insofar as scholars focus on "objective structures which are independent of the consciousness and desires of agents and are capable of guiding or constraining their practices or their representations" (Bourdieu 1990:123). Conversely, constructivism focuses on "patterns of perception, thought and action" which are in turn constitutive of these very same social structures (Bourdieu 1990:123; Dressler 2001). Early medical anthropological work in international health grew out of a constructivist perspective, which focused on how cultural patterns, perceptions, and related behaviors affected disease risk in the community (e.g., Paul 1955). The work of Farmer, Singer, and others, was intended to add to, or in some cases correct, this narrow, often apolitical focus on culture and behaviour through explicating the structural forces that constrain local agency and produce glaring health inequities. However, while individuals and communities may be severely constrained in their responses to globalization and disease, patterns of and responses to illness and disease in communities require attention to local subjectivities. The key challenge, only partially met in global health, is to integrate this conceptual, theoretical, and methodological divide (Dressler 2001). Emerging methodologies and perspectives, ranging from multi-sited ethnography (Biehl 2007; Petryna 2002; Scheper-Hughes 2000, 2005), to studies of cultural consonance in the context of stress and disease (Dressler 2001), to social-ecological and evolutionary theoretical perspectives (Goodman and Leatherman 1998; Janes and Chuluundorj 2004; Leatherman 1994; Thomas 1998), represent promising attempts to bridge, though only partially, structuralist and constructivist models of health inequities. Krieger's model of "ecosocial epidemiology" (Krieger 2001) might also be usefully employed in anthropological approaches to global health (Nichter 2008). This model addresses the interplay among exposure, resilience, and susceptibility at meso- and macro-scales across the lifecourse.

Although anthropologists have engaged with many of the core themes of health equity studies in global public health, they lag in taking up some emerging concerns. Gaps are apparent in the domain of environmental change, affecting and affected by global processes. Examples range from climate change (Baer and Singer 2009), to specific problems such as microbial resistance (Orzech and Nichter 2008). Many of the models of human impacts of climate change point to the need for more research to identify factors that affect the vulnerabilities of local populations in the context of political economy (Intergovernmental Panel on Climate Change 2007). We anticipate that in the next decade medical anthropology will begin to investigate more systematically the relationship of global environmental transformations to health. We expect to see greater convergence of scholarly concerns among researchers who focus on global health and others who focus on local to global ecological and environmental challenges (Baer and Singer 2009).

GLOBAL STUDIES OF SCIENCE AND TECHNOLOGY

In his writing on the various cultural dimensions of globalization, Arjun Appadurai (1996:34) invoked the term "technoscape" to describe the "global configuration … of technology, and the fact that technology, both high and low, both mechanical and information, [that] moves at high speeds across various kinds of previously impervi-

boundaries." In the context of global health, technologies include medicines, lical devices, machines, medical procedures, a corpus of knowledge about the ly and its constituent parts, and the full array of practices and procedures for creat- g and applying health-relevant knowledge. Together these might be seen as comprising the many dimensions of biomedical science as it is developed and applied in developed countries. Questions central to investigation of global science concern how paradigms, practices, and results are negotiated and unfold far from their places of origin (Adams et al. 2005). As many have noted, the products and purported benefits of science and technology are unevenly distributed, with some sites and groups having greater access than others (Ginsburg and Rapp 1995b; Inhorn 2003). Lack of access is not only a consequence of economics; it is also political and ideological. This was evidenced by the actions of former South African President, Thabo Mbeki, who critiqued orthodox interpretations of the etiology of HIV, and questioned the validity of conventional treatment regimens, thus, according to some, and at a great cost in lives and suffering, considerably exacerbating the South African epidemic. As Fassin (2007) argues, Mbeki's actions resonated with South Africans' distrust of Western hegemony, expanding the viral theory of HIV to encompass poverty and disadvantage.

Examples of key works in this area include: the local impact of biomedical research practices, such as those involving translation of the ethical principles of scientific research, especially clinical trials, in specific cultural contexts (Adams et al. 2005; Petryna 2005); the circulation of medicalized objectifications of body and behaviour, such as those having to do with sexuality in this era of HIV (Parker 2000; Pigg and Adams 2005); the transformations of local beliefs and understandings about the body, life, and death that are entailed by the globalization of human organ replacement therapies (Lock 2001; Marshall and Daar 2000); local acceptances of and resistance to contraceptive technologies (Maternowska 2006); the complex local/global dynamics of organ transplantation (Cohen 2005; Scheper-Hughes 2000, 2005), and cases illustrating complexities of corporate practices, medicalization, and the politics of biomedical knowledge through the interwoven dynamics of drug production, marketing and sales practices, the classification of disease, and patterns of clinical practice (Applbaum 2006; Hayden 2007; Singer and Baer 2008). Other work relevant to global health that focuses on science and technology, but is not specifically framed in terms of health, includes studies on food security and related technologies (Stone 2002).

A prominent area of research has focused on the globalization of reproductive and prenatal diagnostic technologies (Browner and Sargent 2009; Ginsburg and Rapp 1995a; Inhorn 2003, 2005, 2007). Writing of the globalization of treatments for infertility, Inhorn (2003) observes that, "[l]ocal considerations, be they cultural, social, economic, or political, shape and sometimes curtail the way in which these Western-generated technologies are both offered to and received by non-Western subjects" (p. 1844). Cultural or religious proscription of procedures such as donor insemination has led to increased global demand and rapid circulation of more expensive technologies such as *in vitro* fertilization (Inhorn 2003). In Egypt, for example, men and women contending with infertility are confronted by constraints that are deeply embedded in local social and cultural contexts. These "arenas of constraint" include local understandings of reproductive biology, social and economic barriers to access, gender dynamics within marriage, and local understandings of Islam (Inhorn 2003: 844, 2005, 2007).

The global technoscape has also set into motion people, for example the export of physicians and nurses (the "brain drain") from low income countries to rich countries (Pfeiffer and Nichter 2008), and "medical tourists" and others who travel to places where desired technologies exist or are affordable (Kangas 2002).

Bioscience is not the only set of ideas about bodies, physiology, and health that circulate globally. There are also "countervailing creativities," whereby what were formerly "local" and "non-Western" engage both the imagination and the markets at the center of the world system (Høg and Hsu 2002). This is the case for Asian medicines, both brought by immigrants and practiced by immigrant communities, but also adopted by "New Agers" and others challenging the dominance of conventional biomedicine. In their places of origin and in their global circulation, the content and practice of these medical traditions are transformed (Høg and Hsu 2002; Janes 2002). In many cases these processes of transformation involve at their core the commoditization of medicinal substances, which is in turn based on the reduction of complex systems of diagnosis, explanation, and healing to the exchange of material things (Janes 1999).

Van der Geest and colleagues (1996) have made the important point that commodities produced by science – machines, techniques, tools, and medicines – have social lives. Each has a biographical trajectory: they are produced, marketed, distributed, consumed or used, and, ultimately, have an effect on the people who use them. At each stage a particular set of actors are involved, and a different "regime of values" is invoked (van der Geest et al. 1996:156). Referring specifically to pharmaceuticals, van der Geest et al. (1996) set forth a research agenda to investigate the social relations of actors, the values and cultural assumptions that each brings to their stage of the biographical process. It is a useful framework to investigate the inherently social process by which technology is produced globally and distributed and consumed locally, with important consequences for health and well being.

Medicines – *materia medica* - are at the heart of much of what we might define as "medical technologies." Although medicines, especially pharmaceuticals, were often as not ignored as a focal topic by medical anthropologists in the first decades of the discipline, work by van der Geest and other anthropologists in the 1980s and 1990s initiated a "florescence" of research on their uses in the context of global influences, and factors affecting their production, distribution, demand, and consumption (Trostle 1996; van der Geest et al. 1988, 1996). This trend continues, spurred in part by the ethical and practical challenges represented by the need for people everywhere who live with HIV/AIDS to receive treatment (Farmer et al. 2001; Robins 2009; Whyte et al. 2006). Addressing the problem of access to treatment requires investigating pharmaceutical governance, trade practices, patent protection, and distribution channels, and alternative industries and markets, as well as local organizations and the cultural and ritual properties of medicines (Hayden 2007; Kim 2009; Mather 2006; Oldani 2004). As anthropologists reflect on adverse medication use, including overuse, inappropriate use, and errors in getting the medication and its delivery to a patient right, they increasingly situate these practices within global institutional and perceptual systems (Nichter 2008).

One outcome of the global circulation of expert, biomedical knowledge is the creation of novel social forms or arrangements that develop around particular diseases or therapeutic programmes (Biehl 2007; Lee 2003a; Nguyen 2005; Rose and Novas 2005). In the context of HIV, notes Nguyen, these groups are "more than social movements articulated around objectives," but are a "complex biopolitical assemblage, cobbled together from global flows of organisms, drugs, discourses, and technologies of all kinds" (Nguyen 2005:125). Specifically Nguyen considers the degree to which the global AIDS industry, particularly the constellation of technoscientific understandings of prevention and treatment, is translated locally by groups and organizations to mobilize a response to the epidemic. Similarly, Petryna (2002) shows how the Chernobyl disaster and its impacts on health provided an avenue for affected individuals, joined by a biologically mediated identity, to make claims on the state for resources. The development of therapeutic groups is increasingly entangled with the industry of health development (Nguyen 2005:25). This form of citizenship represents those evolving subjectivities, politics, and ethics that result from the globalization of biomedical developments and discoveries (Ecks 2005; Rose and Novas 2005).

INTERNATIONAL HEALTH POLICY

A scholar of the development of European social policy suggests that in its ideal form the essence of policymaking is for a group, presumably of experts, authorities, or delegates, to puzzle out solutions to particular problems on society's behalf (Heclo 1974). Nichter (2008) suggests that in doing so, policymakers simplify and frame problems in a way that limits the thinking about possible solutions. He suggests that these representations of reality comprise "master narratives" that dominate health and development policy (Nichter 2008:2). Lee and Goodman (2002) argue further that the networks of so-called experts in global health tend to be fairly small, but are positioned strategically to create and successfully advocate for solutions to key international agencies. They show how World Bank health reform policy, now dominant throughout the world, grew out of the work of a relatively small network of individuals who represented a handful of non-governmental organizations, research centers and universities located in Washington, Boston, London, and Geneva. This group acted on the basis of a set of core beliefs or representations that held that market institutions offered better and more efficient solutions to providing health care than did inefficient and bureaucratic government institutions (also Janes 2004; Janes et al. 2006). Such networks comprise what are in international relations and globalization literatures termed "epistemic communities" (Adler and Haas 1992). In the context of global health, these communities are comprised of loose networks of actors who develop common frameworks of knowledge, values, and beliefs which they draw on in creating public health policy. As many critics have observed, epistemic communities tend to represent the interests, at least implicitly, of the global capitalist class (Singer and Castro 2004). The power of these communities has expanded along with the increasing prominence of philanthropies and super-NGOs on the global scene, and the decreasing power of states. It is notable that these networks extend into major universities, especially in the fields of economics and public health (Lee and Goodman 2002).

Anthropologists' policy-oriented studies focus on critiques of policy makers and the policy-making process. Van der Geest (2008) critiques an over-emphasis in global health domains on pharmaceutical policies as a solution, commenting about the "lip service "and culture of policy makers whose mandate is to produce planning reports and documents (e.g., about essential medicines, their distribution, etc.) but are not concerned about program implementation:

> The culture of policymakers is mainly the production of documents. A well composed text, delivered before the deadline to the Minister to cite in his speeches or accounts to higher authorities is indeed the first priority of policymakers. Having accomplished this makes them feel satisfied. The actual realization of the plans in health care is the responsibility of others (p. 313).

Hardon (2005) also is critical of policy makers, claiming that their work often entails a focus on "magic bullets." Recent policy shifts reflect a growing acknowledgement in the pharmaceutical and policy sectors that people without economic resources or literacy can and do use HIV/AIDS treatments appropriately, and an increasing adoption of an equity ethic, favoring broader access to pharmaceuticals through, for instance, changes in patent protection and pricing of medicines. Although many more people now have access to previously far too expensive treatments, other problems have cropped up. The price of pharmaceuticals is still extremely high for people on the margins of the economy, and entire family networks may experience cash depletion and food insecurity as they shift the household economy to procure medicines for a family member who is ill (Whyte et al. 2006).

On the face of it, a knowledge or technology translation program based on reputable change theories and found effective in one or a few settings merits broad diffusion in a region or globally. Yet the trend in scale-up endeavors and the optimism behind them, if not carefully implemented, run counter to what medical anthropologists typically advocate: that we must cautiously and painstakingly adapt programs and policies to local socio-cultural realities (Orchard et al. 2009). As Hardon (2005) states in a discussion of current approaches to HIV/AIDS: "Though different in policy content, the prevention and treatment policies have in common that they pay little attention to the local socio-cultural realities in sub-Saharan Africa that ultimately determine their success" (p. 601). "One size never fits all." Model research settings characterize the sites for many published studies that meet scientific peer-review criteria, and findings may thus have serious limitations for real-world dissemination. And as Biehl (2007) demonstrates, to have the desired effect, any policy will have to deal with local institutional practices, the lives of a multitude of diverse and differently situated actors, and socio-cultural issues such as stigmatization whose forms are profoundly local.

The global circulation of expert knowledge produces particular relations of power between policy makers and policy subjects. The collapse of the primary care initiatives developed at Alma Ata in 1978, the resurgence of selective forms of primary care and vertical public health programs, and the ascendency of the World Bank as the principal health policy making institution provides a glimpse of how these processes work themselves out (Janes 2004, 2008; Janes et al. 2005; Lee and Goodman 2002; Paluzzi 2004). Deploying a set of strategies to reframe health and health care in narrow technical terms (i.e., the development of the Disability Adjusted Life Year, or DALY) subject to the principles of classical economics, a relatively small group of individuals crafted an approach to health care that removed it from public governance and placed it largely in the hands of the market, complementing and completing the processes of structural adjustment begun in the 1980s (Farmer 2003; Farmer and Castro 2004; Janes 2004; World Bank 1993). Employing, though implicitly, a utilitarian approach to health reform, where health itself is framed primarily as a technical problem with identifiable technical solutions, earlier, rights-based frameworks were largely displaced by others beholden to a market ethic (Janes 2008). The result has been increasing inequities and contradictions at local levels, for example reforms that mandate selling medicines to poor people who cannot afford them (Keshavjee 2004). Although it is notable that the World Health Organization is currently attempting to reclaim the high ground on health reform and reassert the principles of primary care originally formulated at Alma Ata (World Health Organization 2008), it remains to be seen whether rights-based approaches will be able to "trump" current policies that champion market based solutions and view publicly provided care as undesirable, inefficient, and expensive.

Population and reproductive policy is an important area where deeply held beliefs about the causes and consequences poverty, and the role of scientific development and expert knowledge of demographic processes in remediating poverty, have come to drive health and social policy (Maternowska 2006). For example, in a series of works focusing on population policy in China, Greenhalgh (2005) has shown how the development of coercive family "planning" practices linked a version of Western population science with socialist planning and party-led community mobilization. China's leaders drew on Western population science to frame the Chinese population as "abnormal" and "in crisis," and to establish the logic for a coercive family planning project designed to achieve "demographic modernity." This program of population control, resulting in the egregious excesses of a sterilization campaign in 1983, was linked, according to Greenhalgh, with "China's entry into global capitalist and scientific circuits ... and the nation's dreams of becoming a global economic power and ethical member of the world community of nations" (p. 369). Although the International Conference on Population Development held in Cairo in 1994 urged countries to move away from a narrow focus on fertility targets and to respect and protect women's rights to make an informed choice about their reproduction, in many countries oppressive and coercive regimes of family planning have continued, directed primarily at poor women (Castro 2004; Maternowska 2006; Morsy 1995).

As noted, much of the critique of policy cites failure to appreciate local social and cultural contexts as a central contributor to failure (e.g., Whiteford and Manderson 2000). Ironically, though, development work appears to have taken a page from the anthropologists' notebook: community mobilization and participation in health programs has come to dominate much development language (Morgan 2001). Representations of these social forms – households and communities – and entailed methods for including and/or targeting such forms in public health programs – are increasingly commonplace. Generated at a global level, and based, often as not, on relatively superficial ideas about the "local" and "traditional," these representations may overemphasize the capacity of communities to collaborate with planners, assume the existence of cooperative institutions, and they often leave important issues relating to power and conflict under-examined (Jambai and MacCormack 1996;

Janes 2004; Nichter 1995, 2008). Underlying these formulations are important development-oriented ideologies that ascribe to communities the capacity and necessity to be responsible for health and social welfare in the context of a weakening state (Janes 2004). Critics of these ideologies point to the fact that communities are dynamic and fluid, may be divided along class lines, may have very few resources and a great many competing needs, and may be highly marginalized, both socio-economically, and politically; at a given historical moment, they may be neither ready nor able to increase their responsibility over social and other determinants of health and health care. Regardless, the failure of communities to marshal sufficient resources to sustain and support health development efforts may be met with victim-blaming (Pearce and Davey Smith 2003). Community participation, though, remains an alluring strategy for those committed to more organic, "bottoms-up," and social justice oriented approaches to health development (Morgan 2001; Nichter 1999). The lesson here for anthropologists is twofold: we should maintain a commitment to elucidating local contexts and fully engaging communities, and avoid contributing to superficial, occasionally romantic, visions of what communities can and cannot do.

The Social Relations of Global Health Development

Market-oriented development strategies initiated in the health sector since the 1980s have systematically reduced the size and reach of government public health services. As a result, a number of private organizations, grouped collectively under the general heading of "civil society" have become the cornerstone of health development. In its most common usage, the term includes all organizations not formally considered part of government or individual households (Walt et al. 1999). As employed by institutions such as the World Bank, civil society encompasses non-governmental organizations (or NGOs), trade unions, faith-based organizations, indigenous peoples' movements, and foundations. In contrast to the more general category of civil society, NGOs are commonly defined as private voluntary organizations that pursue activities to relieve suffering, promote the interests of the poor, protect the environment, provide basic social services, or undertake community development. Although civil society organizations are thought to operate largely outside of the private, for-profit sector, there is often a considerable overlap of public and private interests and goals – through foundations, charitable arms of corporations, for-profit health care organizations, and so on. Because the large, international NGOs are often the preferred implementing agencies for donors – they are able to comply with standards for proposal writing, program planning, monitoring and evaluation – they have developed into a large and largely uncoordinated group of agencies operating in parallel, and sometimes in competition with, the public health sector, creating and sustaining what Buse and Walt (1997) refer to as an "unruly mélange" (Pfeiffer 2003, 2004).

Despite their prominence in health development, NGOs have just begun to gain attention as social and cultural phenomena in their own right (Abramson 1999; Markowitz 2001; Pfeiffer 2003, 2004; Redfield 2005). Pfeiffer (2003, 2004) has documented how in Mozambique the operation of NGOs, instead of strengthening health services, may have in fact had the opposite effect, undermining local control of health programs and recruiting public sector employees away from public health service. International NGO competition for skilled local personnel, offering salary supplements and per diems for field activities, can seriously compromise the public sector. Pfeiffer also gives us a glimpse of the social dynamics of NGOs, observing that in the interaction between the elite, educated technicians from the rich countries and community members living in extreme poverty, the exercise of power is laid bare. Like Pfeiffer, we ask whether the same quantity of aid, distributed through ministries of health rather than through private institutions, might have a more positive effect on health and social outcomes.

The expansion of NGOs is but one example of a growing number of transnational institutions that have become active in global health. Along with existing bilateral donors, intergovernmental institutions, and public private partnerships, these include economic interest groups, large philanthropic organizations, and multinational pharmaceutical companies. Increasingly the effective practice of global health, regardless of disciplinary orientation, requires not just understanding how to work effectively at a local level to improve health and well being; it involves skills needed to work across these many, and often competing, interest groups (Adams et al. 2008). Lumping these skills under the term "health diplomacy," Adams and colleagues (2008) write that:

> Successful health development efforts have depended on functional and respectful relations among all the stakeholders, including donor and recipient governments, health care providers, local political leaders, and fieldbased NGOs. A capable health diplomat must have a sophisticated understanding of the structures, programs, approaches, and pitfalls surrounding these relationships to achieve success, whether working in the clinical setting or at the policymaking table (p. 319).

They suggest that medical anthropologists are well-suited to engage in explorations of the politics of health diplomacy, policymaking, and agenda setting. However, to do so requires commitment to a different kind and level of ethnographic research than that with which most anthropologists are comfortable. Such research would involve asking about the power dynamics and politics that drive health development, both locally and globally. Here the subject of study might be informational flows and decision-making processes among networks of policy makers working at local, national, and global levels (e.g., Lee and Goodman 2002).

CONCLUSIONS

The escalation of sociopolitical factors that promote and sustain inequities in global health indicate that the global health crisis is worsening. For anthropologists addressing this area, global health involves a focus on the factors and forces of globalization, identifying how these affect health in local to global social arenas. Our work encompasses all peoples, not only those who live in the low-to-middle income countries that have been the primary areas of concern for international health practitioners over the past century or so. Yet it is clear that globalization has produced winners and losers: peoples in many resource-poor settings have experienced assaults on their health that far exceed those faced by the middle and upper classes in the developed countries. A girl born in some countries can expect to live for 80 years, but less than 45 years if she is born in others. Within countries there may be similar gradients linked to social location, gender, and ethnicity (Commission on the Social Determinants of Health 2008). There is a moral and an ethical imperative to challenge these vast inequities.

We have encapsulated contributions into four main areas of research and practice. In the first of these, through ethnographic analysis of health inequities, anthropologists have added considerable depth to the project of identifying the social determinants of health (Commission on the Social Determinants of Health 2008). By specifying links among local life worlds and the global forces of neoliberal development, anthropologists have laid bare the lines of power, exploitation, and violence. Although more conceptual development is needed, this work has pointed to inherent flaws in health development programs that do not take poverty and environmental degradation, their (often overlapping) root causes and consequences, as the most important problems.

Second, and now a rapidly growing area of research, is the study of global technoscience. Here anthropology focuses on the circulation of technology as well as the bundles of meanings, representations, and understandings that together constitute biomedical science in wealthy countries at the center of the global economy. The goals of research here are twofold: to analyze the cultural context of science and its products, and, then, to understand how science, as a social and cultural product, engages the local, where it is transformed and transforms, through being adopted, used, and resisted. Theoretically complex, this research area nevertheless has simple, direct, and profound implications for global health problems related to access to medicine and technology, the impact of science on conceptions of the body, ethical issues related to experimentation, the commoditization of body parts, identity, and emerging processes of governance.

Third, an investigation of the globalization of western bioscience facilitates interrogation of entailed policies. How are policies made? Who makes these policies, and what ideologies, discourses, representations, and systems of knowledge do they draw upon in crafting decisions? How do policies made by global communities of practice work themselves out, and to what effect, in highly variable local settings and contexts? Here, as with the study of the global circulation of science and technology, the focus is on examining the unintended consequences of policy for locals, reflecting on the fact that for the poor and vulnerable, it is an "unlevel playing field" (Whiteford and Manderson 2000).

Fourth, it is clear from analysis of global health policy making that the social institutions of global health governance have been transformed. The proliferation of non-state actors and neoliberal development practices that engage an imagined civil society has produced a complex mix of groups and organizations at state and community levels. Successful health development entails both coordinating across this "unruly mélange," and understanding the social and cultural effects of its various operations. Yet there is much we do not understand about how civil society operates in global health. The principal questions appear to be whether private organizations operating in parallel to the state foster, or compromise, positive health outcomes, and whether they in fact contribute to reducing, or increasing, health inequities.

In line with H.G. Wells' caution, "Human history becomes more and more a race between education and catastrophe" (1920), we find ourselves concerned about anthropology's contributions to concrete solutions, educational and otherwise. We ask: Is anthropology contributing in substantive ways to the kinds of engagement and interventions that promise to reduce health inequities, foster social justice, and address the challenges to global health presaged by global climate change, habitat destruction, and mass species extinction, as well as the forces and contradictions of the global capitalist system? We believe that it is imperative for medical anthropology to re-prioritize our calling, moving from the interpretive, micro-anthropological modes characteristic of much late 20th century cultural anthropology, to highlight how social realities are contextualized in and generative of the macro-anthropological realities of global troubles writ large: the complex, maladaptive, diplomatic, material and biological constraints affecting us, the planet, and our health (Corbett 1999). As many preeminent anthropologists have appealed to the discipline in the past (e.g., Rappaport 1993; Scudder 1999), our efforts now more than ever should reflect an engaged anthropology with applications of our vision at its center. It is time we engage more with problem solving, although well armed with precautions and past lessons in mind.

There are promising examples, and the work that many researchers have done lends itself clearly to appropriate engagement and interventions. We are mindful of the several generations of anthropologists who, largely external to the academy, through hard work at community to policy levels, through clear and principled commitment to socially and culturally relevant public health efforts, have made a difference. These efforts are, in many ways, both the foundation and backbone of current medical anthropology, and constitute in large measure the substance of promise and hope that we hold out to our students. Yet we also worry that many medical anthropologists hesitate in applying insights gained in their research to making a difference. Especially for those anthropologists firmly ensconced in the academy, critique short of action may unfortunately be the easiest and more comfortable path to professional success.

Anthropologists' work in global health is diverse, spanning a broad spectrum of topics, methods, and voices. Conceptualizations of global health are a work in progress, and have consequences for the construction, translation, and exchange of knowledge as well as the foci of our research. Beyond being researchers, anthropologists have a role in generating and bringing about solutions. It is time we relax our disciplinary insularity and adopt interdisciplinarity as a hallmark of who we are. Exclusionary allegiance to our own literature, fear of breaching the expectations of colleagues in academia, and an excessive disciplinary tendency to introspection about what anthropologists as such have to offer, what unique niche we have or should occupy, may threaten our readiness and capacity to contribute to solutions that are so urgently needed. Among scholars, anthropologists should stand out as having the breadth of education (biology, culture, material life, history, etc.) and experiences in the world to address the challenges to health that humans and other beings on the planet face in our times. The global political economic system appears to be unravelling, and the news about transformations in the global environment is very bad. These have everything to do with health, and should be the targets that the next generation of research addresses. To do this effectively, we believe, requires anthropologists to be more interdisciplinary and collaborative, to attend more closely to the literature generated externally to anthropology, and to engage more directly and deliberately in proposing and participating in solutions.

NOTE

1   As this discussion suggests, NGOs are highly variable in terms of scope, geographic scale, and strength of ties both to local communities and international organizations. The diversity of these organizations defies simple definition. Much of the work cited here refers primarily to private development organizations who are either inter- or transnational in scope (e.g., Family Health International, CARE, World Vision), or who are local implementing organizations that depend on international donors for funding and direction.

REFERENCES

Abramson, David, 1999 A critical look at NGOs and civil society as a means to an end in Uzbekistan. Human Organization 58:240–250.

Adams, Vincanne, Suellen Miller, Sienna Craig, Sonam Nyima, Lhakpen Droyoung, and Michael Varner, 2005 The challenge of cross-cultural clinical trials research: case report from the Tibetan Autonomous Region, People's Republic of China. Medical Anthropology Q 19(3):267–289.

Adams, Vincanne, Thomas E. Novotny, and Hannah Leslie, 2008 Global health diplomacy. Medical Anthropology 27(4):315–323.

Adler, Emanuel, and Peter M. Haas, 1992 Epistemic communities, world order, and the creation of a reflective research program. International Organization 46(1):367–390.

Appadurai, Arjun, 1996 Modernity at Large : Cultural Dimensions of Globalization. Minneapolis: University of Minnesota Press.

Applbaum, Kalman, 2006 Educating for global mental health: the adoption of SSRIs in Japan. In Global Pharmaceuticals: Ethics, Markets, Practices. Adriana Petryna, Andrew Lakoff, and Arthur Kleinman, eds. pp. 85–110. Durham NC: Duke University Press.

Baer, Hans, and Merrill Singer, 2009 Global Warming and the Political Ecology of Health: Emerging Crises and Systemic Solutions. Walnut Creek CA: Left Coast Press.

Baer, Hans, Merrill Singer, and Ida Susser, 2003 Medical Anthropology and the World System. Westport CT: Praeger.

Biehl, Joao, 2006 Pharmaceutical governance. In Global Pharmaceuticals: Ethics, Markets, Practices. Adriana Petryna, Andrew Lakoff, and Arthur Kleinman, eds. pp. 206–239. Durham NC: Duke University Press.

Biehl, Joao, 2007 Will to Live: AIDS Therapies and the Politics of Survival. Princeton NJ: Princeton University Press.

Bourdieu, Pierre, 1990 In Other Words: Essays Towards a Reflexive Sociology. Stanford CA: Stanford University Press.

Bourgois, Phillipe, and Nancy Scheper-Hughes, 2004 Comment on "An Anthropology of Structural Violence," by Paul Farmer. Current Anthropology 45(3):317–318.

Briggs, Charles L., and Clara Mantini-Briggs, 2003 Stories in a Time of Cholera: The Transnational Circulation of Bacteria and Racial Stigmata in a Venezuelan Epidemic. Berkeley: University of California Press.

Browner, Carole H., and Carolyn F. Sargent, In press, 2009 Reproduction, Globalization, and the State. Durham NC: Duke University Press.

Burawoy, Michael, 2000 Grounding globalization. In Global Ethnography: Forces, Connections, and Imaginations in a Postmodern World. Michael Burawoy, Joseph A. Blum, Sheba George, Zsuzsa Gille, Teresa Gowan, Lynne Haney, Maren Klawiter, Steve H. Lopez, Sean O. Riain, and Millie Thayer, eds. pp. 337–350. Berkeley: University of California Press.

Buse, Kent, and Gill Walt, 1997 An unruly mélange? Coordinating external resources to the health sector: a review. Social Science and Medicine 45(3):449–463.

Butt, Leslie, 2002 The Suffering Stranger: Medical Anthropology and International Morality. Medical Anthropology 21(1):1–24.

Castro, Arachu, 2004 Contracepting and childbirth: the integration of reproductive health and population policies in Mexico. *In* Unhealthy Health Policy: A Critical Anthropological Examination. Arachu Castro and Merrill Singer, eds. pp. 133–144. Walnut Creek CA: AltaMira Press.

Clair, Scott, Merrill Singer, Francisco Bastos, Monica Malta, Claudia Santelices, and Naline Ebertoni, 2009 The Role of Drug Users in the Brazilian HIV/AIDS Epidemic: Patterns, Perceptions and Prevention. *In* Globalization of HIV/AIDS: An Interdisciplinary Reader. Cynthia Pope, Renée White, and Robert Malow, eds. pp. 50–58. New York: Routledge.

Cohen, Lawrence, 2005 Operability, bioavailability, and exception. *In* Global Assemblages: Technology, Politics, and Ethics as Anthropological Problems. Aihwa Ong and Stephen J. Collier, eds. pp. 79–90. Malden MA: Blackwell.

Comaroff, Jean, and John Comaroff, eds., 2001 Millenial Capitalism and the Culture of Neoliberalism. Durham NC: Duke University Press.

Commission on the Social Determinants of Health, 2008 Closing the Gap in a Generation: Health Equity Through Action on the Social Determinants of Health. Geneva: World Health Organization.

Corbett, Kitty K., 1999 A short sweep of the global situation: environmental crisis and the place of anthropology. High Plains Applied Anthropologist 20(2):168–178.

Desjarlais, Robert, Leon Eisenberg, Byron Good, and Arthur Kleinman, eds., 1995 World Mental Health: Problems and Priorities in Low-Income Countries. Oxford: Oxford University Press.

Dressler, William W., 2001 Medical anthropology: toward a third moment in social science? Medical Anthropology Quarterly 15: 455–465.

Dressler, William W., and James Bindon, R., 2000 The health consequences of cultural consonance: cultural dimensions of lifestyle. American Anthropologist 102:244–260.

Ecks, Stefan, 2005 Pharmaceutical citizenship: antidepressant marketing and the promise of demarginalization in India. Anthropology and Medicine 12(3):239–254.

Evans, Mike, Robert C. Sinclair, Caroline Fusimalohi, and Viliami Liava'a, 2001 Globalization, diet, and health: an example from Tonga. Bulletin of the World Health Organization 79(9):856.

Farmer, Paul, 1999 Infections and Inequalities: The Modern Plagues. Berkeley CA: University of California Press.

Farmer, Paul, 2001 Infections and Inequalities : The Modern Plagues. Berkeley CA: University of California Press.

Farmer, Paul, 2003 Pathologies of Power: Health, Human Rights, and the New War on the Poor. Berkeley CA: University of California Press.

Farmer, Paul, and Arachu Castro, 2004 Pearls of the Antilles? Public health in Haiti and Cuba. *In* Unhealthy Health Policy: A Critical Anthropological Examination. A. Castro and M. Singer, eds., pp. 3–28. Walnut Creek CA: AltaMira Press.

Farmer, Paul, J. Simmons, and M. Connors, 1996 Rereading social science. *In* Women, Poverty, and AIDS: Sex, Drugs, and Structural Violence. P. Farmer, M. Connors, and J. Simmons, eds. pp. 147–206. Monroe ME: Common Courage Press.

Farmer, Paul, Fernet Léandre, Joia S. Mukherjee, Marie Sidonise Claude, Patrice Nevil, Mary C. Smith-Fawzi, Serena P. Koenig, Arachu Castro, Mercedes C. Becerra, Jeffrey Sachs, Amir Attaran, and Jim Yong Kim, 2001 Community-based approaches to HIV treatment in resource-poor settings. The Lancet 358(9279):404–409.

Fassin, Didier, 2007 When Bodies Remember: Experiences and Politics of AIDS in South Africa. Berkeley CA: University of California Press.

Feldman, Douglas A, ed., 2008 AIDS, Culture and Africa. Gainesville FL: University Press of Florida.

Ferguson, Anne 2005 Water reform, gender, and HIV/AIDS: perspectives from Malawi. *In* Globalization, Water, and Health: Resource Management in Times of Scarcity.

L. M.Whiteford and S. Whiteford, eds. pp. 45–66. Santa Fe NM: School of American Research Press.

Ginsburg, Faye, and Rayna Rapp, eds., 1995a Conceiving the New World Order: The Global Politics of Reproduction. Berkeley CA: University of California Press.

Ginsburg, Faye, and Rayna Rapp, eds., 1995b Introduction. *In* Conceiving the New World Order: The Global Politics of Reproduction. Faye Ginsburg and Rayna Rapp, eds. Berkeley CA: University of California Press.

Goodman, Alan, and Thomas Leatherman, eds., 1998 Building a New Biocultural Synthesis: Political–Economic Perspectives on Human Biology. Ann Arbor MI: University of Michigan Press.

Greenhalgh, Susan, 2005 Globalization and population governance in China. *In* Global Assemblages: Technology, Politics, and Ethics as Anthropological Problems. Aihwa Ong and Stephen J. Collier, eds. pp. 354–372. Malden MA: Blackwell.

Gutierrez, Emily C. Zielinski, and Carl Kendall, 2000 The Globalization of Health and Disease: The Health Transition and Global Change. *In* The Handbook of Social Studies in Health and Medicine. Gary L. Albrecht, Ray Fitzpatrick, and Susan Scrimshaw, eds. pp. 84–99. Thousand Oaks CA: Sage.

Hardon, Anita, 2005 Confronting the HIV/AIDS epidemic in sub-Saharan Africa: policy versus practice. International Social Science Journal 57(186):601–608.

Hayden, Corinne P., 2007 A generic solution? Pharmaceuticals and the politics of the similar in Mexico. Current Anthropology 4(4):475–495.

Heclo, Hugh, 1974 Modern Social Politics in Britain and Sweden: From Relief to Income Maintenance. New Haven CT: Yale University Press.

Høg, Erling, and Elisabeth Hsu, 2002 Introduction to special issue: 'countervailing creativity: patient agency in the globalisation of Asian medicines. Anthropology and Medicine 9(3):205–221.

Inhorn, Marcia C., 2003 Global infertility and the globalization of new reproductive technologies: illustrations from Egypt. Social Science and Medicine 56(9):1837–1851.

Inhorn, Marcia C., 2005 Gender, health, and globalization in the Middle East: male infertility, ICSI, and men's resistance. *In* Globalization, Women, and Health in the Twenty-First Century. I. Kickbush, K. A. Hartwig, and J. M. List, eds. pp. 113–125. New York: Palgrave Macmillan.

Inhorn, Marcia C., ed., 2007 Reproductive disruptions : gender, technology, and biopolitics in the new millennium. New York: Berghahn Books.

Inhorn, Marcia C., and Peter J. Brown, eds., 1997 The Anthropology of Infectious Disease: International Health Perspectives. Amsterdam, The Netherlands: Gordon and Breach.

Institute of Medicine, 1997 America's Vital Interest in Global Health: Protecting our People, Enhancing our Economy, and Advancing our International Interests. Washington: National Academy Press.

Institute of Medicine, 2009 The US Commitment to Global Health: Recommendations for the New Administration. Washington: National Academy Press.

Intergovernmental Panel on Climate Change, 2007 Climate Change 2007: Impacts, Adaptation, and Vulnerability. Fourth Assessment Report. Martin Parry, Osvaldo Canziani, Jean Palutikof, Paul van der Linden, and Clair Hanson, eds. Cambridge: Cambridge University Press.

Jambai, Amara, and Carol MacCormack, 1996 Maternal health, war, and religious tradition: authoritative knowledge in Pujehun District, Sierra Leone. Medical Anthropology Quarterly 10(2):270–286.

Janes, Craig R., 1999 The health transition and the crisis of traditional medicine: the case of Tibet. Social Science and Medicine 48:1803–1820.

Janes, Craig R., 2002 Buddhism, science, and market: the globalisation of Tibetan medicine. Anthropology and Medicine 9(3):267–289.

Janes, Craig R., 2004 Going global in century XXI: medical anthropology and the new primary health care. Human organization: Journal of the Society for Applied Anthropology 63(4):457–471.

Janes, Craig R., 2008 An ethnographic evaluation of post-Alma Ata health system reforms in Mongolia: lessons for addressing health inequities in poor communities. *In* Anthropology in Public Health. R.A. Hahn and M. Inhorn, eds. chapter 23. New York: Oxford University Press.

Janes, Craig R., and Oyuntsetseg Chuluundorj, 2004 Free markets and dead mothers: the social ecology of maternal mortality in post-socialist Mongolia. Medical Anthropology Quarterly 18(2):102–129.

Janes, Craig R., and Kitty K. Corbett, 2009 Anthropology and global health. Annual Reviews of Anthropology 38:167–183.

Janes, Craig R., Oyuntsetseg Chuluundorj, Casey E. Hilliard, Khulan Janchiv, and Kimberley Rak, 2006 Poor medicine for poor people? Assessing the impact of neoliberal reform on health care equity in a post-socialist context. Global Public Health 1:5–30.

Kangas, Beth, 2002 Therapeutic itineraries in a global world: Yemenis and their search for biomedical treatment abroad. Medical Anthropology 21:35–78.

Kawachi, Ichiro, and Sarah Wamala, 2007 Globalization and Health: Challenges and Prospects. *In* Globalization and Health. I. Kawachi and S. Wamala, eds. pp. 3–15. New York: Oxford University Press.

Kearney, Michael, 1995 The local and the global. Annual Review of Anthropology 24: 547–565.

Kendall, Carl, 2005 Waste not, want not: grounded globalization and global lessons for water use from Lima, Peru. *In* Globalization, Water, and Health: Resource Management in Times of Scarcity. L. M. Whiteford and S. Whiteford, eds. pp. 85–106. Santa Fe NM: School of American Research Press.

Keshavjee, Salmaan, 2004 The contradictions of a revolving drug fund in post-Soviet Tajikistan: selling medicines to starving patients. *In* Unhealthy Health Policy: A Critical Anthropological Examination. A. Castro and M. Singer, eds. pp. 97–114. Thousand Oaks CA: AltaMira Press.

Kickbusch, Ilona, 2000 The development of international health policies – accountability intact? Social Science and Medicine 51(6):979–989.

Kim, Jim, 2009 Transcultural medicine: a multi-sited ethnography on the scientific-industrial newtworking of Korean medicine. Medical Anthropology 28(1):31–64.

Kleinman, Arthur, 1988 Social Origins of Distress and Disease: Depression, Neurasthenia, and Pain in Modern China. New Haven CT: Yale University Press.

Koplan, Jeffrey P., T. Christopher Bond, Michael H. Merson, K. Srinath Reddy, Mario Henry Rodriquez, Nelson K. Sewankambo, and Judith N. Wasserheit, for the Consortium of Universities for Global Health Executive Board, 2009 Towards a common definition of global health. The Lancet 373:1993–1995.

Krieger, Nancy, 2001 Theories for social epidemiology in the 21st century: an ecosocial perspective. International Journal of Epidemiology 30(4):668–677.

Leatherman, Thomas L., 1994 Health implications of changing agrarian economies in the southern Andes. Human Organization 53:371–379.

Lee, Kelley, 2003a Globalization and Health: An Introduction. New York: Palgrave Macmillan.

Lee, Kelley, 2003b Introduction. *In* Health Impacts of Globalization: Towards Global Governance. Kelley Lee, ed. pp. 1–12. New York: Palgrave MacMillan.

Lee, Kelley, Suzanne Fustukian, and Kent Buse, 2002 An Introduction to global health policy. *In* Health Policy in a Globalizing World. Kelley Lee, Kent Buse, and Suzanne Fustukian, eds. pp. 3–17. Cambridge UK: Cambridge University Press.

Lock, Margaret, 2001 Twice Dead: Organ Transplants and the Reinvention of Death. Berkeley CA: University of California Press.

Macfarlane, Sarah B., Marian Jacobs, and Ephata E. Kaaya, 2008 In the name of global health: trends in academic institutions. Journal of Public Health Policy 29:383–401.

Manderson, Lenore, and Yixin Huang, 2005 Water, vectorborne disease, and gender: schistosomiasis in rural China. *In* Globalization, Water, and Health: Resource Management in

Times of Scarcity. L. M. Whiteford and S. Whiteford, eds. pp. 67–84. Santa Fe NM: School of American Research Press.

Markowitz, Lisa, 2001 Finding the field: notes on the ethnography of NGOs. Human Organization 60(1):40–46.

Marshall, Patricia A., and Abdallah Daar, 2000 Ethical issues in human organ replacement: a case study from India. *In* Global Health Policy, Local Realities: the Fallacy of the Level Playing Field. L. M. Whiteford and L. Manderson, eds. pp. 205–230. Boulder CO: Lynne Rienner Publishers.

Maternowska, M. Catherine, 2006 Reproducing Inequities: Poverty and the Politics of Population in Haiti. New Brunswick NJ: Rutgers University Press.

Mather, Charles, 2006 Medical innovation, unmet medical need, and the drug pipeline. Canadian Journal of Clinical Pharmacology 13(1):e85–e91.

McMichael, Tony, and Robert Beaglehole, 2003 The global context for public health. *In* Global Public Health: A New Era. R. Beaglehole, ed., chapter 1. New York: Oxford University Press.

Morgan, Lynn M., 2001 Community participation in health: perpetual allure, persistent challenge. Health Policy and Planning 16(3):221–230.

Morsy, Soheir A., 1995 Deadly reproduction among Egyptian women: maternal mortality and the medicalization of population control. *In* Conceiving the New World Order: The Global Politics of Reproduction. F. Ginsburg and R. Rapp, eds. pp. 162–176. Berkeley: University of California Press.

Nguyen, Vinh-Kim, 2005 Antiretroviral globalism, biopolitics, and therepeutic citizenship. *In* Global Assemblages: Technology, Politics, and Ethics as Anthropological Problems. A. Ong and S. J. Collier, eds. pp. 124–144. Malden MA: Blackwell.

Nichter, Mark, 1995 Vaccinations in the Third World: a Consideration of Community Demand. Social Science and Medicine 41(5):617–632.

Nichter, Mark, 1999 Project Community Diagnosis: Participatory Research as a First Step Toward Community Involvement in Primary Health Care. *In* Anthropology in Public Health: Bridging Differences in Culture and Society. R. A. Hahn, ed. pp. 300–324. New York: Oxford University Press.

Nichter, Mark, 2008 Global Health: Why Cultural Perceptions, Social Representations, and Biopolitics Matter. Tucson AZ: University of Arizona Press.

Nichter, Mark, and Elizabeth Cartwright, 1991 Saving the children for the tobacco industry. Medical Anthropology Quarterly 5(3):236–256.

Oldani, Michael J., 2004 Thick prescriptions: toward an interpretation of pharmaceutical sales practices. Medical Anthropology Quarterly 18:325–356.

Ong, Aihwa, and Stephen J. Collier, 2005 Global assemblages, anthropological problems. *In* Global Assemblages: Technology, Politics, and Ethics as Anthropological Problems. Aihwa Ong and Stephen J. Collier, eds. Malden MA: Blackwell.

Orchard, Treena, John O'Neil, James Blanchard, Aine Castigan, and Stephen Moses, 2009 HIV/AIDS prevention programming with "traditional" sex workers in rural India: challenges for the empowerment approach in community-sanctioned sex work environments. *In* HIV/AIDS: Global Frontiers in Prevention/Intervention. Cynthia Pope, Renee T. White, and Robert Malow, eds. pp. 82–95. New York: Routledge.

Orzech, Katherine M., and Mark Nichter, 2008 From resilience to resistance: political ecological lessons from antibiotic and pesticide resistance. Annual Review of Anthropology 37:267–282.

Paluzzi, Joan E., 2004 Primary health care since Alma Ata: lost in the Bretton Woods? *In* Unhealthy Health Policy; A Critical Anthropological Examination. A. Castro and M. Singer, eds. pp. 63–78. Walnut Creek CA: AltaMira Press.

Parker, Richard, 2000 Administering the epidemic: HIV/AIDS policy, models of development, and international health. *In* Global Health Policy, Local Realities: The Fallacy of the Level Playing Field. L. M. Whiteford and L. Manderson, eds. pp. 39–56. Boulder CO: Lynn Rienner Publishers.

Parker, Richard, and Anke Ehrhardt, 2001 Through and ethnographic lens: Ethnographic methods, comparative analyses and HIV/AIDS research. AIDS and Behavior 5(2):105–114.

Parker, Richard, Dianne di Mauro, Beth Filiano, Jonathan Garcia, Miguel Munoz-Laboy, and
Robert Sember, 2004 Global transformations and intimate relations in the 21st century:
social science research on sexuality and the emergence of sexual health and sexual rights
frameworks. Annual Reviews of Sex Research 15:362–398.

Paul, Benjamin D., ed., 1955 Health, Culture and Community. Case Studies of Public Reactions
to Health Programs. New York: Russell Sage Foundation Pearce, Neil, and George Davey
Smith, 2003 Is Social Capital the Key to Inequalities in Health? AJPH 93:122–129.

Petryna, Adriana, 2002 Life Exposed: Biological Citizens after Chernobyl. Princeton NJ:
Princeton University Press.

Petryna, Adriana, 2005 Ethical variability: drug development and globalizing clinical trials.
American Ethnologist 32(2):183–197.

Pfeiffer, James, 2003 International NGOs and primary health care in Mozambique: the need
for a new model of collaboration. Social Science and Medicine 56(4):725–738.

Pfeiffer, James, 2004 International NGOs in the Mozambique health sector: the "velvet glove"
of privatization. In Unhealthy Health Policy; A Critical Anthropological Examination.
A. Castro and M. Singer, eds. pp. 43–62. Walnut Creek CA: AltaMira Press.

Pfeiffer, James, and Mark Nichter, 2008 What can critical medical anthropology contribute to
global health? Medical Anthropology Quarterly 22(4):410–415.

Pigg, Stacy Leigh, and Vincanne Adams, 2005 Introduction: the moral object of sex. In Sex
in Development: Science, Sexuality, and Morality in Global Perspective. V. Adams and
S.L. Pigg, eds. pp. 1–38. Durham NC: Duke University Press.

Rappaport, Roy A., 1993 The Anthropology of Trouble. American Anthropologist 95(2):
295–303.

Redfield, Peter, 2005 Doctors, borders, and life in crisis. Cultural Anthropology 20(3):
328–361.

Robbins, Richard, 2007 Global Problems and the Culture of Capitalism, 4th edition. Boston:
Allyn & Bacon.

Robins, Steven, 2009 Foot soldiers of global health: teaching and preaching AIDS science and
modern medicine on the frontline. Medical Anthropology 28(1):81–107.

Rose, Nikolas, and Carlos Novas, 2005 Biological Citizenship. In Global Assemblages:
Technology, Politics, and Ethics as Anthropological Problems. A. Ong and S. J. Collier, eds.
Malden MA: Blackwell.

Scheper-Hughes, Nancy, 2000 The Global Traffic in Human Organs. Current Anthropology
41(2):191–224.

Scheper-Hughes, Nancy, 2005 The last commodity: post-human ethics and the global traffic in
"fresh" organs. In Global Assemblages: Technology, Politics, and Ethics as Anthropological
Problems. A. Ong and S. J. Collier, eds. pp. 145–168. Malden MA: Blackwell.

Scudder, Thayer, 1999 Malinowski Award Lecture. The emerging global crisis and development anthropology: can we have an impact? Human Organization 58(4):351–364.

Simmons, Janie, Paul Farmer, and Brooke G. Schoepf, 1996 A global perspective. In Women,
Poverty, and Aids: Sex, Drugs, and Structural Violence. P. Farmer, M. Connors, and
J. Simmons, eds. pp. 39–90. Monroe ME: Common Courage Press.

Singer, Merrill and Scott Clair, 2003 Syndemics and public health: reconceptualizing disease in
biosocial context. Medical Anthropology Q 17(4):423–441.

Singer, Merrill, 1997 The Political Economy of AIDS. Amityville NY: Baywood Publishing
Company.

Singer, Merrill, 2008 Drugs and Development: Global Impact on Sustainable Growth and
Human Rights. Prospect Heights IL: Waveland Press.

Singer, Merrill, 2009 Introduction to Syndemics: A Systems Approach to Public and Community
Health. San Francisco CA. Jossey-Bass.

Singer, Merrill, and Hans Baer, 1995 Critical Medical Anthropology. Amityville NY: Baywood Press.

Singer, Merrill and Hans Baer, 2008 Killer Commodities: Public Health and the Corporate Production of Harm. Walnut Creek CA: AltaMira/Roman Littlefield Publishers, Inc.

Singer, Merrill, and Arachu Castro, 2004 Introduction. Anthropology and Health Policy: A Critical Perspective. *In* Unhealthy Health Policy; A Critical Anthropological Examination. A. Castro and M. Singer, eds. pp. xi–xx. Walnut Creek CA: AltaMira Press.

Stebbins, Kenyon Rainier, 1991 Tobacco, politics and economics: Implications for global health. Social Science A and Medicine 33(12):1317–1326.

Stone, Glenn D., 2002 Both sides now: fallacies in the genetic-modification wars, implications for developing countries, and anthropological perspectives. Current Anthropology 43: 611–630.

Stuckler, David and Martin McKee, 2008 Five metaphors about global health policy. The Lancet 372:95–97.

Thomas, R. Brooke, 1998 The evolution of human adaptability paradigms: Toward a biology of poverty. *In* Building a New Biocultural Synthesis: Political–Economic Perspectives on Human Biology. A. H. Goodman and T. L. Leatherman, eds. Ann Arbor MI: University of Michigan Press.

Trostle, James, 1996 Inappropriate distribution of medicines by professionals in developing countries. Social Science and Medicine 42:1117–1120.

Trostle, James, 2005 Epidemiology and Culture. New York: Cambridge University Press.

Tsing, Anna, 2000 The global situation. Cultural Anthropology 15(3):327–360.

van der Geest, Sjaak, 2008 Anthropology and the pharmaceutical nexus. Anthropological Quarterly 79(2):303–214.

van der Geest, Sjaak, Anita Hardon, and Susan Reynolds Whyte, eds. 1988 The Context of Medicines in Developing countries: Studies in Pharmaceutical Anthropology. Dordrecht, The Netherlands: Kluwer Academic Publishers.

van der Geest, Sjaak, Susan Reynolds Whyte, and Anita Hardon, 1996 The anthropology of pharmaceuticals: a biographical approach. Annual Review of Anthropology 25:153–178.

Wacquant, Loic, 2004 Comment on: "An Anthropology of Structural Violence," by Paul Farmer. Current Anthropology 45(3):322.

Walt, Gill, Enrico Pavignani, Lucy Gilson, and Kent Buse, 1999 Health sector development: from aid coordination to resource management. Health Policy Plan 14(3):207–218.

Waitzkin, Howard, 2004 At the Front Lines of Medicine. Lanham MD: Rowman & Littlefield.

Wells, H. G., 1920 The Outline of History, vol. 2, chapter 41. Garden City NY: Garden City Publishing Company Inc.

Whiteford, Linda M., and Beverly Hill, 2005 The political ecology of dengue in Cuba and the Dominican Republic. *In* Globalization, Health and the Environment. Greg Guest, ed. pp. 219–238. Oxford: AltaMira Press.

Whiteford, Linda M., and Lenore Manderson, eds., 2000 Global Health Policies, Local Realities: The Fallacy of the Level Playing Field. Boulder CO: Lynne Reinner Publishers.

Whyte, Susan Reynolds, Michael A. Whyte, Lotte Meinert, and Betty Kyaddondo, 2006 Treating AIDS: dilemmas of unequal access in Uganda. *In* Global Pharmaceuticals: Ethics, Markets, Practices. Adriana Petryna, Andrew Lakoff, and Arthur Kleinman, eds. pp. 240–262. Durham NC: Duke University Press.

World Bank, 1993 Investing in Health: World Development Report 1993. New York: Oxford University Press for the World Bank.

World Health Organization, 2008 Primary Health Care: Now More than Ever. Geneva: World Health Organization.

CHAPTER 8

Syndemics in Global Health

Merrill Singer, D. Ann Herring,
Judith Littleton,
and Melanie Rock

INTRODUCTION

In 1997, the Institute of Medicine (IOM) helped advance the growing recognition of health as an intertwined global phenomenon by noting that:

> The health needs of diverse countries are converging as the factors that affect health increasingly transcend national borders. Among those factors are the globalization of the economy, demographic change, and the rapidly rising costs of health care in all countries. In a world where nations and economies are increasingly interdependent, ill health in any population affects all peoples, rich and poor.

Ten years later, the IOM (2008) reported that an eager new generation of philanthropists, students, scientists, private industry leaders, and citizens offer the promise of potential solutions to global health. The health social sciences, including medical anthropology, thus face the challenge of identifying specific ways it can contribute to the emerging global health agenda. An important step in this process is developing concepts "that may serve as useful lenses to bring issues in need of investigation into better focus" (Nichter 2008:157). One of the concepts Nichter recommends for this purpose is syndemics, which has been defined as the concentration and deleterious interaction of two or more diseases or other health conditions in a population, especially as a consequence of social inequity and the unjust exercise of power (Singer 2009b). Syndemics is a useful concept for global health initiatives because of its sensitivity to "environments of risk and agents promoting risk, not just groups at risk and risky behaviors" (Nichter (2008:157) and its ability to focus attention on three fundamental

A Companion to Medical Anthropology, First Edition. Edited by Merrill Singer and Pamela I. Erickson.

intersections in the making of health: synergistic disease interactions that increase the burden of disease beyond mere comoridity, interspecies interactions that lead to emergent diseases, and health and society interactions that support the clustering of multiple diseases in vulnerable populations (Singer and Clair 2003). Syndemics thus offers a pathway for transcending shortcomings of existing health interventions and prevention initiatives in disparity populations (Paluzzi and Farmer 2005). In this chapter we examine existing and emerging applications of the syndemics model in global health research, past and present.

OVERVIEW OF SYNDEMICS

The syndemics approach to understanding disease is rooted in medical anthropology, especially the theoretical framework known as critical medical anthropology. The idea emerged as a response to early research in this field which tended to be narrowly focused on micro-level explanations of health related beliefs and practices and their interface with local ecological conditions, wider cultural configurations, or human psychological factors. The subsequent generation of medical anthropologists, influenced by social movements and broader cultural realignments in the 1960s/1970s, argued that the prevailing theoretical models tended to ignore crosscutting political economic influences on health and on human decision-making and action in the health arena.

The alternative understanding created in response to these limitations – critical medical anthropology – drew attention to the vertical linkages that connect a social group or behavior (or health configuration) to larger political and economic systems and to the arrangement of social relationships they help produce and reproduce over time (Singer 1995). The goal of critical medical anthropology has been not to dismiss the contributions of microanalyses of illness and healing or ecologically influenced accounts of health, but rather: to emphasize the relevance of culture to issues of power, control, and resistance associated with health, illness, and healing, and to rethink nature itself in light of historic anthropogenic (intended and unintended) restructurings of the environment. Further, the critical approach stressed that while human groups engage and are impacted by the environment, they do not simply adapt to it; rather, in thought and in deed they remake it, although never with unlimited ability nor without unintended and unforeseen consequences.

The syndemic orientation was forged as part of this rethinking, and in no small measure in direct response to the global challenges to health and society of the emergent HIV/AIDS pandemic. Specifically, this way of understanding disease recognizes the fundamental biosocial nature of health and that constellations of diseases and other health conditions interact synergistically, in consequential ways. This interaction involves multiple biological and psychosocial channels and mechanisms, including biochemical changes in the immune system, damage to cellular repair processes, and psychopathological effects on behavior. Further, the syndemics orientation emphasizes the ways that social conditions shape disease processes, often through broader environmental mediation. Consequently, the syndemics approach examines both the emergence and nature of "disease concentrations" (i.e., multiple coterminous diseases and disorders affecting individuals and groups) and "disease interactions" (i.e., the

ways in which the presence of one disease or disorder enhances the health consequences of other diseases and disorders). More particularly, this perspective aims to
identify specific pathways through which diseases and other health conditions work
together inside individual bodies and within populations and significantly multiply
thereby the overall health burden of the afflicted. Human social environments, including prevailing structures of social relationship, such as institutionalized inequality and
injustice, as well as socio-genic environmental conditions contribute enormously to
disease clustering, disease spread and interaction, and the interlocking of diseases and
other health conditions into health-threatening syndemic complexes.

SYNDEMIC RESEARCH

Syndemic theory extends the work of health researchers who long ago recognized the
crucial importance of disease interaction in social context. In an important series of
publications on health in New York City, for example, Rodrick and Deborah Wallace
(Wallace 1988, 1990; Wallace and Wallace 1998) drew attention to the "synergism of
plagues" produced by public policies deliberately designed to restrict municipal services in low income neighborhoods so as to pressure residents to move away and free
up land for economic development. The tragic result was a mass movement of people
to new (also poor) areas, overcrowding, and an unraveling of community relationships and social support structures, as well as a set of closely linked epidemics, including tuberculosis, measles, substance abuse, AIDS, low-weight births, and street
violence. Separating these health issues – and thereby overlooking the ways in which
they are intimately connected and mutually enhancing, and ignoring the underlying
social and biological processes involved in their development and clustering – distorts
"on-the-ground" and "in-the-body" realities and fails to address the nature of the
relationship between the health of physical and social bodies.

The term syndemic was first used to label a tripartite health condition of the inner
city poor called SAVA, a product of the complex interactions between substance
abuse, violence and AIDS (Singer 1996). From the syndemic perspective, AIDS, drug
use, and violence in particular social contexts are so entwined, and each is so significantly shaped by the presence of the other two, that it is wrong to conceive of them
as distinct "things in the world." In SAVA, all three disease/health related components interact. Thus there are ways in which drug use interacts directly with AIDS
(e.g., in promoting HIV transmission, disease progression, AIDS-related mortality,
and the development of AIDS-defining illnesses), and both conditions are worsened
as a result (Cook et al. 2008). Similarly, violence and AIDS interact in mutually accelerating ways, such as when the risk of clinical progression of HIV is enhanced by
domestic violence that prevents access to health care or the ability to adhere to HIV
treatment (e.g., Lichtenstein 2006). Drugs and violence also help to propel each
other along their injurious paths (Duke et al. 2006). In addition to these interactions,
the actual expression of a SAVA syndemic is shaped by the local social context, including both the population being affected and the configuration of social conditions they
endure (Singer 2006). It is thus more accurate to recognize the existence of multiple
SAVA syndemics, each driven by its own arrangement of populations, social conditions, and structural relationships (Gonzalez-Guardia 2008).

Stall and co-workers (2003, 2008) have examined SAVA in populations of men who have sex with men (MSM) using a household telephone survey of almost 3,000 men in New York City, Chicago, Los Angeles, and San Francisco. They found that the SAVA syndemic among MSM is rooted in childhood sexual abuse which contributes to the development of depression in adulthood, and subsequent entrance into abusive adult relationships, use of multiple drugs, and high levels of HIV risk and infection. Further, being the victim of homophobic attacks contributes to serious health problems among adult gay men. These psychosocial factors interact and are mutually reinforcing.

Building on the work of Stall and co-workers, Mustanski and colleagues (2007) studied an ethnically diverse community-based sample of 310 young (16–24 year old), self-identified MSM in Chicago. Their analysis of various psychosocial, behavioral and health variables (e.g., regular binge drinking, experiencing partner violence, sexual assault, psychological distress, sexual risk taking and HIV status) led them to conclude: "that the number of psychosocial health problems additively increase risk for HIV among urban YMSM. For example, each problem increased the odds of an HIV positive status by 42% and also increased the odds of sexual health risk behaviors. Multivariate analyses indicate that substance use and being the victim of violence show the strongest relationship to sexual health and HIV risk" (Mustanski et al. 2007:44). This syndemic of psychosocial risk factors underscores the multiple health disparities, higher moribidity, and barriers to care faced by gay and lesbian individuals (Mustanski et al. (2007:39).

Building on the Wallaces' work in New York, Freudenberg and co-workers (2006) point out that public policy decisions in New York City in the mid-1970s were driven by a cost-cutting mission intended, ostensibly, to save money for the city. Instead, these decisions contributed to deteriorating living conditions, a 20% rise in the number of poor people in the city (despite an overall population decrease of 10%), and a significant rise in the health burden of the poor. Tuberculosis rates, for example, rose despite a previous century of declining infection. At the same time, AIDS cases became more frequent, particularly among drug users. Homicide rates accelerated and climbed continuously through 1990. In short, neither was public health prioritized as a social good nor were the significant interactions that occur between health and social issues a basis for making public policy. The fallout from cost-cutting was enormous, fiscally and in terms of socially structured suffering, and sparked a costly tripartite syndemic of HIV, TB, and violence.

An explicit syndemic perspective informs several other studies, such as tobacco-related syndemics (Marshall 2005; Nichter 2008), a sexually transmitted diseases and HIV/AIDS syndemic in disparity populations (Singer et al. 2006), the role of syndemics in the health of inner city populations (Mercado et al. 2007; Singer 1994), syndemic interaction among diabetes, obesity, and periodontal disease (Hein and Small 2007), the HIV and food insecurity syndemic in Southern Africa (Singer 2008), the role of tuberculosis in syndemics (Mavridis 2008), infectious disease syndemics in Canadian Aboriginal populations (Herring and Sattenspiel 2007; Young and Herring 2004), and syndemics and the diseases of global warming (Baer and Singer 2003; Singer 2009a). These and other studies prompted the Centers for Disease Control and Prevention to incorporate the concept into public health prevention initiatives.

An even larger literature examines the negative health consequences of comorbid disease interactions without an explicit syndemics perspective (e.g., Alisjahbana et al. 2006; Abu-Raddad et al. 2006; Cain et al. 2007; Ponce-De-Leon et al. 2004; Sethi 2002). Exemplary research by Tashiro et al. (1987) shows that staphylococci bacteria secrete enzymes that activate the infectivity of influenza viruses in animal models. Virus–bacteria interaction has been reported to be a major cause of severe influenza pneumonia in humans that works in both directions, with bacteria enhancing influenza virulence and the influenza virus promoting the adherence of bacteria to host cells. Under social conditions that promote the transmission and clustering of these two pathogens, deadly global syndemics can ensue, as occurred in 1918 (Singer 2009b).

The term *syndemic*, however, is not synonymous with comorbid or equivalent medical terms (e.g., co-infection, dual-diagnosis). Patients in Hong Kong dually infected with SARS and human metapneumomovirus (HMPV) were found to be no sicker than patients only infected with SARS (Lee et al. 2007). This suggests that comorbid SARS and HMPV either do not interact or that interaction does not lead to excess disease burden. SARS interacts with other diseases, however, such as diabetes or cardiopulmonary disease, resulting in poorer outcomes (Chen et al. 2005).

To date, the syndemics literature has stressed human/environment and human/ human relationships. More recently, a focus on human/animal relationships in syndemic formation has begun to emerge.

ANIMAL–HUMAN CONNECTIONS IN SYNDEMICS

Even though anthropologists argue that people's treatment of and ways of talking about animals represent cultural mirrors (Mullin 1999), medical anthropologists have tended to neglect the importance of animal health and ethnoveterinary practices to human health (but see McCorkle et al. 1996; Nyamanga et al. 2008; Rock and Babinec 2008; Barta 2008; Engel and Engel 2008). The history of anthropological work on animal–human connections, for instance, often refers to Evans-Pritchard's (1960) research with Nuer pastoralists (e.g., Shanklin 1985), but not to *Witchcraft, Oracles and Magic among the Azande* (Evans-Pritchard 1976 [1937]). The Azande study remains "a monument in the history of the anthropology of medicine" (Cambrosio et al. 2000:6), but scant attention has been paid to animal–human connections in Zande beliefs and practical responses to disease specifically, or in health and disease generally.

When teaching this classic study, anthropologists often tell their students that colonial authorities dispatched Evans-Pritchard to investigate the local – seemingly irrational – responses to *trypanosomiasis*, also known as sleeping sickness. These responses included witchcraft accusations and a refusal to move to places where the tsetse flies that spread the infection were sparse. Yet, we suspect, very few anthropologists emphasize that sleeping sickness is a zoonotic disease that afflicts, for example, cattle and donkeys, as well as people. While "the oracles provide[d] an endless supply of 'witches,' thus perpetuating the Zande inclination to consult witch-catching oracles when someone falls sick or suffers misfortune" (Cambrosio et al. 2000:6), contact between infected livestock, wildlife, insect, and people ensured a continuous supply of human cases of sleeping sickness who were identified as victims of witchcraft. Thus attention was directed away from flies, animals, colonial authorities, and local hierarchies, and towards specific individuals. The result was a generalized state of high anxiety in which most sicknesses and deaths were viewed as instances of malevolence (Evans-Pritchard 1976 [1937]:5). *Trypanosomiasis,* moreover, involves sleep disturbances and "various psychiatric and mental symptoms such as anxiety, lassitude and indifference, agitation, irritability, mania, sexual hyperactivity, suicidal tendencies, and hallucinations" (Kennedy 2008:118). Underlying and helping to animate this "synergistic brew" between animal health and human health was inequality within and between human populations, between colonial and local populations, and within the Zande population.

In syndemic fashion, inequality remains fundamental to *trypanosomiasis* morbidity and mortality, for *trypanosomiasis* "continues to pose a major threat to 60 million people in 36 countries in sub-Saharan Africa" (Kennedy 2008:118), where HIV is rife and can interact deleteriously with it (Lloyd-Smith et al. 2008). In addition, people living with both HIV and *trypanosomiasis* may be at elevated risk for drug treatment failure (Pepin et al. 1992). As Kennedy (2008:118) observes, "All four main drugs used for human African trypanosomiasis are toxic, and melarsoprol, the only drug that is effective for both types of central nervous system disease, is so toxic that it kills 5% of patients who receive it," but Western governments, donor agencies and the pharmaceutical industry have shown little interest in developing new drug therapies.

If disrupting "man/tsetse fly contact" is essential for controlling sleeping sickness (Kennedy 2008:124–125), then treating cattle and other infected animals may prove to be a cost-effective and ethical avenue for improving human health (Zinsstag et al. 2007). Animal husbandry practices can help prevent and control *trypanosomiasis,* reducing the likelihood of human cases and improving the productivity of draught animals used in agriculture and for transportation (Mattioli et al. 1994).

Even though medical anthropologists have paid insufficient attention to zoonotic diseases, recognition of the importance of human/animal relationships is growing because many public health problems have their ultimate origins in animal bodies. An estimated 60% of all emerging and re-emerging infectious diseases are zoonotic (Jones et al. 2008), and the socio-economic conditions that drive the distribution of diseases in human populations spill over to animal populations (Jones et al. 2008; Rock et al., 2009). For example, epidemics of tuberculosis in industrializing cities of the 19th century involved both *Mycobacterium tuberculosis* and *Mycobacterium bovis* (Jones 2004). *M. bovis* is often called bovine tuberculosis but can infect nearly all mammals, including people. While infected animals or people can transmit *M. bovis* to each other, people mainly contract it by consuming infected animal-sourced foods, particularly unpasteurized milk and raw or undercooked meat (Ayele et al. 2004).

Worldwide, at least 3% of all pulmonary cases and 9% of all non-pulmonary cases of tuberculosis in people involve *M. bovis* (Ayele et al. 2004). While this pathogen disproportionately affects low-income countries, it also disproportionately affects low-income inhabitants of wealthier countries. In San Diego, for example, researchers found that 1/24 adult human patients with TB-related respiratory disease and 11/24 with non-respiratory disease related to TB were infected with *M. bovis,* and that the infected population was 80% Hispanic (Dankner et al. 1993). Overall, 45% of pediatric human tuberculosis cases in San Diego between 1994 and 2005 involved *M. bovis,* 6% of the adult cases involved *M. bovis,* and 25% of them were also living with HIV (Rodwell et al. 2008:913). Compared with those with *M. tuberculosis,* people with

M. bovis were more than two and half times more likely to die in spite of treatment (Rodwell et al. 2008).

M. bovis is thought to be less virulent for humans than *M. tuberculosis*. In combination with HIV infection, however, *M. bovis* could pose a serious syndemic threat. If the differential virulence between the two pathogens stems from greater susceptibility of human host defenses to *M. bovis*, immunosuppression induced by HIV co-infection could enhance the contagiousness of *M. bovis* (Grange et al. 1994:1565). Indeed, European studies have confirmed human-to-human transmission of *M. bovis* among hospitalized patients with HIV (Guerrero et al. 1997; Samper et al. 1997). Human cases of *M. bovis*, furthermore, cannot be treated with standard drug therapy because *M. bovis* is almost universally resistant to pyrazinamide (PZA), the main antituberculosis drug (Rodwell et al. 2008:910). A strain of *M. bovis* that claimed the lives of at least 20 HIV+ patients in European hospitals has proved resistant not only to PZA, but to 11 different antituberculosis drugs (Guerrero et al. 1997; Samper et al. 1997).

People's reactions to policies put in place to control animal diseases can affect their health, and these perceptions are influenced by power differentials. Canada, for example, is one of many countries to adopt a "test-and-slaughter policy" for *M. bovis* in cattle and other animals that serve as human food, yet wildlife populations are exempt from this policy. Elk infected with *M. bovis* have been sources of infection for cattle that graze near a national park, within which hunting is prohibited (Brook and McLachlan 2006). Cattle farmers living near the park risk losing their entire herd should one of their animals test positive for *M. bovis*. While compensation is offered, farmers understandably fear bureaucratic delays, becoming embroiled in negotiations about compensation, stigma, and lower prices for their cattle or land. Successful measures to control animal-to-human disease transmission, in other words, can lead to mental health concerns such as depression in susceptible individuals and to mistrust and feelings of powerlessness across entire communities. Mistrust and powerlessness are not diseases, but human beings are sensitive to power relations and to the ability to exercise control over their lives such that mortality rates vary along these lines (Nguyen and Peschard 2004).

While animal-sourced foods can transmit infections to humans, they also have beneficial effects by preventing and controlling human diseases through nutritional pathways. The quality of nutrition influences the life expectancy of people with infectious diseases like *M. bovis*, *M. tuberculosis*, HIV/AIDS, or some combination of these. Veterinary expertise has helped reduce the effects of infectious diseases in human populations (Hardy 2002; Jones 2004), not least by improving food safety, yet animal health is largely absent from accounts of public health's history. Animals infected with *M. bovis* and other zoonotic diseases, moreover, are less productive, which affects people's livelihoods and food supply.

Disease interactions, zoonotic or otherwise, are not always deleterious in the sense of a syndemic; they may have protective effects. Such phenomena are referred to as counter-syndemics (Singer 2009a,b). *Trypanosome cruzi* (the protozoa responsible for Chagas disease, the most endemic zoonosis in Latin America), for example, inhibits HIV replication in human placenta, and so might reduce the likelihood of mother-to-child transmission of HIV (Dolcini et al. 2008). The Chagas case also illustrates how a single infection can have both counter-syndemic and syndemic-promoting effects. The co-occurrence of Chagas disease and rheumatic heart disease (caused by

Streptococcus pyogenes infection) among poor, rural children in Latin America enhances the chances that they will die in early adulthood from congestive heart failure because of the lack of access to health care and treatment of their childhood infections (Cubillos-Garzon et al. 2004).

SYNDEMICS IN HISTORY: CASE STUDY 1

Thus far we have underscored the utility of the syndemics concept for identifying pathways through which biological and social phenomena interact and capacitate each other in contemporary settings. The concept also offers a powerful framework for interpreting health in historical contexts. We illustrate this through a consideration of the circumstances that led to entwined epidemics and deteriorating life circumstances in northern Aboriginal communities in Canada. Apart from its ability to illuminate the complex processes through which the disease burden of communities increases through time, application of the syndemics concept allows scholars to speak to larger historical issues, such as the role of introduced pathogens in the demographic history of the Americas.

It is becoming increasingly clear from research on Aboriginal communities in Canada that epidemics of the early 20th century were not simply the result of exposure to new pathogens, but rather the expression of the long-term operation of a multifaceted set of interacting social and biological processes more appropriately interpreted as a syndemic (Herring and Sattenspiel 2007; Stephens 2008). These include: ecological changes associated with the importation of new plant and animal species (including pathogens) imposition of social, political, economic and religious structures by missionaries, traders, and government officials; ever more numerous settlers farming the lands of Aboriginal people; increasing isolation of Aboriginal people from centers of economic and political power; assimilationist policies; and social fragmentation that left Aboriginal groups on the margins of Canadian life (Waldram et al. 2006). In addition, the growth of endemic urban foci for density-dependent diseases, such as measles, and improvements in transportation efficiency allowed a wider spectrum of infectious diseases to travel over long distances (Hackett 1991, 2002), enmeshing northern Aboriginal communities in global disease networks through the confluence of disease pools (McNeill 1976:69 ff.).

At the same time, centuries of hunting and trapping fur for export had depleted animal resources in the Canadian north, eroding the economic foundation of most northern Aboriginal communities. In response, international businesses, such as the Hudson's Bay Company, closed fur trade posts, the hubs of the northern fur economy. Growing intrusions of the Canadian Government, including the system of native reserves, and progressively larger numbers of non-native participants in the northern economy, further undermined social and economic life in the north. Added to the demise of the fur economy, crowding of Aboriginal peoples into reserve housing, the growing concentration of children in government-funded residential schools, and the change from "a portable home within an ecological range, to housing in sedentary settlements" (Preston 1986:245), left many communities impoverished and ever more vulnerable to malnutrition and to diseases spread from elsewhere (Herring et al. 2003; Honigmann 1948; Tisdall and Robertson 1948; Waldram et al. 2006).

During the epidemiologic transition that accompanied this social and demographic transformation (Young 1988), tuberculosis emerged as a major health problem. A study of children in residential schools in the early 20th century, for instance, concluded that TB was the leading cause of death (Bryce 1907). By the 1930s, TB death rates among Aboriginal people in the western provinces of Canada were ten to twenty times higher than the rate for non-Aboriginal people (Stewart 1936). TB also increased susceptibility to other infections (Stone 1926). The relocation of Aboriginal people to reserves with minimal economic resources, and over-crowded houses and schools, allowed tubercular infection to spread rapidly, especially among children (Bryce 1907; Stoops 2008; Waldram et al. 2006). TB soon became a central element in the syndemic conditions that developed on many northern reserves.

The circumstances at the site known as the York Factory, a Cree community located on the western edge of Hudson Bay, illustrates how syndemic processes operated through endemic TB and two acute respiratory epidemics in 1927 (ACCA 1864–1929). From February to April, the York Factory was overwhelmed by a severe epidemic of influenza. The influenza death rate was highest among adults between the ages of 21 and 65, who accounted for 87% of the deaths (120 deaths per 1000). By mid-February, life in the community had ground to a halt; by March, coffin building was a major task. Not only was everyone sick, but the fur trade that year was a disaster. The tragic loss of such a large group of productive adults, which occurred at a vital point in the fur harvest cycle, led to an unusually poor harvest (HBCA 1794–1939), adding additional hardship by cutting the already wobbly economic legs out from under the community that year (Young and Herring 2004).

The following autumn, another virulent epidemic struck. Whooping cough (*Bordatella pertussis*), a highly contagious bacterial disease acquired by droplet infection, swept through the York Factory. The bacteria attach themselves to the cilia in the trachea where they produce exotoxins that kill the ciliated cells and induce inflammation and mucous production that compromise the lungs. The worst effects of whooping cough are felt by children under the age of six, especially among infants and two-year olds (Cherry 1999). Acquired immunity fades with age, however, making adults an important source of this strictly human disease.

The York Factory's autumn whooping cough epidemic erupted in September during another crucial time in the annual cycle when families were preparing for the fall fishery. The epidemic lasted until December (HBCA 1794–1939), taking a heavy toll among children under the age of six (237 deaths per 1000), the group normally affected (Young and Herring 2004; Herring 2008). Two teenage girls also died, indicative of the severity of the outbreak. While children were dying from whooping cough, adults were suffering from what was described as "very bad colds" (HBCA 1794–1939) and more than likely were the source of the whooping cough outbreak (Young and Herring 2004).

In 1927, therefore, we see three respiratory diseases, one endemic (tuberculosis) and two epidemic (influenza and whooping cough), acting together and sequentially to amplify each others' effects on the lungs of the people of the York Factory. The mortality profile that year is effectively described by these three causes: 32% of deaths are attributable to the spring influenza outbreak, 40% to the fall whooping cough outbreak, and another 7% to tuberculosis (Young and Herring 2004). As discussed earlier in this chapter, active tuberculosis can exacerbate influenza infection. Influenza, in turn, enhances bacterial lung disease, impairs normal recovery mechanisms, and impairs the immune system. It can also induce latent TB to erupt. Whooping cough affects the respiratory tract, destroys the respiratory lining, and makes it necessary to cough to remove mucous. This can worsen existing lung disease in the form of tuberculosis. Adults already suffering with TB at the York Factory, in turn, may have been more likely to experience a bout of whooping cough.

Together, these diseases made it more difficult to make a living off the land under the already difficult circumstances of increased competition and resource depletion. Ultimately, the economy was not sustainable. By the 1950s, the York Factory had essentially been abandoned as residents progressively moved out of the area to find a better living in more prosperous southern locations. In short, a series of interacting epidemics were both enhanced by and contributed to the erosion of the local economy and were part of entwined historical, biological and economic processes. Operating synergistically over the long-term, these processes contributed to the eventual abandonment of the York Factory and led to its current status as a heritage site.

The story doesn't end there. Today TB rates in Canada are low (5.0/100,000) (Public Health Agency of Canada 2007) on the global scale and in comparison to the high rates characteristic of the early 20th century. Yet there are residual pockets where the disease flourishes and particular groups in which it continues to take a higher toll, notably among migrants from TB endemic areas and Canadian-born people of Aboriginal descent who, together, account for the largest proportion of contemporary TB cases. The clustering of cases among Aboriginal people becomes even clearer when foreign-born cases are eliminated and only native-born cases considered. In 2005, for example, the TB rate for the Aboriginal population was almost 30 times higher (26.8/100,000) than that for the non-Aboriginal population (0.9/100,000). Aboriginal communities at highest risk for TB remain those in remote locations, with poor housing and crowding, lacking adequate health care, or in the process of implementing new health transfer agreements (Health Canada 1999). In other words, the conditions that underlay the operation of syndemics in the 20th century persist into the 21st, yet the vast majority of studies fail to address the social and economic determinants of this disease's tenacity in Aboriginal populations (Farmer and Jacklin 2008), let alone its interaction with other conditions.

The second case study shifts focus from Canada to the Pacific Islands, but also addresses the role of TB in indigenous and migrant populations.

A CONTEMPORARY SYNDEMIC: CASE STUDY 2

In the study of health problems it at times becomes clear that the health condition being analyzed could be replaced by others and the same patterns and processes would be found (Farmer 1999). Alternatively, synergistic interaction may multiply misery, a process highlighted by the syndemic perspective. A shift in understanding from the former to the latter perspective is illustrated by a recent research project on tuberculosis (TB) in New Zealand.

Although a significant public health issue globally, TB in New Zealand has a relatively low national prevalence of 10 per 100,000 per annum, making it a minor problem. As is the case for Canada, closer examination reveals major disparities by ethnicity, geography, class and history (Das et al. 2006). Interdisciplinary research on tuberculosis in Auckland, New Zealand, using a political ecology framework, elucidated highly variable patterns and experience of TB infection among six different groups: Maori, Pakeha (New Zealanders of European origin), Pacific Islanders, an African refugee group, and Asian immigrants (Park and Littleton 2007). Despite living in the same urban location and utilizing the same health care system, different ethnic groups experienced very different patterns of TB transmission and disease and had very different treatment experiences, termed "local ecologies" (Littleton and King 2008). Beyond TB, the study shows how analysis of an infectious disease can illuminate the experience of social and economic inequality. A diagnosis of TB places patients and their families into prolonged contact with administrative structures, creates social tensions, and highlights the importance of social support or its lack (Anderson 2007). Notably, another disease, Meningococcal B viral infection, shows a similar geographic and economic distribution (Crump et al. 2001). In other words, the study of either of these diseases would have yielded similar findings.

In the case of the Pacific Island group, however, a series of further puzzles materialized. In contrast to the other communities in the study, TB among this group has increased especially among the young (Das et al. 2006). Furthermore there is active transmission from adults to children and from local to foreign born individuals and vice versa, creating a significant future burden of ill health (Das et al. 2006; Littleton et al. 2008; Howie et al. 2005). In the other immigrant communities, TB is most commonly due to reactivation of preexisting infection, often acquired in the home country (Verver and Veen 2006) and in these groups transmission between foreign and locally born populations is small to non-existent (Littleton et al. 2008).

Mexicans living along the Mexican–USA border have a similar pattern of transmission to Pacific Islanders living in Auckland (Restrepo et al. 2007; Littleton et al. 2008). Other similarities occur: both populations are transnational with frequent border crossings, both have marginal economic positions and, at times, equivocal migration status, and, significantly, Mexicans, like Pacific Islanders, experience disproportionately high rates of TB and diabetes mellitus (DM) (Restrepo et al. 2007).

Epidemiologically TB and DM operate synergistically. Along the Texas border, it is estimated that the relative risk of TB disease in a Hispanic person with DM is two times the risk of a person without DM (Restrepo et al. 2007). In addition, the presence of DM changes the traditional epidemiological profile of a TB patient in this population from a young man with a history of incarceration to an older woman introducing a new subset of people to TB disease and opening up new transmission links.

Clinical and experimental studies demonstrate that the syndemic interaction between TB and DM operates in multiple ways (see Stevenson et al. 2007). Preexisting diabetes (DM) serves to increase the risk of TB disease through multiple effects on the immune system including increased bacterial loads among DM patients, lowered production of interferon-γ in diabetics (Martens et al. 2007), and depressed activation of alveolar macrophages (Wang et al. 1999). DM and TB also interact to make treatment of both more difficult, prolonged and with higher failure rates. In an Indonesian study by Alisjahbana et al. (2006), diabetic patients treated with rifampicin have lower plasma levels of the drug than non-diabetics on equivalent treatment. In reverse, active TB disease is associated with difficult glucose control among diabetics (Stevenson et al. 2007). It has also been hypothesized that TB predisposes people to DM through amyloidosis of the pancreatic islet cells which impairs insulin production (Broxmeyer 2005). Finally, there is some evidence of mutual causation via routes such as disorders in Vitamin D metabolism (Chan 2000; Flores 2005; Ustianowski et al. 2005).

Given the evidence for a TB/DM syndemic affecting the Mexican population in the area of the Texas border the question arose: could Pacific Islanders also be affected by a similar syndemic? Stall et al. (2003) identified a need to discover populations that might be at similar risk of syndemic conditions and that is a starting point for planned future research.

At the same time, diseases do not necessarily operate in the same ways since they are produced by local biological and social conditions interacting within a global political economic context. The initial study on TB in Auckland identified the importance of history at the international, national, community, and generation levels (Dunsford 2008). For example, international relations, particularly as they translated into migration policies, had and continue to have a significant impact on requirements for TB testing of immigrants, particularly from different Pacific Island nations and the access to health care of different communities in Auckland (non-permanent residents do not have access to free treatment) (Ng Shui 2006). At the national level, some island nations (e.g., the Cook Islands) achieved very effective control over TB during the 1960s and 1970s thereby reducing the pool of currently infected people. At the community and generation levels, experiences of stigma affect the willingness of people to come forward for contact tracing and treatment (Ng Shui et al. 2008). These complexities, visible in the first study, will almost certainly be salient in the next. Indeed, the Ministry of Health ethnic grouping "Pacific peoples" hides diverse experiences. Some Pacific groups in New Zealand experience similar rates to their home countries, others have higher recorded rates in New Zealand than at home although such rates need to be treated cautiously given the small numbers involved (e.g. the rate of TB in Tuvalu in 2005 was 305 versus 629.3 among Tuvaluan born in New Zealand from 2000 to 2004; the comparable figures for the Cook Islands are 16 versus 34.2 (Das et al. 2006; World Health Organization 2007)). For this reason the planned research will work with two communities both in New Zealand and at home to capture and explain this diversity.

One of the barriers to health improvement in populations is the failure to examine linked phenomena. As Bartlett writes: "experts in TB and experts in HIV infection live in different worlds ... This great divide applies to clinical care, research, and training; it is lessened by the overlap between the two diseases but not as much as it should be" (Bartlett 2007:S125).

In relation to TB and DM in New Zealand this division occurs bureaucratically at the national and local level, while relationships between health and immigration status offer a further difficulty in coordinating effective policy. A syndemic approach to TB is envisaged as a way of assessing and developing inter-sectoral approaches to health while recognizing the transnational lives of research participants and the way risks are concentrated and "buffered" over time.

TB is a historical residue of previous exposure occurring within a new disease environment. Working with Pacific people requires a transnational perspective to explore the continual movement of people, capital, goods, and information across national borders. Such movement is a significant challenge to traditional approaches to health research and policy (Vertovec 1999; Messias 2002). Developing effective strategies to reduce health disparities among transnational populations will require an understanding of: the relationships between migration status and health, life history (inter- and intragenerational), multiple health services, and political economic conditions in the sender and receiver communities. Attention to such factors is built into the syndemic perspective, which is one of the advantages of this approach.

In addition, the syndemic approach offers a means of moving beyond a focus on prevention strategies dealing with proximate causes by drawing attention to the processes that create clusters of disease and noxious living conditions for particular populations. As Stall et al. (2003:941) assert, the basic public health question regarding syndemics is "What are the best approaches to disrupting syndemics so that the health of vulnerable populations is enhanced?"

SYNDEMICS, MEDICAL ANTHROPOLOGY, AND THE FUTURE OF GLOBAL HEALTH

Improving public health remains one of the great challenges of the 21st century. As the World Health Organization (2004:4–7) documents, "Almost 57 million people died in 2002, 10.5 million (or nearly 20%) of whom were children of less than 5 years of age... Of these child deaths, 98% occurred in developing countries. Across the world, children are at higher risk of dying if they are poor." While impressive gains were made in adult health internationally in the last quarter of the 20th century, the subsequent slowdown in the rate of decline in adult mortality has been interpreted by the WHO as a clear warning that further reductions, especially in developing countries, will not be easily realized without changes in contemporary efforts and approaches.

Among the factors contributing to the problem are the forces of globalism that in ways large and small are reshaping the contexts of social life and health everywhere. The ranges of many infectious diseases have increased in part because of more rapid and widespread movement of goods and services worldwide, leading to the global diffusion of pathogens. Included in the global flow of commodities are antibiotics, contributing to their inappropriate use and the development of drug resistant stains of previously controllable infections. Further, as a consequence of resource wars and rural poverty, people move across national boundaries and into concentrated urban centers that facilitate disease onset and transmission. Moreover, as the proportion of elderly people grows in a world in which more than half of the elderly population is found in developing societies (Barrett, in press), we can expect the intersection between infectious and chronic diseases, such as TB and DM, to become an increasingly important health research issue. Understanding the risks that emerge in a changing world requires attention to the kinds of biosocial interactions that are shaping contemporary global health. The syndemic perspective offers one tool for enhancing the armature of public health for its daunting task.

The health of indigenous populations that are socially subordinated within the context of a dominant state structure and political economy is a case in point. In a recent review of the literature, Farmer and Jacklin (2008) point out that in addition to tuberculosis – which we have discussed at some length – other health conditions cluster disproportionately among Aboriginal people in Canada. These include diabetes, cancer and renal failure – all of which, notably, are medical risk factors for TB. At the same time, Aboriginal communities suffer disproportionately from deleterious social conditions, including poverty, poor nutrition, limited access to or use of health care services, homelessness, overcrowding, alcoholism, and drug abuse. These social and health disparities are linked to the historical relationship of indigenous peoples to the wider society. Here we see the intersection of biological and social conditions that gives rise to syndemics, yet the concept has yet to be applied in any meaningful way by health care providers (Farmer and Jacklin 2008). The syndemics perspective asks researchers to consider how disease synergies have come to be channeled into vulnerable populations – and sustained among them – through social inequalities and systems of power. These kinds of relationships have not sprung up de novo but are rooted in historical systems, such as colonial policies and practices, whose effects persist today (Farmer 1999). The continued resonance of historical systems of power into contemporary social relations is exemplified by the excess burden of ill-health among many indigenous populations. We echo Farmer and Jacklin's (2008) call for more participatory and interdisciplinary research that integrates indigenous, biomedical and social science knowledge concerning TB, but in addition suggest that a syndemics perspective is a fruitful avenue for future public health research with disparity populations across the spectrum of human diseases and health conditions.

As suggested, such an approach leads to new frontiers of work for medical anthropologists, such as health problems that transcend the borders of human and non-human animal populations. A starting point in this instance is closer consideration of animal–human connections in our teaching and in our own research. The veterinary community is primed to consider the global reach of socio-economic forces on both animal and human health (Jones et al. 2008; Rock et al., in press; Waltner-Toews 2007; Zinsstag et al. 2006), and also the importance of communication and culture for effective practice (Kurtz and Adams 2009). To date, however, we have come across only a single published report on public health training of social scientists that has involved at least one veterinarian (Good 1992), while the 2008 World Veterinary Congress hosted a standing-room-only crowd for a full-day session on global health. We envision much stronger links between veterinarians and anthropologists, for example, among those working with disadvantaged populations (Obrist et al. 2007) and in regions increasingly affected by climate change (Baer and Singer 2003). Similar opportunities for multidisciplinary approaches in syndemics research may develop with medical historians, biologists, microbiologists, virologists, "wet-lab" epidemiologists, and a range of other health related disciplines confronting the rapidly changing world of global health, past and present.

On the intervention front, the syndemic perspective offers an approach for addressing existing fragmentation in prevention and treatment that is needed to address the multiple and entwined health consequences of social disparities (Walkup et al. 2008). Similarly, medical anthropology skills and training are well-suited to prevention-oriented research because of the subdiscipline's focus on health in social context. The "next wave" of contributions from medical anthropologists to public health should include designing, following, and evaluating efforts to attenuate the syndemic potential of various combinations of disease and other afflictions. Of importance in this regard is a needed focus on the various expressions of syndemic phenomena, including sequential epidemics (in which biosocial changes introduced by one epidemic shapes subsequent epidemics in a population), various kinds of interacting epidemics, such as infectious/noninfectious disease syndemics, counter-syndemics, ecosyndemics (i.e., disease interactions that are mediated by environmental change, such as climate change), and supersyndemics (i.e., two or more independent syndemics that come together and significantly impact a population's health burden), as well as factors that account for the particular patterns of syndemic diffusion (and resistance to diffusion, such as resiliency) within and between populations (Stall et al. 2008).

REFERENCES

Abu-Raddad, Patrick P. Laith, and J. Kublin, 2006 Dual Infection with HIV and Malaria Fuels the Spread of Both Diseases in sub-Saharan Africa. Science 314:1603–1606.

ACCA (Anglican Church of Canada Archives, General Synod Office, Toronto, Canada), 1864–1929. York Factory Burials. Diocese of Keewatin Records, Ms. 217, Reel #2.

Alisjahbana, B., R. van Crevel, E. Sahiratmadja, M. den Heijer, and A. Maya, 2006 Diabetes mellitus is strongly associated with tuberculosis in Indonesia. International Journal of Tuberculosis and Lung Disease 10: 696–700.

Anderson, Anneka, 2007 Migration and Settlement of Indian, Chinese and Korean Migrants in Auckland, a Perspective from Health. Ph.D. dissertation, Department of Anthropology, University of Auckland, New Zealand.

Ayele, W., S. Neill, J. Zinsstag, M. Weiss, and I. Pavlik, 2004 Bovine tuberculosis: an old disease but a new threat to Africa. International Journal of Tuberculosis and Lung Disease 8:924–937.

Baer, Hans, Merrill Singer, and Ida Susser, 2003 Medical Anthropology and the World System. Westport CT: Greenwood Publishing Company.

Barrett, Ron, In press Avian influenza and the third epidemiological transition. In Plagues, Epidemics and Ideas. D. Ann Herring and Alan C. Swedlund, eds. New York/Oxford: Berghann Press.

Barta, Jodi Lynn, 2008 Man's Best Friend: Implications of Tuberculosis in a 16th Century Neutral Iroquois Dog from Canada. In Multiplying and Dividing: Tuberculosis in Canada and Aotearoa, New Zealand. Judith Littleton, Julie Parks, D. Ann Herring, and Tracy Farmer, eds. pp. 23–31. RAL-e: Research in Anthropology and Linguistics No. 3. Department of Anthropology, University of Auckland, New Zealand. Electronic document. http://researchspace.auckland.ac.nz/xmlui/handle/2292/2558/.

Bartlett, John, 2007 Tuberculosis and HIV infection: partners in human tragedy. Journal of Infectious Disease 196(Suppl 1):S124–125.

Brook, R. K., and S. McLachlan, 2006 Factors influencing farmers' concerns regarding bovine tuberculosis in wildlife and livestock around Riding Mountain National Park. Journal of Environmental Management 80:156–166.

Broxmeyer, Lawrence, 2005 Diabetes mellitus, tuberculosis and the mycobacteria: two Millennia of enigma. Medical Hypotheses 65(3):433–439.

Bryce, P., 1907 Report on the Indian Schools of Manitoba and the Northwest Territories. Ottawa: Government Printing Bureau.

Cain, K., N. Kanara, K. Laserson, C. Vannarith, K. Sameourn, K. Samnang, M. Qualls, and J. Varma, 2007 The Epidemiology of HIV-associated Tuberculosis in Rural Cambodia. International Journal of Tuberculosis and Lung Disease 11(9):1008–1013.

Cambrosio, A., A. Young, and M. Lock, 2000 Introduction. In Intersections: Living and Working with the New Biomedical Technologies. M. Lock, A. Young, and A. Cambrosio, eds. pp. 1–16. Cambridge UK: Cambridge University Press.

Chan, T. Y. K., 2000 Vitamin D deficiency and susceptibility to tuberculosis. Calcified Tissue International 66:476–478.

Chen, C., C. Lee, C. Liu, J. Wang, L. Wang, and R. Perng, 2005 Clinical Features and Outcomes of Severe Acute Respiratory Syndrome and Predictive Factors for Acute Respiratory Distress Syndrome. Journal of the Chinese Medical Association 68(1):4–10.

Cherry, J., 1999 Pertussis in the preantibiotic and prevaccine era, with emphasis on adult pertussis. Clinical Infectious Diseases 28(Suppl 2):S107–S111.

Cook, J., J. Burke-Miller, M. Cohen, R. Cook. D. Vlahov, T. Wilson, E. Golub, R. Schwartz, A. Howard, C. Ponath, M. Plankey, A. Levine, and D. Grey, 2008 Crack cocaine, disease progression, and mortality in a multicenter cohort of HIV-1 positive women. AIDS 22(11):1355–1363.

Crump, John, David Murdoch, and Michael Baker, 2001 Emerging Infectious Diseases in an Island Ecosystem: The New Zealand Perspective. Emerging Infectious Diseases 7:767–772.

Cubillos-Garzon, L., J. Casas, C. Morillo, and L. Bautista, 2004 Congestive Heart Failure in Latin America: The Next Epidemic. American Heart Journal 147(3):412–417.

Dankner, W., N. Waecker, M. Essey, K. Moser, M. Thompson, and C. Davis, 1993 Mycobacterium bovis infections in San Diego: A clinicoepidemiologic study of 73 patients and a historical review of a forgotten pathogen. Medicine 72:11–37.

Das, Dilip, Michael Baker, and Lester Calder, 2006 Tuberculosis epidemiology in New Zealand: 1995–2004. New Zealand Medical Journal 119(1243):U2249.

Dolcini, G., M. Solana, G. Andreani, A. Celentano, L. Parodi, A. Donato, N. Elissondo, S. González Cappa, L. Giavedoni, and L. Martínez Peralta. 2008 Trypanosoma cruzi (Chagas' disease agent) reduces HIV-1 replication in human placenta. Retrovirology 5:53.

Duke, Michael, Wei Teng, Scott Clair, Hassan Saleheen, Pamela Choice, and Merrill Singer, 2006 Patterns of Intimate Partner Violence Among Drug Using Women. Free Inquiry in Creative Sociology 34(1):29–38.

Dunsford, Deborah, 2008 A Social History of Tuberculosis in New Zealand from World War 2 to the 1970s. Ph.D. dissertation, Department of History, University of Auckland, New Zealand.

Engel. Lisa, and Gregory Engel, 2008 A Multidisciplinary Approach to Understanding the Risk and Context of Emerging Primate-Borne Zoonoses. In Health, Risk and Adversity. Catherine Panter-Brick and Agustín Fuentes, eds. pp. 52–77. Studies of the Biosocial Society, volume 2. New York/Oxford: Berghahn Books.

Evans-Pritchard, E. E., 1960 The Nuer: A Description of the Modes of Livelihood and Political Institutions of a Nilotic People. Oxford: Clarendon Press.

Evans-Pritchard, E. E., 1976 [1937] Witchcraft, Oracles and Magic among the Azande (Abridged with an introduction by Eva Gillies). Oxford: Clarendon Press.

Farmer, Paul, 1999 Infections and Inequalities: The Modern Plagues. Berkley: University of California Press.

Farmer, Tracy, and Kristen Jacklin, 2008 Matching Research with Evidence: Re-orienting Aboriginal Tuberculosis Research in Canada. In Multiplying and Dividing: Tuberculosis in Canada and Aotearoa, New Zealand. Judith Littleton, Julie Parks, D. Ann Herring, and Tracy Farmer, eds. pp. 85–103. RAL-e: Research in Anthropology and Linguistics No. 3. Department of Anthropology, University of Auckland, New Zealand. Electronic document. http://researchspace.auckland.ac.nz/xmlui/handle/2292/2558/.

Flores, Mario, 2005 A role of vitamin D in low-intensity chronic inflammation and insulin resistance in type 2 diabetes mellitus? Nutrition Research Reviews 18:175–182.

Gonzalez-Guardia, Rosa, 2008 The Syndemic Model for Understanding Substance Abuse, Intimate Partner Violence and HIV/AIDS among Hispanics. Presented at the 8th Annual National Hispanic Science Network on Drug Abuse, Bethesda, Maryland.

Good, M.-J., 1992 Local knowledge: Research capacity building in international health. Social Science and Medicine 35:1359–1367.

Grange, J. M., C. Daborn, and O. Cosivi, 1994 HIV-related tuberculosis due to Mycobacterium bovis. The European Respiratory Journal 7:1564–1566.

Guerrero, A., J. Cobo, J. Fortún, E. Navas, C. Quereda, A. Asensio, J. Cañón, J. Blazquez, and E. Gómez-Mampaso 1997 Nosocomial transmission of Mycobacterium bovis resistant to 11 drugs in people with advanced HIV-1 infection. Lancet 350:1738–1742.

Hackett, F., 1991 The 1819–1820 Measles Epidemic: Its Origin, Diffusion and Mortality Effects upon the Indians of the Petit Nord. M.A. dissertation, University of Manitoba, Winnipeg, Canada.

Hackett, F., 2002 A Very Remarkable Sickness: Epidemics in the Petit Nord, 1670 to 1846. Winnipeg, Canada: University of Manitoba Press.

Hardy, A., 2002 Pioneers in the Victorian provinces: Veterinarians, urban public health and the urban animal economy. Urban History 29:372–385.

HBCA (Hudson's Bay Company Archives, Winnipeg, Canada), 1794–1939 York Factory Post Journal. B.239:a/186–196.

Health Canada, 1999 Tuberculosis in First Nations Communities. Ottawa, Canada: Minister of Public Works and Government Services.

Hein, Casey, and Doreen Small, 2007 Combating Diabetes, Obesity, Periodontal Disease and Interrelated Inflammatory Conditions with a Syndemic Approach. Electronic document. http://www.healthdecisions.org/Dental/News/default.aspx?doc_id=109688/.

Herring, D. A., 2008 Viral panic, vulnerability, and the next pandemic. In Health, Risk and Adversity. C. Panter-Brick and A. Fuentes, eds. New York/Oxford UK: Berghahn Books.

Herring, D. A., and L. Sattenspiel, 2007 Social contexts, syndemics, and infectious disease in northern Aboriginal populations. American Journal of Physical Anthropology 19(2): 190–202.

Herring, D. A., S. Abonyi, and R. Hoppa., 2003 Malnutrition among northern peoples of Canada in the 1940s: an ecological and economic disaster. In Human Biologists in the Archives: Demography, Health, Nutrition and Genetics in Historical Populations. D. A. Herring and A. C. Swedlund, eds. Cambridge UK: Cambridge University Press.

Honigmann, J., 1948 Foodways in a Muskeg Community. Ottawa, Canada: Department of Northern Affairs and Natural Resources, Northern Coordination and Research Centre.

Howie, S., L. Voss, M. Baker, L. Calder, K. Grimwood, and C. Byrnes, 2005 Tuberculosis in New Zealand, 1992–2001: a resurgence. Archives of Disease in Childhood 90(11): 1157–1161.

Institute of Medicine (IOM), 1997 America's Vital Interest in Global Health: Protecting our People, Enhancing our Economy, and Advancing our International Interests. Washington: National Academy Press.

Institute of Medicine (IOM), 2008 The US Commitment to Global Health. Washington: National Academy Press.

Jones, K., N. Patel, M. Levy, A. Storeygard, D. Balk, J. Gittleman, and P. Daszak, 2008 Global trends in emerging infectious diseases. Nature 451:990–993.

Jones, S., 2004 Mapping a zoonotic disease: Anglo–American efforts to control bovine tuberculosis before World War I. Osiris 19:133–148.

Kennedy, P., 2008 The continuing problem of human African trypanosomiasis (sleeping sickness). Annals of Neurology 64:116–126.

Kurtz, Suzanne and Cynthia L. Adams, In press, 2009 Essential education in communication skills and cultural sensitivities for global public health in an evolving veterinary world. Scientific and Technical Review of the World Organization for Animal Health, Special issue, Veterinary education for global animal and public health. Donal E. Walsh, ed. 28(2).

Lee, N, P. Chan, I. Yu, K. Tsoi, G. Lui, J. Sung, and C. Cockram, 2007 Co-circulation of human metapneumovirus and SARS-associated coronavirus during a major nosocomial SARS outbreak in Hong Kong. Journal of Clinical Virology 40(4):333–337.

Lichtenstein, Bronwen, 2006 Domestic violence in barriers to health care for HIV-positive women. AIDS Patient Care STDS 20(2):122–132.

Littleton, Judith, and Ron King, 2008 The political ecology of tuberculosis in Auckland: an interdisciplinary focus. In Multiplying and Dividing: Tuberculosis in Canada and Aotearoa, New Zealand. J. Littleton, J. Park, J. Herring, and T. Farmer, eds. pp. 31–42. RAL-e: Research in Anthropology and Linguistics No. 3. Department of Anthropology, University of Auckland, New Zealand. Electronic document. http://researchspace.auckland.ac.nz/xmlui/handle/2292/2558/.

Littleton, J., J. Park, C. Thornley, A. Anderson, and J. Lawrence, 2008 Migrants and tuberculosis: analyzing epidemiogical data with ethnography. Australian and New Zealand Journal of Public Health 32:142–149.

Lloyd-Smith, J., M. Poss, and B. Grenfell, 2008 HIV-1/parasite co-infection and the emergence of new parasite strains. Parasitology 135:795–806.

Marshall, Mac, 2005 Carolina in the Carolines: A Survey of Patterns and Meanings of Smoking on a Micronesian Island. Medical Anthropology Quarterly 19(4):354–382.

Martens, G., M. Arikan, J. Lee, F. Ren, D. Greiner, and H. Kornfeld, 2007 Tuberculosis Susceptibility of Diabetic Mice. American Journal of Respiratory Cell and Molecular Biology 37:518–524.

Mattioli, R., J. Zinsstag, and K. Pfister, 1994 Frequency of trypanosomosis and gastrointestinal parasites in draught donkeys in The Gambia in relation to animal husbandry. Tropical Animal Health and Production 26:102–108.

Mavridis, Agapi, 2008 Tuberculosis and Syndemics: Implications for Winnipeg, Manitoba. *In* Multiplying and Dividing Tuberculosis in Canada and Aotearoa, New Zealand Judith Littleton, Julie Park, Ann Herring and Tracy Farmer, Eds. pp. 43–53. RAL-e: Research in Anthropology and Linguistics No. 3. Department of Anthropology, University of Auckland, New Zealand. Electronic document. http://researchspace.auckland.ac.nz/xmlui/handle/2292/2558/.

McCorkle, C. M., E. Mathius, T. W. Schillhorn, and Van Veen, eds., 1996. Ethnoveterinary Research and Development. London: Intermediate Technology Publications.

McNeill, W., 1976 Plagues and Peoples. Garden City, NY: Anchor Press/Doubleday.

Mercado, Susan, Kirsten Havemann, Keiko Nakamura, Andrew Kiyu, Mojgan Sami, Roby Alampay, Ira Pedrasa, Divine Salvador, Jeerawat Na Thalang, and Tran Le Thuey, 2007 Responding to the Health Vulnerabilities of the Urban Poor in the "New Urban Settings" of Asia. Paper presented at Improving Urban Population Health Systems, sponsored by the Center for Sustainable Urban Development, July.

Messias, DeAnne, 2002 Transnational health resources, practices, and perspectives: Brazilian immigrant women's narratives. Journal of Immigrant Health 4(4):183–200.

Mullin, M., 1999 Mirrors and windows: Sociocultural studies of animal–human relationships. Annual Review of Anthropology 28:201–224.

Mustanski, Brian, Robert Garofalo, Amy Herrick, and Geri Amy and Donenberg, 2007 Psychosocial health problems increase risk for HIV among urban young men who have sex with men: Preliminary evidence of a syndemic in need of attention. Annals of Behavioral Medicine 34(1):37–45.

Ng Shiu, Roannie, 2006 The Place of Tuberculosis: The Lived Experience of Pacific Peoples in Auckland and Samoa. M.A. dissertation, Department of Geography, University of Auckland, New Zealand.

Ng Shiu, Roannie, Robin Kearns, and Julie Park, 2008 Placing the experience of Pacific peoples living with tuberculosis in Auckland, New Zealand. *In* Multiplying and Dividing: Tuberculosis in Canada and Aotearoa, New Zealand. J. Littleton, J. Park, J. Herring, and T. Farmer, eds. pp. 218–230. RAL-e: Research in Anthropology and Linguistics No. 3. Department of Anthropology, University of Auckland, New Zealand. Electronic document. http://researchspace.auckland.ac.nz/xmlui/handle/2292/2558/.

Nguyen, V., and K. Peschard, 2004 Anthropology, inequality, and disease: A review. Annual *Review of Anthropology* 32:447–474.

Nichter, Mark, 2008 Global Health: Why Cultural Perceptions, Social Representations, and Biopolitics Matter. Tucson: The University of Arizona Press.

Nyamanga, P., C. Suda, and J. Aagaard-Hansen, 2008 The socio-cultural context and practical implications of ethnoveterinary medical pluralism in western Kenya. Agriculture and Human Values 25(4):513–527.

Obrist, B., N. Iteba, C. Lengeler, A. Makemba, C. Mshana, R. Nathan, S. Alba, A. Dillip, M. W. Hetzel, I. Mayumana, A. Schulze, and H. Mshinda, 2007 Access to health care in contexts of livelihood insecurity: A framework for analysis and action. PLoS Medicine, vol. 4, pp. e308. Electronic document. doi:10.1371/journal.pmed.0040308/.

Paluzzi, J., and Farmer, Paul, 2005 The Wrong Question. Development 48(1):12–18.

Park, Julie, and Judith Littleton, 2007 Ethnography Plus. Tuberculosis Research SITES: a journal of Cultural and Social Anthropology 4(1):3–23.

Pepin, J., L. Ethier, C. Kazadi, F. Milord, and R. Ryder, 1992 The impact of human immuno-deficiency virus infection on the epidemiology and treatment of Trypanosoma brucei gambiense sleeping sickness in Nioki, Zaire. The American Journal of Tropical Medicine and Hygiene 47:133–140.

Ponce-De-Leon, Alfredo, de Lordes Garcia-Garcia, Cecilia Garcia-Sancho, Francisco Gomez-Perez, and Jose Valdespino-Gomez, 2004 Tuberculosis and diabetes in southern Mexico. Diabetes Care 27:1584–1590.

Preston, R., 1986 Twentieth-century transformations of the West Coast Cree. Paper presented at the Seventeenth Annual Algonquian Conference/Actes du Dix-Septieme Congres des Algonquinistes, Ottawa, Canada. W. Cowan, ed. Carleton University, Ottawa, Canada: Public Health Agency of Canada.

Preston, R., 2007 Tuberculosis in Canada 2003. Ottawa, Canada. Electronic document. http://www.publichealth.gc.ca/tuberculosis/.

Restrepo, B., S. Fisher-Hoch, J. Grespo, E. Whitney, A. Perez, B. Smith, and J. McCormick, 2007 Type 2 diabetes and tuberculosis in a dynamic bi-national border population. Epidemiology and Infection 135(3):483–491.

Rock, M., and P. Babinec, 2008 Diabetes in people, cats and dogs: Biomedicine and manifold ontologies. Medical Anthropology 27:324–252.

Rock, M., B. Buntain, J. Hatfield, and B. Hallgrímsson, 2009 Animal–human connections, "one health," and the syndemic approach to prevention. Social Science and Medicine 68(6):991–995.

Rodwell, T., M. Moore, K. Moser, S. Brodine, and S.Strathdee, 2008 Tuberculosis from Mycobacterium bovis in binational communities, United States. Emerging Infectious Diseases 14:909–916.

Samper, S., C. Martín, A. Pinedo, A. Rivero, J. Blázquez, F. Baquero, D. van Soolingen, and J. van Embden, 1997 Transmission between HIV-infected patients of multidrug-resistant tuberculosis caused by Mycobacterium bovis. AIDS 11:1237–1242.

Sethi, Sanjeev, 2002 Bacterial Pneumonia. Managing a Deadly Complication of Influenza in Older Adults with Comorbid Disease. Geriatrics 57(3):56–61.

Shanklin, E., 1985 Sustenance and Symbol: Anthropological Studies of Domesticated Animals. Annual Review of Anthropology 14:375–403.

Singer, Merrill, 1994 AIDS and the Health Crisis of the US Urban Poor: The Perspective of Critical Medical Anthropology. Social Science and Medicine 39(7):931–948.

Singer, Merrill, 1995 Beyond the Ivory Tower: Critical Praxis in Medical Anthropology. Medical Anthropology Quarterly 9(1):80–106.

Singer, Merrill, 1996 A Dose of Drugs, a Touch of Violence, A Case of AIDS: Conceptualizing the SAVA Syndemic. Free Inquiry in Creative Sociology 24(2):99–110.

Singer, Merrill, 2006 A Dose of Drugs, A Touch of Violence, A Case of AIDS, Part 2: Further Conceptualizing the SAVA Syndemic. Free Inquiry in Creative Sociology 34(1):39–51.

Singer, Merrill, 2008 The Perfect Epidemiological Storm: Food Insecurity, HIV/AIDS and Poverty in Southern Africa. Anthropology Newsletter (American Anthropological Association) 49(7):12 and 15 October.

Singer, Merrill, 2009a Desperate Measures: A Syndemic Approach to the Anthropology of Health in a Violent City. In Global Health in a Time of Violence. Paul Farmer, Barbara Rylko-Bauer, and Linda Whiteford, eds. Santa Fe NM: SAR Press.

Singer, Merrill, 2009b Introduction to Syndemics: A Systems Approach to Public and Community Health. San Francisco: Jossey-Bass.

Singer, Merrill and Scott Clair, 2003 Syndemics and Public Health: Reconceptualizing Disease in Bio-Social Context. Medical Anthropology Quarterly 17(4):423–441.

Singer, Merrill, Pamela Erickson, Louise Badiane, Rosemary Diaz, Dueidy Ortiz, Traci Abraham, and Anne Marie Nicolaysen, 2006 Syndemics, Sex and the City: Understanding Sexually Transmitted Disease in Social and Cultural Context. Social Science and Medicine 63(8):2010–2021.

Stall, R., T. Mills, J. Williamson, and T. Hart, 2003 Association of Co-occurring Psychosocial Health Problems and Increased Vulnerability to HIV/AIDS Among Urban men who have Sex with Men. American Journal of Public Health 93(6):939–942.

Stall, R., M. S. Friedman, and J. Catania, 2008 Interacting Epidemics and Gay Men's Health: A Theory of Syndemic Production among Urban Gay Men. In Unequal Opportunity: Health Disparities Affecting Gay and Bisexual Men in the United States. R. Wolitski, R. Stall, and R. Valdiserri, eds. Oxford UK: Oxford University Press.

Stephens, Christianne V., 2008 "She was weakly for a long time and the consumption set in": Using Parish Records to Explore Disease Patterns and Causes of Death in a First Nations Community. In Multiplying and Dividing: Tuberculosis in Canada and Aotearoa, New Zealand. Judith Littleton, Julie Parks, D. Ann Herring and Tracy Farmer, eds. pp. 136–150. RAL-e: Research in Anthropology and Linguistics No. 3. Department of Anthropology, University of Auckland, New Zealand. Electronic document. http://researchspace.auckland. ac.nz/xmlui/handle/2292/2558/.

Stevenson, C., N. Forouhi, G. Roglic, B. Williams, J. Lauer, C. Dye, and N. Unwin, 2007 Diabetes and tuberculosis: the impact of the diabetes epidemic on tuberculosis incidence. BMC Public Health 7:234–242.

Stewart, D., 1936 The Red Man and the White Plague. Canadian Medical Association Journal 35:674–676.

Stone, E., 1926 Health and Disease at the Norway House Indian Agency. Reprinted in Native Studies Review 1989 5(1):237–256.

Stoops, M., 2008 Norway House Residential School and Tuberculosis, 1900–1946. In Multiplying and Dividing: Tuberculosis in Canada and Aotearoa, New Zealand. Judith Littleton, Julie Park, D. Ann Herring, and Tracy Farmer, eds. RAL-e: Research in Anthropology and Linguistics No. 3. Department of Anthropology, University of Auckland, New Zealand. Electronic document. http://researchspace.auckland.ac.nz/xmlui/handle/2292/2558/.

Tashiro, Masato, Pawel Ciborowski, Manfred Reinacher, Gerhard Pulverer, Hans-Dieter Klenk, and Rudolph Rott, 1987 Synergistic role of staphylococcal proteases in the induction of influenza virus pathogenicity. Virology 157:421–430.

Tisdall, F., and E. Robertson, 1948 Voyage of the medicine men. The Beaver 28:42–46.

Ustianowski, A., R. Shaffer, S. Collin, R. Wilkinson, and R. Davidson, 2005 Prevalence and associations of vitamin D deficiency in foreign-born persons with tuberculosis in London. Journal of Infection 50(5):432–437.

Vertovec, Steven, 1999 Conceiving and researching transnationalism. Ethnic and Racial Studies 22(2):447–462.

Verver, Suzanne, and Jaap Veen, 2006 Tuberculosis and migration. In Reichman and Hershfield's Tuberculosis: a Comprehensive, International Approach. M. Raviglione, ed. pp. 869–906. New York: Informa Healthcare.

Waldram, J., D. A. Herring, and T. Young, 2006 Aboriginal Health in Canada: Historical, Cultural and Epidemiological Perspectives. 2nd edition. Toronto: University of Toronto Press.

Walkup, James, Michael Blank, Jeffrey Gonzalez, Steven Safren, Rebecca Schwartz, Larry Brown, Ira Wilson, Amy Knowlton, Frank Lombard, Cynthia Grossman, Karen Lyda, and Joseph Schumacher, 2008 The Impact of Mental Health and Substance Abuse Factors on HIV Prevention and Treatment. Journal of Acquired Immune Deficiency Syndrome 47(Supplement 1): S15–S19.

Wallace, Roderick, 1988 A Synergism of Plagues. Environment Research 47:1–33.

Wallace, Roderick, 1990 Urban Desertification, Public Health and Public Order: Planned Shrinkage, Violent Death, Substance Abuse and AIDS in the Bronx. Social Science and Medicine 31: 801–813.

Wallace, Deborah, and Roderick Wallace, 1998 A Plague on your Houses: How New York was Burned Down and National Public Health Crumbled. New York: Verso.

Waltner-Toews, David, 2007 The Chickens Fight Back: Pandemic Panics and Deadly Diseases that Jump from Animals to Humans. Vancouver/Toronto/Berkeley: Greystone Books.

Wang, C.-H., C.-T. Yu, H.-C. Lin, C.-Y. Liu, and H.-P. Kuo, 1999 Hypodense alveolar macrophages in patients with diabetes mellitus and active pulmonary tuberculosis. Tubercle and Lung Disease 79(4):235–242.

World Health Organization, 2004 Global Health Report, 2003. Geneva: World Health Organization.

World Health Organization, 2007 Combating HIV/AIDS and Tuberculosis. Jeju, Republic of Korea. Geneva: Regional Committee for the Western Pacific, World Health Organization.

Young, T., 1988 Health Care and Cultural Change: The Indian Experience in the Central Subarctic. Toronto: University of Toronto Press.

Young, Ann and Ann Herring, 2004 A Syndemic Perspective on Whooping Cough Epidemics at the York Factory. Paper presented at the Canadian Association for Physical Anthropology, London.

Zinsstag, J., E. Schelling, K. Wyss, and M. Mahamat, 2006 Potential of cooperation between human and animal health to strengthen health systems. Lancet 366:2142–2145.

Zinsstag, J., E. Schelling, F. Roth, B. Bonfoh, D. de Savigny, and M. Tanner, 2007. Human benefits of animal interventions for zoonosis control. Emerging Infectious Diseases 13: 527–531.

CHAPTER 9

The Ecology of Disease and Health

Patricia K. Townsend

Writing a quarter of a century ago, in an essay titled "Medical Anthropology: A Critical Appraisal," David Landy (1983:187) claimed that while no single theoretical approach "unites the field and that everyone can agree upon" there was a "broad tacit consensus" that an ecological–evolutionary perspective does provide a central focus to medical anthropology. By the time the "ink had dried" on Landy's critical assessment, the consensus he described had already dissolved. Medical anthropology had grown rapidly and divided into numerous interest groups based on differences in research interests and theoretical commitments. Ecological and evolutionary approaches remained central in physical (biological) anthropology but were marginalized for the rest of the 20th century among the majority of medical anthropologists whose primary orientation was toward cultural anthropology.

In the decades prior to Landy's essay, medical anthropology had taken shape out of a loose collection of ethnographic descriptions of shamans and other healers, applied work in international public health, culture and personality studies, and physical anthropology (Johnson and Sargent 1990:1). Theory was not much discussed, but underlying most applied studies and ethnographic field work was an attachment to cultural relativism and an easy functionalism that assured anthropologists that if they looked deeply and wisely enough, even seemingly irrational behavior, from sacred cows to genital surgeries, made sense in its cultural context. This was the message that teachers of medical anthropology thought they needed to teach to future health workers.

Beyond the local-level studies that anthropologists characteristically produced, when they talked about the big picture of health and disease, anthropologists in the 1950s and 1960s did so from an ecological–evolutionary theoretical perspective, as can readily be seen in several bench mark edited volumes from that era. In 1959 Sol Tax invited 19 promising younger American colleagues to talk about what they found significant in anthropology for a Voice of America broadcast series. The lectures were

A Companion to Medical Anthropology, First Edition. Edited by Merrill Singer and Pamela I. Erickson.

later published as the volume *Horizons of Anthropology*. Steven Polgar wrote "Evolution and the Ills of Mankind." Although his training was as a social anthropologist, he worked as an applied anthropologist, director of international population research for Planned Parenthood. Polgar wrote, "When an anthropologist, reared in the tradition of anthropology which unites the study of social man and physical man, comes to learn about the complex ecological relationships involved in human diseases, it is logical that he should be asking questions about the changes that might have occurred during human evolution" (1964:202). He drew evidence from paleopathology as well as inferences from studies of contemporary humans, treated as representative of hunters and gatherers, farmers, and city dwellers of the past. The general outlines of his lecture have been revisited by medical anthropologists many times since then, increasingly refined with new data and insights.

Another major gathering of anthropologists came together at the University of Chicago in 1965, producing an edited volume, *Man the Hunter*. Discussion at this event evoked Marshall Sahlins' concept of the 'Original affluent society' and other provocative work. Frederick Dunn's paper, "Epidemiological Factors: Health and Disease in Hunters and Gatherers" represented state-of-the-art medical ecology. In it, Dunn developed a comprehensive argument about the relationships between the diversity and complexity of environments occupied by hunters and gatherers and the incidence and prevalence of infectious and parasitic disease among them (Dunn 1968).

An even earlier benchmark essay in medical ecology came out of a series of talks on "environment and man," sponsored by the Anthropological Society of Washington in 1955–1956. The lecture series included such notable anthropologists as Eric Wolf and Betty Meggers. In his paper, "The Ecology of Human Disease," Jacques May referred to his discipline not as "medical anthropology" but as "the geography of disease." Nonetheless, he was as insistent as any anthropologist on the influence of culture on the distribution of disease. From his experience in the 1930s as a medical school professor in French Indo-China, he described the house types that protected the Vietnamese from malaria or exposed them to the disease. More generally, he saw disease as "an expression of temporary maladjustment of the host" to an environmental stimulus. His examples of such stimuli included the cholera vibrio or a deficit of a particular nutrient (May 1957:100).

ADAPTATION AND MALARIA

Physical anthropologist Frank B. Livingstone produced the classic anthropological research on disease ecology in the 1950s in his study of malaria and sickle cell disease in West Africa. Probably no one at the time would have called what Livingstone was doing "medical anthropology," yet this work remains central to the intellectual foundations of the subdiscipline. Livingstone (1958) continues to be cited repeatedly in key texts. What made Livingstone's work the classic case that it has remained for fifty years? It rested on Neo-Darwinism (Darwin's natural selection plus Mendelian genetics), which was the best articulated theory in the anthropological study of disease at the time. Prior to the 1950s, there had been little discussion of the role infectious disease played in biological evolution, but disease distributions in Africa had led

Haldane and Allison to hypothesize that the alleles for certain disorders of hemoglobin afforded protection against malaria (Lederberg 1999). In its homozygous form, the gene produces the disease sickle cell anemia, but individuals who are heterozygous have the sickle cell trait that provides a selective advantage when exposed to *falciparum* malaria. This is an instance of balancing selection, or a *balanced polymorphism*.

Livingstone went on to relate the spread of both *falciparum* malaria and the sickle cell trait to the introduction of iron tools and swidden agriculture in West Africa. By cutting forests, farmers created breeding sites for *gambiae* mosquitos, the major vectors for potentially deadly *falciparum* malaria. Agriculture also increased population densities, increasing the potential for transmitting malaria. Part of the continuing appeal of Livingstone's work is that his argument spans all four traditional subfields of anthropology: biological anthropology, prehistoric archaeology, linguistics (the spread of the Bantu languages), and cultural anthropology (change in farming practices and settlement patterns). This four-field unity was under threat through much of the discipline of anthropology by the end of the 20th century, but it continues to characterize medical anthropology, which aspires to a *holistic* understanding of health problems.

Not all of the adaptations to malaria were genetic: others were behavioral. Medical anthropologists also studied the use of food plants, such as cassava, and herbal medicines as cultural adaptations to malaria and other infectious diseases. Whether or not genetic adaptation can be demonstrated in a given disease, the Livingstone study continues to provide a model for what anthropology can contribute to the study of disease by looking simultaneously at processes of environmental, cultural, and biological change across time and space.

The ecological/evolutionary approach in medical anthropology asserted that human societies constantly change and recreate the physical and biological environment to which they must then adapt through the processes of co-evolution of human biology and culture. Adaptation was a core concept at the outset (e.g., Alland 1970), though it soon became clear to medical ecologists that poverty and powerlessness placed severe constraints on the human ability to adapt, except perhaps in the most egalitarian of social systems. The constraints of poverty were historically manifest in nutritional deficiencies that reduced resistance to infectious disease in the very young. Poverty also increases exposure to toxic substances, occupational risks, and physical violence. The poor also lack equal access to effective medical care.

FORAGERS AND FARMERS

Within the traditional subject matter of anthropology, the most dramatic of the environmental changes associated with cultural evolution were those that occurred at the transition from foraging to farming. These changes included altered land use and settlement patterns, increased human population density, domestication of plant and animal species, and reshaping the physical landscape by drainage, irrigation, and terracing. Close relationships with domesticated animals resulted in humans acquiring some their diseases (zoonoses), including possibly measles, pertussis, smallpox, tuberculosis, taenid tapeworms, as well as *falciparum* malaria (Pearce-Duvet

2006; Wolfe et al. 2007). Some of these diseases may have moved from humans to animals or moved to both humans and domestic animals from rats or wildlife in habitats modified by agriculture. The use of molecular biology to determine relationships has revised our assumptions about several of these diseases, for example, showing that smallpox is closer to camelpox than to cowpox.

All things considered, it is not surprising that the transition from hunting and gathering to agriculture was a main focus in the early years of both medical and environmental anthropology. In understanding the effects of farming on health, anthropologists were not limited to inferences based on studies of living populations. They also had direct access to the remains of the past. In human bones and teeth, paleopathologists found abundant evidence of iron-deficiency anemia, malnutrition, dental caries, shorter stature, and infectious disease associated with the adoption of agriculture (Cohen and Armelagos 1984; Cohen 1989).

Few topics in medical anthropology have grabbed more public attention than the implications of the hunting and gathering past for the health problems of the present. A flood of mass market books and articles explore the implications of our modern sedentary life and diet for bodies evolved for a hunter-gatherer life style. Those writers take up where the anthropologists who devised *The Paleolithic Prescription* left off (Eaton et al. 1988). This *Paleolithic* lifestyle is basically the pattern of diet and activity attributed to the hunter-gatherers of the Kalahari, as they lived in the 1960s when they were studied by Richard B. Lee (1979).

Evolutionary medicine hypothesizes a mismatch between human biological evolution and health conditions in industrialized society. While these ideas are very popular with science journalists and medical consumers, relatively few of them have yet been fully tested by clinicians. The main exceptions are the changes in pediatricians' recommendations for breastfeeding and infant sleeping arrangements. There has been a major expansion in such research, especially by biological anthropologists, since the term "evolutionary medicine" or "Darwinian medicine" was first introduced in the 1990s (Trevathan et al. 2008).

Few anthropologists challenged the assumption that underlies much of evolutionary medicine: the human genome has remained relatively unchanged for several thousand years. Rapid cultural evolution was thought to have replaced the slow process of genetic change in human adaptation. The contrary view – that genetic change accelerated rapidly after the origin of agriculture and civilization – has now been presented in *The 10,000 Year Explosion* (Cochran and Harpending 2009). Acknowledging that complex adaptations, those requiring the coordinated action of several genes, do occur slowly, Cochran and Harpending argue that, nevertheless, natural selection has operated to cause significant genetic change in the past 10,000 years. Rather than requiring complex multi-gene adaptations, this change relies on intense natural selection acting on mutations of *single* genes. These changes can take place very rapidly. Other types of relatively rapid change include the loss of old adaptations and processes such as neoteny – the retention of a juvenile trait into adulthood. Large population size also facilitates more rapid evolution (Hawks et al. 2007).

Though they discuss several types of genetic changes, Cochran and Harpending are particularly interested in the evolution of human intelligence and the capacity for cultural innovation. They argue that the mutations that increased intelligence were favored by natural selection during the medieval period among Ashkenazi Jews, who were confined by prejudice to work as financiers, the only occupation open to them in that era in Europe. These mutations were associated with levels of certain bio-chemical compounds that affect the development of the central nervous system These compounds also cause a group of inherited diseases, including Tay–Sachs disease, among others. This suggests a mechanism of balancing selection in Europe, a process that operates like the sickle cell gene and resistance to malaria in West Africa. In the Ashkenazi case, the mutations affected a different metabolic pathway (sphingolipid storage rather than hemoglobin) and were adapted to the social environment rather than to an infectious disease.

ECOLOGICAL ANTHROPOLOGY: NUTRITION AND HEALTH

Human biologists and bioarchaeologists were not alone in contributing to under-standing the health conditions of hunter-gatherers and tropical forest farmers. Cultural ecologists, geographers, and ecological anthropologists did ethnographic field work in which they attempted to measure the flow of energy through systems and the time and energy input for hunting, gathering, and farming tasks (Lee 1979; Little and Morren 1976; Townsend 1974).

Roy Rappaport's classic work on the Tsembaga Maring of New Guinea measured household food intake over the year. Calories were not the only thing that counted: Rappaport (1968) argued that the protein from domesticated pigs was nutritionally crucial, and that the population of pigs was regulated by rituals. Reading Rappaport's work while still in the field in the Sepik region of Papua New Guinea inspired Townsend to concentrate more on nutrition than she had initially planned as a cul-tural ecologist. The lowland population of foragers that she studied depended on the sago palm for their staple food. Sago is almost pure carbohydrate. Sources of protein and fat were very scarce in their diet, and the people experienced hunger and malnu-trition even in the presence of adequate energy sources. At the same time, the high rates of morbidity and mortality that Townsend observed in the field began the proc-ess of turning her into a medical anthropologist (Townsend 1971).

A wealth of dissertations and monographs describing hunting-gathering and small-scale farming communities was inspired by cultural ecology and ecological anthropology in the 1960s and 1970s. They produced a rich body of data concerning subsist-ence systems, but, the attempt to understand any of these populations as an isolated adaptive system in equilibrium with its environment quickly proved inappropriate (McCay 2008). Even the seemingly most isolated of these communities were integrated into regional systems of trade. Colonial and neo-colonial conquest had introduced diseases, decimated populations, and radically changed settlement patterns in what superficially appeared to be isolated, traditional societies.

In the light of these and other concerns, a few of the leading proponents of eco-logical anthropology disowned some of their own previous analysis (Vayda 2008; Alland 1987; Thomas 1997). Just as cultural ecology, for the most part, gave way to political ecology, an ecology of health gave way to a political economy of health. In any case, most medical anthropologists were now working in urban and industrial settings, where environmental issues and health inequities related to class, race, and place demanded their attention. Medical and cultural geographer Charles Good has pointed out that his discipline experienced similar shifts away from rural and non-Western field settings and toward political economy in the same time frame (Good 2000). Historians also do research at the interface of environment and health in industrial society, producing studies of the "modern malady" of allergy (Jackson 2006) and pesticides in California's Central Valley (Nash 2006) that are fundamentally similar to work in medical anthropology and medical geography.

TECHNOLOGICAL DISASTERS AND TOXIC SITES

The industrial revolution, like the earlier agricultural revolution, fostered a constellation of changes in human health and disease that medical anthropologists seek to understand. It was first of all an energy revolution, with fossil fuels supplying industries that had formerly been limited to the power of humans, animals, wind, and water. Laboratories synthesized thousands of new chemical compounds. Industrial agriculture and mining massively disrupted natural biological and geological cycles.

In the 20th century, the acceleration of technological innovation transformed health care systems as well. Most medical anthropologists are now concerned not with shamans and herbal medicines but with the industrialized system, whether it is called cosmopolitan medicine or western medicine or biomedicine or simply "medicine." Medicine is ever more dependent on laboratory tests, pharmaceuticals, MRIs, CT scans, new generations of joint replacements, and other capital intensive developments.

In industrial and post-industrial society, a major point of intersection between environmental anthropology and medical anthropology is the exposure of humans to new levels of risk from the chemical and physical products and byproducts of industry. The 1978 crisis at Love Canal, a suburban neighborhood in Niagara Falls, New York, was an iconic event in this development. Homeowners discovered that their back yards, basements, and elementary school were built atop a leaking toxic chemical waste dump. Organizing for redress and relocation, the Love Canal Homeowners Association became a major force in the creation of the federal Superfund program for the remediation of toxic waste sites (Townsend 2001).

Love Canal residents, realistically enough, attributed the reproductive problems, cancers, and other diseases that they experienced to their exposure to toxic wastes, though they were to learn through bitter experience how difficult it can be to demonstrate cause and effect in epidemiologically acceptable terms. The population exposed at most Superfund sites is small, appropriate control groups are difficult to establish, the possibly related diseases are relatively rare, and the toxic exposures involve mixtures of chemicals of mostly unknown amounts and durations. Thus the illnesses attributed to toxic exposure at any given site are highly contested, even though the effects produced by particular toxic substances in the laboratory or workplace may be well documented (Packard et al. 2004; Brown 2007). Even more highly contested exposures are those associated with radioactivity (Johnston 2007).

One remedy for the statistical challenge of studying the effect of environmental exposures was offered by physical anthropologists. They used birth weight and growth as more accessible indicators of harmful exposures at Superfund sites. This strategy is effective because everyone born into the exposed population has a birth weight while only a few may develop a particular cancer many years later (Schell 1997).

Medical anthropologists were slower to be attracted to research at Superfund sites than sociologists and journalists. Paradoxically, sociologists researching toxic waste sites behaved much like anthropologists would have, engaging in participant observation in neighborhoods and grassroots organizations. Anthropologists did engage in disaster research, studying for example the technological disasters of Chernobyl in the Soviet Union and Bhopal in India, both of them sudden lethal events, the explosion of a nuclear power plant and a chemical factory. Both events had wider health effects in chronic disease that continued to unfold slowly (Petrayna 2002; Rajan 2002).

Within anthropology, significant research related to industrial toxic exposures is now underway. The work of Larry Schell and his colleagues among the Akwesasne Mohawk is exemplary in this regard. The Akwesasne reserve is adjacent to federal and New York State General Motors and ALCOA Superfund sites. Consuming fish, wildlife, and breast milk exposed people to polychlorinated biphenols (PCBs) and other toxic substances. Studies of Mohawk youth have shown effects of low levels of exposure to PCBs on growth and development, in part occurring through effects on thyroid hormones (Schell et al. 2002, 2007).

The exposure to toxic substances has become an international problem. Daniel Renfrew made a recent epidemic of pediatric lead poisoning in Uruguay the subject of his doctoral research in anthropology (Renfrew 2009). Alexa S. Dietrich (2007, 2009) similarly studied the health effects of air and water pollution in a Puerto Rican center of pharmaceutical manufacturing. These and other recent studies exemplify the growth, in this decade, of a critical environmental anthropology of health.

ENVIRONMENTAL ANTHROPOLOGY AND HEALTH

A series of developments outside of the discipline of anthropology during the 1990s energized a new wave of environmental interest among medical anthropologists at the beginning of the 21st century. The first development was the emergence of the term "biodiversity," first used in a book title in 1988 (Wilson 1988). The new term helped to focus concern about the accelerating loss of species due to human-initiated changes in their habitats. The United Nations Conference on Environment and Development (UNCED, also referred to as the Rio Earth Summit), which was held in Brazil in June 1992, became the occasion for intense media coverage of threats to biodiversity.

The second development was the introduction of the concept of "emerging infectious diseases." The term was coined by Rockefeller University microbiologist Joshua Lederberg (Lederberg et al. 1992). It was highlighted in a 1989 conference on emerging viruses, then in edited scientific volumes, and soon entered popular use in such works as *The Coming Plague* (Garrett 1994) and *The Hot Zone* (Preston 1994).

The third development was the increasing recognition of the seriousness of global climate change, crystallized around the 1997 Kyoto conference. The United States and Australia were laggards in ratifying the Kyoto Protocol, but popular consciousness was finally aroused by the Al Gore's slide shows, film, and book, *An Inconvenient Truth* (2006). Hurricanes in the United States, drought, and wildfires, to which Australian eucalyptus are especially vulnerable, underscored the potential for disaster that had perhaps not been conveyed adequately by the seemingly innocuous phrase "global warming."

All three of these lines of development suggested that anthropogenic change in the global environment was far more extensive than formerly thought. This meant that human-caused extinctions, the introduction of invasive species, changes in land use, toxic emissions, and production of greenhouse gases had now become substantial factors in human health and disease. These changes were now interacting with levels of economic inequality, both within and between countries, which had been rapidly increasing for several decades. By the beginning of the 21st century, the stage was set for a renaissance of interest in ecological approaches in medical anthropology, this time with a more sophisticated integration of the political economy of health.

Biodiversity and human health

Anthropologists were notably absent from the first high profile conference on biodiversity and health. The conference was held in March 1995 in Washington DC with the joint sponsorship of the National Institutes of Health, the National Science Foundation, Smithsonian Institution, National Association of Physicians for the Environment, and the Pan American Health Organization. Although it was a broadly multidisciplinary congress, and much of the material presented at it was concerned with ethnobotany and with the traditional knowledge of indigenous peoples, none of the participants are identified as anthropologists in the published work (Grifo and Rosenthal 1997). Indeed, the main organizer, though familiar with ethnobotany, claimed never to have heard of a field called medical anthropology (Grifo, 1997, personal communication).

The lineal descendant of the 1995 conference is the beautifully illustrated book *Sustaining Life: How Human Health depends on Biodiversity* (Chivian and Bernstein 2008), generously funded by foundations and corporations and sponsored by United Nations agencies. The conversation about biodiversity and health taking place among environmentally concerned physicians and biologists still lacks participant social scientists, despite the existence of highly relevant work in medical anthropology and geography.

The excluded anthropological perspectives are frequently critical of the dominant paradigm on biodiversity and health, as presented by environmentalist physicians and biologists. The dominant paradigm emphasizes the potential of "bio-prospecting" for the discovery of new pharmaceuticals to be used within Western medicine by those with access to that medical system. The dominant paradigm is especially concerned with threatened species in environmental hot spots such as tropical forests and coral reefs, biomes that are high priorities for conservationists. One anthropological critique of the dominant paradigm points out that the vast majority of plants used in traditional ethnomedicine are found not in pristine environments but in disturbed settings (Stepp and Moerman 2001).

Another anthropological critique points out that the indigenous people whose lands and plants are eyed as a target of bio-prospecting for new drugs generally lack access to biomedicine, even to basic immunizations, antibiotics, anti-malarials, in other words, *old* drugs that have long been available elsewhere. Janice Harper's field research shows how particular conservation efforts directed at protecting the lemurs of Madagascar, and primarily funded from sources in developed countries, have failed to protect the health of humans cruelly displaced from park lands (Harper 2002, 2005).

It is perhaps not surprising that such critical perspectives are not always welcome among advocates of the protection of biodiversity on behalf of biomedicine. Yet the field research of anthropologically trained ethnobotanists is widely appreciated. For example, the Hausa of Nigeria are the subjects of the long-term ethnobotanical work of Nina Etkin at the University of Hawaii. In her articles and in *Edible Medicines* (2006) Etkin emphasized the substantial overlap between the knowledge and traditional use of plants as foods and as medicines.

Perhaps the most focused and detailed work on a single set of health conditions and the associated medical ethnobotany used in treating them is the research of Elois Ann Berlin and Brent Berlin (1996) on Maya gastrointestinal disease. Analyzing the medical practices of the Tzeltal and Tzotzil of Highland Chiapas, the Berlins and their colleagues described a sophisticated naturalistic set of diagnostic categories based on differences of symptoms. Detailed ethnobotanical studies identified the plants, and combination of plants, used in treatment of these conditions, and preliminary pharmacological analysis suggested that these herbal medicines were likely to have been empirically effective.

Brent Berlin's doctoral student Glenn Shepard took medical ethnobotany to a new level by comparing the Matsigenka and Yora, two neighboring but linguistically unrelated indigenous societies in the rainforest of southeastern Peru. In his fieldwork, Shepard (2004) identified 740 combinations of a particular medicinal plant with a particular illness that were used in Matsigenka ethnomedicine and 538 in Yora. Despite a similar environment, the two medical systems had relatively little overlap in the species they used, though with more overlap in the alkaloid-rich plant families from which they select most of their herbal medicines. Plants are selected for their sensory qualities, especially odor, taste, and chemical and physical irritation. The terminology of sensory qualities is complex, and the two languages differ from each other and from English (or Spanish) in the way that they classify qualities such as bitter, salty, or pungent. The logic of efficacy underlying the two systems also sharply contrasts, the Yora being homeopathic (selecting plants with sensory qualities similar to the disease agent) and the Matsigenka, allopathic (selecting noxious, unpleasant plants seen as driving out the disease-causing entity). Studies like Shepard's underline the significance of what he terms *sensory ecology*, the complex biocultural process by which humans acquire information about their environment.

Emerging and re-emerging diseases

If physicians and ecologists were willing and able to discuss biodiversity and health without medical anthropologists at the table, they were equally willing to have such conversations about emerging diseases without anthropological insights. The most prominent exception was Paul Farmer, powerfully credentialed in both anthropology and medicine and widely known for his tireless work with AIDS and re-emergent tuberculosis in Haiti and Russia. Farmer publishes prolifically, not only in anthropology journals but in the medical journals, including the CDC (US Centers for Disease Control) journal *Emerging Infectious Diseases* (Farmer 1996).

The concept of "emerging disease" was coined only in the late 20th century, but the phenomenon of disease emergence was not new to anthropologists. Indeed the "old" disease of malaria was an emerging disease at the time of the transition to farming in

West Africa, as the Livingstone study had shown. Human biologists identified several other genetic adaptations to malaria. They included thalassemia, the Duffy blood group system, and G-6PD deficiency. In the wake of these discoveries in the 1950s and 1960s there was intense optimism that genetic adaptations to other diseases such as tuberculosis, schistosomiasis, and smallpox, would soon be identified. But this goal proved elusive in the decades that followed, as Joshua Lederberg wrote: "Outside the domain of malaria and the erythrocyte, the pickings for established polymorphisms in relation to human disease are rather thin" (1999:2).

With the development of genetic sequencing and the explosion of work in genomics, a whole new phase in the work on genetic adaptation to disease (and the role of genes in causing disease) is now under way.

Another emergent disease that engaged early medical anthropologists was kuru, a fatal neurological disease among the Fore of highland Papua New Guinea. The Fore attributed kuru to sorcery. Oral histories, kinship data, and other findings of ethnographic fieldwork in 1961 to 1963 by anthropologists Robert Glasse and Shirley Lindenbaum helped to reveal that the disease emerged about 1920 and might have been transmitted by ritual consumption of infected portions of the brains of deceased relatives (Lindenbaum 2008). After the abandonment of cannibalism in 1957, the incidence of kuru began to decline. Because the disease had a long period of incubation, new cases continued to appear for many years.

Once thought to be a virus, the kuru pathogen was later identified as a new disease entity, a prion. The complexities of kuru, like those of today's newly emerging diseases, could not have been elucidated without multidisciplinary fieldwork and laboratory research and the participation and cooperation of the Fore themselves. Research on kuru provided insights into other prion diseases, including variant Creutzfeldt–Jakob disease, popularly called "mad cow disease."

The most recent development in the history of kuru research is the discovery that heterozygotes for codons 127 and 129 of the human prion protein gene have resistance to kuru and other prion diseases. Researchers who tested survivors of the kuru epidemic suggest that kuru imposed strong balancing selection, and this may have happened more than once in human history (Mead et al. 2008, 2009).

Through their work in international public health, many applied anthropologists were already positioned to contribute effectively to the understanding of emerging infectious diseases in their region of research (Inhorn and Brown 1997). Mark Nichter's research in public health in south Asia led him to work on kyasanur forest disease, which had long been endemic in South India. The disease emerged in epidemic form only following the clearing of forests in a development project that brought workers into closer contact with the tick vectors of the arbovirus (Nichter 1987). Similarly, Barry Hewlett was able to put his African anthropological experience into practice as part of a World Health Organization team sent to contain an outbreak of Ebola hemorrhagic fever in Uganda (Hewlett and Hewlett 2008). Ted Green's work on AIDS in Africa was grounded in an ecological approach that takes indigenous disease concepts and indigenous practitioners seriously for their naturalistic, empirical effects (Green 1999). Plus Linda Whiteford even more explicitly identified her work in Latin America on dengue and cholera as medical ecology (Whiteford 1997; Coreil et al. 1997). Anthropologists working across several countries in Asia have now begun to engage the cultural, social, biological, and ecological contexts of avian flu and

SARS (Kleinman et al. 2008a, 2008b). Similarly, the emergence of a new variant of Influenza A H1N1 virus in 2009 drew critical anthropological attention to the relationships between pigs and people under the conditions of industrial hog farming.

Another aspect of infectious disease emergence that lends itself to an ecological approach is the growing problem of antibiotic and pesticide resistance. Medical anthropologists continue to investigate the interaction of cultural and biological systems that contribute to this global concern (Stephenson 1997; Orzech and Nichter 2008).

The shared feature of the emerging and re-emerging infectious diseases is that they arise from the major changes that human societies are making in the environment that we share with pathogens and vectors. Medical anthropologists specialize in understanding those changed relationships between biology and culture, while other disciplines specialize in studying the biology of the humans, the vectors, or the micro-organisms.

Climate change and health

Since 1993, a small group of physicians have regularly published articles and book chapters forecasting the likely public health risks of continued global warming. Notable among them are Anthony McMichael, Professor of Epidemiology at the London School of Hygiene and Tropical Medicine from 1994 to 2001, and since then at the National Centre for Epidemiology and Population Health at the Australian National University and Paul Epstein, at the Center for Health and the Global Environment at Harvard Medical School.

Several environmental anthropologists including Emilio Moran, Susan Stonich, and Bonnie McCay have taken prominent roles in multidisciplinary discussions of climate change. Although no medical anthropologist has attained similar celebrity as a public intellectual speaking about global climate change, many medical anthropologists through their teaching in the classroom and published texts have called attention to these health risks (McElroy and Townsend 1996:367; Townsend 2004; Baer and Singer 2009).

The strongest contribution of anthropology to the study of global climate change is likely to be its patient accumulation of hundreds of local level small-scale studies, both prehistoric and contemporary, of how human populations have adapted, or failed to adapt, to drastic changes in climate from melting polar ice to encroaching desert edge. Although each study seems a modest contribution by itself, the whole body of work enables significant comparison and understanding. Despite appropriate calls for "studying up" – that is, looking at powerful government and corporate decision makers – most anthropological fieldwork has dealt with relatively powerless and impoverished peoples, precisely those on the front lines of risk for damage from climate change.

Medical ecologists have long noted the *synergism* of stress, disease, and malnutrition, the interaction between them multiplying their impact on an individual organism or a population. This synergism is particularly obvious among young children living in poverty and in populations experiencing famine, the causes of which lie in the interaction of socio-political and biological systems with climate change (McElroy and Townsend 1979:169, 252–253).

Building on this earlier usage, the neologism *syndemics* has recently captured with particular resonance the core idea of the critical medical ecology of health. Introduced by Merrill Singer and his colleagues, it refers to "two or more diseases or health conditions acting in tandem and which can have greater health impact than the sum of their individual contributions" (Baer and Singer 2009:74; see also Singer 2009a, 2009b). By further coining the term *ecosyndemic*, they drew attention to the environmental changes that underlie inter-related patterns of poverty and vulnerability to social ills and disease.

CONCLUSION

In the past two decades, there has thus been a convergence among the approaches labeled biocultural anthropology, medical ecology, and critical medical anthropology. This has produced a critical environmental anthropology of health that is able to take into account the behavior of mosquitoes and worms as well as human actors from grocers, grandmothers, psychiatrists, bureaucrats, to the CEOs of pharmaceutical companies. James Greenberg and Thomas Park forecasted this development in their seminal essay inaugurating the *Journal of Political Ecology*. In it they said: "Political ecology does not amount to a new program for intellectual deforestation, rather it is a historical outgrowth of the central questions asked by the social sciences about the relations between human society, viewed in its bio-cultural complexity, and a significantly humanized nature" (Greenberg and Park 1994:1).

They went on to suggest that it would be most productive to regard the biocultural paradigm, medical ecology, and critical medical anthropology as "variant(s) within a common field of discourse," (1994:5). This prophecy is on its way to being fulfilled.

REFERENCES

Alland Jr, Alexander, 1970 Adaptation in Cultural Evolution: An Approach to Medical Anthropology. New York: Columbia University Press.
Alland Jr, Alexander, 1987 Looking Backward: An Autocritique. Medical Anthropology Quarterly 1:424–431.
Baer, Hans A., and Merrill Singer, 2009 Global Warming and the Political Ecology of Health : Emerging Crises and Systemic Solutions. Walnut Creek CA: Left Coast Press.
Berlin, Elois Ann, and Brent Berlin, 1996 Medical Ethnobiology of the Highland Maya of Chiapas, Mexico: The Gastrointestinal Diseases. Princeton NJ: Princeton University Press.
Brown, Phil, 2007 Toxic Exposures: Contested Illnesses and the Environmental Health Movement. New York: Columbia University Press.
Chivian, Eric, and Aaron Bernstein, 2008 Sustaining Life: How Human Health Depends on Biodiversity. New York: Oxford University Press.
Cochran, Gregory, and Henry Harpending, 2009 The 10,000 Year Explosion: How Civilization Accelerated Human Evolution. New York: Basic Books.
Cohen, Mark Nathan, 1989 Health and the Rise of Civilization. New Haven: Yale University Press.
Cohen, Mark Nathan, and George Armelagos, eds., 1984 Paleopathology at the Origins of Agriculture. Orlando: Academic Press.
Coreil, Jeannine, Linda M. Whiteford, and Diego Salazar, 1997 The Household Ecology of Dengue in the Dominican Republic. In The Anthropology of Infectious Disease: International Health Perspectives. M.C. Inhorn and P.J. Brown, eds. pp. 142–172. London: Routledge.

Dietrich, Alexa S., 2007 The Corporation Next Door: Pharmaceutical Companies in Community, Health, and the Environment in Puerto Rico. Ph.D. dissertation, Emory University.

Dietrich, Alexa S., 2009 Corrosion in the System: The Community Health By-Products of Pharmaceutical Production in Northern Puerto Rico. *In* Killer Commodities: Public Health and the Corporate Production of Harm, M. Singer and H. Baer, eds. pp. 335–366. Lanham MD: AltaMira Press.

Dunn, Frederick L., 1968 Epidemiological Factors: Health and Disease in Hunters and Gatherers. *In* Man the Hunter. R. B. Lee and I. DeVore, eds. pp. 221–228. Chicago: Aldine.

Eaton, S. Boyd, Marjorie Shostak, and Melvin Konner, 1988 The Paleolithic Prescription: A Program of Diet and Exercise and a Design for Living. New York: Harper & Row.

Etkin, Nina L., 2006 Edible Medicines: An Ethnopharmacology of Food. Tucson: University of Arizona Press.

Farmer, Paul, 1996 Social Inequalities and Emerging Infectious Diseases. Emerging Infectious Diseases 2(4):259–269.

Garrett, Laurie, 1994 The Coming Plague: Newly Emerging Diseases in a World out of Balance. New York: Farrar, Straus and Giroux.

Good, Charles M., 2000 Cultural and Medical Geography: Evolution, Convergence, and Innovation. *In* Cultural Encounters with the Environment: Enduring and Evolving Geographic Themes, A. B. Murphy and D. L. Johnson, eds. pp. 219–238. Lanham, MD: Rowman and Littlefield.

Gore, Al, 2006 An Inconvenient Truth: The Planetary Emergency of Global Warming and What We Can Do About It. Emmaus, PA: Rodale Press.

Green, Edward C., 1999 Indigenous Theories of Infectious Disease. Walnut Creek CA: AltaMira Press.

Greenberg, James B., and Thomas Park, 1994 Political Ecology. Journal of Political Ecology 1:1–12.

Grifo, Francesca, and Joshua Rosenthal, 1997 Biodiversity and Human Health. Washington: Island Press.

Harper, Janice, 2002 Endangered Species: Health, Illness, and Death among Madagascar's People of the Forest. Durham NC: Carolina Academic Press.

Harper, Janice, 2005 The Not-So Rosy Periwinkle: Political Dimensions of Medicinal Plant Research. Ethnobotany Research and Applications 3:295–308.

Hawks, John, Eric T. Wang, G. M. Cochran, Henry C. Harpending, and Robert K. Moyzis, 2007 Recent Acceleration of Human Adaptive Evolution. PNAS 104(52):20753–20758.

Hewlett, Barry S., and Bonnie L. Hewlett, 2008 Ebola, Culture, and Politics: The Anthropology of an Emerging Disease. Belmont CA: Thomson Wadsworth.

Inhorn, Marcia C., and Peter J. Brown, eds., 1997 Anthropology of Infectious Disease: International Health Perspectives. London: Routledge.

Jackson, Mark 2006 Allergy: The History of a Modern Malady. London: Reaktion Books.

Johnson, Thomas M., and Carolyn Sargent, eds., 1990 Medical Anthropology: Contemporary Theory and Method. New York: Praeger.

Johnston, Barbara Rose, ed., 2007 Half-lives and Half-truths: Confronting the Radioactive Legacy of the Cold War. Santa Fe NM: School for Advanced Research Press.

Kleinman, Arthur M., Barry R. Bloom, Anthony Saich, Katherine A. Mason, and Felicity Aulino, 2008a Asian Flus in Ethnographic and Political Context: A Biosocial Approach. Anthropology and Medicine 15(1):1–5.

Kleinman, Arthur M., Klein, Barry R. Bloom, Anthony Saich, Katherine A. Mason, and Felicity Aulino, 2008b Avian and Pandemic Influenza: A Biosocial Approach. The Journal of Infectious Diseases 197:S1–S3.

Landy, David, 1983 Medical Anthropology: A Critical Appraisal. *In* Advances in Medical Social Science. J. L. Ruffini, ed., vol. 1, pp. 185–314. New York: Gordon and Breach.

Lederberg, Joshua, 1999 JBS Haldane (1949) On Infectious Disease and Evolution. Genetics 153(1):1–3.

Lederberg, Joshua, R. E. Shope, and S. C. Oaks, 1992 Emerging Infections: Microbial Threats to Health in the United States. Washington DC: National Academy of Sciences.

Lee, Richard Borshay, 1979 The !Kung San: Men, Women, and Work in a Foraging Society. Cambridge UK: Cambridge University Press.

Lindenbaum, Shirley, 2008 Understanding Kuru: the Contribution of Anthropology and Medicine. Philosophical Transactions of the Royal Society: Biological Sciences 363: 3715–3720.

Little, Michael A., and George E. B. Morren, 1976 Ecology, Energetics, and Human Variability. Dubuque IA: W. C. Brown Company.

Livingstone, Frank B., 1958 Anthropological Implications of Sickle Cell Distribution in West Africa. American Anthropologist 60:533–562.

May, Jacques M., 1957 The Ecology of Human Disease. In Studies in Human Ecology. pp. 91–113. Washington: Anthropological Society of Washington and Organization of American States.

McCay, Bonnie J., 2008 An Intellectual History of Ecological Anthropology. In Against the Grain: The Vayda Tradition in Human Ecology and Ecological Anthropology. B. B. Walters, B. J. McCay, P. West, and S. Lees, eds. pp. 11–26. Lanham MD: AltaMira Press.

McElroy, Ann, and Patricia K. Townsend, 1979 Medical Anthropology in Ecological Perspective, 1st edition. North Scituate MA: Duxbury.

McElroy, Ann, and Patricia K. Townsend, 1996 Medical Anthropology in Ecological Perspective, 3rd edition. Boulder CO: Westview Press.

McElroy, Ann, and Patricia K. Townsend, 2009 Medical Anthropology in Ecological Perspective, 5th edition. Boulder CO: Westview Press.

Mead, Simon, Jerome Whitfield, Mark Poulter, Paresh Shah, James Uphill, Jonathan Beck, Tracy Campbell, Huda Al-Dujally, Holger Hummerich, Michael P. Alpers, and John Collinge, 2008 Genetic Susceptibility, Evolution, and the Kuru Epidemic. Philosophical Transactions of the Royal Society: Biological Sciences 363:3741–3746.

Mead, Simon, Jerome Whitfield, Mark Poulter, Paresh Shah, James Uphill, Tracy Campbell, Huda Al-Dujally, Holger Hammerich, Jonathan Beck, Charles A. Mein, Claudia Verzilli, John Whittaler, Michael P. Alpers, and John Collinge, 2009 A Novel Protective Prion Variant that Colocalizes with Kuru Exposure. New England Journal of Medicine 361:2056–2065.

Nash, Linda, 2006 Inescapable Ecologies: A History of Environment, Disease, and Knowledge. Berkeley: University of California Press.

Nichter, Mark, 1987 Kayasanur Forest Disease: An Ethnography of a Disease of Development. Medical Anthropology Quarterly 1:406–423.

Orzech, Kathryn M., and Mark Nichter, 2008 From Resilience to Resistance: Political Ecological Lessons from Antibiotic and Pesticide Resistance. Annual Review of Anthropology 37(1):267–282.

Packard, Randall M., Peter J. Brown, Ruth L. Berkelman, and Howard Frumkin, eds., 2004 Emerging Illnesses and Society: Negotiating the Public Health Agenda. Baltimore: Johns Hopkins University Press.

Pearce-Duvet, Jessica M. C., 2006 The Origin of Human Pathogens: Evaluating the Role of Agriculture and Domestic Animals in the Evolution of Human Disease. Biological Reviews of the Cambridge Philosophical Society 81:369–382.

Petryna, Adriana, 2002 Life Exposed: Biological Citizens after Chernobyl. Princeton: Princeton University Press.

Polgar, Steven, 1964 Evolution and the Ills of Mankind. In Horizons of Anthropology. S. Tax, ed. pp. 200–211. Chicago: Aldine Publishing Company.

Preston, Richard, 1994 The Hot Zone. New York: Random House.

Rajan, S. Ravi, 2002 Missing Expertise, Categorical Politics, and Chronic Disasters. In Catastrophe and Culture: The Anthropology of Disaster. S. M. Hoffman and A. Oliver-Smith, eds. pp. 237–259. Santa Fe NM: School of American Research Press.

Rappaport, Roy A., 1968 Pigs for the Ancestors: Ritual in the Ecology of a New Guinea People. New Haven CT: Yale University Press.

Renfrew, Daniel, 2009 In the Margins of Contamination: Lead Poisoning and the Production of Neoliberal Nature in Uruguay. Journal of Political Ecology 16:87–103.

Schell, Lawrence M., 1997 Using Patterns of Child Growth and Development to Assess Community-wide Effects of Low-level Exposure to Toxic Materials. Toxicology and Industrial Health 13(2/3):373–378.

Schell, Lawrence M., L. Hubicki, A. DiCaprio, M. V. Gallo, and the Akwesasne Task Force on the Environment, 2002 Polychlorinated Biphenyls and Thyroid Function in Adolescents of the Mohawk Nation at Akwesasne. In Human Growth from Conception to Maturity. G. Gilli, L. Benso, and L. Schell, eds. pp. 289–296. London: Smith-Gordon.

Schell, Lawrence M., J. Ravenscroft, M. V. Gallo, and M. Denham, 2007 Advancing Biocultural Models by Working with Communities: A Partnership Approach. American Journal of Human Biology 19(4):511–524.

Shepard, Glenn H., 2004 A Sensory Ecology of Illness and Therapy in Two Amazonian Societies. American Anthropologist 106(2):252–266.

Singer, Merrill, 2009a Ecosyndemics: Global Warming and the Coming Plagues of the 21st Century. In Plagues: Models and Metaphors in the Human 'Struggle' with Disease. D. Ann Herring and Alan C. Swedlund, eds. London: Berg.

Singer, Merrill, 2009b Introduction to Syndemics: A Systems Approach to Public and Community Health. San Francisco: Jossey-Bass.

Stephenson, Peter H., 1997 Environmental Health Perspectives on the Consequences of an Ideology of Control in "Natural" Systems. The Canadian Review of Sociology and Anthropology 34:349–367.

Stepp, John R., and Daniel E. Moerman, 2001 The Importance of Weeds in Ethnopharmacology. Journal of Ethnopharmacology 75:19–23.

Thomas, R. Brooke, 1997 Wandering toward the Edge of Adaptability: Adjustments of Andean People to Change. In Human Adaptability Past Present and Future. S.J. Ulijaszek and R. Huss-Ashmore, eds. pp. 183–232. New York: Oxford University Press.

Townsend, Patricia K., 1971 New Guinea Sago Gatherers: A Study of Demography in Relation to Subsistence. Ecology of Food and Nutrition 1(1):19–24.

Townsend, Patricia K., 1974 Sago Production in a New Guinea Economy. Human Ecology 2:217–236.

Townsend, Patricia K., 2001 Case Study One: Love Canal Superfund Site, Niagara Falls, New York. Society for Applied Anthropology. Electronic document. http://www.sfaa.net/eap/lovecanel.pdf/.

Townsend, Patricia K., 2004 Still Fiddling While the Globe Warms? Reviews in Anthropology 33(4):335–349.

Trevathan, Wenda R., E. O. Smith, and James J. McKenna, 2008 Evolutionary Medicine and Health: New Perspectives. New York: Oxford University Press.

Vayda, Andrew P., 2008 Causal Explanation as a Research Goal: A Pragmatic View. In Against the Grain: The Vayda Tradition in Human Ecology and Ecological Anthropology. B. B. Walters, B. J. McCay, P. West, and S. Lees, eds. pp. 317–367. Lanham, MD: Rowman & Littlefield.

Whiteford, Linda M., 1997 The Ethnoecology of Dengue Fever. Medical Anthropology Quarterly 11(2):203–223.

Wilson, E. O., ed., 1988 Biodiversity. Washington: National Academy Press.

Wolfe, Nathan D., Claire Panosian Dunavan, and Jared Diamond, 2007 Origins of Major Human Infectious Diseases. Nature 447(7142):279–283.

The Medical Anthropology of Water

*Linda M. Whiteford
and Cecilia Vindrola Padros*

"When the well's dry, we know the worth of water"

Benjamin Franklin 1900 [1746].

INTRODUCTION

Two hundred and sixty-two years ago Benjamin Franklin wrote the above aphorism in *Poor Richard's Almanac* as a way to suggest that too often there is a delay between when a crisis occurs and when the full extent of the loss is recognized. We believe that the global water crisis is well recognized, and yet, few effective and sustainable solutions have been found, nor have the consequences yet been fully recognized.

In 2002, 1.1 billion people or 17% of the global population, lacked access to improved water sources (WHO 2004). According to the UNDP, 700 million people located in 43 countries suffer from water stress, and by the year 2025 this figure may be as high as 3 billion people suffering from inadequate and unreliable access to water (2006:14). This scarcity will be unevenly distributed and will take on different connotations according to the location of each country. Even with public health and public relations campaigns to improve the provision of a clean and reliable water supply (i.e., the United Nation's International Decade for Action: Water for Life), access to potable drinking water is still difficult to achieve in many parts of the world like Asia, where approximately 675 million people consume water from inadequate sources (UNICEF et al., 2004 in Moe and Rheingans 2006:41).

In this chapter, we present a review of the medical anthropology of water by connecting the global water crisis and its health consequences with anthropological

A Companion to Medical Anthropology, First Edition. Edited by Merrill Singer
and Pamela I. Erickson.

research and analysis. The chapter includes discussions of water and disease (the bio-medical model), and anthropological social explanation models (social science episte-mology), that are exemplified with cases drawn from our own research. In our conclusion we describe where we hope that the next generation of medical anthro-pologists will take us in trying to resolve the water and health crisis.

Lack of access to potable water, combined with inadequate sanitation, causes or exacerbates significant, enduring and debilitating health problems (Whiteford 2005). According to the World Health Organization, 88% of all diarrheal disease is attributed to unsafe water supply, inadequate sanitation and hygiene, costing the lives of 1.8 million people every year (WHO 2004). Water-related illnesses, such as malaria kill 1.3 million each year, 90% of whom are children under 5 (WHO 2004). In many areas of the world where malaria is endemic, people are continuously infected, developing chronic anemia and experiencing episodes of acute symptoms (Wiley and Allen 2009). There are currently 50 million dengue infections worldwide every year (WHO 2008). Six million people are visually impaired by trachoma, another water-related infection. It can result in blindness after repeated infections and it is a disease implicated by the absence of safe water as people who do not have access to water for hand washing tend to become re-infected in areas where trachoma is endemic (WHO 2004). Another all too common and yet deadly water-borne illness is transmitted through *E. coli* bacteria. *E. coli* causes approximately 400 million diarrheal episodes in children under 5 with more than 700,000 needless deaths each year (Chakraborty et al. 2001; Ford 2006:61). While a considerable range of national and international measures have been employed to reduce rates of water-related morbidity and mortality, few have produced significant and sustained improvement in health outcomes. The Millennium Project, established by the United Nations in 2002 to stimulate government and global agencies to improve the quality of life, and to collect and maintain indicators by which to measure those changes, continues to document the failure to deliver a clean and reliable source of water to much of the world (Millennium Project 2006). Eight targets to reduce pov-erty and disease on a global scale were established as part of the Millennium Development Goals (MDGs) (Millennium Project 2006). In goal number seven, which focuses on ensuring environmental sustainability, water was identified as a critical global need (Millennium Project 2006). Through this goal, the Millennium Project aims to reduce the number of people without access to safe water and sanitation by 50% by the year 2015 (Montgomery and Elimelech 2007:18). Organizations like the United Nations Development Program (UNDP), the United Nations Children's Fund (UNICEF), the World Health Organization (WHO) and the World Bank concentrate on address-ing water shortage and scarcity, as well as the conflicts that arise as a consequence of the inadequate provision of clean water (Whiteford and Whiteford 2005:257). Local gov-ernments and non-governmental organizations also contribute in this endeavor by identifying how international programs can be adapted to suit local water and sanita-tion needs, in order to change the spread of disease (Whiteford and Whiteford 2005).

Anthropologists collaborated in many of these programs in different capacities and their research is instrumental in the study of the use, distribution, and sustainability of water systems. However, little research has explicitly focused on health measures as outcome matrices, thus failing to track the many ways that water leads to the increased spread of disease. In this chapter we will present some illustrations of how medical anthropology can contribute to the study of the complex and political relationships between water and health, and the need for improvement of the living conditions of those groups of people that are deprived of public services. Two examples are presented to suggest the value of anthropology to policy formation and program implementation, as well as to shed light on how anthropologists can shape policy by working both with those who create public policy, as well as with those whose lives are influenced by those policies. The chapter ends with our vision of some future directions medical anthropology research and practice could take to inform understandings of the global nexus between water and health, especially those changes that might direct new ways to prepare students engaged in the resolution of this global crisis. We argue for greater reliance on transdisciplinary training in the search for ways to resolve the water and health crisis, and we suggest that medical anthropologists can play a critical role in that process, particularly when they link their activities in research and teaching to the creation of effective policies.

THE ANTHROPOLOGY OF WATER

Anthropological interest in water dates back to early studies on the control of water in rural areas and the development of irrigation systems. When studying these topics, anthropologists looked at the political and social uses of water by analyzing the institutional requirements and social ties necessary to distribute water (Childe 1953; Coward 1979; Kelly 1983; Steward 1955; Wittfogel 1955, 1957). These mechanisms of water politics became the lens through which anthropologists studied social relations and power differentials (Davis-Salazar 2003, 2006; Fleuret 1985; Gelles 1990; Hunt 1988; Hunt and Hunt 1976; Lansing 1991; Lees 1986; Trawick 2001).

Contemporary studies have incorporated more complex models in order to explain the impact of power relationships on water access and use by looking at these issues from global perspectives (Treitler and Midgett 2007). Contemporary studies have focused on the conflicts over natural geophysical resources (Cortez Lara et al. 2005; Ennis-McMillan 1998, 2002; Guillet 2005; Whiteford and Quesada Aldana 2006; Whiteford and Melville 2002). Anthropologists have long been intrigued by how power imbalances present in these decisions affect the livelihood of local populations. Recently Barbara Rose Johnston (2005) documented the practice of creating "manufactured scarcity" where water is bottled and sold by large multinational corporations with little monetary returning to local peoples, while their water table drops.

Anthropology, because of its focus on the lived experience and the on-the-ground observations of intimate rituals of daily life, offers both methodological and theoretical frameworks particularly appropriate for an analysis of the current global water crisis. A study carried out in Ceceles, Ecuador, Boelens and Doornbos (2001) analyzed peasants' struggle over the right to water, finding that the struggle did not only take place at the level of the community, but also was shaped by larger frameworks where peasants negotiated the community's autonomy and authority. By using action research the authors were able to demonstrate that conflicts related to water are actually struggles over larger culturally and historically embedded decision-making processes (Boelens and Doornbos 2001).

In their 1998 volume, *Water, Culture, and Power: Local Struggles in a Global Context*, Donahue and Johnston analyzed the cultural constructions and power dimensions in the control of water by focusing on the cultural perceptions of water, and its use, its ownership and how those forces intersect with global discourses on development and sustainability. Their work ushered in a revitalized interest in the study of global intersections shaping access and distribution of water. The research of Derman and Ferguson (2003) also moved anthropological research on water forward with their references to the coexistence of multiple "values" of water in order to explain how actors used international, national, and local ideas about water and water access to situate themselves within Zimbabwe's water reform process.

Some authors have focused on the commoditization of water and the effects of this centralization of water management and distribution on the everyday lives of people. Aiyer (2007) for example, analyzed the Plachimada struggle against the Coca-Cola Company within the context of the agrarian crisis in India. In doing so, his study exposed the role of transnational corporations in the centralization of capital and water on a global scale, and the effects of these processes on specific groups of people (Aiyer 2007).

These authors embed their consideration of access to a clean and adequate water supply in a framework of universal human rights. As Derman and Ferguson (2003) indicated, the human rights perspective illuminates representations of water as a common good with contrasting valuations of water as an economic commodity, as a scarce resource, or as a productive utility. What is often missing from these diverse discussions is that despite promoting understanding of the universal need and right for water, many authors fail to make an explicit link between access to potable water and health outcomes (Whiteford and Cortez-Lara 2005).

A MEDICAL ANTHROPOLOGY PERSPECTIVE ON WATER AND HEALTH

We believe that two major threats to world stability are global health disparities, and unequal access to natural resources such as water. In a recent book, the lead author brought together two groups of anthropologists: one group whose primary research focused on water – its management, its distribution, and its allocation – and the policies that shape those practices, and the second group were anthropologists who studied health. The aim of the book was to open a discussion linking anthropological research on water with anthropological research on health, and to demonstrate how global water management directly affects the distribution of disease, and exacerbates disparities in health outcomes (Whiteford and Whiteford 2005). In that book, the authors underlined the ways in which globalization reshapes health and environmental policies, and identified the need to look at the interaction of culture, resources, and power as a more encompassing and global process than had previously (Whiteford and Whiteford 2005:255–256).

Some authors in the book applied a moral economy of health framework to contextualize water as an outcome measure, but also as a stimulus or impetus (Whiteford 2005). This perspective was used because "a moral economy of health framework makes explicit a set of values that honor the obligation to protect common global resources, identify the underlying social and political structures of violence against disenfranchised populations, and defend health as a human right to be protected in global trade and lending agreements" (Whiteford 2005:30). Additionally, it identifies

Table 10.1 Categories of water, sanitation, and hygiene-related diseases.

Category	Description/disease
Water-borne	Caused by the ingestion of water contaminated by human or animal excreta or urine containing pathogenic bacteria or viruses; includes cholera, typhoid, amoebic and bacillary dysentery, and other diarrheal diseases
Water-based	Caused by parasites found on intermediate organisms living in water; includes dracunculiasis, schistosomiasis, and some other helminths
Water-related	Caused by microorganisms with life cycles associated with insects that live or breed in water; includes dengue fever, lymphatic filariasis, malaria, onchoceriasis, and yellow fever
Excreta-related	Caused by direct or indirect contact with pathogens associated with excreta and/or vectors breeding in excreta; includes trachoma and most water-borne diseases
Water collection and storage	Caused by contamination that occurs during or after collection, often because of poorly designed, open containers and improper hygiene and handling
Toxin-related	Caused by toxic bacteria, such as cyanobacteria, which are linked to eutrophication of surface-water bodies; causes gastrointestinal and hepatic illnesses

By courtesy of the American Chemical Society from Montgomery, M. A., and Eimelech, M., 2007, Water and Sanitation in Developing Countries: Including Health in the Equation, *Environmental Science and Technology*, 41:16–24.

local and global frameworks that disenfranchise specific groups of people who then become more exposed to disease than others, and it sheds light on the social and political factors that reify and promote those disparities among groups and their health outcomes (Whiteford 2005:30).

Water is related to health and disease in several critical ways that are important to our discussion in this chapter, in particular we focus on several variables as shaping the global water and health crisis: the level of bacteria/environment pollution in drinking water, the reliability of the water supply, and the accessibility of the water: access, reliability, and portability (see Table 10.1). All human life is dependent on water, and yet we rarely explicitly study human–water beliefs and behaviors. But we do know that people become sick by pathogenic organisms in their water containing bacteria, viruses, protozoa, or helminthes. We know that people's habits and behaviors are shaped by how close or far away their source of water is from where they live; that people's cultural practices reflect how and for what they use water, and that people often fail to understand the multiple and often conflicting relationships between water and health. Water scarcity changes people's behaviors, including how often water is used, how water is stored, and from where water is collected. Water storage patterns (open receptacles, standing water) may increase breeding grounds for larvae, snails, worms and other disease vectors.

One of the first diseases to be traced to contaminated drinking water was cholera, a water-borne bacterial disease that causes debilitating and sometimes deadly, diarrhea (Wiley and Allen 2009:301). The provision of clean water and human waste containment

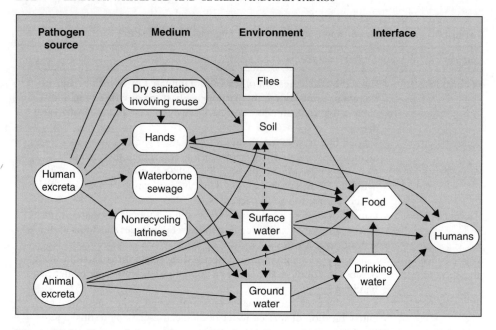

Figure 10.1   Transmission pathways of fecal-oral disease. By courtesy of The National Institute of Environmental Health Sciences and the authors from Pruss, A., Kay, D., Frewtrell, L., and Bartram, J., 2002, Estimating the Burden of Disease from Water, Sanitation, and Hygiene at a Global Level, *Environmental Health Perspectives*, **110**(5):537–542.

and removal reduces the incidence of cholera, as most outbreaks bloom in large populations of people relying on a contaminated water source, coupled with the failure to systematically separate waste water from drinking water (Wiley and Allen 2009; Yacoob and Whiteford 1994:332). Figure 10.1, for instance, indicates how disease is spread from sources of contamination like human and animal excreta to other humans.

Parasites can be transferred to humans as they come in contact with water contaminated with snails that have schistosomiasis or guinea worms (MacCormack 1985:15). People can become infected when bathing, swimming; washing clothing, or drinking contaminated water (Whiteford and Whiteford 2005:10). The spread of this disease is increased where there are bodies of still water, the lack of access to indoor plumbing, and the inability to separate waste water from the water used for consumption, bathing, irrigation of crops, and washing of clothes (Wiley and Allen 2009:306–307).

The spread of diseases like schistosomiasis, where the deposition of schistosome eggs by worms through small cuts in people's feet or hands where worms move into the blood vessels surrounding the bladder or intestines (WHO 2009), is acerbated by changing the environment in which the disease vector (the parasite) and human beings intersect. This may happen when dams to generate hydroelectricity or control water for irrigation are built by damming up rivers, creating still ponds of waters that become ideal breeding grounds for parasites in places where previously the water was free flowing and rapid, thus not ideal breeding areas (Holtz and Kachur 2004; Wiley and Allen 2009:304). The Three Gorges dams in China and the Aswan dam in Egypt tragically exemplify this expansion of disease affiliated with development.

The Aswan Dam was built on the Nile River in the 1960s in order to provide hydro-electricity. The dam allowed nearby farm workers to practice year-round irrigation instead of seasonal irrigation, increasing the amount of agricultural production (McElroy and Townsend 2004; Wiley and Allen 2009). However, the still waters of the dam represented an ideal breeding ground for schistosomiasis and the elimination of seasonal irrigation increased the exposure of the nearby villages to the parasite because there were no more dry seasons to keep the snail population low (McElroy and Townsend 2004:368). Humans continued to use the water thus becoming exposed to the snails carrying the parasites that previously did not live in the water.

The Three Gorges Dam in China represents another example of how the development of dams can cause severe transformation in the ecological landscape leading to the spread of parasitic diseases like schistosomiasis. The Three Gorges Dam was built on the Yangtze River to control flooding (Xu et al. 2000). The upper and lower areas of its reservoir are endemic areas for schistosomiasis and represent adequate breeding grounds for snails (Zheng et al. 2002). However, each area maintained a particular snail subspecies that could be infected by the parasite (Miller 2005). Since the dam was created, the transformations in water levels have changed the snail distributions where the snail subspecies that were in each area have mixed (Miller 2005; Zheng et al. 2002). As a result, higher rates of infection have been found because the parasite has more genetic diversity to choose from (Minter 2005).

Insect vectors also rely on water as a breeding ground as, for instance, when female mosquitoes deposit their larvae in water. Mosquitoes are implicated in the spread of several well known diseases such as dengue, malaria, West Nile virus, filariasis (disease characterized by the lodging of parasitic filarial worms in the lymphatic system which, in conjunction with bacterial infection, causes elephantiasis and genital damage) (WHO 2000), and yellow fever (Whiteford and Whiteford 2005:10). Community water deposits or those surrounding households can become important sources of disease propagation, just as agricultural practices that necessitate clearing large areas of land for farming and irrigation or the flooding of land for the cultivation of crops like rice, also contribute to the spread of these diseases, especially malaria (Holtz and Kachur 2004:138; McElroy and Townsend 2004:369). Current climate changes like global warming will also lead to the spread of diseases like malaria and dengue fever because they are able to survive in northern, more temperate regions where they were not found before (Mayer 2000:12).

Large scale agricultural projects or the construction of dams can also lead to the insertion or reinsertion of malaria through workers that can act as carriers (Holtz and Kachur 2004:138; Packard 1986). As Brown has indicated, the spread of malaria has been linked with seasonal migration and the generation of infrastructure such as roads that can act as enhancers of mobility (1997:132). The creation of dams can also generate transformations in agricultural production. In the case of Tanzania, the de Kalimawe Dam farmers removed cattle from the land closer to the dam in order to use it for agricultural purposes (Wiley and Allen 2009:304). However, this led to the spread of malaria as the mosquitoes that had fed previously on the cattle, now fed on humans (Wiley and Allen 2009:304).

Patterns of water-related diseases are shaped not only by changing the environment, but also by water scarcity, as families reduce the amount of hand washing, bathing, and use of soap or other disinfectants for the washing of fruits and vegetables

(Arar 1998:288; Whiteford and Whiteford 2005:9). It is difficult to fully comprehend our constant and pervasive dependence on water, particularly for those of us who live where we have easy and reliable access to clean water. Research suggests that limited access to a water supply leads individuals to obtain water from compromised sources like surface water, increasing the risk of contracting diarrheal diseases (Plate et al. 2004). Some research even suggests having a water supply available within reasonable distance is more important for good health than the quality of the water (Gorter et al. 1991). According to Gorter et al. (1991), cleanliness and reliability of the water supply may be less important to users, than the distance which they must travel to secure it.

Even when potable water is supplied, if the system is not locally sustainable, it often becomes "bowdlerized" and fails to protect the health of the users. In our research in highland Ecuador, for instance, we found community-based piped water systems in which the community was responsible for their maintenance. The community water council (junta) was in charge of collecting a "water fee" and the monies were to be used to purchase the disinfectant for the water tank that supplied the water for the community.

However, in poor rural communities, tax collection is an unpopular job that no community member wants. No one wants to ask his or her neighbors to pay from what little they have for disinfectant, especially when they cannot see what it was supposed to do. As long as the water continues to be piped into their homes, they saw no need to pay a tax for disinfectant. The result was that, indeed, the money was never collected, the disinfectant was not purchased and water, while still piped, was no longer clean (Whiteford 1997). As a result, the community was exposed to a variety of water-related diseases that could have been avoided.

Clearly, what people believe about water (and about health) is culturally created, but it is also shaped by global economic and political forces, as well as environmental factors. For these reasons, we believe that medical anthropology can significantly contribute to the better understanding of the complex interplay between water and health. We offer two brief cases from our own research to show how medical anthropology was used to identify the causes of the continued reemergence of water-related diseases. The continual re-infestation of cholera in rural highland Ecuador communities is our first example, and in the second case, we show how the analysis of culturally appropriate gender roles unlocked the question of why water tanks were left exposed to mosquitoes, resulting in increases in dengue fever in the urban Dominican Republic.

The Case of Cholera – A Water-borne Epidemic

One of the most devastating cholera epidemics to hit South America took place between 1991 and 1993 (Guthmann 1995). It began in Peru, causing over 9,000 deaths, and spread rapidly to Ecuador where it would affect different regions of the country, particularly the communities in the coast and Andean regions (Izurieta et al. 2000). The immediate response of the government and international health authorities was to control the outbreak in the urban areas of the country through campaigns promoting proper waste disposal and hand-washing. However, the rural, indigenous communities of the Andes did not receive these services and people continued to become infected (Whiteford, in press, 2008b).

During the period of 1994–1995, one of us (Whiteford) worked on a USAID, World Bank funded, bilateral cholera intervention project with an Ecuadorian epidemiologist/physician and a community educator in order to carry out research on why cholera persisted in two Andean provinces long after the epidemic was controlled in the urban centers. Together with the province of Imbabura, Chimborazo and Cotopaxi were among the poorest areas of the country; they had the largest concentration of indigenous people in Ecuador, and the highest rates of cholera at the time (Whiteford 2005).

As part of this project, Whiteford worked with a team from Ecuador to develop what came to be called the Community-Based Participatory Intervention (CPI) project. The project trained community members to identify adult behaviors that could lead to the spread of cholera. The interdisciplinary team was instrumental in creating ethnography of the communities that focused attention on the history and power relations within the affected communities, the training of the adult leadership teams in the communities, the collaborative assessment of re-infestation causes, and the design and implementation of a community-based intervention. Both epidemiology and medical anthropology shaped the project by focusing attention on collecting data on environmental and domestic health behaviors, and developing community-based interventions to change high-risk behaviors. Community education was also instrumental in developing reciprocal educational processes with local people, resulting in enhanced local leadership, improved community based knowledge about disease transmission, and the collaborative design of a locally appropriate and sustainable intervention (Whiteford et al. 1996).

The community-based investigation identified a series of behaviors associated with the continual re-emergence of the disease in the community. Those behaviors were: defecation in fields or areas close to living and eating activities, lack of potable water, the consumption of food prepared, sold, and consumed on the street, and close contact with family members who were labor migrants returning from coastal areas (where sporadic outbreaks of cholera existed). The research also showed that because water was difficult to obtain, many hygiene practices like hand-washing were severely reduced, or abandoned. Furthermore, much drinking water was transported in open air canals and had been contaminated by human, animal, and, in the case of one community, hospital waste.

In the 1990s, most Latin American countries adopted neoliberal economic reforms that resulted in many of the services previously provided by the central government, like provision of water, sanitation, and public health facilities, being transformed into responsibilities of the individual local communities or were placed in the hands of private enterprises (Armada et al. 2001; Assies 2003; Iriart et al. 2001; Lloyd-Sherlock 2004; Peabody 1996). This generalized privatization transformed access to water into a luxury that only a few rural communities could afford (Whiteford 2005). In addition, in Ecuador the harsh economic conditions experienced during this period were particularly severe in the rural areas of the country, leading to the loss of agricultural and other jobs. This caused significant financial difficulties in already poor communities as scarce employment disappeared. In these communities, the result was an increase in the number of men who migrated to the large coastal cities like Guayaquil or Esmeraldas in search of jobs. In coastal areas of Ecuador cholera is endemic; when men returned to their highland home communities for yearly festivals, they often returned carrying the cholera vibrio in them, which was shared as families and friends partook of common pot meals or street food where the vibrio could be easily transmitted.

The suggestions made by the CIP research team resulted in a series of changes, some small like the provision of convenient and hygienic containers to store and serve water, and some larger, changes like leadership training for women and students – two groups traditionally excluded from leadership in these communities. Large or small, these changes were associated with significantly and sustained drops in the rates of cholera in these communities. There were several key elements to the success of the CIP projects: the incorporation of the community in all aspects of the project, the slow pace of the project (12 months) and its follow-up assessment six months later, and the interdisciplinary composition of the team. The most important anthropological contributions that appeared to have had lasting effects were the detailed and personal observations of individual's behaviors over time, the documenting of people's everyday lives, and valuation of local beliefs and practices, the commitment to the local community, and the embedding of the analysis in an understanding of the local in the larger, global context. The clearly and repeatedly demonstrated effectiveness of these anthropological techniques and frameworks make the anthropological perspective crucial to research on the water and health crisis.

THE CASE OF DENGUE FEVER – A VECTOR-BORNE OUTBREAK

Our second example also emphasizes the role played by medical anthropology in shaping the research methods and framework in a project designed to change peoples' water handling practices to reduce the spread of dengue fever. From 1989 to 1990 a team of medical anthropologists (Coreil et al. 1997; Salazar 1993; Whiteford and Coreil 1991) carried out a nine month investigation in a neighborhood called Villa Francisca in Santo Domingo, the capital of the Dominican Republic (Whiteford 1997). The research used an ecological model to identify local beliefs about the causation and prevention of Dengue Fever. In anthropology, ecology is a framework where the relationship between human beings and their environment is seen as mutually reinforcing and studied as a dynamic and fluid process (Fowler 2000; Posey et al. 1984). While the primary objective of the project was to understand what was contributing to the high levels of dengue fever, the team was also interested in learning about local Dominican perceptions and linguistic categories of their biocultural environments, especially at the intersection between water handling and knowledge of disease transmission (Coreil et al. 1997). The project combined this ecological model with a historical and political analysis of the region in order to identify how residents of a particular neighborhood perceived and explained threats of infection of dengue fever. In addition, we wanted to know what public health measures were being taken to protect the population from dengue fever and other water related vector-borne diseases.

Dengue epidemics increased in Latin America and the Caribbean during the 1970s, and between 1980 and 1990 dengue spread rapidly due to the introduction of new virus strains and the presence of multiple serotypes (Gubler 1998:481). As Figure 10.2 shows, there are currently many countries at risk of dengue transmission. Dengue fever symptoms are similar to those of the flu, but longer lasting and they can be more severe. They include fever, severe headache, muscular and joint pain, and rashes

Aedes aegypti Distribution in the Americas

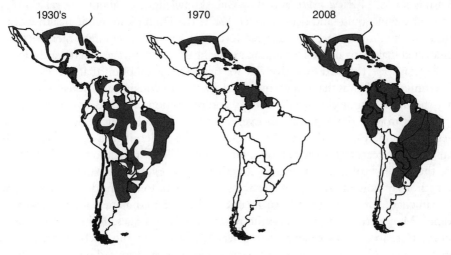

Adapted from Gubler, 1998

Figure 10.2 *Aedes egypti* distribution in the Americas. Adapted by courtesy of the American Society for Microbiology from Gubler, D. J., 1998, Dengue and Dengue Hemorrhagic Fever, *Clinical Microbiology Reviews*, 11(3):480–496.

(WHO 2008). In acute cases, people may be unable to get out of bed due to the severity of their bone pain. In addition, dengue hemorrhagic fever, a serotype spread by the *Aedes egypti* mosquito, can be deadly. Dengue viruses spread from human to human through the biting (blood meal) of infected female *Aedes* mosquitoes in which they pass the virus to humans (WHO 2008). Once the virus enters the human bloodstream, it circulates within the body from two to seven days and during this time other mosquitoes can acquire the virus while feeding on these infected people (WHO 2008).

In the case of the Dominican Republic, increases in the population, uncontrolled urbanization and the increased demand on resources, like land and water for the building of hotels for the burgeoning tourist industry, resulted in the creation of densely populated neighborhoods without piped water systems or latrines (Whiteford 1997; Yamashiro et al. 2004). Furthermore, since most of the water pumps in neighborhoods like Villa Francisca used electrical current, the frequent suspension of electricity equated with the frequent loss of water supply. As a consequence, most people relied heavily on the storage of water in various kinds and sizes of containers in anticipation of such outages. Small water containers were used for drinking and cooking, while water for other (non-drinking) household use was stored in 55 gallon drums outside the house. Those outside containers were rarely covered, and thus provided excellent breeding grounds for *Aedes aegypti*, the vector for dengue fever transmission.

The anthropologists found that the main cause for dengue transmission was not the failure of public health workers to communicate appropriate public health information. Community members in Villa Francisca employed a combination of ethnomedical and biomedical knowledge in order to explain the reproduction and transmission of *Aedes aegypti*, and they were knowledgeable about the relationships between the mosquito and dengue fever. While the Dominican public health workers effectively communicated how dengue fever was spread, community members were dissatisfied that many of the Dominican public health programs geared towards dengue prevention were targeted exclusively at women. The assumption that the Dominican government made was that since women used water for cooking and household chores, they should be responsible for the control and protection of the water storage devices.

Our anthropological research uncovered another variable that we believed contributed to the increase in dengue fever. Our analysis indentified a contradiction that explained the reasons for the failure of families in Villa Francisca to successfully translate the public health messages into effective behaviors. Our research indicated that even though women controlled the water containers found inside the house, men were in charge of the large and usually uncovered water containers found outside the homes. Men were not targeted by the public health messages, and therefore, lacked information about how clean standing water, like that in the uncovered 55 gallon tanks, provided breeding places for the mosquito that transmitted dengue. Failing to have that information, the men saw no reason to cover the tanks after their frequent use (Whiteford 1997). Had the team not employed an anthropological gendered analysis, the gender role differences in expectations and actions as they related to inside/outside might not have been noticed. Once noticed, an appropriate change in to whom the public health message were aimed could be made.

Our anthropological perspective included a political/historical analysis that allowed the team to understand why the Dominican public health campaign had failed. While the Dominican government and the Ministry of Health focused their activities on trying to generate neighborhood responses to common problems with mosquito control (and hence, dengue control), residents refused to accept the responsibility for removing mosquito breeding grounds. They argued that this should be the responsibility of the government (i.e., garbage removal), not the residents. Careful ethnographic and participatory research identified what the residents referred to as the "mala union" between the government and themselves. The people of Villa Francisca distrusted government programs and policies because in the past, the communities had not benefited from them. They saw health campaigns as empty political manipulations, used to win votes but once the election was over, nothing more. As a consequence, members of the neighborhood refused to participate in public health projects. People said they did not see the value of participating in the cleaning or covering of the water tanks when they did not have access to public services like running water, reliable electricity, sewers and drainage systems (Whiteford 1997). These results, generated by applying an anthropological framework and methodologies can be used to improve public health campaigns by understanding the historical context within which they occur.

ANTHROPOLOGY AND WATER POLICY

In this chapter we are describing medical anthropology as the quintessential tool, both methodological and theoretical, to understand the complex and often opaque relationship between the cultural habits of belief and practice, and the biological responses to disease transmission. This is equally true be they cultural practices that lead to the increased incidence of cholera in highland Ecuador, or the "inevitability" of suffering from "bonebreak fever" if one lives in Villa Francisca. We also believe that policy is critical to the application of anthropological research. However, the relationship between anthropology and policy has been neither inevitable nor lineal (Shore and Wright 1997; Whiteford 2008). On the contrary, it has been a complex relationship filled with tensions, failed attempts, and limited successes. Tensions produced when anthropologists interact with professionals from other disciplines, especially those in charge of making policy, because of contrasting theories, methods and even, vocabularies. As Robert Hackenberg noted, problems in the past arose due to the fact that "the donor groups, led by economists who were allied with the policy makers, sought refuge in the obscure macroeconomics of structural adjustment, while anthropologists, submerged beneath postmodern discourse, became equally unintelligible to outsiders" (2002:290). Collaboration cannot take place when each side maintains its own language and neither is willing to listen or adapt their approach.

In spite of these difficulties, there are currently many anthropologists working in different areas of the government and many of them have become decision and policy makers. As Castro and Singer (2004) pointed out, anthropologists have collaborated with policy makers and worked with policies in many different ways. The most common form of participation of anthropologists in policy making has consisted in the provision of research findings, and in some cases, the proposal of recommendations for the elaboration of policies (Singer and Castro 2004:xiii). Anthropologists have analyzed existing policies and searched for ways to make them more effective as well as looked at the effects policies have on peoples' everyday lives (Singer and Castro 2004; Wedel et al. 2005). In fewer cases, anthropologists have even become the policy makers.

There are, however, great opportunities for anthropologists interested in contributing to policy making and implementation (Fiske 2006, 2008; Wulff and Fiske 1987). In this section of the chapter we introduce some ideas about the relationship between anthropology and policy by asking two questions: what are some contributions anthropological research can make to policy, and secondly, what can anthropologists learn from looking at policies and working with policy makers?

Environmental policy, and particularly water policy, brings new challenges for anthropological involvement. First of all, it has a broad scope, varying from one location to another and crosscutting many different areas of public concern such as health, energy, food production, and the protection of ecological systems (Kraft 2001:13). Second, water policy, especially in the USA, has been linked with political decentralization and fragmentation where political actors at the federal, state, and local levels are all involved in the implementation of water policies (Smith 2009:132). Finally, decisions regarding environmental policy can have long-term and irreversible consequences on the climate, biological diversity, and amount of available resources, severely affecting the health of populations on a global scale (Kraft 2001:14; Vig and Kraft 2000).

However, as the examples presented earlier suggest, anthropological research and analysis can provide important contributions to the understanding of the consequences of the failure to provide something as supposedly simple as access of clean water. Much of anthropological research contextualizes analysis with history, embeds it in a discussion of power, and grounds it in cultural understandings. When it is done well, anthropological research makes the marginalized the center of focus, the invisible clearly identified, and moves from description to theory. Policy, we believe, is a way to insert practice into the movement toward theory because, while policy is theoretical, it is also translated into practice and becomes both observable and quantifiable. In our Dominican example, by identifying the invisible water handlers (men who were responsible for the outside water containers), there was an opportunity to shape policy to include men and their water-related roles and practices. The other policy lesson from the Dominican example is the culturally rational response of the Villa Franciscans to the "mala union" of failed promises, and the clarity of a demonstrated reciprocal relationship between the government and the stakeholders.

Contextualization allows anthropologists to identify the conditions in which policies, once they are designed, will operate. In the case of Ecuador, recommendations for policies to control the spread of cholera needed to be framed within the political and economic context of rural highland provinces like Chimborazo and Cotopaxi, and to take into consideration the effects of the neoliberal policies on the provision (and the lack thereof) of public services to already marginalized indigenous communities (Whiteford 2005).

Anthropological research can also look at the historical relationship between policies and specific groups identifying the reasons why policies might not be effective. In other words, it can look at the people for whom policies are directed, as well as the policy makers themselves. As Wedel et al. described: "from an anthropological perspective, what happens in the executive boardroom, the cabinet meeting, or the shareholders' annual general meeting is no less important than that which occurs at the level of the factory floor or locality" (2005:34). By analyzing who makes policies and how they make them, anthropologists show that policies are not neutral, but rather reflect and represent the concepts and ideas of the groups that have the power to make them (Shore and Wright 1997; Wedel et al. 2005). Anthropological research uses a variety of methodological tools that can provide information from a local as well as a global perspective (van Willigen 1984). This is particularly important when referring to water policy because as Vig and Kraft (2000) have indicated, natural resources go beyond country barriers making issues of water pollution or scarcity a global concern. The anthropological bifocal view can inform policy about local realities in the context of larger political arenas. Plus, in many cases, anthropology tries to bring individuals and their communities together to inform policy formation (Treitler and Midgett 2007:141). Ethnographic research is useful in this endeavor because it sheds light on the everyday lives of individuals: "Ethnography is a mode of knowing that privileges experience – often going into realms of the social that are not easily discernible within the more formal protocols used by many other disciplines" (Das and Poole 2004:14). When focused on the formation and institutionalization of policy, ethnography can point to the social relations created through policies, their adaptation to local contexts, and the contradictions that arise when differing interpretations of the same policies intersect (Castells 1996; Mosse 2006).

In other words, anthropological research highlights the local, nuanced, and fine-grained characteristics of social problems that are all too frequently lost in policies. Furthermore, by favoring the perspective of the people in the study, anthropology is more oriented toward increasing the participation of the targeted population in the research process, design of policies, and their actual implementation.

In our cholera example, the medical anthropological analysis identified how tradi-tional decision-making processes and rules of exclusion removed both women and young people from being able to affect water reforms because they were being excluded from access to power. By bringing women and young people into leadership roles in the research process, new avenues for water use and means to interrupt the disease transmission routes were made possible. The spread of cholera was then attacked at multiple levels: introduction of soap and chlorine, the storage of water in closed, spigotted containers, the reduction of consumption of street food, and an understanding of sources of reintroduction of the disease. Furthermore, by enhancing the active participation of all community members, many of those previously excluded groups assumed leadership roles promoting sanitation measures and the consumption of potable water inside their communities. They became advocates for the improve-ment of the living conditions of the region (Whiteford 1997).

CONCLUSION

This chapter was co-authored by a senior medical anthropologist (Whiteford), and a doctoral student in applied medical anthropology (Vindrola Padros). We have used our research and readings to shape this chapter, as they shape the questions we ask and our epistemologies. Plus, as we complete this chapter, we conclude with our vision of some possible future directions in the medical anthropology of water and health. The literature reviewed and fieldwork experiences described in this chapter suggest that if medical anthropologists are to be effective in providing viable solutions to the reduc-tion of diseases transmitted through and by water, they need to receive *transdiscipli-nary* training. By "transdisciplinary" we do not mean participating in teams composed of professionals from different academic disciplines (usually referred to as multidisci-plinary or interdisciplinary). We mean that medical anthropology training needs to include instruction not only in anthropology, but also in other areas such as engineer-ing, public health, medicine, and chemistry, among others.

In the fall of 2000, the Department of Anthropology at the University of South Florida moved in the direction of transdisciplinary training with the inauguration of its anthropology and public health dual degree program, allowing students to cross-train at both the M.A. and Ph.D. levels in applied anthropology and public health. This very effective program allows students to take either an M.A. or Ph.D. in applied anthropology and in one of eight research areas of public health: Environmental Health, Epidemiology, Global Communicable Disease, Healthcare Organizations and Management, Health Policy and Programs, Maternal and Child Health, Public Health Education, and Global Health.

In the spring of 2009, the USF moved into a new experiment in transdisciplinary education with the initiation of a graduate certificate program in *Water, Health, and Sustainability* jointly offered by the College of Arts and Sciences (Departments of Anthropology and Geography), College of Engineering (Departments of Civil and Environmental Engineering and Chemical Engineering), and the College of Public Health (Department of Global Health and Environmental and Occupational Health). This program is directed at graduate students interested in research on the nexus between water and health, and for public health professionals, anthropologists, humanitarian aid providers, engineers, and others interested in addressing health problems associated with inadequate and unclean water. The study program draws from collaborating departments and provides students with transdisciplinary education and training on topics such as the social and cultural dimensions of local and global health, the treatment, testing, and management of water supplies, the role of water as a sustainable resource, the role of water in health and disease, and the engineered environment of water and sanitation.

The certificate is designed to provide students with transdisciplinary training in medical anthropology, epidemiology, global information systems, civil, environmental, and chemical engineering, and geography. Already students are working on transdisciplinary projects such as how to design solar latrines in culturally appropriate and sustainable ways, investigating how cultural conceptions of water shape behavior and sanitation practices, researching how to raise the temperature on waste composting to levels sufficient to kill ascaris (round worm) in sustainable and culturally acceptable forms (focusing on local beliefs and uses of human excreta), experimenting with locally grown plants to extract a substance to filter out dangerous bacteria from water, and developing sustainable water systems for impoverished rural and poor urban areas of Latin America.

Both the authors of this chapter participated in the process of creating this graduate certificate program in *Water, Health and Sustainability* in different ways and capacities, one as a principal investigator and the other as a graduate student. However, our experiences are similar in that we both encountered the difficulties of transdisciplinary inquiry and dialogue, while at the same time as benefitting from its value. We believe that medical anthropology is a critical component to any research on water and health, but we also believe that the subject is so complex and so urgent that medical anthropology alone cannot reduce the number of what Paul Farmer calls "stupid deaths," deaths that need not to happen (Farmer 2003). To stop these stupid water-related deaths, we need to know much more that we can just from anthropology, public health or engineering alone. We conclude this chapter with two brief stories about our "transdisciplinary experiences."

My story (Whiteford)

While I knew that transdisciplinary teaching and research could be immensely productive, I also knew from experience that it often is equally challenging. Even with that knowledge I was constantly surprised by what I, even as the senior anthropologist on the team, failed to anticipate. As this story shows, my experience in our transdisciplinary seminar – as with any fieldwork – was humbling as well as exciting. As we began our water, health and sustainability cross-college seminar, we anticipated paradigmatic, methodological, and terminological barriers. We counted on our common passion and commitment to the subject to help us work through these obstacles. We set up a seminar for members of the group to present reviews of discipline-specific articles that we felt were important for members of the seminar to be exposed to. In part, we wanted to establish some grounding in the "sea" of unknown vocabularies, models, and methods, and even a sense of what was really important to share. The first presentation was on semipermeable membranes and their relative width, densities and chemical compositions and their ability to filter particular wastes. Another presentation focused on the various ways to increase temperature using solar capabilities to a level to kill ascaris parasites and the relative importance of pH, temperature, moisture, biogas digesters, and other things unintelligible to many medical anthropologists.

The anthropology group presentation was focused on participatory research (PAR) methods which we felt was important for our transdisciplinary colleagues to share. The presentation went well. The anthropologists provided great detail on what PAR was, why it was important, and how it was conducted. At the end of the presentation, we offered an anthropological example of how PAR was used to develop community-based support for a water system. When the presentation was over, there was silence in the seminar room. The engineering and public health students and faculty had listened, but the presentation had not generated any discussion or questions. Then one of the engineering faculty raised her hand and asked what kind of water system had been put in, was it a pump, tank, in-ground, gravity based, and was the source a generator, battery, or hand turned? None of the anthropologists knew the answer. These were clearly crucial technical questions, and the anthropologists had not even thought of them. Nor were they addressed in the article.

Her questions focused on the technical response of the project and were central to understanding the case. None of us could answer them. This moment provided an unforgettable example that what different partners in the seminar thought was important to ask, and how different our responses were. Clearly, our narrow disciplinary expertise blinded many of us to a whole array of questions. The seminar in transdisciplinary research once again showed us not only the value of understanding multiple approaches to common problems, but also the hidden obstacles to their resolution. Clearly, expanding our realm of what we considered information was important for all of us.

My story (Vindrola Padros)

During my first semester at USF, Linda invited me to participate in the water, health, and sustainability cross-college seminar. In one of our meetings, a representative from a group of engineering students ("Engineers without Borders") was asked to come in and make a presentation on a project they were designing to provide water to a small community. The representative indicated that they needed collaboration from students and faculty from disciplines outside of engineering, especially anthropologists. I became interested in the project and attended one of their meetings. It was surprising to me how the group had already decided which water system to install in the community without having visited it for an extended period of time and without carrying out an in site investigation of what the community members wanted. I expressed this concern indicating many other things that I thought needed to be taken into consideration like power relationships, gender roles, and government policies. The group of engineers listened patiently to my arguments; however, to them the water system appeared to operate separately from the things I mentioned. I knew this was not the case, but since I had no idea about the operating mechanisms of the water system I could not provide them with specific examples on how the installation and maintenance of the system would be affected if the community did not participate actively in the decision-making process. I did not understand their language and I could not translate my anthropological language into terms they could understand.

As a result, I failed to demonstrate the value of adding an anthropological perspective to the project and some of my proposals were dismissed because they appeared too complex to be carried out in the short time available for the implementation of the water system. Even though in the following meetings our communication improved, the group incorporated social research methodology, and received some suggestions from professors in the Anthropology Department, that experience made me think of the many things that were failed to communicate in attempting to translate concepts to a methodological/technical language I did not understand.

Last words

Medical anthropologists have called our attention to the need to look at the relationship between water and health, and to propose viable solutions to interrupt the spread of infectious diseases. In this chapter we suggest that the relationship between anthropology, water, and policy will represent a valuable factor in this process. Furthermore, anthropologists who have received transdisciplinary training will be well-equipped to participate in the design and implementation of policies and programs that look at the relationship between water and health from multiple perspectives. As we concluded this chapter we offered our own experiences in one new way to approach the remediation of the water and health crisis. We know that there are many other forms and perspectives critical to this discussion, and we look forward to improved health as clean water becomes more equitably distributed across the globe. We believe that there are many lessons to be learned from the medical anthropology of water, as well as from our transdisciplinary partners.

REFERENCES

Aiyer, Ananthakrishnan, 2007 The Allure of the Transnational: Notes on Some Aspects of the Political Economy of Water in India. Cultural Anthropology 22(4):640–658.

Arar, Nedal Hamdi, 1998 Cultural Responses to Water Shortage among Palestinians in Jordan: The Water Crisis and Its Impact on Child Health. Human Organization 57(3): 284–291.

Armada, Francisco, Charles Muntaner, and Vicente Navarro, 2001 Health and Social Security Reforms in Latina America: The Convergence of the World Health Organization, the World Bank, and Transnational Corporations. International Journal of Health Services 31(4):729–768.

Assies, Willem, 2003 David versus Goliath in Cochabamba: Water Rights, Neoliberalism, and the Revival of Social Protest in Bolivia. Latin American Perspectives 30(3):14–36.

Boelens, Rutgerd, and Bernita Doornbos, 2001 The Battlefield of Water Rights: Rule Making Amidst Conflicting Normative Frameworks in the Ecuadorian Highlands. Human Organization 60(4):343–355.

Brown, Peter, 1997 Culture and the Global Resurgence of Malaria: International Health Perspectives. In The Anthropology of Infectious Disease. Marcia Inhorn and Peter Brown, eds. pp. 119–141. London and New York: Routledge.

Castells, M., 1996 The Rise of Network Society. Oxford: Blackwell.

Castro, A. and Merrill Singer, eds., 2004 Unhealthy Health Policy: A Critical Anthropological Examination. Lanham MD: AltaMira Press.

Chakraborty, S., J. S. Deokule, P. Garg, S. K. Bhattacharya, R. K. Nandy, G. B. Nair, S. Yamasaki, Y. Takeda, and T.Ramamurthy, 2001 Concomitant Infection of Enterotoxigenic Escherichia coli in an Outbreak of Cholera Caused by Vibrio cholera 01 and 0139 in Ahmedabad, India. Journal of Clinical Microbiology 39:3241–3246.

Childe. V. G., 1953 New Light on the Most Ancient Near East. New York: Praeger.

Coreil, Jeannine, Linda Whiteford, and Diego Salazar, 1997 The Household Ecology of Disease Transmission: Dengue Fever in the Dominican Republic. *In* The Anthropology of Infectious Disease: International Health Perspectives. Marcia Claire Inhorn and Peter J. Brown, eds. pp. 145–171. London and New York: Routledge.

Cortez Lara, Alfonso, Scott Whiteford, and Manuel Chavez Marquez, eds., 2005 Seguridad, Agua y Desarrollo: El Futuro de la Frontera México-Estados Unidos. Tijuana, Spain: Colegio de la Frontera Norte.

Coward, E. Walter, Jr, 1979 Principles of Social Organization in an Indigenous Irrigation System. Human Organization 38:28–36.

Das, Veena, and Deborah Poole, 2004 State and Its Margins: Comparative Ethnographies. *In* Anthropology in the Margins of the State. Veena Das and Deborah Poole, eds. pp. 3–33. Santa Fe NM: School of American Research Press.

Davis-Salazar, Karla, 2003 Late Classic Maya Water Management and Community Organization at Copan, Honduras. Latin American Antiquity 14(3):275–299.

Davis-Salazar, Karla, 2006 Late Classic Maya Drainage and Flood Control at Copan, Honduras. Ancient Mesoamerica 17:125–138.

Derman, Bill, and Anne Ferguson, 2003 Value of Water: Political Ecology and Water Reform in Southern Africa. Human Organization 62(3):277–288.

Donahue, John, and Barbara Rose Johnston, eds., 1998 Water, Culture, and Power: Local Struggles in a Global Context. Washington: Island Press.

Ennis-McMillan, Michael C., 1998 Drinking Water Politics in Rural Mexico: Negotiating Power, Justice, and Social Suffering. Ph.D. dissertation, Michigan State University Department of Anthropology.

Ennis-McMillan, Michael C., 2002 A Paradoxical Privatization: Challenges to Community-Managed Drinking Water Systems in the Valley of Mexico. *In* Protecting a Sacred Gift: Water and Social Change in Mexico. Scott Whiteford and Roberto Melville, eds. Boulder CO: Lynne Rienner Publishers.

Farmer, Paul, 2003 Pathologies of Power: Health, Human Rights, and the New War on the Poor. Berkeley: University of California Press.

Fiske, Shirley, 2006 Anthropology in Pursuit of Public Policy and Practical Knowledge. National Association for the Practice of Anthropology (NAPA) Bulletin 26:82–107.

Fiske, Shirley, 2008 Working for the Federal Government: Anthropology Careers. National Association for the Practice of Anthropology (NAPA) Bulletin 29(1):110–130.

Fleuret, Patrick, 1985 The Social Organization of Water Control in the Taita Hills, Kenya. American Ethnologist 12(1):103–118.

Ford, Tim, 2006 Emerging Issues in Water and Health Research. Journal of Water and Health 4(Supplement 1):59–65.

Fowler, Catherine, 2000 Ethnoecology: An Introduction. *In* Ethnobotany: A Reader. Paul E. Minnis, ed. pp. 13–16. Oklahoma: University of Oklahoma Press.

Franklin, Benjamin, 1900 [1746] Poor Richard's Almanac. New York: Caldwell.

Gelles, Paul H., 1990 Channels of Power, Fields of Contention: The Politics and Ideology of Irrigation in an Andean Peasant Community. Ph.D. dissertation, Harvard University, University Microfilms, Ann Arbor, MN.

Gorter, A., Sandford, P., Davey Smith, G. and Pauw, J., 1991 Water Supply and Sanitation and Diarrhoeal Disease in Nicaragua: Results from a Case Control Study. International Journal of Epidemiology 20(2):527–533.

Gubler, Duane J., 1998 Dengue and Dengue Hemorrhagic Fever. Clinical Microbiology Reviews 11(3):480–496.

Guillet, David, 2005 Water Management Reforms, Farmer-Managed Irrigation Systems, and Food Security: The Spanish Experience. *In* Globalization, Water, and Health: Resource

Management in Times of Scarcity. Linda Whiteford and Scott Whiteford, eds. pp. 185–208. Santa Fe NM: School of American Research Press.

Guthmann, J., 1995 Epidemic Cholera in Latin America: Spread and Routes of Transmission. Journal of Tropical Medicine and Hygiene 98(6):419–427.

Hackenberg, Robert A., 2002 Closing the Gap between Anthropology and Public Policy: The Route Through Cultural Heritage Development. *Human Organization* 61(3):288–298.

Holtz, Timothy, and Patrick Kachur, 2004 The Reglobalization of Malaria. *In* Sickness and Wealth: the Corporate Assault on Global Health, Meredith Fort, Mary Ann Mercer, and Oscar Gish, eds. pp. 131-–143. Cambridge MA: South End Press.

Hunt, Robert C., 1988 Size and the Structure of Authority in Canal Irrigation Systems. Journal of Anthropological Research 44:335–355.

Hunt, Robert C., and Eva Hunt, 1976 Canal Irrigation and Local Social Organization. Current Anthropology 17:389–410.

International Water Management Institute, 2002 Water – A Scarce Resource? Electronic Document. http://www.lk.iwmi.org/Press/press4.htm#Water-%20A%20Scarce%20Resource?/.

Iriart, Celia, Emerson Elias Merhy, and Howard Waitzkin, 2001 Managed Care in Latin America: The New Common Sense in Health Policy Reform. Social Science and Medicine 52(8):1243–1253.

Izurieta, Ricardo, Tatiana Ochoa, Alberto Narváez, José Racines, Arturo Castro, Verónica Villegas, and José Álvarez, 2000 Cólera en los Andes Ecuatorianos: Factores Ambientales y Etnoculturales de su Transmisión. Electronic document. http://ris.bvsalud.org/finals/ECU-1367.pdf/.

Johnston, Barbara Rose, 2005 The Commodification of Water and the Human Dimensions of Water and the Human Dimensions of Manufactured Scarcity. *In* Globalization, Water, and Health: Resource Management in Times of Scarcity. Linda Whiteford and Scott Whiteford, eds. pp. 133–152. Santa Fe NM: School of American Research Press.

Kelly, William W., 1983 Concepts in the Anthropological Study of Irrigation. American Anthropologist 85(4):880–886.

Kraft, Michael E., 2001 Environmental Policy and Politics. New York: Longman.

Lansing, J. Stephen, 1991 Priests and Programmers: Technologies of Power in the Engineered Landscape of Bali. Princeton NJ: Princeton University Press.

Lees, Susan H., 1986 Coping with Bureaucracy: Survival Strategies in Irrigated Agriculture. American Anthropologist 88(3):610–622.

Lloyd-Sherlock, Peter, 2004 Health Sector Reform in Argentina: A Cautionary Tale. Social Science and Medicine 60:1893–1903.

Mayer, Jonathan, 2000 Geography, Ecology and Emerging Infectious Diseases. Social Science *and* Medicine 50:937–952.

MacCormack, Carol, 1985 Anthropology and the Control of Tropical Disease. Anthropology Today 1(3):14–16.

McElroy, Ann, and Patricia Townsend, 2004 Medical Anthropology in Ecological Perspective. Cambridge MA: Westview Press.

Millennium Project, 2006 UN Millennium Project. Electronic document, http://www.unmillenniumproject.org/.

Minter, Adam, 2005 Breeding Snail Fever. Scientific American 293(1):21–22.

Moe, Christine L., and Richard Rheingans, 2006 Global Challenges in Water, Sanitation and Health. Journal of Water and Health 4:41–57.

Montgomery, Maggie A., and Menachem Eimelech, 2007 Water and Sanitation in Developing Countries: Including Health in the Equation. Environmental Science and Technology 41:16–24.

Mosse, David, 2006 Anti-social Anthropology? Objectivity, Objcetion, and the Ethnography of Public Policy and Professional Communities. Journal of the Royal Anthropological Institute 12:935–956.

Packard, Randall M., 1986 Agricultural Development, Migrant Labor and the Resurgence of Malaria in Swaziland. Social Science and Medicine 22(8):861–867.

Peabody, John W., 1996 Economic Reform and Health Sector Policy: Lessons from Structural Adjustment Programs. Social Science and Medicine 43(5):823–835.

Plate, David, Beverly Strassman, and Mark Wilson, 2004 Water Sources are Associated with Childhood Diarrhoea Prevalence in Rural East-Central Mali. Tropical Medicine and International Health 9(3):416–425.

Posey, Darrell, John Frenchione, John Eddins, Luiz Francelino Da Silva, Debbie Myers, Diane Case, and Peter Macbeath, 1984 Ethnoecology as Applied Anthropology in Amazonian Development. Human Organization 43(2):95–107.

Pruss, Annette, David Kay, Lorna Fewtrell, and Jamie Bartram, 2002 Estimating the Burden of Disease from Water, Sanitation, and Hygiene at a Global Level. Environmental Health Perspectives 110(5):537–542.

Salazar, Diego, 1993 Folk Models and Household Ecology of Dengue Fever in an Urban Community of the Dominican Republic. Ph.D. dissertation, University of South Florida.

Shore, Cris, and Susan Wright, 1997 Anthropology of Public Policy: Critical Perspectives on Governance and Power. London: Routledge.

Singer, Merrill, and Arachu Castro, 2004 Introduction: Anthropology and Health Policy: A Critical Perspective. In Unhealthy Health Policy: A Critical Anthropological Examination. Arachu Castro and Merrill Singer, eds. pp. xi–xix. Lanham MD: AltaMira Press.

Smith, Zachary A., 2009 The Environmental Policy Paradox. Upper Saddle River NJ: Pearson Prentice Hall.

Steward, Julian, ed., 1955 Irrigation Systems: A Comparative Study. Washington; Pan American Union Social Science Monographs.

Trawick, Paul, 2001 The Moral Economy of Water: Equity and Antiquity in the Andean Commons. American Anthropologist 103(2):361–379.

Treitler, Inga, and Douglas Midgett, 2007 It's About Water: Anthropological Perspectives on Water and Policy. Human Organization 66(2):140–149.

United Nations Development Program (UNDP), 2006 Human Development Report. New York: United Nations Development Program.

van Willigen, John, 1984 Truth and Effectiveness: An Essay on the Relationships between Information, Policy and Action in Applied Anthropology. Human Organization 43(3):277–282.

Vig, Norman, and Michael Kraft, eds., 2000 Environmental Policy: New Directions for the Twenty-First Century. Washington: A Division of Congressional Quarterly, Incorporated.

Wedel, Janine, Cris Shore, Gregory Feldman, and Stacy Lathrop, 2005 Toward an Anthropology of Public Policy. Annals of the American Academy of Political and Social Science 600:30–51.

Whiteford, Linda, 1992 Contemporary Health Care and the Colonial and Neo-Colonial Experience: The Case of the Dominican Republic. Social Science and Medicine 35(10): 1215–1223.

Whiteford, Linda, 1997 The Ethnoecology of Dengue Fever. Medical Anthropology Quarterly 11(2):202–223.

Whiteford, Linda, 2005 Casualties in the Globalization of Water: a Moral Economy of Health Perspective. In Globalization, Water, and Health: Resource Management in Times of Scarcity, Linda Whiteford and Scott Whiteford, eds. pp. 25–44 Santa Fe NM: School of American Research Press.

Whiteford, Linda, 2008 The Political Economy of Policy: The Dengue Complex. Keynote paper presentation at the International Conference on Dengue Fever, Phuket, Thailand, October 15–17.

Whiteford, Linda, 2009 Approaches to Policy and Advocacy. In Social and Behavioral Foundations of Public Health. Second edition. Jeannine Coreil, ed., pp 311–322 Thousand Oaks CA: Sage Publications.

Whiteford, Scott, and Sergio Quesada Aldana, 2006 La Ecologia Politica en la Cultura del Agua en Queretaro. Queretaro Spain: Universidad Autonoma de Queretaro.

Whiteford, Linda, and Jeannine Coreil, 1991 Household Ecology of Aedes aegypti Control in the Dominican Republic. Unpublished project report.

Whiteford, Scott, and Antonio Cortez-Lara, 2005 Good to the Last Drop: the Political Ecology of Water and Health on the Border. *In* Globalization, Water, and Health: Resource Management in Times of Scarcity. Linda Whiteford and Scott Whiteford, eds. pp. 231–254. Santa Fe NM: School of American Research Press.

Whiteford, Scott and Roberto Melville, eds., 2002 Protecting a Sacred Gift: Water and Social Change in Mexico. Boulder CO: Lynne Rienner Publishers.

Whiteford, Linda, and Scott Whiteford, 2005 Paradigm Change. *In* Globalization, Water, and Health: Resource Management in Times of Scarcity. Linda Whiteford and Scott Whiteford, eds. pp. 3–15. Santa Fe NM: School of American Research Press.

Whiteford, Linda, C. Laspina, and M. Torres, 1996 Cholera Prevention in Ecuador: Community-Based Approaches for Behavior Change. Activity Report No. 19. Arlington VA: Environmental Health Project.

Wiley, Andrea S., and John S. Allen, 2009 Medical Anthropology: a Biocultural Approach. New York: Oxford University Press.

Wittfogel, Karl, 1955 Development Aspects of Hydraulic Civilization. *In* Irrigation Systems: A Comparative Study. Julian Steward, ed. Washington: Pan American Union Social Science Monographs.

Wittfogel, Karl, 1957 *Oriental Despotism: A Comparative Study of Total Power.* New Haven CT: Yale University Press.

World Health Organization (WHO), 2000 Lymphatic Filariasis, Fact Sheet No. 102. Electronic document. http://www.who.int/mediacentre/factsheets/fs102/en/print.html/.

World Health Organization (WHO), 2004 Water, Sanitation and Hygiene Links to Health: Facts and Figures, Updated November 2004. Electronic document. http://www.who.int/water_sanitation_health/publications/facts2004/en/.

World Health Organization (WHO), 2006 Countries/areas at risk of dengue transmission. Map Production Public Health Imaging. Geneva: World Health Organization.

World Health Organization (WHO), 2008 Dengue and Dengue Haemorrhagic Fever. Fact Sheet No. 117. Electronic document. http://www.who.int/mediacentre/factsheets/fs117/en/.

World Health Organization (WHO), 2009 Schistosomiasis. Epidemiological Situation. Electronic document. http://www.who.int/schistosomiasis/epidemiology/en/.

Wulff, Robert, and Shirley Fiske, 1987 Anthropological Praxis: Translating Knowledge into Action. Boulder CO: Westview Press.

Xu, X, F. H. Wei, X. X. Yang, Y. H. Dai, G. Y. Yu, L. Y. Chen, and Z. M. Su, 2000 Possible Effects of the Three Gorges Dam on the Transmission of Schistosomiasis Japonicum on the Jiang Han Plain, China. Annals of Tropical Medicine and Parasitology 94(4):333–341.

Yacoob, May and Linda M. Whiteford, 1994 Behavior in Water Supply and Sanitation. Human Organization 53(4):330–335.

Yamashiro, Tetsu, Mildre Disla, Angela Petit, Delfis Taveras, Mercedes Castro-Bello, Miguel Lora-Orste, Sonia Vardez, Ana Julia Cesin, Barbara Garcia, and Akira Nishizono, 2004 Seroprevalence of IgG Specific for Dengue Virus Among Adults and Children in Santo Domingo, Dominican Republic. American Journal of Tropical Medicine and Hygiene 71(2):138–143.

Zheng, Jiang, Xue-guang Gu, Yong-long Xu, Ji-hua Ge, Xian-xiang Yang, Chang-hao He, Chao Tang, Kai-ping Cai, Qing-wu Jiang, You-sheng Liang, Tian-ping Wang, Xing-jian Xu, Jiu-he Zhong, Hong-chang Yuan, and Xiao-nong Zhou, 2002 Relationship between the Transmission of Schistosomiasis Japonica and the Construction of the Three Gorge Reservoir. Acta Tropica 82:147–156.

11 Political Violence, War, and Medical Anthropology

*Barbara Rylko-Bauer
and Merrill Singer*

INTRODUCTION

Wealth makes wars and wars make wealth – for some. Poverty fosters violence and violence creates poverty – for many. As Rudolph Virchow observed over 150 years ago, "war, plague and famine condition each other" (Rather 1985:115). Consequently, wars and much violence can best be understood in terms of human structural relationships, or more precisely, in terms of the historic making of social inequalities in local, regional, and global spaces. While disparities of various sorts are now a core defining feature of the world system and considered key determinants of health and well being (Marmot and Wilkinson 2005; WHO 2008), in terms of the wide and troubled sweep of human history "there is nothing normal or inherently inevitable about living with violence, with oppression, with extreme suffering. It is, in fact, an abnormal state of humanness, even if a common one" (Rylko-Bauer, Whiteford, and Farmer 2009b:5).

Over the course of its history, anthropology has had an uneven and varied engagement with violence and war (Nagengast 1994). While a few scholars, such as Eric Wolf (1969), himself a war veteran and leader of the anti-war Teach-In Movement of the Vietnam War era, had already begun developing critical perspectives on violence and war, these issues were not central topics for the discipline when Morton Fried, Marvin Harris, and Robert Murphy (1967) published their edited volume, *War: The Anthropology of Armed Conflict and Aggression.* A decade later, Ashley Montagu (1978) edited the first anthology on nonviolent societies.

Since that time, violence and conflict – and to a lesser extent, peace and nonviolence (Sponsel 2009) – have increasingly become areas of anthropological debate, research, and analysis, expanding from an initial focus on conflict in smaller scale societies to the

A Companion to Medical Anthropology, First Edition. Edited by Merrill Singer
and Pamela I. Erickson.

contemporary examination of global warfare among and within nation/states (Simons 1999). Such work has included political economic analyses of particular wars and acts of political violence (e.g., Harding and Libal 2010; Hills and Wasfi 2010; Kohrt et al. 2010; Nordstrom 1997; Rylko-Bauer 2009), examination of typologies and theories of violence during interludes of active warfare and so-called "peacetime" (Scheper-Hughes and Bourgois 2004b), how the state shapes and manipulates political violence (Coronil and Skurski 2005; Nagengast 1994; Sanford 2003b; Sluka 2000), varied causes and prerequisite structures that promote and perpetuate war and collective violence (Appadurai 2006; Hinton 2002; Lutz and Nonini 2000; Rao et al. 2007); the cultural constructions, meanings, aesthetics, and everyday experiences of political violence at both the individual and group levels (Daniel 1996; Das et al. 2000; Feldman 1991; Manz 2004; Trawick 2002; Whitehead 2004), and the impacts of war and militaries on the environment (Baer 2010).

Anthropologists have also revealed erased histories and hidden connections between local violent realities and the political–economic forces of state and global power, finance, and trade (Binford 1996; Nordstrom 2004a, 2007) and have shown how these are often linked to the everyday structural violence of injustice, racism, disenfranchisement, and poverty (e.g., Bourgois 2003; Farmer 2003, 2004a; Quesada 2009; Scheper-Hughes 1992, 2007; Singer 2006, 2009). They have examined issues of memory, voice, and representation regarding collective violence (Das 2007; Hinton and O'Neill 2009), reflected upon "fieldwork under fire" (Nordstrom and Robben 1995; Van Dongen 2007), assessed who benefits from war (Singer and Hodge 2010a; Waterston 2009a), studied military institutions (Ben-Ari 1998; Simons 1997) and militarism as process and product (Ben-Ari 2004; Gusterson 2007; Lutz 2002), and addressed the traumatic aftermaths of war and violence, including notions of accountability, reparations, and the right to meaningful remedy (Das et al. 2001; Fassin and Rechtman 2009; Johnston and Barker 2008; Johnston and Slyomovics 2009; Sanford 2003a), as well as varying conceptualizations of peace, peacekeeping, and nonviolence (Rubenstein 2008; Sanford and Angel-Ajani 2006). Finally, anthropologists have turned their gaze onto their own discipline's relationship with and involvement in war and political violence, both historically and in the current wars being waged in Afghanistan and Iraq (e.g., Ben-Ari 2004; González 2007b; Gusterson 2007; Price 2000; Schafft 2004). Included in this "turn" is a consideration of the relationship of medical anthropology to war and political violence, the central focus of our concern in this chapter.

Overall, the body of anthropological scholarship on violence and war is impressive, rapidly growing in size and set of authors, and evolving in its range of focus. Much, however, remains to be done. As Veena Das (2008:295) notes, "it is precisely because the reality of violence includes … its potential to both disrupt the ordinary and become part of the ordinary – that the study of violence continues to challenge and channel our disciplinary desires in profound ways." In assessing this topic from the perspective of critical medical anthropology, we see the challenges and potential contributions of an anthropology – and medical anthropology, in particular – of war and political violence as fourfold. The first of these concerns efforts to *denaturalize* these complex phenomena based on an investigation of their socio-historical origins, social distribution, and outcomes. Despite the seeming ubiquity of political violence – since 1945, there have been more than 160 wars with well over 24 million people killed (the great majority civilians), and tens of millions displaced by internal conflict (Pedersen 2002) – what evidence disputes the fairly common assumption that humans are biologically "hard-wired" for violence? What contributions has anthropology made toward an alternative paradigm?

The second challenge involves developing approaches for a critical ethnographic *revisualization* that discloses and renders visible what often is forgotten or unseen. "It is at the point where violence disappears from our field of vision," notes Didier Fassin (2009:116), "that the work of anthropology becomes crucial." What has medical anthropology contributed to our understanding of how and why so much of the world's violence remains invisible, or at least ignored, by those living away from the battlefield in relative peace or undisturbed privilege? What more needs to be done, so that the causes and consequences of war and political violence are not so easily elided? As Lawrence Langer (1997:47) notes, "until we find a way of toppling the barrier that sequesters mass suffering in other regions of the world from the comfort and safety we enjoy far from its ravages," not much will change regarding our ability to address the horrors of our time or prevent those of the future.

A third challenge for anthropology involves *reconceptualizing* political violence and war as grave threats to the health and well being not only of individuals and families, but ultimately the planet and world order. The Nobel Peace Laureates' *Charter for a World Without Violence* begins with the statement: "Violence is a preventable disease" (Permanent Secretariat of Nobel Peace Laureates Summits 2009). We would rephrase this by characterizing war and violence as *biosocial* diseases, thereby stressing the fundamental role of social relationships and social inequalities in the formation – and prevention – of these destructive processes and events. What are the implications of defining war as disease, both for our discipline and for our understanding of war as an issue of pressing social concern?

By seeking to understand war and political violence as health problems, medical anthropology as *applied* social science has the potential to contribute to the fourth, and greatest, challenge of all – creating strategies for healing and recovery that put us on the path toward "a world without violence." Are there concrete examples of anthropologists working against war and political violence, of using disciplinary methods and insights to help heal the wounds of armed conflict and promote peace as a public health issue?

Our goals for this chapter are to describe the contours of an emergent medical anthropology against war and political violence by responding to each of these challenges based on the work of contemporary medical anthropologists, indicate gaps in knowledge, and suggest areas for future work within our discipline. While our focus is on war and political violence, we wish to underscore that other types of less visible violence – such as interpersonal, symbolic, normalized, and structural violence, that often get misrecognized as the natural order of the human world (Bourgois 2009:18–20; Scheper-Hughes and Bourgois 2004a) – are also present in war zones. They serve as the precursors and legacies of war, as well as adding layers of suffering during periods of armed conflict. As Panter-Brick (2010:2) points out, "in war-affected settings, not all distress or trauma is directly related to armed conflict, and this is because of a considerable backdrop of 'structural' violence affecting mental health and social functioning in 'everyday' life. ... [resulting from] poverty, social marginalization, and political exclusion." Much, if not most, of the recent medical anthropology literature cited in this chapter incorporates such an awareness of structural violence vis-à-vis war and political violence in its analyses.

The Making of a Medical Anthropology against War

In her 2007 Presidential Address to the Society for Medical Anthropology, titled "Medical Anthropology against War," Marcia Inhorn (2008:421) asked "why is there so little on the medical anthropology of war? What is the cause of our inertia?" Her remarks stemmed from a perceived dearth of engagement with issues in conflict-ridden Iraq: "Few medical anthropologists have examined any aspect of war or its aftermath in Iraq, or other parts of the Middle East" (Inhorn 2008:421). However, they were also directed at the subdiscipline as a whole:

> This is true of other regions as well. As a discipline, we have been faint of heart and lacking moral courage in this arena. In so doing, we have turned away from the brutal realities, the embodied suffering, the psychological devastation, the sexual violence, and the refugee aftermath of war. We have failed to attend to these realities during wartime, and our record of scholarship in war's aftermath is similarly thin. It is not enough to study "structural violence" … War creates poverty, but it also creates many other forms of embodied suffering that require our anthropological attention and our concern (Inhorn 2008:421–422).

While there may not be many medical anthropologists witnessing and documenting war *as it unfolds*, it seems to us that war, conflict, political violence, and their aftermaths have been the long-term focus of a number of our colleagues. Some, noted below, come readily come to mind, and there are others whose work is equally relevant to any discussion of medical anthropology's engagement with this difficult facet of human existence:

- Carolyn Nordstrom (1997, 1998, 2004a, 2007, 2009) has seen war and its consequences first hand while conducting research in Mozambique, Sri Lanka, and Angola. Her writings have set a standard for their insight and compassion.
- Didier Fassin's work on the violence of history and AIDS in South Africa (2007, 2009), as well as studies of the politics of trauma in asylum seeking (with d'Halluin 2007; with Rechtman 2009) are examples of penetrating scholarship that addresses the aftermaths of political violence.
- Linda Green (1999) has chronicled the invisible violence of fear and terror, and how Mayan widows reconstructed their lives and communities in the face of political violence and civil war in Guatemala.
- Barbara Rose Johnston (1994, 2007; with Barker 2008) has mapped the radioactive legacies of nuclear testing and human experimentation during the Cold War and documented the synergistic legacies of political violence, massacre, and international development with regard to the Chixoy Dam project in Guatemala (Johnston 2005).
- Byron Good, Mary-Jo DelVecchio Good and colleagues have assessed psychosocial and mental health impacts of long-term conflict and natural disaster on the lives of people in Aceh, Indonesia (Good et al. 2007; Grayman, Good, and Good 2009).

- Philippe Bourgois (2009) has examined the consequences of civil war and political violence in various Latin American contexts.
- Paul Farmer (1992, 2003, 2004a, 2004b, 2009b) has worked in Haiti since the early 1980s, writing about the health consequences of living in a place of endemic conflict, political violence, and abject poverty.
- Doug Henry (2005, 2006) has conducted research in the midst of conflict, to examine health sector adaptations and conceptions of the body by survivors of war and political violence in Sierra Leone.
- Judith Zur (1996, 1998) has worked on PTSD and the ways that Mayan widows experienced and coped with death, the destruction of life-ways, the loss of identities, and deteriorating health in conflict-ridden Guatemala.

This partial listing (along with other examples referenced in this chapter) is not intended to suggest that Inhorn's critique is unwelcome or unnecessary. In fact, one could say that she caught the crest of a wave of research that is building with each passing year (e.g., Rylko-Bauer, Whiteford, and Farmer 2009a; Singer and Hodge 2010a). In the following pages we present some of this work, with the hopes of building upon Inhorn's critique and thus stimulating even more focus on this critically important area for medical anthropology. If, as we believe, the goal of medical anthropology is to expand and deepen our understanding of health and healing, and to put this knowledge to positive use in human communities globally, then assuredly war is an arena of human suffering and loss that cries out for expanded effort.

DENATURALIZING VIOLENCE

There is a strong tendency in and out of the academy to think of violence and war as natural, even biologically determined human impulses – and there are many reasons why those in positions of power with armies at their command find it beneficial to nurture such a perspective. And yet, as Brian Ferguson (2009:33–36) argues, based on broad ethnographic and ethnohistoric findings, "our species is not biologically destined for war" just as "war is not an inescapable part of social existence." Other disciplines, such as psychology, biology, geography, public health, sociology, and history also offer evidence and alternative paradigms that challenge the notion that violence is an intrinsic, and thus inevitable, aspect of human nature (Pim 2009).

Anthropology's contribution to this debate comes, in part, from an awareness of the relationships between history, biology, and culture informed by a cross-societal focus. The fact that an "overwhelming majority of humans [across cultures] have not been involved directly in any kind of killing" challenges normalizing theories of species-wide biological tendencies toward violence and redirects attention toward theories of culture and power (Sponsel 2009:36). The historical and ethnographic record provides numerous examples of nonviolent societies and cultures and can serve as a source of alternative strategies for contemporary conflict resolution and redistributive justice (Bonta 1996; Dentan 1968, 2008; Fry 2006; Sponsel 2009).

Furthermore, as Gretchen Schafft (2009:52) notes, "before we assert that it is *impossible* to label war abnormal, it is good to remember that once other forms of violence were considered normal and are now, at least in many parts of the world considered aberrations. We can no longer violate, hold in bondage, or attack *at will* children, servants, spouses," and that such actions still occur does not detract from her point that they are not globally considered normative or permissible.

Recent history also offers examples of alternatives to military responses. Since 1949, Costa Rica's constitution forbids a standing military and its resources have instead been directed toward other social sectors such as health care and education. Obviously, many factors contribute to a society's level of health and social indicators, but this may be part of the reason why Costa Rica ranks relatively high, in relation to many other countries of Latin America and the Caribbean, on health status measures: e.g., life expectancy at birth (79), infant mortality rate (10), primary school enrollment/attendance (92%), adult literacy rate (96%), and 54th on the Human Development Index (UNDP 2009; UNICEF 2009).

There are, as well, multiple accounts of compassion across "enemy" lines in the midst of horrifying carnage that suggest the need for alternative understandings of violence in human life (LeShan 2002). Research on conflicts avoided and on peace-making efforts suggest that peace is more than the absence of war (Aureli and de Waal 2000); how peace is constituted after the cessation of violence is critical to the chances of its sustainability (Schafft 2009). Peace is the product of conscious efforts to avoid and settle conflict as well as culturally constituted mechanisms (e.g., various rituals) designed to constrain conflict. Victoria Sanford and H. C. Muggah (2003), for example, have written about Columbia's peace communities, formed by internally displaced people who, upon return to their communities of origin, declared them neutral in the civil conflict and out of bounds to armed individuals or groups. This body of literature calls into question the notion that war or violence are somehow more integral to human nature than peace and cooperation.

In recent years, belief in the existence of an innate cause of war has been bolstered by neurological research (e.g., brain scans) and animal studies observing lethal conflict among neighboring chimpanzee bands. However, while neuroimaging may suggest reasons why some individuals engage more frequently than others in acts of violence (Scarpa and Raine 2007), it cannot explain war, which is a socio-political event and not a product of individual brain structures, proclivities, orientations, or intentions. Similarly, Frans de Waal, who has studied chimpanzee behavior as the director of Yerkes' Living Links Center, questions biological determinism as an explanation of violence. He argues that primates, including humans, are calculating and will abandon aggressive behaviors that do not appear to be serving their interests. "We know a great deal about the causes of hostile behavior in animals and humans ... Yet we know little of the way conflicts are avoided – or how, when they do occur, relationships are afterward repaired and normalized" (de Waal 2007:1). While the notion of reparations is generally associated with efforts to redress the consequences of violence and promote peace, there is also evidence that such processes can promote political transformation by exposing causal links to war and political violence, identifying culpability, and creating unique structures that may serve in future conflict resolution efforts (Johnston and Slyomovics 2009).

There is significant potential for medical anthropology to contribute to advancing our understanding of these issues, including, for example, the role of healing rituals in easing interpersonal and intergroup conflict, and in helping people survive war while creating processes for subsequent peace-building (Erickson 2008; Nichter 1992;

Nordstrom 1998). Similarly, medical anthropologists can expand our knowledge of the ways in which improving health and social disparities can contribute to a reduction in social tensions within and across societies. The *World Report on Violence and Health* (Krug et al. 2002:10) notes that of the estimated 1.6 million violence-related deaths globally in 2000, 91.1 % occurred in low- to middle-income countries.

> Societies with already high levels of inequality, which experience a further widening of the gap between rich and poor as a result of globalization, are likely to witness an increase in interpersonal violence. ... [Similarly] grossly unequal distribution of resources, particularly health and education services, and of access to these resources and to political power ... are important factors that can contribute to conflict between groups (Krug et al. 2002:14, 220–221; see also Stewart 2002).

Finally, anthropologists have had some level of success in challenging other widely held views regarding the human condition and its potential. For example, the American Anthropological Association's (2007a) RACE Project has addressed common biological, genetic, and societal assumptions regarding human variation and the concept of "race," through public outreach using popular media, traveling exhibits, educational materials, and an interactive website. Similar strategies could be applied to the misconceptions regarding the inateness and inevitability of war and political violence.

REVISUALIZING WAR AND POLITICAL VIOLENCE: ANTHROPOLOGY'S "COUNTERGAZE"

The notion of "gaze" as a politically influenced view of the social other – such as the cultural lens that allowed Europeans to see a lesser humanity in the appearance and actions of peoples of color during and following the colonial encounter (Lutz and Collins 1994) – has come, appropriately, to have a negative connotation. Inherent in the notion of gaze as it has been used in social scientific analysis is the existence of an unequal power relationship between the viewer and the viewed, one that often rationalizes violence, both structural and physical. Inherent too is a capacity to "not-see" the violence in front of our eyes, for violence of the most egregious sort to literally disappear from our field of vision (Fassin 2009; Nordstrom 2009).

Even in the case of readily visible, large-scale conflicts, such as war, genocide, massacres, and other atrocities, the complexities of their historical and political–economic causes can be misrepresented or rendered invisible. In fact, the histories of wars are often rewritten (with political intent) even as the immediate memory of their details begins to fade. As Stanley Cohen (2001:4–5) stresses, "There seem to be states of mind, or even whole cultures, in which we know and don't know at the same time."

Writing of the Persian Gulf War, for example, Herman (1995) notes that how the war was presented via the media, and thus largely known by the American public, involved a focus more on our soldiers than on the war itself:

> We could watch them in action as they took off, landed, ate, joked, and expressed their feelings on the enemy, weather, and folks back home... They were part of an extended family, doing a dirty job, but with clean bombs and with the moral certainty of a just cause. The point was not often made that the enemy was relatively defenseless, and in

somewhat the same position as the "natives" colonized, exterminated, and enslaved by the West in past centuries... One of the effects of high-tech warfare, as well as the exclusive focus on "our" casualties, plus censorship (official and self), is that the public is spared the sight of burning flesh.

Such official management of public knowledge, images, and memories facilitates viewing war and political violence as inevitable, acceptable, and even desirable, and contributes to making the enduring devastation and agony they inflict seem routinized and distant, or renders them invisible. Defined "enemies" are never seen for what they are (i.e., people like us, with families and friends, fears and desires), much of the violence (political and structural) that we do to them is concealed, and what we remember later about the conflict is quite limited. Except, of course, for those who have known war up-close. For them, such forgetting is not as easy and rates of enduring trauma (physical, mental, and emotional) from recent conflicts are coming to be recognized as being far higher than has been realized (Hasanović et al. 2006; Lončar et al. 2006; McCue 2007).

The anthropological gaze – or "countergaze" (a seeing not bound to official "truths," perhaps even subverting them) – increases the potential for understanding the realities of war as embodied experience with lasting negative and degrading effects on human well being. This potential is rooted in anthropology's traditional embrace of immersion ethnography, its research commitment to engage the emic perspective and explore the textures of lived-experience, using a holistic framework that highlights interconnections across cultural, social, geographic and political–economic landscapes. These features of anthropology arm the discipline with the tools needed:

- To see war and political violence not as scattered and episodic local events but as "long-term, structural process[es] with different phases, some more visible than others" that span wide geographic distances and recognized political borders (Harding and Libal 2010:59).
- To perceive the ways that "violence configures a society... how long trauma can affect people and the larger social universe they live in, is less well understood" (Nordstrom 2004b:224).
- To locate cultural sources of particular expressions of violence within broader unifying frames of social understanding (Whitehead 2004).
- To comprehend, based on the heartfelt expressions of those on the frontlines of conflict, what violence-related pain, dismemberment, community destruction, and death feel like as human experience and come to mean to people in diverse social locations (Nordstrom 2004a; Rylko-Bauer et al. 2009a).

Of course, anthropologists are also capable of "not-seeing" entrenched and institutionalized violence, the everyday violence that is hidden by power and commerce, violence that arrives in familiar forms, and even emergent atrocity (Franke 1984). This is what Linda Green (1999:58) refers to historically as "anthropology's diverted gaze. What is at stake are the struggles between the powerful and the powerless, and what is at issue for anthropologists is to decide with whom to cast their lot."

A neutral or distanced stance, whether grounded in claims of objectivity, methodological rigor, or theoretical abstraction, is increasingly untenable and indefensible within the narrow confines of our discipline and the broader expectations of society (Rylko-Bauer et al. 2006). In addition, by spending prolonged periods in zones of actual conflict and seeing its diverse impacts on the lives of real peoples, anthropologists are pushed to fully realize the contours of political violence (Inhorn 2008; Omidian 2009). Notes Avram Bornstein (2010:231), ethnographers have come to realize they have an "ethical obligation to document" the violence they witness, especially when, as increasingly is the case, it is carried out by armed combatants against unarmed civilians.

Seeing the raw face of violence, its direct assault on the well being and survival of people immediately known to anthropologists, adds an important dimension to our understanding. While the official gaze on war – the one promulgated by ruling classes, governments, generals, and the like – seeks to make the realities of war more distant, the anthropological countergaze seeks to bring us closer to those realities. For medical anthropologists this means providing the kinds of intimate, contextualized, and integrated accounts of the health consequences of war and political violence (e.g., Manz 2004; Rylko-Bauer, Whiteford, and Farmer 2009a; Singer and Hodge 2010a; Waterston 2009a) that have characterized the study of other kinds of threats to health, ranging from infectious disease (Biehl 2007) to intense poverty (Scheper-Hughes 1992) to anthropogenic environmental degradation (Ayuero and Swistun 2009).

Beyond advancing our knowledge of war, such an understanding has applied value in the movement "to undermine war, to help bring an end to war" (Waterston 2009b:14), even if from our current vantage the precise pathway for achieving that goal remains uncertain. As Waterston (2009b:18) reminds us: "Silencing and blinding are political projects, weapons of the dominant. Speaking and writing are tools of resistance. *Seeing* is a power that might help us off our current, destructive course."

RECONCEPTUALIZING WAR AS A COMPLEX BIOSOCIAL DISEASE

To begin with, we are not promoting the medicalization of violence – a problematic framework that often de-contextualizes, objectifies, de-politicizes, and transforms collective political violence into discreet individual experiences of "trauma-as-pathology" (Kleinman and Desjarlais 1995). War cannot be effectively understood or resisted the way medicine usually is practiced, one patient at a time.

Rather, what is needed is a public health approach to our understanding of war enhanced by critical medical anthropological analysis of health in social context. The starting point of this understanding, argues physician Jerome Marmorstein (2001), is a recognition that: "No matter how war begins, it always ends up to be a devastating form of traumatic disease. Because it kills, injures and disables more people in shorter periods of time than any other known disease, war should be recognized as a true disease epidemic."

The toll of war on health and well being

Indeed, there is a growing body of literature regarding the egregious health consequences of war and violence, much of it coming out of medicine and public health (Abu-Musa et al. 2008; Levy and Sidel 2000; Minayo et al. 2006; Krug et al. 2002;

Taipale et al. 2002), but increasingly out of medical anthropology as well (e.g., Becker et al. 2000; Johnston and Barker 2008; Panter-Brick 2010; Pedersen 2002; Pike et al. 2010).

Moreover, the damage done to human lives in contemporary war is caused most immediately by the spread of disease and hunger from loss of access to food in combat zones, rather than munitions per se (Human Security Research Group 2009). The *Global Burden of Armed Violence* report issued by the Geneva Declaration Secretariat (2008) estimated that for every individual who died violently in the wars fought around the world between 2004 and 2007 (about 600,000), another four died from war-related disease and malnutrition. In this light, war is not just "like disease" but rather disease and hunger have become the most potent weapons in a new era of war, coupled with the use of fear and terror as a means of defeating, dehumanizing, and controlling populations (Nordstrom 1998).

Seeing war through the lens of public health takes us beyond immediate injury and death, by focusing attention on war's full toll and pathology, including its immediate and longer-term impacts on human well being, the wide range of ways it causes damage across gender, age, subgroups, and environments, and the ability of war to trigger other threats to human life. The growing compendium of studies clearly shows that war and political violence affect health and well being of individuals, families, and communities in multiple, intersecting, and synergistic ways, including:

- Inflicting pain, injury, and death not only on combatants, but increasingly on civilian populations who may be targeted as a form of terror and control.
- Increasing the risk of epidemics and incidence of often-deadly infectious diseases.
- Disrupting families and communities of support.
- Displacing populations and exposing them to risks of hunger, disease, trauma, and permanent disability.
- Exposing displaced and occupied populations, in particular women and children, to further violence, such as rape, torture, exploitation.
- Destroying the social and cultural fabric (including a people's history, identity, way of life, and set of values).
- Affecting or damaging the environment (as in "scorched-earth" actions or radioactive contamination from weapons production and use).
- Introducing genetic damage into populations (e.g., as a result of exposure to radioactive materials).
- Destroying political and economic infrastructures, means of livelihood, and life trajectories.
- Limiting access to healthcare and destroying treatment infrastructures.
- Disrupting health information systems and preventive care (e.g., immunizations).
- Diminishing the number of available health care providers.
- Multiplying the stress of living with fear and uncertainty.
- Causing trauma, witnessed or experienced, that manifests itself in culturally mediated physical, mental, and emotional ways.
- Producing individual and collective memories that keep the trauma of violence alive, sometimes over many generations.
- Diverting funds away from public health and other social needs.

This last point merits elaborating because of its widespread ramifications. Diversion of resources is a particularly critical issue for lesser developed countries, since the need for basic social services is especially great because of poverty and underdevelopment. Yet in many instances, the proportion they spend on military expenditures is several times that spent publicly on health and education – even in cases where there are no ongoing conflicts (Ugalde et al. 2000; World Council of Churches 2005). The impact of militarism is significant for wealthier nations, as well. Sidel and Levy (2009:134) observe that "in 2007 the United States ranked first among countries in military expenditures and arms exports, but only 30th in life expectancy at birth and 39th in infant mortality." The USA was also the leader in sales of weapons to developing countries, to the tune of $30 billion dollars.

Medical anthropology's interface with war and political violence

To date, medical anthropology's primary interface with armed conflict and other kinds of violence has been through witnessing, describing, and measuring these acute and enduring health consequences and providing cultural and political economic analyses of how they come to be a painful part of the human condition. This is a critical first step in developing a medical anthropology against war.

Yet how wars begin, from a socio-political perspective, is also vitally important, in the same way that understanding the origins of disease is a fundamental part of public health assessment and response. From the perspective of critical medical anthropology, whatever its proximate causes (e.g., pathogens, trauma, toxins), social relations of inequality and injustice are the distal or ultimate causes of much disease (Baer et al. 2003). Along these same lines, war is to society as disease is to the human body.

Just as health disparities reflect and amplify structurally imposed social disparities, so should we view war as a "pathology of power," to borrow Paul Farmer's (2003) phrase. Moreover, this pathology is damaging to all that are swept up in its pathway. As Carolyn Nordstrom aptly notes, perpetrators, victims, and witnesses alike carry with them the violence they have seen and experienced. In the words of one of her informants, an African medical practitioner working in a battle zone, "this violence sticks to them. … this violence tears at the order of the community. … violence is a dangerous illness.....This violence, it tears them up inside, it destroys the world they care about" (Nordstrom 2004b:228–229). Consequently, the larger tasks before us in the development of a medical anthropology against war include assessing both causality and accountability for war and violence and contributing to the development of strategies that promote peace and reduce the likelihood of future conflict (Waterston 2009b; Singer and Hodge 2010a).

An important step in this process is the recognition of the global and interconnected nature of what Singer and Hodge (2010b:4) call the "war machine," which can help us to move beyond:

a narrow focus on the undeniably considerable and complex public health impacts of bullets, bombs, and battles. In addition to the varied forms of direct armed hostility, the concept of the war machine includes vast war industries and their heavy toll on environments and workers, the international weapons trade that reaps great profit while helping to fuel new conflicts, the "saber-rattling" ideologies and policies that justify and encourage war, and war budgets that rob public treasuries of funds needed for pressing health and social needs.

Clearly, the consequences of war and political violence to health and well being are best seen at the microlevel of "on-the-ground" lived experience.

Anthropology's ethnographic toolkit is especially suited for bringing this into sharp focus and helping to visualize the very real, complex, and enduring impacts of war. However, understanding the broader implications and causal pathways requires also examining forces at the macrolevel and using analytical tools, such as those of critical medical anthropology, to identify the connections between health, war, ideology, and political economy. The emergence of a multisited/multileveled approach within anthropology, one that focuses research simultaneously and interactively at the local- and macrolevels of social action is a fundamental methodological advance for this kind of work.

Medical anthropologists, including many cited in this chapter, have contributed to many facets of this topic by providing multifaceted, crosscultural, and meaning-centered understandings of war and conflict, while at the same time highlighting the socio-structural forces that generate and shape violence and responses to it at both the individual and societal levels. The nature of these contributions can be seen in the analyses medical anthropologists have provided of gendered and ethnic dimensions of violence (Das 2007, 2008; Green 1999; Jenkins 1998): the socio-cultural contexts that give meaning to specific acts of violence and how these are reconceptualized as memory and trauma (Das 2007; Fassin and Rechtman 2009; Ferrándiz 2006); the ways in which political violence is experienced and inscribed on physical and social bodies, including those of children (Fassin 2007; Fassin and d'Halluin 2007; Kleinman et al. 1997; Scheper-Hughes and Sargent 1998); the psychosocial consequences of violence, how these are manifested, and various culturally appropriate efforts toward amelioration and healing (Foxen 2010; Grayman et al. 2009; Pedersen 2006; Zraly and Nyirazinyoye 2010; Zur 1998); the impact of conflict on access to care and resultant adverse outcomes (Varley 2010); the complex web of power, politics, and economies – legal and extralegal – that fuel local conflicts and global profits (Nordstrom 2004a, 2007); the interconnected dynamics of various forms of violence and how they intersect synergistically with history, science, racism, poverty, *and* global politics (Farmer 2003; Johnston 2007; Maternowska 2006; Rylko-Bauer et al. 2009a; Singer and Hodge 2010a).

Exemplary is Maria Olujic's (1998:46) astute analysis in the former Yugoslavia of the ways that war "transforms the individual body into the [targetable] social body as seen in genocidal rapes, ethnic cleansing, and purifying of the blood-lines." Savage brutalities committed against real and accessible individuals serve the cultural function of symbolically attacking and damaging the hated and faceless collective "Other." The greatest atrocity of war, Olujic (1998:46) maintains, is that "individuals are absorbed by the collective actions of the social/political fantasy…lives are destroyed and then discarded as the collective fantasy proceeds." War, all war, is fueled by such cultural fantasy, and hence a task of a medical anthropology against war is analytic assault on "the culture of war" (Desjarlais and Kleinman 1994).

The roles of health care in war

Anthropologists are also making contributions in documenting the complex and at times contradictory roles that health care plays in conflict and post-conflict settings. As Panter-Brick observes (2010:4), "health-related matters are closely interlinked with politics. Health, as a commodity, is hardly value-free, even when social and political will makes health equity a social priority." The recognition of healthcare's potential to contribute to broader agendas of equity, social cohesion, and social justice, which in turn can foster conditions for political stability and peace is not a new notion. Almost thirty years ago, the 34th World Health Assembly declared that "the role of physicians and other health workers in the preservation and promotion of peace is the most significant factor for the attainment of health for all" (WHO 1981).

Over time, this perspective has evolved into a number of frameworks and programs that focus on ways in which the health sector, and in particular health workers at various levels, can contribute not just to mitigating the direct consequences of war and political violence, but also promoting conflict reduction, reconciliation, and peace-building within the context of meeting basic social needs and human rights (Bunde-Birouste et al. 2004; MacQueen and Santa-Barbara 2000). These approaches include the World Health Organization's "Health as a Bridge for Peace" program (WHO 2002) and various "Peace through Health" initiatives (Arya and Santa-Barbara 2008) such as the HEAL Africa projects described by D'Errico et al. (2010) that aim to reduce risk factors for conflict and contribute to long-term rehabilitation in Eastern Congo. Other examples include efforts to limit weapons that are indiscriminate in causing great civilian harm (e.g., initiatives against biological and chemical agents, stun guns, landmines, nuclear weapons), negotiated humanitarian ceasefires (to allow immunization campaigns), and projects aimed at forcing greater accountability for the consequences of war, such as the Iraq Body Count (http://www.iraqbodycount.org).

Others go further, in asserting that for post-conflict countries, investing not only in individual initiatives but in developing a functional, equitable health care system will help "build government capacity, promote social cohesion, and strengthen the social contract, thereby ... reducing the risks of conflict recurrence" (Kruk et al. 2010:90). As James Pfeiffer and colleagues (2008) argue, an important part of this process requires channeling development aid to ministries of health (rather than just to NGOs) and integrating NGOs with the public health sector. Clearly, there are many opportunities for anthropological input, evaluation, as well as constructive critique, within these health and peace-enhancing initiatives (e.g., Lyon et al. 2008).

Medical anthropologists have studied cases where health care served as a means of instilling social solidarity by mobilizing people and communities around broader social issues that get at the root causes of disease, illness, and despair. They have also documented the risks involved in doing so within contexts of political violence, since such actions of self-determination are often construed by those in power as acts of resistance and challenge to the status quo. For example, the Primary Health Care movement that evolved from the historic Alma Ata conference was not simply about access to basic health care "but was also tied to fundamental social restructuring that would improve equity, social justice, and thus *health* itself" (Heggenhougen 2009:182). In countries of great disparities, such as Guatemala, this was perceived as threatening and even revolutionary by those in power. Community health care workers, such as

Kris Heggenhougen's friend, mentor, and key informant, Francisco Curruchiche, were swept up in the political violence and often murdered.

The persecution of health care workers in Guatemala during the 1970s and 1980s, however, is not an isolated case. As the nature of modern warfare and political conflict has changed, the health care system has come to be viewed as a valuable resource, a useful political symbol, and a tool for social control (Ghimire 2009). There are numerous cases where health workers and the healthcare infrastructure have been targeted by combatants, in an effort to terrorize local populations, gain control, or destabilize governments (Brentlinger 1996; Cliff and Noormahomed 1988; Easterbrook 1990; Varley 2010). Despite such setbacks, local populations in many parts of the world continue to struggle to better their lot by resisting oppression through efforts to improve community health and well being. As Duncan Pedersen (2002:181) notes, there are important lessons to be learned from such cases: "The collective responses in confronting extreme violence and death represent a range of critical mechanisms for restoration and survival, which should not be underestimated" (Pedersen 2002:181).

In fact, health care has the capacity to provide a humanitarian space for acting against violence, even in the most extreme contexts. The Nazi era is a historic case that offers both heroic and challenging examples. These include the struggles of Jewish doctors and nurses to provide relief in contexts of extreme deprivation and suffering within the ghettos (Roland 1992) and the efforts of prisoner-doctors (of various religious and ethnic affiliations) assigned to work in Nazi concentration camps, who tried to heal, aid in acts of resistance, and at times even save lives against all odds, thus offering some slender thread of hope (Levi and de Benedetti 2006; Rylko-Bauer 2009). More recently, Carolyn Nordstrom (1998) has written about the ways in which local traditional healing systems served as frameworks of creativity, resistance, and survival during the height (1988 to 1991) of the war in Mozambique.

A more general contemporary example might be humanitarian medical and relief efforts provided by various aid organizations, at times conducted on a massive scale in settings of both short- and long-term crises that often are the intertwined result of natural disasters, wars, and political violence. At the same time, critical analyses by medical anthropologists and others point to "the paradox of humanitarian action" (Terry 2002), namely that relief aid occurs in political, economic, and ideological contexts which can be manipulated for purposes that go against the goals of humanitarian action and may even cause greater harm to already highly vulnerable displaced peoples living in refugee camps. This is partly due to the fact that most relief groups are funded by outside donors who have fiscal and ideological demands that often take priority over the accountability of the NGOs toward the vulnerable populations they serve (de Waal 1997). In addition, since "the link between NGOs and the state is inextricable," the kinds of partnerships that NGOs choose to form (for financial, pragmatic, and operational reasons) can present numerous challenges with regard to accountability, representation, and legitimacy (Campos and Farmer 2003:507).

This is especially true within the realm of global family planning and reproductive rights (Maternowska 2006). For example, Linda Whiteford (2009) explores the ways in which African women, displaced by war and living in refugee camps, are denied access to regular and emergency contraception despite being constantly at risk for rape. She describes this as both a "failure to protect" and a "failure to provide" on the part of relief aid NGOs, who are influenced by the politics of global health policies. Perhaps most destructive has been the Mexico City policy of the United States (initiated in 1984 and reactivated whenever a Republican administration comes to power), which essentially denies funding to NGOs that address (or are perceived as addressing) abortion on any level. The very real needs and suffering of displaced women are secondary, at best, to the fiscal concerns of some NGOs and the ideological expectations of their donors. Moreover, as Peter Redfield (2005:330) notes in his ethnography of *Médecins Sans Frontières* (Doctors without Borders), "amid worldwide zones of repeated disaster, medical humanitarian action offers the promise of preserving existence ... at the possible expense of deferring actions that might support a mode of being more consistent with dignity."

The involvement of health care professionals in contexts of war and political violence also has its dark side. The most notorious and best known is the cooptation of medicine and science during the twelve years of the Third Reich, where racism, oppression, and violence were interwoven in complex ways with the political economy of war (Gutterman 2008; Rylko-Bauer 2009). As Eric Wolf (1999:240) notes, "what remains unique to Germany was the intensive enlistment of the medical establishment in the cause of racial hygiene and the significant role played by German physical anthropologists in that cause." German doctors, nurses, and other health-related professionals aided, abetted, and actively engaged in the racist Nazi agenda of "cleansing" Germany and its occupied territories of populations deemed undesirable and subhuman, by incarcerating, experimenting upon, and ultimately murdering millions of people – most notably Jews, but also the physically and mentally disabled, those deemed social misfits, homosexuals, as well as Poles, Slavs, Roma, Sinti, and other ethnic groups (e.g., Lifton 2000[1986]; Schafft 2004).

While the Holocaust presents us with a unique case, medicine in the service of political violence and repression unfortunately has a long history, predating World War II and continuing into the present (Dadrian 1986; Vesti and Lavik 1991). Indeed, medicine played a fundamental role in rationalizing colonialism and the rampant structural and extensive physical violence it engendered. Jean Comaroff (1993:305), for example, observes that medicine held a core position in the colonization of Africa during the 19th century and that "the development of British colonialism in Africa as a cultural enterprise was inseparable from the rise of biomedicine as a science." By the turn of the 20th century, the colonial narrative concerning the civilizing effects of European presence in Africa increasingly was replaced by a discourse of asserted poor health, unregulated native hygiene, and the polluting nature of African populations. Africans, in short, were equated with dirt, disease, and disorder and were said to be in pressing need of biomedical and hygienic intervention. Thus the indigenous workforce was disciplined and communities forcefully reorganized and relocated during the colonial era "in the name of sanitation and control of disease" (Comaroff 1993:306).

In fact, as Warwick Anderson (2006) stresses, colonial pacification and sanitation were seen as unified processes. Consequently, colonial warfare often was fought under the banner of a war on disease based on the cultural assumption that colonized peoples were inherently contaminating and hence dangerous to colonial soldiers and administrators. Speaking of the Philippines, for example, he notes (Anderson 2006:1) that physicians of biomedicine worked hand-in-glove with colonial administrations

234 BARBARA RYLKO-BAUER AND MERRILL SINGER

to "purify not only… public spaces, water and food, but also the bodies and conduct" of the Filipino people.

More recently, the ongoing US-led wars in Iraq and Afghanistan have brought a particularly abhorrent aspect of medical involvement in state-sponsored violence into sharper focus, namely the role of health care professionals in state-sponsored torture. While such cases have been documented in many parts of the world (British Medical Association 1986, 1992; Cohn 1991; Gould and Folb 2002), the highly publicized use of torture by the US government on detainees from the "global war on terror" (especially during the George W. Bush administration) has raised serious and troubling questions about the role and responsibilities of health professionals. Participation in such acts by medical personnel not only violates international conventions and medicine's established mission to heal and do no harm, but also contributes significantly to the normalization of torture by lending legitimacy to such acts (Danner 2009; Miles 2006; Miles and Marks 2007; Physicians for Human Rights 2005). Some critics have even questioned the very notion of medical professionals working for the military (Sidel and Levy 2003).

Anthropologists are also contributing to these critiques of medical personnel in military interrogations (American Anthropological Association 2007b; González 2007a; Rylko-Bauer 2009), as well as the more general use of medicine and humanitarian aid as an integral part of waging war by "winning the hearts and minds" of local populations – as with US military outreach in Iraq and Afghanistan (Price 2009). A notable example of direct relevance to anthropology is the Human Terrain System (HTS), a counterinsurgency program where social scientists are "embedded" with combat troops to provide information about indigenous cultures and populations that can facilitate decision making with regard to on-the-ground military actions. The involvement of anthropologists in this program has generated intense criticism from within the discipline (e.g., Bickford 2008; González 2008; Omidian 2009), culminating in a report produced by the American Anthropological Association's Commission on the Engagement of Anthropology with the US Security and Intelligence Communities (2009:3), which concluded that:

> When ethnographic investigation is determined by military missions, not subject to external review, where data collection occurs in the context of war, integrated into the goals of counterinsurgency, and in a potentially coercive environment – all characteristic factors of the HTS concept and its application – it can no longer be considered a legitimate professional exercise of anthropology.

Anthropologists have also engaged in critical analyses of the consequences of broader involvement of the military in humanitarian aid, including response to natural disasters, and with regard to peacetime short-term training missions, such as the Medical and Dental Readiness Training Exercises (MEDRETES) that the US military conducts in Latin America. As Abigail Adams (2010:282) notes, "health care itself is mobilized in the service of the war machine, through the MEDRETES' offer of short-term palliative health gains in developing countries" at the expense of long-term investments in the public health care infrastructure. In Guatemala, where she conducted her fieldwork, Adams (2010:299) found that "the exercises reinforce the Guatemalan military's role in nation building and undermine the legitimacy of the appropriate civilian ministries." Even in peacetime, there are foreign troops posted in many countries around the world. Understanding their local health and social impacts (e.g., spread of STIs, environmental pollution, support for or undermining of local public health infrastructure) remains an important arena of work for an applied medical anthropology against war.

Finally, there is a growing recognition that war and other acts of violence also encompass human rights violations. There is an inverse correlation between respect for human rights (including social and economic rights that have a direct impact on health and well being, such as the right to health care, shelter, clean water, sustenance, education, and social security) and risk factors for violence (Gruskin and Butchart 2003; Stewart 2002). Going one step further, Paul Farmer (2003, 2008) has argued that the most effective way of furthering the *global* human rights agenda is to make health (which in its broadest sense also encompasses other social and economic rights) central to this struggle.

APPLYING MEDICAL ANTHROPOLOGY IN ZONES OF WAR AND POLITICAL VIOLENCE

Clearly, anthropologists have been increasingly concerned with witnessing, documenting, and analyzing various facets of war and political violence and how such events impact and intersect with health, well being, and health care delivery. The most difficult question, however, remains largely unanswered: What is to be done?

The final challenge for a medical anthropology against war, then, is the implementation of anthropological insights and methods in the struggle for peace and in efforts to promote human physical, emotional, and social healing in the aftermath of war. In searching for examples of such direct engagement, we discovered a number of noteworthy cases, but not nearly as many as we had expected to find. The following sampling reveals the diversity of applied work by anthropologists (medical or otherwise) that not only seeks to help heal the wounds of violence, but also contribute to social justice, conflict reduction, and peace-building. We begin with an in-depth look at the efforts of Barbara Rose Johnston and Holly Barker (2008) in response to the harm produced by nuclear arms testing, and then briefly describe several other examples of this kind of work.

Redressing the aftermath of violence through accountability and reparations

War does not begin with the first deployment of weapons or the first casualties. Its roots are to be found in the advance preparations for war, including the development and production of weapons. In the case of nuclear weapons, the environmental and health consequences have been severe.

The events leading up to Johnston and Barker's involvement in this arena began in the aftermath of the Second World War as the United States embarked on a highly secret initiative to make additional atomic bombs like those used with such deadly and destructive effect against Japan. Testing took place over a twelve-year period in the Pacific Ocean far from the continental United States, and was focused in the Marshall

Islands, a nation comprised of 29 atolls that was liberated from the Japanese and placed under US control by the United Nations.

Ultimately, a total of 67 atomic and thermonuclear bombs were detonated on land, in the skies, and under the waters of the Marshall Islands. The collective yield of these tests was "108 megatons, the equivalent of more than 7,000 Hiroshima bombs" (Thornburgh et al. 2003:5). The largest of these (codenamed Bravo), a 15-megaton hydrogen bomb detonated on Bikini Atoll, produced a mushroom cloud that spread snow-like radioactive debris and fallout across the scattered island nation. Hard hit by this material, because of a sudden shift in prevailing winds, were the indigenous communities on Rongelap, Ailinginae, and Utrik Atolls. When word reached the global media that casualties had been suffered the United States evacuated survivors to a military base for medical examination. After three months, people from Utrik were allowed to return home.

People from Rongelap, who had had the heaviest exposure, were not allowed to go home. Rather, they were closely monitored in a secret program that came to be known cryptically as Project 4.1, with the intention of increasing understanding of the effects of exposure to nuclear radiation. While placating international concerns about conditions in the Marshall Islands and the health of their inhabitants, some of the motivation for this initiative came from "military questions and needs, rather than … the health treatment needs of the affected population" (Johnston 2009:7). Three years later, despite full knowledge that radiation levels were still dangerously high, the people were given "assurances that the radiation levels on their atoll were safe" and were shipped back to Rongelap (National Research Council 1994:9). The rationale for this decision was that it offered medical and environmental scientists the unique opportunity to track the movement of radiation through the food chain and the build-up of radionuclide burdens in the human body.

This study, conducted by physicians and other researchers affiliated with the Brookhaven National Laboratory (BNL), was kept secret because of concern about "possible adverse public reaction" (Hacker 1994:147). Moreover, in 1995 a US presidential advisory panel concluded that BNL doctors injected Marshall Island residents with radioactive substances without the consent of their patients. According to the panel, "Because there was virtually no therapeutic benefit envisioned, it appears the primary goal of the study was to measure radiation exposures for research purposes, although the knowledge may have been helpful in the clinical care of the patient" (quoted in Maier 2009).

Despite suffering from increasing numbers of diseases like thyroid cancer that were previously unknown to them, as well as high rates of miscarriage and congenital birth defects, the people of Rongelap remained on their contaminated atoll for 28 years, worried but uncertain about the cause of their growing health woes. Then in 1982, a representative of the the US Environmental Protection Agency told residents that radioactive dangers were still present. Subsequent requests to the US government to be evacuated were turned down. Prompted by growing distrust of the government and its physicians, in 1985 the residents of Rongelap quietly arranged to be removed from their island by environmental activists working with Greenpeace, "a move BNL doctors later criticized as unnecessary" (Maier 2009). To date, they have not returned to their homeland, fearful that it still is unsafe to do so.

In 1998, Johnston and Barker were invited to serve as advisors for the Marshall Islands Nuclear Claims Tribunal, which was created by Congressional action to respond to legal claims by Marshallese for damage awards for nuclear testing. As part of their work, they were asked to provide anthropological insight about how damages should be defined and compensation provided to a people who lived outside of a market economy. Specifically, the question they were asked to address was: "Are there precedents or methodologies for indentifying and quantifying the damages associated with the loss of the means to sustain a healthy way of life" (Johnston 2009:5).

In findings presented to the Tribunal in 2001, these researchers stressed that harm to Rongelap included far more than the most obvious cases of radiation burns, poisonings, and cancers, but extended to a long list of symptoms and diseases including immune-deficiency conditions, metabolic disorders, premature aging, and reproductive consequences. They also argued for a broad understanding of the psychosocial traumas suffered by the people of Rongelap, including the humiliation, marginalization, and stigmatization endured because of their exposure to radiation. Further, they asserted that there were critical human rights issues at stake because of the medical research that was conducted on atoll residents (Barker 2007; Johnston and Barker 2008). In 2007, the Tribunal determined that the amount of compensation due to the claimants was $1,031,231,200 covering the costs of island remediation and restoration, compensation for lost property, loss of a healthy way of life, and suffering human experimentation. Unfortunately for the Marshallese people, who feel that they were cruelly treated like human guinea pigs, the Bush administration rejected these damage awards and efforts to collect them in federal court have to date failed. The work of Johnston and Barker, nonetheless, stands as an applied model for the development of a medical anthropology against war.

Additional cases of healing, rebuilding, reconciliation, and resistance

While, many people are familiar with physician/anthropologist Paul Farmer's ongoing applied work (1992, 2003) on health issues in Haiti, perhaps less well known are his efforts (in collaboration with others) to help rebuild Rwanda's public health care system in rural areas that were devastated by the 1994 civil war and genocide. In mid-2005, Partners in Health (PIH, the NGO that Farmer, Jim Yong Kim, and Ophelia Dahl founded) took over a hospital that had been built by a Belgian mining company that left the country decades ago. After the war, the facility sat abandoned until PIH (at the request of the Rwandan Health Ministry) launched its first project in Africa (Inshuti Muy Buzima) to rebuild and open the facility. The goal was to serve more than 200,000 people in that rural region, almost all of them resettled war refugees living in poverty (Farmer 2009a). Their program has now expanded to other sites and includes treatment of landmine trauma, HIV/AIDS that in many cases is the legacy of wartime rape, and providing health care services to inmates imprisoned because of their involvement in the genocide. The program incorporates a comprehensive approach to health, by focusing not only on the provision of care, but also on education, food distribution, improving access to clean water, the building of homes, and job creation – all based on a model of community partnership and involvement. In the process, community members are reaching some level of reconciliation with their horrible past as they work together for a common good (English 2008).

Patricia Omidian (2009) lived and worked in Afghanistan from 1998 to 2008, initially doing research for various NGOs and later working as the country representative for the American Friends Service Committee. Part of her work involved developing a culturally sensitive training program to address trauma, domestic violence and psychosocial needs of Afghan women struggling with both war-related distress and the daily strain of living in difficult social conditions. This kind of applied work is readily replicable in many other war-ravaged settings where women (as well as children) have been specifically targeted for abuse.

Lack of adequate shelter is recognized as a critical factor for health and well being. When this lack is due to a violent act by the state, the harmful impacts on health are multiplied several times over. Witnessing the demolition of a Palestinian family's home by Israeli military forces led anthropologist Jeff Halper (2008) to form the Israeli Committee Against House Demolitions (ICAHD), a non-violent, direct-action group that resists such acts of political violence by rebuilding homes and fostering a "paradigm change within Israeli society" through exhibits, films, workshops, cultural events, and tours of the Occupied Territories (Halper 2001:14).

Additional cases highlight the importance of exhumation and reburial in a society's transition from war to peace (Barkey 2008) and the complexity of such processes with regard to the recovery of historical memory (Ferrándiz 2006), as well as the need for culturally appropriate psychosocial assessments in helping to develop mental health services for populations, such as the Aceh of Indonesia, traumatized by war, political violence, and natural disaster (Good et al. 2007; Grayman et al. 2009). These various examples suggest an important direction for applied efforts in medical anthropology that go beyond description and analysis, by engaging in the difficult tasks of working against war and toward lasting peace (Singer and Erickson 2009).

CONCLUSION: WAR, VIOLENCE AND THE FUTURE OF MEDICAL ANTHROPOLOGY

Plato supposedly stated that "only the dead have seen the end of war" – perhaps he was right (although some attribute the quote to George Santayana). Nevertheless, the better we understand group violence, the greater the potential for a coming generation to see the end of war. We are not utopianists, and nothing witnessed by anthropologists about war in recent decades suggests that the end to war is in sight, and yet, a medical anthropology against war offers a pathway for helping one day to realize that vision.

Our overview of this topic is not meant to be exhaustive. In surveying the literature, we focused on four areas where we feel that anthropology, and in particular medical anthropology, can continue making a significant contribution in understanding the causes, consequences, and response to war and political violence. These include:

- Offering ethnographically informed additions to the growing compendium of studies that challenge the notion of violence as an inevitable, biologically predestined feature of human life.
- Developing approaches in critical ethnographic methods that facilitate revisualizing the complexities and realities of violence, so as to make the many faces of violence, and its consequences, more visible.

- Continuing to expand the growing body of literature that views war and political violence as "pathologies of power," while exploring the role of health care and public health in peace-building.
- Working toward a more engaged involvement that combines theory and praxis so that our witness and analysis have an impact on diminishing the terrible human costs of war and group violence.

Related areas of study might include improving our understanding of human resilience (and not just vulnerability) in the face of the traumas of war, political violence, and the oppression and privation that all too often accompany such events. Examining forms and processes of resilience within various cultural, social, and historical contexts shifts attention from an exclusive focus on marginality and victimization (Panter-Brick 2002) toward understanding local strategies of coping with and resisting violence, sustaining human dignity, and rebuilding life in the aftermath of conflict (Foxen 2010; Nordstrom 1998; Zraly and Nyirazinyoye 2010). In fact, Catherine Panter-Brick (2010:5) predicts that "resilience is the next 'frontier knowledge' in the field of violence and health" and suggests that such research will help identify "under what conditions specific social, political, and health interventions work best to efface the scars of violence."

Another area of study with great potential for impacting the future of war is identifying the root causes of political violence and social conflict, especially the processes that create, foster, and reproduce "Othering" fantasies that focus on differences within and among populations, with the purpose of motivating soldiers and civilians, alike, to commit injustices and atrocities. In addition, we envision future work in the medical anthropology against war as contributing to growing interdisciplinary efforts that develop an understanding of peace and identify strategies for avoiding armed conflict as a way of solving human problems (Panter-Brick 2010).

We also look forward to an expansion in the number and kinds of exemplary cases of medical anthropology being applied to the prevention of war, the resolution of conflicts, the delegitimation of combat as a valid and desirable option, and the development of strategies that increase the likelihood of peace. An important part of such work involves contributing to programs and projects that heal the wounds inflicted by political violence on individual and social bodies and the physical and cultural environments they inhabit.

Critical to all such efforts is the development of focused training – through existing or new graduate programs in medical anthropology – in the critical theory, research methods, ethics, and applications that help foster a medical anthropology of and against war. One strategy would be to integrate existing established programs, such as peace and conflict studies, with programs in medical anthropology. As this chapter demonstrates, health is central to human well being. Health is interconnected with most other facets of culture and arenas of social life (be it education, employment, housing, food production, medical care, family life, religion, the environment), as well as being linked to the potential for social and economic development. Conflicts over resources and power always have multiple consequences for health. There is great potential for medical anthropology, especially, to serve as an integrating and synthesizing framework for studies of war, political violence, peace and health – not only within anthropology, in general, but also cross-disciplinarily.

As this overview has demonstrated, medical anthropology is well on the way to documenting the suffering and injustice inflicted by war and political violence, and in exploring precursors, causal factors, and processes that reconcile violent pasts while building more hopeful futures. The biggest challenge we face, as a discipline, is in translating these experiences and the insights and knowledge gained from them, so as to inform pragmatic action. There are many research questions regarding war and political violence that still need to be addressed, but perhaps the most significant one is: What more can we, as medical anthropologists, contribute through our methods and research, and our resulting theory and knowledge, that helps bring us closer to that stated goal of "a world without violence?"

REFERENCES

Abu-Musa, Antoine A., Loulou Kobeissi, Antoine G. Hannoun, and Marcia C. Inhorn, 2008 Effect of War on Fertility: A Review of the Literature. Reproductive Biomedicine Online 17(supplement 1):43–53.

Adams, Abigail, 2010 Olive Drab and White Coats: US Military Medical Teams Interoperating with Guatemala. *In* The War Machine and Global Health. Merrill Singer and G. Derrick Hodge, eds. pp. 279–304. Lanham MD: AltaMira Press.

American Anthropological Association, Commission on the Engagement of Anthropology with the US Security and Intelligence Communities, 2009 Final Report on the Army's Human Terrain System Proof of Concept Program. Electronic document. http://www.aaanet.org/cmtes/commissions/CEAUSSIC/ upload/CEAUSSIC_HTS_Final_Report.pdf/.

American Anthropological Association, 2007a Race: Are We So Different? Electronic Document. http://www.understandingrace.org/home.html/.

American Anthropological Association, 2007b Statement on Torture. Electronic Document. http://www.aaanet.org/issues/policy-advocacy/Statement-on-Torture.cfm/.

Anderson, Warwick, 2006 Colonial Pathologies: American Tropical Medicine, Race, and Hygiene in the Philippines. Durham NC: Duke University Press.

Appadurai, Arjun, 2006, Fear of Small Numbers: An Essay on the Geography of Anger. Durham NC: Duke University Press.

Arya, Neil and Joanna Santa Barbara, eds., 2008 Peace through Health: How Health Professionals Can Work for a Less Violent World. Sterling VA: Kumarian Press.

Aureli, Filippo, and Fran de Waal, 2000 Natural Conflict Resolution. Berkeley: University of California Press.

Auyero, Javier, and Débora Alejandra Swistun, 2009 Flammable: Environmental Suffering in an Argentine Shantytown. Oxford UK: Oxford University Press.

Baer, Hans, 2010 The Impact of the War Machine on Global Warming and Health: A Political–Ecological Perspective. *In The War Machine and Global Health*. Merrill Singer and G. Derrick Hodge, eds. pp. 157–167. Lanham MD: AltaMira Press.

Baer, Hans, Merrill Singer, and Ida Susser, 2003 Medical Anthropology and the World System. 2nd edition. Westport CT: Greenwood.

Barker, Holly, 2007 From Analysis to Action: Efforts to Address the Nuclear Legacy in the Marshall Islands. *In* Half Lives and Half Truths: Confronting the Radioactive Legacies of the Cold War. Barbara Rose Johnston, ed. pp. 213–248. Sante Fe NM: School for Advanced Research Press.

Barkey, Nanette, 2008 Building Peace in Angola: The Role of the Exhumation Process in Kuito. Human Organization 67(2):164–172.

Becker, Gay, Yewoubdar Beyene, and Pauline Ken, 2000 Memory, Trauma, and Embodied Distress: The Management of Disruption in the Stories of Cambodians in Exile. Ethos 28(3):320–345.

Ben-Ari, Eyal, 1998 Mastering Soldiers: Conflict, Emotions and the Enemy in an Israeli Military Unit. Oxford UK: Berghahn.

Ben-Ari, Eyal, 2004 The Military and Militarization in the United States. American Ethnologist 31(3):340–348.

Bickford, Andrew, 2008, Skin-in-Solutions: Militarizing Medicine and Militarizing Culture in the United States Military. North American Dialogue 11(1):5–8.

Biehl, João, 2007 Will to Live: AIDS Therapies and the Politics of Survival. Princeton NJ: Princeton University Press.

Binford, Leigh, 1996 The El Mozote Massacre: Anthropology and Human Rights. Tucson: University of Arizona Press.

Bonta, Bruce D., 1996 Conflict Resolution Among Peaceful Societies: The Culture of Peacefulness. Journal of Peace Research 33(4):403–420.

Bornstein, Avram, 2010 Hasbara, Health Care, and the Israeli Occupied Palestinian Territories. In The War Machine and Global Health. Merrill Singer and G. Derrick Hodge, eds. pp. 209–239. Lanham MD: AltaMira Press.

Bourgois, Philippe, 2003 In Search of Respect: Selling Crack in El Barrio, 2nd edition. New York: Cambridge University Press.

Bourgois, Philippe, 2009 Recognizing Invisible Violence: A Thirty-Year Ethnographic Retrospective. In Global Health in Times of Violence. Barbara Rylko-Bauer, Linda Whiteford and Paul Farmer, eds. pp. 17–40. Santa Fe NM: School for Advanced Research Press.

Bretlinger, Paula E., 1996 Health Sector Response to Security Threats During the Civil War in El Salvador. British Medical Journal 313:1470–1474.

British Medical Association, 1986 Torture Report. London: British Medical Association.

British Medical Association, 1992 Medicine Betrayed: The Participation of Doctors in Human Rights Abuses. London: Zed Books.

Bunde-Birouste, Anne, Maurice Eisenbruch, Natalie Grove, Michael Humphrey, Derrick Silove, Emily Waller, and Anthony Zwi, 2004, Health and Peace-building: Securing the Future. Sydney, Australia: University of New South Wales Health and Conflict Project and the School of Public Health and Community Medicine. Electronic Document. http://www.med.unsw.edu.au/SPHCMWeb.nsf/resources/AUSCAN_Background_I.pdf/$file/AUSCAN_Background_I.pdf/.

Campos, Nicole Gastineau and Paul Farmer, 2003 Partners: Discernment and Humanitarian Efforts in Settings of Violence. Journal of Law, Medicine and Ethics 31:503–515.

Cliff, Julie and Abdul Razak Noormahomed, 1988 Health as a Target: South Africa's Destabilization of Mozambique. Social Science and Medicine 27(7):717–722.

Cohen, Stanley, 2001 States of Denial: Knowing About Atrocities and Suffering. Cambridge UK: Polity.

Cohn, Jørgen, 1991 Proceedings of the International Symposium on Torture and the Medical Profession. Journal of Medical Ethics 17:S1–S64.

Comaroff, Jean, 1993 The Disease Heart of Africa: Medicine, Colonialism and the Black Body. In Knowledge, Power, and Practice: The Anthropology of Medicine and Everyday Life. Shirley Lindenbaum and Margaret Lock, eds. pp. 305–329. Berkeley: University of California Press.

Coronil, Fernando, and Julie Skurski, eds., 2005 States of Violence. Ann Arbor: University of Michigan Press.

Dadrian, Vahakn N., 1986 The Role of Turkish Physicians in the World War I Genocide of Ottoman Armenians. Holocaust and Genocide Studies 1(2):169–192.

Daniel, E. Valentine, 1996 Charred Lullabies: Chapters in an Anthropography of Violence. Princeton: Princeton University Press.

Danner, Mark, 2009 US Torture: Voices from the Black Sites. New York Review of Books 56(6):69–77.

Das, Veena, 2007 Life and Words: Violence and the Descent into the Ordinary. Berkeley: University of California Press.

Das, Veena, 2008 Violence, Gender, and Subjectivity. Annual Review of Anthropology 37: 283–299.

Das, Veena, Arthur Kleinman, Mamphela Ramphele, and Pamela Reynolds, eds., 2000 Violence and Subjectivity. Berkeley: University of California Press.

Das, Veena, Arthur Kleinman, Margaret Lock, Mamphela Ramphele, and Pamela Reynolds, eds., 2001 Remaking a World: Violence, Social Suffering, and Recovery. Berkeley: University of California Press.

Dentan, Robert Knox, 1968 The Semai: A Nonviolent People of Malaya. New York: Holt, Rinehart and Winston.

Dentan, Robert Knox, 2008 Overwhelming Terror: Love, Fear, Peace, and Violence among Semai of Malaysia. Lanham MD: Rowman & Littlefield.

D'Errico Nikki, Wake, Christopher M, and Wake, Rachel M., 2010 Healing Africa? An Examination of the Peace-building Role of a Health-based NGO Operating in Eastern Democratic Republic of Congo. Medicine, Conflict and Survival 26(2):145–159.

Desjarlais, Robert, and Arthur Kleinman, 1994 Violence and Demoralization in the New World Disorder. Anthropology Today 10(5):9–12.

de Waal, Alex, 1997 Famine Crimes: Politics and the Disaster Relief Industry in Africa. Bloomington: Indiana University Press.

de Waal, Frans, 2007 Chimpanzee Politics: Power and Sex among Apes. Baltimore MD: The Johns Hopkins University Press.

Easterbrook, Philippa, 1990 The Health Impact of "Low Intensity Conflict." Journal of Public Health Policy 11(3):277–280.

English, Bella, 2008 In Rwanda, Visionary Doctor is Moving Mountains Again: Health System Built from the Ground Up. Boston Globe, 13 April, p. A1.

Erickson, Pamela, 2008 Ethnomedicine. Long Grove IL: Waveland Press.

Farmer, Paul, 1992 AIDS and Accusation: Haiti and the Geography of Blame. Berkeley: University of California Press.

Farmer, Paul, 2003 Pathologies of Power: Health, Human Rights, and the New War on the Poor. Berkeley: University of California Press.

Farmer, Paul, 2004a An Anthropology of Structural Violence. Current Anthropology 45(3):305–325.

Farmer, Paul, 2004b Political Violence and Public Health in Haiti. New England Journal of Medicine 350(15):1483–1486.

Farmer, Paul, 2008 Challenging Orthodoxies: The Road Ahead for Health and Human Rights. Health and Human Rights 10(1):1–15. Electronic document. http://www.hhrjournal.org/index.php/hhr/article/view/33/102/.

Farmer, Paul, 2009a "Landmine Boy" and the Tomorrow of Violence. In Global Health in Times of Violence. Barbara Rylko-Bauer, Linda Whiteford and Paul Farmer, eds. pp. 41–62. Santa Fe NM: School for Advanced Research Press.

Farmer, Paul, 2009b Mother Courage and the Future of War. In An Anthropology of War. Alisse Waterston, ed. pp. 164–184. New York: Berghahn Books.

Fassin, Didier, 2007 When Bodies Remember: Experiences and Politics of AIDS in South Africa. Amy Jacobs and Gabrielle Varro, translation. Berkeley: University of California Press.

Fassin, Didier, 2009 A Violence of History: Accounting for AIDS in Post-apartheid South Africa. In Global Health in Times of Violence. Barbara Rylko-Bauer, Linda Whiteford and Paul Farmer, eds. pp. 113–135. Santa Fe NM: School for Advanced Research Press.

Fassin, Didier and Estelle d'Halluin, 2007 Critical Evidence: The Politics of Trauma in French Asylum Policies. Ethos 35(3):300–329.

Fassin, Didier and Richard Rechtman, 2009 The Empire of Trauma: An Inquiry into the Condition of Victimhood. Rachel Gomme, translation. Princeton: Princeton University Press.

Feldman, Allen, 1991 Formations of Violence: The Narrative of the Body and Political Terror in Northern Ireland. Chicago: University of Chicago Press.

Ferguson, R. Brian, 2009 Ten Points on War. *In* An Anthropology of War: Views from the Frontline. Alisse Waterston, ed. pp. 32–49. New York: Berghahn Books.

Ferrándiz, Francisco, 2006 The Return of Civil War Ghosts: The Ethnography of Exhumations in Contemporary Spain. Anthropology Today 22(3):7–12.

Foxen, Patricia, 2010 Local Narratives of Distress and Resilience: Lessons in Psychosocial Well-being among the K'iche' Maya in Postwar Guatemala. Journal of Latin American and Caribbean Anthropology 15(1): 68–89.

Franke, Richard, 1984 More on Geertz's Interpretive Theory. Current Anthropology 25(5):692–693.

Fried, Morton, Marvin Harris, and Robert Murphy, eds., 1967 War: The Anthropology of Armed Conflict and Aggression. New York: Doubleday.

Fry, Douglas P., 2006 The Human Potential for Peace: An Anthropological Challenge to Assumptions about War and Violence. New York: Oxford University Press.

Geneva Declaration Secretariat, 2008 Global Burden of Armed Violence. Geneva, Switzerland: Geneva Declaration Secretariat.

Ghimire, Sachin, 2009 The Intersection between Armed Conflict and the Health Service System in the Rolpa District of Nepal: An Ethnographic Description. Social Medicine 4(3):139–147. Electronic document. http://www.socialmedicine.info/index.php/social-medicine/article/view/342/666/.

González, Roberto J., 2007a Shattered Taboo: Notes on the Incremental Acceptance of Torture. Paper presented at the 106th Annual Meeting of the American Anthropological Association, Washington, November 38–December 2.

González, Roberto J., 2007b Towards Mercenary Anthropology? Anthropology Today 23(3):14–19.

González, Roberto J., 2008 Human Terrain: Past, Present, and Future Applications. Anthropology Today 23(6):21–22.

Good, Mary-Jo DelVecchio, Byron Good, Jesse Grayman, and Matthew Lakoma, 2007 A Psychosocial Needs Assessment of Communities in 14 Conflict-Affected Districts in Aceh. Geneva, Switzerland: International Organization for Migration.

Gould, Chandré, and Peter Folb, 2002 The Role of Professionals in the South African Chemical and Biological Warfare Programme. Minerva 40:77–91.

Grayman, Jesse Hession, Mary-Jo DelVecchio Good, and Byron J. Good, 2009 Conflict Nightmares and Trauma in Aceh. Culture, Medicine and Psychiatry 33:290–312.

Green, Linda, 1999 Fear As A Way of Life: Mayan Widows in Rural Guatemala. New York: Columbia University Press.

Gruskin, Sofia, and Alexander Butchart, eds., 2003 Violence Prevention: Bringing Health and Human Rights Together. Theme Issue. Health and Human Rights 6(2).

Gusterson, Hugh, 2007 Anthropology and Militarism. Annual Review of Anthropology 36:155–175.

Gutterman, Bella, 2008 A Narrow Bridge to Life: Jewish Forced Labor and Survival in the Gross–Rosen Camp System, 1940–1945. New York: Berghahn.

Hacker, Barton, 1994 Elements of Controversy: The Atomic Energy Commission and Radiation Safety, 1947–1974. Berkeley: University of California Press.

Halper, Jeff, 2001 Engaged Anthropology. Anthropology News May:14.

Halper, Jeff, 2008 An Israeli in Palestine: Resisting Dispossession, Redeeming Israel. London: Pluto Press.

Harding, Scott and Kathryn Libal, 2010 War and the Public Health Disaster in Iraq. *In* The War Machine and Global Health. Merrill Singer and G. Derrick Hodge, eds. pp. 59–87. Lanham MD: AltaMira Press.

Hasanović, Mevludin, Osman Sinanović, Zihnet Selimbašić, Izet Pajević, and Esmina Avdibegović, 2006 Psychological Disturbances of War-Traumatized Children from Different Foster and Family Settings in Bosnia and Herzegovina. Croatian Medical Journal 47(1):85–94.

Heggenhougen, H. K., 2009 Planting "Seeds of Health" in the Fields of Structural Violence: The Life and Death of Francisco Curruchiche. *In* Global Health in Times of Violence.

Barbara Rylko-Bauer, Linda Whiteford and Paul Farmer, eds. pp. 181–199. Santa Fe NM: School for Advanced Research Press.

Henry, Doug, 2005 The Legacy of the Tank, the Violence of Peace. Anthropological Quarterly 78(2):443–456.

Henry, Doug, 2006 Violence and the Body: Somatic Expressions of Trauma and Vulnerability during War. Medical Anthropology Quarterly 20(3):379–398.

Herman, Edward, 1995 The Banality of Evil. Electronic document. http://musictravel.free.fr/political/political65.htm/.

Hills, Elaine A., and Dahlia S. Wasfi, 2010 The Causes and Human Costs of Targeting Iraq. *In* The War Machine and Global Health. Merrill Singer and G. Derrick Hodge, eds. pp.119–156. Lanham MD: AltaMira Press.

Hinton, Alexander Laban, ed., 2002 Annihilating Difference: The Anthropology of Genocide. Berkeley: University of California Press.

Hinton, Alexander Laban and Kevin Lewis O'Neill, eds., 2009 Genocide: Truth, Memory, and Representation. Durham NC: Duke University Press.

Human Security Research Group, 2009 Human Security Research Report: The Shrinking Costs of War. Vancouver, Canada: School for International Studies, Simon Fraser University.

Inhorn, Marcia, 2008 Medical Anthropology against War. Medical Anthropology Quarterly 22(4):416–424.

Jenkins, Janis, 1998 The Medical Anthropology of Political Violence: A Cultural and Feminist Agenda. Medical Anthropology Quarterly 12(1):122–131.

Johnston, Barbara Rose, 1994 Experimenting on Human Subjects: Nuclear Weapons Testing and Human Rights Abuses. *In* Who Pays the Price? The Sociocultural Context of Environmental Crises. Barbara Rose Johnston, ed. pp. 131–141. Washington: Island Press.

Johnston, Barbara Rose, 2005 Chixoy Dam Legacy Issues Study. Electronic document. http://www.centerforpoliticalecology.org/chixoy.html/.

Johnston, Barbara Rose, ed., 2007 Half-Lives and Half-Truths: Confronting the Radioactive Legacies of the Cold War. Santa Fe NM: School for Advanced Research Press.

Johnston, Barbara Rose, 2009 Atomic Times in the Pacific. Anthropology Now 1(2): 1–9.

Johnston, Barbara Rose, and Holly M. Barker, 2008 Consequential Damages of Nuclear War: The Rongelap Report. Walnut Creek CA: Left Coast Press.

Johnston, Barbara Rose, and Susan Slyomovics, eds., 2009 Waging War, Making Peace: Reparations and Human Rights. Walnut Creek CA: Left Coast Press.

Kleinman, Arthur, and Robert Desjarlais, 1995 Violence, Culture, and the Politics of Trauma. *In* Writing at the Margin: Discourse Between Anthropology and Medicine. Arthur Kleinman, ed., pp. 173–189. Berkeley: University of California Press.

Kleinman, Arthur, Veena Das, and Margaret Lock, eds., 1997 Social Suffering. Berkeley: University of California Press.

Kohrt, Brandon A., Wietse A. Tol, Judith Pettigrew, and Rohit Karki, 2010 Children and Revolution: Mental Health and Psychosocial Well-Being of Child Soldiers in Nepal. *In* The War Machine and Global Health. Merrill Singer and G. Derrick Hodge, eds. pp.89–116. Lanham MD: AltaMira Press.

Krug, Etienne G., Linda L. Dahlberg, James A. Mercy, Anthony B. Zwi, and Rafael Lozano, eds., 2002 World Report on Violence and Health. Geneva: World Health Organization.

Kruk, Margaret E., Lynn P. Freedman, Grace A. Anglin, and Ronald J. Waldman, 2010 Rebuilding Health Systems to Improve Health and Promote Statebuilding in Post-Conflict Countries: A Theoretical Framework and Research Agenda. Social Science and Medicine 70(1):89–97.

Langer, Lawrence L., 1997 The Alarmed Vision: Social Suffering and Holocaust Atrocity. In Social Suffering. Arthur Kleinman, Veena Das, and Margaret Lock, eds. pp. 47–65. Berkeley: University of California Press.

Levi, Primo, and Leonardo de Benedetti, 2006 Auschwitz Report. Robert S. C. Gordon, ed., Judith Woolf, trans. London: Verso.

Levy, Barry S., and Victor W. Sidel, eds., 2000 War and Public Health, updated edition. Washington: American Public Health Association.

LeShan, Lawrence, 2002 The Psychology of War: Comprehending its Mystique and its Madness. New York: Helios Press.

Lifton, Robert Jay, 2000[1986] The Nazi Doctors: Medical Killing and the Psychology of Genocide. New York: Basic Books.

Lončar, Mladen, Vesna Medved, Nikolina Jovanović, and Ljubomir Hotujac, 2006 Psychological Consequences of Rape on Women in 1991–1995 War in Croatia and Bosnia and Herzegovina. Croatian Medical Journal 47:67–75.

Lutz, Catherine, 2002 Homefront: A Military City and the American Twentieth Century. Boston: Beacon.

Lutz, Catherine and Jane Collins, 1994 The Photograph as an Intersection of Gazes: The Example of National Geographic. In Visualizing Theory. Lucien Taylor, ed. pp. 311–339. New York: Routledge.

Lutz, Catherine and Donald Nonini, 2000 The Economics of Violence and the Violence of Economics. In Anthropological Theory Today. Henrietta Moore, ed. pp. 73–113. Malden MA: Blackwell Publishers.

Lyon, Evan, Jim Yong Kim, and Paul Farmer, 2008 Social Justice and the Responsibility of Health-Care Workers: Observation, Assessment, Action. In Peace through Health: How Health Professionals Can Work for a Less Violent World. Neil Arya and Joanna Santa Barbara, eds. pp. 267–276. Sterling VA: Kumarian Press.

MacQueen, Graeme, and Joanna Santa-Barbara, 2000 Peace Building through Health Initiatives. British Medical Journal 321:293–296.

Maier, Thomas, 2009 Questions and Answers about the Island and the Lab. Newsday.com 21 August. Electronic document. http://www.newsday.com/long-island/li-life/questions-and-answers-about-the-island-and-the-lab-1.1385308?print=true/.

Manz, Beatriz, 2004 Paradise in Ashes: A Guatemalan Journey of Courage, Terror, and Hope. Berkeley: University of California Press.

Marmorstein, Jerome, 2001 War As a Disease Epidemic. Nuclear Age Peace Foundation. Electronic document. http://www.wagingpeace.org/articles/2001/07/00_marmorstein_war-disease.htm/.

Marmot, Michael, and Richard Wilkinson, 2005 Social Determinants of Health, 2nd edition. Oxford: Oxford University Press.

Maternowska, Catherine M., 2006 Reproducing Inequities: Poverty and the Politics of Population in Haiti. New Brunswick NJ: Rutgers University Press.

McCue, Jack, 2007 Enduring Injuries to Brain and Mind: Medical Consequences of the Iraq War. Internal Medicine World Report, May. Electronic document. http://www.imwr.com/issues/articles/2007–05_38.asp/.

Miles, Steven H., 2006 Oath Betrayed: Torture, Medical Complicity, and the War on Terror. New York: Random House.

Miles, Steven H., and Leah Marks, eds., 2007 United States Military Medicine in War on Terror Prisons. Online archive at the Human Rights Library of the University of Minnesota. Electronic document. http://www.umn.edu/humanrts/OathBetrayed/index.html/.

Minayo, Maria Cecília de Souza, Simone Gonçalves de Assis, and Edinilsa Ramos de Souza, 2006 Violence in Today's Society and Its Repercussions on Collective Health. Theme Issue. Ciência and Saúde Coletiva 11(2). Electronic document. http://www.scielo.br/scielo.php?script=sci_issuetoc&pid=1413–812320060002&lng=en&nrm=iso.

Montagu, Ashley, 1978 Learning Non-Aggression: The Experience of Non-Literate Societies. New York: Oxford University Press.

Nagengast, Carole, 1994 Violence, Terror, and the Crisis of the State. Annual Review in Anthropology 23:109–136.

National Research Council, 1994 Radiological Assessments for the Resettlement of Rongelap in the Republic of the Marshall Islands. Washington: National Academy Press.

Nichter, Mark, 1992 Anthropological Approaches to the Study of Ethnomedicine. Langhorne PA: Gordon and Breach Science Publishers.

Nordstrom, Carolyn, 1997 A Different Kind of War Story. Philadelphia: University of Pennsylvania Press.

Nordstrom, Carolyn, 1998 Terror Warfare and the Medicine of Peace. Medical Anthropology Quarterly 21(1):103–121.

Nordstrom, Carolyn, 2004a Shadows of War: Violence, Power, and International Profiteering in the Twenty-First Century. Berkeley: University of California Press.

Nordstrom, Carolyn, 2004b The Tomorrow of Violence. In Violence. Neil L. Whitehead, ed. pp. 223–242. Santa Fe NM: School of American Research Press.

Nordstrom, Carolyn, 2007 Global Outlaws: Crime, Money, and Power in the Contemporary World. Berkeley: University of California Press.

Nordstrom, Carolyn, 2009 Fault Lines. In Global Health in Times of Violence. Barbara Rylko-Bauer, Linda Whiteford and Paul Farmer, eds. pp. 63–87. Santa Fe NM: School for Advanced Research Press.

Nordstrom, Carolyn, and Antonius C. G. M. Robben, eds., 1995 Fieldwork Under Fire: Contemporary Studies of Violence and Survival. Berkeley: University of California Press.

Olujic, Maria B., 1998 Embodiment of Terror: Gendered Violence in Peacetime and Wartime in Croatia and Bosnia-Herzegovina. Medical Anthropology Quarterly 12(1):31–50.

Omidian, Patricia A., 2009 Living and Working in a War Zone: An Applied Anthropologist in Afghanistan. Practicing Anthropology 31(2):4–11.

Panter-Brick, Catherine, 2002 Street Children, Human Rights, and Public Health: A Critique and Future Directions. Annual Review of Anthropology 31:147–171.

Panter-Brick, Catherine, 2010 Conflict, Violence, and Health: Setting a New Interdisciplinary Agenda. Social Science and Medicine 70(1):1–6.

Pedersen, Duncan, 2002 Political Violence, Ethnic Conflict, and Contemporary Wars: Broad Implications for Health and Social Well-Being. Social Science and Medicine 55:175–190.

Pedersen, Duncan, 2006 Reframing Political Violence and Mental Health Outcomes: Outlining a Research and Action Agenda for Latin America and the Caribbean Region. Ciência and Saúde Coletiva 11(2):293–302.

Permanent Secretariat of Nobel Peace Laureates Summits, 2009 Charter for a World Without Violence. Electronic document. http://www.nobelforpeace-summits.org/wp-content/uploads/2009/07/charter-EN1.pdf/.

Pfeiffer, James, Wendy Johnson, Meredith Fort, Aaron Shakow, Amy Hagopian, Steve Gloyd, and Kenneth Gimbel-Sherr, 2008 Strengthening Health Systems in Poor Countries: A Code of Conduct for Nongovernmental Organizations. American Journal of Public Health 98(12):2134–2140.

Physicians for Human Rights, 2005 Break Them Down: Systematic Use of Psychological Torture by US Forces. Electronic document. http://physiciansforhumanrights.org/library/report-2005-may.html/.

Pike, Ivy L., Bilinda Straight, Matthias Oesterle, Charles Hilton, and Adamson Lanyasunya, 2010 Documenting the Health Consequences of Endemic Warfare in Three Pastoralist Communities of Northern Kenya: A Conceptual Framework. Social Science and Medicine 70(1):45–52.

Pim, Joám Evans, ed., 2009 Toward a Nonkilling Paradigm. Honolulu: Center for Global Nonkilling. Electronic document. http://www.nonkilling.org/.

Price, David, 2000 Anthropologists as Spies. The Nation, 20 November, pp.24–27.

Price, David, 2009 Human Terrain Systems, Anthropologists and the War in Afghanistan. Counterpunch, 1 December. Electronic document. http://www.counterpunch.org/price12012009.html/.

Quesada, James, 2009 The Vicissitudes of Structural Violence: Nicaragua at the Turn of the Twenty-first Century. In Global Health in Times of Violence. Barbara Rylko-Bauer, Linda Whiteford and Paul Farmer, eds. pp.157–180. Santa Fe NM: School for Advanced Research Press.

Rao, Aparna, Michael Bollig, and Monika Böck, eds., 2007 The Practice of War: Production, Reproduction, and Communication of Armed Violence. New York: Berghahn Books.

Rather, L. J., ed., 1985 Rudolf Virchow: Collected Essays on Public Health and Epidemiology. Boston MA: Science History Publications.

Redfield, Peter, 2005 Doctors, Borders, and Life in Crisis. Cultural Anthropology 20(3): 328–361.

Roland, Charles G., 1992 Courage Under Siege: Starvation, Disease, and Death in the Warsaw Ghetto. New York: Oxford University Press.

Rubenstein, Robert A., 2008 Peacekeeping Under Fire: Culture and Intervention. Boulder CO: Paradigm.

Rylko-Bauer, Barbara, 2009 Medicine in the Political Economy of Brutality: Reflections from the Holocaust and Beyond. In Global Health in Times of Violence. Barbara Rylko-Bauer, Linda Whiteford and Paul Farmer, eds. pp.201–222. Santa Fe NM: School for Advanced Research Press.

Rylko-Bauer, Barbara, Merrill Singer, and John van Willigen, 2006 Reclaiming Applied Anthropology: Its Past, Present, and Future. American Anthropologist 108(1):178–190.

Rylko-Bauer, Barbara, Linda Whiteford, and Paul Farmer, eds., 2009a Global Health in Times of Violence. Santa Fe NM: School for Advanced Research Press.

Rylko-Bauer, Barbara, Linda Whiteford, and Paul Farmer, eds., 2009b Prologue: Coming to Terms with Global Violence and Health. In Global Health in Times of Violence. Barbara Rylko-Bauer, Linda Whiteford and Paul Farmer, eds., pp. 3–16. Santa Fe NM: School for Advanced Research Press.

Sanford, Victoria, 2003a Buried Secrets: Truth and Human Rights in Guatemala. New York: Palgrave Macmillan.

Sanford, Victoria, 2003b Learning to Kill by Proxy: Colombian Paramilitaries and the Legacy of Central American Death Squads, Contras and Civil Patrols. Journal of Social Justice 30(3):1–19.

Sanford, Victoria, and Asale Angel-Ajani, eds., 2006 Engaged Observer: Anthropology, Advocacy, and Activism. New Brunswick NJ: Rutgers University Press.

Sanford, Victoria and H. C. Muggah, 2003 Peacebuilding in a War Zone: The Case of Columbian Peace Communities. Journal of International Peacekeeping 10(2):107–118.

Scarpa, Angela, and Adrian Raine, 2007 Biosocial Bases of Violence. In The Cambridge Handbook of Violent Behavior and Aggression. Daniel Flannery, Alexander Vasonyi and Irwin Waldman, eds. pp. 151–169. Cambridge: Cambridge University Press.

Schafft, Gretchen E., 2004 From Racism to Genocide: Anthropology in the Third Reich. Urbana IL: University of Illinois Press.

Schafft, Gretchen E., 2009 The Ethical Dimensions of Peace. In Waging War, Making Peace: Reparations and Human Rights. Barbara Rose Johnston and Susan Slyomovics, eds., pp. 31–55. Walnut Creek CA: Left Coast Press.

Scheper-Hughes, Nancy, 1992 Death Without Weeping: The Violence of Everyday Life in Brazil. Berkeley: University of California Press.

Scheper-Hughes, Nancy, 2007 The Gray Zone: Small Wars, Peacetime Crimes, and Invisible Genocides. In The Shadow Side of Fieldwork: Exploring the Blurred Borders between Ethnography and Life, Athena McLean and Annette Leibing, eds. pp. 159–184. Malden MA: Blackwell Publishing.

Scheper-Hughes, Nancy, and Philippe Bourgois, 2004a Introduction: Making Sense of Violence. In Violence in War and Peace: An Anthology. Nancy Scheper-Hughes and Philippe Bourgois, eds. Malden MA: Blackwell Publishing.

Scheper-Hughes, Nancy and Philippe Bourgois, eds., 2004b Violence in War and Peace: An Anthology. Malden MA: Blackwell Publishing.

Scheper-Hughes, Nancy and Carolyn Sargent, eds., 1998 Small Wars: The Cultural Politics of Childhood. Berkeley: University of California Press.

Sidel, Victor W., and Barry S. Levy, 2003 Physician–Soldier: A Moral Dilemma? In Military Medical Ethics, vol. 1. Thomas E. Beam and Linette R. Sparacino, eds. pp. 293–329.

Washington: Office of the Surgeon General at TMM Publications, Borden Institute, Walter Reed Army Medical Center.

Sidel, Victor W., and Barry S. Levy, 2009 The Health Consequences of the Diversion of Resources to War and Preparations for War. Social Medicine 4(3):133–135. Electronic document. http://www.socialmedicine.info/index.php/socialmedicine/article/view/362/663/.

Simons, Anna, 1997 The Company They Keep: Life Inside the US Army Special Forces. New York: Free Press.

Simons, Anna, 1999 War: Back to the Future. Annual Review of Anthropology 28:73–108.

Singer, Merrill, 2006 *The Face of Social Suffering: The Life History of a Street Drug Addict.* Long Grove, IL: Waveland Press.

Singer, Merrill, 2009 Desperate Measures: A Syndemic Approach to the Anthropology of Health in a Violent City. *In* Global Health in Times of Violence. Barbara Rylko-Bauer, Linda Whiteford and Paul Farmer, eds. pp. 137–156. Santa Fe NM: School for Advanced Research Press.

Singer, Merrill and Pamela I. Erickson, 2009 The Future of Medical Anthropology: Meeting Global Health Challenges. Anthropology News 50(9):13, 15.

Singer, Merrill and G. Derrick Hodge, eds., 2010a The War Machine and Global Health. Lanham MD: AltaMira Press.

Singer, Merrill and G. Derrick Hodge, 2010b The Myriad Impacts of the War Machine on Global Health. In The War Machine and Global Health. Merrill Singer and G. Derrick Hodge, eds.. pp. 1–27. Lanham MD: AltaMira Press.

Sluka, Jeffrey A., ed., 2000 Death Squad: The Anthropology of State Terror. Philadelphia: University of Pennsylvania Press.

Sponsel, Leslie E., 2009 Reflections on the Possibilities of a Nonkilling Society and a Nonkilling Anthropology. *In* Toward a Nonkilling Paradigm. Joám Evans Pim, ed. pp. 35–70. Honolulu: Center for Global Nonkilling. Electronic document. http://www.nonkilling.org/.

Stewart, Frances, 2002 Root Causes of Violent Conflict in Developing Countries. British Medical Journal 324:432–345.

Taipale, Ilkka, P. Helena Mäkelä, Kati Juva, Vappu Taipale, Sergei Kolesnikov, Raj Mutalik, and Michael Christ, eds., 2002 War or Health? A Reader. London: Zed Books. Helsinki: Physicians for Social Responsibility.

Terry, Fiona, 2002 Condemned to Repeat? The Paradox of Humanitarian Action. Ithaca NY: Cornell University Press.

Thornburgh, Dick, Glen Reichardt, and Jon Stanley, 2003 The Nuclear Claims Tribunal of the Republic of the Marshall Islands: An Independent Examination and Assessment of its Decision-Making Processes. Washington: Kirkpatrick & Lockhart LLP.

Trawick, Margaret, 2002 Killing and Healing Revisited: On Cultural Difference, Warfare, and Sacrifice. *In* New Horizons in Medical Anthropology. Mark Nichter and Margaret Lock, eds. pp. 266–296. London: Routledge.

Ugalde, Antonio, Ernesto Selva-Sutter, Carolina Castillo, Carolina Paz, and Sergio Cañas, 2000 The Health Costs of War: Can They Be Measured? Lessons from El Salvador. British Medical Journal 321 (7254):169–172.

UNDP (United Nations Development Programme), 2009 Human Development Report 2009. Electronic document. http://hdrstats.undp.org/en/countries/country_fact_sheets/cty_fs_CRI.html/.

UNICEF (United Nations Children's Fund), 2009 State of the World's Children, Special edition. Electronic document. http://www.unicef.org/rightsite/sowc/fullreport.php/.

Van Dongen, Els, 2007 Farewell to Fieldwork? Constraints in Anthropological Research in Violent Situations. *In* On Knowing and Not Knowing in The Anthropology of Medicine. Roland Littlefield, ed. pp. 160–171. Walnut Creek CA: Left Coast Press.

Varley, Emma, 2010 Targeted Doctors, Missing Patients: Obstetric Health Services and Sectarian Conflict in Northern Pakistan. Social Science and Medicine 70(1): 61–70.

Vesti, Peter, and Niels Johan Lavik, 1991 Torture and the Medical Profession: A Review. Journal of Medical Ethics 17:S4–S8.

Waterston, Alisse, ed., 2009a An Anthropology of War: Views from the Frontline. New York: Berghahn Books.

Waterston, Alisse, 2009b Introduction: On War and Accountability. *In* An Anthropology of War: Views from the Frontline. Alisse Waterston, ed. pp. 12–31. New York: Berghahn Books.

Whitehead, Neil L., ed., 2004 Violence. Santa Fe, NM: School of American Research Press.

Whiteford, Linda, 2009 Failure to Protect, Failure to Provide: Refugee Reproductive Rights. *In* Global Health in Times of Violence. Barbara Rylko-Bauer, Linda Whiteford and Paul Farmer, eds. pp. 89–112. Santa Fe NM: School for Advanced Research Press.

WHO (World Health Organization), 1981 34th World Health Assembly. Resolution 34.38. Geneva: World Health Organization.

WHO (World Health Organization), 2002 Report on the Second World Health Organization Consultation on Health as a Bridge for Peace. Escogia, Versoix, 8–9 July. Geneva: World Health Organization. Electronic document. http://www.who.int/hac/techguidance/hbp/Versoix_consultation_report.pdf/.

WHO (World Health Organization), 2008 Closing the Gap In a Generation: Health Equity Through Action On the Social Determinants of Health. Final Report of the Commission on Social Determinants of Health. Geneva: World Health Organization. Electronic document. http://www.who.int/social_determinants/thecommission/finalreport/en/index.html/.

Wolf, Eric R., 1969 Peasant Wars of the Twentieth Century. New York: Harper and Row.

Wolf, Eric R., 1999 Envisioning Power: Ideologies of Dominance and Crisis. Berkeley: University of California Press.

World Council of Churches, 2005 World Military Expenditures: A Compilation of Data and Facts Related to Military Spending, Education, and Health. Electronic Document. http://www.ipb.org/i/pdf-files/World_Council_of_Churches-World_Military_Expenditures_Education_and_Health.pdf/.

Zraly, Maggie and Laetitia Nyirazinyoye 2010 Don't Let the Suffering Make You Fade Away: An Ethnographic Study of Resilience among Survivors of Genocide-Rape in Southern Rwanda. Social Science and Medicine 70(10):1656–1664.

Zur, Judith, 1996 From PTSD to Voices in Context: From an "Experience-Far" to an "Experience-Near" Understanding of Responses to War and Atrocity Across Cultures. International Journal of Social Psychiatry 42(4):305–317.

Zur, Judith, 1998 Violent Memories: Mayan War Widows in Guatemala. Boulder CO: Westview Press.

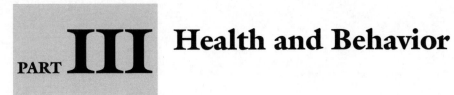

PART **III** Health and Behavior

CHAPTER **12** # Humans in a World of Microbes: The Anthropology of Infectious Disease

Peter J. Brown,
George J. Armelagos,
and Kenneth C. Maes

INTRODUCTION

All humans live in a world full of microbes, including bacteria, viruses, prions, fungi, protozoa, and multi-cellular parasites. Microbes are in our environment and they live on and in our bodies. Over 500 different species of bacteria reside in the normal large intestine, comprising nearly five pounds of the total body weight of adults in low-income countries, but less than three pounds in developed countries (Bengmark 2000). Some microbes are necessary for normal physiological function. However, certain microbes cause infectious diseases that have plagued humanity throughout history. Infections arise when microbes have particular pathogenic biological charac-teristics, when they are "out of place", or when the human host's immune system is vulnerable.

For people in societies with relatively little infectious disease, it is easy to underes-timate how diseases shape human biology, culture, and experience. All humans harbor infections of pathogenic organisms, and suffer the consequences at some time in their lives. The experience of disease is as inescapable as death itself, and coping with dis-ease is a universal aspect of the human existence. Yet the particular diseases that afflict people – as well as the way in which symptoms are interpreted and acted upon – vary greatly across different societies. Cultural notions of "contagion," fear, and stigma have a major impact on the experience of disease, accessibility of care, and hence on

A Companion to Medical Anthropology, First Edition. Edited by Merrill Singer and Pamela I. Erickson.
© 2011 Blackwell Publishing Ltd. Published 2011 by Blackwell Publishing Ltd.

disease course and consequences. Infectious diseases are also exacerbated by political economic factors including poverty and war. Because understanding the interactions between disease, culture, social inequality, and ecology is a productive way of under- standing the human condition, this is an essential intellectual focus for medical anthropologists.

We have three goals in this chapter. First, we describe how the application of specific medical anthropological concepts can provide a nuanced and full understanding of the biocultural etiology, epidemiology, and ecology of infectious disease. Second, we use epidemiological transition theory to demonstrate the importance of social and historical contexts for explaining changes in the prevalence of infectious disease (including epidemics). This is related to "emerging" diseases in the contexts of grow- ing socio-economic inequality, globalization, and urbanization. Finally, we use the example of the HIV/AIDS pandemic in Africa to illustrate three processes: (1) how biological, behavioral and economic factors interact and influence the spread of an infectious disease; (2) how political factors are important for understanding the context of infectious disease; (3) how cultural beliefs and stigmatization can exacerbate the epidemic and complicate interventions for prevention and treatment. The anthropo- logical literature on infectious disease is very large; by necessity we have truncated discussions of some important topics including studies of local ethnomedical beliefs related to infectious disease (see excellent volumes by Nichter 2008; Green 1999).

CULTURE, ECOLOGY AND THE EPIDEMIOLOGY OF INFECTIOUS DISEASE

Culture plays three major roles in determining the patterns of disease and death in a population. First, culture may shape important behaviors (with respect to diet, activity patterns, water use, sexual practices, etc.) that predispose individuals to acquire certain diseases. Second, through cultural practices as varied as agriculture and war, people actively change the nature of their environment in ways that affect their sus- ceptibility to infections. The archeological and historical records clearly demonstrate that anthropogenic environmental changes can have profound effects on disease rates, both positive and negative. Third, cultural models of etiology, patient role and treat- ment (including neglect) influence the way people respond to those who become ill. In this section we focus on the first way and provide some examples of how medical anthropologists have contributed to this field.

Infection, the harmful colonization of a host by a microscopic species that uses the host's resources for its own reproduction, is a necessary but insufficient cause of contagious disease. Infection often does not result in serious disease and death because normal immunologic reactions of the host organism can kill the invading microbes. Many episodes of infectious disease are therefore self-limiting, but serious disease or death is more likely when an infected person is immunologically compro- mised by malnutrition, HIV, or previous disease episodes. Severe infections require clinical treatments like antibiotics or surgical removal of infected parts. Antibiotic resistant strains of infectious agents – the result of anthropogenic changes in the pathogen itself – make treatment difficult or impossible. Some infections can also turn out to be the ultimate cause of chronic disease. For example, peptic ulcers were once thought to be caused by stress but are now recognized to be the result of

H. pylori colonization. Periodontal infections may result in chronic systemic inflammation and cause cardiovascular disease (Demmer 2006), and viral infections like sexually transmitted human papillomavirus (HPV) cause cervical cancer.

Infectious disease prevalence can vary significantly between societies because of differences in culture, social structure, ecological setting, and historical context. This is also the case within a single society, where variations in the kind and severity of diseases afflict individuals of different ages, sexes, social classes, and ethnic groups. Social class – which affects both exposure to pathogens and access to treatment – is particularly salient for many medical anthropologists, because patterns of disease distribution often reflect patterns of socio-economic inequality as well as culturally-coded class-linked behaviors that put individuals at risk.

The three basic variables of descriptive epidemiology – *person, place,* and *time* – are related to the particularities of society and culture. Descriptive epidemiological data are used to identify the causal agent of a disease outbreak; they can also be used in mathematical models to predict the spread of disease. From a medical anthropological perspective, Trostle (2005) has shown that epidemiological data are shaped by the culture of biomedicine, specifically the assumptions inherent in disease pattern categories as well as biases in the collection of information. Epidemiology's emphasis on quantification oversimplifies and obscures the complexities and contingencies of human life and decision-making.

In a similar vein, Turshen (1977) has criticized the traditional, "bourgeois" model of disease ecology that emphasizes the interaction of host, pathogen, and environment, thereby simplifying the notion of environment to a question of climate. This model fails to recognize that "host factors" for disease risk are often the result of social inequalities or political economic policies. For example, people may become more likely to contract HIV because of labor policies that forbid intact families to migrate, as has occurred in southern Africa, just as the shift from HIV infection to full-blown AIDS may be related to malnutrition or access to anti-retroviral therapy. In light of such problems, medical anthropologists have advocated for a "Cultural Epidemiology" which emphasizes variables like social class, social support, cultural beliefs, values, illness labels, norms, and representations (Trostle and Sommerfeld 1996). Weiss (2001) describes Cultural Epidemiology as interdisciplinary research on locally valid representations of illness and their distributions in cultural context; while much of this work focuses on mental illness, it has important ramifications for infectious disease.

An anthropological model of infectious disease ecology must include three levels. First, there is a microbiological level where certain phenotypes of pathogens undergo selection in different environments. Because humans change the environment where pathogens live (for example by using antibiotics as therapy), there is a relentless interaction between host and pathogen that can result in emerging diseases. Most biomedical research concentrates on this microbiological level.

The second level of disease ecology involves individual human behaviors in which the demands of social and economic roles place people at differential risk of contracting disease. Such individual behavior can theoretically be changed to prevent disease transmission. For example, people can boil their water, wash their hands more frequently, or refuse unprotected sex. However, such behavioral choices are not always possible. Most people do not freely choose social roles or behaviors that put them at risk of disease. Most social research in Public Health concentrates on this level.

The third level of disease causation is political and ecological. It refers to larger social and economic forces that constrain individual behaviors and limit access to resources that may improve health. Since the Neolithic Revolution, these roles have been determined by social systems based on structured inequalities of social class and gender. Farmer (2004) refers to these embedded inequalities as "structural violence." Stillwaggon (2005) uses the phrase "the ecology of poverty" to refer to underlying host factors caused by poverty (i.e., worm infections, malaria, malnutrition) that increase the chances that infections will become diseases. Traditional models in epidemiology typically ignore this powerful socio-economic level of disease causation.

INFECTIOUS DISEASE IN HISTORY: EPIDEMICS AND EPIDEMIOLOGICAL TRANSITIONS

In today's world, disease ecology can be viewed as a consequence of four interdependent developments – globalization, urbanization, increased socio-economic inequalities, and emerging disease. Globalization and infectious disease are inextricably linked, and recent anthropological findings suggest this process began millennia earlier than traditionally thought. In recent years, concerns about potential infectious pandemics include: XDR-TB (2006), avian flu (2005), SARS (2003), anthrax (2001), Ebola hemorrhagic fever (2000), plague (1994), cholera (1993), HIV (1982-present), swine flu (1976), and polio (1952). Most of these outbreaks were of limited geographical scope, and some (like SARS, which had a greater geographic range) were controlled by effective public health surveillance and intervention. In April 2009, the global media was riveted by an outbreak of "swine flu" (novel H1N1) in Mexico City, one of the ten largest cities in the world. There was fear that the outbreak represented the beginning of a worldwide epidemic (pandemic) that could cause massive morbidity, mortality, and economic havoc. Fear and stigma continue to be common social reactions to epidemics (Barrett and Brown 2008).

Much of this media attention and public fear is related to the extraordinary historical impact of the 1918 influenza pandemic, which killed an estimated 50 to 100 million people worldwide in a single year; the vast majority of deaths occurred among poor Indian peasants (Barry 2004). But the 1918 influenza pandemic was not an isolated event. Epidemics of infectious disease have been a regular aspect of world history (Watts 1997). The iconic example is the bubonic plague ("black death") which killed an estimated 25–50% of the entire European population in 1347. McNeill (1976) has described such historical epidemics as the result of the "confluence of disease pools" in conjunction with urbanization and global trade, and as repetitive sources of massive mortality, fear, economic decline, and cultural chaos.

While globalization is frequently seen as a product of recent political-economic events, there is abundant evidence that processes of globalization and urbanization began thousands of years ago. Cities first appeared around 6,000 BCE, not long after the Neolithic Revolution. These population centers were marked by ecological conditions (e.g., crowding and poor sanitation) conducive to the transmission of a variety of infectious diseases, to which urban populations developed antibodies. Epidemic diseases can become endemic childhood diseases when urban populations are large enough to sustain ongoing transmission to disease-naïve individuals. McNeill (1976) argues that a Eurasian disease pool coalesced with the expansion of trade between urban centers between 1200 BCE and 500 BCE. The power of urban centers expanded as they "digested" populations they encountered, aided by the process in which the same pathogens endemic in the urban centers caused new epidemics and high mortality in newly contacted groups. In this way infectious diseases cleared the way for the expansion of empires. This was particularly obvious in the European conquest of the New World.

Urbanization continues to be important in regard to infectious disease. The demographic and socio-economic transition of urbanization in the developing world is marked by huge urban slums with inadequate water and sewers, as well as terrible rates of violence (Neuwirth 2005). These large cities are characterized by a pattern of growing social and economic disparity. While modern cities are a healthy environment for the wealthy and middle classes, they represent substantial health risks for the poor.

Three distinct disease transitions have occurred during the course of human history. Contingent on local contexts, these transitions happened in different places and at different times (Barrett et al. 1998; Armelagos and Harper 2005). The first epidemiological transition occurred about 10,000 years ago with a major shift from foraging to agriculture as the basis of subsistence. This transition was marked by a tremendous increase in the prevalence of infectious and nutritional diseases, apparent in the archaeological and paleopathological records (Cohen and Armelagos 1984). The interdependence of epidemiological, nutritional, and demographic changes persists to the present day. Cities have always been the sites of cultural development, creativity, and power, despite poor hygienic conditions that made them "graveyards of humanity," requiring continued immigration from rural areas to maintain their population. Epidemics of infectious disease eventually became a common part of the urban "disease-scape." Outbreaks of cholera, typhoid fever, typhus, smallpox and yellow fever have been described by a number of historians (Johnson 2006; Porter 2007). All of these accounts detail the fear that gripped urban populations during these epidemics, as well as the scientific achievements that occurred as a result of them.

About 150 years ago, some populations in high and middle income nations underwent a second epidemiological transition. This occurred when improved nutrition, basic public health measures and medicine led to a decline in mortality from infectious disease and a rise in noninfectious, chronic, and degenerative diseases. The second epidemiological transition was accelerated by the invention of antibiotics, and this important biomedical development made some scientists predict the end of infectious disease; this has not happened. The poor in low income countries have yet to experience the second epidemiological transition.

History is now marked by the third epidemiological transition, in which many humans now face a resurgence of infectious diseases previously thought to be under control. Many of the resurging pathogens are antibiotic resistant and some, such as tuberculosis, are multi-antibiotic resistant. In addition, a number of novel infectious diseases have been identified (Satcher 1995). There are six factors at the root of the re-emergence of infectious disease in the third epidemiological transition: ecological change, human demographics and behavior, international travel and commerce, technology and industry, microbial adaptation and change, and breakdown in public health measures (IOM 1992). Jones and colleagues (2008) investigated 335 instances of emerging disease from 1940 to 2004 and confirm that emerging diseases are driven by socioeconomic, environmental and ecological factors (see Townsend, this volume).

From an ecological perspective, the third epidemiological transition is the latest revision in human–disease relationship, a direct result of social, economic, and technological change on a global level. Because of the increased speed of global travel and trade, as well as the increased number of travelers, many of the emerging and re-emerging infectious diseases have the potential to be spread rapidly throughout the world. At the same time, the gap between classes within society and differences in wealth between societies continue to widen, accelerating the spread of emerging and reemerging diseases (Armelagos et al. 2005). Farmer (1996) shows how global social inequities are at the center of many emerging diseases (see also Baer et al. 2003). He argues that people in power attempt to make the differential distribution of disease seem "natural" and ignore the history of political violence that brings humans into contact with pathogens. In contrast, the threat of emerging diseases like avian influenza receives a remarkable degree of attention and resources. The possibility of a global pandemic of a novel pathogen is high on the public health agenda, even if it only exists in worst-case simulations and as a nightmare in the public imagination. Glass (2004) has argued that current health priorities are overly focused on unknown risks from new diseases at the expense of known threats such as influenza.

MODES OF INFECTIOUS DISEASE TRANSMISSION REFLECT SOCIAL REALITIES

There is a wide variety of diseases recognized by biomedicine. The World Health Organization's International Classification of Diseases (ICD), currently in its 10th edition, lists 12,420 codes of different diseases. Approximately 200 of these labels refer to infectious and parasitic etiologies, often grouped by their causative agents, including bacteria (e.g., tuberculosis, syphilis), viruses (e.g., HIV, measles), prions (e.g., kuru, Creutzfeldt–Jakob disease), fungi (e.g., candidiasis, ringworm), protozoa (e.g., malaria, giardia), and multi-cellular parasites (e.g., roundworm, filariasis). Communicable infectious diseases can also be grouped by their primary mode of transmission – through water, air, food, direct contact, insects, and sex. In the following section, we use this approach because it emphasizes the social and cultural factors related to how pathogens are spread.

Water

Water-related diseases are extremely important because contamination of drinking water by sewage can result in diarrhea and death by dehydration, particularly in infants; about two million children die from diarrhea-related dehydration each year (Whiteford and Padros, this volume). The "father of epidemiology," John Snow, is best known for his 19th century investigation of a cholera outbreak that was linked to a single drinking water pump (Johnson 2006). Recently, medical anthropologists have made important contributions to understanding cholera outbreaks and their aftermaths in their wider cultural contexts. Briggs and Briggs (2004) provide a detailed ethnographic account of a cholera epidemic in the delta of eastern Venezuela in 1992, in which poor and marginalized indigenous peoples were blamed for the epidemic that killed them. Social processes of racial profiling and stigmatization of the indigenous people, who were not considered "hygienic citizens," caused immense suffering. Similarly, Nations and Monte (1997) provide a powerful ethnographic account of how poor people can actively resist cholera diagnoses that result in social stigma, allocation of blame, and discrimination. The challenge for public health interventions, therefore, is to promote healthy hygienic practices while avoiding fear-driven educational messages and stigmatization.

Water-related diseases like schistosomiasis and guinea worm are caused by parasites that inhabit water during part of their lifecycles. Hewlett and Cline (1997) describe how ethnographic observations of the urinary behavior of boys contributed to a successful intervention targeting schistosomaisis in northern Cameroon. Medical anthropologists and other social scientists have made many contributions to understanding malaria, which is spread by water-borne mosquito vectors (see Williams and Jones 2003; Heggenhougen et al. 2003). Such studies have included a wide variety of approaches to malaria transmission and control, from mosquito densities related to maize agricultural practices in Ethiopia (McCann 2007), to ethnomedical beliefs and mosquito net usage (Winch 2008), to gender and malaria treatment-seeking (McCombie 1996). Others have provided critical analyses of the underlying assumptions of anti-malaria projects (Jones and Williams 2004; Brown 1997). All of these studies have emphasized complex social and cultural contexts.

Air

Air-borne transmission of disease often results in acute respiratory infections (ARI), which are a leading cause of death for children under five living in low-income parts of the world. Viruses and bacteria are spread through the air in droplets produced by coughing and sneezing. Air-borne diseases thrive in the overcrowded and unsanitary living conditions typical of urban poverty and many prisons. ARIs are exacerbated by factors like low birth weight, malnutrition, indoor air pollution, and co-infections. The most important airborne disease is TB; approximately one-third of the world's population is infected with the TB mycobacterium and 95% of these people live in low-income countries, particularly in urban slums. Medical anthropologists have contributed to understanding the context of TB infection and antibiotic resistant TB in Russian prisons (Farmer 2001); Nichter (2008) demonstrated how a combination of ethnomedical beliefs about weak lungs and the stigma of TB diagnosis delays treatment in the Philippines.

Food

Although some food-borne health problems are not caused by infectious agents but rather by toxic additives, food-borne diseases are often the result of ingesting food contaminated with microbes like salmonella (Tauxe 1997). Both water-borne and food-borne diseases are ultimately linked to poor sanitation and a fecal–oral route of transmission. Some food-borne diseases like *E. coli* O157:H7 and BSE ("mad cow disease") are considered to be newly emerging because they are either biologically novel or newly recognized. Unclean foods are often associated with institutional kitchens and industrial food processing centers, which are notorious for "cutting corners" on food safety. Food-borne diseases therefore represent a growing public health problem worldwide. BSE is caused by an industrial "feed-lot" practice of feeding protein made from the brains of slaughtered cows to those being fattened. Using a combination of political-economic and interpretive methods, Dunn (2008) has analyzed why the Caucasus Republic of Georgia has an extremely high prevalence of botulism; the collapse of the state-owned food packaging system was one significant factor.

Contact

Infectious agents are also spread by direct (kissing, shaking hands) or indirect (shared clothing, doorknobs, blood transfusions) contact. Hansen's disease – traditionally known as leprosy – represents the historical archetype of stigmatized diseases; medical anthropologists have studied the process of stigmatization and efforts for the elimination of this bacterial disease, which causes limb numbness and secondary infections (White 2009). Some germs in our environment are ubiquitous and only cause infections in particular circumstances. For example, Staph bacteria are commonly carried on the skin and can be transmitted either directly or indirectly, posing a problem when they enter the body through a cut. Many of these infections can be prevented through basic hygiene practices like hand-washing, but this can be difficult in low-resource settings. Although it is difficult to transmit, there have been recent outbreaks of a form of Staphylococcus whose evolved resistance to broad-spectrum antibiotics (Chambers 2005) is associated with pigs that are regularly fed diets including antibiotics. There are many zoonotic diseases that are spread from animals to humans; transmission is thought to initially occur by direct contact with an infected animal, and later person-to-person. Anthropologists have contributed to understanding the exotic prion disease of kuru, found only in the South Fore people of Papua New Guinea, thought to be transmitted by the ingestion of infected human brains (Lindenbaum 2001). A more likely route of transmission, however, was through direct contact with the bodies of kuru victims during mortuary rituals when the prion entered new hosts through small cuts or conjunctiva (Steadman and Merbs 1982).

Sex

Sexual contact is the most important route of infection for HIV/AIDS, the largest infectious disease pandemic facing the contemporary world. Sexually transmitted infections (STIs) can result from infected fluid entering the body of an uninfected person through micro-abrasions caused by vaginal or anal intercourse. Transmission through oral sex or direct contact with sores or chancres on the genitals is also possible. Over thirty STIs have been identified, caused by bacteria (e.g., gonorrhea, syphilis), viruses (e.g., HIV, herpes, human papilloma virus (HPV)), and parasites (e.g., trichomoniasis). In some individuals, STIs can have few or no symptoms. Global estimates of new STIs per year (incidence) approach 340 million, of which 2.5 million are new HIV infections. Because they are often the recipients of infected seminal fluids, women are more likely to become infected through sexual intercourse, and the consequences of STIs are often much more serious (e.g., pelvic inflammatory disease which causes infertility). Moreover, STIs can be vertically transmitted (from pregnant mother to baby) either during gestation or at birth; there are a wide array of negative health affects for infected newborns. Medical anthropologists have studied the contexts and consequences of STIs, particularly through the lenses of gender inequalities and stigmatization (Inhorn and Brown 1997; Singer et al. 2006). STIs often imply immoral behavior; this may become a reason for delaying treatment or failing to disclose the infection to a sex partner. We return to the central question of stigma associated with sexual transmission of HIV below.

THE HIV/AIDS PANDEMIC IN AFRICA ILLUSTRATES COMPLEX BIOLOGICAL, POLITICAL AND CULTURAL INTERACTIONS

The HIV/AIDS epidemic in Africa is an excellent example of how the interactions between biology, behavior, political economy and culture, must all be included in an anthropological model of disease ecology. The history of HIV/AIDS also illustrates how cultural beliefs and social stigmatization exacerbate the epidemic and can block effective interventions for prevention and treatment.

Jonathan Mann distinguished between three separate epidemics of HIV/AIDS – the invisible virus, followed by AIDS, and the public response (Mann 1987, 1999). Treichler (1988) also foresaw that the "third epidemic" – the epidemic of social, cultural, economic, and political responses – would be the most explosive and difficult to control, suggesting that human behavior is more dangerous than the virus itself. History has shown this prediction to be true. From the standpoint of affected individuals, medical anthropologists have affirmed the third epidemic's significant impact on human suffering (see Singer and Erickson, this volume).

A distinction can be made between HIV and AIDS epidemics because of a peculiarity of the virus' interaction with the human immune system that delays onset of opportunistic infections and other symptoms for up to a decade. The idea of the third epidemic, on the other hand, reflects a human rights and biocultural approach to understanding the pandemic, emphasizing the infectious spread of AIDS-related fear and stigmatization among human societies, from rural farming and urban slum communities to national ministries and multinational pharmaceutical corporations. The idea of the third epidemic encourages medical anthropologists and other social scientists to put more effort into the study and control of fear, stigmatization, apathy, violence, and meaning, as well as economic and organizational structures to fund and guide the epidemic response (Pope et al. 2009; Wallace and Fullilove 2008).

The first epidemic – that of HIV infection – was unique in its invisibility, which facilitated its early spread in Africa and across oceans. Phylo-geographic analysis can reconstruct the molecular evolution and originally silent spread of various HIV strains through Africa since the late 1970s with some degree of confidence (Iliffe 2006). If the third epidemic of stigmatization had never spread, HIV and AIDS epidemics would still have been difficult to reverse in Africa, due to the fact that HIV is an extremely syndemogenic disease (Singer 2009), thriving where human immune systems are weakened by poverty, malnutrition, and other infectious parasites. But instead, communities, governments, and global institutions often behaved with fearful apathy and violence, encouraging the spread of an opportunistic, syndemogenic virus.

Iliffe (2006) provides an historical understanding of how HIV/AIDS transmission, progression, prevention, and treatment in Africa have been shaped by neglect and discrimination, as well as by positive action to address these threats to individual and social health (see also Coriat 2008; Feldman 2008; Whelehan 2009). Understanding this process starts with appreciating that while HIV/AIDS has infected and killed millions, it has also been the impetus for fervent social response. Early in the epidemic (and still today), stigmatization and lack of concerted public health efforts compelled many families and civil society organizations to take prevention and support into their own hands. By the late 1980s it was clear that epidemics of stigmatization and blame on local and international scales were exploding. Villagers in Haiti and elsewhere blamed "witches" (Farmer 2006), many Africans blamed Western scientists (Rödlach 2006), Americans and Europeans blamed homosexuals, drug users, Haitians and Africans (Herek and Glunt 1988; Sabatier 1988), men blamed women, women blamed other women, rural Ethiopian farmers blamed urban dwellers. Human rights advocates of many creeds and nationalities fought back, blaming World Bank and IMF structural adjustment programs, bilateral and multinational trade agreements, and pharmaceutical giants, for keeping many poor countries poor (Poku and Whiteside 2004; Schoepf et al. 2000).

National and international bodies, including private pharmaceutical corporations, have formulated and reformulated policy in response not only to the underlying epidemiology of HIV/AIDS, but also to economic interests and claims for social justice by fed-up and well-organized advocates, such as the AIDS Support Organization (TASO) in Uganda (Ibembe 2009) and the Treatment Action Campaign (TAC) in South Africa, (D'Adesky 2004; Fassin 2007). By the first decade of the 21st century, this process led to increased treatment access in *some* areas of sub-Saharan Africa, for *some* people, reshaping HIV/AIDS epidemics. The goal of universal access by 2010 (WHO 2006) still faces cultural, social, economic, and physical barriers, which loom larger in the current global economic recession.

According to UNAIDS' 2007 Global AIDS Report (most recent statistics), an estimated 33.2 million people worldwide are living with HIV. In Africa the incidence has slowed in recent years, but worldwide an estimated 2.5 million were *newly* infected with HIV in 2007 and approximately 2.1 million people died of AIDS. Much of the deadliness of the epidemic in sub-Saharan Africa has to do with a deadly synergy between HIV and TB. Tuberculosis is the world's greatest infectious killer of women of reproductive age and the leading cause of death among people with HIV/AIDS; this is a good example of what Singer has identified as a syndemic (Singer 2009; Singer et al., this volume). A generalized epidemic exists in sub-Saharan Africa, where HIV/AIDS and TB are the leading causes of death for adults and infection rates are equal between men and women.

Though HIV is relatively difficult to transmit, women, as recipients of infected semen during intercourse, are at greater biological risk of infection. Yet this biological fact explains only a fraction of the increased risk of infection for women in sub-Saharan Africa. Epstein (2007) has recently argued that "concurrency" in sexual networks is a cause of the spread of HIV. Concurrency may be contrasted with serial monogamy, in which people have only one sex partner at a given time. Simultaneous sexual relations link individuals in a network that can spread infection, even when a minority of the people involved has sex with multiple partners. This is particularly important during the limited symptom-less period of elevated viral load after initial HIV infection when people cannot know they are infected (unless tested). The number of sexual partners at any one time increases risk of infection. However, the assumption that women infected with HIV must have multiple sex partners is wrong; most women in Africa adhere to norms of monogamy and are infected by their husbands (Farmer 2001). The notion of concurrency is similarly applicable to the direct and indirect sharing of needles and other drug paraphernalia by IDUs.

Most public health interventions for HIV/AIDS in Africa have focused on changing the behavior of individuals to limit sexual partners and avoid unprotected sex through condom use. The oft-repeated ABC slogan – abstain, be faithful, use condoms – has generally been ineffective in the African context, given the lack of emphasis on overcoming the cultural and other barriers to condom use (Ibembe 2009; Susser 2009). The introduction of condoms is more than a simple transfer of technology. An emphasis on sexual behavior change (e.g., abstinence) exaggerates the ability of individuals to choose particular behaviors and largely ignores the power of social and economic constraints that shape behavior. For example, the ABC message might be considered a cruel joke to an African woman whose only "risk behavior" is having sex with her husband. Given cultural perceptions of male privilege that extend to sexual relations, the economic dependence of women, and the positive value placed on fertility, a woman's request that her husband or lover use a condom may be impossible and even dangerous. Women may find it difficult, if not impossible, to limit their sexual partners when sex is used as a means for economic survival and emotional fulfillment. In this context, the risk of AIDS somewhere down the line may not seem quite as "risky" in light of the perceived immediate consequences of partner reduction.

Women engaged in commercial sex work have typically been depicted as reservoirs of HIV infection rather than as links in broader networks of HIV transmission. Medical anthropologists have criticized interventions aimed at "prostitutes" for assuming that the goal is to protect men from women, and for ignoring the role of male clients in the transmission of HIV (de Zalduondo 1991). From a historical perspective, the structure of colonially created urban centers with large male populations and few females produced social and economic consequences that affected the dynamics and networks of both commercial and non-commercial sexual relations. Similarly, the history of apartheid labor policies and the homeland system in South Africa, which placed large groups of miners far away from their families, created patterns of commercial sex work that exacerbated the spread of HIV (Campbell 2003; Fassin 2007).

Castro and Farmer (2005) argue that generating a wealth of information about men's and women's knowledge and attitudes about HIV/AIDS, while ignoring the larger social processes that have allowed HIV to spread much faster among marginalized populations, leads to desocialized theories of stigmatization and interventions that have little hope of reducing AIDS-related stigma on a larger scale. Recent meta-analysis suggests that interventions aimed at educating the general population about HIV transmission and increasing tolerance have little positive effects (Brown et al. 2003; Jewkes 2006). Likewise, attempts to "educate" people with HIV/AIDS about the need to get tested and access other services have failed in the absence of eliminating the economic barriers people face in accessing public health services. This suggests that education and "sensitization" are insufficient (Buseh and Stevens 2006) and must be coupled with providing quality care at low cost and reducing economic inequalities.

As noted above, "Highly Active Anti-Retroviral Therapy" (HAART) has become accessible to some populations in sub-Saharan Africa in recent years. HAART is a striking example of how drugs can be both pharmacologically and socioculturally active (Biehl 2007; Whyte et al. 2006). HAART curbs HIV replication and immune system breakdown, prolonging life and also affecting the likelihood of further trans-mission over the life course (Law et al. 2001). While the life-prolonging effect is a host–virus interaction operating primarily at the level of immunology and cell biology, HAART's role in transmission acts at the biological, life history, and social-psychological levels. HAART prevents transmission by decreasing a person's viral load, diminishing the probability of transmission during sexual intercourse, birth, and breastfeeding (Bartlett and Gallant 2005). Yet HAART also affects transmission likelihood by giving hope and adding sexually active life-years (and in some cases years of risky drug use) to individuals living with HIV/AIDS. When HAART becomes available, many of those who know they are HIV+ and those who suspect it are motivated to personally face their fears, seek testing to know their status, disclose their status to those they trust, and change their behavior to avoid transmitting the virus to others.

Yet some people living with HIV/AIDS, especially many youths and adolescents, may not maintain safe sex and safe (in terms of HIV transmission) drug use behavior. These are not simple cases of ignorance that can be fixed with education, especially in the case of youths and adolescents who may have been on HAART since infancy or early childhood and are entering adolescence like "normal" young adults. These issues have been addressed by medical anthropologists in Brazil (Abadia-Barrero 2004; Clair et al. 2009). In many sub-Saharan African locales, children with HIV/AIDS have only recently gained access to HAART, and many still lack access to treatment. In addition, prevention of mother-to-child transmission programs remains limited, fostering the continued reproduction of children with HIV.

Nowhere have the political-economic factors in the spread of HIV/AIDS been more obvious than in the case of South Africa. When AIDS came to southern Africa, testing methods had been developed and prevention strategies were clearly under-stood. This scientific knowledge posed a great opportunity; the epidemic could have been curtailed by prompt political and public health action. This did not happen, and the result is that South Africa now has one of the highest HIV prevalence in the world. The central figure in this tragedy was President Thabo Mbeki, who rejected scientific consensus by denying that HIV was the cause of AIDS and therefore anti-retroviral (ARV) drugs were not useful for patients. In a nuanced anthropological analysis, Fassin (2007) explains the cultural and historical underpinnings of Mbeki's view that AIDS was a disease of poverty and that the appropriate government response was therefore poverty alleviation, palliative care, and improved nutrition (see also Butler 2005). Mbeki made several policy decisions that sparked international contro-versies; the most important was not to accept freely donated nevirapine for the pre-vention of vertical transmission of HIV from mother to child. This decision triggered powerful protests from political activists from around the world, largely organized by South Africa's Treatment Action Campaign (TAC). In 2002, Mbeki's decision about nevirapine was overturned by the South African High Court and treatment was begun in 2003. Chigwedere and colleagues (2008) estimate that the delay in treatment programs in South Africa resulted in the loss of 330,000 lives.

The political obstacles that the suffering and dying millions and their advocates have had to overcome to gain access to HAART involve a clash between worldviews (Farmer and Castro 2004; Moatti et al. 2003). Paradoxically, worldviews based on resource scarcity and cost-efficiency found among wealthy bureaucrats, have been confronted by worldviews based on abundance held by those deprived of economic security. Human rights and treatment advocates have had to respond to arguments that the majority of Africans are too poor, uneducated or afraid of stigmatization, that their governments too corrupt, and that their health systems too weak, to manage effective HAART without causing widespread anti-retroviral resistance or simply wasting drugs (Irwin et al. 2003). The idea of HAART as a copyrightable commodity like any other on the "free market" (Abadia-Barrero 2004; d'Almeida et al. 2008) has been confronted by arguments to treat HAART as a global public good essential for the healthy functioning of local, national, and global social bodies (Singer and Castro 2004).

Successful examples of scale-up of HAART access in Africa should not suggest that these ideological differences have been resolved on a global scale. In terms of equitable or "universal" distribution, success has not yet been achieved (Biehl 2006; Coriat 2008; Desclaux 2004; Pope et al. 2009). Only a minority of those who need HAART get it. Underfunding of local health delivery systems and efforts to treat HAART as a copyrightable global commodity still prevail on a global scale (Craddock 2009; Petryna et al. 2006; van Niekerk 2005).

Jewkes (2006) suggests that a shift in focus is needed in the effort to reduce AIDS-related stigmatization, from the innumerable examples of failure to the growing number of successes in non-discrimination and decent care. Around the world, non-discriminatory, compassionate caregiving is culturally motivated by religious beliefs and universal human instincts; successes are often translatable and shareable across religious and cultural traditions (Karpf et al. 2008). This highlights the importance of how religion and public health will interact in the future, evolving out of a troubled past in which religious institutions were seen to promote stigmatization and obstruct HIV prevention and care (Defert 1996).

It is crucial for medical anthropologists to recognize that alleviating poverty and reducing inequality on global and national scales requires changing ideological or cultural models of what is economically beneficial and moral. This is not an easy task, since cultural models that underlie behaviors that exploit and socially marginalize other humans are reinforced by emotional capacities for greed and fear. On the other hand, cultural models that underlie decent and non-discriminatory care are reinforced by emotional capacities for compassion and pragmatic goals of social well being. The HIV/AIDS pandemic and the drama of our response to it have highlighted these seemingly dualistically opposed human capacities. Perhaps the development and spread of positive human responses to AIDS can be conceptualized as another epidemic, in a sense competing with the "third epidemic" of stigmatization and apathy for human hosts and resources. A key challenge to medical anthropologists is to understand these processual epidemics by paying attention to human psychology, behavior, culture, and political economy in addition to infectious pathogen and host biology.

REFERENCES

Abadia-Barrero, C. E., 2004 Happy children with AIDS: The paradox of a healthy national program in an unequal and exclusionary Brazil. *In* Unhealthy Health Policy: A Critical Anthropological Examination. A. Castro and M. Singer, eds. pp. 163–176. Walnut Creek CA: AltaMira Press.

Armelagos, G., and K. Harper, 2005 Disease Globalization in the Third Epidemiological Transition. *In* Globalization, Health and the Environment: An Integrated Perspective. G. Guest, ed. pp. 27–33. Walnut Creek CA: AltaMira Press.

Armelagos, G., M. Ryan, and T. Leatherman, 1990. The Evolution of Infectious Disease: A Biocultural Analysis of AIDS. American Journal of Human Biology 2:353–363.

Armelagos, G., T. Leatherman, M. Ryan, and L. Sibley, 1992 Biocultural Synthesis in Medical Anthropology. Medical Anthropology 14:35–52.

Armelagos, G., P. J. Brown, and B. Turner, 2005 Evolutionary, historical and political economic perspectives on health and disease. Social Science and Medicine 61:755–765.

Baer, H., M. Singer, and I. Susser, 2003 Medical Anthropology and the World System. 2nd edition. New York: Praeger.

Barrett, R., and P. Brown, 2008 Stigma in the Time of Influenza: Social and Institutional Responses to Pandemic Emergencies. Journal of Infectious Diseases 197:S34–S37.

Barrett, R., C. W. Kuzawa, T. W. McDade, and G. J. Armelagos, 1998 Emerging and re-emerging infectious diseases: the third epidemiologic transition. Annual Review of Anthropology 27:247–271.

Barry, J., 2004 The Great Influenza: The Epic Story of the Deadliest Plague in History. New York: Viking.

Bartlett, J. G., and Gallant, G., 2005 Medical Management of HIV Infection 2005–2006. Baltimore: Johns Hopkins Medicine Health Publishing Business Group.

Bengmark, S., 2000. Bacteria for optimal health. Nutrition 16:611–615.

Biehl, J., 2006 Pharmaceutical Governance. *In* Global Pharmaceuticals: Ethics, Markets, Practices. Petryna, A., A. Lakoff, and A. Kleinman, eds. pp. 206–239. Durham NC: Duke University Press.

Biehl, J., 2007. Will to Live: AIDS Therapies and the Politics of Survival. Princeton NJ: Princeton University Press.

Briggs, C. L, and C. Mantini-Briggs, 2004 Stories in the Time of Cholera: Racial Profiling during a Medical Nightmare. Berkeley: University of California Press.

Brown, L., K. Macintyre, and L. Trujillo, 2003 Interventions to reduce HIV/AIDS stigma: What have we learned? Aids Education and Prevention 15(1):49–69.

Brown, P. J., 1997 Malaria, *Miseria*, and Underpopulation in Sardinia: the "Malaria Blocks Development" Cultural Model. Medical Anthropology 18:239–254

Buseh, A. G., and P. E. Stevens, 2006 Constrained but not determined by stigma: resistance by African American women living with HIV. Women and Health 44(3):1–18.

Butler, A., 2005 South Africa's HIV/AIDS Policy 199402004: How Can It Be Explained? African Affairs 104/417:591–614.

Campbell, C., 2003 Letting Them Die: Why HIV/AIDS Prevention Programmes Often Fail. London: James Curry.

Castro, A., and P. Farmer, 2005 Understanding and addressing AIDS-related stigma: From anthropological theory to clinical practice in Haiti. American Journal of Public Health 95(1):53–59.

Chambers, H., 2005 Community-associated MRSA-resistance and virulence converge. New England Journal of Medicine. 352(14): 1485.

Chigwedere P., G. Seage, S. Gruskin, T. Lee, and M. Essex, 2008 Estimating the Lost Benefits of Antiretroviral Drug Use in South Africa. Journal of Acquired Immune Deficiency Syndrome. 49:410–415.

Clair, S., M. Singer, F. I. Bastos, M. Malta, C. Santelices, and N. Bertoni, 2009 The role of drug users in the Brazilian HIV/AIDS epidemic: patterns, perceptions, and prevention. In HIV/AIDS: Global Frontiers in Prevention/Intervention. C. Pope, R. T. White, and R. Malow, eds. pp. 50–58. New York: Routledge.

Coriat, B., ed., 2008 The Political Economy of HIV/AIDS in Developing Countries: TRIPS, Public Health Systems and Free Access. Cheltenham UK: Edward Elgar.

Craddock, S., 2009 AIDS and the politics of violence. In HIV/AIDS: Global Frontiers in Prevention/Intervention. C. Pope, R. T. White, and R. Malow, eds. pp. 279–291. New York: Routledge.

D'Adesky, A., 2004 Moving Mountains: The Race to Treat Global AIDS. London: Verso.

d'Almeida, C., L. Hasenclever, G. Krikorian, F. Orsi, C. Sweet, and B. Coriat. 2008 New antiretroviral treatments and post-2005 TRIPS constraints: first moves towards flexibilization in developing countries. In The Political Economy of HIV/AIDS in Developing Countries: TRIPS, Public Health Systems and Free Access. B. Coriat, ed. pp. 25–51. Cheltenham UK: Edward Elgar.

Defert, D., 1996 AIDS as a challenge to religion. In AIDS in the World II: Global Dimensions, Social Roots and Responses. J. Mann and D. Tarantola, eds. pp. 447–452. New York: Oxford University Press.

Demmer, R., and M. Desvarieux, 2006 Peridontal infections and cardiovascular disease: the heart of the matter. Journal of the American Dental Association 137.

de Zalduondo, B., 1991 Prostitution Viewed Cross-Culturally: Towards Recontextualizing Sex Work in AIDS Research. Journal of Sex Research 28:223–248.

Desclaux, A., 2004 Equity in access to AIDS treatment in Africa: Pitfalls among achievements. In Unhealthy Health Policy: A Critical Anthropological Examination. A. Castro and M. Singer, eds. pp. 115–132. Walnut Creek CA: AltaMira Press.

Dunn, E., 2008 Postsocialist Spores: Disease, Bodies and the State in the Republic of Georgia. American Ethnologist 35:243–258.

Epstein, H., 2007 The Invisible Cure: Africa, the West, and the Fight Against AIDS. New York: Farrar, Straus and Giroux.

Farmer, P., 1996 Social inequalities and emerging infectious diseases. Emerging Infectious Diseases 2:259–269.

Farmer, P., 2001 Infections and Inequalities: the Modern Plagues. Berkeley: University of California Press.

Farmer, P., 2004 An Anthropology of Structural Violence. Current Anthropology 45:305–325.

Farmer, P., 2006 AIDS and Accusation: Haiti and the Geography of Blame. 2nd edition. Berkeley: University of California Press.

Farmer, P., and A. Castro, 2004 Pearls of the Antilles? Public health in Haiti and Cuba. In Unhealthy Health Policy: A Critical Anthropological Examination. A. Castro and M. Singer, eds. pp. 3–28. Walnut Creek CA: AltaMira Press.

Farmer, P., and A. Kleinman, 1988 AIDS as human suffering. Daedalus 118(2):135–160.

Fassin, D., 2007 When Bodies Remember: Experiences and Politics of AIDS in South Africa. Berkeley: University of California Press.

Feldman, D., 2008 AIDS, Culture, and Africa. Gainesville FL: University Press of Florida.

Glass R., 2004 Perceived threats and real killers. Science 304 (5673):927.

Green, E., 1999 Indigenous Theories of Contagious Disease. Walnut Creek CA: AltaMira Press.

Heggenhougen, K., V. Hackenthal, and P. Vivek, 2003 The Behavioural and Social Aaspects of Malaria and its Control : An Introduction and Annotated Bibliography. Geneva: TDR, World Health Organization.

Herek, G. M., and E. K. Glunt, 1988 An epidemic of stigma – Public reactions to AIDS. American Psychologist 43(11):886–891.

Hewlett, B., and B. Cline, 1997 Anthropological contributions to a community-based schistosomiasis control project in northern Cameroun. Tropical Medicine and International Health. 2(11):25–36.

268   PETER J. BROWN, GEORGE J. ARMELAGOS AND KENNETH C. MAES

Ibembe, P., 2009 The evolution of the ABC strategy of HIV prevention in Uganda: Domestic and international implications. *In* HIV/AIDS: Global Frontiers in Prevention/Intervention. C. Pope, R. T. White, and R. Malow, eds. pp. 246–255. New York: Routledge.

Iliffe, J., 2006 The African AIDS Epidemic: A History. Athens OH: Ohio University Press.

Inhorn, M., and P. J. Brown, 1997 The Anthropology of Infectious Disease: International Health Perspectives. New York: Gordon and Breach.

IOM (Institute of Medicine), 1992 Emerging Infections: Microbial Threats to Health in the United States. Washington: The Institute of Medicine.

Irwin, A. C., J. Millen, and D. Fallows, 2003 Global AIDS: Myths and Facts. Cambridge MA: South End Press.

Jewkes, R., 2006 Beyond stigma: Social responses to HIV in South Africa. Lancet 368(9534):430–431.

Johnson, S., 2006 The Ghost Map: The Story of London's Most Terrifying Epidemic – and How It Changed Science, Cities, and the Modern World. New York: Riverhead.

Jones, C., and H. Williams, 2004 The Social Burden of Malaria: What Are We Measuring? American Journal of Tropical Medicine and Hygiene 71(2):156–161.

Jones, K., N. Patel, M. Levy, A. Storeygard, D. Balk, J. Gittleman, and P. Daszak, 2008 Global trends in emerging infectious diseases. Nature 451:990–993.

Karpf, T., J. T. Ferguson, R. Swift, and J. Lazarus, eds., 2008 Restoring Hope: Decent Care in the Midst of HIV/AIDS. New York: Palgrave Macmillan for the World Health Organization.

Law, M. G., G. Prestage, A. Grulich, P. Van de Ven, and S. Kippax, 2001 Modelling the effect of combination antiretroviral treatments on HIV incidence. Aids 15(10):1287–1294.

Lindenbaum, S., 2001 Kuru, Prions, and Human Affairs: Thinking About Epidemics. Annual Review of Anthropology. 30:363–385.

Mann, J., 1987, Statement at an informal briefing on AIDS to the 42nd session of the United Nations General Assembly, New York.

Mann, J., 1999 The future of the global AIDS movement. Harvard AIDS Review. Spring:18–21.

McCann, J., 2007 Maize and Grace: Africa's Encounter with a New World Crop, 1500–2000. Cambridge MA: Harvard University Press.

McCombie, S., 1996 Treatment seeking for malaria: A review of recent research. Social Science and Medicine 43:933–945.

McNeill, W. H., 1976 Plagues and Peoples. Garden City, New York: Anchor/Doubleday.

Moatti, J.-P., T. Barnett, Y. Souteyrand, Y.-A. Flori, J. Dumoulin, and B. Coriat, 2003 Financing efficient HIV care and antiretroviral treatment to mitigate the impact of the AIDS epidemic on economic and human development. *In* Economics of AIDS and Access to HIV/AIDS Care in Developing Countries. Issues and Challenges. J.-P. Moatti ed. pp. 247–265. Paris: Agence Nationale de Recherches sur le Sida.

Nations, M., and C. Monte, 1997 "I'm Not Dog, No!": Cries of Resistance Against Cholera Control campaigns in Brazil. *In* The Anthropology of Infectious Disease: International Health Perspectives. M. Inhorn and P. Brown, eds. pp. 439–481. New York: Gordon and Breach.

Neuwirth, R., 2005 Shadow Cities: A Billion Squatters, a New Urban World. New York: Routledge.

Nichter, M., 2008 Global Health: Why Cultural Perceptions, Social Representations and Biopolitics Matter. Tucson AZ: University of Arizona Press.

Omran, A. R., 1971 The epidemiologic transition: A theory of the epidemiology of population change. Millbank Memorial Fund Quarterly 49:509–538.

Petryna, A, A. Lakoff, and A. Kleinman, 2006 Global Pharmaceuticals: Ethics, Markets, Practices. Durham NC: Duke University Press.

Poku, N., and A. Whiteside, eds., 2004 The Political Economy of AIDS in Africa. Aldershot,UK; Burlington VT: Ashgate.

Pope, C., R. T. White, and R. Malow, 2009 Global convergences: Emerging issues in HIV risk, prevention and treatment. *In* HIV/AIDS: Global Frontiers in Prevention/Intervention. C. Pope, R. T. White, and R. Malow, eds. pp. 1–8. New York: Routledge.

Porter, D., 2007 Health, Civilization and the State. New York: Taylor and Francis.

Rödlach, A., 2006 Witches, Westerners, and HIV: AIDS and Cultures of Blame in Africa. Walnut Creek CA: Left Coast Press.

Sabatier, R., 1988 Blaming Others: Prejudice, Race, and Worldwide AIDS. Washington: Panos Institute and New Society Publishers.

Satcher, D., 1995 Emerging Infections: Getting Ahead of the Curve. Emerging Infectious Diseases 1:1–6.

Schoepf, B., C. Schoepf, and J. Millen, 2000 Theoretical therapies, remote remedies: SAPs and the political ecology of poverty and health in Africa. *In* Dying for Growth: Global Inequality and the Health of the Poor. J. Y. Kim, J. V. Millen, A. Irwin, and J. Gershman, eds. pp. 91–126. Monroe ME: Common Courage Press.

Singer, M., 1989 The Limitations of Medical Ecology: The Concept of Adaptation in the Context of Social Stratification and Social Transformation. Medical Anthropology 10.

Singer, M., 2009 Introduction to Syndemics: A Systems Approach to Public and Community Health. San Francisco: Jossey-Bass.

Singer, M., and A. Castro, 2004 Introduction – Anthropology and health policy: A critical perspective. *In* Unhealthy Health Policy: A Critical Anthropological Examination. A. Castro and M. Singer, eds. pp. xi–xx. Walnut Creek CA: AltaMira Press.

Singer, M., P. I. Erickson, L. Badiane, R. Diaz, D. Ortiz, T. Abraham, and A. M. Nicolaysen, 2006 Syndemics, Sex and the City: Understanding Sexually Transmitted Diseases in Social and Cultural Context. Social Science and Medicine 63(8):2010–2021.

Sleigh, J., and M. C. Timbury, 1998. Notes on Medical Bacteriology. New York: Churchill Livingstone.

Steadman, L., and C. Merbs, 1982 Kuru and Cannibalism? American Anthropologist 84:611–625.

Stillwaggon, E., 2005 AIDS and the Ecology of Poverty. New York: Oxford University Press.

Susser, I., 2009 AIDS, Sex, and Culture: Global Politics and Survival in Southern Africa. Chichester UK; Malden MA: Wiley-Blackwell.

Tauxe, R., 1997 Emerging Foodborne Diseases: An Evolving Public Health Challenge. Emerging Infectious Disease 3(4).

Treichler, P., 1988 AIDS, homophobia, and biomedical discourse: An epidemic of signification. *In* AIDS: Cultural Analysis/Cultural Activism. D. Crimp, ed. pp. 31–70. Cambridge MA: MIT Press.

Trostle, J., 2005 Epidemiology and Culture. New York: Cambridge University Press.

Trostle, J., and J. Sommerfeld, 1996 Medical Anthropology and Epidemiology. Annual Review *of Anthropology* 25:253–274.

Turshen, M., 1977 The Political Ecology of Disease. Review of Radical Political Economics 9:45–60.

UNAIDS, 2007 Global AIDS Update. Geneva: UNAIDS/WHO. Electronic document. http://data.unaids.org/pub/EPISlides/2007/2007_epiupdate_en.pdf/.

UN-HABITAT, 2008 State of the World's Cities 2008/2009. United Nations Human Settlements Programme (UN-HABITAT). New York: United Nations.

van Niekerk, Anton A., 2005 Principles of global distributive justice and the HIV/AIDS pandemic: Moving beyond Rawls and Buchanan. *In* Ethics and AIDS in Africa: The Challenge to our Thinking. A. A. Van Niekerk and L.M. Kopelman, eds. pp. 84–110. Claremont, South Africa: David Philip.

Wallace, R., and M. T. Fullilove, 2008 Collective Consciousness and its Discontents: Institutional Distributed Cognition, Racial Policy, and Public Health in the United States. New York: Springer Science and Business Media.

Watts, S., 1997 Epidemics and History: Disease, Power and Imperialism. New Haven CT: Yale University Press.

Weiss, M., 2001 Cultural epidemiology: an introduction and overview. Anthropology and Medicine 8: 5–29.

Whelehan, P., 2009 The Anthropology of AIDS: A Global Perspective. Gainesville FL: University Press of Florida.

White, C., 2009 An Uncertain Cure: Living with Leprosy in Brazil. Brunswick OH: Rutgers.

Whiteside, A., 2008 HIV/AIDS: A Very Short Introduction. New York: Oxford University Press.

Whyte, S., M. Whyte, L. Meinert, and B. Kyaddondo, 2006 Treating AIDS: Dilemmas of Unequal Access in Uganda. *In* Global Pharmaceuticals: Ethics, Markets, Practices. A. Petryna, A. Lakoff, and A. Kleinman, eds. pp. 240–262. Durham NC: Duke University Press.

Williams, H., and C. Jones, 2003 A critical review of behavioral issues related to malaria control in sub-Saharan Africa: what contributions have social scientists made? Social Science and Medicine 59:501–523.

Winch, P. J., 2008 The Role of Anthropological Methods in a Community-Based Mosquito Net Intervention in Bagamoyo District, Tanzania. *In* Anthropology in Public Health. R. Hahn and M Inhorn, eds. pp. 44–62. New York: Oxford University Press.

Woolhouse, M., 2008 Epidemiology: emerging diseases go global. Nature 451:898–899.

World Health Organization, 2006 Progress on Global Access to HIV Antiretroviral Therapy – A Report on "3 by 5" and Beyond. p. 80. Geneva: World Health Organization.

World Health Organization, 2007 International Classification of Disease. 10th edition. Geneva: World Health Organization.

CHAPTER 13

Sexuality, Medical Anthropology, and Public Health

Pamela I. Erickson

"In the beginning was sex and sex will be in the end... sex as a feature of man and society was always central and remains such..."

Goldenweiser 1929:1, quoted in Vance 1991:875.

THE FRAUGHT LEGITIMIZING PROCESS IN SEX RESEARCH

If there were ever a topic in need of an anthropological perspective, it is sexuality and reproductive health. For too many years, the field of public health has gone unchallenged in applying an epidemiological method to understand sex and reproduction within a rational model of individual health behavior (e.g., the Theory of Reasoned Action – Ajzen and Fishbein 1975, 1980; the Health Belief Model – Becker 1974, Rosenstock 1966; the Information-Motivation-Behavioral Skills Model – Fisher and Fisher 2002) or prevention strategies for sexually transmitted infections (STIs) and HIV/AIDS and unintended pregnancy without fully recognizing the highly emotional and often contested individual interpersonal behavior associated with human sexual relationships. The role of romantic love and sexual desire as the social and emotional contexts of sexual behavior has been especially absent from the public health discourse on reproductive health. This is a rather astounding fact, considering that most people have had personal experience with romantic, passionate love or the obsession of lust and the powerful feelings they can evoke. Nevertheless, most prevention programs continue to rely on rational choice models for individual behavior change that assume people have the agency and capacity to achieve the desired behavior within the context of their sexual behavior that generally involves two or more individuals. But in matters of the

A Companion to Medical Anthropology, First Edition. Edited by Merrill Singer and Pamela I. Erickson.

heart, sometimes the mind gives in to the body and people may engage in sexual pleasures that can lead to undesired outcomes.

Moreover, sexual expression and reproduction are patterned by the social, political, and economic institutions of the societies in which they occur and the scripts (Gagnon and Simon 1987; Kimmel 2007) for these behaviors are not always shared by policy makers, health providers, researchers, and the target population whose behavior they are seeking to modify. Over three decades working in clinical settings, intervention programs, and sexual and reproductive health research, I have often found myself joking with colleagues that we design prevention programs as though we had never been young and inexperienced, in love or in lust (at any age), compromised by a specific situational context, or torn between social expectations and individual desires. With respect to sexual and reproductive health, public health has long proceeded within a scientific, rational model aimed at the individual. This model has not been wildly successful in preventing STIs or unintended pregnancy but has had some success with HIV/AIDS prevention where the stakes are considerably higher.

We should not be too sanguine about anthropology's disciplinary contributions to sexual and reproductive health within the domains of human sexuality, eroticism, and romantic love, however. As Vance (1991:875) noted almost two decades ago "Anthropology as a field has been far from courageous or even adequate in its investigation of sexuality." Although we like to point to Malinowski's (1987 [1929]) work on the Trobriand Islands as a marker of the discipline's long interest in human sexuality, the truth is that there has been precious little work on the topic between his writings, Mead's work in Samoa and New Guinea (1928, 1930, 1950 [1935]) and the more recent flood of research on sexual behavior and sexual meanings within anthropology since the 1980s (Lyons and Lyons 2004; Parker and Easton 1998).

Whatever their shortcomings, and they have been criticized by many, Malinowski's and Mead's contributions were key to presenting the West with information on the sexual behaviors of non-Western peoples without exoticizing and distancing them from our own. They presented sexuality in social context and took a relativistic stance to behavioral differences. Moreover, and perhaps most bold of any of their assertions, they suggested that the West had much to learn from the study of human sexual expression in different societies.

Although both Malinowski and Mead were proponents of the liberalization of sexuality in America, their contributions to the reproductive health debates of the times over contraception, sex education, and companionate marriage went largely unnoticed by other anthropologists (Lyons and Lyons 2004). In the 1920s, those who advocated the idea of companionate marriage stressed access to contraception, sex education, divorce by mutual consent for the childless, marriage counseling for those with children who wanted to divorce, and alimony laws that reflected the increasing economic independence of women. Today, these "beliefs are so common among ordinary middle class people in England and North America that it is difficult to appreciate how controversial they once were." (Lyons and Lyons 2004:171). At the time they were roundly condemned for their implication that sex could be divorced from reproduction, marriage, and monogamy.

Two decades later, the tour de force study of cross-cultural sexual behaviors in 191 societies by Ford and Beach (1951) was published. This book summarizes then extant anthropological knowledge on human and primate sexual behavior. The authors, like Malinowski and Mead before them, took a relativistic stance in their documentation of the variability in social arrangements for sexual and reproductive behavior in different cultural groups and drew parallels with the behavior of other mammals as well (e.g., both homo- and heterosexual behaviors, monogamous or serial pair bonding, different arrangements for parental care of infants and juveniles, etc.).

It would be another three decades before the next anthropological foray into human sexuality. Thus, if there were ever a topic so central to social and cultural life that was neglected by anthropology for so long, it is surely human sexuality.

CULTURAL BARRIERS TO THE STUDY OF SEXUALITY

We should not be too hard on ourselves for our oversight of sexuality and sexual behavior from the 1950s to the 1980s. Few other disciplines dared to address human sexual behavior during that time period either, except for medicine and psychiatry and then only from a purely clinical perspective. Sex was simply not perceived as a legitimate research area for the social sciences until Alfred Kinsey's ground breaking work. Kinsey, a biologist by training, exploded into the public eye with the publication of his first volume, *Sexual Behavior in the Human Male* (Kinsey et al. 1948) and the second, its female counterpart (Kinsey et al. 1953) five years later. These works reported findings from the first serious research on the actual sexual behaviors of contemporary American men and women. Kinsey's work scandalized the nation and was very controversial at the time. Even today there are those who vilify his work as the onslaught against him by political conservatives and the Christian after the debut of the 2004 movie about his life and work, *Kinsey* (Fox Searchlight Pictures 2004), attests (see SIECUS 2004).

Kinsey's work was followed over a decade later by gynecologist Masters and psychologist Johnson's (1966) volume, *Human Sexual Response*, and their later volumes on sexual inadequacy (1970) and homosexuality (1979). With the publication of these texts, the cultural taboo on serious academic research about sexual behavior was significantly breached if not fully broken. At the same time these volumes were published, Alex Comfort, the inventor of the modern sex manual, published his best seller, *The Joy of Sex* (1972), and women spurred by the feminist movement began to claim authoritative knowledge to speak for themselves regarding their sexuality with the publication and subsequent updates of *Our Bodies Ourselves* (Boston Women's Collective 1973). These books highlighted the sea change towards greater sexual freedom and experimentation in the cotidian lives of Westerners during the 1960s and 1970s. This era, now known as the "sexual revolution," witnessed the rise of the feminist and gay and lesbian social movements that contested the status quo of male and heterosexual dominance as well as conservative, prudish attitudes about sex.

Interest in sexuality was also apparent in sociology. In 1973 Gagnon and Simon published *Sexual Conduct* (2005 [1973]), the first serious sociological work on sexuality in America. The core of their approach challenged the view that sex was natural (biological) and suggested that the phenomenon was better understood within a social and symbolic context (Plummer 2005). In addition, they attempted to deconstruct sexual categorizations as over-simplistic devotion to the idea of sexual types. Their text was foundational for the development of the social constructionist and "new sexuality studies" perspectives in American sociology.

Five years later, the first of Foucault's three volumes of work on human sexuality (1978, 1985, 1986) was published in English. These works had an enormous impact on the development of postmodernist anthropological theory and emerging sexuality studies during the latter part of the 20th century. Like Gagnon and Simon, Foucault proposed the fundamental idea that sexuality is socially constructed. Moreover, he attacked the commonly held idea that sex is something that in earlier periods, particularly the 19th century, was repressed and that modern peoples have fought to liberate. Foucault suggests that sex, rather than a natural act, is a complex idea produced by social practices and by the way we talk and write (discourse) about it. Thus, sex in the latter 19th century began to signify a wide range of things that are potentially quite different: sexual acts, biological distinctions, parts of bodies, psychological reactions, and, above all, social meanings. Taken together, these conducts, sensations, and biological functions created something different, an artificial unity called "sex" that came to be treated as fundamental to the identity of the individual. For example, in earlier periods, acts of sexual intercourse between individuals of the same sex were stigmatized, but under our new understanding of sex, the stigmatization shifted to the core identities of those involved in such behaviors. The "homosexual" was created, and the polar ends of a continuum from same sex to opposite sex desire were set up as homosexual and heterosexual. In our Western propensity for dualism the core identities were seen as completely distinct, and the heterosexual, procreating couple was naturalized and validated by the discourse of the time. Heterosexuality was socially constructed as the normal, healthy, valid, and valued status, while homosexuality was portrayed as unnatural and perverse. Foucault's great contribution was the identification of the role of power and discourse to the maintenance of this fiction.

Yet, even with this resurgence of interest in human sexuality in the 1970s and the energy of the developing post-modern theoretical perspective, as a primary research interest, sex was largely eschewed by anthropologists as well as other social science disciplines for another ten years or more. In particular, it seems, anthropology was disinclined to legitimate scholars who engaged the topic of human sexuality as a serious and worthy topic of anthropological inquiry (Lyons and Lyons 2004; Usher 2009; Vance 1991). Indeed, most of us who have worked in this area, especially in the early years but even today, have felt the subtle but insidious estimation that our academic interest in pursuing studies of sexuality denotes some kind of personal prurient interest or perversion (Usher 2009; Vance 1991), or perhaps worse, a subversion of male, heterosexual privilege. As Vance comments "students [in the 1980s] interested in the topic perceive that they must rediscover past generations' work on their own" (Vance 1991:875). Today, however, there are entire courses on human sexuality within the anthropology curriculum and textbooks written especially for them (Ferber et al. 2009; Lancaster and di Leonardo 1997; Middleton 2002; Nanda 2000; Robertson 2005). The mainstreaming of sexuality studies in the social sciences has begun to neutralize the subtle disapproval of earlier times and to make the study of sexuality an integral part of the discipline.

REDISCOVERING SEX IN THE 1980S

Medical anthropology, the usual but not exclusive site of anthropological concern for issues of sexuality and reproductive health, emerged as a subdiscipline on the heels of the large scale involvement of anthropologists in international health and development programs aimed at improving the health and economic conditions of the peoples in the developing countries of the world, the traditional cultures studied by anthropologists. During this era, the major theoretical paradigms in medical anthropology included the positivist biological–evolutionary, ecological, materialist perspectives, and the humanist perspectives of feminism and cultural interpretation. Evolutionary anthropologists were busy explaining human sexuality within the paradigm of reproductive fitness, ecological scholars were explaining culture, health, and reproduction as adaptation to specific environments, and cultural materialists were explaining everything in terms of access to or control of resources. Feminists focused on deconstructing male dominance and humanistic cultural anthropologists were intent on describing and interpreting cultural knowledge and systems. Many medical anthropologists in the 1970s and 1980s, especially women, were addressing birth and reproduction (see Sargent and Gulbas, this volume). However, in none of these areas was sexuality and sexual meaning the focus of study.

In the long silence of anthropological inquiry into sexuality from the 1950s to the 1980s, anthropologists grappled only obtusely with sexuality, subsuming it under reproduction and the subjugation of women under the (then) new feminist agenda. These second wave feminist scholars changed Western notions of the naturalness of patriarchy and male dominance (issues of gender and power) forever by highlighting the unnecessary subjugation of women based on their reproductive role as mothers. Contesting feminist assertions that there was nothing natural about patriarchy, sociobiological and evolutionary oriented anthropologists (and psychologists) interpreted human sexuality in light of reproductive fitness considerations (see Small 1995; Symonds 1995). For these evolutionary anthropologists, the male strategy was to impregnate as many females of high biological quality (i.e., young, clear skin, shining hair, wide hips, large breasts, etc.) as possible to ensure continuation of his genetic line. Female strategy was to find one mate and secure his investment in her/their children long enough to ensure mating, birth, and economic support for at least six to seven years (the time it took a child to become semi-self sufficient).

Many anthropologists adhered to a cultural influence model in their writings on sexuality. In this paradigm, sexuality and gender are often blended or conflated, gender, sexuality, and gender systems, are assumed to be connected, and sexual acts have a stable and universal significance (Vance 1991). Illustrating this perspective as well as the "gender wars" in anthropology in the 1960s–1970s was a volume edited by Marshall and Suggs (1971) that did not have one female contributor and whose major theme was to counter the threat to Western male identity (and authority) that had surfaced in the many works of feminist scholars after the first wave of feminism (Lyons and Lyons 2004). Feminists took aim at the subjugation of women on the basis of biology, and defenders of traditional male identity retaliated by marshaling cultural and biological arguments for male dominance and the sexual objectification of women's bodies.

The hostile stalemate between these two factions was palpable and set the stage for a paradigm shift. Ortner and Whitehead's (1981) volume, *Sexual Meanings: The Cultural Construction of Gender and Sexuality,* signaled both a rediscovery of sex by anthropology and a reorientation of ways to understand it by liberating it from naturalistic assumptions. Ortner and Whitehead set out to incorporate gender in order to counter the male bias in anthropological texts up to that time, to focus on sex and its meaning, and to link the personal to the political. The volume also engaged other issues of the times – such as gender equity and sexual freedom – and reflected the pressing political implications of "compulsory heterosexuality" that privileged male genital-centric response over the more diffuse female response (Rich 1980). Even though this volume set out to engage sexuality and meaning cross-culturally it was curiously devoid of a sense of the erotic and sensuous in portraying sexuality in non-Western settings perhaps out of a concern for contributing to the sexploitation of Third World peoples or as a means to avoid the stigma associated with academic work on sex. Yet, it provided a new way of interpreting old themes.

In these opposing theoretical perspectives – cultural influence, socio-biology, feminist, cultural construction – there was little room for a more nuanced biocultural understanding of human sexuality. The race was on to make sexuality all natural or all social. Although most anthropologists recognize that both biology and culture are important to understanding human nature and human sexuality, the entrenchment and bitterness of taking "sides" in this civil war between the positivists and postmodernists made it almost impossible for either side to take the other's arguments very seriously. This, I believe, eroded the influence that anthropologists might have had when HIV/AIDS came on the scene and made the study of sexual behaviors and especially the understanding of why people do what they do sexually so important for protecting sexual and reproductive health.

Mass movements that aimed to liberalize sexual attitudes towards STIs, prostitution, masturbation, and the sexual double standard in the early part of the 20th century used grassroots techniques to advance their agendas. As Vance (1991) notes, these "problematic" sequelae of sex were increasingly subsumed under a larger health agenda that fomented regulatory interests on the part of the state. The development of the social construction perspective within the social sciences provided a strong critique of sex and sexuality as biological entities within the positivist paradigm. The new message (old to us now): sexuality is mediated by historical and cultural factors that produce different sexualities in different times and places with different meanings (Vance 1991). Sexual acts, identities, and communities are never fixed. Taken to its logical extreme, some even posited that desire itself is socially constructed.

HIV/AIDS AND THE NEED FOR SEX INFORMATION

It was the advent of HIV/AIDS in the early 1980s (the virus was not identified until 1983) and its rapid rise to global pandemic status, that created the global research machine (i.e., dedicated research funds both nationally and internationally, specialized journals, conferences and meetings) to investigate what, how, when, with whom, and why people do what they do sexually. Because there is no vaccine to prevent infection with HIV or drugs to cure AIDS once a person becomes infected, prevention of transmission is the only viable strategy to contain the spread of the disease. Such prevention depends largely on changing sexual behaviors, the major route of infection in the world today (UNAIDS 2008), as well as the social, political, and economic environments that foster and exacerbate risk behaviors. It quickly became apparent, however, that we did not have enough information about the actual sexual behavior of Americans (or of people in any other society) to design effective interventions, the last study of this kind having been Kinsey's work more than three decades earlier and before the behavior changes that accompanied the sexual revolution of the 1960s and 1970s. Data on the parameters of sexual contact in the general population (with whom, how often, how many partners, what kind of sex, etc.) were desperately needed by epidemiologists to understand HIV transmission and to model the epidemic and by health providers to inform the design of prevention efforts. Studies of sexual behavior patterns among designated high risk groups (e.g., commercial sex workers, gay men, injection drug users, crack cocaine users) in the early part of the epidemic had already been of immense value to understanding HIV transmission, but there was nothing like this for "ordinary" heterosexual citizens.

In 1987, the call for a national survey of the sexual behavior of Americans was issued by the National Institute for Child Health and Development (NICHD), which was greeted with enthusiasm and relief by the health and research communities alike. However, the proposed research sparked the same controversies as the Kinsey studies four decades earlier, and the much needed investigation of American sexual behavior was quashed by Congress (Laumann et al. 1994a). The study was ultimately funded by private foundations (Robert Wood Johnson Foundation, Henry J. Kaiser Family Foundation, Rockefeller Foundation, Andrew Mellon Foundation, John D. and Catherine T. McArthur Foundation, New York Community Trust, American Foundation for AIDS Research, Ford Foundation) and resulted in the publication of the much needed information on Americans' sexual behavior (Laumann et al. 1994b), which is now over a decade old. These events revealed that little had changed about the controversial nature of sex studies and how bitterly divided Americans continue to be over the appropriateness of sex as a topic of study, even while HIV/AIDS continues to grow in importance globally. Although there are periodic surveys of the sexual behavior of American youth and the fertility behavior of American women, no data are regularly collected on the sexual behavior of the general population in the United States.

The national sex survey (Laumann et al. 1994b) results were important not only for the wealth of data on American sexual behavior, but also for their contextualization within the social aspects of sex. The study itself was designed by a multidisciplinary team and in addition to an exhaustive array of sexual behaviors also addressed issues of age, gender, race/ethnicity, social class, and religion and their relationship to sexual behavior. The team brought a social science perspective to both the design and interpretation of data on sexual behavior. These researchers recognized that sex occurs within relationships and that people are part of sexual networks. Most importantly, they drew on three social theories to guide their work: scripting (cultural rules for sexual conduct); economic choice; social network theory. Thus, they moved the study of human sexuality away from the traditional focus in reproductive health on individual sexual behavior towards a more holistic understanding of sex and social arrangements. This is important because it promoted the idea in the health research community that sex was social and cultural as well as biological. The need to understand the meaning and social structuring of sexual behavior was as important as understanding what people do and how often.

DECONSTRUCTING IRRATIONAL SEXUAL "CHOICES"

Many of the pressing contemporary questions in sexual and reproductive health are related to the non-rational (from the health professional's perspective) choices people make. Why do people "choose" to engage in sexual behaviors that put them at risk for unintended pregnancy, STIs, and HIV/AIDS despite having knowledge of those risks? How can people say that "it [sex] just happened" as though they had no role or agency in a voluntary act? Why do people not protect themselves from STIs with condoms? Why do women continue to get pregnant "unintentionally"? To answer these questions anthropologists seek to understand the social, political–economic, psychological, and emotional context of sexual behavior and people's lived experiences. This emic perspective is what has been largely missing from two decades of sex research conducted under the umbrella of public health and medicine. We know a lot about sexual behaviors but still very little about how people go about making (or not making) decisions about sex. Indeed, it is not clear the extent to which conscious decisions are, in fact, the force that guides sexual behaviors. Strangely, we are awash in information about sexual behavior and its outcomes, but we know far less than we need to know to help people understand and alter their own behavior to achieve optimal sexual and reproductive health. Anthropology and its qualitative methods can answer some of these vital questions and by doing so, it can also call attention to the broader social, cultural, political, and economic forces that impinge on an individual's ability to make decisions and follow through behaviorally to meet their own goals with respect to sexual and reproductive health and behavior.

CLEAVAGES AND CAMPS: 1980S AND 1990S

The vast cleavages that came in the 1980s and 1990s between the positivist, postmodern, and activist perspectives were set in motion by the social movements of the 1970s and the paradigm shift within cultural anthropology (as well as sociology and the humanities) to the emerging social constructionist and phenomenological theoretical perspectives that rejected positivist ways of knowing and stressed the uniqueness of each person's social construction of reality. The emergence of a third, boldly political perspective called Critical Medical Anthropology (CMA) in the early 1980s (Singer 1986; Morsy 1996; Singer and Baer 1995; Baer et al. 1997; Baer and Singer 2009) amplified these internal debates. Anthropologists who embraced the CMA perspective insisted that we needed to consider the social, economic, and political context to truly understand culture and behavior. They pointed to the hegemony of biomedicine and the role of social inequality in shaping culture and behavior. In the arena of sexual risk, critical medical anthropologists raised important questions about the role of power and inequality in the health disparities rapidly documented worldwide in the wake of HIV/AIDS (e.g., access to prevention resources, effects of policing practices, impact of gender inequalities, effects of self-medication to address the hidden injuries of structural violence, the impact of physical and emotional violence).

The bitter struggle among these factions weakened the discipline's applicability and accessibility within the health field, which did not share our interest in these theoretical debates and had difficulty reading our literature. However, it also produced a remarkable intellectual debate within anthropology about the nature of what we know, how we know it, and what we should do with it. These three perspectives (positivist, post-modernist, critical) have had reverberations throughout the social sciences, the humanities, and to a lesser extent the sciences, although CMA came well before public health embraced the social origins of disease and social justice agenda promoted today in health disparities research (Farmer 2005; Krieger 2001, 2003).

The emerging dominance of the social constructionist perspective in cultural anthropology simultaneously reduced anthropology's ability to be relevant to medicine and public health and increased our ability to understand the nuances of sexual and reproductive behavior in terms of lived experience, process, performance, and social context. In particular, the content and language of the post-modern paradigm often precluded a genuine understanding among those outside the discipline of the important points being made by anthropologists. This reduced the exposure of much important theoretical writing on sexuality and gender issues outside the social sciences. The works that made their way into the health arena were those that could translate the jargon of anthropology for the health field (primarily applied anthropologists working in HIV/AIDS). The incredible impact that Paul Farmer has had outside anthropology lies in his ability to reach out to the medical and public health audience in a language they grasp to bring home important messages about the impact of structural violence on the health and well being of people throughout the world.

More recently, the bitterness and divisiveness of these theoretical battles have subsided somewhat, and there seems to be a genuine search for a more holistic paradigm that has proven to be one of anthropology's enduring strengths. We increasingly hear calls for a biosocial-cultural approach to health problems within medical anthropology (see Singer 2009 and Singer and Clair 2003 on syndemics; Baer and Singer 2009 on global warming). I see these hybrid approaches – feminist and critical, qualitative and quantitative, ethno-epidemiological, ecological and critical – especially in the dissertation proposals and the field work of younger anthropologists.

SEXUALITY , REPRODUCTION, GENDER DIVERSITY, LOVE, AND QUEER THEORY

There has been a virtual explosion of literature related to the broader issue of sexuality in medical anthropology since the late 1990s. The number of teaching texts, in particular is impressive and situates the topic of human sexuality in its broadest sense firmly as a primary topic in the pedagogy of anthropology today. There have been introductory primers on sexuality (Middleton 2002; Nanda 2000), histories of the study of sexuality within anthropology (Lyons and Lyons 2004), and a number of excellent readers on sexuality, gender, love, and GLBT (gay, lesbian, bisexual, transgender) themes (Ferber et al. 2009; Jankowiak 1995, 2008; Lancaster and di Leonardo

1997; Padilla et al. 2007; Robertson 2005) as well as reviews of clinical ethnography and sexual culture (Herdt 1999) and the sexuality of anthropologists in the field (Markowitz and Askenazi 1999). These teaching texts attest to the salience of sexuality and reproduction in anthropology. The intersection with reproductive health is more nuanced and contested within anthropology, but has been essential to the impetus to question the status quo in medicine and public health approaches to sex, gender, and contextualization of lived experiences.

Women's health

Women's reproductive health is one of the older and larger subfields of study (Inhorn 2006). At first studies were concerned primarily with the cross-cultural investigation of childbirth and midwifery, but rapidly expanded with the changing medical technology of reproduction to include contraception, infertility, biomedicalization of conception and birth, adolescent and "elderly" (from the biomedical perspective, this is defined as women over age 35) pregnancy and parenting, menopause, abortion, benign neglect, surrogate mothers, fostering, single motherhood, multipartnered fertility, female genital cutting, sexually transmitted infections, HIV/AIDS, sex work, eating disorders, rape, and intimate partner violence. Engagement with health disparities and political economy as well as interpretive, feminist, and social construction perspectives has contributed to a rich and varied canon of work in this area (see Inhorn 2006; Parker and Easton 1998).

Men's health

Men's reproductive health, except as it relates to HIV/AIDS, has been oddly neglected by anthropologists (and the health field). As the default status (i.e., heterosexual male), it has not been problematized until relatively recently. There is a new interest in issues of heterosexual male identity (Guttman 1996), male infertility issues (Inhorn and van Balen 2002), male genital cutting (Immerman and Mackey 1998), and STIs among heterosexual males (Lichtenstein and Schwebke 2005). As topical interests follow the broader medicalization of men's health, we are now seeing or will soon see more studies of body image and eating disorders, use of performance-enhancing drugs, erectile dysfunction and its treatment, and the use of sex-enhancing pharmaceuticals. It is high time to we brought the heterosexual male under the gaze of anthropologists in one of the only arenas where he has been neglected, his reproductive health.

Other-gendered health

In writing about women's and men's health I struggled with the obvious heterosexual "normalcy" of their construction in the wider culture where gender and reproduction are conflated and heterosexuality is privileged. We do not yet have the language to disentangle ourselves from this conundrum, but we do have the vibrant field of "queer theory" to assist us in this endeavor. In fact, queer theory was developed to destabilize gender categories and to break free of the oppressive hetero-normativity that pervades discussion of sexual and reproductive behavior (Warner 1993). It situates the most stigmatized sexual identities as central to the production of knowledge because normalcy is always defined in opposition to deviance (Butler 1993). The last 15 years or so have seen the rise of an impressive body of work about humans who do not indentify themselves at the "heterosexual only" pole of what is now widely viewed as a continuum of orientations from heterosexual to homosexual. Even this dimension of hetero-homo-sexual does not do justice to this literature because, aside from gay and lesbian at the homosexual pole, there are other sexualities that may not fit on this binary dimension at all such as transsexual, transgenderist, and third sex identities. Queer theory and its literature have had a tremendous impact on the way we think about gender, social arrangements, and sexuality (see Nanda 2000; Robertson 2005).

Love, romantic passion, and the revival of companionate marriage

It was relatively recently that anthropologists turned their attention to human emotions (Lutz and White 1986). Indeed, it was only a little more than a decade ago that Jankowiak (1995) proposed the idea that romantic passion is a universal human experience. Prior to this edited volume, the "study of romantic passion (or romantic love) as it is experienced in non-Western cultures is nonexistent" (Jankowiak 1995:1). Thus, only recently have anthropologists begun to look closely into human sexuality as a personal, emotional experience and to expand our investigations beyond the role of sex as a means of reproducing the species, ordering social relations through kinship, and spreading disease. This is rather astounding given the preoccupation with passionate love in popular culture throughout the ages and the increasing globalization of Western notions of love, romance, and marriage.

Jankowiak's' edited volumes (1995, 2008) firmly established the existence of romantic love in a wide variety of cultures. There is no doubt that all peoples are capable of experiencing love in all its aspects from obsession to companionate domesticity. Indeed, many cultures view being in love as a form of temporary insanity that wreaks havoc with ordered social life. Indeed, science has recently corroborated what most people know instinctively, that love and attraction are not under voluntary control. The neural systems responsible for emotion and intellect are separate (Lewis et al. 2001).

My own work on love and teen pregnancy among Latinas in East Los Angeles (Erickson 1998, 1998–1999) was innovative in drawing attention to the role of emotion, social context, and structural factors in producing the public health "problem" of early childbearing. I was among the first anthropologists/public health professionals to stress the importance of love, emotion, and sexual attraction in studies of teen pregnancy (Erickson 2006). I was by no means alone, however, in drawing attention to the importance of love for sexual behavior (see Hatfield and Rapson 1996). The last decade has seen a growing interest among anthropologists in the globalization of love and companionate marriage (Hirsch and Wardlow 2006; Padilla et al. 2007). This literature shows that love has become a critical element of modernity. Young people the world over are increasingly desirous of choosing their own mates and having meaningful, supportive, emotionally close relationships with their spouses. Studies show that their encounters with these possibilities begin in the viewing of Western movies or through listening to Western music genres.

Sex tourism, Internet matchmaking, and cybersex

Cutting edge topics that make use of our globalized world, digital communication devices, the Internet, and virtual reality are now being subjected to the anthropological gaze. These include the use of sex-enhancing recreational drugs, sex tourism, cybersex, use of the Internet and digital technologies for connecting (e.g., eHarmony, Match.com) and communicating (chat rooms, cell phones), *Second Life* (Linden Lab) and other virtual realities, and use of computer-aided distance sex (cameras, devices that can be manipulated by a partner from his/her computer). The digital age has brought us new and interesting ways to find mates, explore sexuality, role play, and have virtual sex. Many of these technologies can be adapted to commercial sex exchanges, perhaps making sex safer if less physically intimate.

CONTEXTUALIZING SEXUAL BEHAVIOR FOR THE HEALTH FIELD

By the beginning of the 21st century there was a vast amount of information on sexual behaviors and practices, but far less on the social context of that behavior. This resulted in the paradoxical situation in which there was much factual information, but it was divorced from any attachment to meaning and context. Today, in public health we know what people do, with whom, and how often, but we do not understand why they do what they do, especially when they have the knowledge they need to avoid undesirable outcomes (STI, HIV, unintended pregnancy). Thus, because of the disconnection between behavior and meaning, the health field was hobbled in its attempts to prevent the spread of HIV/AIDS as well as other STIs and unintended pregnancy, the three scourges of sex. Despite the surge of research on sexual behavior in the 1980s and 1990s, curiously little theory was produced within public health that could speak to the need for interventions that worked or explain why people behaved "irrationally" (from the point of view of prevention) when it came to sex. In addition, much of this research also suffered from the profound impact of the sex negativity that persists in western culture (Plummer 2005) as well as our binary ideas of the "normal" dichotomy between male/female and homosexual/heterosexual and the privileging of heterosexuality, especially male heterosexuality, in social arrangements (Usher 2009). The deconstruction and critique of these core Western perspectives on sexuality became the central activity of the anthropology of sexuality in the 1980s and1990s.

In retrospect, this short history of the public health and anthropological approaches to the study of sexuality highlights the difference between medicine's focus on biology and individual behavior and social science's focus on their social determinants. Despite some good work by anthropologists, many of whom were practicing rather than academic anthropologists, with targeted populations (gay men, commercial sex workers, Latina teen mothers) that did incorporate both meaning-centered and broader understandings of the social, political, and economic context of sexuality and sexual behavior (e.g., Bolton 1992 on HIV and promiscuity; Carrier 1989 on homosexuality in Mexico; De Zalduondo and Bernard 1995 on commercial sex workers; Erickson 1998, 1998–1999 on Latina teen mothers), the sexual and reproductive health research machine and its reliance on survey methods, largely failed to address the complexity of human motivations, the social and cultural constraints, and the political and economic necessities that impinge on sexual behavior.

Just as biomedicine focuses on the individual body, its diseases and their treatments, much sex research has focused on discrete behaviors of individuals that expose those individuals to risk and the need to change their behavior. Work by social scientists during the first wave of HIV/AIDS research legitimized the power of qualitative methods for understanding sexual behavior in social context, but it did not lead to easily implemented social interventions. The most successful safer sex campaign of the early phase of the epidemic in the United States was mounted by the gay community that was first afflicted and affected by the disease. As HIV made its way into the drug-using and heterosexual populations, there were fewer successful campaigns. Another community endeavor, the Kaiser Family Foundation/BET "wrap it up" campaign that promoted condom use for STI and pregnancy prevention, reached minority youth making condom use normative in new or casual sexual relationships (Kaiser Family Foundation 2009; Singer et al. 2006). However, no prevention strategy has been successful in overcoming the fact that condom use drops propitiously among people in serious relationships, leaving intimates vulnerable to infections (Singer et al. 2006; Sobo 1995).

TRANSLATING KNOWLEDGE TO ACTION

The anthropological literature on sexuality and reproduction has much relevance for sexual and reproductive health. At the macro-level, it calls attention to the diversity of social arrangements for sexual expression, the existence of sexual subcultures that may have different health risks from the other groups, and the extent to which political–economic factors affect the ability of people situated in different contexts to exercise their sexual and reproductive rights and desires. At the micro-level, it provides a rich description of the ways that sex, love, and reproduction play out in peoples' lives. There is a deep need for a meaning-centered understanding of sexuality in the health field in order to develop interventions that speak to the real needs and concerns that people have about protecting their health. Although we now have a better understanding of why people do what they do, we need to develop a means to translate this knowledge into action. Anthropologists can make valuable contributions to the development of a sexual and reproductive health paradigm that can accommodate the biosocial-cultural nature of human sexual experience within the holistic context of individual motivation, couple negotiation, family influences, community norms, government constraints, and global political economy.

REFERENCES

Ajzen, Icek, and Martin Fishbein, 1975 Belief, Attitude, Intention, and Behavior: An Introduction to Theory and Research. Reading MA: Addison-Wesley.
Ajzen, Icek, and Martin Fishbein, 1980 Understanding Attitudes and Predicting Social Behavior. Englewood Cliffs NJ: Prentice Hall.
Baer, Hans, and Merrill Singer, 2009 Global Warming and the Politcal Ecology of Health. Emerging Crises and Systematic Solutions. Walnut Creek CA: Left Coast Press.

Baer, Hans, Merrill Singer, and Ida Susser, 1997 Medical Anthropology and the World System. A Critical Perspective. Westport CT: Bergin & Garvey.

Becker, Marshall H., 1974 The Health Belief Model and Personal Health Behavior. Health Education Monographs 2:324–473.

Bolton, Ralph, 1992 AIDS and Promiscuity: Muddles in the Models of HIV Prevention. Medical Anthropology 14:145–223.

Boston Women's Health Collective, 1973 Our Bodies Ourselves. New York: Simon & Schuster.

Butler, Judith, 1993 Initiation and Gender Insubordination. In The Lesbian and Gay Studies Reader. Henry Aberlove, Michele Barale and David Halperin, eds. pp. 307–320. New York: Routledge.

Carrier, Joseph, 1989 Sexual Behavior and the Role of AIDS in Mexico. In The Aids Pandemic: A Global Emergency. Ralph Bolton, ed. pp. 37–50. New York: Gordon & Breach.

Comfort, Alex, 1972 The Joy of Sex. A Cordon Bleu Guide. New York: Simon and Schuster.

De Zalduondo, Barbara, and H. Russel Bernard, 1995 Meanings and Consequences of Sexual-economic Exchange: Gender, Poverty, and Sexual Risk Behavior in Urban Haiti. In Conceiving Sexuality: Approaches to Research in a Poatmodern World. Richard G. Parker and John H. Gagnon, eds. pp. 157–180. London and New York: Routledge.

Erickson, Pamela I., 1998 Latina Adolescent Childbearing in East Los Angeles. Austin TX: University of Texas Press.

Erickson, Pamela I., 1998–1999 Cultural Factors Affecting the Negotiation of First Sexual Intercourse among Latina Adolescent Mothers. International Quarterly of Community Health Education 18(1):121–137.

Erickson, Pamela I., 2006. The Role of Romantic Love in Sexual Initiation and the Transition to Parenthood among Immigrant and US-Born Latino Youth in East Los Angeles. In Modern Loves. The Anthropology of Romantic Courtship and Compassionate Marriage. Jennifer S. Hirsch and Holly Wardlow, eds. pp. 118–134. Ann Arbor MI: University of Michigan Press.

Farmer, Paul, 2005 Pathologies of Power: Health, Human Rights, and the New War on the Poor. Berkeley: University of California Press.

Ferber, Abby L., Kimberly Holcomb, and Tre Wentling, 2009 Sex, Gender, and Sexuality. The New Basics. An Anthology. New York: Oxford University Press.

Fisher, Jeffrey. D., and William A. Fisher, 2002 The Information-Motivation-Behavioral Skills Model. In Emerging Theories in Health Promotion and Practice. Richard. DiClemente, R. Crosby and M. Kegler, eds. pp. 40–70. San Francisco: Jossey Bass Publishers.

Ford, Clelland S., and Frank A. Beach, 1951 Patterns of Sexual Behavior. New York: Ace.

Gagnon, John H., and William Simon, 1987 Sexual Theory: A Sexual Scripts Approach. In Theories and Paradigms of Human Sexuality. James H. Geer and William T. O'Donahue, eds. pp. 363–383. New York: Plenum Press.

Gagnon, John H., and William Simon, 2005 [1973] Sexual Conduct. The Social Sources of Human Sexuality. New Brunswick NJ: Aldine Transaction.

Guttman, Matthew, 1996. The Meanings of Macho: Being a Man in Mexico City. Berkeley: University of California Press.

Hatfield, Elaine, and Richard L. Rapson, 1996 Love and Sex. Cross-Cultural Perspectives. Boston: Allyn and Bacon.

Herdt, Gilbert, 1999 Clinical Ethnography and Sexual Culture. Annual Review of Sex Research 10:100–119.

Hirsch, Jennifer S., and Holly Wardlow, eds., 2006 Modern Loves. The Anthropology of Romantic Courtship and Companionate Marriage. Ann Arbor MI: University of Michigan Press.

Immerman, Ronald S., and Wade C. Mackey, 1998 A Biocultural Analysis of Circumcision. Social Biology 44(3–4):267–273.

Inhorn, Marcia C., 2006 Defining Women's Health: A Dozen Messages from More than 150 Ethnographies. Medical Anthropology Quarterly 20(3):345–378.

Inhorn, Marcia C., and Frank van Balen, 2002 Infertility around the Globe: New Thinking on Childlessness, Gender, and Reproductive Technologies. Berkeley: University of California Press.

Jankowiak, William, ed., 1995 Romantic Passion. A Universal Experience? New York: Columbia University Press.

Jankowiak, William, ed., 2008 Intimacies. Love and Sex across Cultures. New York: Columbia University Press.

Kaiser Family Foundation, 2009 RAP-IT-UP, BET. Electronic document. http://www.kff.org/entpartnerships/bet2/.

Kimmel, Michael, ed., 2007 The Sexual Self. The Construction of Sexual Scripts. Nashville TN: Vanderbilt University Press.

Kinsey, Alfred C., Wardell B. Pomeroy, Clyde E. Martin, and Paul H. Gebbhard, 1948 Sexual Behavior in the Human Male. Philadelphia: Saunders.

Kinsey, Alfred C., Wardell B. Pomeroy, Clyde E. Martin, and Paul H. Gebbhard, 1953 Sexual Behavior in the Human Female. Philadelphia: Saunders.

Krieger, Nancy, 2001 Theories for Social Epidemiology in the 21st Century: An Ecosocial Perspective. International Journal of Epidemiology. 30(4):668–677.

Krieger, Nancy, 2003 Does Racism Harm Health? Did Child Abuse Exist Before 1962? On Explicit Questions, Critical Science, and Current Controversies: An Ecosocial Perspective. American Journal of Public Health 93(2):194–199.

Lancaster, Roger N., and Micaela di Leohardo, eds., 1997 The Gender/Sexuality Reader. Culture, Histpry, Political Economy. New York: Routledge.

Laumann, Edward O., Robert T. Michael, and John H. Gagnon, 1994a A Political History of the National Sex Survey of Adults. Family Planning Perspectives 26:84–88.

Laumann, Edward O., John H. Gagnon, Robert T. Michael, and Sturat Michaels, 1994b The Social Organization of Sexuality. Sexual Practices in the United States. Chicago: The University of Chicago Press.

Lewis, Thomas, Fari Amini, and Richard Lannon, 2001 A General Theory of Love. New York: Random House.

Lichtenstein, Bronwen, and Jane R. Schwebke, 2005 Partner Notification Methods for African American Men Being Treated for Trichomoniasis: A Consideration of Main Men, Second Hitters, and Third Players. Medical Anthropology Quarterly 19(4):383–401.

Lutz, Catherine, and Geoffrey M. White, 1986 The Anthropology of Emotions. Annual Review of Anthropology 15:405–436.

Lyons, Andrew P., and Harriet D. Lyons, 2004 Irregular Connections. A history of Anthropology and Sexuality. Lincoln NB: University of Nebraska Press.

Malinowski, Bronislaw, 1987 [1929] The Sexual Life of Savages in North-Western Melanesia. Boston: Beacon Press.

Markowitz, Fran, and Michael Ashkenazi, eds., 1999 Sex, Sexuality, and the Anthropologist. Champaign-Urbana IL: University of Illinois Press.

Marshall, Donald, and Robert C. Suggs, eds., 1971 Human Sexual Behavior: Variations in the Ethnographic Spectrum. Studies in Sex and Society. New York: Basic Books.

Masters, William H., and Virginia E. Johnson, 1966 Human Sexual Response. Boston: Little, Brown.

Masters, William H., and Virginia E. Johnson, 1970. Human Sexual Inadequacy. Boston: Little, Brown.

Masters, William H., and Virginia E. Johnson, 1979 Homosexuality in Perspective. Boston: Little, Brown.

Mead, Margaret, 1928 Coming of Age in Samoa. New York: William Morrow.

Mead, Margaret, 1930 Growing Up in New Guinea. New York: William Morrow.

Mead, Margaret, 1950 [1935] Sex and Temperament in Three Primitive Societies. New York: Mentor.

Middleton, DeWight R., 2002 Exotics and Erotics. Human Cultural and Sexual Diversity. Long Grove IL: Waveland Press.

Morsy, Soheir A., 1996 Political Economy in Medical Anthropology. *In* Contemporary Theory and Method. Revised edition. Carolyn F. Sargent and Thomas M. Johnson, eds. New York: Praeger.

Nanda, Serena, 2000 Gender Diversity. Crosscultural Variations. Long Grove, IL: Waveland Press.

Ortner, Sherry B., and Harriet Whitehead, 1981 Sexual Meanings. The Cultural Construction of Gender and Sexuality. Cambridge UK: Cambridge University Press.

Padilla, Mark B., Jennifer S. Hirsch, Miguel Muñoz-Laboy, Robert E. Sember, and Richard G. Parker, eds., 2007 Love and Globalization. Transformations of Intimacy in the Contemporary World. Nashville TN: Vanderbilt University Press.

Parker, Richard G., and Delia Easton, 1998 Sexuality, Culture, and Political Economy: Recent Developments in Anthropological and Cross-Cultural Sex Research. Annual Review of Sex Research 9:1–19.

Plummer, Ken, 2005 Permanence and Change: Sexual Conduct – Thirty Years On. Foreword. *In* Sexual Conduct. The Social Sources of Human Sexuality. 2nd edition. John H. Gagnon and William Simon, eds. pp. ix–xxi. New Brunswick NJ: Aldine Transaction.

Rich, Adrienne, 1980 Compulsory Heterosexuality and Lesbian Existence. Signs: Journal of Women in Culture and Society 5(4):631–660.

Robertson, Jennifer, ed., 2005 Same-Sex Cultures and Sexualities. An Anthropological Reader. Malden MA: Blackwell Publishing.

Rosenstock, Irwin M., 1966 Why People Use Health Services. Milbank Memorial Fund Quarterly 44:94–124.

SIECUS (Sexuality Information and Education Council of the United States), 2004 The Far-Right's Fight against Kinsey. Electronic document. http://www.siecus.org/index.cfm?fuseaction=Feature.showFeature&featureid=1182&pageid=483&parentid=478/.

Singer, Merrill, 1986 The Emergence of a Critical Medical Anthropology. Medical Anthropology 17(5):128–129.

Singer, Merrill, 2009 Introduction to Syndemics: A Systems Approach to Public and Community Health. San Francisco: Jossey-Bass.

Singer, Merrill, and Hans Baer, 1995 Critical Medical Anthropology. Amiytyville NY: Baywood Publishing Company.

Singer, Merrill, and Scott Clair, 2003 Syndemics and Public Health: Reconceptualizing Disease in Bio-Social Context. Medical Anthropology Quarterly 17(4):423–441.

Singer, Merrill, Pamela I. Erickson, Louise Badiane, Rosemary Diaz, Dugeidy Ortiz, Traci Abraham, and Anna Marie Nicolaysen, 2006 Syndemics, Sex, and the City: Understanding Sexually Transmitted Diseases in Social and Cultural Context. Social Science and Medicine 63(8):2010–2021.

Small, Meredith F., 1995 What's Love Got to Do with It? The Evolution of Human Mating. New York: Anchor Books.

Sobo, Elisa J., 1995 Choosing Unsafe Sex: AIDS Risk Denial among Disadvantaged Women. Philadelphia PA: University of Pennsylvania Press.

Symons, Donald, 1995 Beauty Is in the Adaptations of the Beholder: The Evolutionary Psychology of Human Female Attractiveness. *In* Sexual Nature, Sexual Culture. Paul R. Abramson and David D. Pinkerton, eds. pp. 80–118. Chicago: University of Chicago Press.

UNAIDS (Joint United Nations Programme on HIV/AIDS), April 2008 Fast Facts about HIV Prevention. Electronic document. http://www.unaids.org/en/KnowledgeCentre/Resources/FastFacts/.

Usher, Jane, 2009 Sexual Science and the Law: Regulating Sex – Reifying the Power of the Heterosexual Man. *In* Sex, Gender, and Sexuality. The New Basics. An Anthology. Abby L., Kimberly Holcomb, and Tre Wentling, eds. pp. 377–416. New York: Oxford University Press.

Vance, Carole S., 1991 Anthropology Rediscovers Sexuality: A Theoretical Comment. Social Science and Medicine 33(8):875–884.

Warner, M., ed., 1993. Fear of a Queer Planet: Queer Politics and Social Theory. Minneapolis: University of Minnesota Press.

FURTHER READING

Frayser, Suzanne G., 1985 Varieties of Sexual Experience. An Anthropological Perspective on Human Sexuality. New Haven CT: HRAF Press.
Suggs, David N., and Andrew W. Miracle, eds., 1993 Culture and Sexuality. A Reader. Pacific Grove CA: Brooks/Cole Publishing Company.

FURTHER READING

CHAPTER 14

Situating Birth in the Anthropology of Reproduction

*Carolyn Sargent
and Lauren Gulbas*

INTRODUCTION

After more than 30 years of ethnographic research, the anthropology of birth has a well-established, empirically based literature. Case studies from both preindustrial and industrialized societies have provided data for considering the diversity found in "ways of knowing" about and managing birth. Researchers have explored the negotiation between high- and low-technology birthing systems, as well as how women in heterogeneous societies embrace and adapt diverse models for maternity. Although early research on childbirth in cross-cultural perspective was heavily descriptive, the now substantial scholarship in this area has emphatically demonstrated the theoretical significance of the "anthropology of birth." At the same time that we acknowledge the extensive literature on birth, it is important to recognize that anthropological studies of childbirth represent an important component in the broader anthropology of reproduction, rather than a distinct subfield. Accordingly, discussion of anthropological research on birth is most meaningfully situated in this more comprehensive domain, which encompasses a diverse array of issues concerning such themes as fertility and infertility, pregnancy and birth, miscarriages and abortions, reproductive technologies, genetics and disabilities.

Our aim in this chapter is not to provide a comprehensive review of the literature that has been published on the anthropology of birth. Several excellent and exhaustive reviews are already accessible (Davis-Floyd 2003; Davis-Floyd and Sargent 1997; Ginsburg and Rapp 1991, 1995; Inhorn and Birenbaum-Carmeli 2008; Lock 1993). With this in mind, this chapter begins with an assessment of the anthropological study

A Companion to Medical Anthropology, First Edition. Edited by Merrill Singer and Pamela I. Erickson.

of childbirth in the context of a large and sophisticated body of research on reproduction, more broadly construed.

Over the past twenty years, numerous scholars have argued powerfully that the study of reproduction is central to theory in anthropology (see Browner and Sargent 1996; Davis-Floyd and Sargent 1997; Franklin and Ragone 1999; Ginsberg and Rapp 1995; Rapp 2001). As Franklin and Ragone (1982:2) observe, "… an important genealogy of modern anthropology can readily be traced through its relationship to a core set of ideas related to reproduction." Similarly, Browner and Sargent (1996) note that the study of reproductive meanings and practices, including ethnographies of childbirth, demonstrates how reproduction reflects and shapes core societal values and structures. For example, studies of birth in cross-cultural perspective offer rich data for medical anthropologists as they explore the changing face of medicine, whether through the emergence of evidence-based obstetrics (Wedland 2007), the humanist tradition in American birthing practices (Davis-Floyd 2003), the discursive idiom of natural birth in the practice of midwifery (MacDonald 2006), or the functioning of gender hegemony in the production of motherhood (Davis-Floyd 2004). As studies of birth grow to encompass a broader range of theoretical issues, from the experience of infertility to the global flows of biotechnologies, such research becomes key to understanding how childbirth – like other reproductive processes – shapes and reshapes social, moral, and political landscapes (Browner and Sargent 1996; Lock 1997; Kleinman et al. 1997).

From Feminist Activism to Women's Health

The rise of feminism and the proliferation of gender studies in the 1970s reinvigorated and transformed scholarship on childbirth, setting the stage for the emergence of an anthropology of childbirth that was inherently political. Feminist activists and anthropologists engaged in a mutually enriching dialogue that ultimately contributed to the revolutionalizing of women's health care in the United States. The rich ethnographic and theoretical scholarship on reproduction in general, and childbirth in particular, is thus a product of a dialectic between 20th century popular health and feminist movements and scholarship in the area of women's health (Browner and Sargent 1996).

Scholars across disciplines have looked to anthropology for comparative and historical perspectives on women's health, the female body, and the politics of reproduction. An enduring objective central to the feminist project in medical anthropology has been the critical analysis of the "rise of male institutional domination over reproduction and the female patient" (Browner and Sargent 2007:233) and the documentation of the biocultural patterning of reproductive practices across cultures. In the context of these conceptual and political dynamics, anthropologists generated a foundational literature of cross-cultural, ethnographic studies of childbirth.

Bridgette Jordan's *Birth in Four Cultures* (1978) represented a milestone in the anthropology of birth, producing the standard for a new generation of empirically grounded comparative studies of birthing systems while simultaneously establishing the intellectual legitimacy of anthropological research on human reproduction (Browner and Sargent 2007:234). *Birth in Four Cultures* has been lauded as "instrumental in defining the field of the Anthropology of Birth, as well as in lishing some of its primary methods of cross-cultural comparison, analysis, a. strategies for planning change" (Davis-Floyd 1993:ix). Correspondingly, a number of anthropologists working simultaneously in the 1960s and 1970s (see reviews such as Ginsburg and Rapp 1991; Davis-Floyd and Sargent 1997) made significant developments towards what would later be broadly conceptualized as "the anthropology of birth." Jordan's work, however, is widely considered groundbreaking in its central argument that birth – in both biomedical and local birthing systems – constitutes a cultural production. Her comparison of birth in four cultures, Sweden, Holland, the United States, and among the Maya of Mexico, is a landmark among anthropological studies of reproduction. As a result, Jordan stimulated a broader anthropological interest in how the practices of biomedical obstetrics are culturally shaped and, in addition, legitimized comparative ethnographic research on childbirth (Browner and Sargent 2007; Davis-Floyd and Sargent 1997).

MEDICALIZATION OF CHILDBIRTH AND THE CONTINUED INFLUENCE OF BIOTECHNOLOGIES

Intersecting with feminist activism regarding the female body and reproductive rights, anthropological studies of childbirth both reflect and have generated new investigations of the management of birth. Following Jordan, a central and enduring issue involves birth as a cultural production, as well as the realization that biomedical management of childbirth is also culturally shaped. For this reason, challenges to the biomedical definition of pregnancy, labor and delivery as pathologies necessitating technological expertise and medical surveillance have characterized anthropological studies of childbirth from the 1970s to the present (Michaelson 1988; MacCormack 1994). Much research has documented and critiqued the medicalization of pregnancy and childbirth that has accompanied the global exportation of biomedicine (Davis-Floyd and Sargent 1997; Davis-Floyd 2001; Van Hollen 2003; Roth Allen 2002). Davis-Floyd's compelling classic (2003) *Birth as an American Rite of Passage*, which analyzes the prevalence of "technocratic birth" in the United States has encouraged comparative research on birthing systems worldwide, to examine the promotion of technological interventions during birth as standard practices in diverse societies.

With the rapid pace of innovations in the fields of reproductive science and technology, the cultural/social/political expectations of childbirth are continually shifting (Browner and Sargent 2007:235). As childbearing becomes increasingly "technoscientific" (Dimut and Davis-Floyd 1998:2), the actors involved in the process of childbirth are confronted with a cultural idiom of reproduction that values advanced technology, progress, and expert knowledge. Although this is certainly not a new line of analysis among anthropologists who study childbirth, Jordan's writings on the concept of authoritative knowledge – that knowledge established through interaction which becomes the basis for making decisions and taking actions, the knowledge which "counts" – (Jordan 1993:152) have influenced scholars interested in the production and display of authoritative knowledge in a range of birthing systems (for ethnographic examples of such studies, see Davis-Floyd and Sargent 1997 and Jordan 1983; for a review of related literature, see Ginsburg and Rapp 1991).

The theoretical investigation of authoritative knowledge as it pertains to the contested power relations related to pregnancy and birth thus continues the long-standing anthropological interest in the politics of childbirth. Anthropologists continue to examine the contestation of control over childbirth as a way to explore shifting power relations at multiple levels, from the local to the global (Browner 1986, 2000; Inhorn 2007; Sargent 2007; Browner and Sargent, in Press).

Issues of dominance and resistance reflect another important theme in anthropological studies of medicalization and childbirth. Many scholars have demonstrated how the shift in birth practices, from home-based births attended by midwives to hospital births overseen by obstetric specialists, has been accompanied by a concomitant loss of women's control over the birth experience (Davis-Floyd 2001; Davis-Floyd and Sargent 1997; Sargent and Stark 1989). Some scholars have pursued a meta-analytical approach to this issue, focusing not on the loss of a parturient's control in her birth experience, but on the scholarly interest in narratives of personal control as a reflection of the individualistic values of 20th century Anglo-European societies. Several anthropologists have argued, on the basis of informant narratives of pregnancy or neonatal loss, that the study of infertility and complications surrounding conception, pregnancy, and birth can contribute to more robust models of individual decision-making and control (see Ginsburg and Rapp 1999; Layne 1999).

The focus on "control," which originated in feminist activism of the 1960s and early feminist anthropological engagement with women's health issues, has evolved over the years. Davis-Floyd (2003) and Sargent and Stark (1989), for instance, have shown that there are multiple meanings of "control." Whereas for some scholars and activists, control referred to a woman's decision-making authority in the management of birth (Davis 2007), studies of women's birth experiences in the United States suggest that for many women, "control" during childbirth refers to pain management and remaining "in charge" of personal behavior and emotions such as crying, body movement, anxiety, and other emotional responses.

THE DIALECTIC OF FETAL RIGHTS AND REPRODUCTIVE GOALS

The conceptual distinction between mother and child as discrete entities is central to the ideological "hyper-valuation" (Davis-Floyd 2003) of technology, including not only the routinization of high-tech birth, but also the broadening possibilities for diagnostic testing during pregnancy. This becomes especially problematic regarding a woman's decision to undergo prenatal and genetic testing. Whether the question concerns alpha-fetoprotein testing, ultrasound, or amniocentesis, a mother's choice to forgo diagnostic tests may result in her being seen as selfish and averse to providing her baby the best medical care available (see Browner and Press 1997; Dumit and Davis-Floyd 1998; Rapp 1999). As Lock notes, until recently, there has been "relatively little resistance, in principle, to the development and application of medical technology...Despite the fact that the interests of powerful elites are often directly involved with the creation, manufacture, distribution, and application of medical technology, the assumption that such technologies are inevitably 'good' is widespread" (Lock 1997:209).

The ethical and moral issues surrounding reproductive technologies become even more pronounced in the case of fetal surgery, a new medical specialty that is still in an experimental stage. As Monica Casper documents in her book, *The Making of the Unborn Patient*, "fetal surgery embodies how we think about reproduction, pregnant women, families, and most of all, those tiny dependent occupants of women's bodies – fetuses. Fetal surgery…is intimately connected to other social practices, like abortion politics, in which the personhood and worth of the fetus are salient" (1998:4). The practice of fetal surgery contributes to "the erasure of pregnant women that has occurred as fetuses continue to attract greater attention from health care providers. Despite women's own commitments to securing healthier babies, fetal surgery feeds into cultural preoccupations with maternal–fetal conflict. It fuels rather than resolves ongoing social confusion about where women end and fetuses begin (1998:5)."

Ultimately, Casper's research demonstrates the need to "recast fetal surgery in terms of a women's health agenda…fetal surgery poses a number of serious health risks and consequences for the pregnant women who undergo it…[Yet] pregnant women themselves have been active participants in fetal surgery, selecting a range of interventions for the sake of their fetuses (1998:219)." Thus, there is continued need to reveal how "reproductive medicine both heals and harms women; it both produces and destroys fetuses, it is both palliative and iatrogenic; it both opens and closes reproductive possibilities; it is both a consumer choice and a form of social control; and it both shapes cultural meanings and is a product of culture" (Casper 1998:220).

It is precisely these paradoxes that anthropologists who study pregnancy and childbirth continue to navigate in their research (Morgan and Michaels 1999; Ragone 1994; Davis-Floyd and Dumit 1998). Morgan and Michaels, for example, confront the challenging topic of "fetal subjects." Fetuses, they argue, have come to "occupy a significant place in the private imaginary of women who are or wish to be pregnant" (1999:2). An anthropological perspective has much to tell us in this area of inquiry, given that the meanings associated with conception, the fetus, and life prior to birth are culturally diverse. At the same time, globalization has mediated local meanings of the fetus and fetal personhood. Morgan and Michaels' collection of essays is groundbreaking in its project: to explore the "practices, institutions and discourses that have brought fetuses into the center of reproductive politics" (Morgan and Michaels 1999:5).

The ever-increasing influences of biotechnologies, assisted reproductive technologies, and the medicalization of birth have highlighted the various dilemmas that can take place before, during, and/or after childbirth. In an effort to understand the nuances of reproductive health problems, barriers to safe pregnancy, and the differing and often incompatible reproductive goals among women, men, healthcare practitioners, and the state, scholars have examined the concept of "disrupted reproduction" (Inhorn 2007). Disrupted reproduction, broadly conceived, refers to the multiplicity of ways in which the conventional (i.e., "expected") patterns of conception and birth become problematic (Jenkins and Inhorn 2003). The notion of disrupted reproduction encourages scholarship to unpack what is meant by "normal" birth, in addition to exploring the numerous problems and possibilities associated with reproduction, such as pregnancy loss, genetic screening, disability, and adoption (Landsman 2003; Layne 2002; 2003; Rapp and Ginsburg 2007).

A Note on Low-Technology Birthing Systems

Biomedical obstetrics – its meanings, practices, transformations, and variations – remains an enduring focus in cross-cultural research on birth. The biomedical model for birth that has come to dominate practices in the United States and Western Europe has been exported to much of the developing world, and an increasingly large and important literature focuses on the extent to which local birthing systems accommodate or resist the introduction of new technologies, beliefs, and practices (Dundes 2003; Pranee Liamputtong 2007). Despite the worldwide proliferation of biomedical obstetrics, much research demonstrates the viability of low-tech birth systems and midwifery, and suggests that local birthing systems can be resilient and successful in contesting high-technology obstetrics (Davis-Floyd and Sargent 1997; Laderman 1983; MacCormack 1982; Sargent 1982, 1989). Unfortunately, the language of analysis in childbirth studies often dichotomizes low-technology versus technocratic, or "traditional" versus "modern." As Margaret Jolly points out, this "reduces the diversity of birthing experiences at both ends – since both 'traditional' and 'modern' birthing patterns are quite various, not just in techniques but in their cultural conceptualization and evaluation" (1998:14). Frequently, traditional birthing practices are read as "natural," yet in many parts of the world, childbirth is construed as an event that threatens spiritual well being at both individual and social levels (Rozario 1998). Scholars must remain committed to the study of birthing systems across the technological spectrum. Local-level, theoretically informed ethnographies are imperative in order to develop more fully an analytical language that helps us move beyond binaries and appreciate the complexities of childbirth practices at the local level and in global contexts (Inhorn and Sargent 2006:1).

Midwifery

The subject of midwifery has been a theme in numerous cross-cultural studies of childbirth. Many have focused on the social status of midwives, how individuals select or are recruited for training, the ways that techniques and knowledge are acquired, and the role of the midwife in providing prenatal care, assistance at birth, care for the newborn, and postpartum treatment. The first significant review of this topic was conducted by Cosminsky (1976), who synthesized a body of secondary ethnographic and medical literature to assess the midwife's role at all stages in the birth systems where specialists are active.

Studies of midwifery continue to thrive, providing accounts of local birthing practices and the intricate negotiations that emerge among pregnant women, their familial and social networks, birthing attendants, and biomedical practitioners. In contrast to the early research on the social attributes, training and practices of local midwives, recent ethnographies necessarily address the complex institutional and state politics and policies that shape midwifery practices. Among the issues that have garnered attention over the years, the variations in the social esteem associated with the practice of midwifery has continued to be salient, whether in studies of rural midwives in West Africa (Holloway 2007) or South Asia. Although the status of midwives is a respected one in many societies (e.g., Jamaica, peninsular Malaysia, and large parts of Africa), this is not uniformly the case. For example, the position of midwife (*dai*) in India is reserved for low-caste women due to the perceived unclean nature of birth and bodily fluids (see Jeffery and Jeffery (1993)), who critique the romanticism displayed in some studies of local community midwives. Rozario (1998:161) has noted a similar situation in Bangladesh, where the *dai* has very low social status, and is usually an older woman of low socio-economic status who has received no formal education or training. These women receive little compensation for their labor, although their experience and value as birth attendants is acknowledged.

The role of the Bangladeshi *dai* that Rozario describes is thought to be typical in neighboring areas, and is likely to be common in most parts of South Asia. Towghi (2004) examines shifting government policies toward Pakistani *dais* (local community midwives) since the Declaration of Alma Ata in 1978, which promoted the integration of "traditional healers" in resource-limited national health systems. In the context of evolving international health campaigns, local community midwives in Pakistan serve as family planning agents, as primary care providers, and as birth attendants. Towghi details the multifaceted responsibilities of the *dais* in reproductive and infant health care. Intermittent government initiatives to devalue these local midwives and to replace them with biomedical practitioners have not succeeded, given the important services they continue to provide and the reality that individual *dais* cannot be expected to enhance women's reproductive health without attention to health infrastructure and the reduction of broader structural inequalities.

When considering the status of the midwife from a dynamic global perspective, it is important to note that the proliferation of biomedical facilities has increasingly led women to choose assistance from biomedical practitioners, resulting in a concomitant decline in the social estimation of local midwives (for a valuable collection of articles on midwives' "shifting identities and practices" in global perspective see Davis-Floyd et al. 2001; Cosminsky 2001). The proliferation of such research has helped to challenge stereotypical conceptualizations of midwives who live and work outside North America and Western Europe as highly valued and honored members of society. Recent anthropological accounts of non-Western birthing systems are careful to avoid the romantic bias that midwifery is "a universal, woman-centered tradition, relying on simple or 'appropriate' technology to aid the 'natural' process of birth" (MacDonald 2006:239; see also Michie and Kahn 1996 on the concept of the "natural/unnatural" birth).

Scholarship on midwives is beginning to consider more seriously the ideological relation between so-called natural birth and the practice of midwifery. Margaret MacDonald notes that the concept of "natural birth" is utilized by midwives as a way to critique dominant biomedical models of birth. However, the dichotomy between biomedical obstetrics as "modern science" and midwifery as "natural" does not fully encapsulate the intricacies of childbirth practices. In Canada, midwives work within clinical spaces and must continually negotiate technological intervention as part of the birthing process (MacDonald 2006). Studies of midwifery must grapple with strong cultural binaries that posit nature against medicine. As Davis-Floyd notes, it "has been difficult for an anthropologist to write about midwifery in a way that avoids these value-laden polarities, however crude they are recognized to be. One reason for this is that the judgments embedded in them undergird many of the concrete efforts made around the world either to foster midwifery practice or to replace it with obstetrically managed systems" (2001:108). Overly simplified models of accommodation/resistance to provide a framework for talking about midwives in relation to biomedicine do not capture the flexibility of contemporary midwives or their subtle adaptations to the demands placed by their institutional structures (Davis-Floyd 2001:108–109).

Correspondingly, Davis-Floyd observes that "Around the world the pressures that, a priori, define biomedicine as structurally superior to traditional medicine, doctors as superior to midwives, and professional midwives as superior to folk midwives have not so much supplanted various ethno-obstetric systems with a set of universal 'modern' practices (or resistance to them) as they have produced a multiplicity of practices of accommodation and negotiation" (2001:114). It is within this complex web of practices that midwifery becomes increasingly medicalized through state and international efforts to promote safe motherhood (Geuits 2001; Manderson 1996). By incorporating midwifery into practices of the state, governments are better able to control it. As a result, many government or professionally trained midwives adopt a biomedical perspective (or partially adapt their practices) through a series of required medical training courses. Graduation from these courses is often predicated on successful demonstration of the biomedical model of childbirth, which tends to be counter to a midwifery model (Davis-Floyd 1998).

MISSING MEN

The vast majority of studies on reproduction in general and childbirth in particular focus on women as reproducers, with the unfortunate consequence of reifying the dominant cultural ideology that men are involved in productive activities in the public sector, and women in reproductive, hence "private," labor (Inhorn 2007:9). A potential frontier for research is the investigation of the changing demographics of biomedical practitioners. Male practitioners often bear the blame for the subjugation and control of their female patients. Yet among obstetrics residents, research suggests that female physicians are often more likely than their male colleagues to stress compliance and control over their patients (Zambrana et al. 1987). Given this dynamic, anthropological research on biomedical practitioners must be consistent with a more nuanced feminism that recognizes the fact that women may promote attitudes that challenge the agency and empowerment of other groups of women (Mohanty 1991). Such research will be a more complete realization of what Bridgette Jordan envisioned – a comprehensive assessment of the birthing process that considers the social location of the practitioner with particular attention directed at the intersections among gender, race, and class.

A similar shortcoming in research on the anthropology of childbirth is that studies on related topics such as conception and infertility have attended primarily to women. This has left men out altogether from the vast majority of ethnographic discussions of reproduction (Browner 2000; Inhorn 2007; Gutmann 2007). To date, the existing literature is limited, although there are important perspectives on male participation in childbirth (Ebin 1994; Romalis 1981; Whiteford and Sharinus 1988). Yet it is only recently that scholars have begun to unpack how shifting notions of masculinity impact men's role in childbirth, revealing that men have emotional and personal birth narratives of their own (Reed 2005). As new definitions of fatherhood develop – some of them emphasizing the father as participant rather than outsider – continued research on male involvement in the birth process will contribute to more nuanced understandings of childbirth as an engendered process (Browner 2007:148; Gutmann 2007).

Infertility, an important area of inquiry long neglected in medical anthropological research (see Inhorn and Van Balen 2002), has also generated important recent studies that focus on male reproductive health (Inhorn 2006). Other male reproductive health issues such as men's use of contraception, workplace risks to men's fertility, and HIV/AIDS are receiving greater attention (see, for example, Bledsoe et al. 2000; Dudgeon and Inhorn 2003, 2004; Gutmann 2007). Although anthropological research on fertility and infertility is beyond the scope of this essay, we note the significance of the trajectory within the anthropology of reproduction to encompass men's as well as women's reproductive health.

LOCALES AND LEVELS OF ANALYSIS

When one examines the locales where studies of childbirth and other reproductive health issues are situated, it is evident that certain areas of the globe have become "zones of anthropological theorizing" (Abu-Lughod 1989:280). There is a broad range of studies that touch on most regions of the world and provide historic perspective where it is possible to do so, yet certain regions remain understudied. As Inhorn and Sargent point out, certain "regions of the world have been the focus of medical anthropological scholarship – particularly Latin America; sub-Saharan Africa in the era of HIV/AIDS; the three Asian powerhouses of China, Japan, and India; and North America" (2006:1).

Recent research is beginning to fill in these ethnographic gaps. For example, Rozario and Samuel (2002) provide a noteworthy account of beliefs and practices surrounding childbirth among Tibetan refugees in North India. Despite nearly 40 years living among Indian population, several practices remain distinct. Among Khumbo Tibetans, men are permitted to be present during childbirth, and they are often the ones to assist in the process. Fathers are usually the individuals who cut the umbilical cord. This is entirely different from Indians and Bangladeshis, where the act of cutting the umbilical cord is considered to be so defiling that the mother herself is usually the one to do it. This does not mean that a concept of pollution does not exist among Khumbo Tibetans, but rather the way the belief is put into practice is quite variable (Rozario and Samuel 2002). This research serves as a reminder that even in the era of globalization, further ethnographic research among under-studied communities is warranted in order to detail more fully the organization of local reproductive systems in articulation with broader state and global structures.

Similarly, studies of childbirth in New Guinea are few. Even rarer is research that is longitudinal in design (a concern not limited to research in New Guinea), despite the ability for such research to reveal how local groups navigate global processes. A major exception is the work of Naomi McPherson, who has conducted research among Bariai women from the early 1980s to 2005 (McPherson 1986, 1994, 2006). Her research documents how the spread of Christianity has increased the number of pregnancies among Bariai women while decreasing the amount of time used in "child spacing," both of which place a great amount of physical, emotional, and economical stress upon the mother and family. New Guinea has also experienced an influx of NGOs, and in West New Britain many NGOs have targeted maternal and infant health as areas in need of intervention. Yet the lack of needs-based assessment has led NGOS to place a strong emphasis on technological intervention rather than attending to more pressing concerns that affect mortality, such as malaria, anemia, and low birth weight (MacPherson 2006).

In analyses of childbirth studies conducted around the world, it also becomes clear that the reproductive concerns of individuals living in the Muslim Middle East and Muslim Central Asia have garnered little attention, with the exception of a few notable contributions (Boddy 1989; Gruenbaum 2001; Inhorn 1994, 1996, 2003; Kanaaneh 2002). The publication of a special issue in *Medical Anthropology Quarterly* on "Medical Anthropology in the Muslim World" by Marcia Inhorn and Carolyn Sargent represents one of the first attempts to organize a collection that focuses on reproductive and child health across the Muslim world. This volume is especially valuable because it reveals how birth-related beliefs and practices emerge from the interplay between local medicine and state-sponsored health services, in addition to religious beliefs and gender roles and ideologies.

In addition to noting the specific locales in which we conduct research on reproduction, it is important to recognize the tensions surrounding levels of analysis. The understandable attention devoted to globalization problematizes the personal, the local (and its many meanings) and the state. Pregnancy, childbirth, and other reproductive health issues merit research that addresses articulations and intersections linking local, state, and global dynamics. Such research should include renewed investigation of the role of state institutions, policies, and politics in shaping reproductive meanings and practices.

Recent research has demonstrated, for example, the various ways in which state governments exercise power in the area of reproduction and some of the factors that limit their ability to do so (Browner and Sargent, in press). These studies help to document the variety of state formations and how such formations shape lived experiences. For example, state ideologies are often deployed to compel citizens to "adopt the lifestyles and values of the dominant society" (Browner and Sargent, in press). This process is evident in Cecilia van Hollen's ethnographic work in South India that reveals the multiple ways in which "women's reproductive bodies have become irrevocably linked to colonial and postcolonial state interest" (2003:6). In the context of international concern regarding India's "population explosion," women's fertility reflects not only individual and family strategies, but also national and regional political interests. For example, state efforts to curb population growth, such as encouraging sterilization and the use of IUDs, are often interpreted by women as "a sign of being 'modern'." The conflating of family planning and modernity thus serves government policy objectives as well as personal and local community goals.

LOOKING TO THE FUTURE

Anthropological studies of childbirth, viewed in the context of an anthropology of reproduction, have encompassed a diverse array of topics over the past several decades. These range dramatically from Malinowski's interest in the disposal of the placenta to

Ragone's analysis of surrogate pregnancy. A simplistic assessment of this literature might describe a trajectory beginning with references to exotic reproductive practices, moving to descriptive accounts of meanings and practices associated with birth and midwifery, to analyses of childbirth and authoritative knowledge. Numerous scholars have demonstrated the centrality of research on birth (as well as on related issues such as conception, infertility, and assisted reproductive technologies) to social theory. But rather than representing this trajectory as a unilinear shift from ethnographic studies to theorizing reproduction, we find a scholarly exploration of childbirth that is both ethnographic and theoretical, and that addresses personal, local, state, and global issues. The global flow of biotechnologies has attracted much anthropological attention and will no doubt continue to do so. Yet unanswered questions about the implications of these technologies in everyday life point to the importance of ethnography as a means for explicating the links between the global and the local. Similarly, in spite of the large literature on the professionalization of midwives and the global exportation of biomedical obstetrics, nuanced and fine-textured studies of these issues will remain invaluable in future research on childbirth, a central thematic focus in the anthropology of reproduction.

REFERENCES

Abu-Lughod, Lila, 1989 Zones of Theory in the Anthropology of the Arab World. Annual Review of Anthropology 18:267–306.

Allen, Denise Roth, 2002 Managing Motherhood, Managing Risk. Fertility and Danger in West Central Tanzania. Ann Arbor MI: University of Michigan Press.

Boddy, Janice, 1989 Wombs and Alien Spirits: Women, Men, and the Zar Cult in Northern Sudan. Madison WI: University of Wisconsin Press.

Browner, Carole, 1986 The Politics of Reproduction in a Mexican Village. Signs 11(4): 710–724.

Browner, Carole, 2000 Situating Women's Reproductive Activities. American Anthropologist 102(4):773–788.

Browner, Carole H., and Carolyn Sargent, 1996 Anthropological Studies of Human Reproduction. In Medical Anthropology: Contemporary Theory and Method. C. Sargent and T. Johnson, eds. pp. 219–235. Westport CT: Praeger.

Browner, Carole H., and Carolyn Sargent, 2007 Engendering Medical Anthropology. In Medical Anthropology: Regional Perspectives and Shared Concerns. Francine Saillant and Serge Genest, eds. pp. 233–251. London: Blackwell.

Browner, Carole H., and Carolyn Sargent, In press Introduction. In Reproduction, Globalization, and the State. Carole H. Browner and Carolyn Sargent, eds. Durham NC and London: Duke University Press.

Browner, Carole H., and Carolyn Sargent, eds., In press Reproduction, Globalization, and the State. Durham NC and London: Duke University Press.

Casper, Monica J., 1998 The Making of the Unborn Patient: A Social Anatomy of Fetal Surgery. Piscataway NJ: Rutgers University Press.

Cosminsky, Sheila, 1976 Cross-Cultural Perspectives on Midwifery. In Medical Anthropology. Francis X. Grollig and Harold B. Haley, eds., pp. 229–249. The Hague: Mouton.

Cosminsky, Sheila, 2001 Midwifery across the Generations: A Modernizing Midwife in Guatemala. In Robbie Davis-Floyd, ed. Special Issue on Midwifery, Parts I, II. Medical Anthropology 20(3):345–379.

Davis, Kathy, 2007 The Making of Our Bodies, Ourselves. Durham NC and London: Duke University Press.

Davis-Floyd, Robbie, 2003 [1992] Birth as an American Rite of Passage. Berkeley: University of California Press.

Davis-Floyd, Robbie, 1993 Preface. *In* Birth in Four Cultures: A Cross-cultural Investigation of Childbirth in Yucatan, Holland, Sweden, and the United States. 4th edition. Revised and expanded by R. Davis-Floyd. Prospect Heights IL: Waveland Press.

Davis-Floyd, Robbie, 1998 Types of Midwifery Training: An Anthropological Perspective. *In* Pathways to Becoming a Midwife: Getting an Education. Joel Southern, Jennifer Rosenberg and Jon Tritten, eds. pp. 119–193. Eugene OR: Midwifery Today.

Davis-Floyd, Robbie, 2001 Special Issue on Midwifery, Parts I, II. Medical Anthropology 20(2–3).

Davis-Floyd, Robbie, 2003 [1992] Birth as an American Rite of Passage. Berkeley: University of California Press.

Davis-Floyd, Robbie, 2003 Preface. *In* Birth as an American Rite of Passage. 2nd edition. Berkeley: University of California Press.

Davis-Floyd, Robbie, and Joseph Dumit, eds., 1998 Cyborg Babies: From Techno-Sex to Techno-Tots. London and New York: Routledge.

Davis-Floyd, Robbie, and Carolyn Sargent, 1997 Childbirth and Authoritative Knowledge: Cross-Cultural Perspectives. Berkeley: University of California Press.

Davis-Floyd, Robbie, Sheila Cosminsky, and Stacy L. Pigg, eds., 2001 Daughters of Time: The Shifting Identities of Contemporary Midwives, special triple issue. Medical Anthropology 20(2–4).

Davis-Floyd, Robbie, Stacy Leigh Pigg, and Sheila Cosminsky, 2001 Introduction. *In* Daughters of Time: The Shifting Identities of Contemporary Midwives. Robbie Davis-Floyd, ed. Special Issue on Midwifery, Parts I, II. Medical Anthropology 20(2):105–141.

Dundes, Lauren, ed., 2003 The Manner Born: Birth Rites in Cross-Cultural Perspective. Walnut Creek CA: AltaMira Press.

Ebin, V., 1994 Interpretations of Infertility: The Aowin People of Southwest Ghana. *In* Ethnography of Fertility and Birth, 2nd edition. Carol P. MacCormack, ed. pp. 131–151. Prospect Heights IL: Waveland Press.

Franklin, Sarah, and Helena Ragoné, eds., 1998 Reproducing Reproduction: Kinship, Power and Technological Innovation. Philadelphia: University of Pennsylvania Press.

Geuits, K., 2001 Childbirth and Pragmatic Midwifery in Rural Ghana. Medical Anthropology 20(4):379–408.

Ginsburg, Faye D., and Rayna Rapp, 1991 The Politics of Reproduction. Annual Reviews in Anthropology 20:311–343.

Ginsburg, Faye D., and Rayna Rapp, 1995 Conceiving the New World Order: The Global Politics of Reproduction. Berkeley: University of California Press.

Ginsburg, Faye D., and Rayna Rapp, 1999 Fetal Reflections: Confessions of Two Feminist Anthropologists as Mutual Informants. *In* Fetal Subjects, Feminist Positions. Lynn M. Morgan and Meredith W. Michaels, eds. pp. 279–296. Philadelphia: University of Pennsylvania Press.

Gruenbaum, Ellen, 2001 The Female Circumcision Controversy: An Anthropological Perspective. Philadelphia: University of Pennsylvania Press.

Gutmann, Matthew, 2007 Fixing Men: Sex, Birth Control, and AIDS in Mexico. Berkeley: University of California Press.

Holloway, Kris, 2007 Monique and the Mango Rains. Two Years with a Midwife in Mali. Long Grove IL: Waveland Press.

Inhorn, Marcia C., 1994 Quest for Conception: Gender, Infertility, and Egyptian Medical Traditions. Philadelphia: University of Pennsylvania Press.

Inhorn, Marcia C., 1996 Infertility and Patriarchy: The Cultural Politics of Gender and Family Life in Egypt: Philadelphia: University of Pennsylvania Press.

Inhorn, Marcia C., 2003 Local Babies, Global Science: Gender, Religion, and *In Vitro* Fertilization in Egypt. New York: Routledge.

Inhorn, Marcia C., 2007 Reproductive Disruptions: Gender, Technology, and Biopolitics in the New Millennium. New York: Berghahn Books.

Inhorn, Marcia C., and Carolyn Sargent, 2006 Introduction to Medical Anthropology in the Muslim World. Medical Anthropology Quarterly 20(1):1–11.

Inhorn, Marcia C., and Daphna Birenbaum-Carmeli, 2008 Assisted Reproductive Technologies and Culture Change. Annual Review of Anthropology 37:177–196.

Inhorn, Marcia C., and Frank van Balen, eds., 2002 Infertility Around the Globe. New Thinking on Childlessness, Gender, and Reproductive Technologies. Berkeley: University of California Press.

Jenkins, Gwynne L., and Marcia C. Inhorn, 2003 Reproduction Gone Awry: Medical Anthropological Perspectives. Social Science and Medicine 56(9):1831–1836.

Jeffery, R., and P. Jeffery, 1993 Traditional Birth Attendants in Rural North India: The Social Organization of Childbearing. In Knowledge, Power, and Practice: The Anthropology of Medicine and Everyday Life. Shirley Lindenbaum and Margaret Lock, eds. pp. 7–32. Berkeley: University of California Press.

Jolly, Margaret, 1998 Maternities and Modernities: Colonial And Postcolonial Experiences in Asia and the Pacific. Cambridge UK: Cambridge University Press.

Jordan, B., 1978 Birth in Four Cultures: A Cross-cultural Investigation of Childbirth in Yucatan, Holland, Sweden, and the United States. Montreal Canada: Eden Press.

Jordan, B., 1993 Birth in Four Cultures: A Cross-cultural Investigation of Childbirth in Yucatan, Holland, Sweden, and the United States. 4th edition, revised and expanded by R. Davis-Floyd. Prospect Heights IL: Waveland Press.

Kanaaneh, Rhoda, 2002 Birthing the Nation: Strategies of Palestinian Women in Israel. Berkeley: University of California Press.

Kleinman, Arthur, Veena Das, and Margaret Lock, 1997 Introduction. In Social Suffering. Arthur Kleinman, Veena Das and Margaret Lock, eds. pp. ix–1. Berkeley: University of California Press.

Laderman, Carol, 1983 Wives and Midwives: Childbirth and Nutrition in Rural Malaysia. Berkeley: University of California Press.

Landsman, Gail, 2003 Emplotting Children's Lives: Developmental Delay vs. Disability. Social Science and Medicine 56(9):1947–1960.

Layne, Linda L., 1999 "I Remember the Day I Shopped for Your Layette": Consumer Goods, Fetuses, and Feminism in the Context of Pregnancy Loss. In Fetal Subjects, Feminist Positions. Lynn M. Morgan and Meredith W. Michaels, eds. pp. 251–279. Philadelphia: University of Pennsylvania Press.

Layne, Linda L., 2002 Motherhood Lost: A Feminist Account of Pregnancy Loss in America. New York: Routledge.

Layne, Linda L., 2003 Unhappy Endings: A Feminist Reappraisal of the Women's Health Movement from the Vantage of Pregnancy Loss. Social Science and Medicine 56(9):1881–1891.

Liamputtong, Pranee, ed., 2007 Reproduction, Childbearing, and Motherhood: A Cross-Cultural Perspective. New York: Nova Science Publishers, Inc.

Lock, Margaret, 1997 Displacing Suffering: The Reconstruction of Death in North America and Japan. In Social Suffering. Arthur Kleinman, Veena Das and Margaret Lock, eds. pp. 207–245. Berkeley: University of California Press.

MacCormack, Carol P., ed., 1982 Ethnography of Fertility and Birth. Prospect Heights IL: Waveland Press.

MacDonald, Margaret, 2006 Gender Expectations: Natural Bodies and Natural Births in the New Midwifery in Canada. Medical Anthropology Quarterly 20(2):235–256.

Mohanty, Chandra Talpade, 1991 Cartographies of Struggle. In Third World Women and the Politics of Feminism. Chandra Talpade Mohanty, Ann Russo, Lourdes Torres, eds. pp. 1–49. Bloomington IN: Indiana University Press.

Manderson, Lenore, 1998 Health, Illness and the Social Sciences. In Challenges for the Social Sciences and Australia. Prepared by the Academy of Social Sciences in Australia, pp. 251–277. Canberra ACT: Australian Government Publication Services.

Morgan, Lynn M., and Meredith W. Michaels, 1999 The Fetal Imperative. *In* Fetal Subjects, Feminist Positions. Lynn M. Morgan and Meredith W. Michaels, eds. pp. 1–9. Philadelphia: University of Pennsylvania Press.

Rapp, Rayna, 1999 Testing Women, Testing the Fetus: the Social Impact of Amniocentesis in America. New York: Routledge.

Rapp, Rayna, 2001 Gender, Body, Biomedicine: How Some Feminist Concerns Dragged Reproduction to the Center of Social Theory. Medical Anthropology Quarterly 15(4):466–477.

Reed, Richard K., 2005 Birthing Fathers: the Transformation of Men in American Rites of Birth. New Brunswick NJ: Rutgers University Press.

Romalis, Shelley, ed., 1981 Childbirth: Alternatives to Medical Control. Austin TX: University of Texas Press.

Rozario, S., 1998 The *Dai* and the Doctor: Discourses on Women's Reproductive Health in Rural Bangladesh. *In* Maternities and Modernities: Colonial and Postcolonial Experiences in Asia and the Pacific. Kalpana Ram and Margaret Jolly, eds. p p. 144–177. Cambridge UK: Cambridge University Press.

Sargent, Carolyn, 1982 The Cultural Context of Therapeutic Choice: Obstetrical Care Decisions among the Bariba of Benin. Cambridge UK: Cambridge University Press.

Sargent, Carolyn, 1989 Maternity, Medicine, and Power: Reproductive Decisions in Urban Benin. Berkeley: University of California Press.

Sargent, Carolyn, 2007 When the Personal is Political: Contested Reproductive Strategies among West Migrants in France. *In* Reproductive Disruptions: Gender, Technology, and Biopolitics in the New Millennium. Marcia C. Inhorn, ed. pp. 165–182. New York: Berghahn Books.

Sargent, C., and Stark, N., 1989 Surgical Birth: Interpretations of Cesarean Delivery among Private Hospital Patients and Nursing Staff. Social Science and Medicine 25(12):1269–1276.

Towghi, Fouzieyha, 2004 Shifting Policies toward Traditional Midwives: Implications for Reproductive Health Care in Pakistan. *In* Unhealthy Health Policy. Merrill Singer and Arachu Castro, eds. pp. 79–97. Walnut Creek CA: AltaMira Press.

Van Hollen, Cecilia, 2003 Birth on the Threshold: Childbirth and Modernity in South Asia. Berkeley: University of California Press.

Wendland, Claire L., 2007 The Vanishing Mother: Cesarean Section and "Evidence-Based Obstetrics." Medical Anthropology Quarterly 21(2):218–233.

Whiteford, L., and Sharinus, M. 1988 Delayed Accomplishments: Family Formation among Older First-Time Parents. *In* Childbirth in America. Karen L. Michaelson, ed. pp. 239–253. South Hadley MA: Bergin and Garvey.

Zambrana, Ruth E., Wendy Mogel, and Susan S. M. Scrimshaw, 1987 Gender and Level of Training Differences in Obstetricians' Attitudes Towards Patients in Childbirth. Women and Health 12(1):5–24.

FURTHER READING

Bourgeault, Ivy Lynn, Cecilia Benoir, and Robbie Davis-Floyd, 2004 Reconceiving Midwifery. McGill: Queen's University Press.

Craven, Christa, 2005 Claiming Respectable Motherhood: Homebirth Mothers, Medical Officials, and the State. Medical Anthropology Quarterly 19(2):194–215.

Fraser, G. J., 1995 Modern Bodies, Modern Minds: Midwifery and Reproductive Change in an African–American Community. *In* Conceiving the New World Order: The Global Politics of Reproduction. Faye D. Ginsberg and Rayna Rapp, eds. pp. 42–59. Berkeley: University of California Press.

Handwerker, W. Penn, ed., 1990 Births and Power: Social Change and the Politics of Reproduction. Boulder CO: Westview Press.

Kaufert, P., and O'Neil, J., 1993 Analysis of a Dialogue on Risks in Childbirth: Clinicians, Epidemiologists, and Inuit Women. *In* Knowledge, Power, and Practice: The Anthropology of Medicine and Everyday Life. Shirley Lindenbaum and Margaret Lock, eds. pp. 32–55. Berkeley: University of California Press.

Kay, Margarita A., 1982 Anthropology of Human Birth. Philadelphia PA: F. A. Davis.

Press, Nancy, and Carole H. Browner, 1997 Why Women Say Yes to Prenatal Diagnosis. Social Science and Medicine 45(7):979–989.

Ram, Kalpana, and Margaret Jolly, eds., 1998 Maternities and Modernities: Colonial and Postcolonial Experiences in Asia and the Pacific. Cambridge UK: Cambridge University Press.

Sargent, Carolyn, and Caroline Brettell, eds., 1996 Gender and Health: An International Perspective. Upper Saddle River NJ: Prentice-Hall.

CHAPTER 15

Nutrition and Health

David A. Himmelgreen,
Nancy Romero Daza
and Charlotte A. Noble

INTRODUCTION

Most anthropologists would agree that the human experience is in great part shaped by food and nutrition and that human evolution and culture are inextricably linked together because of this. As Kandel and colleagues note "food by virtue of its pivotal place in the human experience is, at once, a bundle of energy and nutrients within the biological sphere, a commodity within the economic sphere, and a symbol within the social and religious spheres" (Kandal et al. 1980:1). As a result, the study of food and nutrition is found throughout the subfields of anthropology. Our goal in this chapter is to provide a synthesis of current scholarship on the role that food and nutrition have on health, disease, and illness. There is an expansive literature that crosscuts the four subfields in American anthropology (archaeology, biological anthropology, cultural anthropology, and linguistics). Because of space limitations and of our respective research interests, we will focus our attention on the scholarship and scholarly debates within cultural anthropology and biological anthropology. We limit our examination of the literature to roughly the last ten years, thereby casting a spotlight on key topics and issues which anthropologists have addressed during the waning moments of the previous century and continue to examine today. This is by no means a comprehensive review, but rather a selective discussion of what appears to be the prevailing themes in the anthropology of food and nutrition at this time.

Three major themes will be covered in this chapter. First, we will examine the influence of globalization on food choices and nutritional health. As part of this discussion, we will review the literature on migration and immigration in relation to dietary acculturation and nutritional status. A second theme to be addressed is gender. Here the emphasis will be on gender inequalities, economic insecurity, and cultural beliefs as factors in nutritional health. The third theme will focus on biocultural approaches to

A Companion to Medical Anthropology, First Edition. Edited by Merrill Singer and Pamela I. Erickson.

issues such as the fetal or developmental origins of life history and the reconsideration of the origins of Type 2 diabetes. For example, there is growing evidence that prenatal stress and birth outcomes are associated with the development of chronic diseases later in life. If this is true, it will force us to rethink our definitions of health and the ways in which diseases can be prevented in the future. In the last part of this chapter, we discuss how this anthropological knowledge can be applied to address nutritional health in present day populations.

Theme I: Globalization, Diet, Lifestyle, and Obesogenic Environments

The rise of the global market economy along with the rapid spread of new technologies has had a significant impact on the diets, lifestyles, and health of many populations worldwide (Martin 2005; Popkin 2002). A major emphasis on anthropological analysis of food and nutrition has been the effects of the economic and social changes brought about by globalization on the nutritional health of various groups. Studies show a clear association between globalizing economies and changes in food consumption patterns and in level of physical activity (Popkin and Gordon-Larsen 2004). The introduction of highly processed carbohydrate-dense foods that are high in fat or sugar along with decreases in physical activity often result in increased rates of overweight and obesity and associated risk for cardiovascular disease and type 2 diabetes. In their 2005 study, Leatherman and Goodman examine the impact of tourism on the dietary patterns of four Mayan communities in the Yucatan. As they demonstrate, despite the economic benefits local residents derive from the tourism-based economy in the area, they become increasingly dependent on processed food, including Coca Cola, at the expense of locally produced items. These changes have resulted in higher rates of adult overweight and obesity and in growth stunting among children. On a similar vein, Himmelgreen and colleagues (2006) examine the impact of tourism in diet delocalization (i.e., reliance on foods that are not locally produced) and changing dietary patterns in Monteverde in rural Costa Rica. Their studies show that the shift from an economy based on agriculture and dairy farming to one dependent on the tourism industry has led to the reduced consumption of fresh fruits and vegetables and higher intake of carbohydrate and fat-laden foods. Importantly, the seasonal nature of tourism in the area has increased levels of food insecurity, especially among households and individuals who are employed in the tourist industry.

In a review of studies from the developing world, Popkin (2006) examines the overall trend in increases of obesity and overweight resulting from a constellation of factors related to globalization. While multinational food companies play a major role in deleterious changes in food habits in many areas of the world, Popkin emphasizes the impact of other aspects such as the increase in technology that has reduced the need for physical energy expenditure in work and transportation. Citing evidence from China, for example, he illustrates increases in body mass index related to involvement in less labor intensive jobs, and to the growing trend in the purchase of cars for transportation. An equally important factor is the notable change in systems of food distribution, which has led to the displacement of small local food markets by multinational corporations that distribute mass produced, highly processed food items at the expense of locally produced foods.

Through the presentation of specific case studies from around the world, Hawkes (2006) examines the impact that the market integration associated with globalization has on food consumption patterns at the global level. By focusing on processes such as foreign investment in food production, food marketing and advertising, and global trade policies such as NAFTA, Hawkes illustrates the complex interaction of economic and social factors that lead to the transformation of traditional diets and the introduction of obesogenic food items. More importantly, Hawkes brings attention to the fact that the "Coca-colonization" process so clearly evident in many areas of the world brings about not only the homogenization of diets (e.g., more people eating highly processed foods), but at the same time contributes to diet diversification. While, as she points out, diversification is believed to be beneficial, in reality those benefits may only be available to people with more economic resources, while those who are poor, may be more likely to experience the homogenization towards unhealthy diets. Thus, Hawkes concludes that while the nutrition transition model is accurate, it does not capture all the complexities of the homogenization and differentiation of dietary patterns that may occur simultaneously as a result of globalization processes.

As seen in the above discussion, the relationship between economic change, obesity, and health is of central importance to the examination of globalization. It is equally important to studies that analyze processes of acculturation of diverse groups to the social and economic milieu of their host countries (Gray et al. 2005; Pollard et al. 2008; Mellin-Olsen and Wandel 2005; Renzaho and Burns 2006; Ulijaszek 2003). Many studies address these issues among Hispanics, the largest minority group in the United States (Gordon-Larsen et al. 2003; Monarrez-Espino et al. 2004; Himmelgreen et al. 2004, 2005, 2007; McArthur et al. 2001). In a 2001 study, McArthur and colleagues use an ecological framework to examine the factors that affect the level of maintenance and change in dietary patterns among Argentinean and Mexican immigrants living in Eastern North Carolina, one of the states with the fastest growing Hispanic population. Factors contributing to changes in diet included higher levels of affordability of food items, such as meats and fruits, and generational differences in food preference, with the younger generation showing a marked preference for American-style foods. The authors highlight the role of schools in influencing dietary choices among immigrant children. Equally important are structural factors such as demanding work schedules and limited access to transportation which increase reliance on canned and highly processed foods available at supermarkets or higher priced neighborhood stores. (McArthur et al. 2004).

Using selected case studies, Palinkas and Pickwell (1995) illustrate changes in dietary patterns among a small number of Cambodian refugees in San Diego, California. The authors highlight the role played by children as agents of change, as they influence their parents' food consumption patterns in a way that favors American foods (e.g., macaroni and cheese, hotdogs, hamburgers) at the expense of traditional Cambodian dishes that are low in fat and include large amounts of fruits and vegetables (for a similar analysis of the role of immigrant children on dietary selection, see Duque-Paramo's (2004) study of Colombian children in Tampa, Florida).

In a study of Puerto Rican women living in Hartford, Connecticut, Himmelgreen and colleagues (2005) examined whether length of time in the United States, language use, and birth place – as proxy measures of acculturation – were associated with dietary patterns. While overall frequency of fresh fruit and vegetable consumption is low for this sample, there are also differences in consumption according to degree of acculturation. For example, length of time living in the USA is positively associated with the frequency of soda and fruit drink consumption. Moreover, women in households where English is the primary language report a higher frequency of soda and fruit drink consumption when compared to their counterparts living in bilingual and monolingual Spanish-speaking households. The frequency of snack food consumption is also higher among bilingual speakers than among mono-lingual Spanish-speakers. In addition to dietary differences by level of acculturation, body mass index (BMI) increases with the length of time that these women have been living in the USA and obesity prevalence is highest (40%) among women living in the USA for 10 or more years and lowest (29%) for women living in the USA for less than one year (Himmelgreen et al. 2004). Interestingly, women born in Puerto Rico but living in the USA are more likely to have higher BMIs than their counterparts born in the USA or elsewhere. This finding may have implications with regard to the influence that the USA has on diet and lifestyle in Puerto Rico.

The specific impact of post-migration changes in the diet and nutritional well being of children is explored by Renzaho (2004) in his study of sub-Saharan immigrants in Australia. Increases in sedentary behavior, television watching, and consumption of nutritionally poor but highly desired "foods for white people" (Renzaho 2004:108) heighten the risk for overweight and obesity among immigrant children and their parents. However, as Renzaho explains, many sub-Saharan African populations show a preference for large body sizes, which are associated with wealth and health. Consequently, immigrants may not see obesity as a problem, but rather as a desirable result of prosperity in their host countries. This poses challenges to programs that intend to curb obesity and overweight among immigrant groups. Renzaho calls for the examination of cultural, historic, and economic factors that may lead to these perceptions among immigrants, and for the design of culturally appropriate interventions to reduce the risk of nutritional problems among these groups. Notably, Morrison and colleagues (2007) call attention to the fact that while obesity and overweight are important health issues among migrants, these problems tend to be less common among very recent immigrants who are just starting their lives in their new communities, and who may be more likely to experience food scarcity and "undernutrition." The authors identify gaps in the provision of services that directly address nutrition and health-related needs of recent immigrants, especially in communities with considerable cultural and linguistic diversity.

The vulnerability of children to nutrition-related problems has been studied in the context of poverty and at the levels of the household and the school. In an analysis of dietary patterns among children from Eastern Kentucky, Crooks (2003) examines the sale of snacks in an elementary school with a high percentage of students of low socioeconomic status (as determined by their qualifying for reduced-price or free lunches). The availability of highly processed snacks, including soft drinks, counters the school's attempts to provide nutritious foods to its students through the school cafeteria. Nevertheless, school officials justify the sale of such snacks on the basis of the income it provides to supplement the small budget on which the school operates. Thus, as Crooks illustrates, the nutritional well being of children attending this school is compromised by the very real needs of the school to obtain supplemental funds for necessities including paper, computers, and even food items provided through the school lunch program. This decision of the school administration to accept the "better of a bad choice" (Crooks 2003:195) points to the very real structural factors that have a detrimental impact on the nutritional health of children in poor communities around the United States, and highlights the very real dilemmas schools face when government support is not enough to meet the basic needs of the student body.

In an ethnographic study of dietary patterns among low-income Latino families in Brooklyn, Kaufman and Karpati (2007) provide an in-depth analysis of structural and cultural factors that increase the risk for overweight and obesity among children. As the authors demonstrate, dependence on government assistance often translates into uneven patterns of food consumption that follow predictable cycles each month: at the beginning of the month, when financial aid arrives, households tend to consume adequate, or even excessive, amounts of food; when money runs out, they must rely on strategies such as the purchase of less expensive and often nutritionally inadequate food items, which are often shared with relatives. Reliance on local *bodegas* (i.e., small neighborhood shops) that provide credit allows families to "get by," but increase their food-related debt, thus further affecting the household ability to secure food in the incoming monthly cycle. An additional factor that appears to play a role in children's propensity to overweight and obesity is the sharing of food items between "not live-in" fathers and their offspring. As the authors state, during visitation, fathers often provide their children with so-called comfort foods such as candy, desserts, and fast foods that offer little in terms of nutritional value. Cultural norms that consider fatness in children to be desirable and a sign of good health and the use of food as instant gratification also contribute to the problem of overweight and obesity among young children. In a more general note, Lindsay and colleagues (2006) offer a comprehensive review of the literature to illustrate the role that parents can play in the prevention of obesity in their children. The authors provide evidence of the influence of parental behaviors in the creation and maintenance of eating and physical activity patterns for children from infancy through adolescence and analyze different strategies for weight control among children. The authors called for the integration of parent involvement in weight control initiatives designed by schools, wellness centers, and community organizations. Likewise, recommendations are made for the inclusion of modules that educate parents on the prevention of childhood obesity in well established programs such as WIC, Head Start, and even birthing classes.

The complexities inherent in the process of dietary change during acculturation are further illustrated by attempts to adapt customary food intake to the realities of new home-settings. For example, Renne (2007) focuses on the dynamic interaction between changing dietary patterns and ethnic/cultural identity among West Africans living in the United States. She examines the process by which these immigrants "reinvent" food traditions in order to maintain their links to their natal communities and cultures, while operating in the fast-paced setting of American cities. In order to do so, West African immigrants rely on highly processed versions of traditional African foods, produced by a burgeoning industry that targets individuals who "idealize the labor intensive techniques of African food preparation, yet pride themselves in their modern US lifestyles" (Renne 2007:623). As Renne points out, the mass produced food items which are sold frozen or in powder form are convenient in terms of preparation, but do not come close to the taste and/or texture of original food stuffs. Nevertheless, by playing on strong associations of specific foods with childhood and traditional family memories, the producers of these items have captured an extensive and profitable market. Citing Phillips (2006), Renne describes this process as "culture-making" by which West African immigrants can simultaneously assume their role as global citizens and yet preserve valuable connections to local tradition, norms, and family groups in their native countries.

The impact of globalization on the transformation of dietary patterns and food production systems is examined at a more general level by Pingali and Khwaja (2004) in their analysis of the consequences of economic change, population growth, migration to urban centers, and involvement of women in the labor force in India. By focusing on demand and supply of food products, the authors emphasize the increasing diversification of diets which include preference for Western-style foods that are convenient to prepare, and the increase on fats, sugars, and animal products. In turn, this demand affects systems of supply, as small-farm workers are forced to adopt strategies that allow them to successfully compete with powerful food producers that are better able to respond to the public desire for diet diversification. The authors present examples of such strategies that have been successfully adopted by other populations in India, and make recommendations for action by the national government to address the emerging needs of food producers in India. Gadio and Rakowski (1999) offer a similar analysis of the impact of local and global processes on the ability of local residents (especially women) in a Senegalese village to engage in agricultural production of three types: subsistence agriculture, agriculture for local sale, and export-driven agriculture. The authors emphasize the disadvantages faced by women who are often excluded from the most profitable type of agricultural activities and bear the burden of subsistence agriculture. Gadio and Rakowki make a call for government and non-government organizations to provide more opportunities for women to participate in highly profitable export agricultural activities. Likewise, Bee (2000) examines gendered policies that dictate the level of participation of women in the production of export grapes in Chile. Women engage in the labor intensive cultivation and packing of the grapes, and often face health risks related to exposure to pesticides and other chemicals in the field. At the same time, they, and their male counterparts, continue engaging in subsistence-level agriculture and negotiating their identities as both food producers and wage-laborers in the grape-export economy. The author highlights the need for research to better understand the impact of export expansion on the ability of local residents to attend simultaneously to the demands posed by their wage employment and their subsistence strategies.

The prominence of global markets has led to an increase in factory employment in many developing countries. Moreno-Black and Homchampa (2007) provide a detailed analysis of the dietary patterns of Thai industrial workers. As they describe, despite their general knowledge about the benefits of a balanced diet and of the consumption of three daily meals, industrial workers find themselves unable to adopt healthy dietary patterns. Factors such as highly structured schedules with limited breaks, long working hours, and long distances between factories and family homes, lead to the skipping of meals or to the consumption of ready-made foods sold by local canteens or street vendors. The authors stress the need for the Thai government to increase the nutritional quality and hygiene standards of these establishments, as part of the existing effort to improve the nutritional health of Thai citizens, and call for further study of the health impact of structural factors associated with factory work.

THEME II: GENDER ISSUES AND NUTRITIONAL HEALTH

Anthropologists have examined the relationship between nutrition and gender issues in both domestic and international settings. Several lines of inquiry can be identified in this arena of research, covering evolutionary, cultural, political–economic, and symbolic perspectives, among others. A major topic of research has been the examination of the potential impact gender inequalities have on the nutritional health of different segments of the population in various areas of the world. For example, DeRose and colleagues (2000) conducted an extensive review of the literature to examine whether differences in the status of women affect the allocation of food resources, and thus the nutritional status of women and girls. While some researchers demonstrate that in settings where there is a marked preference for males, women and girls may be at a disadvantage in the allocation of quality foods (Haddad et al. 1997; Gupta 1987; Gittelsohn et al. 1997), De Rose and colleagues conclude that despite common assumptions about the relationship between gender-determined low status and negative nutritional health, there is no conclusive evidence to support such a link. Rather, they postulate that gender inequalities manifest themselves in a multiplicity of spheres such as education, employment, leisure, and access to health care services – the latter being of critical importance – and that this very complex interaction of factors, rather than access to food by itself, is responsible for the reported inequalities in overall health outcomes (including higher morbidity and mortality) between men and women throughout the developing world (see also Pelletier 1998; Basu 1989). However, according to De Rose and colleagues, what is clear in the literature is that two specific groups of women, pregnant and lactating women, are in fact at a clear nutritional disadvantage when compared not only to men, but also to other women in their communities. The authors argue for increased attention to the needs of these subpopulations, especially in settings where women must continue heavy manual labor during pregnancy and lactation.

More nuanced studies that focus on food security rather than on food intake or food allocation per se, illustrate a clear impact of gender inequalities. For example, drawing on data from an Ethiopian study on adolescent health and well being, Hadley and colleagues (2008) examine differences in levels of food insecurity among a sample of over 2,000 youth from urban, semi-urban, and rural areas. Results indicate that there were no differences in individual-level "food insecurity" among youth from "food-secure" households. However, in food-insecure households, female youth were more likely to report experiencing food insecurity than were their male counterparts. This pattern holds even in cases of brother/sister dyads. Hadley and colleagues speculate that these differences may in part relate to differential buffering in which boys, who are more highly valued than girls, are better protected in households that experience food shortage. Other factors that account for these findings include boys' increased opportunities for mobility outside the household – through education, employment, and socialization – that afford them a better chance to secure food outside of their family home, thus minimizing the impact of food insecurity.

Anthropologists have also examined the impact of gender on susceptibility to nutrition-related diseases. For example, Brenton (2000) analyses differences in morbidity and mortality related to Pellagra in the Southern United States between 1900 and 1950. While Pellagra was decisively a disease of poverty (see Brenton 1998 for a historic overview of pellagra and of the unintended impacts of food relief efforts that may compromise nutritional status), rates of morbidity and mortality followed clear gender and sex patterns. As Brenton reports, pellagra-related mortality and morbidity rates among women were more than double those among men. Using a biocultural framework for the analysis of these data, Brenton identifies biological factors that increase susceptibility for women (i.e., the role of estrogen in inhibiting transformation of tryptophan amino acid to vitamin B niacin). However, equally important are gender-based practices that favored men and children, while disadvantaging women in the distribution of nutritionally rich foods at the household level.

During the last decade, there has been some anthropological research on eating disorders. Although problems such as *anorexia nervosa* and *bulimia* also affect males, most cases are still found among women (Singer and Singer 2007). Researchers are moving away from a focus on the United States and Europe, to examine the multiplicity of factors that contribute to the emergence of these conditions in less developed areas of the world, especially in those that are undergoing economic and social transitions (Gooldin 2008; Lester 2007). In a study on a small group of women from Curaçao, Katzman and colleagues (2004), for example, identify Anorexia Nervosa (AN) on women who struggle in defining their identity as individuals of mixed heritage who are economically and socially mobile. According to the authors, these women exhibit higher levels of anxiety and perfectionism as they try to come close to the ideals of the white economic elite and move away from the image of the "typical Curaçao women…[characterized as] fat, black…nonglobal…[and] not health-concerned" (Katzman et al. 2004:478). Given the fact that all the cases of *anorexia nervosa* in this study occur among women who had traveled abroad for extended periods of time, the authors identify difficulties of reintegration and re-entry as possible risk factors for eating disorders. At the same time, they call for more attention to biological factors that may contribute to individuals' ability to deal with stress brought about by social change.

Disordered eating can be described as eating irregularities, for example, periodic binge eating and food intake restrictions or exaggerated cravings that occur in the absence of other symptoms associated with specific eating disorders. While we are not aware of any anthropological literature that solely focuses on disordered eating per se, there has been research done in which disordered eating has been an outcome variable. For example, based on the belief that "the experience of food insecurity and hunger is, at its core, an experience of suffering," Chilton and Booth (2007:117) attempt to broaden the framework for the examination of food-related issues. The authors analyze the perceptions of food insecurity in the context of stress and violence among African–American women in Philadelphia. Chilton and Booth provide qualitative evidence of the consumption of alcohol and drugs and disordered eating (especially food intake restrictions) as a way of coping with the stress generated by violence at both the individual and the community levels. In talking about the relationship between food insecurity and health, study participants differentiate between "hunger of the body and hunger of the mind" and stress the link between mental health needs – including the need to deal with present and past victimization– and patterns of food intake. The authors present a comprehensive model for the analysis of food insecurity in vulnerable populations that are exposed to chronic stress, poverty, and discrimination. This type of study underscores the need for more research on the potential association between stress-related triggers and periodic binge eating in poverty environments where there is a high degree of economic insecurity, violence, crime, and alcohol and substance abuse. Such endeavors might provide insight into the high rates of obesity found among some inner-city minority populations.

Romero-Daza and colleagues (1999) also examine dietary intake among women who are highly vulnerable to discrimination and violence as a result of their involvement in drug use. In their mixed-methods study in Hartford, Connecticut, the authors illustrate the impact of different drugs in patterns of food cravings and food aversions among users of cocaine, marihuana, heroin, and speedballs (i.e., a mixture of cocaine and heroin). As part of this study the authors also compare dietary intake, food (in) security, and nutritional status between the drug users and a case-control sample of non-drug users. Findings show that the drug users were more likely to be food insecure, eat fewer meals during a typical week, and have poorer nutritional status (as measured by weight, body mass index, upper arm circumference, total upper arm muscle and fat area) when compared to the matched non-drug users. Further, the drug users report a higher frequency of consumption of sweets/desserts than the control group (Himmelgreen et al. 1998), suggesting a drug-related food craving and possibly a pattern of disordered eating. More importantly, the findings show that the drug users make a concerted effort to ensure that their children and other dependents have access to adequate foods. The findings suggest that drug-using women are aware of the impact that drugs have on dietary patterns and that, contrary to stereotypes, they are proactive to ensure the nutritional well being of their children. The authors make recommendations for the incorporation of nutrition interventions in substance abuse programs.

THEME III: NUTRITION AND HEALTH IN BIOLOGICAL ANTHROPOLOGY

For many years the fetus was viewed as the perfect parasite, fully protected from the outside environment, growth and development unabated, sometimes at the expense of its mother's own health. Yet the epidemiological data painted a very different picture – low birth weight, preterm birth, intrauterine growth retardation, and high infant mortality in stressful biocultural environments. While the association between poor prenatal nutritional status and birth outcomes is now well documented, there is growing evidence showing that early life under-nutrition affects human biology resulting in phenotypic plasticity and increases the risk for metabolic diseases later on in adult life (Kuzawa and Pike 2005). In 2005, the *American Journal of Human Biology* published the Wiley-Liss Plenary Symposium on Fetal Origins of Developmental Plasticity, a compilation of articles which "showcase the many exciting research questions that converge on the problem of early environments and their lasting effect on the phenotype" (Kuzawa and Pike 2005:3). The "Barker Hypothesis," also known as the fetal origins hypothesis or fetal programming hypothesis, is based on an epidemiological study in Europe showing a correlation between birth outcomes and coronary heart disease and mortality later on in life (Barker 1994) and the incidence of type 2 (adult-onset) diabetes (Barker 1995). While these findings spurred the interests of epidemiologists into looking at chronic disease factors early in life, human biologists (and others in biological and medical anthropology) were intrigued by these results in terms of human life history stages and "their potential value in understanding pathology" (Ellison 2005:17).

Recently, there has been a concerted effort to examine whether the underlying developmental plasticity in metabolism and physiology associated with early life nutrition and stress (Adair et al. 2001; Kuzawa and Adair 2003) reflects an evolutionary adaptive function beyond the pathophysiology that occurs later on in life (Kuzawa 2005). For example, are low birth weight and chronic disease in later life indicators of pathology or are they the result of the organism's phenotypic plasticity which allows for adjustment to environmental conditions at a given point in time (Ellison 2005)?. The fetal origins/ fetal programming hypothesis can be examined in the context of life history which could be defined as "the strategy an organism uses to allocate energy towards growth, maintenance, reproduction, raising offspring to independence, and avoiding death" (Bogin 2006:296). There is also a more practical application for the study of early life nutrition and stress because of its implications for the prevention and treatment of metabolic diseases. The International Society for Developmental Origins of Health and Disease, comprised of scientists from many disciplines including anthropology, is dedicated to promoting the study of these disorders that "originate through unbalanced nutrition *in utero* and during infancy" (International Society of DOHaD:1).

A recent review article by Bogin and colleagues (2007) addresses the following question regarding life history trade-offs in human growth under adverse biocultural conditions: "are the costs of human growth and development when living under adversity evidence of accommodation or, even adaptation, or are these costs evidence of suffering and failures of biological competence?" (Bogin et al. 2007:631). In addition to malnutrition (under- and over-nutrition), structural violence presents an array of adverse biocultural conditions (e.g., poverty, exposure to infections, gender inequality, religious/ethnic oppression, crime and violence, war, and heavy workloads) that have the potential to negatively impact growth (e.g., stunting, wasting, overweight, and obesity) and increase the risk for disease at various stages of life history. The authors point out that while one group of researchers uses "developmental programming" (DP) (aka the fetal origins/fetal programming hypothesis) to explain the consequences of these biocultural interactions, another group prefers to use the phrase "predictive adaptive response." (PAR) (Gluckman and Hanson 2005, cited by Bogin et al. 2007). The DP groups tends to view such phenotypic plasticity or alterations in growth as having permanent maladaptive effects, while the PAR group considers these changes at two levels of adaptation: (1) "short-term adaptive responses for immediate survival," and (2) "predictive responses required to ensure postnatal survival to reproductive age," according to Bogin and colleagues (2007:631). In their review of the literature, the authors discover that there are life history trade-offs in human growth even under good biocultural conditions. Under adverse conditions these trade-offs result in poor growth, physical activity constraints, poor reproductive outcomes, and increased mortality. They conclude by calling for further development of human life history theory including accommodation for a greater range of biocultural sources of adversity in the model.

The rising rate of type-2 diabetes has reached epidemic proportions in the United States and in a growing number of developing countries (Zimmet et al. 1997). For many clinicians and researchers, the staggering rates of type-2 diabetes found among some Native American and other population subgroups, points to a genetic explanation for this metabolic disease. Within biological anthropology, Neel's "thrifty genotype" hypothesis has been used to explain how a change in the physical environment since the Paleolithic age has resulted in an adaptive response to food scarcity becoming maladaptive in the current environment where food is plentiful throughout the year. No longer do these groups experience the "feast or famine conditions" of the past where selection favored individuals with a "quick-insulin trigger" for energy storage as fat when food was plentiful to be liberated later on when there was food scarcity. Although there is some evidence in support of the "thrifty genotype," there are other possible models for understanding the high rate of diabetes, especially among Native Americans and Latinos. In a review of the literature, Benyshek et al. Johnson (2001) propose the fetal-origin model (fetal origins/fetal programming hypothesis) as an alternative to the "thrifty genotype." Citing Hales and Barker (1992), the authors suggest that under-nutrition *in utero* leads to low birth weight and eventually to the development of type-2 diabetes. Alterations of metabolism and physiology reflect an adaptive response to low energy availability through quick insulin trigger, allowing for early survival, but compromising health through low-birth weight. In their review, which includes in-depth case studies of Native American groups such as the *Pima* and the *Dogrib*, Benyshek and colleagues provide support for the use of the fetal-origin model and suggest that the "thrifty genotype" fails to explain why other Native American groups that should have a high incidence of type-2 diabetes do not. Instead, they suggest that historical conditions relating to poverty, racism, and marginalization need to be taken into account in trying to understand and address this phenomenon. As the authors state "the difference between low (type-2 diabetes) prevalence Native American populations... and high prevalence populations... is that recent generations of the former have not suffered from extended periods of chronic protein malnutrition followed by a rapid transition to a Western diet and lifestyle" (Benyshek et al. 2001:45). This is an area of research ripe for more study using both the biocultural perspective and political economy of health theory. Aside from discovering the biocultural mechanism involved in this process and building theory, there are very practical applications in terms of social justice and public health in pursuing this line of research.

CONCLUSION

As shown throughout this chapter, the human experience is greatly influenced by food and nutrition and there is a complex dialectic between human biology and culture in relation to nutrition and health. In a review of the biological and cultural anthropology literature dating back approximately 10 years, three salient themes are discussed: (1) the influence of globalization on food choices and nutritional health through processes such as the expansion of food markets, increased technology for transportation and work, and population movement in the form of economic-based migration and tourism; (2) gender inequalities as they affect food allocation, risk for diet-related diseases, and disordered eating in highly stressful environments characterized by violence and poverty; (3) theories such as the fetal or development origins of life history and the predictive adaptive response and their usefulness for the reconsideration of the origins of type-2 diabetes; This chapter is not intended to be a comprehensive review but rather its purpose is to provide a synthesis of some of the scholarship on the role that food and nutrition have on health, disease, and illness.

Based on this review, it is clear that global markets, increasing connectedness among people, and technology are having an impact on local and commercial food production. With dietary delocalization there is an increasing reliance on commercially processed "empty-calorie" foods. Whether the slow food movement (not discussed here) or other similar social movements take root during the upcoming decades will determine the extent to which dietary delocalization continues in the future. The research shows that food choices and lifestyle are intertwined and that there is a complex process operating in the food transition that involves both the homogenization of diets and dietary diversification (along socio-economic lines). Although there is the potential to improve nutritional health as a result, the findings suggest otherwise with the rising rates obesity and metabolic diseases in industrialized and developing countries. Special attention needs to be paid to the impact that shifts from subsistence agriculture to involvement in industrial work have on the nutritional health of factory workers, especially in light of very demanding and extended long schedules and the tendency towards sedentary work activities. As changes in food production and intake continue to occur in response to global economic transformations, care must be taken to protect those groups at highest risk for nutritional problems: young children, pregnant and lactating women, the elderly, and individuals going through the initial stages of acculturation in new settings.

As anthropologists, our attention needs to be focused on efforts to contextualize food and nutrition issues in the broader framework of social justice. To do so, we need to be cognizant of the fact that nutrition problems are very often a manifestation of deeper underlying economic and social inequalities. We need to question why, for example, in a country as rich as the United States, schools in poor areas are forced to supplement meager budgets with the sale of foods that are clearly detrimental to their students? Why individuals and families in many areas of the developing world must abandon their subsistence activities in favor of industrial employment that caters to the demands of global markets? Why, in the absence of adequate prevention, treatment, and social support, people affected by drug addiction, mental problems, and chronic violence must also suffer the ill effects of disordered eating?

More importantly, we must apply our knowledge to finding solutions to urgent problems such as the alarming increase in rates of type-2 diabetes among children, a population that was, until recently not affected by the disease. Similarly, an issue of critical importance that has recently received some attention from anthropologists (Himmelgreen et al. n.d.; Himmelgreen and Romero-Daza 2008; Mazzeo 2008; Singer 2008, 2009) is the synergism between food insecurity and malnutrition on the one hand, and HIV/AIDS on the other. Research from other fields has shown that inadequate access to food compromises the immune function of individuals making them more vulnerable to HIV infection and hastening the progression of HIV disease for those already positive. Moreover, in resource-poor settings, there is an increased risk for the transmission of HIV among individuals who engage in transactional sex for survival. The HIV virus has the potential to adversely affect nutritional status

(Scrimshaw and SanGiovanni 1997) through reduced absorption of nutrients in the intestinal tract, altered nutrient storage, and insufficient food intake (Semba 1998; Beisel 1996). Likewise, malnutrition, be it mild under nutrition, severe protein energy malnutrition, or micronutrient deficiencies, can heighten the risk of infection, including increased susceptibility to HIV viral strains. In addition, there is now ample evidence that malnutrition has a role in the earlier onset of AIDS-related illnesses in people living with HIV, increases the susceptibility to the disease among non-infected people, and facilitates vertical transmission (Kottler et al. 1998; Suttmann et al. 1995; Fawzi et al. 2002; Tang 2003). Given the weight of this evidence, it is imperative to shift our focus to potential ways of minimizing the ill effects of malnutrition and food insecurity on the overall health and well being of individuals affected by the disease. While AIDS treatment programs in the Global North provide nutrition education and access to enhanced nutrition, our efforts should be concentrated on the creation of programs that address the structural factors that put individuals at risk for poverty, food insecurity, and HIV.

ACKNOWLEDGEMENTS

We would like to express our gratitude to our graduate assistants who helped us with the literature review for this article. Our thanks go to Charlotte Noble, Hannah Helmy, Adriane Seibert, Sarah Smith, and Geraldina Tercero.

REFERENCES

Adair, Linda S., and Penny Gordon-Larsen, 2001 Maturational Timing and Overweight Prevalence in US Adolescent Girls. American Journal of Public Health 91(4):642–644.
Barker, David J. P., 1994 Mothers, Babies and Disease in Later Life. London: British Medical Journal Books.
Barker, David J. P., 1995 Fetal Origins of Coronary Heart Disease. British Medical Journal 311:171–174.
Basu, Alaka M., 1989 Is Discrimination in Food Really Necessary For Explaining Sex Differentials in Childhood Morality? Population Studies 43(2):193–212.
Bee, Anna, 2000 Globalization, Grapes and Gender: Women's Work in Traditional and Agro-Export Production in Northern Chile. The Geographical Journal 166(3):255–265.
Beisel, William R., 1996 Nutrition in Pediatric HIV Infection: Setting the Research Agenda. Nutrition and Immune Function: Overview. Journal of Nutrition 126 (supplement 10):S2611–S2615.
Benyshek, Daniel C., John F. Martin, and Carol S. Johnston, 2001 A Reconsideration of the Origins of the Type-2 Diabetes Epidemic Among Native Americans and the Implications for Intervention Policy. Medical Anthropology 20(1):25–64.
Bogin, Barry, 2006 The Evolution of Human Growth. In Human Growth and Development. Noël Cameron, ed. pp. 295–320. London: Academic Press.
Bogin Barry, Silva M. Varela, and Luis Rios, 2007 Life History Trade-offs in Human Growth: Adaptation or Pathology? American Journal of Human Biology 19:631–642.
Brenton, Barrett P., 1998 Pellagra and Nutrition Policy: Lessons from the Great Irish Famine to the New South Africa. Nutritional Anthropology 22(1):1–11.
Brenton, Barrett P., 2000 Pellagra, Sex and Gender: Biocultural Perspectives on Differential Diets and Health. Nutritional Anthropology 23(1):20–24.

Chilton, Mariana, and Sue Booth, 2007 Hunger of the Body and Hunger of the Mind: African American Women's Perceptions of Food Insecurity, Health and Violence. Journal of Nutrition Education and Behavior 39(3):116–125.

Crooks, Deborah L., 2003 Trading Nutrition for Education: Nutritional Status and the Sale of Snack Foods in an Eastern Kentucky School. Medical Anthropology Quarterly 17(2): 182–199.

DeRose, Laurie F., Maitreyi Das, and Sara R. Millman, 2000 Does Female Disadvantage Mean Lower Access to Food? Population and Development Review 26(3):517–547.

Duque Páramo, Maria Claudia, 2004 Colombian Immigrant Children in the United States: Representations of Food and the Process of Creolization. Ph.D. dissertation, Department of Anthropology, University of South Florida.

Ellison, Peter T., 2005 Evolutionary Perspectives on the Fetal Origins Hypothesis. American Journal of Human Biology 17(1):113–118.

Fawzi, Wafaie, Gernard Msamanga, Donna Spiegelman, Boris Renjifo, Heejung Bang, Saidi Kapiga, Jenny Coley, Ellen Hertzmark, Max Essex, and David Hunter, 2002 Transmission of HIV-1 through Breastfeeding among Women in Dar es Salaam, Tanzania. Journal of Acquired Immune Deficiency Syndrome 31(3):331–338.

Gadio, Coumba Mar, and Cathy A. Rakowski, 1999 Farmers' Changing Roles in Thieudeme, Senegal: The Impact of Local and Global Factors on Three Generations of Women. Gender and Society 13(6):733–757.

Gittelsohn, Joel, Meera Thapa, and Laura T. Landman, 1997 Cultural Factors, Caloric Intake, And Micronutrient Sufficiency in Rural Nepali Households. Social Science and Medicine 44(11):1739–1749.

Gluckman, Peter D., and Mark A. Hanson, 2005 The Fetal Matrix. Cambridge UK: Cambridge University Press.

Goodin, Sigal, 2008 Being Anorexic. Medical Anthropology Quarterly 22(3):274–296.

Gordon-Larsen, Penny, Kathleen Mullan Harris, Dianne S. Ward, and Barry M. Popkin, 2003 Acculturation and Overweight-related Behaviors Among Hispanic Immigrants to the US: the National Longitudinal Study of Adolescent Health. Social Science and Medicine 57(11):2023–2034.

Gray, Virginia B., Jeralynn S. Cossman, Wanda L. Dodson, and Sylvia H. Byrd, 2005 Dietary Acculturation of Hispanic Immigrants in Mississippi. Salud Pública de México 47(5):351–360.

Gupta, Monica Das, 1987 Selective Discrimination against Female Children in Rural Punjab, India. Population and Development Review 139(1):77–100.

Haddad, Lawrence, John Hoddinott, and Harold Alderman, 1997 Intrahousehold Resource Allocation in Developing Countries: Models, Methods, and Policy. Baltimore MD: Johns Hopkins University Press.

Hadley, Craig, David Lindstrom, Fasil Tessema, and Tefara Belachew, 2008 Gender Bias in the Food Insecurity Experience of Ethiopian Adolescents. Social Science and Medicine 66(2):427–438.

Hales, C. Nicholas, and David J. P. Barker, 1992 Type 2 (Non-insulin Dependent) Diabetes Mellitus: The Thrifty Phenotype Hypothesis. Diabetologia 35:595–601.

Hawkes, Corinna, 2006 Uneven Dietary Development: Linking the Policies and Processes of Globalization with the Nutrition Transition, Obesity and Diet-related Chronic Diseases. Globalization and Health 2(1):4.

Himmelgreen, David A., and Nancy Romero-Daza, 2008 Food Security and the Battle Against HIV/AIDS. Anthropology News 49(7):13–14.

Himmelgreen, David A., Rafael Pérez-Escamilla, Sofia Segura-Millán, Nancy Romero-Daza, Mihaela Tanasescu, and Merrill Singer, 1998 A Comparison of the Nutritional Status and Food Security of Drug-using and Non-drug-using Hispanic Women in Hartford, Connecticut. American Journal of Physical Anthropology 107:351–361.

Himmelgreen, David A., Rafael Pérez-Escamilla, Dinorah Martinez, Ann Bretnall, Brian Eells, Yukuei Peng, and Angela Bermudez, 2004 The Longer You Stay, The Bigger You Get: Length of Time and Language Use in the US are Associated with Obesity in Puerto Rican Women. American Journal of Physical Anthropology 125(1):90–96.

Himmelgreen, David A., Ann Bretnall, Rafael Perez-Escamilla, Yukuei Peng, and Angela Bermudez, 2005 Birthplace, Length of Time in the US, and Language are Associated with Diet Among Inner-City Puerto Rican Women. Ecology of Food and Nutrition 44(2):105–122.

Himmelgreen, David A., Nancy Romero-Daza, Maribel Vega, Humberto Brenes Cambronero, and Edgar Amador, 2006 "The Tourist Season Goes Down But Not the Prices." Tourism and Food Insecurity in Rural Costa Rica. Ecology of Food and Nutrition 45(4):295–321.

Himmelgreen, David A., Nancy Romero-Daza, Elizabeth Cooper, and Dinorah Martinez, 2007 "I Don't Make the Soups Anymore": Pre- to Post-Migration Dietary and Lifestyle Changes Among Latinos Living in West-Central Florida. Ecology of Food and Nutrition 46(5):427–444.

Himmelgreen, David, Nancy Romero-Daza, Sharon Watson, Ipolto Okello-Uma, David Sellen, and David Turkon, n.d. Sowing the Seeds for Health in Africa: Fighting AIDS and Food Insecurity in Lesotho. University of South Florida, unpublished MS.

International Society for Developmental Origins of Health and Disease (International Society of DOHaD), n.d. Electronic Document. http://www.mrc.soton.ac.uk/dohad/.

Kandal, Randy F., Gretel H. Pelto, and Norge W. Jerome, 1980 Introduction. In Nutritional Anthropology: Contemporary Approaches to Diet and Culture. Norge W. Jerome, Randy F. Kandel and Gretel H. Pelto, eds. pp. 1–12 Pleasantville NY: Redgrave Publishing.

Katzman, Melanie A., Karin M. E. Hermans, Daphne Van Hoeken, and Hans W. Hoek, 2004 Not Your "Typical Island Woman": Anorexia Nervosa is Reported Only in Subcultures in Curaçao. Culture, Medicine and Psychiatry 28(4):463–492.

Kaufman, Leslie, and Adam Karpati, 2007 Understanding the Sociocultural Roots of Childhood Obesity: Food Practices Among Latino families of Bushwick, Brooklyn. Social Science and Medicine 64(11):2177–2188.

Kottler, Donald P., Karen Rosenbaum, Jack Wang, and Richard N. Pierson, 1998 Studies of Body Composition and Fat Distribution in HIV-infected and Control Subjects. Journal of Acquired Immune Deficiency Syndrome 20(3):228–237.

Kuzawa, Christopher W., 2005 The fetal origins of developmental plasticity. Are maternal cues reliable predictors of future nutritional environments? American Journal of Human Biology 17(1):1–4.

Kuzawa, Christopher W., and Linda S. Adair, 2003 Lipid profiles in an adolescent Filipino population: relationship to birth weight and maternal energy status during pregnancy. American Journal of Clinical Nutrition 77(4):960–966.

Kuzawa, Christopher W., and Ivy L. Pike, 2005 Introduction. In Fetal Origins of Developmental Plasticity. Theme issue. American Journal of Human Biology 17(1):1–4.

Leatherman, Thomas L., and Alan Goodman, 2005 Coca-colonization of diets in the Yucatan. Social Science and Medicine 61(4):833–846.

Lester, Rebecca, 2007 Critical Therapeutics: Cultural Politics and Clinical Reality in Two Eating Disorder Treatment Centers. Medical Anthropology Quarterly 21(4):369–387.

Lindsay, Ana C., Katarina M. Sussner, Juhee Kim, and Steven Gortmaker, 2006 The Role of Parents in Preventing Childhood Obesity. The Future of Children, Childhood Obesity 16(1):169–186.

Martin, Greg, 2005 Editorial: Globalization and Health. Globalization and Health 1:1.

Mazzeo, John, 2008 A Triple Threat in Rural Zimbabwe. How Drought, HIV/AIDS, and Poverty Endanger Food Security. Anthropology News 49(7):14.

McArthur, Laura H., Ruben P. Viramontez Anguiano, and Deigo Nocetti, 2001 Maintenance and Change in the Diet of Hispanic Immigrants in Eastern North Carolina. Family and Consumer Sciences Research Journal 29(4):309–335.

McArthur, Laura H., Ruben Anguiano, and Kevin H. Gross, 2004 Are Household Factors Putting Immigrant Hispanic Children at Risk of Becoming Overweight: A Community-Based Study in Eastern North Carolina. Journal of Community Health 29(5):387–404.

Mellin-Olsen, Tonje, and Margareta Wandel, 2005 Changes in Food Habits among Pakistani Immigrant Women in Oslo, Norway. Ethnicity and Health 10(4):311–339.

Monarrez-Espino, Joel, Ted Greiner, and Ramiro Caballero Hoyos, 2004 Perceptions of Food and Body Shape as Dimensions of Western Acculturation Potentially Linked to Overweight in Tarahumara Women of Mexico. Ecology of Food and Nutrition 43(3):193–212.

Moreno-Black, Geraldine, and Pissamai Homchampa, 2007 At the Factory, at the Table: Dietary Beliefs and Practices of Thai Industrial Workers. Ecology of Food and Nutrition 46(3-4):313–337.

Morrison, Sharon D., Lauren Haldeman, Sudha Shreeniwas, Kenneth J. Gruber, and Raleigh Bailey, 2007 Cultural Adaptation Resources for Nutrition and Health in New Immigrants in Central North Carolina. Journal of Immigrant and Minority Health 9(3):205–212.

Palinkas, Lawrence A., and Sheila M. Pickwell, 1995 Acculturation as a Risk Factor for Chronic Disease among Cambodian Refugees in the United States. Social Science and Medicine 40(12):1643–1653.

Pelletier, David L., 1998 Malnutrition, Morbidity, and Child Mortality in Developing Countries. In Too Young to Die: Genes or Gender? United Nations, ed. pp. 109–132. New York: Department of Economic and Social Affairs, Population Division, United Nations.

Phillips, Lynne, 2006 Food and Globalization. Annual Review of Anthropology 35(1):37–57.

Pingali, Prabhu, and Yasmeen Khwaja, 2004 Globalisation of Indian Diets and the Transformation of Food Supply Systems. Inaugural Keynote Address presented at the 17th Annual Conference of the Indian Society of Agricultural Marketing, Hyderabad, India, February 5–7.

Pollard, Tessa M., Nigel Unwin, Colin Fischbacher, and Jagdip K. Chamley, 2008 Differences in Body Composition and Cardiovascular and Type 2 Diabetes Risk Factors between Migrant and British-born British Pakistani Women. American Journal of Human Biology 20(5):545–549.

Popkin, Barry M., 2002 An Overview on the Nutrition Transition and Its Health Implications: The Bellagio Meeting. Public Health Nutrition 5(1a):93–103.

Popkin, Barry M., 2006 Technology, Transport, Globalization and the Nutrition Transition Food Policy. Food Policy 31(6):554–569.

Popkin, Barry M., and Penny Gordon-Larsen, 2004 The Nutrition Transition: Worldwide Obesity Dynamics and Their Determinants. International Journal of Obesity 28(Supplement 3):S2-S9.

Renne, Elisha, 2007 Mass Producing Food Traditions for West Africans Abroad. American Anthropologist 109(4):616–625.

Renzaho, André M. N., 2004 Fat, Rich and Beautiful: Changing Socio-cultural Paradigms Associated with Obesity Risk, Nutritional Status and Refugee Children from Sub-Saharan Africa. Health and Place 10(1):105–113.

Renzaho, André M. N., and Cate Burns, 2006 Post-migration Food Habits of Sub-Saharan African Migrants in Victoria: A Cross-sectional Study. Nutrition and Dietetics 63(2):91–102.

Romero-Daza, Nancy, David A. Himmelgreen, Rafael Pérez-Escamilla, Sofia Segura-Millán, and Merrill Singer, 1999 Food Habits of Drug Using Puerto Rican Women in Inner City Hartford. Medical Anthropology 18(3):281–298.

Scrimshaw, Nevin S., and John Paul SanGiovanni, 1997 Synergism of Nutrition, Infection, and Immunity: An Overview. American Journal of Clinical Nutrition 66(2):464S–477S.

Semba, Richard D., 1998 The Role of Vitamin A and Related Retinoids in Immune Function. Nutrition Review 56(1 part 2):S38–S48.

Singer, Merrill, 2008 The Perfect Epidemiological Storm: Food Insecurity, HIV/AIDS, and Poverty in Southern Africa. Anthropology News 49(7):12 and 15.

Singer, Merrill, 2009 Introduction to Syndemics: A Systems Approach to Public and Community Health. San Francisco CA: Jossey-Bass.

Singer, Merrill and Elyse Singer 2007 Eating Disorders. In The Encyclopedia of Epidemiology, pp. 293–295. Thousand Oaks CA: Sage.

Suttmann, Ulrich, Johann Ockenga, Oliver Selberg, Linda Hoogestraat, Helmuth Deicher, and Manfred James Müller, 1995 Incidence and Prognostic Value of Malnutrition and Wasting in Human Immunodeficiency Virus-infected Outpatients. Journal of Acquired Immune Deficiency Syndromes 8(3):239–246.

Tang, Alice M., 2003 Weight Loss, Wasting, and Survival in HIV-positive Patients: Current Strategies. AIDS Reader 13(supplement 12):S23–S27.

Ulijaszek, Stanley J., 2003 Trends in Body Size, Diet and Food Availability in the Cook Islands in the Second Half of the 20th Century. Economics and Human Biology 1(1):123–137.

Zimmet, Paul Z., and Kurt George M. M. Alberti, 1997 The Changing Face of Macrovascular Disease in Non-insulin-dependent Diabetes Mellitus: An Epidemic in Progress. The Lancet 350(S1):S1–S4.

CHAPTER **16**

Anthropologies of Cancer and Risk, Uncertainty and Disruption

Lenore Manderson

PROLOGUE

Cancers occur worldwide. While there are variations in their epidemiology, including the prevalence of genetic risk factors, types, incidence and distribution of cancers, treatment options and outcomes, the diseases are together unique in the fear that they engender, as possibilities and as diagnosed disease, and in the silence that surrounds them. I begin by drawing on Lorraine Yap's ethnography of breast cancer in the Philippines, and summarize one woman's experience:

> Luzviminda discovered a breast lump. It was small and not painful, and so she paid little attention to it. She believed that it was a cyst, caused by hardened breast milk from breastfeeding her children. After some months, however, she mentioned the lump to relatives. They kept asking if she were not afraid, that it might be cancer? They kept asking her this question, and she became *nerbiyos* (nervous) that this was possible. She said that she was afraid of having the lump cut out of her breast because it might spread even more. But her cousin worked as a midwife at the regional hospital, and reassured Luzviminda of her help, and so Ludzviminda gathered up the 'strong will' (*lakas na toob*) to see a doctor at the hospital. By then the lump was much bigger. Luzviminda wanted to be treated by medicines, but the surgeon told her it was best that it be removed. She was then told to take the excised lump to the pathology laboratory, and to collect it a few weeks later. Luzviminda was diagnosed with Stage II breast cancer (Yap 1999: 83).

Luzviminda's account resounded with those of other women with breast cancer. Women ignored lumps, or diagnosed them as harmless cysts or boils, or tumours as symptoms worsened: the size of the lump or their breast increased; they experienced

A Companion to Medical Anthropology, First Edition. Edited by Merrill Singer and Pamela I. Erickson.
© 2011 Blackwell Publishing Ltd. Published 2011 by Blackwell Publishing Ltd.

pain; they developed multiple lumps; the lump was red, inflamed, ulcerous, bleeding, oozing or malodorous. At this point, women might seek advice from a traditional healer, self-treat with herbal medicine, or consult a medical doctor. Further action often depended on household resources, with women balancing the known costs of seeing particular doctors, and the costs of surgery, an associated hospital stay and medicine weighed against their own perceptions of the seriousness of their condition. Many women delayed, fearing that surgery would be painful and would cause the cancer to spread, and that it was a portent of death; they were *hiya* (ashamed) of the disease, worried that they would be abused by the doctor for their delayed presentation, and concerned that the lump was caused by sorcery (Yap 1999).

Luzviminda's case was not extreme. In undertaking her research, Lorraine Yap came across many women with patent evidence of breast disease who, for various social, economic and emotional reasons, delayed seeking medical care. The outcomes of surgery and longer-term changes in disease further confused women: adjuvant therapy, continued medication (e.g., Tamoxifen), lymphedema, and in many cases, metastatic cancer and death. Those who refused surgery, who chose to remain outside of the hospital system, were further disadvantaged; without access to morphine, their last days were often profoundly distressing (Yap 1999:274).

This is not unique to the Philippines. Elizabeth Bennett (2001), writing of death and dying in Northeast Thailand where cholangeocarcinoma (bile-duct cancer) is especially prevalent, recounts many poignant stories of painful deaths of people sent home from hospitals to die, and the impotence of their grieving, watchful families. The nearest source of morphine, available in the region only by injection, is often too far way to be worth the trip. There are common themes in these two studies: paralyzing fear of cancer; confusion of cause, diagnosis, and treatment; the over-determination of household and local economics on decision-making and outcome; the limitations of rural and district health services in resource poor settings; the reluctance of doctors to tell patients that they have cancer, and for patients who know their diagnosis, for them to tell it to others. Cancer is shrouded in secrecy. Similar factors operate in highly industrialized settings, with prevention, screening, timely and accurate diagnosis, and quality of care varying by social and economic gradient. Medical anthropology has much to contribute, everywhere, to understanding the factors that affect vulnerability, screening, diagnosis and treatment, and palliative care (Manderson 1999). In this chapter, I summarize this work, offer specific examples to illustrate it, and identify opportunities for future work.

BACKGROUND

Long-lasting "chronic" conditions now predominate both in highly industrialized and industrializing low- and middle-income countries. This has been due to the development of effective surgical, pharmaceutical, and other interventions to slow the progression of disease, and to prevent co-morbidities and inhibit complications and consequent loss of function, as well as to changes in environmental factors influencing the epidemiology of disease (Manderson and Smith-Morris 2010). Most of these conditions are non-communicable. The most common are cardiovascular disease resulting in stroke and heart disease, and type-2 diabetes, both of which are routinely associated with "life style" – sedentary occupations and over-nutrition (see Himmelgreen and Romero-Daza, this volume). Cancers are the other condition which, with cardiovascular disease and diabetes, contributes more than any other conditions to severe morbidity and extended medical care, and as cause of death, in most highly industrialized countries.

These conditions are often life-long. With the introduction of anti-retroviral therapy, HIV infection too is a life-long condition, controllable although not curable. Hence life-long conditions may be now either communicable or non-communicable. But cancers are an exception to other prevalent diseases in terms of cause and outcome. It was widely assumed that cancers were non-communicable until relatively recently, but it is now clear that various viruses, bacteria, and parasites contribute to the development of some cancers – HPV (Human Papilloma Virus) and cervical cancer, for instance, schistosomiasis, and bladder cancer. In addition, cancers can be caused by genetic factors, as illustrated by the association of an abnormal BRCA1 or BRCA2 gene and breast, ovarian, prostate, and other cancers. Plus, they can be caused by physical, chemical, and biological agents, and by "life style," including notably the role of tobacco in lung and oral cancers. Still, the causes of many other cancers are unknown. Anthropology has a role in identifying possible causes, particularly where familial and local history and epidemiology suggest the abnormal presence of an environmental toxin, an infectious agent yet to be identified, or the possibility of genetic risk factors. Iman Roushdy-Hammady (2004) was referring to physical environmental and genetic co-factors for the development of the fatal asbestos-related disease mesothelioma, when she argued for the development of a medical anthropology of cancer, but her comments hold good for most environmental and other cancers.

Cancers also differ from other chronic conditions by their management. Other highly prevalent chronic conditions, such as cardiovascular disease, have gained with the technological developments of the late 20th and early 21st century – keyhole surgery, life-saving enduring stents, short stays in hospital and life-long medication with limited side effects. Other long-term conditions are well managed by "life-style" changes to diet and exercise, and medication. But the medical interventions for cancer remain invasive and disturbing, and their effectiveness at times uncertain both in the short- and longer-term. Cancers such as thyroid, prostate, endometrial and testicular cancer, and melanomas, have high relative survival rates depending on early diagnosis, but other cancers, particularly those where abnormal cell growth is rapid yet symptoms of illness, diagnosis and treatment delayed, may result in early death. Hence, despite relatively good prognoses for many types of cancer, diagnosis is commonly regarded as a death sentence and consequently, much feared and at times deeply stigmatized. Medical anthropologists have worked to understand the contexts in which causes of cancer proliferate, to shape preventive interventions, to make sense of resistance to their messages, and to map the journeys of human suffering.

THE MEANING OF RISK

Sandra Gifford's article, 'The Meaning of Lumps' (1985), offers important insights into the cultural differences that exist between epidemiologists, surgeons, and patients in understanding risk, and in interpreting and acting on ambiguous signs and equivocal test results. Other long-term conditions have considerable ambiguity also in terms of disease progression, severity, deterioration, and life expectancy (Maynard 2006). But cancer is particularly problematic because of the ways that people are identified as and interpret being "at risk." In Gifford's example, the uncertainty of health outcome derives from the possibility that benign fibrocystic disease might become cancerous. In a clinical setting, epidemiological statements of probability are transformed, and with this, so is the uncertainty of outcome for a consulting surgeon and any individual woman. The ground shifts, and women are faced with a simpler, absolute decision regarding prophylactic mastectomy. Women with mutations of the BRCA1, faced with an estimated 85% risk of developing breast cancer by age 70, receive the same advice.

A benign lump in a breast, in Giffford's example, or some other confusing sign – a questionable pathology report from a Pap smear, a "suspicious" lesion or a dark mole, or an uncertain diagnosis such as "pre-cancer" – creates ongoing uncertainty for patients and their families and friends. This uncertainty, like that associated with having a genetic risk factor, influences decision-making in relation to preventive action and screening; it also often has the effect of positioning the at-risk individual as already having the disease. This has been explored especially in industrialized country settings. Kaja Finkler (2000), in particular, has illustrated how family and kinship relations are medicalized through explanations of the inheritance of genetic disease and related risk factors. As she highlights, this results in two contradictory responses: a sense of control, insofar as knowledge of elevated risk influenced women's health behavior, and a sense of fatalism, that the development of disease was now inevitable. Through their interpretation and internalization of risk, the consequence for some women is to be hyper-vigilant. Others are motivated to take radical preventive steps such as prophylactic mastectomy, either because they truncate risk of disease and presence of disease, or because the gap between the two is perceived to be sufficiently close as to cause continuing anxiety.

Press and colleagues (2005) argue that women's decisions for surgery to reduce risk depend upon whether they regard surgery as preventing breast cancer disease, or of the surgery mimicking the "illness" of breast cancer. In some cases, as Finkler suggests, the anxiety is caused by not knowing. Such anxiety is not always misplaced. Rebel (pseudonym), an Australian participant in my own research, had a complicated family history of cancer: her mother and her mother's three sisters had all had breast cancer, one of these women had also had ovarian cancer and bowel cancer; her mother's two brothers had both died of lung cancer. Her mother's oncologist invited women in the family to participate in a genetic study; during this period Rebel's sister, at 29, was also diagnosed with breast cancer:

> We kind of stuck at it for two years and then they called us and said that they'd found a gene and wanted to take another blood test, just to find out whether it was correct or not, and that's it, we were diagnosed. But prior to that I had already made the decision, whether I was a carrier or not, to have this (prophylactic mastectomy) done because I just felt that too many people in the family had had it and sometimes I feel you just can't trust medicine.

Rebel and her sister made an appointment to see a surgeon, who

> sat us down and explained everything to us, what was the procedure, what could happen if the prostheses or the expanders sort of like, what do you call it? ... your body may reject it, so that could happen which means we've got to go back in and remove them

and treat the infection and so forth. And I was just sitting there listening and she (sister) turned around and said to me "You don't want to hear this. You just want to go in tomorrow and have it done." And I said, "Yes. I do. I'm ready now," and he (doctor) said, "Well, let's wait for your genetics." I said, "I don't want to wait for genetics. I want to go in there and do what I need to do. Even if we didn't do this type of surgery, this bilateral mastectomy, I'll go in there and have my breasts removed totally. It wouldn't faze me at all." I just feel like, especially after everything I've been through, life's too precious ... And after seeing my aunty die, when she knew she wasn't well and she never told anybody, and she knew she had lumps on her breasts and never said anything, and it was too late for her ... I didn't want to be like that (interview transcript, 2002).

But risk is not always and only tied to epidemiology and genetic risk factors. Both Whittaker (1996) and Boonmongkon and colleagues (2001) illustrate that, although empirically the prevalence of reproductive tract infections is low, women in Northeast Thailand self-report high rates of gynecological problems and associated fears of cervical cancer. This impacts on family life and sexual relations, affects health care seeking patterns and expectations from health staff, and results in self-treatment of various over-the-counter drugs. Whittaker (1996:207) provides the example of Grandma Phai, who fears that her *maat khaaw* (vaginal discharge) will develop into cancer, and so she has been treated with analgesics, tetracycline injections, herbs and antibiotics, consulting with hospital staff, private and government clinic doctors, and other local healers in an effort to resolve her problem. Since all women have some discharge varying in appearance during menstrual cycles, the association between "white discharge" and cancer risk implies to women in this area of study that all women are at risk.

UNDERSTANDING CAUSES

The introduction of the notion of risk by clinicians to their patients into everyday discourse is only one way by which people understand the development of cancer. Much research in medical anthropology has been inspired by Kleinman's explanatory model framework. Local cosmologies contribute to lay etiologies of disease. With increasing familiarity everywhere with biomedical practice, technology and theory, however, these explanations are offered in conjunction with biomedical explanations as underlying more proximate reasons for disease. Within local nosologies, cancers may be one of many conditions clustered together by common cause. As Yeo and colleagues (2005) illustrate for Chinese families in Australia, cancer may be seen as the consequence of past misdeeds and moral debt (analogous to *karma* in Buddhist theology), to retribution, fate or God's will, the disharmony of natural energy (*fengshui*), evil, misfortune or bad luck, offence to gods, deities or ancestors, or the ill-will of others. Similar compendia of the multiple causes of different diseases, including but not unique to cancers, exist in various settings: illness may be a consequence of failure to adhere to moral, spiritual, or behavioral prescriptions; to misdeeds in a past or present life; to sorcery or witchcraft; to supernatural spirits like *phii* and *djinn*.

Pimpawun Boonmongkon's study on cervical cancer among women in Northeast Thailand illustrates the conjunction of ideas of risk, etiology, and pathophysiology, including "cultural" and social factors. Village women identify twelve distinct ways in which cervical cancer might be contracted. Clustered, these include reproductive health matters (e.g., certain contraceptives, abortion); "ethnogynecological" concerns (e.g., bad blood, bad uterus); sexual health matters (sexually transmitted infection and sexual intercourse despite a "uterus" problem); other bodily pathologies (ulcers, tumors); economic and environmental factors (hard work, pollution) (Boonmongkon et al. 1999; Gatune and Nyamongo 2005). The dilemma facing these women, one echoed in other contexts, is that many of these putative causes are beyond their control. Even so, many attend for Pap smears, believing that this will allow the diagnosis and appropriate treatment of any reproductive tract infection. The extensive delay between screening and the return of the pathology results means that women continue without receiving appropriate health care where indicated, worried that the symptoms will result in cancer or that they already have cancer (Boonmongkon et al. 1999; Wood et al. 1997).

Complicated etiologies apply equally to other cancers, with biomedical and other risks frequently compounded by social and historical factors. This amalgamated etiology is not unique to rural and resource-poor settings. Scanlon and colleagues (2006), for instance, illustrate the influence of historical, cultural, social, and economic factors in the UK; for Irish immigrants, family experiences of cancers, "stigma" and "secrecy," the limitations of health care available in rural Ireland, and living and working conditions after migration, all influenced Irish understanding of cancers and their interactions in the UK with medical services.

Italian women, surveyed to provide baseline data for a mammography screening program, highlight the link between understanding disease, including cause, and willingness to participate in screening (Gordon et al. 1991). Women included as causes of breast cancer trauma (e.g., being hit), failure to fulfil socially valued roles or to adhere to local, Catholic norms, and the "sorrows, stress and worries of everyday life." In very few cases, women referred to "hereditary factors" and were concerned that the disease could be contagious. Women attributed the development of cancer neither to God nor destiny, but rather, emphasized the protective value of eating and living well since "we write our own destiny" (Gordon et al. 1991:914–916). The attention to the stresses of everyday life reappears in various ethnographic accounts of cancer. Both immigrant and Australian-born women in Melbourne diagnosed with gynecological cancer (primarily ovarian and endometrial cancers) emphasised stress in their own public and domestic, physical, and emotional lives, as a dominant factor contributing to cancer (Manderson et al. 2005). This is consistent with popular etiologies of various other non-communicable and chronic conditions (Manderson and Kokanovic 2009; Pohlman and Becker 2006; Whittaker and Connor 1998).

THE PROBLEM WITH SCREENING

Screening programs are based on the proposition that the early identification of anomalies will enable prompt treatment and cure. Consequently, much anthropological effort has been directed to support breast and cervical screening programs in particular, in order to encourage women to present for screening regularly, in line with national policy. In the Italian and Irish examples above, fear of disease, unfamiliarity or negative experiences with the health system, and understandings of cancer disease as neither preventable nor treatable, influenced willingness to present for screening. In the study conducted in Italy, undertaken in 1990, women conceptualised cancer as painful and frightening

> involving terrible "suffering" and "an inevitable death" (that was) "slow," "disfiguring," "conscious," and "decaying." Cancer was most often depicted as an aggressive, destructive, malign, external force that attacks the good, healthy, positive part of a person ("an animal that eats, that devours you slowly, slowly") or as cells that are "out of control," "in disharmony," "aggressive, crazy cells that at a certain point begin to work for the devil … a factory for the enemy" (Gordon et al. 1991:914).

These women also held to the general belief that discourse about a disease could produce it, and not surprisingly they held to the idea that health education practices and screening – talking about and looking for cancer – had the power to precipitate its development (Gordon 1990; Gordon, et al. 1991).

In general, the research highlights variations in people's willingness to participate in screening programs depending on their acceptance of the possibility of non-symptomatic disease, and the ability of technicians to identify it (Martinez 2005). Participation in breast and cervical cancer screening is also influenced by familiarity with the services and the procedures, knowledge of age at which women should enroll into and exit from screening programs, frequency of screening, embarrassment regarding and discomfort associated with the procedure, and perceptions of the links between screening, cell abnormality, cancer, and death (O'Brien et al. 2009). For cervical cancer screening, too, beliefs about risk factors, particularly sexual license, and the relevance of sexual activity and patterns of partnering, also deter many women from participating in screening programs if they are expected by others to be sexually inactive. These factors are ubiquitous (Chavez et al. 2001; Gatune and Nyamongo 2005; Hubbell et al. 1996; Jirojwong and Manderson 2001; Wood et al. 1997).

One of the few published anthropological monographs on cancer is Jessica Gregg's book *Virtually Virgins* (2003). The economic and environmental living conditions of women in the *favela* of Recife, Northeast Brazil, and dominant ideas of female sexuality and normative heterosexuality that shape both sexual relationships and understandings of cancer, provide the backdrop to sexual and reproductive health, risk factors for cervical cancer, and the impact of its diagnosis on women. Cervical cancer is seen as the consequence of women's "promiscuity," for many, a survival strategy, and of their failure to have regular Pap smears. Here, in sharp contrast to the Italian data, cancer screening is seen as preventive, not diagnostic nor causal.

Contextual and health system factors influence willingness to present by influencing access. These include the availability of screening services at times suitable to women, without the need for them to take time off work; the location of screening services; the availability of women providers to undertake the smears, attitudes to lay midwives, trained midwives and doctors (Schneider 2006); social risks for unmarried women in presenting for screening; embarrassment and physical discomfort associated with examination; the direct and indirect costs related to attending for the procedure. Most of these factors are cultural aspects of biomedicine, not of the people who present for screening or care.

My collaborative research with Indigenous women in Queensland, Australia, provided extensive evidence of health service shortcomings that largely explained women's reluctance to attend. In most centers, fixed services were located in public hospital outpatient departments, not exclusively used for women's health. Women often shared waiting areas and consultation rooms with clients attending sexual health programs. Acoustics separating waiting areas and consultation rooms were sometimes poor, windows unscreened, doors lacked locks, hygiene was questionable, and nurse and doctor practitioners insensitive. Women frequently spoke of medical practitioners interrupting a Pap smear procedure to take a non-urgent telephone call, and health personnel and secretarial staff walking into and out of the consultation room when vaginal examination and screening were in process (Kirk et al. 1998). None of these are cultural factors; they would discourage any woman from attending. The exception is the absence of women-only waiting and examination space for communities that separate "men's business" and "women's business" discursively, spatially and clinically. This breach was one repeated by mobile screening services. In one community, women's health services operated next to the (Indigenous) Lands Council Office, where men sat on the front verandah observing the women, profoundly embarrassed, presenting for women's business.

Cultural, social and institutional factors may influence willingness to participate in other screening programs, although the literature is limited. In explaining African–American women's reluctance to screen for breast cancer, Lende and Lachiondo (2009) maintain that personal considerations of screening and embodied understandings of the body, together with the quality of doctor/patient interactions, influence women's decisions about screening. Australian Aboriginal women offer similar reasons, and depending on region, also cite lack of familiarity with the procedures and purpose and other situational and service-related factors (Kirk et al. 2000). Skin checks, relatively routine in Australia because of its high skin cancer rates, are treated as unproblematic, and lay understandings of different carcinomas and keratoses remain unexplored. Bowel cancer screening is potentially problematic because people are required to submit stool samples; the health education efforts to encourage this for other conditions (e.g., for schistosomiasis mansoni, s.japonicum, and helminth infections) reflect the difficulty of doing so. Similarly, there is virtually no social science research on more invasive procedures. Yet biennial screening colonoscopy is routinely advocated in industrialized country settings to reduce colorectal cancer incidence and mortality, and from a clinical standpoint, colposcopy is essential for women with abnormal Pap smear results to examine the cervix, vagina and vulva for different infections, and menopausal-related and precancerous cell changes. Embarrassment regarding the specific area of the body (vulva, anus), worry that concern was misplaced, and fear of the possibility of cancer and its attendant suffering, all discourage people from presenting for care in diverse populations with varying types of cancers (Smith et al. 2005).

FEAR, DELAY AND TRUTH TELLING

Across populations, the paramount fear of the diagnosis of cancer, and its attendant suffering, discourages people from presenting with symptoms early. As suggested above, diagnoses can be confusing and procedures unclear. The institutional settings, technologies, and practitioners, and the lexicon of oncology itself – dysplasia, neoplasm, biopsy, malignancy, invasiveness, metastasis, adjuvant therapy, targeted radiation, nuclear medicine, cryoablation, mass and stage – mean that people diagnosed with precancerous cells or with cancer, and their families, "spin" into a world unfamiliar organizationally, technologically, and culturally. This is not confined to peoples from cultures and social environments with limited exposure to cosmopolitan care. All people with signs of cancer disease hurtle into a totally medicalized culture, which combined with anxieties and bodily ailments, strips them of all power. Some women spend extended periods of time trying to have their reports of bodily anomalies taken seriously (Markovic et al. 2004a). Others simply avoid or walk away from such situations of loss of control, either because of previous poor experiences with health services or a wider distrust of institutions and services rooted in colonialism and racist practice (Jirojwong and Manderson 2001; Oh and Park 2004).

The next step after cancer screening is to communicate the results, confusing because the result may be "negative" (and therefore good), ambiguous and requiring further investigation, or "positive" (and so, counter-logically, bad). Although it appears a relatively straightforward path from biopsy, smear, X-ray or sample to pathology laboratory and back, in many countries this is not simple: mobile services may be irregular, there may be few pathology laboratories, few people with the skills to interpret results, delays in transmitting samples and returning results, and so on. Again, the best examples relate to women's health. Below, I summarize the experience of one Indigenous woman living in far west Queensland, Australia, who like other women in remote areas, must travel up to a day to receive secondary level care:

> Rose found a lump in December. When she rang the nearest hospital, she was reminded tersely that it was the Christmas holiday period, and she'd have to make an appointment for January. When the flying doctor service came to her small township for a routine visit, she was given a referral to see a doctor in a larger neighboring town; he referred her for mammography at a regional center. Rose was 10 minutes late for the mammogram because of delays due to road works on the highway. The breast screen staff refused to see her, and she was obliged to return the following week. She was told that the mammogram would be faxed through to another center. Three weeks later, when Rose had still not heard, she began to ring the hospital, each time to be advised that the results had not yet been received. When the flying doctor returned again, he made an appointment for her at the hospital. She went back, but was turned away because her results had still not been received. The flying doctor pursued this on her behalf. Six weeks after her first appointment, she was advised that the results were negative. But, as she recalled, "the thing is the hospital jigged me around that much that I didn't know if I was going to die or not for that month and a half. I got my kids and I didn't know if I was going to drop dead or not. The female doctor didn't say nothing to me about what it was or what is wasn't ... (Kirk et al. 2000:21).

Notwithstanding the conventions of contemporary practice in industrialized settings, upon diagnosis, health providers and patients face two ethical–medical dilemmas. Health providers must decide what to tell patients, and what advice to offer them in terms of treatment, care, and prognosis. In response, patients must make relatively quick decisions about the medical and surgical interventions, and if they are told or surmise that they have cancer, they must also decide whether to tell others. The ethnographic accounts of disclosure, truth telling, and decision-making demonstrate the profound difficulties that all people face in this context. There are no clear lines to guide the actors. In their account of disclosure and silence, for instance, Deborah

Gordon and Eugenio Paci (1997) note the uneven and changing practices in this regard. Many doctors continue to withhold or provide elusive statements of diagnosis, within a narrative of what the authors characterize as embedded in social relations; they opt to advise kin and respect their wishes about advising the patient: "His wife asked me and the other physicians not to tell him anything, but he continually asks questions regarding his illness. When he comes to the clinic I reassure him and he leaves feeling much more secure and tranquil…I never told the patient he had a tumor or a metastasis, but that he had a tumor that was not malignant, but not benign either" (Gordon and Paci 1997:1437).

In Tuscany, doctors often emphasized the importance of not disclosing and not offering a prognosis, because they felt the patient would be demoralized if they knew, because they (doctors) would suffer if they caused the patient sorrow, or because the trajectory of illness was not for them to make: "Life is made in such a way that one does not know when one is born and when one dies" (Gordon and Paci 1997:1439).

Elsewhere too, there is ambivalence about disclosure. Elizabeth Bennett (1999) situates the indirect practices around diagnosis and prognosis in Northeast Thailand in local concepts of *kamlancai*, will power or spirit, and the importance of preventing patients from fear and demoralization. Joe Kaufert (1999:418) makes the same point when he describes the cultural prohibitions against "bad news" among First Nations people in Manitoba, Canada, to avoid robbing patients of "strength and courage" to deal with the disease, and the wish to transmit news of impending death gradually and indirectly. Similarly in Northern Tanzania, as described by Harris and colleagues (2003), physicians opted for indirect ways of disclosing, in ways consistent with local discursive styles. Although practices of truth telling are often related to cultural preference and sensitivity (Carrese and Rhodes 2000; Markovic et al. 2004b; Turner 2005), physicians often temper disclosure because of their own assessment of their patients' resilience, resource limitations, lack of treatment options, and patient poverty.

Patients who are given their diagnosis frequently report their inability to make sense of information provided to them at the time of disclosure, because of the limited time the clinician spends with the patient, because of the use of biomedical language, and because of the patient's own sense of shock and inability to focus (Friis et al. 2003). Two Australian Aboriginal women who had had breast disease recalled:

> They sit down, they talk to you, but the words that they say to you, you know, they don't put it in terms how I'd understand. A lot of women are frightened. It's just the fear of finding out I've got cancer. Where do I go, what do I do, who do I talk to? Once you're in hospital, that is when everyone comes to you, but you want that all before you go in. I want the options before I go in (Kirk et al. 2000:24).

While making sense of their diagnosis and its implications for everyday family and social life, patients may chose to withhold disclosure from intimate others, and so also make treatment decisions on the advice of their oncologist without the support of family or friends. Although Freedman (2002) suggests that oncology physicians have moved from a standpoint of authority to one of collaboration with patients, with some shifting of power to enable people to weigh up options regarding the scale of the surgery and/or other treatment, and for breast cancer, surgical preparation for breast reconstruction or a decision to have (or not have) an external prosthesis. Our work with older women with gynecological cancer indicates that in the end, women feel that they have no choice but to accept the advice of their oncologist (Markovic et al. 2006). Viable alternative treatment and decision-making depends on the type of cancer, its management, stage, and the possibility of cure. The pathway is often confusing when the differences between cancers are poorly understood. Chemotherapy may precede surgery to reduce the size of a tumor so that surgery is possible; in other cases early surgery is essential. At various points during the aggressive treatment of cancer, further decision-making takes place, complicated by variable positive or disappointing reports of progress and by the side effects of treatment. I turn to this aspect now.

Unsettling Identity and Everyday Life

The urgency of action and the uncertainty of outcome mean that most people who have been diagnosed with cancer must make quick decisions about medical interventions, from which time their world is defined increasingly by the clinic. Now, "lived time" is measured by the timing of various procedures, recovery from each of these, test results, their interpretation, and consequent decisions. Routine social and economic life is reduced to anxious visits by family and friends, displaced by unfamiliar interactions and negotiations with various care professionals. Contingent ideas of time dominate the discourse: whether and when to have surgery, chemotherapy and radiation, waiting times for post-operative procedures and between each round of adjuvant therapy, and the possibility, timing, and outcome of bone marrow or peripheral blood stem cell transplantations.

This consciousness of time continues for cancer survivors too, as Hansen and Tjornhoj-Thomsen (2008) see anticipated in cancer rehabilitation programs. Here, the dominant illness narrative of recovery, adaptation and hope, which they gloss as "sick–helped–cured," is replaced by a new narrative, "sick–helped-as-if-cured," to take account of the contingencies of cancer prognosis (cf. Warren and Manderson 2008). Cancer survivors experience further time disruptions and its appropriation in various ways. In the immediate term, cancer disrupts time and life, awareness of time increases, time is verbalized and reflected (including in interactions between doctors and patients, as in *How much time do I have?* In the longer-term, survivors prioritize their use of time and make decisions about how to "spend" the time they have (Rasmussen and Elverdam 2007). Ideas of time, estimates of survival and life expectancy, continue to shadow the lives of survivors; the years from diagnosis and various survival-significant reviews mark remission or recovery. People who have had cancer, and their families, must learn to live with uncertainty through acts of resistance and endurance (Honkasalo 2007; De Graves and Aranda 2008).

At the same time, in the first months after treatment, and in the ensuing years, people who have had cancer must also deal with and adapt to the embodiment of the disease and treatment. The body carries visible and psychological scars, often extensive, from medicine's artillery: scars from surgery, burns from radiation, nausea and hair loss from chemotherapy, memory loss, amputation. These side effects do not all fade with time, and the enduring disfigurement and demands of managing the body and bodily functions explain some of the fear and stigma associated with cancers

(Manderson 2005). The side effects create difficulties, too, ideationally and at the level of everyday speech. In working with women with breast cancer, I have written of the complex tasks facing women when speaking of different stages of the embodied past and present, within different discourses (medical, sexual, maternal) and perspectives (Manderson and Stirling 2007). Women necessarily move from one noun to another, talking about the breast, the scar, the mastectomy, the chest and the "breast-that-was" as they search for the precise term for a body part that carries multiple meanings.

Far more attention has been given to women than to men in relation to cancer and the embodiment of gender. Men largely manage their bodies as absent or "silent" compared with women until they must deal with frank disease (Kelly 2009), and consequently they may ignore early signs of disease. But dramatic, unusual symptoms, such as blood in urine or pain on ejaculation in the case of prostrate cancer, or changes in the shape of the testes and/or breasts for testicular cancer, lead men in search of prompt diagnosis. Men then must manage the medicalization of their bodies as they try to make sense of the existential threat of cancer, and both short- and longer-term physical changes, as occurs with prostate cancer for instant, in the context of reduced testosterone that accompanies androgen deprivation therapy (ADT). Men who lose only one testicle do not lose sexual function in theory, but must revise notions of a "normal" masculine body and make sense of the specific excision. Men who have had prostate cancer must manage the side effects of radical prostatectomy and ADT. For some, changes in bladder and bowel functions or incontinence, as well as impotence or impaired sexual function, present continued psychological as well as practical difficulties. As Oliffe (2006) illustrates, participants must reformulate notions of "hegemonic masculinity" to make sense of their own functional body changes and their everyday management.

The performative tasks of gender are not limited to the "sexed body," however. With other kinds of cancer too, men must redefine and re-enact their masculinity and sexuality, re-establishing old behaviours and practices while learning new ways to present themselves. As I have illustrated (Manderson and Peake 2005), by re-engaging in everyday masculine-associated pursuits, men found ways to (re)establish their identity; for example, by dressing each day as if going to work, even if they were to stay at home and were living on a disability pension; taking their children to sporting and other social events; having a drink at the pub. These were tasks that allowed men to maintain normality in face of the abnormal events that had forced a detour in their lives.

CONCLUSION

I have omitted as much as I have covered in this chapter. I have not addressed end-stage disease, palliative care, death and dying, yet death is the persistent specter for people who have cancer, and for their families. I have said little about caregiving, although this is part of the cultural context and lived experience. I have said almost nothing of children and cancer. And I have left untouched several prevalent cancers – of the lung, colon, bladder, and other organs, tissues and systems. My disease focus largely reflects the skewing of the extant literature, in part an outcome of feminist advocacy on women's cancers. But public health imperatives and their politics also shape knowledge. Funds flow for applied research to diseases for which there are population-based screening programs; anthropologists have been less involved even where prevention is seen as a simple matter of social marketing – to prevent tobacco smoking to reduce the incidence of lung cancer and cardiovascular disease, for example (but see Marshall 2008; Mehl 1999; Nichter 2003).

But perhaps more importantly, I have not discussed in this chapter what anthropology does so well – to situate diseases in historic, social and structural context, within a web of relationships of kinship, community, nation, political economy, and globalization. An anthropology of cancer, beyond the individual, his or her tight networks, local constructions of illness, and the diagnosis and management of disease, must attend to how people are exposed to pathogens, to questions of environmental management and the action or inaction in face of risk, to the cultural acceptability of legislation to shore up health education in the application of prevention and screening programs, and to the politics of access to care. There are few studies on the science industry, the role of government, cancer research, or the political economic interests that are its "propellers." Adriana Petryna's ethnography, *Life Exposed* (2002), deals with the aftermath of the Chernobyl nuclear power accident in the then Soviet Ukraine. She locates radiation-related cancers, suffering, deaths and their "underreporting," in the context of a collapsing nation state. In telling this story, and in juxtaposing biological citizenship and human rights with official sensitivities and the politics of science, she demonstrates how medical anthropology can bring together institutions, politics, and the circumstances of ordinary lives. We need more studies of this kind. Gregg's study of cervical cancer, sex, and survival in Brazil, Finkler's of genetics and kinship in the United States, both also provide signposts to the kind of research that we need to better understand cancer, and so to best know how to work across disciplines and fields to reduce the suffering that cancer diseases precipitate.

REFERENCES

Bennett, Elizabeth, 1999 Soft Truth: Ethics and Cancer in Northeast Thailand. Anthropology and Medicine 6(3):395–404.

Bennett, Elizabeth, 2001 The severed heart: Terminal illness and palliative care in Northeast Thailand. The University of Melbourne.

Boonmongkon, P., M. Nichter, and J. Pylypa, 2001 Mot Luuk problems in Northeast Thailand: why women's own health concerns matter as much as disease rates. Social Science and Medicine 53(8):1095–1112.

Boonmongkon, P., J. Pylypa, and M. Nichter, 1999 Emerging fears of cervical cancer in Northeast Thailand. Anthropology and Medicine 6(3):359–380.

Carrese, J. A., and L. A. Rhodes, 2000 Bridging cultural differences in medical practice – The case of discussing negative information with Navajo patients. Journal of General Internal Medicine 15(2):92–96.

Chavez, L. R., J. M. McMullin, S. I. Mishra, and F. A. Hubbell, 2001 Beliefs matter: Cultural beliefs and the use of cervical cancer-screening tests. American Anthropologist 103(4):1114–1129.

De Graves, S., and S. Aranda, 2008 Living with hope and fear – The uncertainty of childhood cancer after relapse. Cancer Nursing 31(4):292–301.

Finkler, Kaja, 2000 Experiencing the New Genetics: Family and Kinship on the Medical Frontier. Philadelphia PA: University of Pennsylvania Press.

Freedman, T. G., 2002 'The doctor knows best' revisited: Physician perspectives. Psycho-Oncology 11(4):327–335.

Friis, L. S., B. Elverdam, and K. G. Schmidt, 2003 The patient's perspective – A qualitative study of acute myeloid leukaemia patients' need for information and their information-seeking behaviour. Suppportive Care in Cancer 11(3):162–170.

Gatune, J. W., and I. K. Nyamongo, 2005 An ethnographic study of cervical cancer among women in rural Kenya: is there a folk causal model? International Journal of Gynecological Cancer 15(6):1049–1059.

Gordon, D. R., 1990 Embodying illness, embodying cancer. Culture, Medicine and Psychiatry 14:275–297.

Gordon, D. R., and E. Paci, 1997 Disclosure practices and cultural narratives: Understanding concealment and silence around cancer in Tuscany, Italy. Social Science and Medicine 44(10):1433–1452.

Gordon, D. R., A. Venturini, M. R. Delturco, D. Palli, and E. Paci, 1991 What Healthy Women Think, Feel and Do About Cancer, Prevention and Breast-Cancer Screening in Italy. European Journal of Cancer 27(7):913–917.

Gregg, Jessica L., 2003 Virtually Virgins Sexual Strategies and Cervical Cancer in Recife, Brazil. Stanford: Stanford University Press.

Hansen, H. P., and T. Tjornhoj-Thomsen, 2008 Cancer Rehabilitation in Denmark: The Growth of a New Narrative. Medical Anthropology Quarterly 22(4):360–380.

Harris, J. J., J. Shao, and J. Sugarman, 2003 Disclosure of cancer diagnosis and prognosis in Northern Tanzania. Social Science and Medicine 56(5):905–913.

Honkasalo, M. L., 2008 Enduring as a mode of living with uncertainty. Health Risk and Society 10(5):491–503.

Hubbell, F. A., L. R. Chavez, S. I. Mishra, and R. B. Valdez, 1996 Beliefs about sexual behavior and other predictors of Papanicolaou smear screening among Latinas and Anglo women. Archives of Internal Medicine 156(20):2353–2358.

Jirojwong, S., and L. Manderson, 2001 Beliefs and behaviors about Pap and breast self-examination among Thai immigrant women in Brisbane, Australia. Women and Health 33(3–4):47–66.

Kaufert, Joseph M., 1999 Cultural mediation in cancer diagnosis and end of life decision-making: the experience of Aboriginal patients in Canada. Anthropology and Medicine 6(3):405–421.

Kelly, Daniel, 2009 Changed men: The embodied impact of prostate cancer. Qualitative Health Research 19(2):151–163.

Kirk, M., E. Hoban, A. Dunne, and L. Manderson, 1998 Barriers to and Appropriate Delivery Systems for Cervical Cancer Screening in Indigenous Communities in Queensland. Final Report. Brisbane, Australia: Queensland Health and The University of Queensland.

Kirk, M., C. McMichael, H. Potts, E. Hoban, D. C. Hill, and L. Manderson, 2000 Breast Cancer: Screening, Diagnosis, Treatment and Care for Aboriginal and Torres Strait Islander Women in Queensland. Final Report. Brisbane, Australia: Queensland Health, The University of Queensland and The University of Melbourne.

Lende, D. H., and A. Lachiondo, 2009 Embodiment and breast cancer among African-American women. Qualitative Health Research 19(2):216–228.

Manderson, L., 1999 Introduction: New perspectives in anthropology on cancer control, disease and palliative care Anthropology and Medicine 6(3):317–321.

Manderson, L., 2005 Boundary breaches: The body, sex and sexuality post-stoma surgery Social Science and Medicine 61(2): 405–415.

Manderson, L., and R. Kokanovic, 2009 "Worried all the time:" Distress and the circumstances of everyday life among immigrant Australians with type 2 diabetes. Chronic Illness 5(1):21–32.

Manderson, L., and S. Peake, 2005 Men in motion: The performance of masculinity by disabled men. In Bodies in Commotion: Disability and Performance. P. Auslander and C. Sandahl, eds. pp. 230–242. Wisconsin MI: University of Michigan Press.

Manderson, L., and C. Smith-Morris, eds., In press, 2010 Chronic Conditions, Fluid States: Chronicity and the Anthropology of Illness. New Brunswick NJ: Rutgers University Press.

Manderson, L., and L. Stirling, 2007 The absent breast: Speaking of the mastectomied body. Feminism and Psychology 17(1): 75–92.

Manderson, L., M. Markovic, and M. Quinn, 2005 "Like roulette": Australian women's explanations of gynecological cancers. Social Science and Medicine 61(2):323–332.

Markovic, M., L. Manderson, N. Wray, and M. Quinn, 2004a "He is telling us something": women's experiences of cancer disclosure in Australia. Anthropology and Medicine 11(3):325–339.

Markovic, M., L. Manderson, and M. Quinn, 2004b Embodied changes and the search for gynecological cancer diagnosis. Medical Anthropology Quarterly 18(3):376–396.

Markovic, M., L. Manderson, and M. Quinn, 2006 Treatment decisions: A qualitative study with women with gynaecological cancer. Australian and New Zealand Journal of Obstetrics and Gynaecology 46(1):46–48.

Marshall, M., 2009 Carolina in the Carolines: A survey of patterns and meanings of smoking on a Micronesian Island. Medical Anthropology Quarterly 19(4):365–382.

Martinez, R. G., 2005 "What's wrong with me?": cervical cancer in Venezuela – living in the borderlands of health, disease, and illness. Social Science and Medicine 61(4):797–808.

Maynard, R. J. 2006 Controlling death – Compromising life: Chronic disease, prognostication, and the new biotechnologies. Medical Anthropology Quarterly 20(2):212–234.

Mehl, G., T. Seimon, and P. Winch, 1999 Funerals, *big matches* and *jolly trips*: 'contextual spaces' of smoking risk for Sri Lankan adolescents. Anthropology and Medicine 6(3): 337–357.

Nichter, M., 2003 Smoking: what does culture have to do with it? Addiction 98: 139–145.

O'Brien, B. A., J. Mill, and T. Wilson, 2009 Cervical Screening in Canadian First Nation Cree Women. Journal of Transcultural Nursing 20(1):83–92.

Oh, H. S., and H. A. Park, 2004 Decision tree model of the treatment-seeking behaviors among Korean cancer patients. Cancer Nursing 27(4):259–266.

Petryna, A., 2002 Life Exposed: Biological Citizens after Chernobyl. Princeton: Princeton University Press.

Pohlman, B., and G. Becker, 2006 "Stress knocks hard on your immune system": Asthma and the discourse on stress. Medical Anthropology 25(3):265–295.

Press, N., S. Reynolds, L. Pinsky, V. Murthy, M. Leo, and W. Burke, 2005 'That's like chopping off a finger because you're afraid it might get broken': Disease and illness in women's views of prophylactic mastectomy. Social Science and Medicine 61(5):1106–1117.

Rasmussen, D. M., and B. Elverdam, 2007 Cancer survivors' experience of time – time disruption and time appropriation. Journal of Advanced Nursing 57(6):614–622.

Roushdy-Hammady, I., 2004 Contested etiology: Cancer risk among two Anatolian populations in Turkey and Europe. Culture, Medicine and Psychiatry 28(3):315–339.

Scanlon, K., S. Harding, K. Hunt, M. Pettigrew, M. Rosato, and R. Williams, 2006 Potential barriers to prevention of cancers and to early cancer detection among Irish people living in Britain: A qualitative study. Ethnicity and Health 11(3):325–341.

Schneider, Suzanne D., 2006 On the periphery of midwifery: A critical analysis of a community-based cancer screening program in Mexico. Human Organization 65(4):362–373.

Smith, L. K., C. Pope, and J. L. Botha, 2005 Patients' help-seeking experiences and delay in cancer presentation: a qualitative synthesis. Lancet 366(9488):825–831.

Turner, L., 2005 From the local to the global: Bioethics and the concept of culture. Journal of Medicine and Philosophy 30(3):305–320.

Warren, M., and L. Manderson, 2008 Constructing hope: Discontinuity and narrative construction of recovery in the rehabilitation unit. Journal of Contemporary Ethnography 37(2):180–201.

Whittaker, A., 1996 White blood and falling wombs: Ethnogynaecology in Northeast Thailand. *In* Maternity and Reproductive Health in Asian Societies. P. Liamputtong Rice and

L. Manderson, eds. pp. 207–225. Chur, Switzerland: Harwood Academic Press/Gordon and Breach.

Whittaker, A., and L. Connor, 1998 Engendering stress in Australia: The embodiment of social relationships. Women and Health 28(1):97–115.

Wood, K., R. Jewkes, and N. Abrahams, 1997 Cleaning the womb: Constructions of cervical screening and womb cancer among rural Black women in South Africa. Social Science and Medicine 45(2):283–294.

Yap, Lorraine, 1999 A map of the human breast: An anthropological enquiry into the management of female breast cancer in La Union, the Philippines. The University of Queensland.

Yeo, S. S., B. Meiser, K. Barlow-Stewart, D. Goldstein, K. Tucker, and M. Eisenbruch, 2005 Understanding community beliefs of Chinese–Australians about cancer: Initial insights using an ethnographic approach. Psycho-Oncology 14(3):174–186.

CHAPTER 17

Generation RX: Anthropological Research on Pharmaceutical Enhancement, Lifestyle Regulation, Self-Medication, and Recreational Drug Use

*Gilbert Quintero
and Mark Nichter*

INTRODUCTION

In this chapter we call for ethnographies of self-administered legal drugs in the United States, for which little anthropological research has been conducted to date. We focus on the range of use, misuse, and abuse of prescription drugs having psychoactive properties, cosmetic pharmacology (Kramer 1993), and drug foods (Jankowiak and Bradburd 1996). Considerable anthropological research has investigated illegal drug and alcohol use (Hunt and Barker 2001; Nichter et al. 2004), and after many years of neglect, research on tobacco use is well underway (e.g., Nichter 2003a; Nichter et al. 2009a, 2009b, 2010; Stromberg 2007). We draw from this literature and argue that it is not possible to understand trends in the use, perception, and representation of any one type of psychoactive substance without understanding it in relation to other

A Companion to Medical Anthropology, First Edition. Edited by Merrill Singer and Pamela I. Erickson.

substances in a given historical, geographic, and global context. We join colleagues in calling for research that examines the social, symbolic, economic, and political context in which drug use occurs (Agar and Reisinger 2001; Anglin and White 1999; Helman 1981). Such research needs to be attentive to the complex life cycle of medications from drug development and marketing to shifting patterns of use, misuse, and abuse (Cohen et al. 2001; Snelders et al. 2006; Van der Geest et al. 1996).

Why direct attention to the social life of prescription psychoactive drugs (PPDs) at this juncture in time? It is presently estimated that these drugs are "misused" by more Americans than any other drugs except for marijuana. The "misuse" of PPDs without a prescription has been the subject of several national and collegiate surveys and has received considerable press coverage including sensationalist accounts characterizing prescription drug misuse as epidemic among today's "Generation RX." Approximately 46 million Americans (20 % of the population) are reported to have used PPDs "non-medically" during their lifetimes, including almost 15 million in 2002 (Colliver et al. 2006). Pain relievers are the most commonly abused prescription drugs, followed closely by tranquilizers, sedatives, and stimulants (McCabe et al. 2006). Although these data are at times informative, they are too often uncritically circulated by media and other sources with little attention to understanding the socio-cultural and political-economic factors driving these trends.

Several research issues beg anthropological inquiry. These include consumer issues such as who uses specific drugs, when, and why, as well as drug preferences, combinations, and substitutions at times of unavailability. Supply side commodity chain issues call for consideration of the extent to which demand for specific classes of drugs is driving supply, and the degree to which ready or diminished supply, availability, and the cost of various drugs drives demand and shifts in patterns of use (Singer and Mirhej 2004). These considerations include the many factors influencing drug distribution, inclusive of how proactive legal and regulatory bodies are in controlling drug distribution routes, penalties for use and trafficking, and so on. It has been pointed out, for example, that harsh penalties promoted by the "War on Drugs" may be leading to the displacement of illicit drugs by licit drug misuse (UN Office of Drugs and Crime 2008). Other issues that require investigation are shifts that may be occurring in the social representations of illicit and licit drugs and how stereotypes of users have changed over time. These representations may be simultaneously influenced by drug education campaigns and news coverage, drug advertisements and the popular media, and the burgeoning networking and information sharing activities afforded by the Internet (Gordon et al. 2006). These myriad factors influence patterns of use, as well as perceptions of risks and benefits associated with particular drugs.

Anthropological examination of PPD misuse and abuse needs to consider both patterns of self-use and prescription practice. An emerging literature reveals PPD prescription patterns as biosocial and political-economic as well as medical phenomena (Singer 2008). The push–pull dynamics influencing prescription-giving as a feature of doctor–patient interaction has been well documented. In the case of PPDs, both physicians and patients are exposed to representations of the effects of drugs through aggressive marketing to practitioners and direct-to-consumer advertising (Montagne 2001; Cohen 2008; Conrad and Leiter 2004; Oldani 2008). This includes the increased visibility of drugs on the Internet associated with cosmetic pharmacology, i.e., using drugs to enhance one's social performance. Two areas in need of ongoing study are "diagnosis bracket creep," related to the expanding claims of drug effectiveness for problems they were not originally intended to treat, and "looping effects" (Kirmayer and Raikhel 2009; Nichter and Vuckovic 1994). In the latter case, information about the prevalence of a medical problem is fostered by the availability of drugs to treat the condition, such that the problem appears to be more and more common, in turn promoting increased drug use. Prime examples are the feedback loops promoting the diagnosis and treatment of ADHD (Conrad and Potter 2000; Singh 2004) and depression (Healy 1997, 2004). Wolf-Meyer (2009) has recently characterized sleep as yet another area where a new generation of medicines has led to a proliferation of new medical disorders such as "extreme daytime sleepiness," which in turn drives demand for new medicines – a phenomenon he aptly labels "pharmakon."

Increased visibility of psychological problems and medications is clearly a "double-edged sword." On the one hand, it decreases stigmatization of problems and promotes consumer agency, which in a best-case scenario increases the likelihood of diagnosis and receiving appropriate treatment (Smardon 2007). On the other hand, it is problematic in three major ways. First, it increases diagnostic inflation and the medicalization of psychosocial problems marked by somatic states associated with the stresses and annoyances of life (cf. Horwitz and Wakefield 2007; Timimi 2004) for which pharmaceutical companies have aggressively promoted products (Conrad 2005; Smith 2005). Second, it fosters diagnosis by treatment. Third, it opens the floodgates to opportunistic diagnosis for secondary gain. Secondary gain is sought by both individuals and those managing problem populations with limited human services resources. For example, school systems can procure benefits in the form of special resources from the diagnosis of student behavior problems such as ADHD. Another example would be nursing home operators using medications to render institutionalized elderly more passive and easier to manage (Beers et al. 1988; Ray et al. 1980).

Control of problem individuals and populations through the use of prescription drugs raises additional issues. Pharmaceuticals may be used to medicalize somatic idioms of distress by individuals whose symptoms are signs of psychosocial discord (Nichter 1981). On a larger scale, pharmaceuticalization may be employed to suppress population-wide states of suffering associated with structural violence. In the latter case, drugs may be used both to mask physical and psychological complaints and to deflect responsibility for illness caused by unhealthy living or working conditions onto individuals. In these cases, victims are asked to assume responsibility for managing "their problems" through medications. The tactics of masking and deflecting may serve to reduce the chances of political activism on the part of people who might come to share a sense of biosociality through common suffering.

The role of substances in everyday life

Anthropologists studying patterns of substance use/abuse investigate how they map onto other social trends, agenda, and coping needs. We live in an era of rapid globalization characterized by a "flexible accumulation" mode of production that demands both labor elasticity and "re-skilling," and shifts in body regulation and performance. Patterns of food and drug consumption enable workers to be in synch with changing work schedules that in turn demand alteration of circadian rhythms and local biology (Nichter 2008). In today's world, there is an ever increasing need to prime oneself to be alert at different times of the day, and to engage in productive sleep at night (Brown 2004). The consumption of drug-foods from high octane coffee and caffeinated soft drinks to energy supplements and stimulants are on the rise as is the consumption of sleeping medications, calming teas, and investment in therapeutic mattresses, music tapes, and so on as enablers of productive relaxation. Drugs that stimulate work performance or enable sleep coexist with drugs to cope with pain associated with strenuous and repetitive work tasks, drugs to treat depression associated with low job satisfaction, and so on.

Work and leisure time have become compressed and intensified in a setting where we are expected to "multitask" more often, are immediately accessible to more people through an array of communication technologies, and where the potential for instant gratification and hyper-stimulation is available "24/7/365." We experience "time-famine" both at work and at home (Jabs and Devine 2006; Vuckovic 1999), but paradoxically must contend with growing feelings of boredom as a malaise of modernity associated with unrealized expectations of leisure, stimulation, and arousal (Brisett and Snow 1993; Conrad 1997; Klapp 1986; Stromberg et al. 2007). Youth have multiple avenues of stimulation open to them in today's network society where they have ready access to high speed Internet and cell phones, yet boredom is cited time and again as a primary reason for drug use.

Just as work requirements have altered, leisure activity demands have shifted. Partying, clubbing, and gaming often extend well beyond 2:00 a.m. and require substances that allow one to stay awake, even while intoxicated. A five and a half billion dollar drug "food-energy" drink market has grown exponentially in the last decade to meet the needs of those under 30 years of age. Hundreds of aggressively marketed brands of energy drinks offer consumers caffeine doses ranging from 100 to 500 mg per can or bottle – most well in excess of the 77 to 150 mg typically offered in a six ounce cup of coffee. These products are marketed conspicuously for a combination of psychoactive, performance enhancing, and stimulant effects. In keeping with consumer demand, energy drinks are promoted as a means to improve performance, endurance, concentration, and reaction speed as well as enhance one's ability to drink and dance (or engage in other leisure activities) all night. "Alcohol-energy" drink combinations are now popular worldwide, although they place users at medical risk, and some companies have gone so far as to overtly market their products as a legal alternative to illicit drugs through such names as "Cocaine and Blow" (Reissig et al. 2008).

Emerging adults use these products to obtain an edgy experience just as some of their parents use high-caffeine products to gain an edge in the workplace. It is notable that recent research suggests a pathway from the use of energy drinks to non-medical prescription stimulant use. In other words, the consumption of energy drinks is identified as a gateway to other substance abuse (Collins et al. 1997; Arria et al. 2008; Packaged Facts 2007). Although more research is required to determine whether or not a direct correlation exists, it is apparent that youth are being socialized to "feel a need for speed" in many domains of their lives.

Another notable trend affecting drug use is that more domains of our lives are being governed by the dictates of advanced liberalism, which valorizes self-care, regulated choices, and active responsibility (Rose 1999). This has fostered the use of drugs as resources to assist people in better adapting to social norms, roles, expectations, and socially desirable states. Ironically, there has been astounding growth in the consumption of prescribed stimulants, mood stabilizers, and antidepressants by adults as well as children of younger and younger ages, at the same time as the government has publicly waged a "War on Drugs" (Cohen et al. 2001). Americans (physicians and the public) appear to be growing more comfortable with the pharmaceutical management of behavioral problems as cosmetic pharmacology (Martin 2006).

The point we wish to make is that we are at a time when the use of medical fixes is becoming far more socially acceptable among young and old alike, whether they are prescribed by doctors, acquired through personal networks or over the Internet, purchased as food supplements or drug-foods, or secured in drugstores as "prescription strength" proprietary drugs. Anthropologists studying drug use must become cognizant of not just increases in recreational drug use by young people (Parker et al. 1998), but broader and deeper forms of pharmaceuticalization that affect all demographic groups in a wide variety of ways.

Anthropologists attempting to understand pharmaceutical practices will have much to investigate in the future. In the remainder of this chapter, we suggest directions for research that can enable a more highly nuanced understanding of the social life of PPDs. We draw attention to the use of drugs for three different purposes: physical and mental enhancement, self-medication, and recreational use. We briefly introduce two concepts that may prove productive in the study of recreational PPD use as at once risky yet self-regulated. We then discuss the need to scrutinize survey data and investigate the social impact of drug prevention and surveillance programs.

EMERGING DRUG USE TRENDS IN SOCIO-CULTURAL CONTEXT

Personal enhancement drugs and self-medication

One important trend in contemporary drug consumption involves the increased popularity of substances for enhancement, i.e., the practice of strategically consuming drugs in order to better meet life challenges and/or as self-improvement. This includes everything from the use of dietary supplements to smart drugs and energy drinks to doping as a means to improve athletic performance. Enhancement also involves the use of drugs to improve social, emotional, and sexual performance in keeping with cultural norms, values, and expectations. By taking enhancement drugs, individuals experience greater flexibility in their range of behavior, albeit often at a cost to their physical health. In historical perspective, society has undergone a sea change in the last 50 years from a condition of "pharmacological Calvinism" characterized by a general mistrust of drugs and underpinned by moral values of abstinence, to a state of "psychotherapeutic hedonism" and the creation of "neurochemical selves" that emphasizes drug-facilitated enhancement of personal interrelations, experiences, and aspects of self (Klerman 1972; Rose 2003; Williams et al. 2008). The use of drugs to address a multitude of conditions is normalized to the point that there are now calls for the legal sanctioning of functional drug use for healthy individuals with no recognized medical problem, however loosely defined. Thus, a recent commentary in a widely known scientific journal argues for the "responsible" use of cognitive-enhancing drugs by individuals who seek to increase performance and do not suffer from any biomedical disease (Greely et al. 2008). At the same time other commentators argue that society has a moral obligation to "enhance" human evolution with whatever technological means available, including the use of performance-enhancing drugs (Harris 2007).

The growing availability of enhancement drugs is generating ethical debates about fair play and societal demarcation of boundaries that delineate conditions when, where, and why enhancement is culturally sanctioned. Should use of cognitive performance enhancing drugs be sanctioned when doping in sports is deemed unethical? What about the ripple effects of some people using performance enhancing drugs in a competitive academic or work environment? Will the uptake of drugs by some individuals push others to use them for fear of being left behind? Studies which suggest that prescription stimulants (e.g., Ritalin and Adderall) are especially being used by college students at institutions that are more academically competitive may indicate such a trend (McCabe et al. 2005). These environments have become laboratories for experimentation in "neuroenhancement" (Talbot 2009). The possibility arises for soft coercion to take place in work environments. In the future, will employers encourage employees to take medicines to be more efficient? Compulsory consumption of stimulants has been condoned by the military for some time during times of conflict and heightened vigilance (Babkoff and Krueger 1992).

Newly emerging professional organizations such as the Neuroethics Society are testament to the growing visibility of the ethical issues attendant to the proliferation and use of performance enhancing drugs. At the moment, over 40 neuroenhancing drugs are under development. One of the most promising drugs in this category is modafinil. Sold under several trade names, the drug is approved by the Food and Drug Administration for treatment of excessive daytime sleepiness associated with narcolepsy, shift sleep disorder, and obstructive sleep apnea/hypopnea. Modafinil has also been found to raise executive functions, improve memory, and effectively address desynchronosis (i.e., "jet lag") with few side effects. The off-label popularity of the drug in our society could be huge and garner large profits for its manufacturer. It remains to be seen how popular this drug will become. In part this may depend on media representations of the drug (Williams et al. 2008). But among youth, Internet chatter may supersede press coverage as a form of influence.

In addition to improving memory or focus, many other enhancement drugs are being used to boost the immune system, improve sleep, and achieve greater physical prowess. Two prime examples of the latter are the use of steroids and erectile dysfunction (ED) drugs. Up to 12% of high school males report lifetime use of steroids (Yates et al. 1990; Kutscher et al. 2002), and the use of ED drugs like Viagra, intended for older males, is increasingly being sought after by males in their 20s–30s (Fisher et al. 2006; Vares and Braun 2006) in an environment where the immediate benefits of such drugs are thought to outweigh the long-term risks.

Anthropologists investigating the rising popularity of drugs such as Ritalin and Viagra need to pay careful attention to slippage between enhancement recreation and self-medication. What begins with experimentation to determine if a drug can enhance one's experience may result in triggering diagnosis by treatment. If one finds they can focus or remember better on Ritalin, or have less sexual inhibition after taking Viagra, does this cause them to conjecture if they have an undiagnosed problem for which they should now self-medicate? Interviews conducted by the authors with college students suggest that this is occurring.

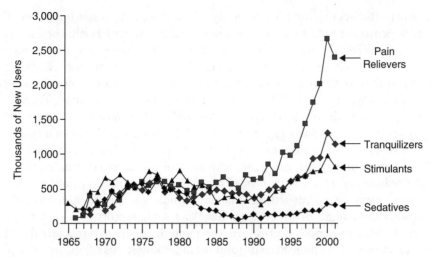

Figure 17.1   Results from the 2001 National Household Survey on Drug Abuse: Volume I. Summary of National Findings, 2002. By courtesy of The Substance Abuse and Mental Health Services Administration, Rockville MD, USA.

How does advertising impact how individuals think about themselves as "having a problem?" An important area for ongoing study will be the impact of direct-to-consumer marketing on the popularity of such drugs as Viagra (and drugs marketed as "Viagra for the mind") for both enhancement and self- medication. Conrad and Leiter (2004) provide a case study of Viagra that illustrates how pharmaceutical interests operate to create medical markets through strategic advertising campaigns intentionally crafted to create demand and expanded market niches for new products. The results of such advertising efforts are quite impressive, with some studies suggesting that the icon of the blue Viagra tablet is nearly as recognizable as the sign for Coca Cola (Vares and Braun 2006).

Recreational drug use of prescription drugs

The non-medical use of several categories of prescription drugs, including pain relievers, tranquilizers, and stimulants, has grown steadily in recent years (see Figure 17.1). Although survey terminology often makes it difficult to ascertain the motivations behind this misuse, recreational purposes drive much of this growth. A number of factors are contributing to the growing socio-recreational popularity of prescription drugs. Pharmaceuticals are readily obtainable from leftover prescriptions, peer-networks, or family members (as well as burglary, theft of prescription pads, doctor shopping, and warehouse diversion, etc.), and knowledge regarding dosages, uses, and effects are easily attained. Individuals gain indirect knowledge from family members and friends as well as media messages and also often have direct personal experience of medical uses of pharmaceuticals that they extend to socio-recreational domains. It is no coincidence that the most widely legitimately prescribed classes of pharmaceuticals – pain relievers and stimulants – are also misused at the highest rates. Name brand medications provide a predictable experience, unlike many illicit drugs where the quality, intensity or purity of the drug is a greater unknown. They are developed and tested by reputable manufacturers, not by home chemists or in garage laboratories, and are subject to regulations that enhance their aura of respectability. PPDs provide a relatively social acceptable and safe means for relatively risk-adverse youth to participate in social life and at the same time offer more established users a way to wean off hard street drugs and improve performance. There is no need to associate with socially marginal, "sketchy" dealers in order to gain access to these drugs and it is less daunting to consider explaining the presence of medications to law enforcement authorities as opposed to a bag of cannabis. In economic terms, pairing prescription narcotic analgesics with alcohol is seen as a cost efficient way to attain intoxication on the cheap, instead of paying for overpriced drinks in addition to a cover charge in a club setting. Media accounts and health education efforts highlighting the danger of street drugs may lead some sectors of society to prefer more predictable prescription drugs. At the same time, street vernacular for PPDs such as OxyContin ("hillbilly heroin") and Ritalin ("kiddie coke") incorporate pharmaceuticals into the recreational drug use scene. There is also the mixing of so-called hard street drugs, like heroin, with pharmaceuticals like tranquilizers for desired effects. Clearly, PPDs possess an impressive flexibility that encompasses not only a range of socio-recreational uses, but a variety of self-medication and functional utility as well.

Anthropological studies of recreational uses of prescription drugs need to be considered in context. The menu of substances utilized for recreational purposes has substantially expanded over the last three decades. Foremost among these are prescription opioids. Data from the 2002 National Survey on Drug Use and Health indicates that almost 30 million persons reported lifetime non-medical use of prescription pain relievers (NSDUH 2004). Typical users were young adults who were male and white. Longitudinal trends show that the number of new non-medical users of prescription pain relievers increased from 600,000 in 1990 to more than 2 million in 2001 – a threefold rise in little more than a decade. These upswings in misuse generally parallel increases in the legitimate medical use of this drug class (Gilson et al. 2004). Newly developing trends suggest that narcotic analgesics may be particularly attractive to young females from lower socio-economic positions (Sung et al. 2005). These trends are also more pronounced among users of illicit street drugs and other classes of pharmaceuticals, suggesting that prescription pain relievers are becoming well integrated into recreational drug use repertoires among a wide range of users (Vivian et al. 2005).

Benzodiazepines ("downers," "goofballs") are another important class of commonly misused pharmaceuticals. Survey data on consumption patterns among college students suggest a great deal of variability that invites anthropological investigation. McCabe et al. (2005) report misuse rates at different institutions ranging from 0 to 20% of the student population. Non-medical use of this class of drugs was more likely to occur among Anglo–American college students who also reported higher rates of other health risk behaviors. Survey data has also revealed regional variations and racial differences in non-medical use of prescription benzodiazepines. Specifically, these drugs were used less frequently in colleges in the North Central region of the USA, and were less likely at historically black colleges and universities. Anthropological studies are needed that can explore gendered and ethnic preferences in drug choice among young adults (Harrell and Broman 2009).

Edgework and harm reduction

Two concepts may assist anthropologists in better documenting patterns of PPD use: "edgework" and "harm reduction." Edgework refers to forms of voluntary risk-taking in which an individual edgeworker attempts to skillfully negotiate the boundaries of risk (Hunt et al. 2007). An edgeworker is at once attracted to the sensation of "being on the edge" as an intense form of pleasure, and the accomplishment of being able to avoid a bad or disastrous experience. Edgework is exemplified by extreme sports and extreme drinking games and may underlie some forms of prescription drug taking alone or with alcohol to boost one's "high." Edgework involving prescription drug use among college students often takes place in environments in which binge drinking is also occurring. For example, "polydrug" use also allows one to experience the edge at parties, raves and other contexts where particular drugs are taken to achieve altered states that complement certain types of music and dancing.

Harm reduction (Nichter 2003b) is often a component of edgework. In the present context, harm reduction refers to behavior one engages in to reduce the negative effects of taking a particular drug. Harm reduction has been amply reported in the illicit drug literature (Hunt et al. 2007; Bardhi et al. 2007), where it may involve a range of behaviors including staying well hydrated while taking ecstasy to balancing out the extreme effects of one kind of drug by the use of another such as using pre-scription tranquilizer to mellow out a bad drug experience, or enabling one to sleep when too wired from using a stimulant. Harm reduction may also entail taking a "quality control" brand labeled PPD to get high rather than a street drug whose properties are unpredictable, or employing a hierarchy of risk mentality when making choices about what drugs to take, and how (Connors 1992).

Limitations of survey data

Much of our current state of knowledge about PPDs and other substances is severely restricted by the limits of available drug surveillance and information systems. In terms of surveys, we have a great deal of data on a limited demographic range of users com-prised largely of high school and college students. Far less is known about other age groups, non-whites, and those from lower socio-economic populations. We know rela-tively little about the working poor, youth out of school, the elderly, housewives, and those suffering from co-morbid conditions that compel them to self-medicate. Even less is known regarding variability in basic consumption patterns and their relation to the contexts within which use and misuse take place. For instance, surveys tend to gloss socio-recreational and self-medication behaviors under the broad category of "misuse" even though these types of consumption address very different needs and often take place in distinct social contexts. The heterogeneity of individuals described as "misus-ers" in standard drug surveillance systems makes it virtually impossible to interpret the clinical implications of these data or to come to a relatively objective decision regarding the true extent and character of problems associated with various types of pharmaceuti-cal use (Barrett et al. 2008). Survey statistics also conflate patterns of PPD misuse by both novice-opportunistic users of drugs and more experienced users.

Drug information systems such as the National Survey on Drug Use and Health and the Monitoring the Future Survey are also quite limited in the extent to which they provide resolution regarding how the use of one drug is influenced by the use of another. Operational definitions of polydrug use, for instance, have almost exclusively been based on the use of multiple drugs within a 30-day time window, whether or not this use is taking place in simultaneous or sequential manner that is socio-culturally significant. Adopting these 30-day prevalence rates as a standard for defining and investigating polydrug use raises the risk of ignoring cultural time frames and sequences that shape drug use and have important implications for its study and interpretation. A more productive approach might draw attention to temporal and developmental frames organized around life phases and social processes, roles associated with identify projects and imagine management, life transitions, shifting activity sets and peer groups and so on (Quintero 2009; Schensul et al. 2005). Standard survey method-ologies also tell us little regarding drug substitution patterns, especially instances where pharmaceuticals are substituted for harder street drugs such as cocaine, or where common pain relievers (hydrocodone) are used by some individuals as an alter-native to marijuana or other street drugs (Bardhi et al. 2007; Quintero et al. 2006).

Although there have been forward thinking contributions made by ethnographic drug surveillance systems (Singer et al. 2006), popular media representations of drug use problems are predominated by quantitative surveys that warrant careful anthropological investigation. Rising rates of prescription drug abuse, for instance, have been steadily reported in the public health and medical literature. These reports commonly rely on surveys focused on lifetime prevalence of drug abuse. The press in turn characterizes these rising rates of abuse in sensationalized terms phrased in moral panic rhetoric to gain attention. Such uncritical use of data may have unintended side-effects. For example, it has been suggested that sensationalistic press coverage of OxyContin played a role in fostering experimentation with the drug among youth (Inciardi and Good 2007).

Anthropologists need to be attentive to social agendas driving the biocommunica-bility (Briggs and Hallin 2007; Briggs, this volume) of drug information and the manner in which data about risk can unintentionally place populations at risk. Aggregating once-in-a-lifetime prevalence data and very low level prescription drug abusers with those who routinely take drugs may inadvertently lead youth to think that these forms of use are far more prevalent than actually is the case. Mimi Nichter has made this argument regarding the reporting of "ever smoker" prevalence rates (Nichter 2000). This reporting of high prevalence rates of ever smokers may lead youth to conclude that a majority of young people smoke. The actual state of affairs, however, is far more complex. While almost 70% of youth experiment with tobacco, far fewer move on to become regular smokers. Anthropologists need to critically assess aggregate data and how it is utilized and interpreted. Looking beyond aggre-gate data we need to investigate drug use transitions and the factors that lead to dif-ferent endpoints, be this experimentation, casual low-level use, or sustained prescription drug use (Hurwitz 2005; Schensul et al. 2000).

Anthropological considerations of prevention and surveillance programs

Another topic that demands serious anthropological investigation is social response to drug prevention interventions in institutional settings and in the home. In the United States, the Substance Abuse and Mental Health Services Administration had a preven-tion budget of $533 million for 2009 (ONDCP 2008), a figure devoted to prevention programs that highlight the dangers of using both legal and illegal drugs, from tobacco to methamphetamine. Universal prevention programs are widely integrated into pedagogical institutions and at least one popular program, Drug Abuse Resistance Education (DARE) claims coverage in 75% of the school districts in the United States (DARE 2009).

These prevention efforts operate in parallel with a growing number of drug use surveillance programs, which do not just ask youth about their drug use in surveys but employ random drug tests. For example, in June 2008 the Office of National Drug Control Policy announced $5.8 million in grants to 49 schools in 20 states to support random school drug testing programs (ONDCP 2008). Many of these testing programs are directed at athletes and others involved in extracurricular activities and focus on marijuana use. One result is that youth divert their consumption to drugs like alcohol that are not tested and which are ostensively legal. It is noteworthy that these testing procedures are being implemented even though evidence suggests that they do little if anything to curb drug use (Yamaguchi et al. 2003).

In addition, a variety of home testing kits are now available enabling parents to detect drug use through urine or hair samples, the breath, or nail clippings. These test kits are marketed as an economical and fast means for parents to monitor their children's drug use and have become a multimillion dollar a year industry (Moore and Haggerty 2001).

What is the impact of these prevention and surveillance programs on the drug-related attitudes and practices of young people? What issues of trust arise that may influence social relations and attitudes toward schools among youth? Research suggests that they have unintended repercussions that warrant further analysis. A review of the so-called "boomerang effects" of drug prevention programs suggests that these efforts can have the counterproductive effect of actually increasing alcohol use and use of drugs not being tested for (Ringold 2002). An issue for anthropological inquiry is the extent to which the demonization of street drugs in prevention programs has the unintended side effect of making "legal" drugs appear more attractive. To what extent does bad press about the unpredictable quality of street drugs and the unsavory character of dealers lead youth to think prescription drugs are more desirable especially given growing ease of access?

This raises another area for anthropological investigation: documenting routes of drug access and pharmaceutical sharing. Data from the National Survey on Drug Use and Health (2006) indicates that 56% of non-medical users of pain relievers obtain them directly from friends or relatives and over 80% of these sources receive these medications from their own doctors. In other words, these relatively short supply chains are organized around fundamental social networks. A recent review of prescription stimulant misuse confirms these trends (Wilens et al. 2008): a meta-analysis of lifetime diversion rates indicates that 16–29% of individuals with legitimate prescriptions had been approached to share their medications at least once. Medical users of stimulants are thus commonly asked to give, trade, or sell medications to individuals in their social networks for multiple purposes, including improving concentration and alertness, as well as more recreationally oriented uses. Certain groups, especially whites, members of fraternities and sororities, and those with low grade point averages, are the most likely to participate in diversion. These findings invite consideration of the exchange value of medications. For instance, ethnographic work with young adult college students indicates that sharing of pharmaceuticals is an important social activity – it reaffirms existing relations and facilitates the formation of new, even if temporary, interactions especially in "party" settings. Beyond sharing for recreational use, these drug exchanges may enable self-medication for those undiagnosed with a condition they later have or imagine they have after consulting a self-help site such as WebMD. Wilens and company (2008), for example, note that individuals with undiagnosed ADHD utilize social networks to self-medicate.

Co-substance use is yet another high-priority research topic for anthropologists. Even a cursory examination of contemporary drug use trends indicates that studies focusing on the consumption of single drugs (e.g., alcohol, tobacco) in isolation are naive. Indeed, in the case of tobacco, the large majority of initiation experiences are under the influence of alcohol (Acosta et al. 2008) and the vast majority of college smokers consume the majority of their cigarettes with alcohol in party settings (Dierker et al. 2006). A similar situation may hold true for prescription drug use. Survey research suggests that polydrug use is fairly common among college students and involves a range of pain, stimulant, sedative, and sleeping medications (McCabe et al. 2006). Anthropological studies of recreational PPD use need to be attentive to differences between intentional and opportunistic polydrug use.

Contemporary trends in drug use underscore the need for careful anthropological assessment of prominent models of drug behavior such as the "gateway theory of drug transition." This theory proposes a connection between the early use of specific "gateway" drugs by an individual and later use of other "harder" drugs. Only a very small set of drugs – alcohol, tobacco and marijuana – have been characterized as gateway substances for the purpose of such analyses. Given what we know about the wide variety of drugs and drug foods being used in American culture at present, is it plausible to confine such analyses to just three drugs? To what extent does medically sanctioned pharmaceutical use during adolescence influence subsequent likelihood or willingness to use other substances in the future as a means of problem solving or achieving shifts in emotional states? To what extent does the use of energy drinks predispose latter licit and illicit use of prescription stimulants (Arria et al. 2008)? Should we be confining the study of gateway phenomena to chains of drug use or looking to other sources of influence? It is apparent that youth are being socialized to "feel a need for speed" in many domains of their lives.

CONCLUSION

By way of a conclusion let us briefly point to the timeliness of this topic. Historical data make it clear that times of crises and rapid social transitions are often associated with changes in drug use, especially in the social strata most dramatically impacted. The collapse of the former Soviet Union, with its attendant rise in mortality and morbidity associated with alcohol and heroin use, provides only one of the most recent and telling examples of these interrelationships (Shkolnikov et al. 2001).

Ethnographic research is called for during these troubled times of economic uncertainty when unemployment, the fear of job losses, the specter of mounting credit card debt and mortgage payments, and decreases in fixed income by the elderly are giving rise to widespread psychological angst. It is likely that the somatic experience and amplification of distress will be on the rise at the same time a larger percentage of the

US population is left without recourse to health care due to the loss of insurance, or longer delays before the insured can access care given an overburdened health care system. How will people cope with the somatic and psychological suffering that accompanies conditions of joblessness, hopelessness, and boredom? Will increases in negative states of "being in the world" associated with a growing state of anomie lead to greater self-use as well as greater prescribed use of psychoactive drugs? Will use of illicit drugs for self-treatment of depression/anxiety, sleeplessness, and temporary escape from problems become more common, or will people increasingly turn to self-use of prescription drug use if it is readily available? An ethnography of Generation RX is called for that speaks to time, place, governance, need, and pleasure.

REFERENCES

Acosta, Michelle C., Thomas Eissenberg, Mimi Nichter, Mark Nichter, Robert L. Balster, and the Tobacco Etiology Research Network (TERN), 2008 Characterizing Early Cigarette Use Episodes in Novice Smokers. Addictive Behaviors 33(1):106–121.

Agar, Michael H., and Heather S. Reisinger, 2001 Trend Theory: Explaining Heroin Use Trends. Journal of Psychoactive Drugs 33:203–212.

Anglin, Mary K., and Jill Collins White, 1999 Poverty, Health Care, and Problems of Prescription Medication: A Case Study. Substance Use and Misuse 34:2073–2093.

Arria, Amelia M., Kimberly M. Caldeira, Kevin E. O'Grady, Kathryn B. Vincent, Roland R. Griffiths, and Eric D. Wish, 2008 Energy Drink Use is Associated with Subsequent Non-medical Prescription Stimulant Use among College Students. Paper presented at the American Public Health Association Annual Meeting. San Diego, CA.

Babkoff, Harvey, and Gerald P. Krueger, 1992 Use of Stimulants to Ameliorate the Effects of Sleep Loss During Sustained Performance. Military Psychology 4(4):192–205.

Bardhi, Flutura, Stephen J. Sifaneck, Bruce D. Johnson, and Eloise Dunlap, 2007 Pills, Thrills and Bellyaches: Case Studies of Prescription Pill Use and Misuse among Marijuana/Blunt Smoking Middle Class Young Women. Contemporary Drug Problems 34(1): 53–101.

Barrett, Sean P., Jessica R. Meisner, and Sherry H. Stewart, 2008 What Constitutes Prescription Drug Misuse? Problems and Pitfalls of Current Conceptualizations. Current Drug Abuse Reviews 1:255–262.

Beers, Mark, Jerry Avorn, Stephen B. Soumerai, Daniel E. Everitt, David S. Sherman, and Susanne Salem, 1988 Psychoactive Medication Use in Intermediate-Care Facility Residents. Journal of the American Medical Association 260:3016–3020.

Briggs, Charles L., and Daniel C. Hallin, 2007 Biocommunicability: The Neoliberal Subject and its Contradictions in News Coverage of Health Issues. Social Text 25(4):43–66.

Brissett, Dennis and Robert P. Snow, 1993 Boredom: Where the Future Isn't. Symbolic Interaction 16:237–256.

Brown, Megan, 2004 Taking Care of Business: Self-Help and Sleep Medicine in American Corporate Culture. Journal of Medical Humanities 25(3):173–187.

Cohen, David, 2008 Needed: Critical Thinking about Psychiatric Medications. Social Work in Mental Health 7(1):42–61.

Cohen, David, Michael McCubbin, Johanne Collin, and Guilhème Pérodeau, 2001 Medications as Social Phenomena. Health 5(4):441–469.

Collins, L., J. Graham, and S. Rousculp, 1997 Heavy Caffeine Use and the Beginning of the Substance Use Process. In The Science of Prevention. M. Bryant, M. Windle and S. West, eds. pp. 79–99. Washington: American Psychological Association.

Colliver, James D., Larry A. Kroutil, Lanting Dai, and Joseph C. Gfroerer, 2006 Misuse of Prescription Drugs: Data from the 2002, 2003, and 2004 National Surveys on Drug Use and Health (DHHS Publication No. SMA 06–4192. Rockville MD: Substance Abuse and Mental Health Services Administration, Office of Applied Studies.

Connors, Margaret M., 1992 Risk Perception, Risk Taking, and Risk Management among Intravenous Drug Users: Implications for AIDS Prevention. Social Science and Medicine 34(6):591–601.

Conrad, Peter, 1997 It's Boring: Notes on the Meanings of Boredom in Everyday Life. Qualitative Sociology 20(4):465–475.

Conrad, Peter, 2005 The Shifting Engines of Medicalization. Journal of Health and Social Behavior 46:3–14.

Conrad, Peter, and Valerie Leiter, 2004 Medicalizations, Markets and Consumers. Journal of Health and Social Behavior 45(Extra Issue):158–176.

Dierker, Lisa, Elizabeth Lloyd-Richardson, Marilyn Stolar, Brian Flay, Stephen Tiffany, Linda Collins, Steffani Bailey, Mark Nichter, Mimi Nichter, Richard Clayton, and the Tobacco Etiology Research Network (TERN), 2006 The Proximal Association between Smoking and Alcohol Use among First Year College Students. Drug and Alcohol Dependence 81:1–9.

Drug Abuse Resistance Education (DARE), 2009 DARE America Annual Report, 2007. Electronic document. http://www.dare.com/home/documents/DAREAmericaAnnual07.pdf/.

Fisher, Dennis G., R. Malow, R. Rosenberg, G. L. Reynolds, N. Farrell, and A. Jaffe, 2006 Recreational Viagra Use and Sexual Risk among Drug Abusing Men. American Journal of Infectious Diseases 2:107–114.

Gilson, Aaron M., Karen M. Ryan, David E. Joranson, and June L. Dahl, 2004 A Reassessment of Trends in the Medical Use and Abuse of Opioid Analgesics and Implications for Diversion Control: 1997–2002. Journal of Pain and Symptom Management 28:176–188.

Gordon, Susan M., Robert Forman, and Candis Siatkowski, 2006 Knowledge and Use of the Internet as a Source of Controlled Substances. Journal of Substance Abuse Treatment 30:271–274.

Greely, Henry, Barbara Sahakian, John Harris, Ronald C. Kessler, Michael Gazzaniga, Philip Campbell, and Martha J. Farah, 2008 Towards Responsible Use of Cognitive-Enhancing Drugs by the Healthy. Nature. Electronic document. /doi:10.1038/456702a/.

Harris, John, 2007 Enhancing Evolution: The Ethical Case for Making Better People. Princeton NJ: Princeton University Press.

Helman, Cecil G., 1981 'Tonic,' 'Fuel' and 'Food': Social and Symbolic Aspects of the Long-Term Use of Psychotropic Drugs. Social Science and Medicine 158:521–533.

Healy, David, 1997 The Antidepressant Era. Cambridge MA: Harvard University Press.

Healy, David, 2004 Let Them Eat Prozac: The Unhealthy Relationship between the Pharmaceutical Industry and Depression. New York: New York University Press.

Horwitz, A. V., and J. C. Wakefield, 2007 The Loss of Sadness: How Psychiatry Transformed Normal Sorrow into Depressive Disorder. New York: Oxford University Press.

Hunt, Geoffrey, Kirstin Evans, and Faith Kares, 2007 Drug Use and Meanings of Risk and Pleasure. Journal of Youth Studies 10(1):73–96.

Hunt, Geoffrey, and Judith C. Barker, 2001 Socio-Cultural Anthropology and Alcohol and Drug Research: Towards a Unified Theory. Social Science and Medicine 53:165–188.

Hurwitz, William, 2005 The Challenge of Prescription Drug Misuse: A Review and Commentary. Pain Medicine 6(2):152–161.

Inciardi, James A., and Jennifer L. Good, 2007 OxyContin: Miracle Medicine or Problem Drug? In The American Drug Scene: An Anthology. 4th Edition. J. A. Inciardi and K. McElrath, eds. pp. 163–173. Los Angeles: Roxbury.

Jabs, Jennifer, and Carol M. Devine, 2006 Time Scarcity and Food Choices: An Overview. Appetite 47:196–204.

Klapp, Orrin E., 1986 Overload and Boredom: Essays on the Quality of Life in the Information Society. New York: Greenwood Press.

Kirmayer, L., and E. Raikhel, 2009 From Amrita to Substance D: Pharmacology, Political Economy and Technologies of the Self. Transcultural Psychiatry 46(1):5–15.

Klerman, Gerald L., 1972 Psychotropic Hedonism vs. Pharmacological Calvinism. Hastings Center Report 1–3.

Kutscher, Eric C., Brian C. Lund, and Paul J. Perry, 2002 Anabolic Steroids: A Review for the Clinician. Sports Medicine 32:285–296.

Martin, Emily, 2006 The Pharmaceutical Person. Biosciences 1:237–287.

McCabe, Sean E., 2005 Correlates of Nonmedical Use of Prescription Benzodiazepine Anxiolytics: Results from a National Survey of U.S. College Students. Drug and Alcohol Dependence 79:53–62.

McCabe, Sean E., John R. Knight, Christian J. Teter, and Henry Wechsler, 2005 Non-Medical Use of Prescription Stimulants among US College Students: Prevalence and Correlates from a National Survey. Addiction 100:96–106.

McCabe, Sean E., Christian J. Teter, and Carol J. Boyd, 2006 Medical Use, Illicit Use, and Diversion of Abusable Prescription Drugs. Journal of American College Health 54:269–278.

Montagne, Michael 2001 Mass Media Representations as Drug Information for Patients: The Prozac Phenomenon. Substance Use and Misuse 36(9, 10):1261–1274.

Moore, D., and K. D. Haggerty, 2001 Bring it on Home: Home Drug Testing and the Relocation of the War on Drugs. Social Legal Studies 10:377–395.

National Survey of Drug Use and Health (NSDUH), 2004 National Survey of Drug Use and Health. The NSDUH Report: Nonmedical Use of Prescription Pain Relievers. May 21, 2004. Office of Applied Studies, Substance Abuse and Mental Health Services Administration.

Nichter, Mark, 1981 Idioms of Distress: Alternatives in the Expression of Psychosocial Distress: A Case Study from South India. Culture Medicine and Psychiatry 5:379–408.

Nichter, Mimi, 2000 Fat Talk: What Girls and Their Parents Say about Dieting. Cambridge MA: Harvard University Press.

Nichter, Mark, 2003a Smoking: What's Culture Got to do With It? Addiction 98(Supplement 1):139–145.

Nichter, Mark, 2003b Harm Reduction: A Core Concern for Medical Anthropology. In Risk, Culture, and Health Inequality: Shifting Perceptions of Danger and Blame. Barbara Herr-Harthorn and Laury Oaks, eds. pp.13–33. New York: Praeger.

Nichter, Mark, 2008 Coming to Our Senses: Appreciating the Sensorial in Medical Anthropology. Transcultural Psychiatry 45(2):163–197.

Nichter, Mark, and Nancy Vuckovic, 1994 Agenda for an Anthropology of Pharmaceutical Practice. Social Science and Medicine 39:1509–1525.

Nichter, Mark, Gilbert Quintero, Mimi Nichter, Jeremiah Mock, and Sohaila Shakib, 2004 Qualitative Research: Contributions to the Study of Drug Use, Drug Abuse, and Drug Use(r)-Related Interventions. Substance Use and Misuse 39:1907–1669.

Nichter, Mimi, S. Padmawati, M. Danardono, N. Ng, Y. Prabandari, and Mark Nichter, 2009a Reading Culture from Tobacco Advertisements in Indonesia. Tobacco Control. Electronic document. /doi:10.1136/tc.2008.025809/.

Nichter, Mark, Mimi Nichter, S. Padmawati, C.U. Thresia, and Project Quit Tobacco International Group, 2009b Anthropological Contributions to the Development of Culturally Appropriate Tobacco Cessation Programs: A Global Health Priority. In Anthropology and Public Health. R. Hahn and M. Inhorn, eds. Oxford: Oxford University Press.

Nichter, Mimi, Mark Nichter, Asli Carkoglu, Elizabeth Lloyd-Richardson, and the Tobacco Etiology Research Network (TERN), 2010 Smoking and Drinking among College Students: "It's a Package Deal." Drug and Alcohol Dependence 106:16–20.

Office of National Drug Control Policy (ONDCP), National Drug Control Strategy, Annual Report, 2008 Electronic document. http://www.whitehousedrugpolicy.gov/publications/policy/ndcs09/index.html/.

Oldani, Michael, 2008 Deadly Embrace: Psychoactive Medication, Psychiatry, and the Pharmaceutical Industry. In Killer Commodities: Public Health and the Corporate Production of Harm. Merrill Singer and Hans Baer, eds. pp. 283–310. Walnut Creek CA:AltaMira Press.

Olfson, Mark, Marc Gameroff, Stephen Marcus, and Peter S. Jensen, 2003 National Trends in the Treatment of Attention Deficit Hyperactivity Disorder. American Journal of Psychiatry 160:1071–1077.

Packaged Facts, 2007 Energy Drinks in the USA. Rockville MD.

Parker, Howard A., Judith Aldridge, and Fiona Measham, 1998 Illegal Leisure: The Normalization of Adolescent Recreational Drug Use. London/New York: Routledge.

Quintero, Gilbert, 2009 Controlled Release: A Cultural Analysis of Collegiate Polydrug Use. Journal of Psychoactive Drugs 41(1):39–47.

Quintero, Gilbert, Jeffery Peterson, and BonnieYoung, 2006 An Exploratory Study of Sociocultural Factors Contributing to Prescription Drug Misuse Among College Students. Journal of Drug Issues 36(4):903–931.

Ray, Wayne A., Charles F. Federspiel, and William Schaffner, 1980 A Study of Antipsychotic Drug Use in Nursing Homes: Epidemiologic Evidence Suggesting Misuse. American Journal of Public Health 70:485–491.

Reissig, Chad J., Eric C. Strain, and Roland Griffiths, 2008 Caffeinated Energy Drinks – A Growing Problem. Drug and Alcohol Dependence 99:1–10.

Ringold, Debra Jones, 2002 Boomerang Effects in Response to Public Health Interventions: Some Unintended Consequences in the Alcoholic Beverage Market. Journal of Consumer Policy 25:27–63.

Rose, Nikolas, 1999 Powers of Freedom: Reframing Political Thought. Cambridge UK: Cambridge University Press.

Rose, Nikolas, 2003 Neurochemical Selves. Society 41:46–59.

Schensul, Jean, Cristina Huebner, Merrill Singer, Marvin Snow, Pablo Feliciano, and Lorie Broomhall, 2000 The High, the Money, and the Fame: The Social Context of "New Marijuana" Use among Urban Youth. Medical Anthropology 18:389–414.

Schensul, Jean J., Mark Convey, and Gary Burkholder, 2005 Challenges in Measuring Concurrency, Agency and Intentionality in Polydrug Research. Addictive Behaviors 30(3):571–574.

Singer, Merrill, 2008 Drugging the Poor: Legal and Illegal Drugs and Social Inequality. Prospect Heights IL:Waveland Press.

Singer, Merrill, and Greg Mirhej, 2004 The Understudied Supply Side: Public Policy Implications of the Illicit Drug Trade in Hartford, CT. Harvard Health Policy Review 5(2):36–47.

Singer, Merrill, Greg Mirhej, Claudia Santelices, Erica Hastings, Juhem Navarro, and Jim Vivian, 2006 Tomorrow is Already Here, Or Is It? Steps in Preventing a Local Methamphetamine Outbreak. Human Organization 65(2):203–217.

Singh, Ilina, 2004 Doing Their Jobs: Mothering with Ritalin in a Culture of Mother-blame. Social Science and Medicine 59:1193–1205.

Smardon, Regina, 2007 "I'd Rather Not Take Prozac": Stigma and Commodification in Antidepressant Consumer Narratives. Health 12(1):67–86.

Snelders, Stephen, Charles Kaplan, and Toine Pieters, 2006 On Cannabis, Chloral Hydrate, and Career Cycles of Psychotropic Drugs in Medicine. Bulletin of the History of Medicine 90:95–114.

Smith, Richard, 2005 Medical Journals are an Extension of the Marketing Arm of Pharmaceutical Companies. PLoS Medicine 2(5):e138.

Stromberg, Peter, Mark Nichter, and Mimi Nichter, 2007 Taking Play Seriously: Low Level Smoking among College Students. Culture, Medicine and Psychiatry 31(1):1–24.

Sung, Hung-En, Linda Richter, Roger Vaughan, Patrick B. Johnson, and Bridgette Thom, 2005 Nonmedical Use of Prescription Opioids among Teenagers in the United States: Trends and Correlates. Journal of Adolescent Health 37:44–51.

Talbot, Margaret, 2009 Brain Gain: The Underground World of 'Neuroenhancment' Drugs. The New Yorker, April 27: 32–43.

Timimi, Sami, 2004 A Critique of the International Consensus Statement on ADHD. Clinical Child and Family Psychology Review 7:59–63.

United Nations Office of Drugs and Crime, 2008 Making Drug Control Fit for Purpose: Building on the UNGASS Decade. New York: United Nations.

Van der Geest, Sjaak, Susan Reynolds Whyte, and Anita Hardon, 1996 The Anthropology of Pharmaceuticals: A Biographical Approach. Annual Review of Anthropology 25:153–178.

Vares, Tina, and Virginia Braun, 2006 Spreading the Word, but What Word is That? Viagra and Male Sexuality in Popular Culture. Sexualities 9(3):315–332.

Vivian, Jim, Hassan Saleheen, Merrill Singer, Juhem Navarro, and Greg Mirhej, 2005 Under the Counter: The Diffusion of Narcotic Analgesics to the Inner City Street. Journal of Ethnicity and Substance Abuse 4(2):97–114.

Vuckovic, Nancy, 1999 Fast Relief: Buying Time with Medications. Medical Anthropology Quarterly 13:51–68.

Wilens, Timothy E., Lenard A. Adler, Jill Adams, Stephanie Sgambati, John Rotrosen, Robert Sawtelle, Linsey Utzinger, and Steven Fusillo, 2008 Misuse and Diversion of Stimulants Prescribed for ADHD: A Systematic Review of the Literature. Journal of the American Academy of Child and Adolescent Psychiatry 47:21–31.

Williams, Simon J., Clive Seale, Sharon Boden, Pam Lowe, and Deborah Lynn Steinberg, 2008 Waking Up to Sleepiness: Modafinil, the Media and the Pharmaceuticalisation of Everyday/ Night Life. Sociology of Health and Illness 30(6):839–855.

Wolf-Meyer, M., 2009 Precipitating Pharmakologies and Capital Entrapments: Narcolepsy and the Strange Cases of Provigil and Xyrem. Medical Anthropology 28(1):11–30.

Yamaguchi, Ryoko, Lloyd D. Johnston, and Patrick M. O'Malley, 2003 Relationship Between Student Illicit Drug Use and School Drug-Testing Policies. Journal of School Health 73(4):159–164.

Yates, W. R., P. J. Perry, and K. H. Andersen, 1990 Illicit Anabolic Steroid Use: A Controlled Personality Study. Acta Psychiatrica Scandinavica 81:548–550.

FURTHER READING

Anderson, Ben, 2004 Time-Stilled Space Slowed: How Boredom Matters. Geoforum 35:739–754.

Harvey, David, 1989 From Fordism to Flexible Accumulation. In The Condition of Postmodernity: An Inquiry into the Conditions of Cultural Change. pp. 141–172. Oxford: Blackwell.

McCabe, Sean E., 2005 Correlates of Nonmedical Use of Prescription Benzodiazepine Anxiolytics: Results from a National Survey of US College Students. Drug and Alcohol Dependence 79:53–62.

Robison, Linda M., David A. Sclar, Tracy L. Skaer, and Richard S. Galin, 1999 National Trends in the Prevalence of Attention-Deficit/Hyperactivity Disorder and the Prescribing of Methylphenidate among School-Age Children: 1990–1995. Clinical Pediatrics 38:209–217.

Sussman, Steve, Mary Ann Pentz, Donna Spruijt-Metz, and Toby Miller, 2006 Misuse of "Study Drugs": Prevalence, Consequences, and Implications for Policy. Substance Abuse Treatment, Prevention, and Policy 1:15.

Werch, Chudley E. and Deborah M. Owen, 2002 Iatrogenic Effects of Alcohol and Drug Prevention Programs. Journal of Studies on Alcohol 63:581–590.

Whyte, Susan Reynolds, Sjaak Van der Geest, and Anita Hardon, 2002 Social Lives of Medicines. Cambridge UK: Cambridge University Press.

Zaje A.T. Harrell, and Clifford Broman, 2009 Racial/Ethnic Differences in Correlates of Prescription Drug Misuse among Young Adults. Drug and Alcohol Dependence 104:268–271.

CHAPTER 18

Anthropology and the Study of Illicit Drug Use

J. Bryan Page

BACKGROUND

Although medical anthropology as a formal subdiscipline was neither conceived nor launched with the issue of drugs in the forefront of early conversations among the founding mothers and fathers, drugs, because of their salience in Western societies and their growing importance elsewhere in the world, soon became the focus for growing numbers of medical anthropologists. Most of the early discussions of how to frame medical anthropology took place in the late 1960s, featuring Hazel Weidman, Stephen Polgar, David Landy, Dorothea Leighton, George Foster, Marvin Opler, and Otto Von Mering, among others, and the participants were busy formulating approaches to traditional healing practices and biomedical institutions as well as the interfaces between the two. They did not explicitly attend to the specific issue of drug use, nor could they be expected to have done so, given their own interests. Some anthropologists had focused on drug use in non-Western cultural contexts, including Lowie's classic study of tobacco societies among the Crow (1919), LaBarre's studies of (and advocacy for) peyote use (1951), and Schultes' accumulating compendium of herbal exotica from all over the Americas (Schultes 1976; Schultes and Hoffman 1991), but these studies had not been counted among anthropological efforts to understand health-related behavior. At the time that the founders were conceiving of medical anthropology, Marlene Dobkin de Rios was conducting her field work in eastern Peru, where shamanistic use of the concoction called ayahuasca was intended to help patients discover the source of their illness through visions induced by a combination of the biochemicals harmaline and dimethyltryptamine (DMT). Carlos Castaneda had just published his influential dissertation (1968) on indigienous drug

A Companion to Medical Anthropology, First Edition. Edited by Merrill Singer and Pamela I. Erickson.

use in Mexico, which came to be seen as a classic fable of culture contact, rather than a rigorous ethnography. Evidence was accumulating that health seeking and drug taking are inextricably linked in both non-Western and Western cultural contexts, and the new subdiscipline of medical anthropology would soon find that some of its proponents wanted to concentrate their research on drug use of various kinds.

The publication of books such as Castaneda's *The Teachings of Don Juan* (1968), Dobkin de Rios' *The Healing Vine* (1971) and Michael Agar's *Ripping and Running* (1973) demonstrated that these kinds of studies had an audience, both among academics and the reading public. The latter book had an impact that helped to build a new group of medical anthropology researchers because it provided evidence in support of some bureaucrats' opinion that ethnography was an important new tool in the effort to understand, prevent, and treat health and social problems related to misuse of drugs. At the National Institutes of Health (NIH), one bureaucrat in particular, Eleanor Carroll, had advocated for ethnographic approaches to studying drug use, pushing for ethnographic studies of Cannabis outside of the USA and studies of illicit drug use within the country. Agar's book succeeded in convincing her colleagues of the value of supporting additional studies of this nature, focusing on the behaviors of active drug users in their natural social settings. Carroll's energetic pursuit of ethnographic studies succeeded in establishing a niche for them in the newly formed entity, the National Institute on Drug Abuse (NIDA), which ultimately became one of the formal institutes of the National Institutes of Health. Extramural grant review panels at NIDA included anthropologists from their inception, and grant applications received helpful, supportive reviews from these committee members, sometimes over the objections of their quantitatively inclined colleagues.[1]

The staff of the NIDA knew that their efforts to understand illicit drug use faced a dilemma, because the active epidemic of illicit drug use was not amenable to the usual epidemiologic techniques for studying outbreaks of disease. Because the term "illicit drugs" contains words that have much social and cultural value loading, it needs a clear definition. . The term "illicit drug" will appear in this chapter to denote any of a set of preparations (see Page 1999) that can be applied to or ingested into the human body, that change the state of the body and possibly affect behavior, and that are prohibited by the laws of the polity in which the drug's consumers live. This definition is broad enough to cover different forms of consumption and widely variable effects and impacts. The policy decisions that define drugs as illicit are purely acts of the polities' governing bodies, and cannot be reified into any valid assessments of the health risks incurred by using these drugs. As obedient bureaucracies often do, the NIDA was trying very hard to wage the "war on drugs" declared by Richard Nixon in 1974 by finding out how much damage could be attributed to their use. It therefore behooved the agency to leave no stone unturned in the quest for the best sources of information. Ethnographic studies carried out by anthropologists and/or sociologists proved themselves to be very rich sources of information about worlds unknown to the NIDA bureaucrats. At the same time, they ultimately helped to fuel criticism of the "war on drugs" from the formulation of its objectives to the nature of its impact on society.

NIDA's receptivity to ethnographic studies originated when its staff were still part of the Alcohol, Drug Abuse and Mental Health Agency (ADAMHA) segment of the NIH, which funded the original Cannabis projects in Jamaica (Rubin and Comitas 1975),

Costa Rica (Carter et al. 1980) and Greece (Stephanis et al. 1977). The first two of these studies relied heavily on ethnographers, while the third did not. Additional studies involving the ethnography of drug use received support from the NIDA from the inception of that Institute, including additional studies of Cannabis in Costa Rica and Jamaica and the first studies of street-based drug use in the United States. Agar also received a K (supported investigator) award on the strength of his early work in studying heroin users.

ACADEMIC HUNTING-AND-GATHERING

At this juncture (about 1978) in the last quarter of the 20th century, employment for anthropologists and sociologists in academic posts was becoming scarce, and the disciplines tended to favor areas of interest that were consistent with traditional departmental offerings. Courses on the anthropology of drug use were only available at Harvard (offered by Schultes' classes) and the sociology of drug use might have been offered at the University of Kentucky (O'Donnell's class), but they were hardly staples of anthropological or sociological curricula. This circumstance created a time in the late 1970s when a number of developing scholars had, if they wanted to continue doing research on the topic of drug use, to avail themselves of grant funding to remain gainfully employed doing work that truly interested them. Fortunately for these scholars, the NIDA had notable receptivity to their applications to conduct research on drug use. To live from grant to grant was not as stable and secure as having a tenure bearing, "hard money" line in a traditional academic department, but it proved to afford its own rewards. Funded investigators could wield a modicum of power in their home institutions, and the funding agencies solicited their help in reviewing grants and refining the scientific issues in their lines of research. Additionally, once funded they had considerable flexibility and often had funds for assistants, research equipment, and for conference and research travel, resources that became increasingly scarce among academic researchers without external funding.

Once an investigator had succeeded in obtaining grant funding, the possibility of continued funding opened up as the individual developed the requisite skills for building a research program. Among these skills were (1) knowledge of the language with which to frame a research idea clearly, (2) vision to recognize a gap or lacuna in the existing literature in need of filling, (3) proficiency in using the methods necessary to collect and analyze the data that are collected, and (4) resourcefulness in finding outlets for disseminating study results, particularly in peer-reviewed journals.

Merrill Singer's journey into the land of research grants exemplifies the experience of drug researchers who received doctoral degrees in the late 1970s. As he was graduating in 1979 the job market in academia had become extremely difficult, and even though he had not focused on drug studies as a student, he was accepted into a postdoctoral fellowship at George Washington University Medical School in "family factors in alcoholism." This opportunity allowed him to conduct beginning research and continue to formulate the theoretical approach that he would subsequently use in a highly productive career as a researcher in studies of both legal and illicit drug use. After the post-doctoral experience, and a brief period as a visiting assistant professor, tenure-track academic jobs were still rare and hard to land. By way of a second postdoctoral fellowship he was able to find employment in a community-based health research and service organization (CBO) called the Hispanic Health Council. He remained in this position for more than 25 years, becoming the director of research, writing grant applications, and conducting applied community-based research.

In this author's case, again, the academic jobs in 1976 were not abundant, and I applied for a postdoctoral fellowship at the Gainesville Veterans Administration Hospital (GVAH) for the purpose of developing quantitative research skills that would complement ethnographic skills already elaborated in a study of Costa Rican marihuana users. My partner in the field in Costa Rica, Bill True, had been in Miami working for a large epidemiologic project there. As my postdoctoral work ended, he decided to leave Miami (in pursuit of a Masters in Public Health) after receiving a fundable score on a grant application to study drug use among Cubans. I applied for that open position and began what was to be a sixteen-year exercise in academic "hunting-and-gathering" as a research faculty member. The contents of this chapter reflect the accumulated perspectives on illicit drugs that evolved among anthropologist drug researchers during the last quarter of the 20th century and the first decade of the 21st.

MIXED METHODS

The first lesson to the social/behavioral scientist vying to become a funded researcher was that regardless of the degree to which you actually practice, you must be conversant in quantitative methods. This exercise in language acquisition and appropriate usage has the primary function of making the researcher realize where his/her work fits in the research enterprise. Research that combines qualitative and quantitative methods has a large footprint on the conceptual landscape, because one complements the other.

The qualitative side

Inquiry in which the final product provides description of processes as they take place and theory about how those processes work is necessarily qualitative in nature. Its task is not to measure how big or widespread a behavior is, or how often it occurs in large populations. Rather, qualitative inquiry has the charge of attempting to define the extent of the cultural complex under investigation. This charge requires the investigation to focus on behaviors of interest and place them in cultural context, paying attention to relationships among components in the cultural system. The concept of redundancy is crucial to conducting this kind of study, because the investigator will inevitably reach a point in the inquiry when each new collected case sounds like one or more of the previously collected cases. Once the investigator confirms thorough redundancy in a given set of questions, the collection of new data becomes nonproductive, and therefore should be terminated.

For example, my colleague in Valencia, Jose Salazar, conducted his first observations of self-injection behavior among IDUs in that city, describing in great detail the process of obtaining the heroin, taking it to a chutadero (locale used by IDUs to inject themselves), obtaining a receptacle for receiving the drugs (in this first case, a bent soft drink can), placing the drug powder in the indentation of the can, squeezing a lemon found on the premises of the chutadero so that three or four drops fall onto the heroin, squirting water drawn into the needle/syringe drawn from a jar of water found on the premises onto the heroin and lemon juice, and stirring the mixture with the needle tip. He emailed me these notes and I immediately asked, "What about the flame?" I was referring to the procedure for "cooking" the heroin using a match or lighter. "No flame," replied my colleague. Subsequent observations yielded the same sequence, with some variants in which the injector applied vinegar rather than lemon juice. Informal interviews with the IDUs in the chutaderos elicited a consistent explanation that the lemon juice or vinegar helped to liquefy the drugs and eliminate "grumos," or crumbs. By continuing to do observations that focused on the injection behavior in cultural context, we were able to characterize a strong pattern that had not been reported before in the literature. We also analyzed responses to an open-ended question about diluents that formed part of a short-answer questionnaire administered to participants in the study, and the responses to that open-ended item strongly confirmed the observations: Valencian injectors do not "cook" heroin but add either lemon juice or vinegar (Page and Salazar 1999b). In this case, the redundancy of the observed patterns was so emphatic that the investigators quickly formed the hypothesis that lemon juice or vinegar were the only diluents other than water applied to doses of heroin. Analysis of open-ended data quickly confirmed this hypothesis.

In the parallel universe of grounded theory (see Strauss and Corbin 1992), the name for repeated encounters with the same set of patterns is called "saturation of categories," but it speaks to basically the same process presented above. The investigator makes inquiries into several cases of the complex of interest and finds that they are patterned into a limited number of variants, which are recapitulated repeatedly on extending the inquiries to more cases.

In both ethnography and grounded theory the task of the inquiry is to accomplish just that – a definition of the extent of the cultural complex. The Psychiatrist-turned ethnographer did not have to conduct a hundred observations to verify the use of lemon juice in the dissolving of heroin, because this kind of inquiry, seeking new variants of identified patterns, relies on identifying patterns and their variants. As observations continued, he/she saw few variants. To determine how widespread each variant pattern is, we would have had to take a probability sample (more on that later) of several thousand Valencian IDUs and ask them short-answer questions about their drug-using preferences. The results of the open-ended question confirmed the near universality of the practice adequately for purposes of intervention.

Much of the study of illegal drugs begins with the same starting point as the psychiatrist-turned-anthropologist, a moment of curiosity followed by the development of a strategy to find out what kinds of behaviors occur among the people with experience in that cultural complex. The informational staple of this kind of study is a combination of field observations and informal conversations with the actors in the observations, and getting into position for this kind of activity is perhaps the most difficult part of conducting ethnographies of illegal drug use. Consumers of illicit drugs are necessarily reticent when asked by a stranger (even a "professional" one; see Agar 1996) about their drug use, so it takes time and rapport building to become sufficiently trusted to be allowed to observe drug users engaged in consuming their drugs of choice. This task is most laborious if the field researcher is entering the field completely *de novo*, without having any prior presence in the community setting where the drug users live.

The researcher must spend time in the place, telling people what he/she is doing there, e.g. "I'm from the University of _____ and I'm studying people who use *name drug(s)*." A potentially off-putting self-introduction may seem counterproductive at first, because it could send users and dealers scurrying away for fear they had encountered an officer of the law. Nevertheless, after patient and repeated self-presentations in which the researcher reiterates his/her task, place of origin, and specific drug(s) of interest, eventually, someone "from the scene" will approach the researcher and gingerly begin to test whether or not that researcher is from the police. This process is likely to involve the appearance of a "mine canary," or individual who is not particularly valued by people in his/her (usually his) network of drug-related acquaintances. The other participants in the network observe what happens to the expendable character, and if nothing bad happens, they may feel emboldened to approach the researcher. Approaches lead to conversations, further "tests," and eventually, establishment of sufficient rapport to be able to hang out with drug users and watch them use their drugs, occasionally asking discreet questions about what the users' consumption of drugs does for them and to them.[2]

All the while, the field researcher is collecting field notes. The standard format of the field notes collected by an ethnographer of drug use is a prose narrative, which records some orientation features at the beginning, including date, time, and a description of the cultural surroundings. Writers of these notes have great latitude in what they include, but they are trained to focus on a specific set of behaviors, including in their notes features of the cultural context that are relevant to the central topic of the research. They are also trained to avoid making judgments or drawing conclusions as they write. Appearances can deceive, and especially in observing behavior under the influence of a drug, it is very difficult to know exactly which drug is causing the observed behavior. A somnolent person may be nodding from a recent heroin dose or dozing from sleep deprivation. Field notes describe the behavior rather than drawing conclusions. They require systematization, some form of content coding, which can be done a priori for large portions of the data to be collected. For example, it is possible to anticipate that a study of drug use will encounter information on the kinds of preparations used, how they are consumed, and in what kinds of settings, so those codes can be established before putting the study into the field. The coding system will, however, have to allow for the addition of new codes to cover the inevitable emergence of unexpected content. Again, the example of the lemon juice finding (Page and Salazar 1999b) exemplifies a new variant in drug use for which the research project had no a priori code. After this discovery, the project needed to add a code and re-code those materials that contained that kind of information but no code to mark its position in the text. Once the field researcher(s) has(ve) spent time in settings where drug users hang out and drug use related activities take place, having recorded and coded field notes, the process of qualitative analysis can begin. In this process, the investigator uses compiled and coded field notes to find patterns in content and process that can be collated and interpreted to define relationships among behaviors, cultural materials, secular conditions, temporal sequencing, and conversational assessments. The combination of field observations and informal interviews with street-based drug users enabled Koester (1994), for example, to explain why IDUs refused to carry needle/syringes on their persons, which forced them to use the needle/syringes provided by shooting galleries. Careful analysis of contexts in which IDUs operated in Hartford enabled Singer et al. (2001) to gain an understanding of violence and the part that it plays in the everyday lives of IDUs.

The ethnographic data collection and analysis in contexts of illicit drug use versus cultural contexts in which people are not engaged in socially disapproved behavior involves covert behavior, difficulty of access, potential danger both to field investigators and their contacts, and uncertainty of informant quality. First, all potential study participants are hiding their behavior from the rest of the world, and after doing this for some time they have built strategies to keep the rest of the world out of their business. Linguistic distancing (see Bourgois 2003:1977) for example, involves lexical changes that keep the outsider bewildered. Examples of this behavior include the inner city glosses used in Miami by IDUs to denote needles/syringes ("gimmicks"), black tar heroin ("black gunya"), and locales for self-injection ("get-offs"). Awareness of the lexical ins and outs of drug users' conversation can become a highly effective tool in the process of initial contact with participants in a network of drug users. Its key feature in terms of the human relations between researcher and street-drug user is that lexicon presents an opportunity to place the newly established contact into the role of mentor and instructor to the newcomer. In study after study, anthropologists who conduct research on drug users have found that the informant's act of guiding the researcher through a bewildering local lexicon of drug-related terms has cemented the rapport between the informant and the researcher. People like to have their expertise recognized and appreciated, and crafty, long-term drug users are no exception.

As rapport builds and field investigators gain access to the social settings and locales where drug-related activities take place, understanding of covert behavior increases, and so does the danger to both investigators and their contacts. In federally funded studies, the investigator has the prerogative to request a Certificate of Confidentiality from the US Department of Health and Human Services (HHS) which theoretically protects confidential data from officers of the court attempting to pursue criminal behavior. The word "theoretically" reflects the fact that while many certificates have been issued to drug researchers, as of this writing, no such certificate has ever been tested in court. Other aspects of danger include the risk that police will detain the field worker's contacts just because they know what the researcher is studying, the risk that the field worker will be arrested with the drug users being studied, and the risk that the drug user's dealer will accuse the researcher of divulging information to the police. The first is potentially very damaging to the study, because subsequent contacts may refuse further interaction with the researcher. The second may not be a terrible thing, because the shared experience will help convince any doubters among the drug users that the researcher is not a "narc" (narcotics officer), and the researchers should get some excellent field notes, providing perspective on the arrest process. The third risk is potentially fatal, because street drug dealers tend to be defensive and not very patient (see Bourgois 2003:22). *In Search of Respect* (Bourgeois 2003) includes an account of an incident in which, as a young researcher, Bourgois attempted to ingratiate himself with a dealer in the context of a corner conversation by handing him a newspaper article in which Bourgois had been interviewed about his work. Unbeknownst to Bourgois, the dealer did not know how to read, and this incident led to a later threat against the eventuality of Bourgois divulging some fact about the dealers business: "Felipe, let me tell you something, people who get other people busted – even if it's by mistake – sometimes get found in the garbage with their heart ripped out and their bodies chopped up into little pieces ... or else maybe they just get their fingers stuck in electrical sockets. You understand what I'm saying?" (Bourgois 2003:22).

Upon reflection, the dealer recognized that the appearance in the newspaper was potentially a threat to his business, and he warned, not against embarrassing him again, but against further appearances in the news media.

Regarding veracity and reliability of information gathered from key informants in street settings, if researchers relied solely on what their informants told them about what they did, the collected information may be worth little. In street ethnography of illicit drug use, however, the researchers position themselves in the places where the drug users are consuming drugs. A well trained ethnographer will quickly (and diplomatically) question a user's response that does not correspond with what he/she has seen the user doing. In fact, because the user knows that the researcher has been watching and learning, this kind of discordance is fairly rare in ethnographic research, as long as the interview takes place after the field observations. When the interview has taken place first, the respondent may have no idea that the interviewer could be out watching what he/she does, and he/she may have other reasons for misrepresenting his/her actions. For example, after accompanying a key informant to a Miami get-off house (shooting gallery), Page (1993) observed the informant taking a needle/syringe from the coffee can where the house's paraphernalia were stored, yet in a previous interview, the individual had stated that he only used new needles. When Page asked him about this he replied, "But it *was* new!" When drug ethnographers write about triangulation (cf. Bluthenthal 1995), this concordance between self-report and observed behavior is part of what they mean. They also point to the use of extant data sets to enhance understanding of key behavior patterns and population characteristics.

This discussion leads logically into the consideration of quantitative methods in the study of illicit drugs. Especially in the study of these kinds of behaviors, qualitative and quantitative methods are inexorably interrelated. Characteristics of the illicit drug-using populations place severe limitations on what the quantitative researchers can find out by using their methods. The qualitative side has covered questions of access and reliability and veracity of information. In the quantitative side lie additional potentials and capabilities.

The quantitative side

Once the qualitative researchers have gained access to drug using-populations, determined the drugs used, described how they are used, and developed a general understanding of what drug use means to the users, the quantitative side of the investigation still has much to do.[3] The qualitative inquiry, because of its limited size, cannot determine how widespread any of the characterized behaviors are, or the distribution of the various behaviors among users of different demographic types. To obtain this level of information, the quantitative component of a study or research center must develop a strategy for gathering data from the same reticent population of drug users. That reticence is salient in the collection of short answers to large numbers of questions, because the content of the questions is potentially threatening to the privacy of the respondent, and using the standard procedure of selecting households according to the canons of probability sampling (as in Vaillant and Dorfman 2000), the interviewer who shows up at the door of a household to ask questions about drug use has little hope of establishing sufficient rapport to elicit truthful answers from the person who answered their knock or ring of the doorbell. The inferential dilemma of the would-be surveyor in the case of collecting self-reports of illegal drug use lies in the issue of representativeness. According to Vaillant and Dorfman (2000), as well as any number of other survey sampling experts, the reason they engage in what they call "probability sampling," is to identify individuals who are representative of the total number of individuals in the sample. A probability sample is really a targeted variant of the random sample. In a random sample, the researcher attempts to give all units of analysis (usually individual persons, but sometimes households) in the population of these units theoretically equal chances of being included in the sample. A probability sample is usually parsed into socio-demographic categories, and the candidates for participation are selected randomly, that is, using a lottery-like device to select from the total pool of individuals in each category. Rigorous probability sampling can be very highly efficient at its best, with only 1 or 2% margin of error for samples of the entire United States, selecting between 800 and 1600 people to represent this population in excess of 300 million. If the pollsters who use these techniques (e.g., Gallup, Harris) are asking innocuous questions about what detergent the respondent tends to use or what the respondent thinks of the candidates in an election, they can readily achieve a high degree of accuracy.

That is not the case in drug surveys. In fact the National Household Survey on Drug Use currently uses a quasi-random sample of nearly 80,000 households, and even with a sample up to 100 times as large as the pollsters' samples, the margin of error is too great to report. This sample "over-samples" urban populations and minority populations, in part because of the abiding belief that these populations have great prevalence of drug problems. The framers of the survey recognize the problems involved in eliciting truthful information from people who are used to hiding their drug-using behavior from the rest of the world, but they do not necessarily grasp the capacity of rural and suburban non-minority drug users to conceal their drug use. Although politicians may seek to cite the statistics that are generated from the National Household Survey's data, they are not generally seen as accurate representations of the drug use patterns currently operating in the United States. The data can be useful to some extent (cf. Lai et al. 2000), however, in deriving patterns of drug use etiology.

Because rigorous probability samples do not work in the effort to elicit population-based estimates of drug use, would-be surveyors of drug use are forced to resort to other means to estimate prevalence and frequency of drug-using behavior among illegal drug users. These techniques begin with the heuristic utilization of a phenomenon that occurs naturally among illicit drug users because they need it to continue using drugs – the network of informal social relations. Most street-based studies of illicit drug users have found their way into the world of illegal drug use through obtaining introductions to an expanding web of social connections among active, street-based individuals (e.g., Carlson and Siegal 1988; Koester 1994; Page et al. 1990a,b; Singer et al. 1995; True et al. 1980). This network tracing strategy was very effective in recruitment of "the genuine article," a real drug user of the type sought by the investigator. Nevertheless, the process left those investigators who wanted to make a claim of representativeness with some misgivings about the network-based sampling scheme. To assuage their misgivings, some researchers developed hybrid strategies called variously "snowball sampling," (Biernacki 1987) or "ethnographic targeted sampling" (Carlson et al. 1994) in which the investigator used observational reconnaissance to identify zones of a community where drug-use activities have been observed and then developed a system of markers to identify the various zones by use characteristics (e.g., mixed residential and commercial, residential, commercial only, etc.), recruiting in each zone via networks among the identified drug users living there. This strategy could produce a simulacrum of a representative sample, based on the effort to draw study participants from different kinds of city zones. Nevertheless, it still does not meet the criterion of providing a fully representative sample of drug users, which, under the current legal circumstances, is not possible. "Seed" strategies for sampling drug users and other "hidden" populations have also succeeded in recruiting drug users as study participants, explicitly engaging them as recruiters of their acquaintances (Weeks et al. 2002).

In all of these variants of the network tracing strategy for identifying and recruiting active, street-based drug users into a survey study, the investigators have succeeded in recruiting large numbers of participants in various cities in the United States (Booth et al 1991; McCoy et al. 1990; Singer et al. 1991) and elsewhere in the world (cf. Finlinson et al. 1993; Page and Salazar 1999b; Singer 2008). With a system for recruitment and follow-up in place, researchers have also engaged large cohorts of street-based users into longitudinal studies (e.g., Latkin et al. 1996).

With the collection of responses to ethnographically framed survey questions in large numbers, researchers on illicit drug use, especially as related to the AIDS epidemic, have been emboldened to publish their findings in a tone that infers generalizability. The factor that enables them to have confidence in asserting their inferences is the large number of respondents that they are able to recruit. Although they have only the vaguest of estimates to define the sizes of the populations of drug users that they study, they can have confidence in their estimates of prevalence, for example (e.g., Bluthenthal et al. 2004; Friedman et al. 2006) because if one assumes that the estimated size of the total population of, say, IDUs is ten thousand, the network samples that have more than one thousand participants in them will account for as much as 10% of the total population of interest. As we have already seen, even a 1% sample of drug users is astronomic in size compared to rigorously framed probability samples. Further enhancing the inferential heft of these estimating techniques is the association of solid ethnography with the recruitment and retention of the study samples.

Most of the investigators involved in population-based studies of illicit drug use and its attendant risks will readily concede that in the study of drug using patterns, qualitative approaches cannot thrive without quantitative studies, and vice versa. Each brings an essential perspective into the study of illicit drug use, helping the other to overcome the considerable barriers and constraints that face research on this topic. What have the qualitative and combined research projects found out about their primary topic? The following section will review key findings.

WHAT WE KNOW AND HOW WE KNOW IT

Two major headings help to delineate the findings of anthropological studies of illicit drug use: consequences of drug use and socio-cultural significance of drug use. As the two headings are not mutually exclusive, some studies will have contributed both to knowledge about consequences and to theories that unify knowledge into explanatory models. Therefore, I shall proceed drug-by-drug, explaining what is known about consequences first and then presenting the socio-cultural significance of the drug according to the investigator(s). The array of drugs that I have elsewhere (Page 1999) called the "big five" will begin the list. We include two legal drugs, alcohol and tobacco, in the list, because they are not legal for one important group of consumers: children under the age of eighteen (or for alcohol, 21).

Alcohol   Because it is ubiquitous, affecting the human condition in practically every corner of the world, alcohol has come under the scrutiny of pre-anthropology scholars, early anthropologists, and current anthropologists. In this scrutiny, the anthropologists and their colleagues have described literally hundreds of different patterns of consumption, from palm wine to pulque, from gin to aguardiente. In this reportage, it has become clear that in general, distilled spirits, regardless of cultural context, carry more severe health consequences than fermented beverages. The distilled spirits' high content of alcohol (up to 97% by volume) presents toxic doses of alcohol readily to drinkers. Nevertheless, Heath's (1958) ethnography of alcohol use among the Camba in lowland Bolivia questions whether health consequences are inevitable as a result of bouts of heavy drinking.

The health consequences of illicit alcohol consumption in the United States among underage youth are demonstrable, primarily in two forms – automobile accidents and alcohol poisoning. Although the underage illicit drinkers have not been at it long enough to incur the common consequences of alcohol use such as cirrhosis and peripheral neuropathy, they are especially vulnerable to death and injury due to driving while intoxicated. Ironically, because the developed nations that have strict constraints on eligibility for driving do not as a rule allow teenagers to drive at all, they do not have the same problem as the USA in youthful intoxicated drivers, despite these countries' lenient approaches to availability of alcohol to minors. In episodes of what has come to be called "binge drinking" (Van Wersh and Walker 2009), drinkers sometimes engage in practices that lead to achieving toxic alcohol levels in the bloodstream. In extreme cases, the rapid "chugging" (gulping down as fast as possible) of distilled spirits enables the chugger to remain conscious long enough to attain lethal levels of alcohol, a toxin, in their bloodstream before passing out (Marcus 2000). Qualitative investigations of the patterns of underage drinking among student-age young people are beginning to increase as of this writing, (cf. Abbott-Chapman et al. 2008; Clapp et al. 2000; Van Wersch and Walker 2009) in Australia, the United States, and the United Kingdom, respectively, and some have attended to these health consequences (e.g., Coleman and Cater 2005; Nygaard et al. 2003). Some anthropological work on this question among African–American and Haitian youth (e.g., Strunin 1999, 2001), however, has elicited strong attitudes against drinking to the point of intoxication. Although it is prudent to meet societal cost estimates with some skepticism, the analysis conducted by Miller et al. (2006) merits notice, as it estimated nearly $62 billion in societal costs for underage drinking, primarily in the "ripple effect" of accidental injuries and deaths. All of these societal impacts are highly proximal to the behaviors that set them in motion, literally coming to pass within hours of the drinking behavior itself. In this way the social impact of underage drinking differs drastically from that of underage smoking.

Tobacco   Among all drugs, licit and illicit, tobacco has the strongest dossier in dealing death to its users, yet new users flock to it from the ranks of the very young. For the first five or six years of use, young cigarette smokers are breaking the law, and their long-term prospects give reason to believe that a subset of young smokers eventually transfer the skills learned while engaging in covert drug use to additional drug using patterns. Lai et al. (2000) found in an analysis of National Household Survey data that individuals who had begun to smoke tobacco before the age of fourteen were nine times as likely to use cocaine later in life as people who used tobacco after that age. They were also 21 times as likely to have smoked crack cocaine as their less drug-precocious peers. In a field strewn with bitter ironies, one of the most poignant belongs to tobacco use among youth: of all the drugs they may be willing to try in their drug-using careers, the one that will most likely kill them is tobacco – the one that is most accessible. Underage smokers may survive a few sorties in automobiles under the influence of alcohol or other drugs, and they may even survive a run of cocaine impairment, but if they keep smoking tobacco throughout, they are very likely to die before their time from the sequelae of tobacco smoking. Therein lies the difference between alcohol and tobacco in terms of societal impact among underage (and therefore illicit) consumers of these drugs. The health consequences of tobacco require years of chronic smoking to begin to manifest themselves in the majority of cases. This fact, coupled with the truncate life spans of humans before the 20th century shielded tobacco use from scrutiny as the serial killer that it now has been proven to be. Only when people began on average to live longer than 38 years did the full array of health damages attributable to it come to light. Medical anthropologists have been at the forefront in the latter part of the 20th and early 21st centuries in defining the broad societal impacts of tobacco use and marketing worldwide (cf. Nichter and Cartwright 1991; Stebbins 2001; Wakefield et al. 2003), taking the approach that continued aggressive marketing of tobacco is tantamount to structural violence against the world population. These and other authors' structural sensibilities are products of their experience in examining smoking behaviors at the ethnographic level in contexts around the world (Marshall 1981, 1991; Nichter 2003; Nichter et al. 2004; Page and Evans 2004; Seguire and Chalmers 2000; Singer et al. 2007). In these works, the ethnographic view of tobacco use and its uptake in culturally varied populations of young people suggests that prevention efforts that focus on individual responsibility fail to address the full array of cultural influences on smoking behavior.

Cannabis   Most controversial among the Big Five Drugs, cannabis use has been the object of social opprobrium in Western societies throughout human history. Its effects on health have been elusive, because with a background of strongly held political opinions about its effects dating back to the time of the Crusades (the other medieval ones) both "sides" have introduced "noise" to the system of assessing risks to users. It became clear in the 1970s that an individual who is intoxicated with an effective (i.e. enough to elicit a self-report of feeling "high") dose of cannabis has no more business operating an automobile or high-speed machinery than does a person intoxicated with alcohol. With regard to the other purported deleterious effects of cannabis, however, the evidence has hardly been conclusive, as testified the predominantly null results found in studies of Jamaican Cannabis users (Rubin and Comitas 1975) and of Costa Rican working class males (Carter et al. 1980).

On the question of respiratory health, it has been difficult to disentangle the effects of tobacco from those of cannabis, because the majority of cannabis users worldwide use tobacco concomitantly at more or less the same rate. Indeed, the relationship is so close that it opens the question of whether or not cannabis use increases risk of tobacco use. On the question of brain function, it is clear that several aspects are impaired during the acute effects of cannabis (yet another argument for not driving under the influence), but the residuals of those effects are extremely subtle, despite the well known tendency of delta-9 tetrahydrocannabinol (THC) to deposit in the brain and other fatty tissue (Fletcher et al. 1996). Nevertheless, it has been possible through sophisticated cognitive testing to detect subclinical differences between cannabis users and non-users.

The societal impact of cannabis use has not received the same attention from anthropologists that tobacco's impact has. It is in fact considerable. Cannabis use has, as most anthropologists working in universities can attest, become normative for a substantial subset of college students. Although these users remain relatively immune to the consequences of the drug's continued illicit status, their contemporaries in minority communities, where cannabis is a staple in the poly-drug patterns found there, are subject to arrest and imprisonment, often for possession of small amounts. This kind of action by police keeps jails and prisons full of minority youth who start criminal careers while serving time for what some scientists would class as a minor offense. Meanwhile, trafficking activities generate cash for growers and dealers throughout the world as they market a plant that will grow practically anywhere under a wide variety of conditions for as much as $800 per ounce (when sold in units smaller than one ounce). Estimates of this cash impact vary wildly, but it is at least in the tens of billions of dollars in the United States alone.

Another cost of the current US policy on cannabis can be found in the younger generations' distrust of government sanctioned efforts to prevent harmful patterns of drug use (unpublished data collected in 2001 on the University of Miami campus). The "drug education" efforts have tended to exaggerate the negative effects of cannabis on health, and because many young people find the government's "information" on cannabis to be faulty, they reject other information that may be more valid than that circulated about cannabis. This process has consequences to the public health far beyond those due to cannabis use.

The contested impact of cannabis on health notwithstanding, it is still desirable to prevent use of the drug by underage youth and anyone operating a machine because of the acute effects it exerts in the four or five hours after ingestion (Crancer et al. 1969). The current circumstance in which large numbers of youth distrust government-backed prevention efforts militates against the success of attempts to reduce harm (such as auto accidents associated with cannabis' acute effects). Therefore, the current policy in the United States, for example, is in a dilemma. If the old patterns of exaggeration and disinformation persist, then the would-be preventers will not have the opportunity to deliver effective messages against driving under the influence of cannabis.

Medical marihuana, as implemented in California, presents an intriguing but confused set of conditions. Some patients with diseases including glaucoma, asthma, cancer, fibromyalgia, and arthritis, among others, have reported mitigation of symptoms, pain, or discomfort report mitigation of their symptoms after smoking marihuana. California enacted legislation in 2002 establishing a system of licensing for the distribution of the drug to people claiming to need it to treat personal health conditions. Because the system has difficulty differentiating between the patient in medical need of the drug and the private citizen in search of a "buzz," this system has come under much criticism and it has encountered considerable resistance from the Federal Government. State Proposition 215 has survived its first test in the State Supreme Court, but more tests are in store in the push–pull between state and federal jurisdiction. Federal authorities have continued to conduct "raids" on licensed "Medical Marihuana" establishments despite the court ruling in its favor. The only ethnographic study of this phenomenon appeared in 1998 (Feldman and Mandel 1998), and its conclusions found these establishments to provide additional therapeutic help for the patients because their clienteles formed support groups. Medical marihuana "clubs" merit much more attention from ethnographers to determine their impact on surrounding communities.

Opioids   One of the most ancient of the drug alkaloids known to humankind is morphine. Its regular use leads to an inexorable craving which, if not satisfied, transforms into a sickness. Because this particular alkaloid relieves pain in the user, it has had myriad medical uses, especially after Western chemists determined how to make it water-soluble. Close examination of how people use opioids finds that the health consequences of regular use are tied primarily to the restrictions placed on them, rather than any intrinsic quality.

O'Donnell and Jones (1969) found that the dangerous practice of intravenous opioid use (morphine sulfate and heroin) grew out of tightening restrictions on prescribed opioids after World War II combined with restrictions on injection paraphernalia. The former action necessitated intravenous injection in order to feel the "jolt" associated with large intramuscular injection (the practice when access to opioids was relatively unrestricted). The latter necessitated use of contaminated paraphernalia by multiple drug injectors, because "works" (needle/syringes) were hard to come by. In both cases, the health risks emanated not from the toxic nature of the drug, but from the restrictions placed on it by the authorities. Intravenous injection requires considerably more care and concentration than intramuscular injection. In conditions where the drugs have been mixed with adulterant often in a haphazard manner, the risk of overdose is substantial, and the danger of lethal overdose is further heightened by the intravenous route of administration.

Most studies of heroin users (including Agar 1973) have focused so much on the dangers associated with the illegality of street opioid use that they have not given much attention to determining whether or not the long-term practice of taking opioids carries any serious health risks. Indeed, the risks associated with opioid injection are primarily related to infectious disease (HIV, syphilis, bacterial endocarditis, septicemia, cellulitis, and Hepatitis B and C, among others) because IDUs have limited access to needle/syringes, and also because they are given to reusing other contaminated pieces of paraphernalia (cf. Page et al. 2006).

The societal impact of opioid use appears to be strongly related to its illegality. Effectively, most adults in the developed world have had at least one exposure to legal opioids in situations of medical pain or gastric distress without any long-term use or medical sequelae as consequences of that exposure. On the other hand, street opioid users, even when they use the same preparations as the legal users (e.g. diverted Percodan or Percocet) still face problems related to injection paraphernalia and purity/potency of the drugs to be used. As with cannabis, morphine in its various guises is not especially expensive or difficult to produce (albeit more difficult than cannabis). Its price is inflated by the premium of risk that traffickers have to absorb in order to be delivered to the market. Would not the treasure being spent on enforcement and interdiction be better spent on framing effective prevention programs instead? This question is likely to re-occur as the wars on drugs drag on around the world.

Ethnographic study of opioids has taken place in India (Sharma 1996), noting a growing pattern of self-injection behavior there. Despite two decades of efforts to warn the public about the dangers of self-injection, the Canadian youth described in Roy et al.'s (2008) ethnographic account of taking up injection continue to initiate the practice. Other countries are known to have similar growth in heroin use, from Russia to China, but published articles on the ethnography of these patterns are sparse. In Western Europe and Australia, ethnographies by Albertin and Iniquez (2008), Page and Salazar (1999a,b), McElrath (2001), Gamella (1994), and Maher et al. (2007) address questions of availability of needles/syringes, impact of policy on risk behaviors, and the process of diffusion of self-injecting behavior.

Cocaine   Of all of the Big Five drugs, cocaine is by far the most seductive, earning it the street name "girl." Health consequences associated with its use include malnutrition, obsessive compulsive behavior, paranoid ideation, HIV infection, and other sexually transmitted diseases (STDs). Cocaine users may choose, as can morphine users, from three different ingestion routes: intranasal, intravenous, or smoked. Cocaine's acute effects have by far the shortest duration of any of the Big Five – not more than 20 minutes (injected or snorted) and less than five minutes for smoked cocaine base, and that, coupled with its euphoric effects, is what makes cocaine the object of the user's obsession. It is also what leads to health risks in users. If one is injecting every 20 minutes, one continues to worsen the risk of infection with each repetition using paraphernalia of unknown origin (Campbell 1990). If one is smoking at five minute intervals, the money to pay for those doses must be found quickly and efficiently – a demand that leads some women crack users into a vortex of highly frequent sexual contact, risking all manner of STDs (cf. Carlson and Siegal 1988).

Mental health aspects of cocaine use are related to obsessive compulsive behavior, usually occurring during the acute effects of the drug, but often continuing long after those effects have worn off. Paranoid ideation is possibly the most health threatening mental impact of cocaine use, because it causes users and using dealers to arm themselves and suspect everyone of treachery (Morningstar and Chitwood 1987). No drug in the pharmacopoeia except alcohol is more associated with death by gunshot wound than cocaine. The patterns of cocaine use range from only using on special occasions to taking as much as the user can get, all the time. The latter pattern is more frequent among cocaine users than for consumers of any other drug. Morningstar and Chitwood (1987) noted that with high availability, cocaine use was capable of accelerating and careening out of control relatively quickly, sometimes in as few as six weeks. This process tends to impoverish the user and alienate his/her friends and family. The process also has similar duration whether the user is a well-to-do architect or a street dealer/user.

One epidemiologic feature of cocaine presents a ray of hope in a landscape where whole countries' political and legal systems are disrupted and corrupted by the drug's popularity and high price: cocaine epidemics appear to collapse of their own weight after a decade or so. This kind of collapse occurred first in the early twentieth century (Musto 2004), and was in the process of re-occurring in the early 1980s when the advent of crack cocaine gave access to the "cocaine high" to an entirely different demographic segment in the United States. Even that epidemic collapsed by the early 1990s, leaving a residue among the marginalized poor in inner cities (Hamid 1992). Word gets around among users that cocaine use leads to ruined lives and family relations, and individuals' experiences of rapid decline and abject dependence provide aversive evidence of cocaine's dangers. The crack epidemic provided strong examples of this process, so that by 1995 in Miami, eleven years after its emergence and spread through the youth of inner city neighborhoods, the only crack users to be found in these same neighborhoods were middle-aged street people. "Crackhead" had become a derogatory term applied by young people to the demented derelicts whom the youths placed in the same category as drunken bums.

This drug's illegality, however, does not give would-be reformers an easy target for changing policy. Like the other illegal Big Five drugs, its price is wildly inflated relative to its cost of production, but reduction of that price would not diminish the danger to users appreciably. De-criminalization and controlled distribution for personal consumption could alleviate much of the corrupting influence that cocaine-related money has in countries like Colombia, Bolivia, and Peru, but users would be no less vulnerable to the patterns of accelerated use that come with high availability. During the previous epidemic, prices were reasonable according to the standards of the times (Musto 2004), but users still had financial problems because of it. The question of whether or not to decriminalize cocaine needs to be weighed at the highest levels of policy formation and guided by the very best evidence behavioral science can provide.

CONCLUSIONS

Human beings ingest myriad preparations intended to improve some aspect of their existence. Humans living in organized polities have for various reasons prohibited use and distribution of some of these preparations but have fostered and encouraged the development and marketing of others. The differentiation between condoned and prohibited drugs has never followed rational assessments of risks and benefits to the public health in association with use of any drug. Rather, the polities' attempts to control access to some drugs or prohibit certain kinds of drug use have complex backgrounds of interethnic distrust, racism, xenophobia, media hype, political resume-building, disinformation, and selective concern for health and public safety. Currently, the polities that prohibit drugs couch their primary objections to the use of illicit drugs in concerns for health and public safety, but they have not reflected on how policy came to this point, and what the alternatives might look like.

Most medical anthropologists who study illicit drugs developed their skills by exercising their abilities to analyze qualitatively the patterns of behavior practiced by active, non-incarcerated consumers of illicit drugs. In so doing, they have found that their qualitative work by itself only produced part of the understanding necessary for fully defining the phenomena under study. Quantitative researchers similarly have come to the conclusion that their surveys are insufficient to understand illegal drugs users' behavior. Therefore, combined methods, at minimum joining ethnographic and survey methods, have become the dominant form of medical anthropological research on illicit drug use.

The five major drug categories that have the broadest distribution in human populations, alcohol, tobacco, cannabis, cocaine, and the opioids have been studied to varying degrees to document the health risks that attend their use and their impact on socio-cultural systems in which they are used. Assessment of these two major concerns has tentatively concluded that, with the possible exception of cocaine, most of the health risks identified for illegal drugs are attributable to their illegal status rather than their intrinsic potential for harm. The issue of dependence provides much of the impetus for making the addictive drugs illegal.

NOTES

1   Perhaps it would be accurate to say that the review committees established a *potentially* supportive and helpful environment in which to review applications that proposed ethnographic studies. In some cases, anthropologists serving on these committees expressed more severe criticisms of their fellow anthropologists than their colleagues from other disciplines.

2   In these circumstances, especially with a *de novo* entry into a community setting, it is generally not advisable to show any interest in patterns of traffic among drug users and dealers. People have long memories regarding novel or different actors moving into their territory, and should an untoward event (e.g., arrest, rip-off, or police harassment) happen subsequent to the interloper's inquiries into trafficking activity, the witnesses to these inquiries are inclined to blame the unwanted events on the interloper, whether or not there is any connection between the two things. Therefore, I require the field workers who work for me to avoid asking informal questions about trafficking drugs, because it raises suspicions that they may be police.

3   Not all qualitative work finds its way into questionnaires and interview guides used in surveys of illicit drug users. One of the historically significant sources of tension in the early years of AIDS research among IDUs involved the refusal of some highly placed investigators in NIDA's projects on drug use and AIDS, the National AIDS Demonstration Research grouping of projects, to incorporate sufficient ethnographically derived information in the nationally approved interview instrument for assessing HIV risk among IDUs.

REFERENCES

Abbott-Chapman, J., C. Denholm, and C. Wyld, 2008 Gender Differences in Adolescent Risk Taking: Are They Diminishing? An Australian Intergenerational Study. Youth and Society 40:131–154.

Agar, M., 1973. Ripping and Running. New York: Academic Press.

Agar, M., 1996. The Professional Stranger. San Diego: Academic Press.

Albertin P., and L. Iniguez, 2008 Using drugs: The meaning of opiate substances and their consumption from the consumer perspective. Addiction Research and Theory 16(5):434–452.

Biernacki, Patrick, 1987 Snowball sampling. Sociological Methods and Research 10(2):141–163.

Bluthenthal, R. N., M. R. Malik, L. E. Grau, M. Singer, P. Marshall, and R. Heimer, 2004 Sterile syringe access conditions and variations in HIV risk among drug injectors in three cities. Addiction 99(9):1136–1146.

Booth R., S. Koester, J. Brewster, W. W. Weibel, and R. B. Fritz, 1991 Intravenous-Drug-Users and Aids – Risk Behaviors. American Journal of Drug and Alcohol Abuse 17(3): 337–353.

Bourgois, P., 2003 In Search of Respect: Selling Crack in El Barrio. 2nd Edition. Cambridge UK: Cambridge University Press.

Carlson, Robert G., and Harvey A. Siegal, 1988 The Crack Life: An Ethnographic Overview of Crack Use and Sexual Behavior among African–Americans in a Midwest Metropolitan City. Journal of Psychoactive Drugs 23(1):11–20.

Carlson, R. B., J. Wang, H. A. Siegal, R. S. Falck, and J. Guo, 1994 An ethnographic approach to targeted sampling: Problems and solutions in AIDS research among Injection drug and crack-cocaine users. Human Organization 53(3):279–286.

Castaneda, Carlos, 1968 The Teachings of Don Juan: The Yaqui Way of Knowledge. Berkeley: University of California Press.

Clapp, John D., Audrey Shilhington, and Lance B. Segars, 2000 Deconstructing Contexts of Binge Drinking among College Students. American Journal of Drug and Alcohol Abuse 26(1):139–154.

Coleman, L., and S. Cater, 2005 Underage "binge" drinking: A qualitative inquiry into motivations and outcomes. Drugs – Education, Prevention, and Policy 12(2):125–136.

Crancer, A., Jr, James M. Dille, Jack C. Delay, Jean E. Wallace, and Martin D. Haykin, 1969 Comparison of the Effects of Marihuana and Alcohol on Simulated Driving Performance Science 164(3881):851–854.

Dobkin de Rios, M., 1971 Ayahuasca, the Healing Vine. International Journal of Social Psychiatry 17(4):256–269.

Feldman, H., and J. Mandel, 1998 Providing Medical Marijuana: The importance of cannabis clubs. Journal of Psychoactive Drugs 30(2):179–186.

Finlinson, A., R. Robles, H. Colon, and J. B. Page, 1993 Recruiting and retaining out-of-treatment intravenous drug users in the Puerto Rico AIDS prevention project. Human Organization 52(2):169–175.

Fletcher, Jack M., J. Bryan Page, D. J. Francis, K. Copeland, M. J. Naus, C. M. Davis, Richard Morris, Dina Krauskopf, and Paul Satz, 1996 Cognitive correlates of chronic cannabis use in Costa Rican Men. Archives of General Psychiatry 53:1051–1057.

Friedman, Samuel R., S. Lieb, B. Tempalski, H. Cooper, M. Keem, R. Friedman, and P. L. Flom, 2006 HIV among injection drug users in large US metropolitan areas, 1998. Journal of Urban Health 82(3):434–445.

Gamella, J., 1994 The Spread of Intravenous Drug Use and AIDS in a Neighborhood in Spain. Medical Anthropology Quarterly 8(2):131–160.

Heath, D., 1958 Drinking Patterns of the Bolivian Camba. Quarterly Journal of Studies on Alcohol 19:491–508.

Hamid, A., 1992 The Developmental Cycle of a Drug Epidemic – The Cocaine Smoking Epidemic of 1981–1991. Journal of Psychoactive Drugs 24(4):337–348.

Koester, S., 1994 Copping, Running, and Paraphernalia Laws: Contextual Variables and Needle Risk Behavior among Injection Drug Users. Human Organization 53(3):287–295.

Lai, S., H. Lai, J. B. Page, and C. B. McCoy, 2000 The association between cigarette smoking and drug abuse in the United States. Journal of Addictive Diseases 19(4):11–24.

Latkin, Carl, W. Mandell, D. Vlahov, M. Oziemkowska, and D. Celentano, 1996 People and places: Behavioral settings and personal network characteristics as correlates of needle sharing. Journal of Acquired Immune Deficiency Syndromes 13(3):273–280.

Mahler, L. Li, B. Jalaludin, H. Wand, R. Jayasuriya, D. Dixon, and M. Kaldor, 2007 Impact of a reduction in heroin availability on patterns of drug use, risk behaviour and incidence of hepatitis C virus infection in injecting drug users in New South Wales, Australia. Drug and Alcohol Dependence 89(2–3):244–250.

Marcus, David L.. 2000 Drinking to Get Drunk: Campuses Still Can't Purge Binging Behavior. US News and World Report 128(12):53–54.

Marshal, Mac, 1981 Tobacco Use in Micronesia – A Preliminary Discussion. Journal of Studies on Alcohol 42(9):885–893.

Marshal, Mac, 1991 The 2nd Fatal Impact – Cigarette-Smoking, Chronic Disease, and the Epidemiologic Transition in Oceania. Social Science and Medicine 33(12): 1327–1342.

McElrath, K., 2001 Risk behaviors among injecting drug users in Northern Ireland. Substance Use and Misuse 36(14):2137–2157.

Miller, Ted, R. David, T. Levy, R. S. Spicer, and Dexter M. Taylor, 2006 Societal Costs of underage drinking. Journal of Studies on Alcohol 67(4):519–529.

Musto, David, 2004 America's first cocaine epidemic. In The American Drug Scene. J. A. Inciardi and K. McElrath, eds. pp. 225–229. Los Angeles: Roxbury Press.

Nichter, Mark, 2003 Smoking: What does culture have to do with it? Addiction 98(Supplement 1):139–145.

Nichter, Mark, and E. Cartwright, 1991 Saving children for the tobacco industry. Medical Anthropology Quarterly 5(3):236–256.

Nygaard, Peter, E. D. Waiters, J. Grube, and D. Keefe, 2003 Why do they do it? A qualitative study of adolescent drinking and driving. Substance Use and Misuse 38(7): 835–864.

O'Donnell, J., and Jones, J. P., 1968 Diffusion of Injection Techniques among Narcotic Addicts in the USA. Journal of Health and Social Behavior 9(1):120–130.

Page, J. B., 1993 I'm Protected Somehow: Discrepancies between Knowledge and Action in HIV Prevention. Paper presented at the Annual Meeting of the Society for Applied Anthropology, San Antonio, Texas, March 17–22.

Page, J. B., 1999 Historical Overview of Other Abusable Drugs. In Prevention and Societal Impact of Drug and Alcohol Abuse. R. T. Ammerman, P. J. Ott and R. E. Tarter, eds. pp. 47–63. Mahwah NJ: L. Erlbaum Associates.

Page, J. B, and Sian Evans, 2003 Cigars, cigarillos, and youth: Emergent patterns in subcultural complexes. Ethnicity in Substance Use 2(4):63–76.

Page, J. B., and J. Salazar, 1999a Lemon Juice as a Solvent for Heroin in Valencia, Spain (letter). Substance Use and Misuse 34(8):1193–1197.

Page, J. B., and J. Salazar, 1999b Needle Use in Miami and Valencia: Observations of High and Low Availability. Medical Anthropology Quarterly 13(4):413–435.

Page J. B., P. C. Smith, and N. Kane, 1990a Shooting Galleries, their Proprietors, and Implications for Prevention of AIDS. Drugs and Society 5(1–2):69–85.

Page J. B., D. D. Chitwood, P. C. Smith, N. Kane, and D. C. McBride, 1990b Intravenous Drug Abuse and HIV Infection in Miami. Medical Anthropology Quarterly 4(1):56–71.

Page, J. B., P. Shapshak, E. M. Duran, G. Even, I. Moleon-Borodowski, and R. Llanusa-Cestero, 2006 Detection of HIV-1 in Injection Paraphernalia: Risk in an Era of Heightened Awareness. AIDS Patient Care 20(8):576–585.

Roy, E., E. Nonn, and N. Haley, 2008 Transition to injection drug use among street youth – A qualitative analysis. Drug and Alcohol Dependence 94(1–3):19–29.

Schultes, Richard Evans, 1976 Hallucenogenic Plants. New York: Golden Press.

Schultes, Richard Evans, and Albert Hoffman, 1991 The Botany and Chemistry of Hallucinogens. Springfield IL: Charles C. Thomas Publisher.

Seguire, M., and K. I. Chalmers 2000 Late adolescent female smoking. Journal of Advanced Nursing 31(6):1422–1429.

Singer, M., 2008 Drugs and Development: Global Impact on Sustainable Growth and Human Rights. Prospect Heights IL: Waveland Press.

Singer, M., N. Romero-Daza, M. Weeks, and P. Pelia, 1995 Ethnography and the Evaluation of Needle Exchange in the Prevention of HIV Transmission. *In* Qualitative Methods in Drug Abuse and HIV Research. Elizabeth Lambert, Rebecca Ashery and Richard Needle, eds. pp. 231–257. National Institute on Drug Abuse Research Monographs No. 157. Washington: National Institute on Drug Abuse.

Singer, M., J. Simmons, M. Duke, and L. Broomhall, 2001 The Challenges of Street Research on Drug Use, Violence, and AIDS Risk. Addiction Research and Theory 9(4):365–402.

Singer, M., G. Mirhej, J. B. Page, E. Hastings, H. Salaheen, and G. Prado, 2007 Black N Mild and Carcinogenic: Cigar Smoking among Inner City Young Adults in Hartford, CT. Ethnicity in Substance Use 6(3/4): 81–94.

Stebbins, Kenyon Ranier, 2001 Going like Gangbusters: Transnational Tobacco Companies "Making a Killing" in South America. Medical Anthropology Quarterly 15(2):147–170.

Stefanis, C., R. L. Dornbush, and M. Fink, 1977 Hashish: A study of long-term use. New York: Raven Press.

Strunin, L., 1999 Drinking perceptions and drinking behaviors among urban black adolescents. Journal of Adolescent Health 25(4):264–275.

Strunin, L., 2001 Assessing alcohol consumption: developments from qualitative research methods. Social Science and Medicine 53(2):215–226.

True, W. R., J. B. Page, M. A. Hovey, and P. L. Doughty, 1980 Marijuana and User Lifestyles. *In* Cannabis in Costa Rica. W. E. Carter, M. J. Coggins and P. L. Doughty, eds. pp. 98–115. Philadelphia: ISHI Press.

Valliant, Richard, and Alan H. Dorfman, 2000 Finite Population Sampling and Inference: A Prediction Approach. New York: John Wiley & Sons, Inc.

Van Wersch, A., and W. Walker, 2009 Binge-drinking in Britain as a Social and Cultural Phenomenon: The Development of a Grounded Theoretical Model. Journal of Health Psychology 14:124–134.

Wakefield, Melanie, Brian Flay, Mark Nichter, and Gary Giovino, 2003 Effects of anti-smoking advertising on youth smoking: A review. Journal of Health Communication 8(3):229–248.

Weeks, Margaret, Scott Clair, Stephen Borgatti, Kim Radda, and Jean Schensul, 2002 Social Networks of Drug Users in High-Risk Sites: Finding the Connections. AIDS and Behavior 6(2):193–206.

FURTHER READING

Bernard, H. Russell, 1995 Research Methods in Anthropology. Walnut Creek CA: AltaMira Press.

Bourgois, P., 1998 The moral economies of homeless heroin addicts: Confronting ethnography, HIV risk, and everyday violence in San Francisco shooting encampments. Substance Use and Misuse 33(11):2323–2351.

Dobkin de Rios, M., 1970 Banisteriopsis Used in Witchcraft and Folk Healing in Iquitos, Peru. Economic Botany 24(35):296–300.

Heath, D., 1991 Continuity and Change in Drinking Patterns of the Bolivian Camba. *In* Society, Culture and Drinking Patterns Reexamined. D. Pittman and H. White, eds. New Brunswick NJ: Rutgers Center of Alcohol Studies.

Heath, D., 2004 Camba (Bolivia) Drinking Patterns: Changes in Alcohol Use, Anthropology and Research Perspectives. *In* Drug Use and Cultural Contexts: 'Beyond the West.' R. Coomber and N. South, eds. pp. 119–136. London: Free Association Books.

Lowie, Robert Harry, 1983 The Crow Indians. Lincoln NB: University of Nebraska Press.

Lowie, Robert Harry, 1919 The Tobacco Society of The Crow Indians. New York: The Trustees.

Page, J. B., 1977 Codes and communication in Costa Rican lower-class society. *In* Drugs, Rituals, and Altered States of Consciousness. B. M. DuToit, ed. pp. 207–214. Rotterdam, The Netherlands: Balkema.

Page, J. B., and P. C. Smith, 1990 Venous Envy: The Importance of Having Usable Veins. Journal of Drug Issues 20(2):291–308.

Schensul, Stephen L., Jean J. Schensul, and Margaret D. LeCompte, 1999 Essential Ethnographic Methods. The Ethnographer's Toolkit, Book 2. Walnut Creek CA: AltaMira Press.

Sharma, H. K., 2000 Sociocultural perspective of substance use in India. Substance Use and Misuse 31(11–12):1689–1714.

PART **IV** Healthwork: Care, Treatment, and Communication

CHAPTER 19

Ethnomedicine

Marsha B. Quinlan

WHAT IS ETHNOMEDICINE?

Ethnomedicine is the area of anthropology that studies different societies' notions of health and illness, including how people think and how people act about well being and healing. Medicine – like language, music and politics – is a subset of culture which is situated locally. Thus, we have British medicine, Bavarian medicine, Massai medicine, Mayan medicine, and so forth. Each society has its own medical style, or medical culture. Beliefs about the body and illness causation, together with societal norms concerning when, why, and who to seek for medical help comprise one's "culture of medicine," or ethnomedicine. Although related societies may share some ethnomedical beliefs, just as linguistic dialects and political circumstances even of close cultures may diverge, so may their medical views. It is safe to assume that there are as many unique medical perspectives, or ethnomedicines, as there are cultures and subcultures. Every society's medicine (the West included) and every type and branch of medicine is "potential fodder" for ethnomedical study (Gaines 1992; Kleinman 1980; Nichter 1992).

The term "ethnomedicine" appears in academic literature with somewhat different meanings. In the American anthropological literature, the "medicine" in "ethnomedicine" usually refers to knowledge and ideas about health and healthcare. In European and biological literature, the "medicine" tends to refer to medication or treatment practices. In fact, the English word "medicine" is not a precise term, but a general one that, in any dictionary, has several related definitions dealing with knowledge about several areas including health, the body, illness causes, prevention, diagnosis and treatment. Just as these types of knowledge are all "medicine" in the English-speaking world, so they are all ethnomedicine when describing the medicine of any particular culture.

A Companion to Medical Anthropology, First Edition. Edited by Merrill Singer and Pamela I. Erickson.
© 2011 Blackwell Publishing Ltd. Published 2011 by Blackwell Publishing Ltd.

As is typical for fields with the "ethno" prefix, ethnomedicine seeks out primarily an "emic" anthropological view, i.e. the perspective of a member of the culture being studied. Emic views are not easy for an outsider to come by because they reflect developmental experience within a particular local framework. Strangely enough, it often takes an outside vantage to clarify an emic system (much as an outside psychotherapist can help untangle patterns from the "noise" in a patient's social history). A foreign researcher who meets medical issues with an outsider's or "etic" perspective can recognize and inquire about cognitive and behavioral models that a native of the culture may take for granted or not notice. Medical anthropologists usually learn emic health views through fieldwork among people from a particular culture (for a fuller consideration of internal logic of the medical system see Spiro 1992).

Ethnomedicine has two basic goals. First, it examines the health related theories and knowledge that people inherit and learn by living in a culture. This information forms the base of a culture's medical common sense, or medical logic that people use to explain and treat their illnesses. Ethnomedicine's other goal is medical translation. We seek not only to understand the medical thinking of one group, but to compare ideas cross-culturally for regional and global understanding. Translation of ethnomedical knowledge is applicable to improve health care delivery for the group studied, or to inform alternative health practices for Western and other societies.

Translation

Ethnomedicine is a touchy subject for many. Examination of varied medical practices attracts some people and repulses others. Alien medical traditions and body image, for reasons unknown, seem to strike at the heart of our ethnocentrism – as particularly odd, wrong-headed, disgusting, or perhaps intriguing. For instance, National Geographic titled a television series that was almost entirely ethnomedical "Taboo." Anthropological translation of these "strange" emic beliefs can make them understandable etically. For Westerners the etic perspective is almost always the bioscientific one.

Browner et al. (1988) propose a way to "combine the emic perspective of ethnomedicine with the etic measures of bioscience"(p. 681). Following their methods, the researcher (1) identifies the health problem and how it is conceivably healed according to locals, (2) objectively assesses the remedy's ability to produce the emically desired effect, and (3) identifies the areas of convergence and divergence between the emic and the etic assessments. For example, these authors suggest that Aztecs envisioned some headaches as the result of a build-up of blood in the head. Many Aztec headache medicines produced nasal bleeding, which was presumably thought to release the feeling of pressure allegedly caused by the excess blood in the head. These medicines were effective in Aztec terms because they achieved the desired result (i.e., a bloody nose). From the etic perspective, Aztec medications have chemical properties capable of causing nosebleeds, though most remain scientifically undemonstrated as headache remedies (Browner et al. 1988:684).

Anthropology's tradition of moving from etic to emic inquiry perhaps obstructed the study of Western medical culture, particularly biomedicine, even though it is one of the world's many ethnomedicines. Only recently, in the late 20th century, have medical anthropologists, informed by other medical systems' perspectives, begun to study and constructively critique (or back-translate) biomedicine as an ethnomedical system (e.g., Hahn and Gaines 1985; Lock and Gordon 1988; Baer 1989; Fabrega et al. 1990; Stein and Stein 1990; Linsk 1993; Good 1998). Ethnomedical research nevertheless persists largely among foreign, minority, and underserved populations.

Knowledge of ethnomedical translation has become increasingly relevant for public health because it identifies beliefs and practices among the foreign, minority, and underserved (Nations 1986; Winch et al. 1996; Hahn 1999; Northridge and Mack 2002; Singer 1981). As mentioned, people tend to be ethnocentric about their medicine – they hold dearly to their own medical traditions. Globalization and the resulting increase in cultural contact leads to medical incongruences. Differences between groups' medical thinking becomes problematic when (1) people from small-scale cultures migrate to developed areas where biomedicine dominates (Dobkin de Rios 2002), (2) illnesses spread to societies that have not experienced the illness before (Green 1999), and (3) Western medicine makes inroads to areas of the globe in which biomedical traditions are new, foreign, and in some cases suspect (Logan 1973; Rubel 1990; Quinlan 2004). Understanding ethnomedical beliefs allows researchers to become medical mediators.

EXPLANATORY MODELS

International public health research particularly embraced Arthur Kleinman's (1980) ethnomedical principle of the "explanatory model" (Coreil et al. 2000; Hooley 2007). Kleinman proposed that every illness has more than one potential cause and description. Bad health leads people to speculate about how they got sick, how it will affect them, and what they can do to make it better (Kleinman et al. 1978). People thus form an explanatory model (EM) of the illness by integrating idiosyncratic thoughts and circumstances with the popular illness ideologies of their culture (Kleinman 1980). Individuals will likely have a somewhat unique EM for each illness event. Further, a patient's EM for an illness will likely differ from his medical practitioner's EM. The closer the cultures of patient and practitioner are, the more presumed convergence in their EMs.

Culture influences construction of EMs through theories and explanatory themes and images. For example, Kleinman notes that Western EMs are filled with war metaphors (e.g., pathogens "invade," and individuals use their "defenses" to "fight," "battle," and hopefully "vanquish" disease); in contrast, Taiwanese metaphors have to do with being hit by ghosts (1980). Cultural ideas – about the nature of the body and illness, but also pervasive cultural philosophies about morality, responsibility, autonomy, powerful forces, and so forth – converge to form an ethnomedical system. This convergence of notions forms a system of "internal logic" for understanding illness. What may be a logical medical determination according to one set of beliefs may seem like a bad idea in the logic of a different ethnomedical system, because each system has its own internal logic (see Levin and Browner 2005). Explanatory models are often so intertwined with other cultural beliefs that identifying ethnomedical theories can be challenging.

Empacho, for example, is a gastrointestinal disorder recognized by Hispanics in Spain, particularly in the Valencia region (Devesa et al. 2005) and throughout Latin

America (Weller et al. 1993). Symptoms of *empacho* include a stomachache; a hard, swollen, or bloated abdomen; cramps; a lack of appetite, and sometimes diarrhea, vomiting, and lethargy (Weller et al. 1993). Mexican–Americans in Texas, Arizona, and New Mexico describe *empacho* as a bolus of food that sticks to the wall of the intestine and causes obstruction (Trotter 1985). A collaborative, multi-site study of four widespread Latino groups finds consistency in beliefs within and between groups (Weller et al. 1993). People in each group attribute *empacho* to some dietary indiscretion, including eating at the wrong time, eating too much, or eating the wrong things (such as spoiled or undercooked food or swallowing non-food items, such as chewing gum). The offending substance becomes lodged in the gastrointestinal tract and starts a blockage. Untreated empacho, may get worse, and sometimes cause death. Massage to dislodge the obstruction is a treatment in all groups (Weller et al. 1993), though regional treatments also include ingesting teas, oils, and purgatives, and dietary restrictions (Pachter et al. 1992; Trotter 1985; Weller et al. 1991). Recognition of *empacho* and its perceived cause and response has been imperative to clinician–patient understanding of gastrointestinal events in multi-cultural areas, and helped to identify toxic remedies sold and taken to treat *empacho* (Baer et al. 1998; Trotter 1985).

The remainder of this chapter introduces the range of traditional topics that have provided a framework for ethnomedical inquiry. Though separated here for the sake of clarity, in real life, the topics comprise conjoined entities in ethnomedical systems.

Ethnomedicine of the body

Body image Across the world, people have different conceptions about the body that anthropologists refer to as "body image" (Fisher and Cleveland 1958). The culture in which we grow up teaches us how to perceive variations that exist between different body types, ages of bodies, states of health, and public or private status of certain body parts or body functions (Helman 2001). Cultures have various norms about who can stand near or touch someone else's body under what circumstances, and ideals of how a beautiful body should look – for example, the amount of fat or muscle preferred, and the propriety of type of clothes or body decoration (jewelry, tattoos, etc.).

Many peoples regard a person's body, not only as an assemblage of physical parts, but as a whole person with social needs, obligations, a reputation to uphold, and a history of various "embodied" lessons and experiences (see Csordas 1994, Finkler 1994, and Scheper-Hughes and Lock 1987 for detailed theoretical discussion of the body as a broad personal concept). Body image may extend beyond the physical body and include obligations to community and family, which can result in concepts of illness that may seem to outsiders to have complex or tangential origins. For example, Kulina infants (Western Amazonia) do not have a body/person of their own and remain as extensions of their parents until they are walking, talking, and eating for themselves. By Kulina internal logic then, the dependant child can be affected by what both parents ingest (Pollock 1996).

Ethnophysiology "Ethnophysiology" (a.k.a. "ethnoanatomy") is the type of body image that refers specifically to cultural notions about body structure and function including perceptions of internal organs and their purpose and placement. Knowing local theories of anatomy and physiology can be key to learning how people in a culture perceive and respond to health issues. Some ethnophysiological ideas appear cross-culturally (Erickson 2008), others are confined to single cultures or to groups of related cultures, as with *empacho* among Hispanics.

Some ethnophysiological theories appear worldwide. For example, there is a globally widespread vision of how menstruation works. Menstruation is a cross-cultural sign of fertility, which is valued the world over; yet nearly all cultures have menstrual taboos (Buckley and Gottlieb 1988). Those prohibitions relate to a nearly worldwide ethnophysiological theory in which peoples tend to view the uterus as a "mechanical" opening and closing vessel-type organ (Hanson 1975) (sometimes referenced with similar opening and closing metaphors such as a flower among the Santal (Carrin-Bouez and Beierle 1998)). In this view, a woman's uterus remains closed for most of the month while blood enters it, and gets trapped. Then, the uterus opens during menstruation, allowing the blood to escape. By this time, the blood is reckoned rotten or polluted – and polluting to others. Some cultures believe that the old blood is bad for the woman herself, for example the Welsh (Skultans 1970) and Iranians (Good 1980). For example, some Welsh women feel "bloated and sluggish" if their menstruation is insufficient to give them a "good clearance" (Skultans 1970). Women in provincial Iran believe that blood that does not escape the body through a heavy period remains in the body causing headaches, joint pain, and darkened skin. Iranians employ cupping and bleeding to extract polluted menstrual blood that remains in the body (Good 1980:149). Menstrual blood is commonly reckoned as polluting to others and avoided. Hundreds of Washington State University students inform me that they feel somewhat uncomfortable even hearing particulars about another's menstrual blood let alone touching it (asking if they would touch it generates disgust-induced laughter and occasional sneers from my students). In South Kanara, India, menstrual blood is taboo not only because it is impure, but because "it is so heating that it could …dry a man's semen, just as the touch of a menstruating woman was heating enough to cause a vine of cooling betel leaves to wilt" (Nichter and Nichter 1996:5). Cultural restrictions on menstruation may range from avoiding food prepared by menstruating women, as in Jamaica (Sobo 1993), women sleeping on separate bedding from their husbands, as in Sri Lanka (McGilvary 1982) to living in designated "menstrual huts," as do the Dogon (Strassman 1992).

Ethnophysiology of the "mechanical uterus" not only explains ubiquitous social restrictions regarding menstruating women as polluting, but influences peoples' concepts regarding fertility and its regulation (Nichter and Nichter 1996). According to this common ethnophysiology, the time that a women may logically become pregnant is while the uterus is reckoned opening and closing before and after menstruation; meanwhile, a woman cannot become pregnant in the middle of her menstrual cycle, because the uterus is considered sealed off. This notion opposes the biological model of the female fertility cycle. So, in the poorest and most rural areas, where birth control is often inaccessible, this ethnophysiology of fertility results in a practiced "rhythm method" (e.g., Maynard-Tucker 1989) that is even less reliable then the biomedically informed version. Further, where birth control is available, women may fear reduced menstrual flow associated with contraceptive use, feeling that they are not properly purging noxious waste from their bodies (de Bessa 2006; Good 1980; Nichter and Nichter 1996; Snow and Johnson 1977).

Spiritual or personalistic and naturalistic explanations   Even though each medical culture is unique, some ethnophysiological principals appear in many ethnomedical systems. In a cross-cultural ethnomedical study, Erickson (2008) found that world ethnomedicines recognize only four basic domains of disease causation: (1) the individual body, (2) the natural world, (3) the social and economic world, and (4) the spiritual world. Plus, within the above areas, there are just three theories for why sickness occurs: (1) imbalance, (2) natural process, and (3) as punishment.

Foster (1976) split disease causation into only two sorts: naturalistic and personalistic. *Naturalistic* illnesses result from exposure to naturally occurring risks in one's environment. This may include germ theory, or a similar contagious notion of "bad air" found in many places, starvation, injury, and being out of balance. *Personalistic* illnesses are those that are blamed on the supernatural intervention of another – be that a human (i.e., witch or sorcerer) or non-human (i.e., a god, ghost, evil spirit, etc.). The sick person with a personalistic illness is not the victim of chance, fate, or the random act of an evildoer. Rather, some existing personal conflict between the perpetrator and his/her victim motivates the evildoer to inflict sickness on an enemy. In Erickson's scheme, Foster's personalistic illnesses would be those explained as punishment by the spiritual world, which may also be motivated by perceived injustices in the social and economic world.

There is some variation in the supposed degree of intent of those who cause personalistic illnesses. For example, Navajo Indians sometimes feared that they were guilty of unconscious witchcraft if they had entertained "bad thoughts" about someone who subsequently died or became ill (White 1930). Similarly, in notions of the "evil eye" (found in Europe, the Middle East, North Africa, and Latin America) a person who possesses the "evil eye" is usually unaware of his/her supernatural powers to curse or inflict sickness on people whom he/she envies or admires (Helman 2001). In these cases the curse may be unintentional, but the conflict between individuals still motivates the perpetrator. Victims of personalistic illness can also vary. For example, a perpetrator might cast an illness not on his enemy but on one of the enemy's loved ones. Anthropologists categorize all sicknesses that locals attribute to conflict-driven supernatural intervention as personalistic illnesses (Foster and Anderson 1978). Unlike a cold that people can trace as it runs through a community, arthritis that occurs with aging, or an injury that has an obvious origin, there is a mysterious and invisible aspect to personalistic illness. Though most cultures do not separate the body and the mind, invisible, brain-related illnesses like seizures and mental illnesses are often assigned to personalistic, spiritual causes, as are those of internal organs.

Humoral explanations: balance   Western cultures are not alone in believing that a well-balanced lifestyle yields a healthy mind and body. Many peoples strive for a "balanced" diet, and some harmony between work and play, rest and exercise, and so forth. In humoral medicine, the most widely known medical belief system in the world (Anderson 1987), people maintain or restore wellness by balancing opposite forces (humors) such as heat and cold, or dryness and wetness. The Chinese forces of yin and yang comprise a humoral system. The South Kanaran Indian characterization of menstrual blood as extremely "heating" is similarly part of the Indian humoral system (Nichter and Nichter 1996).

Latin Americans also have a hot/cold humoral system, which Foster claims may be "the most completely described of all ethnomedical systems" (1994:2). In the hot/cold humoral system, people group mental and physical states, plants, and animals into "hot" and "cold" categories. Here, "cold" or "hot" may refer to the temperature of air or bathing water; however "hot" and "cold" often refer to culturally ascribed symbolic values having nothing to do with thermal state. North Americans similarly refer to chili peppers as "hot" regardless of the temperature at which they are served. Mental states also carry hot or cold labels. The North American view of anger as hot-headedness and indifference as coldness reveals a glimpse of similar symbolic use of heat and cold. People that live by the hot/cold humoral system, believe that the *human* body functions best at a warm state that is in between hot and cold extremes, but that *other* species (plants and animals) function at species-specific hotter and colder states. Heat and cold are reckoned as being transferable: not only can temperatures in the physical environment be absorbed or transferred to the internal and external body, but one can also transfer the humoral quality of something one ingests to one's own body. Becoming too hot or cold can make one sick. People must therefore balance the hot or cold humoral qualities of the foods they eat, and counter humoral forces from the environment and emotions with foods and drinks with the opposite humoral force. Thus, a Dominican who has been working in the hot sun or has experienced a "hot" anger episode (as aggressor or the attacked) must ingest cooling foods such as cucumber and cooling drinks such as coconut water. In humoral systems, illnesses both result from hot/cold imbalances and also are ascribed hot and cold states. Hot illnesses require cold medicines while hot medicines treat cold illness.

Ethnomedicine of the mind: ethnopsychiatry

Ethnopsychiatry is a translational field that examines cultural views on mental illness, and local practices surrounding mental illnesses. Ethnopsychiatry forms a bridge between and fits equally within the purview of both medical anthropology and psychological anthropology. In fact, many peoples of the world do not to separate the processes of the mind and body.

Western Civilization has an ancient, continual habit of separating out stuff that one can see from stuff that one cannot. This idea goes back at least as far as Plato and is also termed "mind-body dualism" and "Cartesian dualism" (for René Descartes, who refined the theory in 1641 (Kenny 1968)). Western culture separates the natural from the supernatural, and the world of ideas and actions from the physical (visible, touchable) world. European languages, for example, have separate terms for the "brain," which is a physical body-part, and the "mind," which is not a body-part (but rather an amorphous brain-based center for thought, perception, emotion, memory, will, and imagination). Like larger Western culture, academic structures distinguish mental from physical, mind from body. For example, anthropology itself traditionally splits Cultural Anthropology, which deals with human behaviors and ideas (minds), from Physical (now Biological) Anthropology, which deals with human bodies. Biomedicine conventionally divides pathologies into mental illness and physical disease. Not surprisingly then, "ethnopsychiatry," which focuses on mental health and mental illness, is somewhat separate from ethnophysiology and the larger ethnomedicine. The area of ethnopsychiatry lets us translate between the biomedicine and ethnomedicine of mental health.

Human brains are essentially the same across the globe, yet mental illness varies with cultures. The language used to express troubles, the experience of symptoms, decisions about treatment, doctor–patient interactions, the practices of care providers, and the likelihood of outcomes such as suicide are all cultural. Culture shapes mental illness in three ways including recognition of an illness, how a problem is expressed, and whether or the degree to which illness manifests at all. As a result, there are worldwide differences in the recognitions and content of mental illness with some conditions appearing universal and some appearing culturally distinct (Kleinman 2004).

Culture and recognition of mental illness   In order for someone to be recognized as ill, he or she must be considered abnormal in the home culture. What might be expected in one culture is deviant in another because norms of behavior, thinking, and feeling vary from culture to culture. Some cultures seem shier, some more strident; some are more violent while others are gentler; some tolerate complaining more than others, and so forth. What might be considered normal drinking in one culture, for example, might be considered pathological in another. Body pain, may or may not be recognized as illness at all, and may or may not be regarded as a sign of emotional troubles. Back pain, for example, is regarded as pathological among some, but it is common, often expected, and rarely considered pathological among the world's laborers (e.g., Goldsheyder et al 2004).

Culture and expression of mental illness   In some societies, illnesses associated with mood or emotion may be expressed largely or only as physical rather than mental symptoms (e.g., back pain, as above). Cross-culturally, the majority of patients in care for major depression (70–80%) first present with somatic (not emotional) complaints (Ebert and Martus 1994). Depressed Chinese people, for example, do not initially seek help for mood troubles; rather they express body discomfort, pain, feelings of inner pressure, dizziness, and fatigue (Kleinman 2004). As most people do not have mind–body dualism, the feedback between physical and emotional problems is recognized and expressed as a single illness. (This is somewhat different than the psychiatric concept of somatization – expression of psychological conflicts with physical symptoms – which implies that the real problem is largely emotional.) Psychological stress generates physical reactions (e.g., muscle contraction) and back pain corresponds to distress, depression, anxiety, and related emotions (Linton 2000). Thus, though laborers may expect back pain due to musculoskeletal stress, back pain may also be a culturally acceptable expression of laborers' culturogenic stress, including working under several bosses, job insecurity, and relative poverty.

Culture shapes the expression of illness etiologies as well as symptoms. In a cross-cultural sample of traditional cultures, hostile social cognition results in accusations and fear of sickness caused by witchcraft (Quinlan and Quinlan 2007), whereas in industrial societies we would expect other routes for hostile social cognition such as hatemongering or unwarranted litigation.

Culture-bound syndromes (CBSs) are mental or behavioral disorders that only occur, or occur in a unique form, within a single culture or constellation of cultures. Within a CBS's home society, the syndrome is a deviant but recognized condition. These conditions are distinctively shaped by local cultural and social contexts, such that Helman (2001) notes that CBSs might also be termed "context-bound disorders."

Table 19.1 Notable culture-bound syndromes.

Syndrome (location)	Description
Amok (Malaysia)	A spree of killing and destruction (as in the expression "run amok") followed by amnesia or fatigue
Dhat (India)	Fear of semen loss through premature ejaculation or leakage into urine
Koro (Asia, including China, Thailand, and India)	Males and occasional females with great anxiety believe that their genitals are shrinking and retracting inside of their body cavity and are bound to kill them by strangling internal organs
Latah (Indonesia and Malaysia)	Highly exaggerated responses to startling including suggestibility and imitative behavior
Pibloktoq, Arctic hysteria (Inuits within the Arctic Circle)	Fatigue, depression, or confusion, followed by a "seizure" of unruly behavior including tearing off clothes, frenzied running, rolling in snow
Susto or *espanto* (Latin America)	Perceived "soul loss" induced by a severe fright to the victim or a friend or relative, which results in diverse and chronic complaints including agitation, anorexia, insomnia, fever, diarrhea, depression, and shyness

Source: The World Health Organization, Geneva, ICD-10, Annex 2. Culture-specific disorders, in The ICD-10 Classification of Mental and Behavioural Disorders: Diagnostic Criteria for Research, Finerman, R., pp. 176–187, 1993.

CBSs are a traditional topic of ethnopsychiatry (and are also termed ethnic psychoses, "culture-specific" disorders, psychoses, or syndromes, and cultural idioms of distress).

An example from the English-speaking world is our folk diagnosis of the "crazy cat lady." In contrast to many parts of the world, Anglophone cultures have a tradition of keeping cats in the home as pets and cuddling with them. While living with cats is normal, up to a point, sharing a radically untidy household with a great number of cats results in the folk diagnosis "crazy cat lady," a Western culture-bound syndrome (see Simons and Hughes 1993).

A small sample of the many CBSs that have been described (see Simon and Hughes 1985) is shown in Table 19.1. As every culture is distinctive, it would be surprising if each society did not have some singular "spin" on the way mental illness occurs there. Some patterns are so shared or similar across cultures, however, that they easily fall into standard diagnostic categories in psychiatric manuals. From the standpoint of biomedical diagnosis, culturally unique patterns are harder to understand, and for that reason, the latest editions of the world's leading psychiatric diagnostic manuals, the American Psychiatric Association's DSM-IV and the World Health Organization's ICD-10, include these illnesses for the first time, but in appendices.

The DSM-IV, and the ICD-10 remain Western academic references, however, largely written by Westerners and geared toward Western or cosmopolitan expressions of mental illness. Each manual calls for additional clinical research on culture-bound syndromes. Others add that future research should empirically investigate the syndromes on their own cultural terms rather than attempt to force the illnesses into Western diagnostic categories (see Guarnaccia and Rogler 1999).

Nervios, a syndrome recognized among Latin American cultures, is the subject of a multi-site study, which compares emic views of *nervios* across four Latino populations – Puerto Ricans, Mexicans, Mexican–Americans, and Guatemalans (Baer et al. 2003). Informants in all sites regard *nervios* as a mostly female condition caused by emotions and interpersonal problems. All sites agree on the symptoms of *nervios* as: depression, sadness, and loss of hope; crying and trembling; insomnia; bad moods and bad tempers. Among these Hispanic cultures who recognize *nervios* the cultural context includes (1) expectations for women's emotionality (Low 1989), and (2) a perceived burden on women because of the many duties of adult daughters, wives, and mothers, as in Saraguro, Ecuador (Finerman 1989). *Nervios* may hence form a sanctioned outlet or coping mechanism for stresses (Finerman 1989) or what Finkler calls "life's lesions" (1994). Almost every informant in the multi-site study considers *nervios* an 'illness,' (Baer et al. 2003). Even though *nervios* has no somatic symptoms, these populations may not regard *nervios* as a 'mental illness' (Baer 1996). Baer and colleagues note that the participants in their *nervios* research, "do not recognize a mind–body distinction, and indeed see a fluid relationship between the physical body and its problems, the mind, emotions, and the spiritual." Thus, *nervios* is simply an "illness." Prayer is the most recommended treatment (Baer et al. 2003).

Organic mental illnesses such as schizophrenia may at first seem unaffected by culture. Schizophrenia may exist around the world and schizophrenics may present with hallucinations, delusions, and feelings of outside influence on bodily functions irrespective of the cultural context. However, as we see in the vast range of culture-bound syndromes, cultural context differently influences the content of hallucinations, delusions, and who or what the schizophrenic perceives to control his or her body. Culture also affects the kind of understanding that the schizophrenic, the family, and the community bring into this suffering.

Culture and occurrence of mental illness If interpersonal relations affect mental health, and cultures prescribe appropriate social interactions, then a population's culture affects its psychological well being (see Quinlan and Quinlan 2007). Culture thus has some effect on mental incidence rates and resilience. It is well-established that genetic factors have a bearing on certain illnesses, such as schizophrenia (Kendler and Diehl 1993). Yet, even genetically based conditions may require an environmental trigger to emerge. (Phenylketonuria (PKU) is a genetic condition in which infants are unable to break down phenylalanine (in many foods including breast milk) so that it accumulates in the body tissues causing severe brain damage and other problems. If an infant with PKU ingests very limited phenylalanine, mental retardation and other disabilities do not develop. The genetic propensity for the PKU-induced mental illness exists at birth, but requires an environmental dietary trigger (see Blau and Erlandsen 2004).) Biomedicine regards schizophrenia as a disorder in which a predisposition – instead of the disease itself – is inherited genetically. Might a cultural schema create a protective or risky environment for such mental illnesses?

In County Kerry, Ireland, the nature of socio-cultural interactions may stimulate madness – including alcoholism, depression, and particularly schizophrenia (Scheper-Hughes 1979). During the mid-1970s, while the Republic of Ireland was undergoing rapid changes including mass migration, it had the world's highest rates of hospitalization for mental illness, with more than half of the diagnoses being schizophrenia – nearly double the normal prevalence for Western societies. County Kerry infants began life with minimal holding or contact, and corporal punishment began during the child's first year. From birth, parental interaction included labeling that encouraged daughters and early-born sons to flourish as they were "reared for export, for emigration" from the village (Scheper-Hughes 2000). Parents (and others) discouraged and derided last-born sons (deemed to become the unmarried caretaker of aging parents and inheritor of the farm), calling them the "black sheep," the "leftover," the "scraping of the pot," and the "runt." The "double-bind" for these rural Irish sons indicated that "You're worthless, you can't live beyond the farm…" and at the same time, "We need you – you're all we have" (Scheper-Hughes 2000). These bachelor sons comprise the majority of those hospitalized for schizophrenia. Mental volatility may also develop in response to the tradition of Irish "double-think, double-speak" (Scheper-Hughes 1979). Here, everyday talk is skilled repartee, an art form thick with metaphor, veiled insults, and ambiguity. Such a social environment may give rise to apprehension and anxiety which create a shaky foundation for mental stability. Though impatient with the verbally inept, villagers are tolerant and implicitly loving of every village "saint." In the local folk taxonomy of behavior, even the very odd are reckoned fine enough, as long as they remain reserved (the cultural norm particularly for men), free of physical or sexual aggression, and properly subordinate to parental and religious authorities. A break with these values indicates madness, which is "uncommonly common" there (Schepper-Hughes 1979). Scheper-Hughes' Irish example demonstrates the possible influence of culture in a population's development and diagnosis of psychopathology.

EXPLANATION AND TREATMENT

There is a link between someone's ethnomedical conceptions of the nature and cause of an illness and what he or she does to prevent that illness or to right the body, should illness occur. The first step in treatment is judging, "what kind of problem is this?" Some problems can be treated on one's own; others need specialist help immediately; others warrant outside care after self-treatment is insufficient.

Health-seeking behavior

When a health issue arises, adults of any culture will consider the nature of their (or a dependant's) problem and weigh it against their cultural understanding of the sickness and mental repertoire of appropriate treatments to try. Assessment begins the "health-seeking process" (Chrisman 1978), in which one tries several options for until the problem is better or all options are exhausted. Most societies are not limited to self-treatment; rather they have some degree of "medical pluralism," or series of treatment options beyond self-treatment, which one tries in a "hierarchy of curative resort" (Romanucci-Ross 1969). Anthropologists sort treatment options into three useful realms of practitioner: professional, popular, and folk (Kleinman 1980). Healers in the "professional" sector require formal training and certification (e.g., medical school and a medical license). The "popular" sector of health care consists of regular people caring for themselves and for their families. Popular treatments are basically common knowledge. Folk healers require training, talents, or experience beyond those available to the population at large, but "folk" practitioners (e.g., an herbalist or traditional midwife) are likely to learn as an apprentice. The three health care sectors can overlap to varying degrees, depending on the society. Also, the relative size and importance of each sector varies across cultures. Some industrial societies may not recognize a folk sector while small-scale groups have no professional sector.

The professional sector of health care includes all licensed or legally sanctioned health care workers. The professional sector includes doctors, dentists, chiropractors, nurses, physical therapists, psychotherapists, dieticians, paramedics, and numerous types of medical technicians. Ethnomedical studies within the professional sector aim to assess communication and willing cooperation between patients and clinicians (e.g., Calvet-Mir et al. 2008), to find best practices for cultural synergy in medicine (Mignone 2007), and to critique standard practices with the goal of improvement (Michaelson 1988).

In industrialized countries with large bureaucracies and legal systems, the professional sector is large. Many jobs that used to be part of the folk sector now require rigorous schooling and certification. This is the case with registered nurse midwives, for example. The Hindu Ayurvedic system of medicine has medical philosophies and practices that differ from those of Western biomedicine. Ayurveda used to be India's primary folk medicine. Now there are several established Ayurvedic medical schools, and since 1970 Ayurveda has been a legal and complementary alternative to Western biomedicine in India (Fulder 1997).

The popular sector is universally and logically the first and most commonly used area of health care. No matter what one's society, it is natural and pragmatic for adults to treat their own ailments (and their dependants') immediately and privately before bothering to seek help from some medical specialist. An estimated 70–90% of health-care takes place in the popular sector (Helman 2001; Kleinman et al. 1978). Variation (between the 70–90%) in peoples' reliance on self-care occurs largely due to discrepancies between communities' accessibility to outside treatment and the acceptability of those options. Travel distance to outside medical care increases likelihood of self-treatment (Quinlan and Quinlan 2007) and competence in home remedies (Nolan and Robbins 1999). Immigrants, particularly undocumented ones, may steer clear of outside health care due to legal issues, language, and social barriers and a preference for traditional, familiar remedies (Waldstein 2008). People also rely more heavily on self-treatment when the quantity and quality of supplies or staff at local facilities are not dependable, or when using specialized care is prohibitively expensive in terms of money or opportunity costs (Quinlan 2004; Wayland 2004). Home health care is literally the most "popular" sector of treatment. Plus, first response to illness can be critical: It may improve, mask, or exacerbate a condition – or create a new problem. Yet, perhaps because it is so ordinary and unobtrusive, the popular sector of health care remains an understudied topic within medical anthropology.

The folk sector of health care tends to be large in non-Western and non-industrialized societies, and it was a large sector of Western health care into the 1900s. This sector includes all of the expert curers who, rather than going through formal schooling for their medical training, learn through self-teaching and exploration, unofficial apprenticeships, and knowledge passed down through kin. Folk healers include (among others) midwives, herbalists, spiritualists, bonesetters, and shamans.

The tacit assumption in much of the medical anthropology and medical ethnobotany research has been that because folk healers are members of particular cultures, and they are medical specialists, their knowledge is the same as knowledge within the popular sector, only more so. It seems that one could most efficiently study local ethnomedicine by speaking with the few folk specialists in a community, rather than deal with sampling issues, or blanketing a population; unfortunately, the assumption may be flawed.

Waldstein and Adams (2006) trace ethnomedical coverage of Tzotzil Maya (in Chiapas, Mexico) and illustrate the problem in treating folk healers as representative of community knowledge. One healer's "rudimentary concepts of anatomy and physiology" led Holland and Tharp to conclude that "the Tzotzil have only vague and elementary knowledge of the human body" (1964:s102). Nash (1967), followed by Fabrega et al. (1970) asserted that ideas about physiology play no role in a curer's diagnosis. Fabrega and Silver (1973) added that Mayan healers neither think about illness in terms of physiology nor have specialized knowledge about the body. One should not, however, conclude from the above statements that Maya generally have little or no physiological knowledge. Mayan *folk* healing is actually a supernatural enterprise; therefore physiology is irrelevant to their practice. Maffi (1994) points out that Mayan folk healers benefit from avoiding natural, physiological explanations, because healers profit only from personalistic, supernatural illnesses. Meanwhile, ordinary Mayans of the *popular* sector do have detailed knowledge of body parts (Berlin and Castro 1988) and a complex ethnophysiological system (Adams 2004). Edward Green (1999) similarly notes a "myth of excessive supernaturalism" regarding African ethnomedicines, which though they are largely spiritual among the folk sector of healing, remain predominantly narturalistic on the popular front.

Ethnomedical systems often intertwine supernatural and natural, and mental and physical healing (Erickson 2008). Folk healers often call on the supernatural. For example, 16th century English midwives' efforts dealt mostly with physical preparation of the mother, baby delivery, and maternal physical restoration, yet they used prayer on their own to improve their practice, and with their patients to improve outcomes (Otten 1993). A Dominican *obeahman*, a sorcerer hired to heal (and to curse), talks to a patient (and often the patient's family) about the patient's physical complaint and also about the patient's present social life and village circumstances. Then the obeahman enters an altered state which involves prayer, discovers the agent that caused the problem, and gives the patient prayers, rituals and medicinal herbs to ward off the problem (personal patient communications). Shamans, found throughout the world, are a sort of curer who work explicitly through spiritual mediation. Shamans, like the obeahman, share the ability to enter a trance and communicate with a spirit world in which there are both good and evil spirits, and they can treat sickness caused by evil spirits. Shamans also tend to share experiential characteristics, such as a spiritual death and rebirth with a calling as a shaman, often coinciding with a near-death experience (Eliade 1972).

Ethnopharmacology
Ethnopharmacology examines drugs or medicines used within a particular culture. In remote and impoverished areas of the world, traditional home and folk remedies persist as the main health care option. Distance from medical facilities, expense, and distrust of physicians can impede rural people's access to biomedical care. In contrast,

self-treatment (or treating one's own dependants) with traditional remedies is accessible and culturally acceptable health care.

About 85% of traditional remedies are herbal (Farnsworth 1988:91). Animal and mineral treatments also exist cross-culturally, but as a minority of treatments. Where I work in Dominica, people boil a chunk of termite nest (with termites) to induce vomiting. They also use salt water for gargling and cleaning wounds and sulfur gathered near volcanic ponds for wounds and fungal infections. About 80% of the total treatments are herbal, and 97% of the salient, common treatments are from plants (Quinlan 2004). Over 70% of the world's population (Pei 2001) relies mainly on traditional herbal medications for primary health care (see Balick et al. 2000).

Because most traditional remedies are botanical, ethnopharmacology largely overlaps with ethnobotany – which examines human–plant interrelations. People use plants for multiple purposes. For example, recreational or ceremonial drug plants, like tobacco and marijuana, often have medicinal uses too (Schultes and Hoffman 1992). Multiple uses of single plants may intertwine "medical ethnobotany," with broader ethnobotany. Ginger and garlic are common food seasonings in many cultures, but they are also common remedies. The diet is often not only nutritional but pharmacological (see Etkin 2006; Pieroni and Price 2005). Further, plants have uses beyond ingestion. The Kalinago (Island Caribs) of Dominica not only eat pineapple fruit, but ferment a urinary treatment from pineapple skins; they also use the small, immature fruits to induce abortions, and extract fibers from the leaves to make sewing thread, fishing line, and cords for jewelry (Hodge and Taylor 1956). Ethnobotanists study plants for cultivation, construction, or any use (see Balick and Cox 1996), and thus may or may not be medical anthropologists. Medical ethnobotany is a large part of ethnobotany, though not the majority of that field. Meanwhile, *most* ethnopharmacology is somehow ethnobotanical.

Ethnographic field research is foundational to ethnopharmacology, though a minority of the field (Etkin 2001). Ethnopharmacology is not necessarily anthropological; rather the field synthesizes cultural, botanical, and biochemical inquiry of traditional medicines. Just as many traditional remedies are herbal; many Western pharmaceuticals also have plant origins. The Bayer Company, for example, derived aspirin from salicylic acid in willow bark from which Europeans brewed a traditional rheumatism and headache remedy (Rishton 2008). Ephedrine, digoxin, morphine, and quinine are a few more important drugs, which were discovered through traditional cures and folk knowledge of indigenous people (Gilania and Atta-ur-Rahman 2005), though examples abound. Of the top 150 brand name drugs, 57% contain at least one major active compound that was originally extracted from a plant (Rajasekharan 2006). Ethnopharmacology is thus applied to biomedical drug development via pharmacognosy (chemistry and biology of natural sources). Yet, ethnopharmacology requires understanding EMs about why, when, and how people use a substance.

Lost in translation

Ethics and utility in ethnomedicine   The utility of herbal medications for the people who use them traditionally, as well as for adoption by others, particularly in pharmaceutical form, helps and hurts the anthropological pursuit of medical ethnobotany.

Medical ethnobotany is bolstered by the awareness that, in addition to ethnographic and ecological data gathering, there is a lot of important applied ethnopharmacology to be done. There are copious herbal remedies to be identified and protected, and some of them are potentially beneficial to the world. It is unclear exactly how globalization and modernization are impacting traditional herbal knowledge (see Quinlan and Quinlan 2007), intensifying efforts to learn about remedies before cultures change or die out. At the same time, the potential for someone (e.g., a pharmaceutical company) to profit from ethnopharmacological findings presents ethical issues concerning intellectual property rights of the study populations. Anthropologists must work in concert with their subjects, carefully assuring benefit sharing and maintaining collaborators' intellectual property rights. Pharmaceutical researchers have not always been attentive to these issues. Consequently, medical ethnobotany can be a politically charged issue. The best intended research may be stonewalled with accusations of "biopiracy" (see Berlin and Berlin 2004). Plus, because plants are emically inseparable from EMs of the illnesses they treat, insiders may perceive inquiry of even non-botanical ethnomedicine as biopiracy, if not cultural piracy. Again this calls for translation from ethnomedical researchers. Here, rather than translating from a local study community to the academic one, we must translate our academic goals to our study community and their local organizations. Researchers may circumvent political troubles with preemptive diplomacy and cooperation, not only within the study population (per tradition), but with local government and non-governmental organizations who act as watchdogs for local communities (see Code of Ethics on the International Society of Ethnobiology website).

Besides drug discovery, local cultural conservation efforts can benefit from ethnomedical research. The Dominican elders I work with do not question the effectiveness of their medical traditions and herbal medicines. They say that pharmaceutical tablets are condensed herbs (in many cases this is essentially true). Elders appreciate my systematic record of traditional practices so that the younger generations, who seem to have less interest in (or need for) learning local medicines now, may have access to self-reliant treatments when they have children of their own to treat, get old or sick, or if their currently limited access to pharmaceuticals becomes even less attainable. Elders even feel vindicated by my reports of phytochemistry of the plants they use because they present a convincing case to Dominican youth, who, in a rapidly modernizing culture, may be more skeptical of traditional remedies and attracted by new pharmaceuticals. Outside substantiation supports their cultural preservation from within.

Meaning and efficacy in ethnomedicine   The West has not always taken the effectiveness of ethnomedicines seriously, and has waged, "extensive and impassioned debate… about whether botanical medicines are efficacious" (Etkin and Elisabetsky 2006:7). For the audience inclined to dismiss local remedies as purely symbolic or bunk, it is convenient to point to the growing body of results that demonstrate bioscientific therapeutic actions of traditional plant remedies (e.g., Quinlan 2004). Although identifying bioactive phytochemicals does indicate that a plant is likely effective, lack of literature on a plant, or researcher failure to identify its active chemicals does not indicate that a plant is not effective (Moerman 2007). To use pharmacology to buoy a culture's traditional medical knowledge is constructive. For outside scientists to attempt to "validate" traditional medicines through biochemistry is a mistake. If a treatment is popularly used within a culture, it is obviously "valid" within that culture, in that it is truly used. Privileging biomedical knowledge is not only ethnocentric, but does not account for the myriad elements of healing that bioscience has yet to learn.

Writing-off treatments with negative chemical results, little consensus about their use, or even untested plants is a logical as well as a scientific error. For one thing, a scientist can miss an important plant constituent for numerous reasons (see Etkin and Elisabetsky 2006:5–8). Or, the pharmacologist may be testing for the wrong medicinal activity. For example, antibiotics cure sinusitis, but we recently learned that most sinusitis is self-limiting with congestion well-controlled (Mölstad 2003). A few years ago, a plant that showed no antibiotic activity may have been dismissed as a poor sinusitis treatment, despite having been a good decongestant, or perhaps having a quality that we still do not know cures sinusitis, just as we did not previously understand that decongestants treat sinusitis effectively. Some plants may be effective in that they stimulate the immune system rather than target a particular pathogen or symptom.

Cross-culturally, medical ethnobotanists have observed that some popular remedies have organoleptic properties (or perceived sensory qualities such as taste, appearance, and odor that relate to the plant's medical function), which may be taken as a "signature" (literally, a "sign from nature"). For example, several peoples use blood-red plant infusions to build blood, such as after childbirth. Red color, in addition to looking like blood, may indicate elements such as iron that aid metabolic functions. Organoleptic qualities may be passed down as explanations of plants that work and certainly are mnemonic devices. (After seeing a fire-roasted banana, one will not likely forget its use as a laxative.) Further, a sensory cue may add to the plant's symbolic appeal ergo its ultimate effectiveness.

In ethnopharmacology, particularly ethnomedical ethnopharmacology, there is much more to a medicine than the chemicals it possesses: medicines have cultural and symbolic meanings that play into their healing, even affecting the drug's biological effect on the human body (Moerman and Jonas 2002). Taking any medication can produce a healing psycho-physiological response (thus clinical drug trials must compare results of patients using the tested drug against the results of patients taking a placebo, rather than compare taking the tested drug with taking nothing). Cultural beliefs about medicines (form, color, dosage), as Moerman (2007) notes can affect the efficacy of a placebo: four placebo tablets work better than two; blue placebos generally make better sleeping aids than red placebos; inert injections work better than inert tablets (in the USA, but not in Europe). Similar additive effects occur when the medicine is not a placebo. Post-operative patients who receive medications face-to-face from a clinician report about one third as much pain as patients receiving the same medication secretly via a computer-controlled intravenous line (Moerman 2007). Moerman (2002) terms this medical augmentation through cognition, the "meaning effect," which is like the "placebo effect" but with emphasis on the symbolic value of medications for placebos and non-placebos alike. A loved one's hug is bioactively "inert," yet it has a biological response: It increases levels of the hormone oxytocin and reduces blood pressure (Grewen et al. 2005). If a plant with an organoleptic cue and cultural salience functions purely as a placebo (which is a hard call to make) it is still ethnographically and medically important.

CONCLUSION

Ethnomedical systems are comprised of all of these domains – ethnophysiology, ethnopsychiatry, and ethnomedical treatment – but they are usually treated as distinct spheres of inquiry with different kinds of anthropologists specializing in each. This separation is an academically practical but artificial one since these branches of ethnomedicine are natural complements, and usually not discretely bounded. For many people, the mental and physical realms of illness are inseparable. Western culture views mind and body as distinct, other cultures rarely do. In most cultures, people are simply sick, not physically ill or mentally ill. By definition, these fields – ethnopsychiatry and ethnomedicine – examine emic perspectives on illness, and so, unless the research is taking place in Western culture where body and mind are distinct, ethnopsychiatry *is* ethnophysiology, and vice versa. The bond between ethnopsychiatry and ethnophysiology is clear, and both of these ethnomedicines are permeated with treatment traditions whose use only makes sense in terms of cultural ideas about the body/mind.

In sum, ethnomedicine examines local ideas and behaviors surrounding how to stay well, and how to treat sickness. Anthropologists examine the diversity of ethnomedical beliefs and practices between individual cultures, and compare ethnomedical trends at the regional and global levels. Ethnomedicine seeks to understand the internal logic of medical systems. We can then apply ethnomedical understanding to several kinds of cultural translation. When we study popular and folk explanatory models, we translate that ethnomedical logic to academics and clinicians with the goal of better treatment through improved cultural understanding. When we study clinicians, we can translate critical findings for potential patients and policy makers with the goal of making professional medicine more user-friendly and efficient. We also need to translate the aims of ethnomedicine to the public, local organizations, and governments so that people are aware of the potential humanitarian outcomes of applied ethnomedical study.

ACKNOWLEDGEMENTS

Thank you Pamela Erickson and Merrill Singer for honoring me with the opportunity to join this excellent volume. Thank you also Rob Quinlan for your many thoughtful suggestions.

REFERENCES

Adams, Cameron L., 2004 The Ethnophysiology of the Tzeltal Maya of Highland Chiapas. Ph.D. dissertation, University of Georgia.
Anderson, Eugene, N. Jr, 1987 Why Is Humoral Medicine So Popular? Social Science and Medicine 25(4):331–337.
Baer, Hans A., 1989 The American Dominative Medical System as a Reflection of Social Relations in the Larger Society. Social Science and Medicine 28(11):1103–1112.
Baer, Roberta D., 1996 Health and Mental Health among Mexican American Immigrants: Implications for Survey Research. Human Organization 55(1):58–66.

Baer, Roberta D., Javier Garcia de Alba, Rosa Mares Leal, Anarosa Plascencia Campos, and Neill Goslin, 1998 Mexican Use of Lead in the Treatment of Empacho: Community, Clinic, and Longitudinal Patterns. Social Science and Medicine 47(9):1263–1266.

Baer, Roberta D., Susan C. Weller, Javier Garcia de Alba Garcia, Mark Glazer, Robert Trotter, Lee Pachter, and Robert E. Klein, 2003 A Cross-Cultural Approach to the Study of the Folk Illness Nervios. Culture, Medicine and Psychiatry 27(3):315–337.

Balick Michael J., and Paul A Cox, 1996 Plants People and Culture: The Science of Ethnobotany. New York: Scientific American Library.

Balick, Michael J., Fredi Kronenberg, Andreana L. Ososki, Marian Reiff, Adriane Fugh-Berman, Bonnie O'Connor, Maria Roble, Patricia Lohr, and Daniel Atha, 2000 Medicinal Plants Used by Latino Healers for Women's Health Conditions in New York City. Economic Botany 54(3):344–357.

Berlin, Brent, and Elois Ann Berlin, 2004 Community Autonomy and the Maya ICBG Project in Chiapas, Mexico: How a Bioprospecting Project that Should Have Succeeded Failed. Human Organization 63(4):472–486.

Blau N., and H. Erlandsen, 2004 The Metabolic and Molecular Bases of Tetrahydrobiopterin-responsive Phenylalanine Hydroxylase Deficiency. Molecular Genetics and Metabolism 82: 101–11.

Browner, C. H., Ortiz de Montellano, B. R., Rubel, A. J., 1988 A Methodology for Cross-Cultural Ethnomedical Research. Current Anthropology 29(5):681–701.

Buckley, Thomas, and Alma Gottlieb, 1988 A Critical Appraisal of Theories of Menstrual Symbolism. In Blood Magic: The Anthropology of Menstruation. T. Buckley and A. Gottlieb, eds. 1–54. Berkeley: University of California Press.

Carrin-Bouez, Marine, and Beierle, John, 1998 Cultural Summary: Santal. New Haven CN: HRAF.

Calvet-Mir, Laura, Victoria Reyes-García, and Susan Tanner, 2008 Is There a Divide Between Local Medicinal Knowledge and Western Medicine? A Case Study among Native Amazonians in Bolivia. Journal of Ethnobiology and Ethnomedicine 4:18.

Chrisman, Noel J., 1978 The health-seeking process: An approach to the natural history of illness. Culture, Medicine and Psychiatry 1(4):351–377.

Coreil, Jeannine, Carol A. Bryant, J. Neil Henderson, Melinda S. Forthofer, and Gwendolyn P. Quinn, 2000 Social and Behavioral Foundations of Public Health. Thousand Oaks CA: Sage.

Csordas, Thomas J., 1994 Embodiment and Experience. London: Cambridge University Press.

de Bessa, Gina Hunter, 2006 Ethnophysiology and Contraceptive Use among Low-income Women in Brazil. Health Care for Women International 27(5): 428–452.

Devesa Jorda, F., J. Pellicer Bataller, J. Ferrando Ginestar, A. Borghol Hariri, M. Bustamante Balen, J. Ortuno Cortes, I. Ferrando Marrades, J. Luit Sala, M. Sintes Marco, A. Nolasco Bonmatf, and J. Fresquet Febrer, 2005 Persistencia de Una Pràctica de Medicina Màgico–religiosa para la Cura del Empacho entre los Enfermos que Acuden a Consultas Externas de Digestivo (Persistence of a magic–religious ritual to treat indigestion among patients attending a gatroenterology outpatient clinic). Gastroenterología y hepatología 28(5):267–274.

Dobkin de Rios, Marlene, 2002 What We Can Learn From Shamanic Healing: Brief Psychotherapy with Latino Immigrant Clients. American Journal of Public Health 92(10):1576–1581.

Ebert, D, and P. Martus, 1994 Somatization as a Core Symptom of Melancholic Type Depression: Evidence from a Cross-cultural Study. Journal of Affective Disorders 32(4):253–256.

Eliade, Mircea, 1972 Shamanism: Archaic Techniques of Ecstasy. Princeton, N.J.: Princeton University Press.

Erickson, Pamela I, 2008 Ethnomedicine. Long Grove IL: Waveland Press.

Etkin, Nina L., 2001 Perspectives in Ethnopharmacology. Journal of Ethnopharmacology 76(2):177–182.

Etkin, Nina L., 2006 Edible Medicines: An Ethnopharmacology of Food. Tucson AZ: University of Arizona Press.

Etkin, Nina L., and Elaine Elisasabetsky, 2006 Ethnopharmacology: An Overview. In Encyclopedia of Life Support Systems (EOLSS). E. Elisabetsky and N. L. Etkin, eds. Developed under the Auspices of UNESCO. Oxford UK: Eolss Publishers. Electronic document. http://www.eolss.net/.

Fabrega, Horacio, Jr, and Daniel B. Silver, 1973 Illness and Shamanic Curing in Zinacantan: An Ethnographic Analysis. Stanford CA: Stanford University Press.

Fabrega, Horacio, Jr, D. Metzger, and C. Williams, 1970 Psychiatric Implications of Health and Illness in a Mayan Indian Group: A Preliminary Statement. Social Science and Medicine 3:609–626.

Fabrega, Horacio, Jr, Chul W. Ahn, James Boster, and JuanMezzich, 1990 DSM III as a Systemic Culture Pattern: Studying Intracultural Variation among Psychiatrists. Journal of Psychiatric Research 24(2):139–154.

Farnsworth, N. R., 1988 Screening Plants for New Medicines. In Biodiversity. E.O. Wilson, ed. pp. 83–97. Washington: National Academy Press.

Finerman, Ruthbeth, 1989 The Burden of Responsibility: Duty, Depression, and Nervios in Andean Ecuador. In Gender, Health and Illness: The Case of Nerves. D. L. Davis and S. M. Low, eds. New York: Hemisphere/Taylor & Francis.

Finerman, Ruthbeth, 1993 Annex 2: Culture-specific Disorders. In The ICD-10 Classification of Mental and Behavioural Disorders: Diagnostic Criteria for Research, pp. 176–187. Geneva: World Health Organization.

Finkler, Kaja, 1994 Women in Pain: Gender and Morbidity in Mexico. Philadelphia: University of Pennsylvania Press.

Fisher, Seymour, and Sidney Cleveland, 1958. Body Image and Personality. Princeton: D. VanNostrand.

Foster, George M., 1976 Disease Etiologies in Nonwestern Medical Systems. American Anthropologist 78:773–782.

Foster, George M., 1994 Hippocrates' Latin American Legacy: Humoral Medicine in the New World. Langhorne PA: Gordon & Breach Science Publications.

Foster, George M., and Barbara Gallatin Anderson, 1978 Medical Anthropology. New York: John Wiley & Sons, Inc.

Fulder, Stephen, 1997 The Handbook of Alternative and Complimentary Medicine. 3rd edition. Oxford: Oxford University Press.

Gaines, Atwood D., 1992 Ethnopsychiatry: The Cultural Construction of Psychiatries. In. Ethnopsychiatry: The Cultural Construction of Professional and Folk Psychiatries. A. D. Gaines, ed. pp. 3–49. Albany NY: State University of New York Press.

Gilani, Anwarul Hassan, and A. Atta-ur-Rahman, 2005. Trends in Ethnopharmacology. Journal of Ethnopharmacology 100(1–2):43–49.

Goldsheyder D, S. S. Weiner, M. Nordin, and R. Hiebert, 2004. Musculoskeletal Symptom Survey among Cement and Concrete Workers. Work 23(2):111–121.

Good, Mary- Jo DelVecchio, 1980 Of Blood and Babies: The Relationship of Popular Islamic Physiology to Fertility. Social Science and Medicine 14(b):147–156.

Good, Mary- Jo DelVecchio, 1998 American Medicine: The Quest for Competence. Berkeley: University of California Press.

Green, Edward C., 1999 Indigenous Theories of Contagious Disease. Walnut Creek CA: AltaMira Press/Sage Publications.

Grewen, Karen M., Susan S. Girdler, Janet Amico, and Kathleen C. Light, 2005 Effects of Partner Support on Resting Oxytocin, Cortisol, Norepinephrine, and Blood Pressure Before and After Warm Partner Contact. Psychosomatic Medicine 67:531–538.

Guarnaccia, Peter J., and Lloyd H. Rogler, 1999 Research on Culture Bound Syndromes. American Journal of Psychiatry 156(9):1322–1327.

Hahn, Robert A., ed., 1999 Anthropology in Public Health: Bridging Differences in Culture and Society. New York: Oxford University Press.

Hahn, Robert A., and Atwood D. Gaines, 1985 Physicians of Western Medicine: Anthropological Approaches to Theory and Practice. Boston/Norwell MA: Kluwer Academic Publishers (for USA and Canada). Dordrecht, The Netherlands: D. Reidel Publishing Company (elsewhere).

Hodge, W. H., and Douglas Taylor, 1956 The Ethnobotany of the Island Caribs of Dominica. Webbia 7:513–643.

Holland, William R., and Roland G. Tharp, 1964 Highland Maya Psychotherapy. American Anthropologist 66:41–52.

Hanson, F. Allan, 1975 Meaning in Culture. London/ Boston MA: Routledge and Kegan Paul.

Helman, Cecil G., 2001 Culture, Health and Illness. 4th Edition. London: Arnold.

Hooley Jill M., 2007 Expressed Emotion and Relapse of Psychopathology. Annual Review of Clinical Psychology 3:329–352.

Kendler, K. S., and S. R. Diehl, 1993 The Genetics of Schizophrenia : A Current, Genetic-epidemiologic Perspective. Schizophrenia Bulletin 19(2):261–285.

Kenny, Anthony, 1968 Descartes: A Study of His Philosophy. New York: Random House.

Kleinman, Arthur, 1980 Patients and Healers in the Context of Culture. Berkeley: University of California Press.

Kleinman, Arthur, 2004 Culture and Depression. New England Journal of Medicine 31:10.

Kleinman, Arthur, Leon Eisenberg, and Byron Good, 1978 Culture, Illness and Cure: Clinical Lessons from Anthropologic and Cross-cultural Research. Annals of Internal Medicine.

Levin Betty W., and Carole H. Browner, 2005 The Social Production of Health: Critical Contributions from Evolutionary, Biological and Cultural Anthropology (Introduction). Social Science and Medicine 61:745–750.

Linsk, Joseph A., 1993 American Medical Culture and the Health Care Crisis. American Journal of Medical Quality 8(4):174–180.

Linton, Steven J., 2000 A Review of Psychological Risk Factors in Back and Neck Pain. Spine 25(9):1148–1156.

Lock, Margaret, and Debora Gordon, eds., 1988 Biomedicine Examined. Dordrecht, The Netherlands: Kluwer Academic Publishers.

Logan, Michael H., 1973 Humoral Medicine in Guatemala and Peasant Acceptance of Modern Medicine. Human Organization 32(4):385–395.

Low, Setha M., 1989 Gender, Emotion and Nervios in Urban Guatemala. Healthcare for Women International 10(2–3):187–196.

Maffi, Luisa, 1994 A Linguistic Analysis of Tzeltal Maya Ethnosymptomatology. Ph.D. dissertation, University of California at Berkeley.

Maynard-Tucker, Gisele, 1989 Knowledge of Reproductive Physiology and Modern Contraceptives in Rural Peru. Studies in Family Planning 20(4):215–224.

McGilvary, D.B., 1982 Sexual Power and Fertility in Sri Lanka. In Ethnography of Fertility and Birth. C. MacCormack, ed. London: Academic Press.

Michaelson, Karen L., ed., 1988 Childbirth in America: Anthropological Perspectives. Westport CN: Bergin & Garvey.

Mignone, Javier, Judith Bartlett, John O'Neil, and Treena Orchard, 2007 Best Practices in Intercultural Health: Five Case Studies in Latin America. Journal of Ethnobiology and Ethnomedicine 3:31.

Moerman, Daniel E., 2002 Meaning, Medicine and the "Placebo Effect". Cambridge UK: Cambridge University Press.

Moerman, Daniel E., 2007 Agreement and Meaning: Rethinking Consensus Analysis. Journal of Ethnopharmacology 112(3):451–460.

Moerman, Daniel E., and Wayne B. Jonas, 2002 Deconstructing the Placebo Effect and Finding the Meaning Response. Annals of Internal Medicine 136(6):471–476.

Mölstad, Sigvard, 2003 Reduction in Antibiotic Prescribing for Respiratory Tract Infections Is Needed! Scandinavian Journal of Primary Health Care 21(4):196–198.

Nash, J., 1967 The logic of behavior: Curing in a Maya Indian town. Human Organization 26:132–140.

Nations, Marilyn K., 1986 Epidemiological Research on Infectious Disease: Quantitative Rigor or Rigormottis? Insights from Ethnomedicine. In Anthropology and Epidemiology.

C. R. Janes, R. Stall and S. M. Gifford, eds. pp. 97–124. Dordrecht/Boston: D. Reidel/ Kluwer Adademic Publishers.

Nichter, Mark, 1992 Introduction. *In* Anthropological Approaches to the Study of Ethnomedicine. Mark Nichter, ed. pp. ix–xxii. Amsterdam, The Netherlands: Gordon and Breach Publishers.

Nichter, Mark, and Mimi Nichter, eds., 1996 Anthropology and International Health: Asian Case Studies. Amsterdam, The Netherlands: Gordon and Breach Publishers.

Nolan, Justin M., and Michael C. Robbins, 1999 Cultural Conservation of Medicinal Plant Use in the Ozarks. Human Organization 58(1):67–72.

Northridge, Mary E., and Richard Mack, Jr, 2002 American Journal of Public Health 92(10): 1561.

Otten, Charlotte F., 1993 Women's Prayers in Childbirth in Sixteenth Century England. Women and Language 16(1):18–21.

Pachter, L. M., B. Bernstein, and A. Osorio, 1992 Empacho in a Mainland Puerto Rican Clinic Population. Medical Anthropology 13(4):285–299.

Pei, S. J., 2001 Ethnobotanical Approaches of Traditional Medicine Studies: Some Experiences from Asia. Pharmaceutical Botany 39:74–79.

Pieroni, Andrea, and Lisa L. Price, eds., 2005 Eating and Healing: Traditional Food as Medicine. New York: Haworth Press.

Pollock, Donald, 1996 Personhood and Illness among the Kulina. Medical Anthropology Quarterly 10(3):319–341.

Quinlan, Marsha B. 2004. From the Bush: The Frontline of Health Care in a Caribbean Village. Belmont, CA: Wadsworth.

Quinlan, Robert J., 2007 Human Parental Effort and Environmental Risk. Proceedings of the Royal Society B: Biological Science 274(1606):121–125.

Quinlan, Marsha B., and Robert J. Quinlan, 2007a Modernization and Medicinal Plant Knowledge in a Caribbean Horticultural Village. Medical Anthropology Quarterly 21(2):169–192.

Quinlan, Robert J., and Marsha B. Quinlan, 2007b Parenting and Cultures of Risk: A Comparative Analysis of Infidelity, Aggression, and Witchcraft. American Anthropologist 109(1):164–179.

Rajasekharan, P. E., 2006 Potential of Plant Derived Pharmaceuticals. Science Tech Entrepreneur. Electronic document. http://www.techno-preneur.net/information-desk/sciencetech-magazine/magazine-index.htm/.

Rishton, Gilbert M., 2008 Natural Products as a Robust Source of New Drugs and Drug Leads: Past Successes and Present Day Issues. The American Journal of Cardiology 101(10, Supplement 1):S43–S49.

Romanucci-Ross, Lola, 1969 The Hierarchy of Resort in Curative Practices: the Admiralty Islands, Melanesia. Journal of Health and Social Behavior 10:201–209.

Rubel, Arthur J., 1990 Compulsory Medical Service and Primary Health Care: A Mexican Case Study. *In* Anthropology and Primary Care. J. Coreil and J. D. Mull, eds. Boulder CO: Westview Press.

Scheper-Hughes, Nancy, 1979 Saints, Scholars, and Schizophrenics: Mental Illness in Rural Ireland. Berkeley: University of California Press.

Scheper-Hughes, Nancy, 2000 Ire in Ireland. Ethnography 1(1):117–140.

Scheper-Hughes, Nancy, and Margaret Lock, 1987 The Mindful Body: A Prolegomenon to Future Work in Medical Anthropology. Medical Anthropology Quarterly (1):6–41.

Schultes, R. E., and Hofmann, A. 1992 Plants of the Gods. Rochester VT: Healing Arts Press.

Simons, Ronald C., and Charles C. Hughes, eds., 1985 The Culture-Bound Syndromes. Dordrecht, The Netherlands: D. Reidel.

Simons, Ronald C., and Charles C. Hughes, 1993 Culture-bound Syndromes. *In* Culture, Ethnicity, and Mental Illness. Albert Gaw, ed. pp. 75–99. Washington: American Psychiatric Press.

Singer, Merrill, 1981 The Social Meaning of Medicine in a Sectarian Community. Medical Anthropology 5(2):207–232.

Skultans, Veida, 1970 The Symbolic Significance of Menstruation and the Menopause. Man (New Series) 5(4):639–651.

Snow, L. F., and S. M. Johnson, 1977 Modern Day Menstrual Folklore: Some Clinical Implications. Journal of the American Medical Association 237(25):2736–2739.

Sobo, Elisa J., 1992 Unclean Deeds: Menstrual Taboos and Binding Ties in Rural Jamaica, In Anthropological Approaches to the Study of Ethnomedicine. M. Nichter, ed. pp. 101 – 126. New York: Gordon and Breach Publishers.

Sobo, Elisa J., 1993. One Blood: The Jamaican Body. Albany NY: State University of New York Press.

Spiro, Melford E., 1992 On the Strange and Familiar. In Recent Anthropological Thought. Anthropological Other or Burmese Brother? M. E. Spiro, ed. pp. 53–70. New Brunswick NJ: Transaction Press.

Stein, Howard F., and Margaret A. Stein, 1990 American Medicine as Culture. Boulder CO: Westview Press.

Strassman, Beverly, 1992 The Function of Menstrual Taboo among the Dogon: Defense against Cuckoldry? Human Nature 3(2):89–131.

Trotter, Robert T., II, 1985 Greta and azarcon: A survey of episodic lead poisoning from a folk remedy. Human Organization 44(1):64–72.

Waldstein, Anna, 2008 Diaspora and Health? Traditional Medicine and Culture in a Mexican Migrant Community. International Migration 46(5):95–117.

Waldstein, Anna, and Cameron Adams, 2006 The Interface Between Medical Anthropology and Medical Ethnobiology. Journal of the Royal Anthropological Institute (Special Issue) 12:95–117.

Wayland, Coral, 2004 The Failure of Pharmaceuticals and the Power of Plants: Medicinal Discourse as a Critique of Modernity in the Amazon. Social Science and Medicine 58(12):2409–2419.

Weller, S. C., T. K. Ruebush, and R. E. Klein, 1991 An Epidemiological Description of a Folk Illness: A Study of Empacho in Guatemala. Medical Anthropology 13(1–2):19–31.

Weller, Susan C., Lee M. Pachter, Robert T. Trotter II, and Roberta D. Baer, 1993 Empacho in Four Latino Groups: A Study of Intra- and Inter-Cultural Variation in Beliefs. Medical Anthropology 15:109–136.

White, Leslie A., 1930 A Comparative Study of Keresan Medicine Societies. In Proceedings of the 23rd International Congress of Americanists, 1928. New York. pp. 604–619.

Winch, P. J., A. M. Makemba, S. R. Kamazima, M. Lurie, G. K. Lwihula, Z. Premji, J. N. Minjas, and C. J. Shiff 1996 Local Terminology for Febrile Illnesses in Bagamoyo District, Tanzania and its Impact on the Design of a Community-based Malaria Control Programme. Social Science and Medicine 42(7):1057–1067.

FURTHER READING

American Psychiatric Association, 1994 Diagnostic and Statistical Manual of Mental Disorders. 4th edition (DSM-IV). Washington DC: American Psychiatric Association.

Helman, Cecil G., 1978 "Feed a Cold, Starve a Fever" – Folk Models of Infection in an English Suburban Community, and their Relation to Medical Treatment. Culture, Medicine and Psychiatry 2(2):107–137.

Hooker, Shirley D., Linda Holbrook Freeman, and Pamela Stewart, 2002 Pet Therapy Research: A Historical Review. Holistic Nursing Practice 17(1):17–23.

Larcom, Joan Clayton. 1980 Place and the Politics of Marriage: the Mewun of Malekula, New Hebrides/Vanuaaku. Ann Arbor MI: University Microfilms International.

Lomask, Milton, 1979 Aaron Burr: The Years from Princeton to Vice President, 1756–1805. New York: Farrar, Straus and Giroux.

Murdock, George P., and Douglas R. White, 1969 Standard Cross-cultural Sample. Ethnology 8:329–369.

Stevens, Rosemary, 1966 Medical Practice in Modern England. The Impact of Specialization and State Medicine. New Haven CT: Yale University Press.

World Health Organization, 1993 The ICD-10 Classification of Mental and Behavioural Disorders: Diagnostic Criteria for Research. Geneva: World Health Organization.

CHAPTER 20

Medical Pluralism: An Evolving and Contested Concept in Medical Anthropology

Hans A. Baer

INTRODUCTION

In contrast to indigenous or tribal societies, each of which has a more or less coherent medical system that is an integral part of the larger socio-cultural system, complex or state societies manifest the coexistence of an array of medical subsystems or a pattern of medical pluralism that is part and parcel of their socially stratified and culturally diverse nature. From this perspective, the medical system of a complex society consists of the totality of medical subsystems that generally compete with one another but sometimes exhibit cooperative, collaborative, and even co-optative relationships with one another. While various sociologists and geographers have employed the concept, anthropologists have gone further than any disciplinary group to apply and develop this concept. Indeed, despite the fact that medical sociologists have written a great deal about biomedical dominance over complementary and alternative medical systems, particularly in developed societies, they have tended to eschew the concept of medical pluralism as is evidenced by the fact that neither Cockerham and Ritchey (1997) and White (2006) included it in their extensive listing of terms utilized in medical sociology. Exceptions are Cant and Sharma (1999) and Goldstein (2004).

Some historians have begun to express an interest in utilizing the concept of medical pluralism. Ernst observes:

A Companion to Medical Anthropology, First Edition. Edited by Merrill Singer and Pamela I. Erickson.
© 2011 Blackwell Publishing Ltd. Published 2011 by Blackwell Publishing Ltd.

Medical historians have only slowly come to avail themselves of the conceptual and empirical insights of anthropological scholarship in non-European cultures... With social history of medicine came a focus on medical alternatives or 'heterodoxies', folk medicines, 'quackery', as well as on 'the patient's view'... Critical publications on the history of colonial medicine, and the present vigour and challenge of fashionable subaltern and post-colonial theories eventually caused social historians of medicine, too, to draw on anthropological perspectives and to consider the development of non-Western medical paradigms and indigenous medicine worthy subjects of historical analysis (Ernst 2002:2).

Ernst (2002) has edited an anthology titled *Plural Medicine, Tradition and Modernity, 1800–2000* which includes essays by historians as well as representatives from other disciplines, including anthropology and sociology, who examine medical pluralism in various societies, including The United Kingdom, India, German East Africa, Swaziland, South Africa, China, and the Maori of New Zealand. She aptly notes that "The cross-fertilization between medical anthropology and medical history certainly constitutes a welcome development" (Ernst 2002:2). In time given their growing interest in complementary and alternative medicine and integrative medicine (Baer and Coulter 2008), it is possible that sociologists also will more fully embrace the concept of medical pluralism than they have until now.

CHARLES LESLIE AND MEDICAL PLURALISM

Charles Leslie is well known for his organizational skills as both a symposium convenor and editor. In 1971 he organized an interdisciplinary Wenner Gren Foundation conference that met at Burg Wartenstein in Austria on Asian medical systems. Presentations from the conference resulted in a Leslie'seminal edited volume *Asian Medical Systems*. As a result, at least within anthropology, Charles Leslie was the first to conceptualize and apply the notion of medical pluralism in a systematic way. In his Introduction to *Asian Medical Systems*, he observes: "[M]edical systems are pluralistic structures of different kinds of practitioners and institutional norms. Even in United States, the medical system is composed of physicians, dentists, druggists, clinical psychologists, chiropractors, social workers, health food experts, masseurs, yoga teachers, spirit curers, Chinese herbalists, and so on" (Leslie 1976a:9).

Leslie, however, recognized that medical pluralism is an ancient phenomenon. He observes that "All the civilizations with *great tradition* medical systems developed a range of practitioners from learned professional physicians to individuals who had limited or no formal training and who practiced a simplified version of the great tradition medicine" (Leslie 1974:74). In his introductory essay to *Asian Medical Systems*, while noting that folk healers practice throughout the world practice, he noted that Asian countries, such as China, India, Japan, and Sri Lanka, are the only places where the "educated continue [their] learned traditions" (Leslie 1976a:1). Conversely, Leslie argued that the medical systems of Asian countries are quite pluralistic. In the case of China, he observes: "Practitioners ranged from physicians who had undergone long periods of training to individuals with little education who practiced a simplified version of the great tradition. Other healers co-existed with these practitioners, their arts falling into special categories: bone-setters, surgeons, midwives, snake-bite curers, shamans, and so on" (Leslie 1976a:3).

Historically, biomedicine has tended to refer to itself as *scientific medicine*, a notion that persists in the form of evidenced-based medicine which often functions as a device by which biomedicine seeks to control and even co-opt various complementary and alternative medical systems that have become very popular in recent decades in developed societies. However, Leslie insisted that biomedicine has no monopoly on science and that Chinese, Ayurvedic, and Arabic exhibit scientific characteristics in that: "They involve the rational use of naturalistic theories to organize and interpret systemic observations. They have explicit, orderly ways of recording and teaching this knowledge, and they have some efficacious methods for promoting health and for curing illness" (Leslie 1976a:7).

In his introductory essay, Leslie (1976a:6) acknowledged the fact that biomedicine or "cosmopolitan medicine progressively subordinates other forms of practice," an assertion that he demonstrated in other works to be the case in South Asia and others, including various sociologists (Willis 1989), have demonstrated to be the case around the world.

In his contribution to *Asian Medical* Systems, Leslie (1976b) created the first detailed delineation of a specific system of medical pluralism, namely the one in India. He identified eight more or less distinct medical sub-systems in the Indian medical system, namely (1) classical Ayurvedic medicine, (2) classical Yunani medicine, (3) the "syncretic medicine of traditional culture, which evolved among learned practitioners from the 13th to the 19th centuries," (4) contemporary professionalized Ayurvedic and Yunani medicine, (5) cosmopolitan medicine or what generally is referred to within medical anthropology today as biomedicine, (6) folk medicine consisting of midwives, bonesetters, various types of religious healers, and other specialists, (7) popular-culture medicine as embodied within the "institutions of mass society," and (8) homeopathy (Leslie 1976b:358–359). While there is the danger in delineating various medical subsystems of implying that each of them is a clearly demarcated entity, Leslie (1976b) recognized that in reality there is often a considerable amount of cross-fertilization between competing medical sub-systems, a process under which they draw from each other: "[I]n the modernization of Asian medicine has not been one-way process in which Ayurvedic and Yunani physicians have borrowed ideas and institutional forms from so-called Western medicine. Cosmopolitan medicine institutions have themselves developed in a distinctive manner because Ayurvedic and Yunani institutions were there, doing medical jobs Indian society wanted and needed to be done" (Leslie 1976b:366).

Leslie organized a second pivotal conference in 1977 in Washington, DC, under the auspices of the National Science Foundation and the Wenner Gren Foundation. Many of the papers at the conference touched upon medical pluralism and most of them were published in 1978 in a special issue of *Social Science and Medicine* on "Theoretical Foundations for the Comparative Study of Medical Systems" (See Leslie 1978). The conference and the subsequent special issue explored "concepts for analyzing the complex systems composed of plural medical traditions" and explored these traditions from a "broad historical and comparative perspective" (Leslie 1978:66).

In 1980 Leslie went onto to edit a special issue of *Social Science and Medicine* on "Medical Pluralism in World Perspective." In the introductory essay to the issue, he not only makes a case for the theoretical significance of the concept of medical pluralism but also for its applied utility in his observation: "Fundamental comparative research on pluralistic structures of medical systems would be an instrument of planning and also a technique for training personnel to design such programs in a realistic manner." While essays in this special issue included contributions by several anthropologists, it also included essays by a sociologist, a historian, a geographer, and a medical ethicist. Indeed, among the anthropologists who contributed to this special issue were Ronnie Frankenberg (1980), Mark Nichter (1980), H. K. Heggenhougen (1980), Margaret Lock (1980), Joan Koss (1980), and Sheila Cominsky (Cominsky and Scrimshaw 1980), all of whom went onto to become well known names in medical anthropology. While the essays in this special issue focused on societies outside the United States, such as India, Malaysia, and Guatemala, the essay by Joan Koss (1980) focused on *espiritismo* in Puerto Rico, a territory of the United States. Her essay and Leslie's following remark in this special issue reminded anthropologists that medical pluralism is an integral component of US society:

> A division of labor exists in every medical system between practitioners who represent different traditions. This in the United States clinical psychologists, yoga teachers, health food experts and Christian Science healers follow various forms of therapy... For some illnesses and kinds of patients [cosmopolitan medicine] provides less effective care than one or another alternative therapy (Leslie 1980:193).

The articles in this special issue highlighted the strong tendency around the world for the biomedical profession to resist the use of alternative medical systems, the notion that alternative practitioners are on the whole no more often "charlatans" than are biomedical practitioners; and that comparative research on medical pluralism has the potential to be an useful tool in health care planning.

Leslie organized a third conference in 1985 in Washington, DC, again sponsored by the Wenner Gren Foundation as well as the Department of Anthropology at the Smithsonian Institution, on "Permanence and Change in Asian Health Care Traditions." Selected papers from the conference were published in a special issue of *Social Science and Medicine* guest-edited by Beatrix Pfleiderer and in *Paths to Asian Medical Knowledge* co-edited by Charles Leslie and Allan Young (1992).

In recognition of not only his contributions to the study of Asian medical systems and medical pluralism but medical anthropology, Mark Nichter and Margaret Lock co-edited a series of essays in honor of Leslie. In the introductory essay to the volume, Lock and Nichter succinctly summarize Leslie's contribution to medical pluralism and medical revivalism:

> Charles Leslie's own work on medical pluralism focused primarily on Ayurvedic practitioners and the conflict and accommodation that were apparent as they were increasingly confronted with cosmopolitan medicine. He was able to show conclusively how self-conscious attempts at revivalism of an "authentic" Ayurvedic tradition were closely associated with nationalism and were in large part responses to perceived threats by forces of modernization and, by implication, "westernization," emanating from both inside and outside India. This is a topic that is of ongoing importance to scholars of Asia and elsewhere (Lock and Nichter 2002:7).

THEORETICAL PERSPECTIVES INTERPRETATIONS OF MEDICAL PLURALISM

Within medical anthropology, three rather distinctive theoretical perspectives have emerged, namely cultural interpretivism, the medical ecology, and critical medical anthropology (Baer et al. 2003). Each of these theoretical perspectives has manifested itself in an array of examinations of medical pluralism. In this section, I provide an overview of some of these.

Cultural interpretive or phenomenological analyses

Chrisman and Kleinman (1983) developed a widely used model that recognized three overlapping sectors in health care systems. Actually, Kleinman (1978) first presented a sketchier version of this model in an article that appeared in the 1978 special issue of *Social Science and Medicine* on "Theoretical Foundations for the Comparative Study of Medical Systems" edited by Charles Leslie. In Kleinman's model, the popular sector consists of health care conducted by sick persons themselves, their families, social networks, and communities. Kleinman, who has conducted research in Taiwan, estimates that 70–90% of the treatment episodes on that island occur in the popular sector. The folk sector encompasses healers of various sorts who function informally and often on a quasi-legal or sometimes an illegal basis. Examples include herbalists, bonesetters, midwives, mediums, and magicians. The professional sector encompasses the practitioners and bureaucracies of both biomedicine and professionalized heterodox medical systems, such as Ayurveda and Unani in South Asia and Traditional Chinese medicine or naturopathy, homeopathy, and Western herbal medicine in Europe, North America or Australasia. Chrisman and Kleinman observe that the three sectors in their model are not mutually exclusive ones but in reality overlap with one another. Helman (2007) applies the sectorial model of health care systems to the UK, which ranges from hospital doctors and general practitioners working under the auspices of the National Health Service to osteopaths, chiropractors, and naturopaths to diviners and religious healers of various sorts.

Emiko Ohnuki-Tierney (1984), a native Japanese anthropologist, discusses medical pluralism in contemporary Japanese society in the context of a broader examination of Japanese health related activities and beliefs. She clearly situated her perspective within symbolic anthropology and maintains that she examines "health related practices and concepts from the perspective of how they are organized according to the 'logico-meaningful' structure of the culture" (Ohnuki-Tierney 1984:3). Ohnuki-Tierney (1984:212) asserts that "[p]erhaps the single most important factor in the success of medical pluralism today is that each system has become so thoroughly embedded in Japanese culture and society." In addition to discussing popular health related beliefs and practices, she identifies two formal medical systems in Japanese society, namely *kanpo* and biomedicine, and various religious institutions that incorporate health practices. *Kanpo* relies heavily upon the regulation of daily habits, including dietary ones, and the administration of herbal medicines.

Since 1875, a physician can practice *kanpo* only after having obtained training in allopathic medicine or biomedicine. Ironically, Ohnuki-Tierney, who employs a functionalist view of socio-cultural systems, does not elaborate upon the fact that *kanpo* in essence has become a subordinate or adjunct medical subsystem within the hierarchical structure of Japanese medical pluralism. Allopathic medicine was first introduced into Japan by the Dutch during the late 18th century but took on a German cast during the Meiji period which started in 1868. Biomedical physicians, who tend to be male, often have their offices in their homes and employ their wives as pharmacists or receptionists. They generally see patients on a "first-come, first-serve" basis. Virtually all Japanese biomedical physicians practice more than one speciality. Japanese hospitals expect family members to be actively involved in patient care, which entails a family member staying with the patient, attending to his or her needs, receiving visitors, and providing meals.

Various Japanese religious institutions also cater to health care needs. Shamanism persists in remote mountainous areas but has been subsumed into the "new religions" that appeared in Japan following World War II. Conversely, major religious institutions play a significant role in health maintenance, although the Japanese do not label the service provided by temples and shrines as medical treatment per se. According to Ohnuki-Tierney (1984:124), the "number of shrines in Japan is phenomenal, and in fact has been increasing for some time." Regular bus tours to temples and shrines often target elderly people who have experienced strokes or suffer from hemorrhoids and other chronic ailments. Ishirki Shrine in the Osaka region is known for the treatment of tumors and Nakayama Temple specializes in matters related to childbirth and infancy, including "easy and safe delivery, the healthy growth of children, and memorial services for aborted fetuses" (Ohnuki-Tierney 1984:141). Whereas Buddhist temples focus on various aspects of death, such as funerals and memorial services, Shinto shrines focus on matters related to birth, growth, and marriage. The Japanese turn to their deities and buddhas for health, prosperity, traffic safety, and other secular concerns.

Ohnuki-Tierney asserts that medical pluralism in Japan has shifted in terms of the influence of its constituent medical subsystems:

> During the premodern periods biomedicine was absent, and both institutionalized religions and *kanpo* played significant roles in health care. During the modernization period, promotion of biomedicine became a national policy, and at least at the institutional level it became the dominant system, and the practice of *kanpo* was officially discouraged. After the beginning of the postmodern period, the dominant role of biomedicine has eroded, especially with the revival of *kanpo* among the general public (Ohnuki-Tierney 1984:221).

Also, in the contemporary era, a prototypical patient varies in terms of how much he or she relies upon the three major medical subsystems over the course of his or her illness career (Ohnuki-Tierney 1984:220–221). In terms of health maintenance, the prototypical patient relies on all three medical sub-systems more or less co-equally. During the acute stage of an illness, the prototypical patient relies heavily upon biomedicine, secondarily upon *kanpo*, and the less upon religious institutions. In the case of chronic, degenerative, or fatal illness, the prototypical patient still relies heavily upon biomedicine but is likely to turn more upon both *kanpo* and religious institutions for chronic conditions or transitions in the life cycle, such as birth, marriage, and death.

Medical ecological or biocultural analyses

By and large, medical ecologists or medical anthropologists with a biocultural perspective have tended not to grapple with the concept of medical pluralism. A notable exception is Horacio Fabrega (1997), who has developed an elaborate scheme of medical systems from a biocultural approach. Indeed, his *The Evolution of Sickness and Healing* probably still constitutes the most comprehensive delineation of the biomedical approach in medical anthropology. He asserts that medicine centers around sickness and healing – an observation made by many medical anthropologists. He defines *healing* as "the culturally meaningful social responses aimed at undoing or preventing the effects of disease and injury" (Fabrega 1997:ix). For Fabrega, the integration of sickness and healing is a natural byproduct of human evolution. He introduces the acronym SH, a notion that has not been widely adopted, for referring to a hypothesized biological adaptation for sickness and healing. He maintains that chimpanzees exhibit some basic behaviors, such as the use of leaves to wipe themselves and the use of leaf napkins to dab at bleeding wounds, associated with the SH, but also observes that they exhibit some non-SH responses, such as aversion to and exploitation of sick group members. Fabrega suggests that many of the SH characteristics of chimpanzees existed in early hominid societies and that SH became more refined during the Neanderthal stages, as is implied by the presence of healing fractures in some Neanderthal remains. Asserting that "SH constitutes the foundational material for elaboration of medicine as a social institution," he posits that the provider of SH in early human societies was a highly insightful individual who possessed an elaborate knowledge of the social organization of his or her society (Fabrega 1997:70). Fabrega then introduces the notion of *meme*: a unit of cultural information which is stored in the brains of individuals and passed onto others through enculturation. With regard to sickness and healing, medical memes serve as mechanisms for orienting to, thinking about, and responding to disease and injury. Unfortunately, while the concept of medical meme may be a useful heuristic device, he provides no concrete evidence that it has any physical reality.

Fabrega characterizes SH in foraging societies as family and small-group oriented, based upon "non-systematized knowledge," and focused on immediate restoration of well being or accommodation to death through ritual activities and social practices. Village-level societies exhibit a higher prevalence of infectious diseases and a decline in general health compared to foraging societies. SH is characterized by the presence of specialized healers, elaborate healing ceremonies attended by community members, and an expansion of the sick role manifested, for example, in growing attention to psychosocial needs and sick individuals. In terms of disease and medical ecology, chiefdoms, pre-state, and early state societies are characterized by less nutritious and balanced diets, increased prevalence of bacterial, viral, and parasitic infections, and lower general health and well being than foraging and village-level societies. They also exhibit a high prevalence of gastrointestinal infections which contribute to a very high infant and adult mortality rate. However, individuals who survive into adulthood tend to live longer lives than people in small-scale societies. According to Fabrega, chiefdom, pre-state, and early state societies exhibit the beginnings of the "institution" or "system" of medicine which includes (1) an elaborate corpus of medical knowledge which continues to embrace aspects of cosmology, religion, and morality, and (2) the beginnings of medical pluralism, manifested by the presence of healers, including general practitioners, priests, diviners, herbalists, bonesetters, and midwives who undergo systematic training or apprenticeships.

Empires and civilizations exhibit the beginnings of industrialization, considerable growth of mercantilism and commerce, social classes and occupational specialization, and ethnic, linguistic, religious, and economic diversity. These societies are characterized by high infant and child mortality rates, a growing prevalence of chronic diseases (e.g., diabetes, heart disease, hypertension, cancer), widespread malnutrition, periodic plagues, and a higher prevalence of psychiatric disorders. Conversely, adult life expectancy probably increased among the more affluent members of empires and civilizations. According to Fabrega, SH in these societies is characterized by a complex pattern of medical pluralism consisting of two tiers: (1) an official, scholarly, academic medical system oriented to the care of the elites, and (2) a wide array of less prestigious physicians and folk healers who treat subordinate segments of society. The state plays an increasing role in medical care by hiring practitioners for elites and providing free or nominal care for the poor, especially during famines and epidemics. The literate or "great" medical tradition includes the formation of a medical profession, the beginnings of clinical medicine, and increasing commercialization of the healing endeavor.

SH in modern European societies is characterized by the emergence of biomedicine as a dominant and hegemonic profession which is characterized by patterns of secularization, scientific knowledge, biological reductionism, the emergence of the hospital as the center of healing and research, and the universalization of categories of sickness. Fabrega (1997:19) asserts that the functions and aims of a medical system are shaped by systemic forces or the "dominant powers" in a society. At the same time, medical pluralism manifests itself in the continuing existence of "unorthodox practitioners, providers of 'alternative medicine'" (Fabrega 1997:135) who are held in contempt by biomedical physicians. Despite the ongoing pattern of biomedical dominance in post-modern societies, ones characterized by corporate globalization and an emphasis on consumerism, a growing public recognition of the limitations of biomedical reductionism has led to the "pursuit of alternative, unorthodox, Eastern, and holistic healing practices" (Fabrega 1997:179). Many individuals in post-modern societies regard health as an achieved status obtained through education, prevention, and lifestyle. According to Fabrega (1997:141), post-modern societies manifest an "obsessive preoccupation with health and fitness," thus resulting in the phenomenon of the "worried well."

Fabrega is to be commended for presenting a comprehensive framework that delineates the relationship between levels of socio-cultural integration and their associated conceptions of sickness and healing. However, referring only to modern European societies, without recognizing "modern Asian societies" or "modern African societies" seems rather "Eurocentric". Furthermore, his typology ignores developing societies.

Critical perspectives on medical pluralism

From a critical perspective, medical pluralism tends to reflect hierarchical relations in the larger society. Patterns of hierarchy may be based upon class, caste, racial, ethnic, regional, religious and gender distinctions (Baer et al. 2003; Singer and Baer 2007).

Medical pluralism flourishes in all state or complex or state societies, whether pre-industrial, industrial, or post-industrial, and tends to mirror the wider sphere of class and social relationships. Since the early 20th century, it is perhaps more accurate to say that national health care systems are *plural* rather than *pluralistic* in that bio-medicine came to exert a dominant status over heterodox and folk medical systems. In reality, plural medical systems may be described as *dominative* in that one medical system, namely biomedicine, enjoys a pre-eminent institutional status vis-à-vis other medical systems. While within the context of a dominative medical system one system attempts to exert, with the support of strategic social elites, dominance over other medical systems, people are quite capable of the dual or multiple use of distinct medical systems.

The dominant status of biomedicine is legitimized by broad practice acts that grant it a monopoly over certain medical practices, and limit or prohibit the practice of other types of healers. Nevertheless, biomedicine's dominance over rival medical systems has never been absolute. The state, which primarily serves the interests of the corporate class, must periodically make concessions to subordinate social groups in the interests of maintaining social order and the corporate mode of production. As a result, certain heterodox practitioners, with the backing of satisfied patients and influential patrons, have been able to obtain legitimation in the form of full practice rights (e.g., homeopathic physicians in the United Kingdom, osteopathic physicians in the USA, and Ayurvedic and Unani practitioners in India) or limited practice rights (e.g., chiropractors, naturopathic physicians, and acupuncturists in North American societies, many European societies, and Australasia). In contrast to the United States, osteopathy in other countries, such as the UK, Australia, and New Zealand, continues to function as primarily manual medical system with limited practice rights. Lower social classes, racial and ethnic minorities, emerging subcultures, and women often have utilized complementary and alternative medical systems as a forum for challenging not only biomedical dominance but also, to a degree, the hegemony of the corporate class and its political allies. Homeopathy in 19th century America would have constituted an exception to this tendency in its practitioners and patients often were drawn from the upper and upper middle classes, but it became absorbed into conventional medicine during the early 20th century for a variety of complex historical and social structural reasons (Kaufman 1971). Conversely, chiropractic and herbal medicine appear to have found both its practitioners and patients initially among rural and working-class peoples, especially the former for those doing physical labor.

Despite the fact that alternative medical systems may over time achieve a certain semblance of legitimacy and professionalization in the form of licensure laws, statutory registration, government support for training and research programs, popularity among the general public, and media coverage, these gains entail the growing pressure on natural medicine providers to accommodate a reductionist theory that is compatible with both corporate ideology and the conventional medicine's model of institutional organization. Unless they are part of a major societal transformation, competing medical systems must accommodate themselves to what Wallace (1956) terms "specialized interest groups" (e.g., organized conventional medicine, corporate and government elites, and health policy decision-makers) if they are to survive and prosper. These systems will remain weak even as they grow. According to Saks (1994:100), "while access to the alternatives to medicine may be expanded, the traditional monopolistic power base of the orthodox profession still seems highly likely to dilute the scope of what is available, even at a time when the profession is coming under ever greater challenge in an increasingly market-based society."

As professionalized heterodox medical systems, osteopathy, chiropractic, and probably naturopathy initially held out the promise of improved social mobility to thousands of working class and lower-middle class individuals as well as members of our social categories, including in some instances women and in the case of US osteopathic medicine Jews (Baer 2001). In attempting to enter the medical marketplace, as Larkin (1983:5) asserts, "innovatory groups in medical science often commence with low status, particularly through their involvement in activities [e.g., spinal manipulation or colonic irrigation] previously regarded as outside of the physician's or surgeon's role." As the new medical system grows, it accumulates:

> More and more members who are interested in making a good living and in raising their status in the outer world. In the health sphere, this means that they become more concerned with obtaining respectable (or at least respectable-looking) credentials, providing services that more clearly follow the medical model, and eventually even developing relationships with the orthodox medical world (Roth 1976:40–41).

There are historical exceptions to these patterns as evidenced by hydropathy and homeopathy which appealed to the upper and middle classes during the 19th century in Europe and North America. Hydropathy remains a very strong tradition throughout much of central Europe and was for a time incorporated into naturopathy in North America, but has become in large part a marginal modality in the latter.

I have developed a model of medical pluralism in the United States that recognizes biomedicine's institutional and economic hegemony and power differences within plural medical systems. This model is referred to as the *dominative medical system* because of the fact that biomedicine exerts dominance over other medical or therapeutic system (Baer 1989, 2001). This scheme is based on the thesis that the principal practitioners of each medical subsystem tend to be drawn from specific classes, racial and ethnic categories, and genders depending on their status in the larger society.

In my own work, I have applied the notion of dominative medical system to medical pluralism in both the United States and more recently Australia (Baer 2001, 2004, 2008a; Singer and Baer 2007). A diverse mixture exemplifying medical pluralism characterized the United States from the colonial times until the early 20th century; while regular physicians were often predominant, homeopathic, eclectic and physiomedical physicians and other "irregular" professional practitioners provided a significant portion of medical care and held positions of social respectability and of income status equivalent to conventional MDs. The domination of biomedical physicians in economic status, institutional pre-eminence and growing acceptance by the general public as medical authorities was not established until the 1930s and later. Thus, the US dominative medical system, which emerged in the mid-20th century, consists of the levels depicted in Figure 20.1. With some modification, the model of the dominative medical system can be applied to other societies.

As a result of corporate support for biomedicine, its practitioners came to consist primarily of white, upper- and upper-middle class males, although, largely due to affirmative action programs, women entered into biomedicine in increasing numbers

---

Biomedicine

Osteopathic Medicine (a parallel medical system focusing on primary care)

Professionalized Heterodox Medical Systems
  Chiropractic
  Naturopathic medicine
  Chinese medicine and acupuncture

Partially Professionalized or Lay Heterodox Medical Systems
  Naturopathy
  Homeopathy
  Herbalism
  Bodywork
  Body-mind medicine
  Direct-entry midwifery

Anglo–American Religious Healing Systems
  Spiritualism
  Seventh-Day Adventism
  New Thought healing systems (Christian Science, Unity, Religious Science,
  etc.)
  Pentecostalism
  Scientology
  New Age healing

Folk Medical Systems
  European–American folk medicine
  African–American folk medicine
  Vodun
  Curanderismo
  Espiritismo
  Santeria
  Chinese–American folk medicine
  Japanese–American folk medicine
  Hmong–American folk medicine
  Native–American healing systems

Figure 20.1   The USA Dominative Medical System. Figure by Hans A. Baer.

as did some Asian–Americans, African–Americans, and Hispanic–Americans. As professionalized heterodox medical systems, osteopathy, chiropractic, and naturopathy held out the promise of improved social mobility for thousands of white-middle- and working-class individuals, most of whom were males, who were denied access to biomedicine due to the structural barriers created by the Flexner Report of 1910. Osteopathic medicine, gutted of its traditional principles and practices and co-opted by biomedicine, eventually evolved into a parallel medical system with full practice rights in all 50 states and the District of Columbia as a result of the paucity of primary care physicians created by the increasing trend toward specialization in biomedicine. In contrast, chiropractic, which in part had its roots in osteopathy, eventually evolved into the foremost professionalized heterodox medical system in the United States (Baer 1987). Many of the prejudices against chiropractic could be viewed as derived from, or at least reflective of, class and urban-rural biases against those who did physical labor and found benefit in hands-on therapies. Anglo–American religious healing systems provided outlets for white women seeking therapeutic roles, except in the notable instances of the physiomedical and eclectic professions which included women from their inception in the 1830s and 40s. Whereas Christian Science served this role largely for upper-middle-class women, Spiritualism and Unity did so for lower-middle-class women. Finally, folk medical systems, including midwifery and Thomsonian herbalism, have enabled working class and rural people from various ethnic groups, particularly people of color and often females, to provide lower-cost and culturally appropriate therapy for individuals at the lowest echelons of US society.

Even when biomedical physicians express an interest in Complimentary and Alternative Medicine (CAM), often under the rubric of integrative medicine, they often continue to view CAM practitioners who work in their clinics as their inferiors or subordinates. Ellen J. Salkend (2005) found this to be the case in her study of the Holistic Medicine Institute (pseudonym), a Midwestern US suburban clinic operated by four biomedical physicians who hired several CAM practitioners on a part-time basis who are expected to carry out various labor-intensive therapies.

Paralleling my own efforts to examine medical pluralism at the national level in two developed societies, Libbet Crandon-Malamud, provided a critical analysis of medical pluralism in a single community in the Bolivian *altiplano* (see Koss-Chionino et al. 2003 for an anthology in her memory). In her book *From the Fat of Our* Souls, Crandon-Malamud (1991) examined power relations embedded in the Bolivian dominative medical system in Kachitu (pseudonym), the center or *municipio* for a canton consisting of some 16,000 Aymara Indians dispersed over 36 *communidades* situated at about 13,000 feet elevation and several miles from Lake Titicaca. At the time of her research in the late 1970s, the town proper had a population of about 1,000 people consisting of three ethnoreligious groups: (1) Aymara campesinos, (2) the Methodist Aymara, and (3) Catholic *mestizos*.

> Crandon-Malamud described ethnic dynamics in Kachitu in the following terms: By the 1970s, as social divisions multiplied, the content, meaning, and significance of mestizoness, Aymara Indianness, Catholicism, and membership in the Methodist church were being culturally redefined within an environment of political and economic instability and radically changing social relations. The resulting confusion left Kachitu, and throughout the altiplano, resources are scarcer than they have ever been in Bolivian history (Crandon-Malamud 1991:19–20).

Kachitunos utilized the local plural medical system for purposes of establishing their sense of cultural identity and obtaining the few resources available to them. According to Crandon-Malamud (1991:138), Kachitunos utilized medical dialogue and curative strategies in order to "make alliances, disassociate themselves from others, exchange resources, and try to forge new identities that will open opportunities and improve their lives under conditions of extreme and seemingly unrelenting national economic contraction, regional peripheralization, and local marginalization." The three medical ideologies in Kachitu, namely shamanism, mestizo home care, and biomedicine, serve as options that address different types of ailments. Thus, "All things being equal, if one has tuberculosis, one goes to the physician in the Methodist clinic; if one suffers from *khan achachi* [sickness emanating from a phantom], one goes to the *yatiri*; if one has a stomach upset, one resorts to *medicinas caseras*" (Crandon-Malamud 1991:202–203). Medical dialogue served as an idiom by which a person defined his or her ethnic identity in the larger context of Bolivian society. For instance, mestizos who found themselves downwardly mobile within the shifting Bolivian political economy could gain access to greater health care by turning to Aymara medicine.

As people elsewhere, Kachitunos, regardless of their social standing, tend to be pragmatic rather than therapeutic purists when it comes to seeking medical treatment. Kachitunos utilized medical dialogue as a mechanism for empowerment in the face of external hegemonic forces, including that of biomedicine. Unfortunately, this medical dialogue served as rather limited form of empowerment and in reality functioned more as a coping mechanism within the larger context of the Bolivian political economy. At any rate, medical pluralism in Kachitu constituted one of many microcosms of the Bolivian dominative medical system – a national system that includes a diversity of biomedical practitioners, herbalists, midwives, and indigenous healers.

THE STANCE OF VARIOUS NATIONAL SOCIO-CULTURAL SYSTEMS TOWARD MEDICAL PLURALISM

The degree of medical pluralism manifested in any particular complex or state society is highly. As illustrated in Figure 20.2, Murray Last (1996) systematically addresses this reality in his delineation of three "broad types of regulatory systems that help to determine politically the nature of a state's medical culture" that in turn shape the degree of medical pluralism that exists in a particular society.

The Soviet Union constituted the prototypical example of the exclusive system in that biomedicine was the only medical subsystem that was legally recognized. Many socialist-oriented developing countries also followed the Soviet model and viewed "traditional medicine" as class-divisive and a "feudalistic practice" that prevented people from "having a proper scientific understanding of their condition and pandering instead to superstition" (Last 1996:381). The French model is followed in not only

Exclusive Systems: *medical monopolies*
- Marxist model
- French model
- American model

Tolerant Systems: *medical markets*
- British model
- German model

Integrated Systems: *Asian pluralism*
- Indian and Chinese models
- Third World model

Figure 20.2   Types of regulatory systems impacting upon medical pluralism. Figure by Hans A. Baer.

France but various Francophone developing countries and some Latin American countries and "starts from the premise of centralized state control with all unlicensed healers illegal" (Last 1996:381). The American model, in which biomedicine enjoys full practice rights in all 50 states and the District of Columbia, in reality does not function as a full blown exclusive system in that various other medical subsystems, including chiropractic, naturopathic medicine, acupuncture, and Chinese medicine, massage therapy, and direct-entry midwifery, enjoy limited practice rights in all or many states. Osteopathic medicine has evolved into a parallel medical system to bio-medicine in that since the early 1970s it has enjoyed full practice rights in all 50 states and the District of Columbia.

Great Britain and various Anglophone countries, including Australia and New Zealand, employ *common law* in permitting a wide array of medical subsystems to coexist with biomedicine and allow them a wide scope of practice, barring procedures that are covered under statutory registration. In the UK, Australia, and New Zealand, statutory registration exists in all political jurisdictions not only for biomedical physicians but also osteopaths and chiropractors. Conversely, naturopaths, Western herbalists, religious healers, and folk healers practice under common law. In Germany, biomedicine has for long been divided into *Schulmedicizin* ("school medicine") and *Naturheilkunde* ("natural medicine")(Roth 1976). By obtaining additional training in the form of short courses and apprenticeships, biomedical practitioners, such as my cousin who obtained her medical degree from the University of Heidelberg, can become practitioners of *Naturheilkunde*. Conversely, Germany tolerates the existence of *Heilpraktikers* or partially professionalized heterodox practitioners who are the rough equivalent of naturopaths in the USA, Canada, Australia, New Zealand, South Africa, and India. According to Last,

> [Heilpraktikers] merely have to pass an examination to show that they know the state law regulating medical practice; the actual content of the expertise they claim to exercise is not otherwise restricted or examined... Schools, however, to teach would-be practitioners the relevant, legal information to pass the examination (Last 1996:385).

As Leslie has illustrated, biomedicine coexists with various professionalized indige-nous medical systems, such as Ayurveda, Siddha, and Unani as well as homeopathy, a Western import. According to Last (1996:385), "[o]ther, less systematic therapeutic systems survive without professionalization on the margins of the national medical culture and meeting specific needs that the various formal systems cannot adequately provide for." While in theory biomedicine and traditional Chinese medicine are inte-grated and on an equal footing in China, in reality the former has a considerably higher status and is funded more heavily than the latter. During the Maoist era, bare-foot doctors, which were highly touted as paragons of revolutionary dedication, served as medical auxiliaries trained in both biomedicine and Chinese medicine. Only about 13% hospitals focus on traditional Chinese medicine. Traditional Chinese med-icine is more extensively employed in remote rural areas than in urban areas or in rural county hospitals close to urban areas. Last (1996:386) argues that plural medical sys-tems of many developing or Third World societies are integrated in the sense that biomedicine is not clearly dominant over heterodox medical subsystems that include a "very large number of local practitioners of traditional medicine, bonesetters, midwives, barber-surgeons, and so forth who have always tried to meet the health needs of the community" and a "wide spectrum of modern alternative therapies alongside a market in medical drugs imported, sometimes unmarked and instruction-less, from all over the world."

MEDICAL SYNCRETISM AND THE TRANSNATIONALIZATION AND GLOBALIZATION OF MEDICAL SYSTEMS

Various anthropologists have criticized a strong tendency in the study of medical plu-ralism to discuss the relationship among allegedly discrete medical subsystems because it downplays the phenomenon of medical syncretism in which health practitioners and patients often blend together beliefs and practices from different medical traditions (Poole 2005:38–51; Lewis 2007). Furthermore, patients often do not clearly sub-scribe to one set of medical beliefs or another. Based upon interview and focus group research in Oceanport (pseudonym), a socio-economically diverse suburb of a New South Wales city, Connor (2004) found that 27 (24%) of her 111 subjects indicated that another household member had engaged in a pattern of "mixed therapy regi-mens" – a scenario in which "people may be using multiple types of therapists and therapies simultaneously, or shift from one type of therapy or practitioner to another in seeking to resolve their health problems." In a similar vein, immigrant groups often tend to engage in "mixed therapy regimens" in which they move back and forth between biomedicine and folk medicine. This pattern is poignantly illustrated in Anne Fadiman's (1997) account of the conflict faced by a Hmong family who encountered a confrontation between themselves and a small California county hospital over the care of their daughter who had been diagnosed of epilepsy. While the Hmong do turn to biomedicine for many health problems, they often also continue to rely on the *txiv neebs*, the "great plea bargainer for the soul, the preeminent champion in the struggle for the demonic" as did the family in this captivating account of a cultural class between a refuge family and biomedicine (Fadiman 1997:281).

Medical syncretism is illustrated in modern Ayurvedic medicine which is drastically different from the system delineated in its classic texts. It has a long tradition of syn-creticism, which has drawn heavily upon the Galenic (Unani) concepts of Islamic medicine. Both professionalized Ayurvedic and Unani medicine have incorporated aspects of biomedicine. Homeopathic practices have become a standard part of Ayurvedic medicine. Leslie, who has for long engaged in this type of research, recog-nizes the syncretic nature of medical pluralism: "Ayurveda and Yunani tibia also bor-row from each other, homeopathic medicine is used by many vaidyas... in another direction entirely, some practitioners combine Ayurveda with tantric ritual" (Leslie 1992:196).

Ferzacca (2001:210) views medical pluralism in Yogyakarta, an educational center in Central Java, as a "social practice that produces hybrid [i.e., a mixture of traditional and modern] forms of medicine" utilized by people who lead "hybrid lives." Indeed, as Alter (2005a:2) observes in the introduction to his anthology on *Asian Medicine and Globalization*, "there is a tremendous amount of historical, theoretical, applied, and practical overlap between key concepts in the various medical systems of Asia" and various forms of "Western" medicine, not only biomedicine but also homeopathy and naturopathy, which have been incorporated into traditional Asian medical systems. Zhang (2007) also illustrates the hybridity between biomedicine and traditional Asian medicine in his analysis of patients switching back and forth between taking Viagra and Chinese medicinal herbs in the treatment of impotence. In his discussion of Ayurvedic acupuncture in modern India, Alter (2005b:42) asserts that in reality "all forms of medicine are theorized as transcultural systems." While Ayurveda has often been viewed as an example of Indian nationalism, it is a system that has diffused to other parts of the world, including the United States where it has become incorporated within the rubric of holistic medicine or complementary and alternative medicine (Baer 2004:74–78).

Many traditional Asian medical systems have been quickly globalizing and diffusing to Western developed societies. Janes (2002:268) argues that Tibetan medicine has become increasingly commodified and globalized as is evidenced by the establishment of private Tibetan medical clinics in major Chinese cities and its engagement with a "Western interest in Eastern spirituality and holistic healing." In embracing neoliberalism, China has been marketing both traditional Chinese medicines and Tibetan medicines overseas. Developments in Korean medicine, which historically drew heavily from Chinese medicine, also reveal processes of hybridity, commodification, and globalization. Kim (2009:32) has examined how three Korean medicine practitioners "actively attempted to scientize, globalize, and industrialize their clinical knowledge by associating with two laboratories and a biotech company that reached beyond local and national boundaries." The commercialized products, particularly weight loss and skin medications, mixed Korean medicine, biomedicine, and cosmetic techniques and were sold to high-status Korean women not only in Seoul but even Los Angeles and New York, two US cities with relatively large Korean populations. Chinese medicine has become very popular not only in the United States (Baer 2004:46–51) but also in Australia where it is taught in numerous private colleges, some of them Chinese medicine colleges per se and others colleges of complementary medicine or natural therapies, and in three public universities in 2000 (Baer 2007).

CONCLUSION

Brodwin (1996:15) asserted that the "study of medical pluralism had reached a theoretical impasse" because efforts to categorize plural or dominative medical systems "often produced rigid functionalist typologies or broke down in a welter of incomparable terms." While indeed many medical anthropologists turn to concerns such as the political economy of health, biomedical hegemony, complementary and alternative medical systems in Western societies, reproduction, the body, the social dynamics of clinical encounters, biotechnology, substance abuse, AIDS, syndemics, and the impact of global warming on health, a perusal of medical anthropology journals indicates that the anthropological examination of medical pluralism is well and alive. Indeed, an increasing global interest in indigenous medical systems and Western heterodox medical systems, such as naturopathy, has accompanied the spread of HIV/AIDS, a topic of major anthropological research (Hollen 2005). Complementary and alternative therapies have come to be viewed not so much as cures for HIV/AIDS but as strategies that potentially bolster the auto/immune system and help patients to better cope with a debilitating disease (Baer 2008b). Furthermore, various anthropologists, including Brodwin (1996), continue to examine how power relations shape plural medical systems. In short, medical pluralism is a topic that continues to be of central concern in medical anthropology.

REFERENCES

Alter, Joseph S., 2005a Introduction: The Politics of Culture and Medicine. *In* Asian Medicine and Globalization. Joseph S. Alter, ed. pp. 1–20. Philadelphia: University of Pennsylvania.

Alter, Joseph S., 2005b Ayurvedic Acupuncture – Transnational Nationalism: Ambivalence about the Origin and Authenticity of Medical Knowledge. *In* Asian Medicine and Globalization. Joseph S. Alster, ed. pp. 21–44. Philadelphia: University of Pennsylvania Press.

Baer, Hans A., 1987 Divergence and Convergence in Two Manual Systems of Manual Medicine. Medical Anthropology Quarterly 1:76–93.

Baer, Hans A., 2001 Biomedicine and Alternative Healing Systems in America: Issues of Class, Race, Ethnicity, and Gender. Madison WI: University of Wisconsin Press.

Baer, Hans A., 2004 Toward an Integrative Medicine: Merging Alternative Therapies with Biomedicine. Walnut Creek CA: AltaMira Press.

Baer, Hans A., 2007 The Drive for Legitimation in Chinese Medicine and Acupuncture in Australia: Successes and Dilemmas. Complementary Health Practice Review 12:87–98.

Baer, Hans A., 2008a The Australian Dominative Medical System: A Reflection of Social Relations in the Larger Society. Australian Journal of Anthropology 19:252–271.

Baer, Hans A., 2008b Comparsion of Treatment of HIV Patients in Naturopathic and Biomedical Settings. Complementary Health Practice Review 13:182–197.

Baer, Hans A., and Ian Coulter, 2008 Taking Stock of Integrative Medicine – Broadening Biomedicine or Co-option of Complementary and Alternative Medicine. Introduction to Special Issue on Integrative, Complementary and Alternative Medicine: Challenges for Biomedicine? Health Sociology Review 17:331–341.

Baer, Hans A., Merrill Singer, and Ida Susser, 2003 Medical Anthropology and the World System: A Critical Perspective. 2nd edition. Westport CT: Praeger.

Brodwin, P., 1996 Medicine and Morality in Haiti. Cambridge UK: Cambridge University Press.

Cant, Sarah, and Ursula Sharma, 1999 A New Medical Pluralism? Alternative Medicine, Doctors, Patients, and the State. London: Taylor & Francis.

Chrisman, Noel J., and Arthur Kleinman, 1983 Popular Health Care, Social Networks, and Cultural Meanings: The Orientation of Medical Anthropology. *In* Handbook of Health, Health Care, and the Health Professions. David Mechanic, ed. pp. 589–591. New York: Free Press.

Connor, Linda, 2004 Relief, Risk and Renewal: Mixed Therapy Regimens in an Australian Suburb. Social Science and Medicine 59:1695–1705.

Crandon-Malamud, Libbet, 1991 From the Fat of Our Souls: Social Change, Political Process, and Medical Pluralism in Bolivia. Berkeley: University of California Press.

Cockerham, William C., and Ferris J. Ritchey, 1997 Dictionary of Medical Sociology. Westport CT: Greenwood Press.

Cominsky, Sheila, and Mary Scrimshaw, 1980 Medical Pluralism on a Guatemalan Plantation. Social Science and Medicine 14B:267–278.

Ernst, Waltraud, 2002 Plural Medicine, Tradition and Modernity: Historical and Contemporary Perspectives: Views From Below and From Above. *In* Plural Medicine, Tradition and Modernity. Waltraud Ernst, ed. pp. 1–18. London: Routledge.

Fabrega, Horacio, 1997 Evolution of Healing and Sickness. Berkeley: University of California Press.

Fadiman, Anne, 1997 The Spirit Catches You and You Fall Down: A Hmong Child, Her American Doctors, and the Collision of Two Cultures. New York: Farrar, Straus and Giroux.

Ferzacca, Steve, 2001 Healing the Modern in a Central Javanese City. Durham NC: Academic Press.

Frankenberg, Ronald, 1980 Medical Anthropology and Development: A Theoretical Perspective. Social Science and Medicine 14B:197–207.

Goldstein, Michael S., 2004 The Persistence and Resurgence of Medical Pluralism. Journal of Health Politics and Law 29:925–945.

Heggenhougen, H. K., 1980 Bomohs, Doctors and Sinsehs – Medical Pluralism in Malaysia. Social Science and Medicine 14B:235–244.

Helman, Cecil G., Culture, Health, and Illness. 5th edition. London: Wright.

Hollen, Cecilia Van, 2005 Nationalism, Transnationalism, and the Politics of "Traditional" Indian Medicine for HIV/AIDS. In Asian Medicine and Globalization. Joseph S. Alter, ed. pp. 88–106. Philadelphia: University of Pennsylvania Press.

Janes, Craig R., 2002 Buddhism, Science, and Market: The Globalisation of Tibetan Medicine. Anthropology and Medicine 9:341–363.

Kaufman, Martin, 1971 Homeopathy in America: The Rise and Fall of a Medical Heresy. Baltimore MD: Johns Hopkins University Press.

Kim, Jongyoung, 2009 Transcultural Medicine: A Multi-Sited Ethnography on the Scientific-Industrial Networking of Korean Medicine. Medical Anthropology 28:31–64.

Kleinman, Arthur, 1978 Concepts and a Model for the Comparsion of Medical Systems as Culture Systems. Social Science and Medicine 12:85–93.

Koss, Joan D., 1980 The Therapist-Spiritist Training Project in Puerto Rico: An Experiment to Relate to the Traditional Healing System to the Public Health System. Social Science and Medicine 14B:255–266.

Koss-Chioino, Joan D., Thomas Leatherman, and Christine Greenway, eds., 2003 Medical Pluralism in the Andes. London: Routledge.

Larkin, Gerald, 1983 Occupational Monopoly and Modern Medicine. London: Tavistock.

Leslie, Charles M., 1974 The Modernization of Asian Medical Systems. In Rethinking Modernization. John Poggie, Jr and Robert N. Lynch, eds. pp. 69–107. Westport CT: Greenwood Press.

Leslie, Charles M., 1976a Introduction. In Asian Medical Systems. Charles L. Leslie, ed. pp. 1–17. Berkeley: University of California Press.

Leslie, Charles M., 1976b The ambiguities of medical revivalism in modern India. In Asian Medical Systems. Charles M. Leslie, ed. pp. 356–367. Berkeley: University of California Press.

Leslie, Charles M., 1978 Introduction to Special Issue on Theoretical Foundations for the Comparative Study of Medical Systems. Social Science and Medicine 12:65–67.

Leslie, Charles M., 1992 Interpretations of illness: syncretism in modern Ayurveda. In Paths to Asian Medical Knowledge. Charles Leslie and Allan Young, eds. pp. 177–208. Berkeley: University of California Press.

Leslie, Charles M., and Allan Young, eds., 1992 Paths of Asian Medical Knowledge. Berkeley: University of California Press.

Lewis, Gilbert, 2007 Medical System and Questions in Fieldwork. In Knowing and Not Knowing. Ron Littlewood, ed. pp. 28–38. Walnut Creek CA: Left Coast Press.

Lock, Margaret, 1980 Organization and Practice of East Asian Medicine in Japan: Continuity and Change. Social Science and Medicine 14b:245–253.

Lock, Margaret, and Mark Nichter, 2002 Introduction: From documenting medical pluralism to critical interpretations of globalized health knowledge, policies, and practices. In New Horizons in Medical Anthropology: Essays in Honour of Charles Leslie. Mark Nichter and Margaret Lock, eds. pp. 1–34. London: Routledge.

Nichter, Mark, 1980 Layperson's Perception of Medicine as Perspective into the Utilization of Multiple Therapy Systems in Indian Context. Social Science and Medicine 14B:225–233.

Ohnuki-Tierney, Emiko, 1984 Illness and Culture in Contemporary Japan. Cambridge: Cambridge University Press.

Poole, Robert, and Wenzel Gessler, 2005 Medical Anthropology: Understanding Public Health. Maidenhead, UK: Open University Press.

Roth, Julius A., with Richard R. Hanson, 1976 Health Purifiers and Their Enemies: A Study of the Natural Health Movement in the United States with a Comparsion to Its Counterpart in Germany. New York: Prodist.

Saks, Michael, 1994 The Alternatives to Medicine. *In* Challenging Medicine. Jonathan Gabe, David Kelleher and Gareth Williams, eds. pp. 84–102. London: Routledge.

Salkend, Ellen J., 2005 Holistic Physicians' Clinical Discourse on Risk: An Ethnographic Study. Medical Anthropology 24:325–347.

Singer, Merrill, and Hans A. Baer, 2007 Introducing Medical Anthropology: A Discipline in Action. Walnut Creek CA: AltaMira Press.

Wallace, Anthony F. C., 1956 Revitalization Movements. American Anthropologist 58: 264–281.

White, Kevin, 2006 The Sage Dictionary of Health and Society. London: Sage.

Willis, Evan, 1989 Medical Dominance. Revised edition. St. Leonards, NSW, Australia: Allen & Unwin.

Zhang, Everett Yuehong, 2007 Switching between Traditional Chinese Medicine and Viagra: Cosmopolitanism and Medical Pluralism Today. Medical Anthropology 26:53–96.

CHAPTER 21

Biotechnologies of Care

Julie Park and Ruth Fitzgerald

Recent anthropological work on biomedical technologies, deals with personhood (Squier 2004), processes of identity formation (Martin 2007), the varied forms of human and non-human connectedness (Rock and Babinec 2008), the impacts of political economies on health technologies and healing performances (Delvecchio Good 2001), economic exchanges based on human tissue trading (Waldby and Mitchell 2006; Thacker 2005) and the context-specific elaboration of moral worlds of treatment (Battles and Manderson 2008). Our focus for this chapter is instead to explore biotechnology and care because much of the recent work attends to the "high tech/low touch" end of the biotechnology spectrum. While assemblages such as tele-medicine, the new genetics, reproductive medicine, new imaging modalities, and transplant surgeries have been enthusiastically investigated by anthropologists; this has often left the analysis of the mundane caring techniques and technologies at the low-tech end of the spectrum to be conducted by the natives. A further characteristic of this recent literature has been the sustained focus on the hybrid personhood devel-oped between patients and technologies, leading to something of a neglect of the similarly complex but under-researched personhoods created between practitioners and technologies, or both groups together. By combining our recent work in the specific local context of Aotearoa/New Zealand however, we have the opportunity to think anthropologically about some of these less studied issues. Furthermore by selecting a perspective from outside the USA and the UK, we can, in doing so, reflect our interests in local biologies (Lock 2001) and also in voice and dominance in the field of medical anthropology itself.

To begin with some definitions, the word "biotechnology" encompasses material devices designed for specific medical functions and the techniques for using them which include the "background practices and treatment rituals in which a given device acquires its meaning" (Brodwin 2000:2). Brodwin writes that value and meaning are

A Companion to Medical Anthropology, First Edition. Edited by Merrill Singer and Pamela I. Erickson.

not inherent in technologies, but are created through their social life which is complex, and may include people and groups who never participate in these technologies but for whom they are meaningful nonetheless. Embryo research is such an example in which a variety of publics comment (often forcefully) on the ethical implications of such work without the experience of parenting or an engagement in research programs making use of such material. Our use of biotechnology draws from these understandings and adds to them Foucaultian theorizing about biopower which produces powerful effects in the bodyself and in social life. Reflecting this perspective, we have chosen to define biotechnology in the broad sense of technologies that intervene in life, rather than the narrower sense of technologies that themselves comprise living organisms.

Care is another complex concept involving care for, care of and care about. It speaks simultaneously to the hopes of patients and the competencies of workers (Fitzgerald 2008a), and has an expansive meaning in regard to affect, while also containing the meaning of "troubles" or "worries" and the ambivalence of thoughts on institutionalized care. As noted long ago in Dr. Johnson's Dictionary, it also has a thread of meaning related to frugality and thrift – so apposite in today's discussion of contemporary healthcare allocation. Anthropologists have been slow to analyze its breadth of meanings. Taylor (2008) and Cohen (2008) for instance have discussed aspects of the "bittersweet" of caring relationships and the nature of personhood for people living with cognitive impairments. Borneman (1996) has argued that relations of care might form the basis for a reconceptualization of kinship in a form which denies the unversalist framing of such connection in terms of dominance and subjugation. As Mol (2008) notes, the term is eloquent in its depth and breadth to convey the complexity of both the experience and the provision of cosmopolitan medicines. She suggests that part of the reason for the contemporary focus on rational choice as a default moral position in medicine, and the prominence of efficiency-based tropes of clinical management (e.g., EBM, Managed Care, TQM) is because of the silencing of the previously prominent language of care to describe best moral practice and the "good" of the patient. Her study of diabetes care in the Netherlands attempts to provide a primer in the language of care in one specific context in relation to one instance of the spread of technologies, as some of our own work has attempted in relation to certain New Zealand health workers (Fitzgerald 2004, 2008b) or patients (Park 2005, Searle et al. 2007).

Circuits of care have been the objects of anthropological attention in the study by Biehl (2007) of the networks of activists and international aid organizations, which first provided access to anti-retroviral therapies (ARVs) for indigent street dwellers in Brazil. In some ways this event was a groundbreaking triumph of the delivery of "high tech" pharmaceuticals by a developing country to its population; as prostitutes and street dwellers took over abandoned buildings to develop "houses of support" as distribution points for ARVs. The very success of the system, however, caused the cycle of exclusion from treatment for the poorest of the poor, to begin once again; as the non-governmental organizations began to develop their own logics of outcomes, measurements, and evidence of efficacy to justify their continued funding of these establishments. The language of care became effaced by the language of efficiency, and the "houses of support" were renamed "houses of passage." While some of the original members of the houses of support could grasp the technology of ARVs and use this pharmaceutical care of the self to transform themselves into models of Brazilian citizenship – actively distancing themselves from the culture of street life – many more could not. A similar circuit in and out of care has been described for stroke victim survivors in the USA who progress along rehabilitation pathways until they "plateau" at a certain level of physical ability which initiates the survivor's exit from active therapy and insertion into the maintenance strategies of geriatric care (Kaufman 1988).

Care is a component of the concepts of biosociality (Rabinow 1996) and genetic citizenship (Heath et al. 2007) which are foundational to anthropological studies of biotechnology. Petryna's (2002) account of the explicit mobilization of private suffering towards public and political purposes (including access to state funded "care" for victims of the Chernobyl disaster) is a case in point. The full potential of anthropological attention to both biotechnology and care, we suggest, is just emerging. It is in ethnographic research with its emphasis on sustained and highly contextualized study that the local specificities of the forms and practice of care emerge, along with its politicized and contested meanings: anthropologists are professionally and methodologically well placed to open up the black boxes of "biotechnology" and "care." Hamdy, for instance, poignantly sums up the interconnectivities of these concepts in her study of poor Egyptians under dialysis treatment, whose own interpretations of the causation of their illness lies in being: "connected to machines that are themselves connected to state infrastructure and its not always reliable delivery of skills, labor and power" (Hamdy 2008:556).

Brodwin recognized the political aspect of biotechnologies when he cited the argument that biotechnologies are powerful because they legitimate dominant social institutions while simultaneously hiding this function. He suggested that they do this via a relationship with science that naturalizes social and political forces. Our approach in Aotearoa/New Zealand suggests, perhaps surprisingly, that scientific views of biotechnologies are not always as dominant as one might expect. Such powerful interests may be silenced by competing and more strident voices, such as managerialism in hospital bureaucracies, or the newly created specialism of bioethics, as in debates around new reproductive technologies. Taking as our starting point the new arrangements of social life that biotechnologies can produce, we will consider three of what is a much larger variety of nodes of the socio-technical system of biotechnology and care: community, hospitals, and embodied contexts. Our final substantive section concerns the public discourses that pertain to all these contexts.

COMMUNITY CONTEXT

Ethnographic research with people who are in the community care of professional others can yield paradoxical results. Participants in some studies downplay the technological/surveillance aspects of care, while others (see below) interpret aspects of home help, for example, as home invasion. Essén (2008) points out that despite considerable debate and many expressions of concern about e-surveillance, there are few empirical studies of the experience of those being surveilled in the health field. She approached her study of elderly people at home who had agreed to trade in their "panic buttons" for e-surveillance systems aware of the contingent nature of surveillance technology and its ability to be experienced as constraining or enabling. One person did experience the technology as an invasion of privacy, but the others found that because it allowed them to stay in the privacy of their own homes, where they were free from the intrusion of unwanted others often experienced in rest homes, it provided freedom, privacy and was enabling. Indeed, the advanced technology was seen as a better way for their health personnel to care for them, being more reliable and flexible than the manual alarms that it replaced. The relationship with their caregiver was paramount and the e-technology appeared to be understood as an effective conduit for that relationship. The subtlety of electronic intrusions may also be at play here, or cultural differences in concepts of privacy, home and care, for a recent Ph.D. dissertation from the University of Otago by Hale suggests that for New Zealand Seniors, it was the residential care facility that was far more favored as the site of personal care delivery than the homeplace. This counterintuitive finding becomes reasonable once the casual psychic brutality of being assessed for personal competencies in the "real" versus "virtual" world are revealed. For instance, one participant described how the (home) visiting Occupational Therapist (OT) asking her to first undress and then dress again in her direct view in order to assess her ability. "Why couldn't she take my word for it?," the participant reflected in remembered anguish. As Hale notes, the humiliation is vivid precisely because it occurs within the home where one expects peace of mind and autonomy. For many of Hale's participants, perceptions of the meaning of place were acute, and such indignities were more easily accommodated within the residential care facility – a site composed of a complex blurring of public and private space to which residents had already become well adjusted. This is a fascinating example of the importance of social context in the emerging meanings of technologies.

Essén's participants' positive experiences of surveillance technology are similar to that of Pakeha (New Zealanders of "European" descent) and Maori (indigenous) patients in New Zealand receiving directly observed therapy (DOT) for tuberculosis. The organizational technology of DOT is used to increase adherence to the six-month-plus course of anti-tubercular drugs that people with active TB disease need to take. Successful TB treatment relies on completion of this course. In New Zealand, DOT usually involves visits by the Public Health Nurse to the patient at a mutually agreed place. Yet, rather than interpreting the visits of the DOT workers as surveillance, many patients interpreted them as part of a key relationship in their lives, one that, in some cases, quite literally saved their lives.

Dale, a middle-aged Pakeha man, emphasized the moral economy of care, loyalty, and appreciation: "You're grateful, you play the game, you've a sense of loyalty. [My PHN] made it easy, she didn't judge me, she understood" (Dale, 57 years, reflecting on his TB treatment) (Searle et al. 2007:57). Oh's work with Maori TB patients found similar themes, "All study participants described PHNs as supportive, informative, and caring throughout patient treatment" (Oh 2008:74). A typical comment from Oh's conversations with Maori TB patients, this one made by an older woman, was "[PHN] is very supportive, good. When I'm having down days, moody, sick of it all, [PHN] would pick me up and say, 'You and me go have a coffee'". The alliance or "being with" of the Public Health Nurses not only encouraged the patient to complete the treatment but provided support, advice and practical help, for example, in dealing with the stigma of tuberculosis or with housing needs.

Collegial relationships between patients and carers using communication technology can also transform potential surveillance technology into a technology of partnership, creating, and reinforcing community, as Essén found in Sweden. Palm pilots for hemo-philia are another example. People with hemophilia in developed countries now mostly treat themselves at home by infusing clotting factor made from human blood or genet-ically engineered recombinant clotting products two or three times a week. For many years it was a struggle for boys, their parents and men to keep track of this in paper diaries, along with the batch numbers of their products, bleeding episodes and other relevant incidents. The advent of palm pilots allows people with hemophilia to record this information electronically and this is instantly transmitted to their treatment centre and possibly to the pharmaceutical company or research trial. Studies of this new tech-nology report that the electronic communication is usually enthusiastically received and experienced as a highly superior method of keeping track of treatments, bleeds and such (Arnold et al. 2005). Reports from individuals reinforce this positive reception. *Voyage* (2006), the Newsletter of the "Passport to wellbeing program" of the Canadian Hemophilia Society contains a story from a 10 year old boy who writes about how get-ting and learning to use a palm pilot was an exciting new step for him, part of learning to infuse himself and becoming more grown up. He comments on the speed, conven-ience and the close, if indirect, contact it provides with his nurse.

The relationship with the treatment centre, "feeling part of the health care team," and an understanding of the benefits of close monitoring of this expensive and some-times difficult treatment, seems to dominate the technology's reception. In addition, the experience of contaminated product in the past, which led to some people with hemophilia being infected with viruses, has alerted the hemophilia community to the importance of recording batch numbers and being very attentive to product recall. In this instance, rather than surveillance being the experience, the exchange of informa-tion among the "team" is a great benefit of the technology, with convenience run-ning a close second. Keeping a close eye on the amount of product consumed is an aspect of good citizenship for people with hemophilia in New Zealand who are very aware that their treatment is funded through the taxes of fellow citizens (Park and York 2008).

HOSPITAL CONTEXT

In a hospital context, material and organizational technologies interact with profes-sional practices to create technologies of care that have complex implications for patients. Neo-liberal reform of the health sector, often adopted as part of broader "structural adjustment" programs, is a forceful technology of care that has reconfig-ured expectations and practices for both hospital workers and their communities in all parts of the globe (Foley 2009; Maupin 2008). Hospitals have not only absorbed information technology and engaged in the redeployment and multi-skilling of their workforce, but the length of stay for patients has decreased while the severity of con-ditions from which they suffer has increased. Keating and Cambrosio (2003:18) also suggest that since the 1950s the incorporation of biomedical science "platforms" or laboratories into the central organization of hospitals has marked a change in the practice of hospital medicine away from the study of gross pathological specimens and toward the study of ordinary biological markers in disease processes. As a result, new and more complex biological entities have emerged and biomedical technologies have become further enmeshed in the performance of routine clinical examinations and diagnosis. As Malone's (2003) study of distal and proximal nursing in the United States makes clear, these rearrangements of hospital life have very immediate consequences for nursing but the implications go well beyond this professional group. They affect all sectors of a modern hospital including managerial, clinical, and service staff, and patients (Fitzgerald 2004).

Malone argues that nursing in the United States is vulnerable to managerial and material technologies because it is based on "taken-for-granted" proximity to patients. This proximity has several dimensions, including physical, narrative, and moral: respectively, physical care and touch, knowing the patient through listening, and "being for" the patient, which may involve acting on their behalf. As she points out, this day-to-day proximity to patients makes possible tasks such as bathing or back-rubs, listening to stories and witnessing distress, and mediating the patient's world view to others when the patient is not able to do so him/herself. Yet in many parts of the Western world re-structured health care systems have greatly changed the spatial-temporal nexus of nurse–patient relationships. Factors such as a more "flexible" work-force (which reduces continuity of care), shorter in-patient stays, managerialism (which stresses efficiency according to standardized care plans), highly structured and limited reporting using abstract categories, as well as more sophisticated material technology, have all played a part in reducing the time that nurses have in close contact with patients. As depicted by Malone, nurses instead monitor and respond to streams of information produced by advanced technical equipment. Less skilled health workers tend to carry out tasks that used to be central to nursing practice, to the creation of healing relationships with patients and information-rich collegial relationships with other nurses. In this context, taking time to listen to distressed patients can be construed as time *out* from the real nursing task of "managing the technical tasks necessary for discharge production" (Malone 2003: 2322). Malone notes that "distal nurses," i.e., those who do not engage with patients but see nursing as a technical pursuit, are perfectly co-adapted to current trends in United States health care. However, their effectiveness as healers is less clear. A tension between proximal and distal nursing as Malone calls it or care and competence (Good 1994) has long been recognized in medical anthropology literature, particularly in studies on the training of health professionals. Much reflective writing speaks of the difficulties of balancing both these dimensions in their practice. What is new, as suggested in Malone's work, is the routine production and selection of distal nurses and nursing practices by health care organizational and managerial structures, enabled by advanced medical and electronic equipment. Pickles (1999), writing of his experience in Intensive Care in England, warns that the valorization of science and technology in nursing may cause nurses to pay too much attention to their equipment and less attention to caring for and about their patients. Yet caring for the lived body, rather than the object body, Pickles suggests, is more complex and demanding than the technical machine-focused tasks, and more central to nursing's emphasis on the whole person. As Spitzer (2004) describes for Canadian obstetrical nurses, cost cutting, partly due to the ever-increasing costs of hospital technology and pharmaceuticals, has primarily been achieved by reducing nursing staff numbers. Not only does this create pressures for more distal nursing in general, but it appears to increase inequality of care. Nurses tended to avoid minority group patients, whom they perceived would take up too much of their precious time. Accounts of nursing cultures from non-Western nations are still very limited in number and scope, but as Henderson warned in a reflective essay in 2004, nursing is fluid and varied between nations as well as within them. Thus these accounts must be seen as relevant to the neo-liberalizing "West," rather than universal.

This tension in care is discussed in the context of two New Zealand hospitals by Fitzgerald (2004). At the time of her study (1997–1998), the New Zealand health care system was in the grip of a managerialist phase in a series of health sector restructurings which had had devastating effects on health-workers' morale and on institutional memory. Fitzgerald developed two ideal type models of care, based on her extensive participant observation and interviews. Type One care, exhibited by a variety of clinical workers was based in technical competence but was focused on the embodied patient and the relationship with the patient. Type Two care, exhibited by managers, administrators, and computer experts, was focused on the hospital and its systems. While this included patients, it was patients in the abstract, for example patients as a category: "regular" or "special," or "satisfied customer" or "angry customer." Rather than the tensions between the more abstract and the more relational forms of care being experienced within single practitioners or within professional groups, the organizational technology "divided the labour of care" between two clusters of health workers who did not communicate, with important ethical consequences for quality of care and, at worst, for patient survival. The introduction of computerized and minutely monitored timetables, careplans, operating theatre rosters and automated supply ordering offered only one perspective of the "health" of the system. For example, while rational and cost effective, the use of "just in time" ordering for hospital supplies left clinical staff unable to provide the material bases of care when faced with rapid fluctuations in the numbers attending in their daily clinics.

The transfiguration of scientists into care workers is another outcome of biotechnology's uptake into cosmopolitan medicine. Technologists who carry out tests on cells obtained through amniocentesis, provide examples of (science) practitioners who practice multi-layered caring but whose ethical contributions are overlooked. This test (extensively investigated by Rapp (e.g., Rapp 1988; Rapp et al. 2001) requires the careful culture of fetal cells over several days. In 2004, Finlay engaged in participant observation with a national sampling of cytogeneticists who work in the hospital laboratories in New Zealand to understand the stresses and challenges of their work. The answers were revealing for amongst their pleasures, cytogeneticists routinely drew upon the personification of the fetal cell cultures, calling them their "little babies," and worrying that their "tootsies were warm enough" – certainly a new variety of life form within the hospital incubators. Similarly, Finlay et al. (2004) found that the incubator alarms had been hooked up to baby monitors in many laboratories. The study also revealed that despite the highest professional standards of practice, these scientists found their work to be ethically troubling. Amongst their concerns were anxieties that the complex results that their work produced were not well comprehended by local doctors who were advising their patients on the "meaning" of the result. The cytogeneticists also routinely tolerated a much wider degree of genetic difference as "normal" than members of the public with whom they came into contact, and were perplexed at the increasing pathologization of this "normal" human variation to which they understood their jobs contributed. In sum, they saw themselves as middlemen and women, unable to discuss their concerns, whose solace was a meticulous professionalism in all interactions, perfect scientific technique, and the resolution of their ethical concerns via the internalization of their roles as "allowing women the right to choose."

EMBODIED CONTEXTS

As well as providing information about new arrangements of professional groups around scientific practices, ethnographic research also provides opportunities to explore the lived experiences of engaging with biotechnologies at more individualized levels, and decades of rich work from medical anthropologists now exist for biotechnologies of reproduction (Becker 2000; Franklin and Roberts 2006), genetics (Rapp et al. 2001; Pálsson and Rabinow 2005; Lock 2009), and human organ transfers (Cohen 2005; Sharpe 2006; Scheper-Hughes 2009). Biotechnologies combine in interesting and unexpected ways with humans and successful explanations of these puzzling new arrangements are often produced by opening up the black box of the biotechnology itself. Consider for a moment the workings of the erectile enhancement drug Viagra.

In a New Zealand study of around 60 men and women with experience of erectile dysfunction and its treatment with the drug Viagra, Potts (Potts et al. 2004:699) notes that the drug "Viagra is a device (or technology) which itself is coded with various social and cultural understandings about sexuality and masculinity." The actions of Viagra can certainly be described biomedically in terms of increasing blood flow, etc. However Potts et al. (2004) argue that Viagra also "flows" through interconnecting channels of ideas of penis/vagina penetrative sex as the "normal" mode of sexual expression (allowing for the pathologization of decreasing erectile function in older men), and dominant assumptions of female sexuality as passive and receptive (thus authorizing men's clinics to exclude female partners from clinical discussions of impotence). The drug also creates different personhoods between the male with and without Viagra to the extent that some women in her study found their Viagra-enhanced partners unrecognizable – "yucky...predatory... demanding... intrusive."

There are parallels here in this materially dispersed yet interconnecting subjectivity and its surprising re-routings of agency which evoke Latour's actor network theory, Haraway's cyborg politics, Canguilhem's rejection of the organic/machine distinction, and Merleau Ponty's classical example of the embodied self as inescapably immersed within and a part of the world which it perceives. Of these approaches to conceiving the new subjectivities which emerge from the interplay between humans and biotechnologies, it seems surprising that so little medical anthropological work explicitly explores cyborg identities (as developed through Haraway's scholarship), apart from early work in cyborg anthropology (Downey et al. 1995). This is especially so because cyborg identities created through medical practice often produce particularly intense and polarized views of the nature of "good care." For instance the bioethicist Nelson (2000), in his study of the cyborg ventilator/baby Michael, explains how the presence of technology changes perceptions of the human connected to it and how the cyborg identity of the child becomes more prominent to medical and nursing staff than it does to the child's mother. As Nelson (2000) recounts, the resulting interpretive battle between the mother and clinical staff over the significance of

Michael's "weeping"/ "tearing" as he "suffered"/ "exhibited the reflex action of any intubated ventilator assisted person" is better understood (and perhaps assuaged) by investigating the interpretive dilemmas of cyborg existence than through determinations of the "facts of the matter" according to biological science.

In another instance of deliberate engagement with the cyborg personhoods which biomedical technologies produce, Hogle (1995), in her study of organ transfers in multiple ethnographic locations in contemporary Germany, explores the context dependent elaboration of cyborgs from the combinations of sustaining drugs and fluids that are pumped into people existing in a state of supported brain death prior to the collection of their organs for transfer to another person. Such cyborgs problematize the meaning and timing of social death through their existence, and create points of conflict over good "care" of the neomort as different chemical cocktails will sustain certain interior organs at the expense of diminished quality in other organs. Deciding which set of fluids to run through the neomort has consequences for several networks of potential transplant recipients, their families and medical teams.

However, not all writers have endorsed the use of cyborg subjectivity as a theoretical term in medical anthropology, for example Cherney (1999), in his discussion of cochlear implant technology, has formulated a critique from the perspective of "Deaf Culture." Drawing on deep readings of several classic science fiction tales of "cyborg spaceships" (constructed of the human central nervous systems from disabled people who are trained from childhood to prepare to be integrated into spaceships as adults), Cherney successfully convinces that the cyborgs of science fiction futures are constructed from the same discriminatory grid of "normal" versus "other" that pervades contemporary political economies. For instance, in all these brain ship novels, no able-bodied person ever steps forward to "become" a brain ship. To compound this, those born with pronounced cognitive developmental disorders are never cared for and allowed a life; instead, they are terminated after cognitive testing reveals a level of mental ability that does not equate to an arbitrary "usefulness." Clearly, a brain ship should not be understood to offer the liberatory potential of Haraway's cyborg politics, and Cherney suggests that the popular use of the term confounds its suitability for analytical work. As it is mostly used in fiction, "cyborg" reinforces one's lack of physical abilities rather than de-emphasizing their importance, with cyborg technology being the compensatory "quick fix" to "nearly as good" as "normal."

Cherney goes on to explain the development of cochlear implant technology and its controversial use in young US children as an example of the dominant oralist culture using futuristic cyborg arguments to override the identity politics arguments from members of "Deaf Culture" who have no wish to hear and whose sign language performs all the rich requirements of any language. Disconcertingly, the majority of consenting cochlear implant/person cyborgs according to Cherney has been those members of the Deaf community who were born with hearing: i.e., only a small segment of the diverse Deaf world. Laing's (2006) writing about the diversity of Deaf Culture in New Zealand supports Cherney's concerns.

So, what should we (as a diversely "abled group") make of Cherney's insights, especially, given that so many accounts focus on the production of cyborg identities for patients, excluding clinical staff from the resulting cybernetic caring networks? As Casper (1995) noted, in her work on "technomoms" and "technofetuses," when studying critically the significance of certain biotechnologies one must always consider *in whose interests* the resultant cyborg identities have been created. For Viagra/Men the answer from Potts would be Phizer, for Cochlear Implants/Recently Deaf People, while Cherney suggests it is oralist culture. Are medical anthropologists then, through their discursive and research-based focus on cyborg/patients rather than cyborg/practitioners, shoring up heroic views of medicine in which intact superheroes manipulate complex machinery entirely to their will in order to cure? To allow cyborg subjectivity into ethnographic constructions of health *practitioners'* practice would allow for the unsettling drift of agency outwards from doctors and onwards through complicated, politically specific cybernetic loops of technologies and people including scientists, technicians, paramedical support staff, and machines.

One overlooked example of caring cyborgs are Medical X-ray Workers, the Medical Imaging Technologists who work with radiation (and other intrusive technologies of imaging) to produce a variety of X-rays and other images for diagnosis. In Fitzgerald's (2004) study, the X-ray department was spoken of as the "blood and guts" department of the hospital for their routine involvement in emergency assessment work for casualties and medical emergencies. As a group, the workers were not held in high regard, a situation compounded by their willing acceptance of Total Quality Management into their working lives as the top level management at that time set about "re-engineering" the workplace. At a personal level, their reputation was for brusque efficiency and lack of empathy since their work frequently involved contorting patients into very painful positions in order to get the best quality X-rays to aid in the diagnosis of their medical problems.

In agreement with this imputed public persona is the uncomplimentary published anthropological literature about X-ray workers. For example in Taylor (2000), the sonographers/technologists are described as judgemental and racist. While in Mitchell and Georges' 1997 Montreal study of women's experiences of ultrasound in pregnancy, we learn how certain women, classified as "not nice mothers," received truncated information about their fetus, occasionally even deliberately wrong information. Burri (2007:118–119), in observing workers in an MRI scanner notes the cold communication via microphone with the patient, the repetitive commanding nature of the instructions by the technologist and the ritually empty platitudes of "well done" when the person complies.

Against these damning commentaries we now place the words of the New Zealand study participants who when asked if they "cared" about their patients replied forthrightly that they most certainly did. As one worker mentioned: "It's an experience thing, a lot of the junior staff don't get it right… like it depends how good your people skills are … but you have to be able to read people to do this job and a lot of my skills I have learnt from dealing with people over the last ten years." This disjunction between appearances and personal beliefs can be bridged by thinking more carefully about the technologists as cyborg entities linked into their imaging machines, for much of the technologists' most potent work of care, in the sense of affect, is invisible to the patient, colleagues and many anthropologist observers! For instance, the radiographers most clearly and regularly demonstrated empathetic concern for their patient's discomfort through the manipulation of their machinery rather than towards the patient directly. In this world of enforced pain and delayed diagnosis, speed and dexterity are themselves compassionate instruments of care. Senior workers, without mentioning to the patient, and working only by silent agreement with each other, routinely changed or reduced the sequence of films during the procedure from those requested on the X-ray request form in order to not unnecessarily prolong a person's agony. One worker noted, when directly questioned about this informal habit, that it was a cruelty to "do all these tests for no (good) reason." However, such changes of technique left the staff member exposed to significant censure should the resulting truncated set of films provide inadequate diagnostic information. In the cybernetic care loop of X-ray work in New Zealand, we suggest that the time pressure, which is a constant feature of such work in the department (with its resultant pressure on caring), is resolved through the cybernetic re-routing of affect towards the patient via the technologist's attention to their imaging equipment, its rapidly dextrous manipulation, and the risky addition or subtraction of "extra" images in the pursuit of a diagnosis. These silent acts of mechanized kindliness and moral practice are part of that unspoken logic of care which Mol (2008) suggests require more study by anthropologists in various locations around the world.

A variety of other publics have *also* been commenting on the moral practices which biotechnologies such we have been discussing can generate. These public comments pertain to all three contexts that we have discussed, demonstrating the importance of biotechnology in public imaginations.

DISCURSIVE PUBLIC CONTEXTS

Inhorn (2008:186) has suggested that Assisted Reproductive Technologies "are a key symbol of our times, representing the growing prominence of biotechnologies in the configuration of individual, familial and collective identities." Biotechnology in general, and ARTs in particular, have been a focus for legislative debates, public submissions, and government-appointed commissions in most Western countries. As Inhorn notes, the religion/science terms in which these debates are often addressed leaves "a moral vacuum to be filled by ethicists and lawyers" (2008:184), while in other jurisdictions, religion may very directly guide the way ARTs are implemented, or not. In the New Zealand debates, in addition to the features noted by Inhorn, what is particularly striking is the observable contrasts in the principles used for ethical decision-making or ethical prescription depending on where the individuals or groups voicing their opinions are located (Fitzgerald 2009; Gillett 2009; Glover and Rousseau 2007; Park 2009). New Zealand completed its ART legislation in 2004, well after a Royal Commission on Genetic Modification (1991) reported. The public written submissions made to the Select Committee in 2003 included two major discourses, one Christian identified, the other science-medicine identified. A more minor discourse was aligned with a disability rights framing. Briefly, the Christian identified discourse referred to God, church teaching or Christianity to support arguments or positions taken, such as the claim that an embryo is a human being from conception. The science-medicine discourse invoked scientific justifications, for example justifying a claim to the timing of individuation by reference to embryological development, or supporting new procedures because science needed to advance. The disability rights discourse framed disability as a social construction, rather than the result of medical or health problems. Within all three discourses there were expressions of fear and caution that ARTs were challenging the boundaries of "normal humanness." Some saw

ARTs as having the potential towards eugenic selection and commodification of humans. The desire to have children was naturalized in the submissions, and, particularly in the Christian-identified ones, "natural kinship" was seen as being challenged. Issues of human rights, identity, and the rights of offspring to know their origins emerged as important issues (Park et al. 2008).

What is of interest here is that the majority of the submissions have been made by individuals or groups who had interests in but no personal experience of ART. Few actually debated issues. Rather, many just asserted a particular perspective on aspects of the impending legislation, such as that reproduction is the realm of nature or the divine and should not be tampered with by humans. Different views were sometimes acknowledged, but usually only to be dismissed. Except for the academic submissions, and a few Christian-identified ones, little scientific evidence was provided for positions taken. These submissions on the Bill were to the Parliamentary Health Committee. Participants in the subsequent debates in Parliament who had been members of this Committee referred several times to the quality of the Committee's debate and the care members had taken to comprehend the perspectives presented through oral and written submissions from the public and officials. These debates showed an unusually careful and cooperative approach to what virtually all Members of Parliament saw as an important and sensitive moral and human issue (McLauchlan et al., in press. It was notable that parliamentarians drew on their own experiences and those of their constituents so that in these debates, much more so than in the submissions, there was representation of the views of those intimately involved with these issues. Members respectfully acknowledged that different people had deeply held views on a range of matters relating to ART and that Parliament could work on those areas on which some agreement could be reached.

When comparing the approaches revealed in the submissions and in the Parliamentary Debates with those gained through ethnographic research with various affected groups in the community, it is clear that the Parliamentary Debates were much more closely aligned with, for example, discourses in the hemophilia community than were the submissions, revealing the situated nature of bioethics and the value of anthropological approaches to understanding what Scully et al. (2006) call "ordinary ethics."

A paradoxical outcome of the NZ Human ART (HART) Act (2004) is that it espoused a guidelines approach which devolved future deliberations on unresolved issues, or new issues, to appointed committees which did not meet in public, although some of them, such as the Bioethics Council /Toi te Taiao (dis-established in 2009) conducted public consultation on a range of issues, including reproduction. One such exercise in public consultation and private deliberation resulted in the publication of the report "Who Gets Born? Pre-birth Testing" (http://www.bioethics.org.nz). The Council reached the conclusion that there is no "ethical" reason against sex selection for non-medical reasons. This conclusion was in opposition to the almost unanimous stance against non-medical sex-selection in both the HART submissions and the Parliamentary Debates as well as in the committee's own highly promoted deliberative encounters with citizens (29–30, 35, *contra* see p.27). To have proposed a recommendation so out of line with widely-shared community concerns suggests the problem of imagining "bioethics" as somehow outside the social, i.e., as a form of naturalised discourse that Brodwin (2000) warned against.

These community concerns which led to such a unanimous opinion against sex selection were complex. They included concerns specific to sex and gender, such as a strong wish for legal protection against selection based on sex that might favor boys. In such a multicultural society as New Zealand there was some fear that such selection might be widely practiced in some migrant communities. This concern was closely aligned with the defense and protection of gender equality. There was also concern that what was often seen as a rather trivial issue, namely so called "family balancing" in terms of sex, trivialized the traumas of HART which should be used only for "serious" issues. Finally, allowing sex selection ignored the widespread understanding of "baby as gift," a metaphor used in the Bioethics Council deliberative process and their Report, but not explored. Babies are widely understood as gifts, and as such, are to be accepted, whatever their sex: "You don't look a gift horse in the mouth."

Trotter (2006) warns that "participatory democracy" can lead to the wielding of power by a few over many, with the façade of consensus and deliberation leading to the acceptance of such rulings. Goven (2003), discussing plant genetic technologies, where New Zealand participants' views in deliberative processes are overshadowed by economic and scientific modes of understanding, concurs. In the human domain we suggest that bioethics deliberations may overshadow the social and cultural concerns of communities and citizens (Pálsson 2007:130), and replace the role of science as the hegemonic discourse. This realizes the fears expressed throughout the HART Debates by many Members about relying on non-representative, unelected groups for bioethical recommendations. The deliberations and reports of specialist bioethics councils are valuable but, as argued by social researchers from Muller (1994) to Scully et al. (2006), they need to be complemented by knowledge of "ordinary" ethics, which ethnographic research is in an excellent position to provide.

An outstanding example is provided by Franklin and Roberts (2006) who in their ethnography of preimplantation genetic diagnosis (PGD) in the UK describe PGD as a way of caring for the grief-stricken. This biotechnology is being employed for social and psychological reasons. They describe the heartbreak of parents who have had their children die from genetic disorders, or mothers who have multiple terminations when tests show the fetus is affected, and who just want to know that their baby will not suffer from this genetic disorder. This sober account of the careful decision-making of would-be parents and the cautionary counsels of doctors and nurses who are engaged in their care is a far cry from some of the popular debates, and indeed the New Zealand HART submissions, which use notions of designer babies and "slippery" slopes to indicate careless and even frivolous approaches to reproduction.

Conclusion

Noting the rich, multi-sited, ethnographic literature which examines biotechnology and care in diverse areas of the world, we hope that future work will expand the study of the more taken-for-granted aspects of bio(medical)technologies as well as increase the variety, location, and complexity of the fieldwork being undertaken. The sophisticated familiarity with the anthropology of technology literature (and of social studies of science) which underpins contemporary work in this field predicts that more profound anthropological insights will derive from detailed studies of the most taken-for-granted and banal of devices.

Our chapter has suggested that one example of these taken-for-granted biotech-nologies is relationships of care. These technologies of care may be very diffusely located within networks of human and nonhumans. The technician manipulating an X-ray machine with speed and silent compassion, or working with DNA analysis with absolute precision, is involved in an ethics of care no less than a proximal nurse or a diabetes patient learning to test their own blood sugar level. An ongoing challenge for health care systems is how to incorporate the voices of all these carers along with the voices of community members with their "ordinary ethics" into grounded discussions of the dynamic and unexpected consequences of the new life forms and assemblages of biotechnology.

ACKNOWLEDGMENTS

We thank Ally Palmer (funded by a University of Auckland Summer Scholarship) for invaluable research assistance for this chapter.

REFERENCES

Arnold, E., N. Heddle, S. Lane, J. Sek, T. Almonte, and I. Walker,2005 Handheld Computers and Paper Diaries for Documenting the Use of Factor Concentrates Used in Haemophilia Home Therapy: A Qualitative Study. Haemophilia 11(3): 216–226.

Battles, H. T., and L. Manderson, 2008 The Ashley Treatment. Furthering the Anthropology of/on Disability. Medical Anthropology Quarterly 27(3):219–226.

Becker, G., 2000 The Elusive Embryo. How Women and Men Approach New Reproductive Technologies. Berkeley: University of California Press.

Biehl, J., 2007 Will to Live: AIDS Therapies and the Politics of Survival. Princeton: Princeton University Press.

Borneman, J., 1996 Until Death Do Us Part: Marriage/Death in Anthropological Discourse. American Ethnologist 23(2):215–235.

Brodwin, P., 2000 Introduction. Biotechnology and Culture: Bodies, Anxieties, Ethics. In P. Brodwin, ed. Pp. 1-26. Bloomington: Indiana University Press.

Burri, R. V., 2007 Sociotechnical Anatomy Technology, Space, and Body in the MRI Unit. In Biomedicine as Culture: Instrumental Practices, Technoscientific Knowledge and New Modes of Life. R. V. Burri and J. Dumit, eds. pp.109–121. London: Routledge.

Casper, M. J., 1995 Fetal Cyborgs and Technomoms on the Reproductive Frontier: Which Way to the Carnival? In The Cyborg Handbook. C. H. Gray, H. Figueroa-Sarriera and S. Mentor, eds. pp. 183–202. New York; Routledge.

Cherney, J. L., 1999 Deaf Culture and the Cochlear Implant Debate: Cyborg Politics and the Identity of People. Argumentation and Advocacy 36(1):22–34.

Cohen, L., 2005 Operability, Bioavailablity, and Exception. In Global Assemblages. Technology, Politics, and Ethics as Anthropological Problems. A. Ong and S.J. Collier, eds. pp. 79–90. Malden MA: Blackwell Publishing.

Cohen, L., 2008 Politics of Care. Medical Anthropology Quarterly 22(4):336–339.

Delvecchio Good, M. J., 2001 The Biotechnical Embrace. Culture Medicine and Psychiatry 25(4):395–410.

Downey, G. L., J. Dummitt, and S. Williams, 1995 Cyborg Anthropology. In The Cyborg Handbook. C. H. Gray, H. Figueroa-Sarriera and S. Mentor, eds. pp. 341–346. New York: Routledge.

Essén, A., 2008 The Two Facets of Electronic Care Surveillance: An Exploration of the Views of Older People Who Live with Monitoring Devices. Social Science and Medicine 67(1): 128–136.

Finlay, S., Fitzgerald, R. and Legge, M., 2004 Cytogeneticists' Stories around the Ethics and Social Consequences of their Work: A New Zealand Case Study. New Zealand Bioethics Journal 5(2):13–24.

Fitzgerald, R., 2004 The New Zealand Health Reforms: Dividing the Labour of Care. Social Science and Medicine 58(2):331–341.

Fitzgerald, R., 2008a Rural Nurse Specialists: Clinical Practice and the Politics of Care. Medical Anthropology 27(3):257–282.

Fitzgerald, R., 2008b Biological Citizenship at the Periphery: Parenting Children with Genetic Disorders. New Genetics and Society 27(3):251–266.

Fitzgerald, R., 2009 PGD, The Right to Choose, Disability and the New Zealand Organization for Rare Disorders (NZORD). Paper presented at the Society for Medical Anthropology Annual Meeting, Yale University, New Haven CT, September 24–27. Electronic document. http://www.otago.ac.nz/anthropology/anth/people/fitzgerald.html/.

Foley, E. Ellen, 2009 The Anti-Politics of Health Reform: Household Power Relations and Child Health in Rural Senegal. Anthropology and Medicine 16(1):61–71.

Franklin, S., and C. Roberts, 2006 Born and Made: An Ethnography of Pre-Implantation Genetic Diagnosis. Princeton: Princeton University Press.

Gillett, G., 2009 Indigenous Knowledges: Circumspection, Metaphysics and Scientific Ontologies. SITES 6(1):95–115.

Glover, M., and B. Rousseau, 2007 Your Child is Your Whakapapa: Maori Considerations of Assisted Reproduction and Human Relatedness. SITES 4(2):117–136.

Good, B. J., 1994 Medicine, Rationality, and Experience. Cambridge UK: Cambridge University Press.

Goven, J., 2003 Deploying the Consensus Conference in New Zealand: Democracy and De-Problematization. Public Understanding of Science 12(4):423–440.

Hamdy, S. F., 2008 When the State and Your Kidneys Fail: Political Etiologies in an Egyptian Dialysis Ward. American Ethnologist 35(4):553–569.

Heath, D., R. Rapp, and K.-S. Taussig, 2007 Genetic Citizenship. *In* A Companion to the Anthropology of Politics. D. Nugent and J. Vincent, eds. pp. 152–157. Malden MA: Blackwell Publishing.

Hogle, L. F., 1995 Tales from the Cryptic: Technology Meets Organism in the Living Cadaver. *In* The Cyborg Handbook. C. H. Gray, H. Figueroa-Sarriera and S. Mentor, eds. pp. 203–216. London: Routledge.

Inhorn, M. C., and D. Birenbaum-Carmeli, 2008 Assisted Reproductive Technologies and Culture Change. Annual Review of Anthropology 37(1):177–196.

Kaufman, S. R., 1988 Toward a Phenomenology of Boundaries in Medicine: Chronic Illness Experience in the Case of Stroke. Medical Anthropology Quarterly 2(4):338–354.

Keating, P., and A. Cambrosio, 2003 Biomedical Platforms: Realigning the Normal and the Pathological in Late-Twentieth-Century Medicine. Cambridge MA: MIT Press.

Laing, T., 2006 Migrating to a Deaf World: A Model for Understanding the Experiences of Hearing Parents and Deaf Children. SITES Special Section. Tricia Laing, ed. 3(1):75–99.

Lock, M., 2001 The Tempering of Medical Anthropology: Troubling Natural Categories. Medical Anthropology Quarterly 15(4):478–492.

Lock M., 2009 Demoting the Genetic Body. Anthropologica 51(1):159–172.

Malone, R. E., 2003 Distal Nursing. Social Science and Medicine 56(11):2317–2326.

Martin, E., 2007 Bipolar Expeditions: Mania and Depression in American Culture. Princeton: Princeton University Press.

Maupin, J. N., 2008 Remaking the Guatemalan Midwife: Health Care Reform and Midwifery Training Programs in Highland Guatemala. Medical Anthropology 27(4):353–382.

McLauchlan, L., J. MacCormick, and J. Park, In press "Quiet as lambs": Communicative Action in the New Zealand Parliamentary Debates on Human Assisted Reproductive Technology.

Mitchell, L. M., and E. Georges, 1997 Cross-Cultural Cyborgs: Greek and Canadian Women's Discourses on Fetal Ultrasound. Feminist Studies 23(2):373–401.

Mol, A., 2008 The Logic of Care: Health and the Problem of Patient Choice. New York: Routledge.

Muller, J. H., 1994 Anthropology, Bioethics, and Medicine: A Provocative Trilogy. Medical Anthropology Quarterly 8(4):448–467.

Nelson, R., 2000 The Ventilator Baby as Cyborg: a Case Study in Technology and Medical Ethics. In Biotechnology and Culture: Bodies, Anxieties and Ethics. P. Brodwin, ed. pp. 209–33. Bloomington IN: Indiana University Press.

Oh, M., 2008 The Treaty of Waitangi Principles in He Korowai Oranga – Maori Health Strategy: A Critique from the Perspective of TB Care. In Multiplying and Dividing. Judith Littleton, Julie Park, Ann Herring and Tracy Farmer, eds. pp. 71–82. Auckland, RAL-e 3. Electronic document. http://researchspace.itss.auckland.ac.nz/handle/2292/2558/.

Pálsson, G., 2007 Anthropology and the New Genetics. Cambridge UK: Cambridge University Press.

Pálsson, G, and P. Rabinow, 2005 The Iceland Controversy: Reflections on the Transnational Market of Civic Virtue. In Global Assemblages. Technology, Politics, and Ethics as Anthropological Problems. A. Ong and S.J. Collier, eds. pp.91–103. Malden MA: Blackwell Publishing.

Park, J., 2005 Beyond His Sisters and His Cousins and His Aunts: Discourses of Hemophilia and Women's Experiences in New Zealand. In A Polymath Anthropologist: Essays in Honour of Ann Chowning. H. C. Gross, H. D. Lyons and D. A. Counts, eds. pp. 97–104. Auckland, New Zealand: RAL 6.

Park, J., 2009 Concepts of Human Nature, Personhood and Natural/Normal in New Reproductive Technology Discourses in New Zealand. Anthropologica 51:173–186.

Park, J., and D. G. York, 2008 The Social Ecology of New Technologies and Hemophilia in New Zealand. Auckland: RAL8. Electronic document. http://www.arts.auckland.ac.nz/departments/index.cfm?P=11661/.

Park, J., L. McLauchlan, L., and E. Frengley, 2008 Normal Humanness, Change and Power in HART: Auckland, New Zealand: RAL-e 2. Electronic document. http://researchspace.auckland.ac.nz/handle/2292/2395/.

Petryna, A., 2002 Life Exposed: Biological Citizens After Chernobyl. Princeton: Princeton University Press.

Pickles, A., 1999 Nurse versus Technician: The Dilemma of Intensive Care Nursing. Nursing in Critical Care 4(3):148–50.

Potts, A., V. Grace, N. Gavey, and T. Vares, 2004 'Viagra Stories': Challenging 'Erectile Dysfunction'. Social Science and Medicine 59(3):489–499.

Rabinow, P., 1996 Essays on the Anthropology of Reason. Princeton: Princeton University Press.

Rapp, R., 1988 Chromosomes and Communication: The Discourse of Genetic Counseling. Medical Anthropology Quarterly 2:143–157.

Rapp, R., D. Heath, and K.-S. Taussig, 2001 Genealogical Dis-Ease: Where Hereditary Abnormality, Biomedical Explanation, and Family Responsibility Meet. In Relative Values. S. Franklin and S. McKinnon, eds. pp. 384–409. Durham NC: Duke University Press.

Rock, M., and P. Babinec, 2008 Diabetes in People, Cats and Dogs: Biomedicine and Manifold Ontologies. Medical Anthropology, 27(4):324–352.

Scheper-Hughes, N., 2009 Making Anthropology Public. Anthropology Today 25(4):1–3.

Scully, J. L., T. Shakespeare, and S. Banks, 2006 Gift Not Commodity? Lay People Deliberating Social Sex Selection. Sociology of Health and Illness 28(6):749–767.

Searle, A., J. Park, and J. Littleton, 2007 Alliance and Compliance in Tuberculosis Treatment of Older Pakeha People in Auckland, New Zealand. International Journal of TB and Lung Disease 11(1):7277.
Sharp, L. A., 2006 Strange Harvest. Organ Transplants, Denatured Bodies, and the Transformed Self. Berkeley: University of California Press.
Spitzer, D. L., 2004 In Visible Bodies: Minority Women, Nurses, Time, and the New Economy of Care. Medical Anthropology Quarterly 18(4):490–508.
Squier, S. J., 2004 Liminal Lives: Imagining the Human at the Frontiers of Biomedicine. Durham NC: Duke University Press.
Taylor, J. S., 2000 Of Sonograms and Baby Prams: Prenatal Diagnosis, Pregnancy, and Consumption. Feminist Studies 26(2):391–418.
Taylor, J. S., 2008 On Recognition, Caring, and Dementia. Medical Anthropology Quarterly 22(4):313–335.
Thacker, E., 2005 The Global Genome. Biotechnology, Politics and Culture. Cambridge MA: MIT Press.
Trotter, G., 2006 Bioethics and Deliberative Democracy: Five Warnings from Hobbes. Journal of Medicine and Philosophy 31(3):235–250.
Waldby C., and R. Mitchell, 2006 Tissue Economies. Blood, Organs and Cell Lines in Late Capitalism. Durham NC and London: Duke University Press.

FURTHER READING

Henderson, V., 2004 The Concept of Nursing. Journal of Advanced Nursing 53(1):21–34.
Royal Commission on Genetic Modification, 1991 Report of the Royal Commission on Genetic Modification. Wellington, New Zealand: Ministry for the Environment. Electronic document. http://www.mfe.govt.nz/.

CHAPTER 22

Social Interaction and Technology: Cultural Competency and the Universality of Good Manners

Kathryn Coe, Gail Barker, and Craig Palmer

INTRODUCTION

In the United States today, the increasing diversity of the population has directed a great deal of attention toward cultural competency in all arenas that involve social interaction. Cultural competency training in the health care arena has been regarded as being of particular importance as interactions are often enduring and intense. Many definitions of cultural competency exist and those definitions depend upon the individual who is the focus – patient, doctor, nurse, public health worker. Generally, however, discussions of cultural competency focus on the health care professional, not the patient, and a commonly accepted definition states that cultural competency refers to "a set of congruent behaviors, attitudes, and policies that enable systems, agencies, and professionals to work effectively in cross-cultural situations" (Cross et al. 1989: iv). Brach and Frasier (2000) have added to that definition, stressing that practitioners must have the skills to work in cross-cultural situations. The need for the development of such a workforce has been emphasized formally many times (see the Report of the Committee for the Future of Primary Care, IOM 1994; Pew Health Professions Commission Report 1995).

Driving this current interest in cultural competency is the assumption that it, along with the development of a more diverse workforce, will help reduce health disparities

A Companion to Medical Anthropology, First Edition. Edited by Merrill Singer
and Pamela I. Erickson.

(O'Neil 2008a). However, although "there is substantial research evidence to suggest that cultural competency should in fact work" (Brach and Frasier 2000:181), there currently is, as Ed O'Neil has recognized (2008b), no commonly understood framework for teaching, evaluating or understanding cultural competence. "Health care systems," as Brach and Frasier echo (2000: 181), "have little evidence about which cultural competency techniques are effective and less evidence on when and how to implement them properly." Today, the teaching of cultural competency tends to draw on a knowledge-based paradigm that encourages learning about other unique cultures in order to better appreciate and communicate with individuals from that culture (O'Neil 2006b). The other approach, one less widely used, is experiential, focusing on the social relationship between the health professional and the patient (O'Neil 2008b).

In this paper, we take a close look at cultural competency trainings and attempt to identify – by conducting a search on the Human Relations Area Files (HRAF), using manners as the key word – what elements are missing that might be of critical importance, particularly in a world in which social interactions are increasingly technologically mediated. We argue that manners are a key issue in the management of successful social interactions. We also argue that even through there are culturally unique aspects to manners (e.g., certain cultural groups may not make eye contact), there is, surprisingly, considerable cross-cultural agreement on what constitutes good manners (while some American Indians may not make eye contract, listening carefully is of central importance to traditional tribal people). That is, not only does the concept of manners exist in all cultures, but there are also certain aspects of social interactions (i.e., good manners) encouraged in all cultures, while others (i.e., bad manners) are discouraged. We describe some of these universal aspects of manners and argue that the recognition of their existence makes an important contribution to the concept of cultural competency and has practical implications for improving interactions via new technologies (e.g., internet, cellular devices, videoconferencing). We suggest that one reason technologically mediated interactions are notorious for causing unintended offense, is that people are often unaware of how important signs of good manners are in social interactions. Thus, we conclude that making students (i.e., future health providers) more aware of the universal aspects of manners, and training them to incorporate ways of signaling good manners in the rapidly developing field of technologically mediated interactions will improve health care in a world in which social interactions are increasingly cross-cultural and technologically mediated.

PERCEIVED IMPORTANCE OF AND METHODS FOR TEACHING CULTURAL COMPETENCY

The story related in *The Spirit Catches You* (Fadiman, 1998) makes clear that there is a need for cultural knowledge, that is learning facts about cultures other than our own. Lia Lee, when the story began, was a three-month old Hmong child with epilepsy. To control the seizures, her doctors prescribed a complex regimen of medication. Lia's parents, however, who felt that the disease was a result of Lia "losing her soul," did not give her the medication partially because of a disconnect between their concepts of the cause and treatment of disease and those of the health care system in the USA and partially because the drug therapy was very complex and mysterious and the side-effects were grim.

This example makes clear that not only is culture a critical social determinant of health, but that a lack of understanding of culture plays an important role in health disparities. If Lia's providers had understood certain important cultural factors, Lia might never have been removed from the care of her family, the recommendations made by doctors might have been made in a quite different style, her parents might have followed the recommendations, and the final outcome predictably could have been quite different. However, its seems clear that while having some knowledge of the unique aspects of culture is important, necessary one could say, it is not sufficient. Tervalon and Murray-Garcia (1998:119), tell the story of an African–American nurse who, when caring for a middle aged Latina several hours post-surgery, ignored the patient's discomfort and moans. When a Latino physician asked the nurse why the patients was experiencing significant post-operative pain, the nurse dismissed his concern, explaining to him that in her cross-cultural nursing class, she had learned that Latinas over express "the pain they are feeling." When such interactions take place over a technologically mediated telemedicine system, the issues are yet more complex.

While knowledge of unique cultural facts is important, it is not always clear what aspects and how much information about a culture the provider needs to possess in order to work or behave in a culturally competent manner. The emerging field of medical humanities seems to be based on the assumption that a very broad understanding of culture is important. According to the Webpage of the Drew University Medical Humanities Program, it involves "engaging all aspects of human culture–science, history, ethics, philosophy, literature, religion, art – in a discursive dialogue centered on what medicine means in relation to the individual and society." While attractive and quite possibly effective, this comprehensive cultural approach takes years, not the hours, days or weeks of coursework that most cultural competency trainings involve.

Although language is another important aspect of culture, language fluency, perhaps because of the time investment required, is not included in the comprehensive listing above nor is it addressed in cultural competency trainings. Several studies have reported that shared language is important and that patients are more comfortable if they share a common language with their physician. A survey of Hispanic patients indicated that 42% reported that they factored language into their choice of a physician (Saha et al. 2000). There is a difference, however, between patients factoring in language in their choice of a provider and their comfort with and compliance with that provider and his/her medical recommendations. To provide an example, the English and Americans share a language; however, an American in England will lack "understanding of the subtler aspects of daily interaction in Britain... which are often completely invisible to them" (Edwards 2000). The same might be said of a Californian who finds him/herself in Vermont. Having a common language does not imply that other aspects of culture will be shared, and we can also assume that English-speaking patients are not always compliant with the recommendations of English-speaking providers, just as Spanish-speaking providers do not always have compliant Spanish-speaking patients. Clearly more than speaking a common language, even when that fluency is combined with mastery of certain cultural facts, must be involved in developing and maintaining a trusting relationship between a patient and provider that might lead to such things as patient compliance and that might have the potential to reduce health disparities.

CULTURAL COMPETENCY AND THE UNIVERSALITY OF GOOD MANNERS

One factor that is missing in most discussions of cultural competency is manners, the often unspoken standards and rules that govern or guide human behavior in social interactions. We suggest that the concept of cultural competency could benefit by a more in depth and explicit analysis of manners. Tervalon and Murray-Garcia (1998) began to touch on the importance of good manners in cultural competency when they wrote that cultural humility should guide interactions between the health care professional and the patient. Humility, they write is a prerequisite to cultural understanding, as by adopting this stance, "the physician relinquishes the role of expert to the patient, becoming the student of the patient with a conviction and explicit expression of the patient's potential to be a capable and full partner in the therapeutic alliance" (p. 120). Cultural humility, thus, would involve such things as patient-focused interviewing that "uses a less controlling, less authoritative style that signals to the patient that the provider values what the patient's agenda and perspectives are" (p. 120). In other words, good listening skills are important, as are methods, such as humility, that tell people that what they say is important for us to hear.

The standard anthropological conception of manners is concisely stated by Franz Boas, widely known as the "father of American Anthropology," in the foreword to the most widely known anthropological book of all time:

> Courtesy, modesty, good manners, conformity to definite ethical standards are universal, but what constitutes courtesy, modesty, good manners, and ethical standards is not universal. It is instructive to know that standards differ in the most unexpected ways. It is still more important to know how the individual reacts to those standards (Franz Boas in the foreword to *Coming of Age in Samoa* by Margaret Mead, 1928).

This view positions manners as a universal aspect of human life, but as a universal aspect that also differs widely between cultures. It is compatible with the standard approach to cultural competence that focuses on cultural differences that make each culture "unique." Although cultural differences in manners are unquestionably important, we suggest that focusing exclusively on cultural differences in manners deflects attention from underlying universal aspects of human social interaction that are very relevant to improved social interactions and to health care. That is, in contrast to both the statement by Boas and current conceptions of cultural competence, we hold that ethnographic evidence indicates that not only is *some* concept of manners universal, but certain specific core values are included in concepts of manners in all known cultures.

Searching for universals in the ethnographic literature is often difficult because, as the anthropologist Maurice Bloch once asserted, it is a "professional malpractice of anthropologists to exaggerate the exotic character of other cultures" (1977:285). Don Brown later commented that this is highly regrettable because "universals not only exist but are important to any broad conception of the task of anthropology" (1991:5)." We suggest that the concept of cultural competence is one of the subjects where exclusively focusing on cultural differences, and neglecting cultural similarities and universals, is regrettable. For example, it is commonly assumed that manners are highly susceptible to change and will vary greatly depending upon geographical location, social stratum, occasion, and other factors.

We argue that these assumptions are regrettable because there is some reason, as the following examples show, to believe that there is a fundamental core to manners that holds across cultures. To convince anyone that a reconceptualization of cultural competence that expands to include universal aspects of culture is important and useful, it is first necessary to demonstrate that cultural universals include aspects of manners that could be useful to attempts to improve health care services, especially in an increasingly technologically mediated world. In order to do that, we must first discuss the definition of manners.

Manners can be defined as a subset of rituals and taboos (see discussion in Visser 1992). Rituals are stereotyped forms of social cooperation while taboos are forbidden behaviors; the term "ritual" comes from the Sanskrit "rta" (Heinze 2000:1), which refers to both "art" and "order." A ritual, according to Goodman (1988:31), "is a social encounter in which each participant has a well rehearsed role to act out." While rituals may have many different functions, an underlying function may be to initiate, maintain, or increase non-stereotyped forms of cooperation (Steadman and Palmer 2008:61; Leibovich 2009). Following from this, a function of taboos is to protect the initiation or maintenance of cooperative social relationships against behaviors that have the potential to damage cooperation. Rituals and taboos often go together in that they prescribe that a certain behavior should take place, and that one or more alternative behaviors should not take place, in a given social situation.

Manners are distinguished from other rituals and taboos in that they are usually simple and frequently occurring rituals and taboos, as opposed to more complicated and infrequent rituals and taboos. Handshakes when meeting someone, or saying "please" before every request are typical manners. In contrast, many of the rituals and taboos involved in the funeral of a king or president may only take place every decade, may be incredibly elaborate, and may last for days, weeks, or longer. These rare and elaborate rituals and taboos involved in such funerals would not be called manners; while the rituals and taboos in the funeral that also commonly occur in everyday life would be called manners.

We suggest that many types of manners are important because they are, among other things, a form of greeting rituals that concern how cooperative interactions are started among previously unknown and/or non-cooperating individuals when they first come into close physical proximity (Palmer and Pomianek 2007). These types of manners are particularly important to the topic of this paper because this is exactly the situation that occurs whenever a health provider meets a previously unknown patient and/or patient's family members (whether or not from another "culture"). We also suggest that good manners guard against behavior that would damage the cooperative social relationship once it has formed.

As the following examples show (see Table 22.1), we believe that there is a fundamental core to manners that holds across cultures. The apparent universality of manners suggests they have had important consequences for social relationships and

Table 22.1 Ethnographic examples of manners by category.

Altruism, kindness	Sherpas: "The sentiments of tolerance and consideration for the interests and feelings of others, which are central to Sherpa morality, find their outward expression in courtesy and good manners" (Fürer-Haimendorf 1964:285)
	Sherpas: "food is probably nowhere a simple matter of energy and calories … hosts required by etiquette to demonstratively beseech guests to eat and drink" (Stevens 1990:134)
	Ibo: "Like the white man too, he trains his children to be kind, honest and gentle" (Leith-Ross 1934:224)
	Ashanti: "By Ashanti standards a good girl … is ready to *help* older people and go on their errands" (Sarpong 1977:83)
Respect for authority, including elders	Ashanti: "By Ashanti standards a good girl … is not gloomy but smiles when talking to her elders, is ready to help older people and go on their errands" (Sarpong 1977:83)
	Banyoro: "Such values as respect for elders, good manners, chastity, hard work, martial spirit, courage, discipline, honesty, good neighborliness and truthfulness were inculcated" (Uzoigwe and Skoggard 2003:6)
	Buganda: "Their idea of mpisa (custom, habit, conduct) subsumes a variety of approved behaviors that children are expected to acquire. Mpisa includes such things as being obedient to authority figures; not interfering in adult conversation; not eating while walking on the road; greeting people properly; interfering in adult conversation; being amiable; sitting properly (for children and women); and many other things. … (Kilbride and Kilbride 1974:303)
	Dogon: "They must use terms of respect in speaking to old people. One of the principal things taught the child is the manner of speaking to the persons whom he meets, to those who are related to him by blood or by marriage and to those who are not allied to him at all … One teaches children to keep quiet in the presence of strangers and to make themselves heard only if they are spoken to. They must use terms of respect in speaking to old people" (Paulme 1940:13–14)
	Umbundu: "Children are supposed to learn 'table-manners' by watching and imitating their elders" (Childs 1949:141)
Listening carefully	Dogon: "To cut someone off while speaking is a serious breach of manners: words that have not been able to follow their normal path are repressed in the spleen where they are represented by the dark blood found there" (Calame-Griaule 1986:55)
Humility and modesty	"Courtesy, modesty, good manners, conformity to definite ethical standards are universal" (Franz Boas in the foreword to *Coming of Age in Samoa* by Margaret Mead, 1928)
Restraint	Azande: "*bear hunger well*, and it is bad manners to seem eager to eat" (Baxter and Butt 1953:17)

Table 22.1 *(cont'd)*

	Nuer: "Once scarified, moreover, a man was expected to demonstrate greater self-control in matters of hunger and thirst by conforming to an elaborate set of 'table manners' designed to suppress all signs of daar (greed)" (Hutchinson 1996:200)
	!Kung: "… good manners in eating express restraint.… I found it moving to see so much restraint about taking food among people who are all thin and often hungry, for whom food is a source of constant anxiety. We observed no unmannerly behavior, no cheating and no encroachment about food. Although informants said that quarrels had occasionally occurred in the past between members of a band …" (Marshall 1961:235)
	!Kung: "… the cultural constraint against drawing sharp differentiations among people leads the !Kung to shun such determinations as winner, prettiest, and most successful, or even best dancer, hunter, healer, musician, or bead-maker" (Shostak 1981:108)
	Sherpas: "Even in lay etiquette, as opposed to religious practice, every child is taught, and every adult feels, some responsibility for controlling their greedy impulses, if not by actually extinguishing them, then at least by masking them with good manners …" (Ortner 1978:100)
	Sherpas: "Here also food is not simply offered and accepted, but instead is ritually refused at least three times, with hosts required by etiquette to demonstratively beseech guests to eat and drink. It is more than bad manners to ask for food or to admit hunger, rather these are things which cannot be mentioned and one must abide in patience until food is offered no matter how famished one may be, and then reject it with enthusiasm" (Stevens 1990:134)
Greets people in an appropriate fashion	Ashanti. "By Ashanti standards a good girl is one who greets people" (Sarpong1977:83)
	!Kung: "When a visitor comes to the fire of a family who are preparing food or eating, he should sit at a little distance, not to seem importunate, and wait to be asked to share" (Marshall 1961:235)
	!Kung: "In !Kung society good manners require that, when !Kung meet other !Kung who are strangers" (Marshall 1961:235)

thus for human survival. Despite the surface variability of the actual words and bodily movements that compose the manners of a society, there are clear universal commonalities in what manners communicate. In the next section, we will apply these examples to the health care setting.

BIOLOGY, LEARNING AND GOOD MANNERS

The existence of similar proper manners across cultures – the well-conducted Ibo is as clearly recognized as the cultured man in any other country (Brasden 1966) – should not be taken to indicate that manners are automatic or "innate." Although the learning of manners tends to often be informal in the sense that the manners themselves tend to be non-catalogued, and no formal system of punishment is likely to exist for the breach of manners, manners are clearly a form of behavior that must be learned. Once again we find universal patterns in how this learning takes place.

Even though manners lack formality, or are uncatalogued, guidance into good manners begins early. As "the appropriate customs are well known, in fact they are part and parcel of daily life" (Brasden 1966:161), the teaching of manners is a central part of childhood. The Tiv claim that "Inculcating children with proper manners and attitudes begins very young" (Bohannan and Bohannan1958:379). Children are often taught manners by watching and modeling their parents and other elders. Manners are often taught at meals. The Sherpas use practice and proverbs to "give the certain guidelines to the young boy or girl to learn the manner in terms of dealing way of eating, drinking, sitting, talking, serving, receiving through his or her cultural way" (Kumwar 1989:191). According to the Umbundu: "[t]he undoubtedly greater effectiveness of that traditional training over the accomplishments of formal western schooling in manners, morals or 'civics' should lead us to investigate the possibility of making use of the traditional method. Social behavior can only be effectively taught in real-life situations" (Childs 1949:141).

THE BREAKDOWN OF CULTURE AND LOSS OF MANNERS

The fact that the learning of manners typically requires extensive and prolonged contact between offspring and parents, or at least children and adults, implies that manners are not inevitable. It also implies that teaching good manners may be time consuming, perhaps requiring the use of regular reminders. Another implication here is that when there is a disruption of traditional patterns of interaction, or a breakdown in parent–child relationships, manners are particularly vulnerable. Thus, manners are likely to be lost, or at least changed, when extensive and intensive cultural contact occurs. This is, of course, exactly what has transpired at an increasing rate through the last several centuries of human existence. Thus it is not surprising to find many reports of traditional patterns of manners failing to be transmitted from elders to the new generation. For example, the Ibo:

> have rules for the regulation of conduct applicable to almost every detail of life. Habits are naturally engendered and developed; they are a subconscious part of the native's being and, amongst the older generation, it is a rare thing to find one failing to observe the traditional rules of conduct. The code of etiquette had a definite place in the social life of the people, but the disintegrating forces of a transition period are plainly visible, and the old system of conduct and etiquette is rapidly losing its significance and its hold upon them. A generation is springing up with a disposition to cast off the manners and traditions of its ancestors. This is a source of no little concern to the old people and for many obvious reasons it is much to be regretted (Brasden 1966:266).

The loss of traditional forms of manners among many populations is a previously unappreciated aspect to the process of globalization. What it means is that not only are people coming into contact with people who have different manners, as the conventional view of the relationship between manners and cultural competency might expect, but people who know little about or are without manners are increasingly coming in contact. Further, this contact between individuals who have lost at least some of their traditional manners is increasingly taking place through new forms of technology. New forms of communication technology increase the chances of misunderstanding and non-cooperation in two ways. First, certain aspects of manners cannot be communicated through the technology. For example, visual signals involving body posture that communicate humility are not transmitted through text-only forms of technology (e.g., email or texting) and are less clear in teleconferencing. Thus, even if these aspects of manners have survived through the generations, they are ineffective in the new technological environment. Second, it often takes some period of time for new ways of communicating proper manners through the unique aspects of the new technology to be developed and learned by users.

APPLYING THE KEY ELEMENTS OF GOOD MANNERS

All of these characteristic elements of good manners are important to health care providers because the interactions between patients, health providers, public health practitioners, and other individuals not only are often enduring and intense, but they are increasingly likely to involve individuals who have not learned the basics of traditional manners, but who must interact in an increasingly technology-based environment. In this section we provide examples for how the specified characteristics of traditional good manners can influence such things as the provider–patient interaction, including patient compliance and patient perceptions of the curing capabilities of the provider.

Altruism and kindness

As was mentioned in the introduction to this paper, the examples of good manners listed in Table 22.1 were identified when doing an HRAF search using the key word "manners." Closer examination of the terms, however, indicates that altruism is not a term that merely describes a particular type of behavior: it is a cross-culturally encouraged moral or ethic. Historically, studies of morals have focused on the possible motivation of the altruist (is that altruist actually behaving selfishly?) (see discussion in Nagel 1978). However, if we ignore possible motivation and focus on the identifiable and measurable characteristics of behaviors referred to as altruistic, we find that altruistic individuals are characterized by good manners. More specifically, altruists are cooperative (Farrelly et al. 2007), generous and willing to help others even if the other is a stranger and even if they incur a cost in so doing (Midlarsky and Kahana 1988; Lee et al. 2005), are humble (Tervalon and Murray-Garcia 1998), and have a strong sense of social responsibility, are respectful of authority, and are self-restrained and nurturing (Ribal 1963).

The importance of these characteristics in a social interaction is described in a paper by Ware and Schneider (1975) who explain that a demonstration of courtesy and respect and kindness are key characteristics of the health care providers that patients like and that, perhaps surprisingly, that patient's feel can cure or heal them. Paul Starr and Paul Friedson, in their book on *The Social Transformation of American Medicine* (1982) describe altruism, and its identifiable behaviors, as a key element of health care professionalism. They explain that professionalism is not a divine right of health care professionals; it is a: "legal, institutional, and moral privilege that is granted by society and that must be earned by health care providers through observing certain standards of behavior, including… (1) Altruism: Professionals are expected to resolve conflicts between their interests and their patient's interests in favor of the patients" (quoted in Blumenthal 1994:253).

Casalino continues this discussion (1999:1148), writing that "[i]f professionalism were defined as putting patients' interests above one's own, then it would be possible to study the degree to which physicians take specific actions that improve the quality of care but for which they are not rewarded." It would also be possible, one could hypothesize, to identify differential effects – such as patient compliance and patient confidence in his/her provider – between altruistic (and well-mannered) providers and providers who do not exhibit such traits.

While the word "altruism" seems to encompass the behaviors we refer to as good manners, an interesting exception might be the rules that encourage respect for elders and hierarchies. One would expect altruism to lead to respect for everyone, without special attention paid to certain members of a society. In an important sense, this is true. The relationship between a health care provider and a patient, however, is necessarily hierarchical. Clear asymmetries in knowledge and information exist between these two actors, as patients rely on the knowledge of their providers to heal them (Casalino 1999). The health care professional, in turn, relies on the responsiveness of the patient. Good manners, including the humility of the provider and the listening responsiveness of the patient, however, are what seem to level the playing field, in that such a provider sends a message to the patient that the patient and provider are important partners in this act of healing and preventing disease (see discussion in Tervalon and Murray-Garcia 1998).

Historically, the holders of traditions, and their enforcers were the elders. In terms of the co-evolution of traditions and human biology, it would make sense for the elders to encourage responsiveness to their influence, as they, at least theoretically, are the ones who would be most likely to attempt to protect the interests and wellbeing of their younger descendants, the less influential member of any hierarchy. In other words, this responsiveness to certain forms of hierarchical relationships (e.g., when the more influential individual demonstrates such things as generosity, concern, and humility) may be wired into the human brain or, at least, an important and very ancient inherited tradition and set of behaviors. If true, then the good manners associated with such a hierarchy would be essential for trust to develop.

Today the situation between a provider and a patient is increasingly complex and will continue to become even more complex as the interactions increasingly will take place through technology that prohibits the communication of some important forms of manners, assuming both partners practice good manners. Technologies might be so new that individuals involved may not have had the time to learn them or to master or acquire the manners unique to them. This can lead to frustration and failed communication. We now turn to a more detailed analysis of this situation.

Technology, the Future, and Good Manners

Communication is a basic aspect of life and for humans the development of language greatly facilitated communication. Over time, as populations increased and humans began to migrate, they developed methods for communicating over distances, with

Table 22.2   Three technology-based communication modalities and methods.

Broadcast Communication (one-way communication)	Interactive Communication	"Store-and-Forward" Communication
Possibly smoke signals, drum, whistle, and petroglyphs (date unknown)	Possibly smoke signals, drum and whistle, pigeons, runner (date unknown)	Possibly petroglyphs (date unknown)
Radio (1895)	Wireless Telegraph (1837)	Telephone Answering Machine (1960)
Television (1927)	Telephone (1876)	Internet (1973)
Internet (1973)	Cellphone (1973)	Voicemail (1986)
—	Videoconference (1964)	Videostream (2000) Podcast(2004)
—	Text Message (1997)	Text Message (1997)
—	Voice over IP (2004)	—

sender and receiver in different places. Messages initially were carried by runner, pigeons, or horsemen or sent via smoke signals, drums, and whistles. It was time consuming and slow to get a message to a distant recipient; at times the message (and even the messenger) got lost in the process. As humans began to develop technology in order to communicate faster and over greater distances, they created such things as lanterns, mirrors, and flags or semaphores (Wikipedia Semaphore 2008). As technology continued to develop messages could be sent greater distances; however, a layer of complexity was added to the universality of good manners. Visual and auditory feedback cues were not as clear, intonations, and subtleties of language were lost, messages were misinterpreted, and imperfect behaviors were magnified.

Today, we have entered the era of telecommunication, or "the assisted transmission of signals for the purpose of communication" (Wikipedia Telecommunication 2008). This type of communication involves three basic modalities: broadcast, interactive, and "store-and-forward." Broadcast communication is a one-way communication used to distribute information through audio and/or video signals (Wikipedia Broadcasting 2008). Interactive communication refers to a simultaneous real-time exchange of information between individuals at [at least] two locations (Federal Register 1998). "Store-and-forward" communication is the transmission of data and/ or images from one location to another where information can be queued up to review immediately or at a later time (Federal Register 1998). Table 22.2 illustrates the three technology-based telecommunication modalities and identifies examples of individual communication devices and the year each device was invented.

Some devices like the Internet can be a broadcast device disseminating information, an interactive device for live interaction using Voice over Internet Protocol (VoIP), or as a "store-and-forward" device where messaging can be posted and retrieved at a later time. Another dual-device is text messaging, which can be performed as either an interactive or "store-and-forward" activity depending on the timing of a reply.

In the late 1990s, broadband communication backbones became available to the mass market and the result was not only the expansion of telecommunication but a facilitation of global interactions (Ng et al. 2004). With this expansion, the complex relationship between technology, culture, and communication became more impor-

Table 22.3 The ABCs of etiquette.

Appearance	Dress, clothing, body language, gestures
Behavior	Custom, eating or dining, protocol, negotiation
Communication	Greetings/farewell, introductions, tone, intonations, listening

tant, and although much has been widely published about this connection (al-Gahtani et al. 2008), a universal set of rules of engagement for "tele-etiquette" or "tele-manners" has not been fully vetted.

Manners and etiquette involve three elements that together define the rules of engagement for good behavior (Hofstede 1996). Table 22.3 illustrates the ABCs of etiquette that transcend all cultures and technical modalities.

New rules of engagement that are based on core values also allow for incorporation of more peripheral values. Table 22.4 provides a preliminary list of new rules of engagement by type of technology: text messaging, teleconferencing, and on-line classroom (national and international), with the ABCs of etiquette involved.

Already cell phones and cell phone devices are being used in some places for health care related activities, for example, as reminders to take medications or make an appointment. Although the communication technologies described above all exist today, predicting future technology use and types of the future is complex. The industry is moving so quickly that it is undoubtedly true that some, indeed many, of the technologies and devices that we will use in the near and distant future do not yet even exist as concepts. But certainly we can anticipate that communication devices will become smaller, faster, cheaper, and more portable. Communication devices will also be fully integrated within the health care system(s). With the advancement of artificial intelligence and decision-support software, answers to important health related questions could be available to patients "on demand." It is also probable that medical error rates and costs will be reduced because the human factor, which is where errors occur, will be removed from the process. Technology will be moved closer to the patient and will be user-friendly. Yet these systems will be secure and privacy-protected.

If we bring together this rapid growth of technology with good manners, the apparently universal values of self-restraint in consumption of tea, coffee or a meal, or listening carefully and not interrupting: altruism, nonviolence, respect for authority (especially elders), valuing kin (e.g., be careful who you criticize; one may criticize his/her own kin, but not the kin of others), and humility are all clearly related to initiating and/or maintaining cooperative social relationships regardless of the technology used. This is an important fact to health care providers interested in cultural competency because successfully providing health care requires cooperation between the provider, the patient and often other people who have social relationships with the patient. Hence, the values found throughout the ethnographic literature are likely to provide at least a rough guide for the behavior of health care providers *regardless of the technology involved or the culture of their patients.*

The value of these universal manners may become increasingly important as health care interactions increasingly incorporate, and become dependent upon, new technologies.

Table 22.4 New rules of engagement.

Type of technology	Type of engagement	Numbers of individuals involved in interaction	Rules of engagement	ABC element involved
Text message	Message sent by one body to a second body or group of individuals. Response may not be indicated	1 to many	If a response is required, involves active listening, in the sense of reading and understanding, and responding to the message appropriately and accurately. Self-restraint, in the sense of not over-reacting to messages	B,C
Tele-conferencing	Interactive communication involving video and audio technology	1 to many	Formal greetings and, introductions, attempting to monitor when someone wishes to speak, pausing for others to speak, restraint from interrupting and sidebar conversations, active listening, and formal farewell	A,B,C
On-line classroom, national program	"Store and forward"	1 to many	Same as text messaging plus understanding (and patience) that responses are not immediate. Attention must be paid to clearly and politely articulate questions and answers	B,C
On-line classroom, international program	"Store and forward"	1 to many	Same as on-line classroom regular program plus appreciation of and patience with language barriers, timeline differences and local custom requirements	B,C

This is because no culture has established specific forms of manners for interacting through such rapidly changing technologies. As a result, finding new ways of interacting via these technologies without damaging or preventing enduring cooperative social relationships will have to be devised for interactions with *all cultures* if the health care of the future is going to be successful. The manners found universally in all cultures that have just been described, that can be identified in ethnographies, are likely to be the best guide available for the creation of these new manners, or for placing a new emphasis on the traditional manners, that can guide social interactions in the new technology and they can form the basis for incorporating culturally unique factors into conversations and social interactions that occur via technology.

REFERENCES

al-Gahtani, S. S., G. S. Hubona, and J. Wanty, 2008 Journal of Information Technology (IT) in Saudia Arabia: culture and the acceptance and use of IT. ScienceDirect. Information and Management 44(8):681–691, December 2007. Electronic document (Science Direct). http://www.sciencedirect.com/science?_ob=ArticleURL&_udi=B6VD0-4R0CPY1-1&_user=5679161&_rdoc=1&_fmt=&_orig=search&_sort=d&view=c&_acct=C000059541&_version=1&_urlVersion=0&_userid=5679161&md5=71bcc5549a73a9a0f67a47842494b9d7/.

Baxter, P. T. W., and Audrey Butt, 1953 The Azande, and Related Peoples of the Anglo–Egyptian Sudan and Belgian Congo. London: International African Institute.

Bloch, Maurice, 1977 The past and the present in the present. Man (NS) 12:278–292.

Blumenthal, David, 1994 Commentary. The vital role of professionalism in health care reform. Health Affairs Spring (I):252–256.

Boas, Franz, 1928 Preface to Margaret Mead's *Coming of Age in Samoa*. New York: William Marrow and Company.

Bohannan, Paul, and Laura Bohannan, 1958 New Haven CN: Human Relations Area Files.

Brown Donald, 1991 Human Universals. New York: McGraw-Hill.

Brach, Cindy, and Irene Fraser, 2000 Can Cultural Competency Reduce Racial and Ethnic Disparities? A Review and Conceptual Model. Medical Care Research and Review 57(Supplement 1):181–217.

Brasden, George T., 1966 Niger Igos: A Description of the Primitive Life, Customs and Animistic Beliefs, etc., of the Ibo People of Nigeria. London: Cass.

Calame-Griaule, Geneviève, 1986 Words and the Dogon World. Philadelphia: Institute for the Study of Human Issues.

Casalino, Lawrence, 1999 The unintended consequences of measuring quality on the quality of medical care. New England Journal of Medicine 241(15):1147–1150.

Childs. Gladwyn Murray, 1949 Umbundu kinship and character: being a description of social structure and individual development of the Ovimbundu of Angola, with observations concerning the bearing on the enterprise of Christian missions of certain phases of the life and culture descriptions. London: Oxford University Press.

Cross, T. L., B. Bazron, K. Dennis, M. Issacs, and M. Benjamin, 1989 Towards a Culturally Competent System of Care: A Monograph on Effective Services for Minority Children Who Are Severely Emotionally Disturbed. Washington: CASSP Technical Assistance Center, Georgetown University Child Development Center.

Edwards, Jane, 2000 The "other Eden": Thoughts on American Study abroad in Britain.

Frontiers: The Forum on Education Abroad. Electronic document. www.frontiersjournal.com/issues/vol6/vol6-06_Edwards.htm/.

Fadiman, Ann, 1998 The Spirit Catches You and You Fall Down. New York: Farrar, Straus & Giroux.

Farrelly, Daniel, John Lazarus, and Gilbert Roberts, 2007 Altruists attract. Evolutionary Psychology 5(2):313–329.

Federal Register, 1980 Department of Health and Human Services, Health Care Financing Administration. Medicare Program: Payment for Teleconsultations in Rural Health Professional Shortage Areas. Federal Register (22 June 1998) 63(119):33883.

Fürer-Haimendorf, Christoph von, 1964 The Sherpas of Nepal: Buddhist Highlanders. London: John Murray.

Goodman, Felicitas, 1988 Ecstasy, Ritual and Alternate Reality: Religion in a Pluralistic World. Bloomington IN: Indiana University Press.

Heinze, Ruth-Inge, 2000 The Nature and Function of Rituals: Comparing a Singapore Chinese with a Thai Ritual. *In* The Nature and Function of Rituals: Fire from Heaven. Ruth-Inge Heinze, ed. pp. 1–24. Westport CT: Begin and Garvey.

Hofstede, Geert., 1996 Cultures and Organizations, Software of the Mind: Intercultural Cooperation and its Importance for Survival. New York: McGraw-Hill.

Hutchinson, Sharon Elaine, 1996 Nuer Dilemmas: Coping with Money, War, and the State. Berkeley: University of California Press.

Kilbride, Philip L., and Janet E. Kilbride,1974 Sociocultural Factors and the Early Manifestation of Sociobility Behavior among Baganda Infants. Berkeley: University of California Press.

Kumwar, Ramesh Faj 1st, 1989 Fire of Himal: An Anthropological Study of the Sherpas of Nepal Himalayan Region. Jaipur, India: Nirala Publications.

Lee, Dong, Chul Kang, Jee Lee, and Sung Park, 2005 Characteristics of exemplary altruists. Journal of Humanistic Psychology 45(2):146–155.

Leibovich, Mark, 2009 Looking for peace, love and manners in Washington. Electronic Document. nytimes.com/business. http://www.nytimes.com/2009/01/11/weekinreview/11leibovich.html/.

Leith-Ross, Sylvia, 1934 African Women: a Study of the Ibo of Nigeria. London: Faver and Faver, Limited.

Marshall, Lorna, 1961 Sharing, Talking, and Giving: Relief of Social Tensions among !Kung Bushman. London: Oxford University Press.

Midlarksy, Elizabeth, and Eva Kahana, 1988 Who helps? Attitudes and characteristics of elderly altruists. Paper presented at the 41st Annual Meeting of the Gerontology Society. Electronic document. http://eric.ed.gov/ERICDocs/data/ericdocs2sql/content_storage_01/0000019b/80/1e/88/e4.pdf/.

Nagel, Thomas, 1978 The Possibility of Altruism. Princeton: Princeton University Press.

Ng, A., D. Lu, C. K. Li, and H. Chan, 2004 A strategic perspective on future residential broadband market. ScienceDirect Technovation 24(8):665–669. Electronic document (ScienceDirect). http://www.sciencedirect.com/science?_ob=ArticleURL&_udi=B6V8B-4-C2R32X-B&_user=56761&_rdoc=1&_fmt=&_orig=search&_sort=d&view=c&_acct=C000059541&_version=1&_urlVersion=0&_userid=56761&md5=49c32fc4b79065ed2a6c302ce38440ff/.

O'Neil, E., 2008a Centering on the Case for Diversity and Cultural Competence, UCSF Center for the Health Professions. Electronic document. http://www.futurehealth.ucsf.edu/archive/from_the_director_0502.htm/.

O'Neil, E., 2008b Centering on a Deeper Look at Cultural Competence, UCSF Center for the Health Professions. Electronic document. http://www.futurehealth.ucsf.edu/archive/from_the_director_0706.htm/.

Ortner, Sherry B., 1978 Sherpas Through Their Rituals. London: Cambridge University Press.

Palmer, Craig T., and Christina Pomianek, 2007 Applying Signaling Theory to Traditional Cultural Rituals: The Example of Newfoundland Mumming. Human Nature 18(4):295–312.

Paulme, Denise, 1940 Social Organization of the Dogon (French Sudan). Paris: Éditions Domat-Montchrestien, F. Loviton et Cie.

Ribal, J. E., 1963 Character and meanings of selfishness and altruism. Sociology and Social Research 47:311–321.

Sarpong, Peter, 1977 Girls' Nobility Rites on Ashanti. Tema. Ghana: Ghana Publishing Corporation.

Shostak, Marjorie, 1981 Nisa: The Life and Words of a !Kung Woman. Cambridge MA: Harvard University Press.

Starr, P., and P. Friedson, 1982 The Social Transformation of American Medicine. New York: Basic Books.

Steadman, Lyle B., and Craig T. Palmer, 2008 The Supernatural and Natural Selection: The Evolution of Religion. Boulder CO: Paradigm Publishers.

Stevens, Stanley F., 1990 Sherpa Settlement and Subsistence: Cultural Ecology and History in Highland Nepal. Ph.D. dissertation, Ann Arbor, MI.

Tervalon, Melanie, and Jann Muray-Garcia, 1998 Cultural humility versus cultural competence: A critical distinction in defining patient training outcomes in multicultural education. Journal of Health Care for the Poor and Underserved 9(2):117–125.

Uzoigwe, G. N. and Ian Skoggard, 2003 Cultural Summary: Banyoro. New Haven CN: HRAF.

Visser, Judith, 1992 The Rituals of Dinner. New York: Penguin.

Ware, John, and Mary Snyder, 1975 Dimensions of patient attitudes regarding doctors and medical care services. Medical Care 13(8):669–682.

Wikipedia, Broadcasting, 2008 Electronic document. http://en.wikipedia.org/wiki/Broadcasting/.

Wikipedia, Semaphore line, 2008 Electronic document. http://en.wikipedia.org/wiki/Semaphore_line/.

Wikipedia, Telecommunication, 2008. Electronic document. http://en.wikipedia.org/wiki/Telecommunications/.

FURTHER READING

Department of Health and Human Services, Health Care Financing Administration, 1998 Medicare Program: Payment for Teleconsultations in Rural Health Professional Shortage Areas. Federal Register (22 June 1998) 63(119):33883.

Fürer-Haimendorf, Christoph von, 1984 The Sherpas Transformed: Social Change in a Buddhist Society of Nepal. New Delhi, India: Sterling.

Saha, Somnath, Sara H. Taggart, Miriam Komaromy, and Andrew Bindman, 2000 Do Patients Choose Physicians of their Own Race. Health Affairs 19(4):76–85.

Biocommunicability

CHAPTER **23**

Charles L. Briggs

INTRODUCTION

This chapter forms part of an ongoing project that seeks to provide a new conceptual departure for medical anthropology by opening up a field of study that centers on biocommunicability. It joins research in medical anthropology to linguistic anthropology, critical discourse analysis, and media studies, but its goals go beyond simply linking preexisting approaches and areas of research. By linking biopolitics to constructions of "information" and "communication," it challenges forms of boundary-work (Gieryn 1983) that have limited the scope and depth of conversations between linguistic and medical anthropologists. My goal is to provide medical anthropologists with a new way of conceptualizing their object of study and a framework for exploring how contemporary phenomena are created and circulate.

In the case of many diseases, epidemics, medications, and interventions, we experience them first – and often primarily – through their public representations that appear in the news and other media forms, on-line, and in advertisements. Indeed, many medical objects become spectacular, in Debord's sense: "images detached from every aspect of life merge into a common stream" (1995[1967]:2). This process is even more complex in that many of the aspects of life that we study are designed in such a way as to be attached to particular sorts of representations that move through specific circuits, reach particular sorts of publics, and be interpreted and embodied in particular sorts of ways. With the continual emergence of new digitally based technologies, it becomes increasingly difficult to keep track of these forms of spectacularlization. What I am most concerned with here are the ways that representations of biomedical objects contain cartographies of the sites where they were produced, how they are traveling, and where, how, and by whom they are to be received. These projections necessarily simplify complex circulatory practices, drawing on models of

A Companion to Medical Anthropology, First Edition. Edited by Merrill Singer and Pamela I. Erickson.

communication that often lag far behind changes in technologies, circuits, and modes of production and reception. At the same time that these projections place themselves vis-à-vis some dimensions of these processes, they obscure others. I argue here that what we take to be biomedical objects are hybrid forms that inscribe these cartographies on their material surfaces; as we focus on the objects themselves, their spectacularization – and the forms of subjectivity, materiality, biosociality, affect, and ethics associated with them – get, to use Ralph Ellison's (1972:152) powerful phrase, "hidden right out in the open."

There are, I think, some important implications for medical anthropology, which I attempt to tease out here. One is that we, as in our various guises, are located in multiple ways in relation to these circuits. Another is that we, as scholars and as participants in policy-making, news production, and practices, help (re)produce these trajectories at the same time that we are affected by them. Nevertheless, in drawing attention to the spectacular features of biomedical objects, we often fail to appreciate the forms of detachment and reattachment that help render them spectacular; the cartographies inscribed on their surfaces often get erased in the course of analysis. A number of notable exceptions come to mind, cases in which medical anthropologists have attended carefully to spectacularization. Nevertheless, we have lacked an analytic guide for revealing how these processes work and thus to suggest how researchers can document them, thereby revealing important dimensions as to how medical objects are made and transformed. My goal here is to lay out this framework, even if in a preliminary fashion.

(BIO)MEDICALIZATION AND LINGUSTIFICATION

Much work in medical anthropology and medical sociology has scrutinized processes of medicalization, pointing to the expansion of medical authority, institutions, and practices into new and broader areas of social life (Conrad 1972; Lock 2003; Zola 1972). Clarke et al. suggest that the last several decades have witness a shift to biomedicalization, such that the scope of medicalization is increasingly extended through a focus on the proper management of health and illness as "individual moral responsibilities to be fulfilled through improved access to knowledge, self-surveillance, prevention, risk assessment, the treatment of risk, and the consumption of appropriate self-help/biomedical goods and services" (2003:162). At the same time that medicalization and biomedicalization create new social and epistemological connections, however, they involve boundary-work, in Gieryn's (1983) terms, defining particular modes of producing knowledge regarding bodies, pathogens, space, subjectivities, and social relations as contained with the boundaries of medical authority and excluding others as ignorance, superstition, popular belief, or politics.

This process has not been charted in relation to what I will refer to as "linguistification." Latour (1993) argued that modernity was born in the 17th century through the emergence of a sharp contrast between nature and society and the emergence of separate epistemologies for understanding and controlling them – science and politics. What he fails to see is that language was invented as a distinct sphere during this same period. John Locke (1959[1690]:483) closed the *Essay Concerning Human Understanding* by separating nature, politics, and language as "the three great provinces of the intellectual world, wholly separate and distinct one from another." Getting credit for being rational and deemed worthy of political participation entailed separating not only science from politics but both from knowledge of language (Bauman and Briggs 2008). In the early 20th century, Ferdinand de Saussure (1959[1916]) argued that a modern discipline of linguistics must be founded precisely on these relations of purification (in Latour's 1993 sense of the term). Like medicalization, linguistification separates out particular areas of social life, draws boundaries around them, defines forms of expertise that can legitimately interpret them, and then continually extends their power by drawing more and more objects and subjects within their purview. Forms of linguistic distinction (matters of "accent," specialized vocabularies, professional literacy practices, etc.) become valuable as forms of symbolic capital (Bourdieu 1991) precisely because they are viewed as being elements of a linguistic "code" that simply serves as a tool for communication. The power and seeming autonomy of linguistification was greatly extended in the 20th century through cybernetics and communication theory and, more recently, through cultural and political–economic constructions of "information technologies" and "communication technologies." Dimensions of social life could be converted into "information" or "communication" and then quantified, standardized, transmitted, and received.

Let me start with an example familiar to many medical anthropologists in suggesting how linguistification operates in the creation of biomedical objects. Rethinking statistics and biomedical modes of classification has constituted a productive boundary object between philosophy, history, science studies, and medical anthropology. Ian Hacking (1990) argued that relations between statistics and "society" shifted in the 18th and 19th centuries; systematically collecting numbers about people and making them public changed how individual and collective identities are created and even the notion of "society" itself. Geoffrey Bowker and Susan Leigh Star (1999) examined categories that underline the production and circulation of statistics, focusing on the International Classification of Diseases. They argue for the central role of two processes. First, how categories and numbers enter and leave institutions involves negotiations between forms of authority, efforts to keep a job or climb the ladder, and political threats and opportunities, thereby imbuing them with complex indexical histories that get multiplied as they travel. On the other hand, the authority of categories and numbers is contingent on their seemingly context-free nature; complex indexical histories are thus rendered invisible as statistics circulate.

I confronted the strikingly contradictory character of categories and statistics while researching the Latin American cholera epidemic. Clara Mantini-Briggs and I had interviewed clinicians and epidemiologists in a Venezuelan rainforest, the Office of the National Epidemiology in Caracas, the World Health Organization's (WHO) Global Cholera Task Force in Geneva, and elsewhere. But the complexities of categories and statistics came home to me when we interviewed Dr. John Schwartz, a Pan American Health Organization (PAHO) epidemiologist. Schwartz helped take cholera morbidity and mortality statistics sent by national PAHO offices and construct the statistical summaries sent to the WHO. A bearded, friendly fellow, Schwartz had been up all night with a new baby when Clara and I visited him in 1998, but he patiently detailed how the PAHO "sent out the standardized definitions, the reports came up, and they put them in a system." He noted that after several years, a new national epidemiologist in Brazil "notified us and said, "gee, you guys have to reduce the number of cases by 200,000 because we only report confirmed cases." So, that's what we did in 1993. We tried to clarify in greater detail each country's definitions, how they were utilizing their definitions." In other words, PAHO epidemiologists had no idea that each country defined cholera cases and deaths differently. What was constructed as "the Latin American cholera epidemic" transformed a heterogeneous assortment of categories, sites, and practices into a seemingly homogeneous set of facts (see also Trostle 2005).

Like statistics, medical objects are shaped by the circuits that they have traveled and their indexical histories. New diseases, technologies, treatments, and the like do not spring directly into labs, clinics, and living rooms any more than epidemiological statistics jump from bodies onto maps and tables. How we perceive SARS, avian flu, the April 2009 outbreak of A(H1N1) "swine flu," new medications, and other objects is tied indexically to how they get linked to clinical trials, the stature of the conference in which it is presented and the journal in which it is published, the reputations of the scientists involved, who funds the research, who reports it in which newspaper and/or on which television station, and how is advertised and marketed. It takes a lot of work – and in some cases, a lot of capital – in each site to bring drugs "to market" or create public spectacles around far away epidemics. How we perceive a medical object – whether we actually get the disease or take the pill – is closely shaped by forms of authority that have shaped it, the circuits it has traveled, the social, political–economic, and epistemological terrains it has traversed, and how it has been shaped in such a way as to appeal to particular publics in particular ways; the indexical histories it has accumulated get inscribed on its surface (such as US advertisements for pharmaceuticals).

The processes of biomedicalization involved in creating new objects works hand-in-hand with linguistification. Both (bio)medicalization and linguistification play distinct but highly complementary roles in creating a boundary between object and representation, between a disease or drug and the way it is written up in professional journals and portrayed on the news media and in advertising. They generate the sense of a pre-existing object that is then cast into language and image. Representations are then placed into "communicative" circuits that exist apart from those inhabited by pathogens and pills. The only necessary link between the two lies with a politics of truth – the representations must reproduce the important aspects of the object without error or distortion. Skeptics, such as critics of the pharmaceutical corporations and for-profit healthcare providers, play a special role in maintaining these boundaries by "crying foul" either when the gap seems too wide, such as when clinically crucial information is withheld, or too narrow, such as when biomedical objects seem to have been produced for particular discursive effects – rather than biomedical results. In this latter regard, Cori Hayden's research on the marketing of less-expensive drugs as being "similar" rather than generic is fascinating. If the two drugs are medically identical, critics ask, why do they have different names and are marketed distinctively? If they are not medically equivalent, how can they be discursively represented as the same? Both clinical medicine and public health policies claim to be based on "evidence," facts that speak for themselves. Linguistification helps to keep objects in biomedical realms and representations in communicative ones – even as my interviews with public relations and marketing professionals for the biotechnology and pharmaceutical industries suggest that they play increasingly important roles in deciding which drugs and devices will be developed, when clinical trials will take place, when conference presentations will be made and articles published, hire the medical writers to draft them, work closely with reporters to publicize them, and work closely with advertising professionals throughout (see Healey 2006). Like biomedicalization, the more effective the linguistification practices in creating the sense that objects and representations are separate, the greater the power of their intimate co-production.

LINGUISTIFICATION IN THE ANALYSIS OF NARRATIVES IN MEDICAL ANTHROPOLOGY

I see two ways that linguistification operates in medical anthropology. The first actively advances the work of linguistification, often even when the focus of the analysis is on discursive representations. A second, to which I turn below, scrutinizes both (bio) medicalization and linguistification.

Since narrative research foregrounds how illness, health, and bodies are discursively represented, it provides a fruitful site for examining how medical anthropologists engage issues of (bio)medicalization and linguistification. Arthur Kleinman and Nancy Scheper-Hughes are two of the most widely respected members of the field, and they have brought the analysis of narratives to the center of medical anthropology. Because they have contributed distinctive approaches to the field, as based respectively in phenomenology and political economy, I think it particularly interesting to explore some similarities in the way they define and analyze narratives.

Kleinman's *The Illness Narratives* has been one of the most widely read books in medical anthropology since it was published over two decades ago, and it has influenced clinical medicine as well. Distinguishing between a focus on disease, which privileges practitioners' perspectives and biomedical reductionism, from one on illness, the individual's "lived experience of monitoring bodily processes" (1988:3), Kleinman argues for the obligation of clinicians to document the experience of illness; he criticizes medical education for erasing patient perspectives and focusing on disease. The Preface provides an origin narrative for Kleinman's own recognition of the centrality of illness-centered perspectives as two patients taught the neophyte physician the interpretive and therapeutic power of illness narratives. He argues, particularly for the treatment of chronic diseases, that "the sensitive solicitation of the patient's and the family's stories of the illness, the assembling of a mini-ethnography of the changing contexts of chronicity" (1988:10) is "a core task in the work of doctoring" (1988:xiii).

What is an illness narrative, where does it come from, and what is the ethnographer/clinician's role in its production and circulation? Kleinman (1988:4) charts a process that starts in the patient's interior, in "the lived experience of monitoring bodily processes." Drawing on cultural and personal models, patients and family members use "plot lines, core metaphors, and rhetorical devices" to create stories (1988:49). Clinicians mediate this movement from inside to outside, helping to "piece together the illness narrative as it emerges from the patient's and the family's complaints and explanatory models" (1988:49). The order and coherence that narratives imbue in illness experiences would thus seem to be provided, in part, by physician–interlocutors. For Kleinman, narratives perform crucial functions in illness and healing, enabling "sick persons to order, communicate, and thereby symbolically control symptoms" (1988:49). To leave the patient's social world and enter the world of clinical medicine (and medical anthropology, it would seem), the narrative requires assistance from professionals who "must interpret it in the light of the different models of illness meanings – symptom symbols, culturally salient illnesses, personal and social contexts." Although the treatment of chronic disease may present somewhat more extended opportunities for patients to tell their stories, changes in healthcare in the United States since 1988 have, unfortunately, anything but expanded the opportunities for patients to narrate and their physicians to listen.

While lauding the way that Kleinman's book helped turn narratives into central components of research in medical anthropology, I would like to point out a contradiction that might be surmounted in order to enhance the value of narratives in medical anthropology. A number of authors have critiqued the notion that illness narratives take patients' interior models of illness and make them accessible to clinicians (Mattingly 1998). Mishler (1984) and Waitzkin (1991) argue that narratives emerging in doctors–patient interactions do not spring directly from illness experiences but are co-produced, shaped by great differences of power. Indeed, patients' narratives often incorporate biomedical epistemologies, sometimes as a means of shaping their reception by physicians (Singer et al. 1988). Taussig (1992[1980]) argues that patient-centered uses of narratives can erase awareness of the broader political economy of illness and health care. These critiques also tend to reify doctor–patient interviews as sites for the emergence of narratives. Cicourel (1992) examines the social lives of patient narratives as they emerge within and move through multiple interviews, consultations, practices of inscription, and classrooms. Inside and outside of clinical settings, each telling is informed, as Bakhtin's work (1981) would suggest, by intertextual links to previous renditions and to medical records, diagnostic tests, and material circulated through the news, advertisements, or, increasingly, the Web.

Byron Good (1994) suggests that it is not just the content of narratives but the performativity associated with their narration and the practices of reception that shape illness experiences. Nevertheless, like forms of erasure required by epidemiological categories and statistics, the contours of the "pragmatics of illness narratives," as he refers to them (1994:158), are erased when stories are lodged in summaries or transcripts that are edited in such a fashion as to strip away features that tie them to interviews and to the history of their circulation. But these rich indexical histories represent patients' efforts to place themselves vis-à-vis the production and circulation of knowledge about them, and patients often use narratives in casting themselves as knowledge-producers. Such representations of knowledge claims are always multiple and often competing. If they position themselves as the privileged conduit through which patients' inner worlds become legible and are articulated vis-à-vis perspectives articulated by professionals, medical anthropologists (and clinicians) enter this contested field by declaring their authority over the process and delegitimize the claims of patients and their relatives, following Taussig (1992[1980]), as expressions of a reified subaltern consciousness. Moreover, they potentially overlook how patients attempt to shape how their stories will be recontextualized in future contexts and what effects will accrue to them (see Briggs and Bauman 1992).

A second example comes from Nancy Scheper-Hughes' exemplary and celebrated work on organ transplant, which has revealed how unethical and illegal practices of organ procurement threaten the lives of poor donors and sometimes even recipients. Scheper-Hughes is centrally concerned here with narratives. She notes that "rumors and urban legends" have a global distribution and produce real social effects, such as popular resistance to new consent laws and even acts of violence against foreigners accused of kidnapping children for their organs (2002:32). Since discourse about shady practices is suppressed, "Above all, we are trying to pierce the secrecy surrounding organ transplantation and to 'make public' all practices regarding the harvesting, selling and distribution of human organs and tissues." Scheper-Hughes details how organ brokers, the mainstream media, and biomedical professionals foster the circulation of sentimental stories about organ recipients but suppress knowledge of the biomedical, psychological, and social difficulties that donors face. Her account is a detective story through ten countries, traversing "alien and, at times, hostile and dangerous territory" (2002:35), using stories as her clues.

Scheper-Hughes' work has brought the centrality of narrative to the fore so powerfully that it might be worthwhile to reflect on how their collection, analysis, and insertion into medical anthropology are conceived here. Her work projects narratives as sparked by biomedical events, the extraction and circulation of organs, and the social contexts in which organs are procured. Scheper-Hughes (2002:55) defines the discursive epicenter quite precisely: "organ donors represent a social and semiotic zero." From there, accurate representations of these events should radiate outwards through open discussion, accurate media accounts, and professional discourses to global publics. Her narrative builds tension by seeing this linear, natural, and necessary process as disrupted by the transplant industry's suppression of donor voices and the distortion of events by popular sectors through rumors, "urban legends," and sensationalist press stories. Narratives form the vehicles of circulation. The ethical violation involved in obstructing this linear flow parallels that of transplants that violate the rights of donors and their families. Thus, starting with the "social and semiotic zero" of donors' narratives, described as "an ideal place for a critical medical anthropologist dedicated to 'following the bodies' to begin" (2002:55), the project involved the monumental task of locating transplant stories that get locked in place and working with mainstream journalists, including reporters of *60 Minutes* and the *New York Times,* and bringing poor donors to visible public forums (such as academic symposia) in order to circulate suppressed stories. This view of discourse as springs from events and radiating continuously outwards towards waiting publics rests on language ideologies (Schieffelin et al. 1998) that have formed a key part of modern political and social projects in Europe since the seventeenth century (Bauman and Briggs 2003).

For Scheper-Hughes, narratives become ethnographic tools, but the social lives of narratives never become an object of ethnography. Although locating narrators willing to talk about illegal organs trading is difficult, collecting stories seems uncomplicated: narrators just seem to agree, like a Brazilian woman whose kidney was apparently stolen, "to share her bizarre medical story with me" (Scheper-Hughes 2002:36). Stories seem be preexisting objects that are located by ethnographers and then given to them, rather than being co-produced by narrators and audiences, including fieldworkers, as extensive research would suggest (see Duranti and Brenneis 1986). Once collected, the first step seems to be to assess their truth values, placing the researcher as the arbiter of their status as valuable revelations of suppressed information *versus* problematic rumors, urban legends, and cover-ups, a rather elite position in relation to the politics of truth (Foucault 1980). One of the strongest features of Scheper-Hughes' work is her attention to political economy as she reveals how "organs flow from South to

North, from poor to rich, from black and brown to white, and from female to male bodies" (2002:45), but we learn little about how stories are lodged in political–economic inequalities that structure who gets to narrate, whose narratives become authoritative, which narratives circulate through which types of channels, who gets to circulate them, and which stories affect policies and practices (Briggs 2004). A Lockean dichotomy between words and things that denies the materiality of language and discourse (see Keane 2007) expels narratives from the material realm occupied by bodies, organs, and capital, in short, advances the work of linguisticification. Once again, I want to frame my comments on Kleinman and Scheper-Hughes not as criticism but in suggesting how their admirable work, which has established the centrality of narratives to medical anthropology, could be used even more fruitfully.

I noted above that there are also numerous examples from the medical anthropology literature in which scholars have attended to the relationship between (bio)medicalization and linguistification. A growing body of research examines issues of mobility, how people, technologies, epistemologies, diseases, cultural forms, etc. are made to seem naturally mobile (Urry 2007) as well as the types of friction (Tsing 2005) that shape the sorts of "grooves" that both make travel possible and route it in particular ways, obstruct mobility (Lakoff 2005), and create global assemblages that juxtapose different widely distributed phenomena in particular ways in concrete spaces (Ong and Collier 2005). In medical anthropology, at the same time that researchers have explored the mobilization of technologies, surgeries, clinical trials, medications, diseases, and biomedical epistemologies, many have paid careful attention to the role of discursive forms in this process and how representations become (im)mobile.

Baer et al. (2003[1997]) and Swora (2001) examine how Alcoholics Anonymous regiments modes of telling and listening to personal narratives, thereby shaping perceptions of alcoholism as a disease that individuals must overcome rather than the product of broader social, historical, and political economic relations. Paul Farmer (1992) carefully traces the development of cultural forms for representing HIV/AIDS in Haiti and the United States, shaping perceptions and policies as the disease was increasingly located in a "geography of blame." Stacy Pigg (2001) traces how Nepalese discussions of HIV/AIDS and sexuality bear indexical traces of the NGOs, interests, and ideologies that shaped their circulation, thereby hierarchicalizing modes of reception. Lawrence Cohen's *No Aging in India* explores how discourses of Alzheimer's, dementia, and gerontology moved iteratively as figures of pathology and exchanges of legitimate forms of suffering between diseased and care-giving bodies (1998:49). Rather than tracking a global conduit from Europe and the United States to India, Cohen scrutinizes portrayals of Alzheimer's in scientific conferences, medical journals, supermarket tabloids, news magazines, and medical training programs, attending to obstacles to mobility and unintended effects. Adryna Petryna (2002) explores how Chernobyl spread both radiation and categories of radiation illness; becoming a biological citizen seems to involve locating oneself in both these circuits. Cori Hayden (2003) disrupts linear narratives that picture plants and medicinal knowledge as traveling from Mexican villages to US pharmaceutical laboratories, whether as stories of global rip-offs or humanitarian gifts and scientific breakthroughs. The social, legal, and practical difficulties of "bioprospecting" emerge in observations she makes while following scientists and samples. João Biehl (2005) locates the life and death of a Brazilian woman not simply in the dilapidated residential center in which she lived but in the circulation of pharmaceuticals and stories about her told by family members, staff, fellow patients, her diaries and poetry, and medical records.

These few examples attest to explorations by medical anthropologists of the complex co-constitutive relations between medical objects and modes of representation. They suggest growing awareness that ethnographic work requires scrutinizing the social lives of documents, images, narratives, statistics, diagnostic results, and other forms. This trajectory has greatly advanced study of biopolitics (Foucault 1997), biosociality (Rabinow 1992), bioavailability (Cohen 2005), biological citizenship (Petryna 2002), and shifting definitions of life (Inhorn 2007; Rapp 1999), death (Lock 2003), and the body (Cohen 2005; Scheper-Hughes 2002). What is needed, I think, are analytic frameworks that can similarly help us see how linguistification operates in the production, circulation, and use of biomedical objects.

From Communication to Communicability

Let me draw on a distinction made by Michael Silverstein (1976) in pinpointing what I mean here. Pragmatics refers to the use of signs in particular contexts. In a conversation, for example, how people take turns, build on each others words, shift topics, display attentiveness, and attempt to dominate their interlocutors are issues of pragmatics. At the same time, however, co-conversationalists are constantly commenting on what is being said, framing particular utterances as authoritative, hesitant, or humorous, registering their agreement or disagreement with what the other has said, and pointing to where they think the conversation should go. Metapragmatic dimensions are no less important in other types of discourse. Following Latour (1987) we can say that scientific texts comment metapragmatically on how they are connected to laboratories, analytic practices, and both complementary and competing perspectives; methodological sections, for example, generally project linear and seemingly necessary relations between particular sites (laboratories or populations), modes of extracting knowledge, juxtaposing discursive fragments (statistical tests), and interpreting their significance. Pragmatics and metapragmatics dance a sort of tango, with metapragmatics attempting to control pragmatics in such a way as to shape further circulation of discourse – but without ever fully succeeding.

Much recent work in medical anthropology is what Marcus refers to as "multi-sited"; nevertheless, researchers do not simply work in different places but track the circulation of bodies, technologies, pathogens, etc. between them. As such, medical anthropologists generate a great deal of material on the pragmatics of discourse circulation. Nevertheless, metapragmatics, I think, has been less adequately documented. A clear implication of the above discussion of narrative is medical anthropologists tend to reify their own metapragmatic models of how knowledge is created, circulates, and is received as providing reliable maps of how discourse is moving, enabling them to separate intersecting cultural forms as rumor, sensationalist press, scientific hegemony, and so far; insofar as this occurs, researchers are less concerned with documenting the metapragmatics that organize the knowledge-making and circulating practices of other participants – and the complex ways that different models overlap, interact, and compete.

An example of these metapragmatic cartographies of production and circulation comes from my own work on news coverage of health issues in the United States, conducted in conjunction with media scholar Daniel Hallin, and my collaboration with researchers in six Latin American countries. Clarke et al. (2003) stress that a crucial dimension of the shift to biomedicalization lies in the proliferation of news coverage of health issues, the growing dominance of the biomedical within science news, and the way this material biomedicalizes mass culture. A number of studies have traced how news coverage affects perceptions of particular diseases, especially HIV/ AIDS (Lupton 1997), SARS (Lewison 2008), cholera (Briggs 2003; Briggs and Mantini-Briggs 2003), avian flu (Ungar 2008), Ebola (Joffe and Haarhoff 2002; Ungar 1998), along with public health policies, clinic practices, and popular reactions. Scholars who do not focus on the media generally use news reports in documenting events and gauging official responses and popular perceptions – a precarious move, I would add. Nevertheless, the press is generally implicitly constructed as a means of transporting information or elite views to the public. Journalism and media researchers generally marginalize health news because it appears peripheral to central issues of politics and economics – that is, they biomedicalize it as a separate domain of specialized knowledge that is only relevant to biomedical issues.

Both of these moves spring precisely from the way that knowledge about health is constructed. Until recently, the dominant view pictured biomedical and public health knowledge as constructed in specialized sites (such as laboratories, teaching hospitals, and epidemiologists' offices), initially transmitted through publication in leading journals, transformed into popular discourse by health educators, reporters, and clinicians, and finally received by ignorant but self-interested lay populations (Briggs and Hallin 2007). I refer to such constructions of how knowledge is produced, circulated, and received as *communicability* and, when cast as metapragmatic maps of biomedical knowledge, as *biocommunicability*. Communicability emerges in broadly distributed models, such as the linear model of health news, and in unique cartographies that emerge as particular texts project the very communicative processes in which they are engaged. One of the most common types of health news stories maps the origin of a new treatment or health "risk" in a particular laboratory or hospital, its testing in a clinical trial, its publication in a leading medical journal, and how the reporter, the PI, and other "experts" are interpreting its significance for lay audiences.

In short, communicative dimensions are projected in news stories alongside biomedical objects. These communicable cartographies are generally multiple and often competing. Hallin and I have charted the growing dominance of cartographies focusing on active patient–consumers who cannot simply wait for information to reach them but must seek out information from a wide range of sources and use it in making rational choices – in short, biomedicalized subjects. Another places health issues in public spheres, framing all parties (including pharmaceutical companies, federal regulators, healthcare institutions, and laypersons) as joining policy and ethical debates; readers/ listeners are cast in the role of citizens, not patients or consumers (Briggs and Hallin, in press). These different models often intersect in the same broadcast or article.

The relationship between these communicable cartographies and the pragmatics of news production, which we have documented ethnographically, is not the ideal *versus* the real. The public health officials, pharmaceutical representatives, their public relations consultants, health care professionals, journalists, and laypersons we interviewed were all aware of gaps between the pragmatics and metapragmatics, but these disjunctures shaped very different types of relationships to health news. Hospital administrators and public health officials noted that they pitch "we-are-informing-the-public type" stories to reporters in order to convince a handful of policy makers or funders that the public wants precisely the program they are pushing. Many health reporters are skeptical of profit-driven reports of new drugs or technologies, and they view a great deal of information that is presented for public dissemination as advertisements disguised as science. Nevertheless, they see producing stories that cast themselves as conduits of information between scientists and "the public" as crucial for holding onto rapidly defecting audience members. Finally, many members of racialized populations that are projected as being out of the biocommunicable loop challenge their projected position of ignorance and indifference, pointing out gaps between paternalistic projections of state interest in educating and healing them *versus* how they are often denied the promised services. Nevertheless, political economy is crucial here – working-class members of immigrant and racialized populations meet with little success in getting stories that embody their own communicable cartographies into the mainstream media.

WHAT CAN COMMUNICABLE CARTOGRAPHIES TELL US?

Okay, you may ask, if I study biocommunicable cartographies, what's in it for me? Of late, scholars have explored how biomedical phenomena get spatialized, temporal-ized, mobilized, and objectified (as bounded biomedical objects) and the construc-tions of scale, subjectivities, agency, forms of biosociality, ethics, and affect that shape them. I suggest that many of these same dimensions also enter into the constitution of biocommunicable cartographies. By adumbrating them, I hope to suggest how researchers can document biocommunicability and use these findings in exploring the making of medical objects. I can do little more than lay these issues out schematically here, noting that each feature merits attention in its own right. What is at issue here is, in Silverstein's terms, the metapragmatic dimensions – how communication is rep-resented and attempts to regulate it. These biocommunicable cartographies never provide adequate characterizations of the complex pragmatics involved, which always present excesses that cannot be adequately contained within or erased by these maps. Models, of course, can shape lived reality and achieve important social and political–economic effects without corresponding point-by-point to their related social fields.

In terms of *spatialization*, biocommunicable cartographies project the spaces through which knowledge about health moves. The sense that spaces are socially and epistemologically bounded is generated by according them distinct communicable roles – some become spaces of knowledge production, others of circulation, others of reception, and still others, such as racialized spaces, as simply being off the communi-cable map. In linear biocommunicable models, power can be measured in inverse relation to one's distance from the spatial locus of knowledge production as well as by its *temporalization*; as with gossip, generally speaking the sooner you learn of a major policy or personnel decision, the higher your status – although lower-status actors may get the goods by working in the same spaces with high-status players. In our research on the Venezuelan cholera epidemic, this temporalization was gauged vis-à-vis a projected flow of authoritative information from the WHO to the PAHO to top Health Ministry officials to health professionals of less status to health educators and to "the public" as well as from the capital to "the interior," especially rural areas. Proximity to centers of knowledge production was marked in decreasing order by possession of original WHO or PAHO manuals, original copies of Ministry manuals, photocopies, manuals designed for non-professionals, or pamphlets; institutional status was coded by one's textual location in this projected linear movement of information. Again, I am not asserting that the production, circulation, and reception of knowledge about cholera was indeed linear and unidirectional; Mantini-Briggs and I documented the multiplicity of sites of production, circulation, and reception, at the same time we analyzed how this dominant unilinear biocommunicable cartography created a geography of blame (Farmer 1999) that largely undermined cholera promotion and education efforts (Briggs and Mantini-Briggs 2003).

Logics of *objectification*, which generate discrete biomedical objects (pathogens, vaccines, kidneys, etc.), also generate corresponding "messages," press releases, training manuals, videos, photographs, e-mail listservs, and Web sites. Notions of "information" and "communication" are powerful constructions that encode common communicable models and enact processes of linguistification. Our very language of "production," "circulation," and "reception" produces objectification, here of components of communicative processes, by inviting us to imagine a discrete entity that can be inserted in multiple places and processes. They constitute, in Bowker and Star's (1999:297) terms, boundary objects "that both inhabit several communities of practice and satisfy the informational requirements of each of them. Boundary objects are thus both plastic enough to adapt to local needs and constraints of the several parties employing them, yet robust enough to maintain a common identity across sites." This objectification produces biomedical objects and their representations, such as deaths from vibrio cholera and both news reports and WHO statistics; the distinctness of a new biomedical object is marked by the emergence of new conference papers, journal articles, and news stories about "it." The concept of a potential "avian influenza epidemic," for example, links the A(H5N1) virus, images of Asian bodies and birds, epidemiological charts and maps, and the sense that reporters are standing in China or Indonesia sending images to "us" – creating the image that information and lethal viruses could take the same route. Urry (2007) argues that *mobility* is not an immanent characteristic – elements of the social world must be constructed in ways that make them seem capable of moving in particular ways. We documented, for example, how cholera morbidity and mortality statistics shaped by particular political agendas, gross inequalities in health infrastructures, and the racialization of life and death could be turned into numbers that would seem to travel smoothly along PAHO/WHO epidemiological circuits. Biocommunicable models generally cast scientific facts as being immutable mobiles (Latour 1988), so intrinsically portable that they can go anywhere without requiring additional work or losing their referential stability. Medical knowledge framed as "superstition" or "culture," however, needs to stay in place, although physicians may receive "cultural competency" training, enabling them to travel effectively to the sites in which patients seem to be "incarcerated by culture" (Appadurai 1988). The illicit mobility of knowledge dubbed "rumors," "hoaxes," or "conspiracy theories" must be suppressed. In short, biocommunicable cartographies create both mobilities and immobilities, on which they in turn rely for their plausibility.

Biocommunicable cartographies similarly define *subject-positions* in relation to knowledge circulation. Researchers are the quintessential producers, while clinicians are both receivers – expected to access knowledge in scientific journals – and transmitters, determining what information is relevant for individual patients and turning it into non-technical language. Although both health professionals and journalists pictured reporters as transmitters rather than producers of knowledge, health journalists' perceptions of their own roles ranged from fellow-members-of-the-health-education-team to translators to fraud detectors to the-eyes-and-ears-of-the-public. Some models, as I noted, cast members of "the public" as ignorant, passive receivers of information, others as active consumers of information and drugs, and others as citizens who can rightfully debate matters of health policy. Subject–positions are associated with differing degrees of *agency*, framed as the power to shape the circulation of health knowledge. Different models project agency distinctly – both patient–consumer and public-sphere citizen models, for example, accord laypersons more agency than linear, doctors' orders varieties.

Just as each subject–position is characterized by normative subjectivities, they are marked by distinct *affective states*. Scientists should not display emotions. Reporters can be moved by others' suffering, but their reporting should be "objective." Clinicians should both weigh cold scientific facts and display humanistic benevolence and sensitivity to their patients' emotions. Affectivity is required for patients; they must display the appropriate degree of anxiety when information regarding their own "risk factors" or condition is disclosed and exude the self-interest and self-confidence needed to follow doctors' recommendations. The affective burden on parents is particularly acute. Biocommunicability provides a key means of evaluating the *ethical status* of actors. In dominant models, each participant must play their assigned subject role, display the entailed subjectivity, and express the appropriate type of affect – and everyone must play their assigned role in keeping knowledge about health moving properly. Reporters accused of distorting the facts, researchers who withhold or distort the results of clinical trials, public health officials who do not make important knowledge public, and laypersons who are not listening, don't understand, or fail to transform knowledge into bodily practices are deemed to be unethical. Patients are branded as "noncompliant" or "resistant" when they deem themselves capable of making their own decisions about what knowledge to accept or, even worse, themselves produce knowledge. Social movements often construct the ethics of communicability quite differently. Urban (2001) suggests that a primary obligation for modern subjects is to keep culture in constant motion, and this obligation seems nowhere as intense as in health matters.

Biocommunicable cartographies link researchers, clinicians, reporters, health educators, medical journals, state officials, publics, HMOs, insurers, corporations, and communicative and biomedical technologies in vast networks that seem to constantly shift as new knowledge emerges. They accordingly project forms of *biosociality* through their shared participation in the circulation of biomedical knowledge. If one adopts perspectives associated with actor–network theory, biocommunicable cartographies – whether they appear in articles in scientific journals or press accounts – are key sites in which the role of "actants" is continually charted within actor–networks (Callon 1986; Latour 1987). The ethical character of biocommunicability is associated with these networks – keeping knowledge moving positively affects the health of others, while obstructing or distorting it jeopardizes people downstream, undermining their "right" to biomedical knowledge. This explains the strong ethical condemnation of irresponsible researchers and pharmaceutical companies; when knowledge-producers suppress information, they affect everyone else. At the same time, biocommunicable cartographies limit and segregate biosociality by projecting subjectivities as maximally shared only within biocommunicable subject–positions.

Finally, biocommunicability informs projects of *scale-making*, imagining scalar differences between laboratories, clinical trials, journal articles, national policies, global and local media, international public health organizations, doctor's offices, and living rooms. Biocommunicable cartographies project how, when, and by whom these scales should be jumped. When pharmaceutical corporations prescribe the prescription practices of individual physicians (Oldani 2004), for example, appropriate scale-jumping practices have been violated.

Conclusion

In this chapter, I have laid out a new framework for research in medical anthropology. I think it would be productive to develop a comparative approach to biocommunicabilities that can help us understand how they are lodged in different sites and construct knowledge in relationship to a diverse set of objects, enabling us to explore variations in how they are engaged with the pragmatics of biomedical discourse. Nevertheless, I have been particularly concerned here with showing medical anthropologists who are not interested "in communication" how this approach might enhance their own research.

Why are biocommunicable models and cartographies so productive? Three reasons: First, spatial, temporal, subjective, and ethical are performatively constructed as components of biocommunicability whenever people talk or write about health. Second, insofar as they are modeled on the pragmatic details of particular representations, biocommunicable cartographies purport to be merely descriptive – to be simple reflections of how knowledge about health is actually circulating at that very moment. Spatialities, temporalities, subject–positions, and so forth are thus projected as existing prior to and independently of this circulation process; in other words, they get naturalized. Third, the modernist separation of words and worlds suggests that bodies, pathogens, epistemologies, drugs, and so forth are what is really real; "information" can be true or false, but it does not seem to directly affect the things it represents. In short, by casting themselves as ultimately inconsequential, communicability cartographies can draw attention away from their own powerful effects. They are thus "hidden right out in the open"; although they are overtly marked, attention is directed to the biomedical objects to which they refer. Their important role in constituting biomedical knowledge can thus go largely undetected – even by medical anthropologists.

Communicable cartographies are most powerful when they are most taken for granted. Their powerful role gets opened up for scrutiny when gaps between normative metapragmatics and a specific set of pragmatics are debated – as evident in criticisms of suppressed research results or of pharmaceutical representatives influencing physicians' prescribing practices. Their role in shaping biomedical phenomena is most up for grabs when communicable cartographies themselves are disputed, as when lay social movements claim the right to produce biomedical knowledge that calls the scientific status of knowledge circulated by researchers and public health officials – and their attempts to assert monopolies over the production of legitimate biomedical knowledge – into question. The success of the gay movement in challenging the dominant biocommunicable cartographies of HIV/AIDS discourse, which Steven Epstein (1996) relates to the power of the gay social movement as well as the white, male, and middle-class status of many of these biocommunicable insurgents, created a public space for alternative cartographies that is still being mobilized in new ways.

Here's the "rub": when they deem "communication" to be inconsequential, medical anthropologists naturalize their own commonsense communicable cartographies. Researchers generally reify hegemonic cartographies that cast elite subjects (like themselves) as privileged producers and transporters of knowledge. Even if their cartographies project the circulation of knowledge from oppressed subjects to policy makers, global publics, and global media (as in the trajectories associated with "engaged" or "public" anthropology), they recapitulate rhetorics of ethnographic authority in which ethnographers cast themselves as the only actors who can cross social chasms, sensitively grasp alien perspectives, and transport them around the globe in order to illuminate powerful audiences. A number of things are lost in this process. One is the multiplicity of ways that participants themselves construct and attempt to control how knowledge is constructed, circulates, and is received. Another is how people, including the powerful and the oppressed, resist, manipulate, and appropriate existing communicable cartographies (including those espoused by medical anthropologists). Third, a productive line of research of late has explored how the knowledge-making practices of anthropologists relate to those of other persons (see for example Riles 2004). Insofar as they reify their own communicable cartographies and fail to explore others, medical anthropologists lose valuable insights into the nature and social location of their own work. Finally, if, as I have suggested, many of the phenomena we investigate are biomedical–communicable hybrids, medical anthropologists limit their ability to realize the central goal of seeing how what seem to be actually existing objects – epidemics, drugs, biotech platforms, global clinical trials, and the like – are made and made to seem real.

I end with the issue of social justice, which animates a great deal of contemporary work in medical anthropology, mine included. The cholera epidemic brought home to me the crucial role of biocommunicable cartographies in naturalizing health inequities. That political economy shapes the circulation of discourse about health is obvious – the ways that poor and racialized populations represent disease and death seldom enters mainstream media or policy discussion, except when transformed into reflections of ignorance and powerlessness. Challenging health inequities and promoting social justice would seem to require two distinct but related steps. One consists of challenging the pragmatic contours that accord elites the role of the "primary definers" (Hall et al. 1978) of public discourse about health, as attempted by social movements, alternative media, and community groups that monitor and denounce denigrating representations or reporters' failure to cover stories that dispute elite perspectives. Another is to challenge the communicable cartographies that reserve credit for producing legitimate information about health to elites, thereby erasing the active participation of working-class and racialized populations in producing and circulating knowledge. Indeed, subaltern subjects are often excluded, even as receptors, from dominant biocommunicable cartographies even as they play complex, active roles in the production of crucial knowledge about health. Under the "do no harm" dictum, we should make sure that efforts by medical anthropologists to bring suppressed voices to global publics do not enhance scholars' own (albeit limited) control over the pragmatics and metapragmatics of discourse about health at the expense of efforts by people who enjoy much less access to health, healthcare, and opportunities to make their own biocommunicable interventions into public debates.

REFERENCES

Appadurai, Arjun, 1988 Putting Hierarchy in Its Place. Cultural Anthropology 3(1):36–49.
Baer, Hans A., Merrill Singer, and Ida Susser, 2003[1997] Medical Anthropology and the World System. 2nd edition. Westport CN: Praeger.
Bauman, Richard, and Charles L. Briggs, 2003 Voices of Modernity: Language Ideologies and the Politics of Inequality. Cambridge UK: Cambridge University Press.
Bielh, João, 2005 Vita: Life in a Zone of Social Abandonment. Berkeley: University of California Press.
Bourdieu, Pierre, 1991 Language and Symbolic Power. G. Raymond and M. Adamson, trans. Cambridge MA: Harvard University Press.
Bowker, Geoffrey C., and Susan Leigh Star, 1999 Sorting Things Out: Classification and Its Consequences. Cambridge MA: MIT Press.
Briggs, Charles L., 2003 Why Nation-States Can't Teach People to be Healthy: Power and Pragmatic Miscalculation in Public Discourses on Health. Medical Anthropology Quarterly 17(3):287–321.
Briggs, Charles L., 2004 Theorizing Modernity Conspiratorially: Science, Scale, and the Political Economy of Public Discourse in Explanations of a Cholera Epidemic. American Ethnologist 31(2):163–186.
Briggs, Charles L., and Richard Bauman, 1992 Genre, Intertextuality, and Social Power. Journal of Linguistic Anthropology 2: 131–72.
Briggs, Charles L., and Daniel C. Hallin, 2007 Biocommunicability: The Neoliberal Subject and Its Contradictions in News Coverage of Health Issues. Social Text 25(4):43–66.
Briggs, Charles L. and Daniel C. Hallin, In press Health Reporting as Political Reporting: Biocommunicability and the Public Sphere. Journalism: Theory, Practice, and Criticism.
Briggs, Charles L., and Clara Mantini-Briggs, 2003 Stories in the Time of Cholera: Racial Profiling during a Medical Nightmare. Berkeley: University of California Press.
Callon, Michel, 1986 Some Elements of a Sociology of Translation: Domestication of the Scallops and the Fishermen of St Brieuc Bay. In Power, Action and Belief: A New Sociology of Knowledge. John Law, ed. pp. 196–233. London: Routledge & Kegan Paul.
Cicourel, Aaron V., 1992 The Interpenetration of Communicative Contexts: Examples from Medical Encounters. In Rethinking Context: Language as an Interactive Phenomenon. Alessandro Duranti and Charles Goodwin, eds. pp. 291–310. Cambridge UK: Cambridge University Press.
Clarke, Adele E., Jennifer Fishman, Jennifer Fosket, Laura Mamo, and Janet Shim, 2003 Biomedicalization: Technoscientific transformations of health, illness and US biomedicine. American Sociological Review 68:161–194.
Cohen, Lawrence, 1998 No Aging in India: Alzheimer's, the Bad Family, and Other Modern Things. Berkeley: University of California Press.
Cohen, Lawrence, 2005 Operability, Bioavailability, and Exception. In Global Assemblages: Technology, Politics, and Ethics as Anthropological Problems. Aihwa Ong and Stephen J. Collier, eds. pp. 79–90. Malden MA: Blackwell.
Conrad, Peter, 1972 Medicalization and Social Control. Annual Review of Sociology 18: 209–232.
Duranti, Alessandro, and Donald Brenneis, eds., 1986 The Audience as Co-Author. Special issue of Text 6(3).

Ellison, Ralph, 1972 Invisible Man. New York: Vintage.

Epstein, Steven, 1996 Impure Science: AIDS, Activism, and the Politics of Knowledge. Berkeley: University of California Press.

Farmer, Paul, 1992 AIDS and Accusation: Haiti and the Geography of Blame. Berkeley: University of California Press.

Farmer, Paul, 1999 Infections and Inequalities: The Modern Plagues. Berkeley: University of California Press.

Foucault, Michel, 1980 Power/Knowledge: Selected Interview and Other Writings, 1972–1977. Colin Gordon, trans. New York: Pantheon.

Foucault, Michel, 1997 The Birth of Biopolitics. In Ethics: Subjectivity and Truth, Paul Rabinow, ed. pp. 73–80. New York: New Press.

Gieryn, Thomas F., 1983 Boundary-Work and the Demarcation of Science from Non-Science: Strains and Interests in Professional Ideologies of Scientists. American Sociological Review 48:781–795.

Hacking, Ian, 1990 The Taming of Chance. Cambridge: Cambridge University Press.

Good, Byron J., 1994 Medicine Rationality and Experience: An Anthropological Perspective. Cambridge UK: Cambridge University Press.

Hall, Stuart, Chas Critcher, Tony Jefferson, John Clarke, and Brian Roberts, 1978 Policing the Crisis: Mugging, the State, and Law and Order. London: Macmillan.

Hayden, Cori, 2003 When Nature Goes Public: The Making and Unmaking of Bioprospecting in Mexico. Princeton: Princeton University Press.

Healey, David, 2006 The New Medical Oikumene. In Global Pharmaceuticals: Ethics, Markets, Practices. Adriana Petryna, Andrew Lakoff and Arthur Kleinman, eds. pp. 61–84. Durham NC: Duke University Press.

Inhorn, Marcia, 2007 Reproductive Disruptions: Gender, Technology, and Biopolitics in the New Millenium. New York: Berghahn.

Joffe, H., and G. Haarhoff, 2002 Representations of far-flung illnesses: The case of Ebola in Britain. Social Science and Medicine 54:955–969.

Kleinman, Arthur, 1988 The Illness Narratives: Suffering, Healing and the Human Condition. New York: Basic.

Lakoff, Andrew, 2005 Pharmaceutical Reason: Knowledge and Value in Global Psychiatry. Cambridge UK: Cambridge University Press.

Latour, Bruno, 1987 Science in Action. Cambridge MA: Harvard University Press.

Latour, Bruno, 1988 The Pasteurization of France. Cambridge MA: Harvard University Press.

Latour, Bruno, 1993 We Have Never Been Modern. Catherine Porter, trans. Cambridge MA: Harvard University Press.

Lewison, Grant, 2008 The reporting of the risks from severe acute respiratory syndrome (SARS) in the news media, 2003–2004. Health, Risk and Society 10(3):241–262.

Lock, Margaret, 2003 Medicalization and the Naturalization of Social Control. In The Enclopedia of Medical Anthropology. Volume 1: Topics. Carol Ember and Melvin Ember, eds. New York: Kluwer Academic Publishers/Plenum.

Locke, John, 1959[1690] An Essay Concerning Human Understanding. 2 volumes. New York: Dover.

Lupton, Deborah, 1997 Moral Threats and Dangerous Desires: AIDS in the News Media. London: Falmer Press.

Mattingly, Cheryl, 1998 Healing Dramas and Clinical Plots: The Narrative Structure of Experience. Cambridge UK: Cambridge University Press.

Mishler, Elliot G., 1984 The Discourse of Medicine: Dialectics of Medical Interviews. Norwood NJ: Ablex.

Oldani, Michael J., 2004 Thick Prescriptions: Toward an Interpretation of Pharmaceutical Sales Practices. Medical Anthropology Quarterly 18(3):325–356.

Ong, Aihwa, and Stephen J. Collier, eds., 2005 Global Assemblages: Technology, Politics, and Ethics as Anthropological Problems. Malden MA: Blackwell.

476   CHARLES L. BRIGGS

Petryna, Adriana, 2002 Life Exposed: Biological Citizens after Chernobyl. Princeton NJ: Princeton University Press.

Pigg, Stacy Leigh, 2001 Languages of Sex and AIDS in Nepal: Notes on the Social Production of Commensurability. Cultural Anthropology 16(4):481–541.

Rabinow, Paul, 1992 Artificiality and Englightenment: From Sociobiology to Biosociality. In Incorporations. J. Crary and S. Kwinter, eds. pp. 234–252. New York: Zone.

Rapp, Rayna, 1999 Testing Women, Testing the Fetus: The Social Impact of Amniocentesis in America. New York: Routledge.

Riles, Annelise, 2004 Real Time: Unwinding Technocratic and Anthropological Knowledge. American Ethnologist 31(3):392–405.

Saussure, Ferdinand de, 1959[1916] A Course in General Linguistics. Wade Baskin, trans. New York: McGraw-Hill Book Company.

Scheper-Hughes, Nancy, 2002 Commodity Fetishism in Organs Trafficking. In Commodifying Bodies. Nancy Scheper-Hughes and Loïc Wacquant, eds. pp. 31–62. London: Sage.

Schieffelin, Bambi B., Kathryn A. Woolard, and Paul V. Kroskrity, eds., 1998 Language Ideologies: Practice and Theory. Oxford: Oxford University Press.

Silverstein, Michael, 1976 Shifters, Linguistic Categories, and Cultural Description. In Meaning in Anthropology. Keith H. Basso and Henry A. Selby, eds. pp. 11–55. Albuquerque NM: University of New Mexico Press.

Singer, Merrill, Lani Davison, and Gina Gerdes, 1988 Culture, Critical Theory, and Reproductive Illness Behavior in Haiti. Medical Anthropology Quarterly 2:370–385.

Swora, Maria Gabrielle, 2001 The Creation of Social Structure in Alcoholics Anonymous through Performance of Autobiography. Narrative Inquiry 11(2):363–384.

Taussig, Michael, 1992[1980] Reification and the Consciousness of the Patient. In The Nervous System. pp. 83–109. New York: Routledge.

Trostle, James, 2005 Epidemiology and Culture. Cambridge UK: Cambridge University Press.

Tsing, Anna, 2005 Friction: An Ethnography of Global Connection. Princeton NJ: Princeton University Press.

Ungar, Sheldon, 1998 Hot Crises and Media Reassurance: A Comparison of Emerging Diseases and Ebola Zaire. British Journal of Sociology 49(1):36–56.

Ungar, Sheldon, 2008 Global bird flu communication: Hot crisis and media reassurance. Science Communication 29(4):472–497.

Urban, Greg, 2001 Metaculture: How Culture Moves through the World. Minneapolis MN: University of Minnesota Press.

Urry, John, 2007 Mobilities. Cambridge UK: Polity.

Waitzkin, Howard, 1991 The Politics of Medical Encounters: How Patients and Doctors Deal with Social Problems. pp. 11–48. New Haven CT: Yale University Press.

Zola, Irving Kenneth, 1972 Medicine as an Institution of Social Control. Sociological Review 20:487–504.

FURTHER READING

Bauman, Richard, and Charles L. Briggs, 1990 Poetics and Performance as Critical Perspectives on Language and Social Life. Annual Review of Anthropology 19:59–88.

Briggs, Charles L., 2005 Communicability, Racial Discourse, and Disease. Annual Review of Anthropology 34:269–291.

Good, Byron J., 1990 The Taming of Chance. Cambridge UK: Cambridge University Press.

Joffe, H., and G. Haarhoff, 2007 Christian Moderns: Freedom and Fetish in the Mission Encounter. Berkeley: University of California Press.

Kuipers, Joel C., 1989 "Medical Discourse" in Anthropological Context: Views of Language and Power. Medical Anthropology Quarterly 3(2):99–123.

Scheper-Hughes, Nancy, and Margaret Lock, 1989 The Mindful Body: A Prolegomenon to Future Work in Medical Anthropology. Medical Anthropology Quarterly 1(1):6–41.

CHAPTER **24** # Anthropology at the End of Life

Ron Barrett

Schopenhauer famously stated that "death is the real inspiring genius or the muse of philosophy" (1969[1844]:436). The same could be said for anthropology. Human beings have an odd habit of considering the inevitability of their own mortality, even when such consideration bears no immediate benefits for survival or reproduction. Yet, from an applied perspective, mortality awareness is essential to our overall well-being as we confront the aging of world societies, global health disparities, emerging biomedical technologies, and shifting understandings of good deaths and lives worth living. Given these issues, one might argue that death is a central domain of medical anthropology.

Despite its importance, the topic of death has received only sporadic attention in the medical anthropological literature. The purpose of this chapter is to call for greater interest in the topic by presenting a selective set of examples among the many opportunities for further inquiry. Here, I examine some of the challenges and possibilities of conducting an experience-near ethnography of dying and loss. I then turn to the ideals and realities of a "good death" and its shifting meanings across societies and historical periods. Finally, I explore the process of living while dying to consider the social dynamics of healing in hospital-based biomedicine, and the hospice and palliative care movements.

EXPERIENCE-NEAR THANATOLOGY

"Thanatology" arose with the Death with Dignity movement of the early 1970s as an interdisciplinary category for the study of death, inspiring numerous volumes and two prominent English language journals: *Omega* and *Death Studies*. Yet for all this attention to death, scholars and practitioners in the field have often remarked on its paradoxical

A Companion to Medical Anthropology, First Edition. Edited by Merrill Singer and Pamela I. Erickson.
© 2011 Blackwell Publishing Ltd. Published 2011 by Blackwell Publishing Ltd.

focus on the nature and quality of human life (Byock 1997; Green 2008; Kaufman and Morgan 2005). It is therefore understandable that one such scholar would famously redefine the field as "the study of life with death left in" (Kastenbaum 1993:75).

The prospect of dying as a living human experience should resonate with most anthropologists, personally as well as professionally. We see the personal and professional merged in first-person ethnographies such as Robert Murphy's *The Body Silent*, in which the anthropologist shares his experience of dying from a gradually increasing paralysis as an untreatable tumor grows along his spine (1990). Here, the author speaks of the existential experience of *dis-embodiment* that accompanies the gradual progression of his disabilities:

> To fall quietly and slowly into total paralysis is much like either returning to the womb or dying slowly, which are one and the same thing. With all the bodily stimuli to movement muted and almost forgotten, one gradually loses the volition for physical activity. The growing stillness of the body invades one's apprehension of the world (Murphy 1990:193).

In contrast to his narratives of detachment and silence, Murphy focuses his remaining senses on the suffering of dependency, lost abilities, lost status, and social isolation. Despite the author's stoicism, the reader cannot help but feel the irony of emotional pain amidst the loss of physical sensation. The other irony is that, until his illness, the author could hardly be characterized as an interpretive or reflexive anthropologist. But yet, as both ethnographer and informant, Murphy achieves a level of reflection beyond the prevalent theoretical soliloquies by sharing some of his most intimate experiences of living at the end of life.

As anthropologists, we need not wait until our moments of immanent death to approach the deeper experiences of "life with death left in." Our daily experiences of mortality may suffice. Borrowing the Balinese concept of *negeleh keneh,* Wikan develops the notion of *resonance* as "a joint effort at feeling-thought: a willingness on the part of the author and reader to engage with another world, life, or idea" by means of one's own life experience (Wikan 1990:269). We encounter death and loss throughout our lives. Although these elements of human experience are refracted into a myriad of cultural trajectories, we can still find common – if unspoken – areas of intersection between the hermeneutic horizons of other people.

Thus, many can relate to the ethnographer's puzzled appreciation for cultural differences when Michelle Rosaldo (1980) describes how the tremelo of a Joan Baez song evokes a particular nostalgia among the Ilongot for the lost days of headhunting. But following Michelle Rosaldo's tragic death, many can also appreciate the conflicted emotions of her husband and fellow anthropologist as he resonated with the combined grief and rage described by their informants while recalling *their* losses (Rosaldo 2004). Far from an epiphany on the psychic unity of humankind, the anthropologist–informant is merely asking us to consider a few dimensions of shared experience so as to "achieve a balance between wide-ranging human differences and the modest truism that any two human groups must have some things in common" (Rosaldo 2004:171).

In a similar vein, Panougia's (1996) experimental "anthropography" presents the ethnographer tacking back and forth between her own bereavement and those of her family and informants in Athens, Greece. We might also appreciate the ethnographer's anguish when Shostak (2000) describes her ambivalent reunion with Nisa amidst her personal struggles against breast cancer. Finally, amid Myerhoff's (1978) wonderful portraits of a California Jewish retirement community, we are struck by fateful musings of the ethnographer as she imagines herself in old age without the foreknowledge that her own death will come only seven years later. It is a poignant reminder as we read and write about the ends of life: our own deaths may only be a sentence away.

I was reminded of this while standing on the cremation grounds during fieldwork in Banaras, India. I was conducting a 22-month ethnographic investigation of stigma and healing among the Aghori, a tantric sect that sought to embrace mortality in order to achieve a psycho-spiritual state of nondiscrimination (Barrett 2008). I had been living with an Indian family who were Brahmins by birth and Aghori by choice. Lakshman, the family patriarch, had died that morning after more than ninety years of life, and I joined the family as they performed their funerary duties. Although I had been to the cremation grounds many times, I had never before witnessed the Hindu rite of final sacrifice among people I knew and cared about. As a former hospice nurse, I had helped care for Lakshman during his final days. I felt my own remorse for this remarkable man, as well as guilt for not providing care during his final moments, despite my intuition that I should have visited him the night before. I also felt for his middle-aged sons as they stood in stoic yet misty-eyed silence around the pyre. Then, something remarkable happened. One of the sons, Ramchandra, asked me about human diversity, and commented that he regarded this as a miracle and worldly proof of the existence of God. It was not unlike his previous philosophical reflections except that he now spoke while watching the graphic destruction of his father's body, just after Lakshman's soul was released when his elder brother struck open the skull with a bamboo staff.

What Ramchandra said made sense to me on a cognitive level. But I could not emotionally connect his words with what we were witnessing. I could not imagine doing anything like this when I lost my mother. I had never encountered anything like this as a nurse. Yet, both these experiences helped me connect with Ramchandra in some way. Plus they helped me peel back a few layers of the "hermeneutic onion" between us, if only to appreciate their further depth.

If thanatology is as much about life as death, then we can reasonably expect our examinations of death trajectories to be as diverse as people's lives. Nevertheless, if we approach the topic from the point of our own mortality, then some common ground may be possible. With this recognition, we might achieve some form of cultural resonance, thereby moving a few steps nearer to the lived experience of another death.

THE GOOD DEATH: IDEALS AND REALITIES

In *The Hour of Our Death*, Phillippe Aries analyzes popular depictions of death in French literature from the Middle Ages to the early 20th century (1981).[1] Interpreting these stories as allegorical prescriptions for *ars moriendi* (the art of dying), he traces their historical transformations as reflections of changing social attitudes toward human mortality. Key among them is the medieval baseline he characterizes as "The Tame Death" that marches into the 17th century with an attitude of "indifference, resignation, familiarity, and a lack of privacy" (Aries 1981:26). Here, fictional heroes foresee their immanent demise, confess their sins, and bid their friends and families *adieu* as they face Jerusalem, close their eyes…and die happily ever after.

Regardless of whether such literary deaths were fashionable among the Medieval French, Aries' text is certainly fashionable in the present day academy. I therefore feel obligated to teach some of it in my Death and Dying courses. But I also feel obligated to help cure my students of their immortality, however impossible the task may be. So I juxtapose this tame ideal with the physical realities of dying along a range of different cultural trajectories.

Nuland (1993) presents some of these trajectories, translating the pathophysiology of several common disease processes such as cancer, Alzheimer's, and congestive heart failure into accessible language. More importantly, he sets these processes in motion and relates them to particular narratives that reveal the lived experiences of particular people. There is a stark contrast between Nuland's and Aries' deaths, and if we reasonably presume that human physiology has changed little in the last twelve centuries, then we are left to wonder how people resolve their particular realities of dying with their social ideals of a good death.

Drawing on a much broader range of contemporary media, Green (2008) confronts the changing Euro–American ideals of death and dying following the rise of new medical technologies, the Death with Dignity movements, and recent public traumas such as the 9/11 attacks. It is a daunting task for a single volume, but it poses significant questions and quandaries in the attempt. Green argues that a revival of The Tame Death is seen in the many popular texts, pamphlets, and documentaries that advocate for ideals of individual choice and resistance to the forces of curative biomedicine. These prescriptions for a good death are as pluralistic as their audiences, and perhaps as privileged. Yet at the same time, these ideals convey common themes of nobility, fallibility, and middle-class American populism. Such themes are especially relevant, given the global reach of North American media.

Taking care to note the differences among Anglophone societies, Seale (1998) examines the cultural scripts of professionals, patients, and popular authorities in the recent shifts toward death affirmation and the social construction of good dying. Despite significant cultural variability, these scripts share similar themes with the conception of good deaths in less technologically developed societies such as the Kwahu-Tafo of Ghana and the Kaliai of Papua New Guinea, insofar as they entail a peaceful death by natural causes, supported by family, and following a long and prosperous life (Counts and Counts 2004; Seale 2004; van der Geest 2004). Yet as it can be difficult enough for the affluent to achieve such ideals, these authors note the challenges are further compounded by rising mortality and poverty. Consequently, the scripts for good and bad deaths are constantly shifting just as they are inextricably linked to local and global inequalities.

In a similar manner, Long (2005) examines the multiple scripts and metaphors for "dying one's own way" in contemporary Japanese society. Many Japanese scripts share common themes on the surface, often in the context of *death on the tatami*: dying at home in some traditional way. But imagined traditions take many different forms. For instance, a common script of *rosui*, a gradual death in old age, is contrasted with *pokkuri*, a popular folk script of sudden death. The first allows for gradual adjustment, preparation, and grieving in the context of dying at home while surrounded by family. The second relieves the family of *meiwaku* (burden/trouble) that comes with family caregiving, but simultaneously deprives them of the opportunity to express their love through the performance of filial duties. It is interesting to note gender differences in script preference, with women leaning more toward *pokkuri* suggesting a stronger identity with their own social roles as family caregivers in contrast to the prospect of dependency on others.

Long is careful to point out that these underlying tensions mainly pertain to issues of dependency versus interdependency. The North American ideal of independence can be problematic in Japanese contexts. In the words of one Japanese bioethicist, "To be autonomous and independent as an individual had been regarded as an ego-centric idea, one which does not address the need for people to be dependent on each other in the family, social, economic, and political community" (Long 2005:85). Yet this is not to say that desires for independence are absent in Japanese scripts of dying, only that these desires may collide with more pervasive and opposing expectations – thereby carrying an attendant threat of social isolation.

In India, the good death is exemplified in the pilgrimage to die in Banaras for many Hindu religious communities. As one of the oldest and largest centers of religious pilgrimage, Banaras is a popular destination for people facing the end of life. The city is also home to two very auspicious cremation grounds, both located in the center of the city along the steps (*ghats*) along the Ganges River. Several religious texts refer to Banaras as the Great Cremation Ground, where all who die within its sacred interior (*Kashi*) may achieve instant spiritual liberation (Eck 1983). For all these reasons, a death in Banaras is often considered to be a good death.

This Indian ideal is nevertheless subject to multiple models and conflicting inter-pretations. Justice (1997) explores some of these models in his ethnography of Indian *mutkibhavans* (lit. "liberation houses"), traditional hospices near the river where peo-ple bring their family members to die. These institutions only provide basic lodging and religious services; they do not provide medical management for pain or symptom control. As such, they present an interesting contrast to biomedical institutions which notoriously address the dying process with medications and technical treatments without addressing the meaning of suffering and loss (cf. Kaufman 2005; Kleinman 1988). In the following excerpt, Justice (1997) discusses the ideals of the good death with an attendant, Kapil Deo Singh, who is well versed in the realities of dying in the *muktibhavan*:

CJ: What is a good death?

Singh: One of old age. A person who will die according to his own time, his death time.

CJ: Should one be conscious?

Singh: It is impossible.

CJ: Should one be asleep?

Singh: It is impossible. Death never comes to a sleeping person.

CJ: Should one be taking God's name?

Singh: That is very important. The name of God and donations are the two most important things.

CJ: Should the stomach be empty or full?

Singh: The stomach of somebody dying a good death will always be empty because they will not eat at that time (Justice 1997:228).

This ideal is a much closer approximation to the physiological changes that occur in the final (aka. active or immanent) stages of the dying process for many common diseases, which typically entail a loss of appetite and consciousness (Hallenbeck 2003; Nuland 1993). "Taking the name of God" – that is having one's mind on the divine at the moment of death, can only occur in a psycho-spiritual state in which no other living person has access, and therefore, cannot question. Justice correctly notes that voluntary withdrawal of food and fluids may hasten the dying process. This is not usually accompanied with outward signs of discomfort, but it can often be troubling to family members concerned about withdrawing life support, or for whom food is a vehicle for compassion and care (Justice 1997). Yet here, the ideal of an empty stomach can help reassure the family and attendant caregivers insofar it is bound up with a good death as well as a natural dying process.

Yet even in these sacred contexts, dying in Banaras can be highly problematic. We do not encounter issues of pain and symptom management in the *muktibhavan,* which may be the result of a tendency to admit relatively calm, elderly, and feeble residents. That aside, there is a long-standing ambivalence to suffering in both: (a) traditional contexts, where it may be seen as an opportunity for spiritual growth, or b) in biomedical contexts, where it may be seen as a necessary aspect of curative treatments. In the first instance, Indian traditions of Ayurvedic medicine recognize the role of suffering in the removal of karma. As such, Ayurvedic *vaidyas* have long debated whether physical health is at odds with spiritual health of the body (Weiss 1980). In the second instance, many Indian physicians share with their Western counterparts a strong emphasis on quantity over quality of life (Barrett 2008).

There are also difficult questions about a common lack of curative intervention among the feeble elderly, which are closely tied to cultural norms of dying in old age. Cohen's (1992) study of aging and family in Banaras begins with the question of why there is so little senile dementia in India. Given the prevalence of neglect among his informants, and my own observations in some of the same communities, it could reasonably be argued that senility is absent because the feeble simply do not survive. If we also consider the prevalence of poverty among these families, then we are left to consider an expanded and somewhat inverted definition of benign maternal neglect, or perhaps benign *paternal* neglect.

The World Health Organization (WHO) defines health as "a state of complete physical, mental and social wellbeing and not merely the absence of disease or infirmity" (World Health Organization 1948). We might reasonably consider this as an overarching model for a good death in all human societies, a global prescription for *ars moriendi* not unlike the tame deaths of Aries' European nobility. But this prescription is subject to at least as many interpretations as human communities, and even more negotiations as people confront particular realities in the hours of their deaths. Medical anthropologists have only begun to examine and represent these issues.

DENIAL AND HEALING UNTO DEATH

An expanded concept of health ideally entails a similar expansion of healing across the lifespan, to include the final moments of life. Yet many biomedical structures have historically resisted or constrained such *healing unto death* at the earliest stages of the process: communication about death between healers and patients.

Glaser and Strauss (1965) present a classic sociological analysis of these communication dynamics. Based on fieldwork in several North American hospitals in the early 1960s, these authors examined death trajectories in relation to micro-level interactions between healthcare professionals and their patients and families. Focusing on the theme of death awareness, the authors identified four categories of communication that ranged from mutual denial to mutual acknowledgement. The most prominent of these involved some measure of deception in which patients either failed to resolve their suspicions or collaborated with their physicians in mutual pretense. Patients had little agency in either case.

These observations underscore the loss of personal agency that accompanied the rise of intensive care units and complex medical technologies in American hospitals during the latter half of the 20th century (Rothman 1997). Here, we see parallels between the medicalization of death with the medicalization of birth. Both had long since shifted from home to hospital with family attendants replaced by medical professionals. But the increasing use of electronic monitoring, intravenous medications, and potential surgical interventions created further specialization such that patients and families would feel, or be made to feel, disqualified to make their own decisions.

On paper, it would seem that much has changed in North American hospitals since the Glaser and Strauss study. The rise of the Death with Dignity movement paralleled an increasing number of guidelines and legislation aimed at informed decision-making and patient autonomy (Annas 2004; Starr 1982). Yet there is strong evidence to indicate that in many instances, these principles continue to be inadequately translated into actual clinical practices. In the early 1990s, for example, a large-scale Study to Understand Prognosis and Preferences for Outcomes and Risks for Treatment (SUPPORT) examined these dynamics for about 9,000 patients in five US teaching hospitals over a four-year period. An initial retrospective assessment compared the treatment preferences of about 4,500 terminally ill patients to actual care provided, finding that: (a) more than half of all communicative patients were in moderate to severe pain at least 50% of their last 72 hours of life and, (b) fewer than half the physicians fully understood their patients' preferences not to be resuscitated when such wishes were expressed (Moskowitz and Nelson 1995).

The second phase of the SUPPORT study produced even more striking results. This case-control design compared the aforementioned outcomes for another sample of 4,500 patients divided into two groups with and without a comprehensive set of interventions aimed at improving physician–patient communication, to include additional reports on patient prognoses and treatment preferences and the inclusion of a specifically trained nurse advocate. Tragically, the study found no significant differences between case and control groups for aggressive treatments and pain relief in the last days of life. Communications remained insufficient, power remained in the hands of physicians, and a concerted effort to improve the situation had failed completely.

From an anthropological perspective, we might reasonably critique the SUPPORT study for taking a biomedical approach to a fundamentally cultural problem. Indeed, the SUPPORT interventions seem little different from the clinical checklists generated by cultural competency programs to address complex issues of inequality and difference in biomedical settings (Kleinman and Benson 2006). These problems instead call for a *constructively* critical medical anthropology that builds on ethnographies of communication and power within particular clinical settings.

Kaufman (2005) presents a rich ethnography of micro-interactions and decision-making between professionals, patients, and families facing the end of life in several North American hospitals. Far from a simple critique, the author demonstrates the complex ways that health professionals as well as patients are constrained by the structures of hospital bureaucracy. Patients do not know what to want, physicians do not know what to say, and nurses are still caught in the middle. Kaufman presents dozens of stories and narratives, all involving some liminal purgatory of death-in-life combined with an ever-present impetus to *move things along*.

Time is a dominant theme in these death-in-life trajectories. Things *move along* variable trajectories and at variable rates. Even when medical providers openly acknowledge the inevitable, there may be coercion and conflict over the time needed for families to process this information. Such is the case for the family of a comatose woman with end-stage abdominal cancer as expressed in a conversation between the patient's daughter, surgeon, and family physician (Kaufman 2005:52):

Family physician:	If you decide to let go, if you decide to accept the inevitable, is another way to say it, to give her dignity.
Surgeon:	As her primary surgeon, I need from you the code status. She is being resuscitated right now with drugs. She can't make an informed decision. Should she be shocked? Defibrillated? We need to know yes or no. You can say, "Don't go higher on the drugs." We could dial them down. For me, the main issue is shocking the heart. It's not active, it's just saying that if her heart stops, you wouldn't want to do this. I'd like a decision from you before this conference is over.
Daughter:	We need time to think about that and we'd like to consult with you. (She breaks down and cries.)
Family physician:	We respect that. You don't have to make that decision now.

The patient dies in the ICU two weeks later, her family at the bedside. Like so many of these examples, the ethnographer leaves us with a sense of tragedy, of something gone wrong. But like many of Kaufman's informants, we cannot easily identify the problem. We hear multiple medical voices, both coercive and caring, just as we see multiple axes of inequality and power exchange. The ethnographer then helps to orient us, providing us with some useful frameworks ranging from the internal struggles of people unprepared to test their earlier beliefs and expectations to the specific realities of dying in a hospital, to the political economy of health care organizations.

Comparing these dynamics with the earlier work of Glaser and Strauss, we see historical continuities as well as important differences. There is a greater openness and expanded language for talking about death. Yet, paradoxically, recent innovations in lifesaving technology have stretched the boundaries of life and death into an ambiguous continuum. At the same time, changes in the health care funding have segmented the temporal continuity of dying trajectories into a series of billable procedures, just as they have reorganized and redefined the roles of clinical care (Good et al. 2004; Kaufman 2005). Healing unto death has never been so complex.

Hospice Care in England and the United States

The aforementioned examples underscore the fact that biomedicine does not comprise a single monolithic culture. Anthropologists often approach biomedical systems as cultural or ethnomedical systems (see Fabrega 1975; Kleinman 1978; Erickson 2008). It is imperative we do so with the recognition of cultural diversity within and between societies and clinical settings (Hahn 1995; Payer 1988). The hospice and palliative care movements are important cases in point, comprising their own distinctive ethnomedical traditions at their imagined centers, blurring boundaries at their peripheries, and subject to a myriad of local interpretations.

The hagiography of the modern hospice movement traces its origins to places of refuge for medieval European pilgrims (Kastenbaum 2001). But despite a few medical forerunners in the 19th and early 20th centuries, the present movement had its beginning in 1965, when Cicely Saunders first broke ground for St. Christopher's Hospice in Sydenham, England. Built to address the comprehensive needs of the dying in South London communities, St. Christopher's quickly become the prototype for hospice organizations around the world (Clark et al. 2005).

Building on her experience as a nurse, social worker, and physician, Saunders wrote down a set of guidelines that became a template for the subdiscipline of palliative biomedicine. Yet even with these biomedical tools, St. Christopher's represented a different kind of healing model, emphasizing holism, family-centered care, and community participation well before these concepts had become "buzzwords" in medical parlance. I would argue that such changes were possible because this hospice was a homesteader in unoccupied medical territory.

Many proponents of the St. Christopher model argue that, while hospice includes the *practice* of palliative care, the two are distinct as *institutions* (Stoddard 1992). Unlike hospices, palliative care units arose within hospital settings and are therefore governed by the same structures. Whereas, most hospices treat only those patients who have forgone curative treatment, palliative care institutions treat all manner of patients, including those without a terminal prognosis (Hallenbeck 2003). Situated at the crossroads of curing and caring, palliative care often serves as a repository for illness trajectories not otherwise addressed by conventional biomedical specialties.

These trajectories include patients with chronic conditions such as congestive heart failure, chronic renal failure, and chronic obstructive pulmonary disease. In these cases, dying is typically a continuous process entailing years of gradual decline without the punctuated moments that could clearly delineate the biomedical categories of "chronic" and "terminal." In theory, US Medicare provides hospice benefits for any patient having a medical prognosis of less than six month to live. Yet in practice, it can be very difficult to even roughly estimate when a patient will die (Hallenbeck 2003). Under these circumstances, few patients make the transition from hospital to hospice, or if they do so, it is only in the very last days of life.

These issues are especially poignant among historically disadvantaged communities. For instance, a National Mortality Followback Survey reveals that African–Americans are less likely to utilize hospice than the general populace, even when accounting for education, income, access to healthcare, and the presence of a living will (Greiner et al. 2003). The two most-cited explanations for this phenomenon are distrust of a predominantly *white* medical system (Winston et al. 2005; Burrs 1995), and specific religious beliefs surrounding issues such as, the relationship between human and divine agency, the role of miracles in medicine and, the purpose of human suffering (Matsuyama et al. 2007; Kumasaka and Miles 1996; Johnson 1992). Of course these explanations are not exclusive of one another, but closer ethnographic research is needed for a better understanding of the inequalities and ideologies that underlie this kind of phenomenon. Such investigations could make important social as well and theoretical contributions, insofar as they can inform policies and programs aimed at reducing human suffering in marginalized populations.

Despite a few notable studies, there is a dearth of ethnographic literature on hospice and palliative care, which is surprising given the questions posed by their translation into diverse communities and cultural settings around the world. Hospice and palliative care are pivotal in the ongoing debates over euthanasia in the Netherlands and Belgium, which have different organizational approaches to hospice, and where some question whether patients would opt for assisted suicide if they already had good symptom management (Broeckaert and Janssens 2002).

A large-scale retrospective study revealed little increase in the demand for euthanasia or physician-assisted death in the decade following its official recognition by the Dutch government in 1990 (Onwuteaka-Phillipsen et al. 2003). But it is not clear whether these data could be attributed to adequate symptom management. Indeed, there is evidence to suggest that the Dutch have not developed its hospice services to the same degree as other Euro–American countries. Despite its progressive reputation, the Netherlands did not establish standalone hospices until the early 1990s, more than a decade after its Western European neighbors (Clark et. 2000). This is largely attributed to the fact that the Dutch already had a well-established home care system in place, and the government felt it could adopt hospice principles without creating new institutions. However, my interviews with Dutch hospice providers found that, although care providers work well across institutions, much of their efforts are impeded by bureaucratic disputes.

The Netherlands also faces the challenge of under-utilization, particularly among Moroccan and Turkish immigrants. My recent pilot study of two Dutch hospice organizations found that Moroccan and Turkish immigrants comprised less than 2% of their patient populations, despite representing more than 20% of their surrounding communities. My informants attributed part of this to religious differences between these Muslim majority communities and Christian majority providers. These perceived differences may have been enhanced by the uniquely Dutch phenomenon of "pillarization" whereby the government promotes religious tolerance, but maintains structures of segregation between different ethnic communities (Spiecker and Steutel 2001). But as with the principle of "separate yet equal" in the American Jim Crow laws, these policies may have also created antagonism and distrust between communities. Preliminary discussions between one Dutch hospice and Moroccan community members reveal a common perception that the hospice could be a means of denying medical resources that would otherwise be provided to people of European origin. As in the case of many African–Americans, a history of discrimination among non-European immigrants may be a significant factor in their underutilization of hospices.

The hospice model has undergone some interesting transformations while adapting to non-Western contexts. For instance, one Nepali hospice admits patients regardless of whether they know about their terminal prognosis (Gongal et al. 2006). In these instances, the hospice decision is typically made by senior family members in a manner reminiscent of the jural decision-making described by Janzen (1978). Here, patients are asked whether they wish to know their prognoses, and when they decline, the information is provided to family decision-makers. Similar issues arise in Japan, where disclosure remains controversial despite the proliferation of hospices (Long 2005). Both scenarios present multiple dimensions of death awareness, and opportunities to compare death trajectories and family dynamics for those with varying degrees of mortality consciousness.

Hospice presents classic questions of health provision and access in the underdeveloped communities of sub-Saharan Africa (Harding and Higginson 2005). Some may argue that provision of hospice services should be of lesser priority than the provision of other health resources, such as anti-retroviral (ARV) medications for HIV/AIDS. However, it should be noted that ARVs are not permanent cures; they are not effective for all patients, and they do not negate the need for palliative treatment for people with HIV-related cancers. Here, it is important to consider the lessons of NGOs such as "Partners in Health," who have achieved much greater adherence to ARV treatment when their programs address more comprehensive sets of health needs identified by the local communities themselves (Farmer 2004). With these lessons in mind, it would be reasonable to consider whether these needs might include the relief of suffering and the burden care for terminally ill family members.

Finally, medical anthropologists can examine inequalities in hospice provision among societies where these institutions are ostensibly well developed. Inequalities arise in the work of Lawton (2000), who contributes a vivid and critical ethnography of dying in an English hospice. Here, many patients suffer with social isolation, physical pain, and the loss of dignity, despite the promise of a good hospice death. The author notes that this tragic disjuncture is partly attributed to an unrealistic promise; death trajectories are unpredictable and complete relief is elusive under the best of circumstances. But these circumstances could also be attributed to years of underfunding for community-based services by the National Health Service (Ham 2009). Funded through an independent charity, St. Christopher's was an exception to the public state of hospice care at the time[2] – a model for the world perhaps, but not for all communities in the United Kingdom.

CONCLUSION

When Schoepenhauer proposed that death is the muse of philosophy, he had hoped the consequent understanding would palliate human anxieties about our inevitable mortality (1969[1844]). This application seems problematic for anthropology, but a better understanding of our mortality may help to improve the quality and quantity of human life. Human mortality is closely tied to people's perceptions of risk and vulnerability; in turn, these perceptions inform daily health decisions and practices. At larger scales, a better awareness of death can inform health policies and the equitable distribution of health resources. Plus the question of suffering prompts further examination of what we mean by human health.

Human mortality and the dying experience can serve as a beginning and entre to any anthropological investigation of health, illness, or healing. It focuses the cultural dynamics and political economies of biomedical healing into sharp relief. It is closely surrounded by the latest technological innovations, and the conflicts and ambiguities that accompany them. The Death with Dignity Movement begat the field of thanatology and new ethnomedical systems in the form of hospice and palliative care. Death is universal fact of our biological existence, yet our cultural experiences of dying are varied as any other aspect of our lives.

If death trajectories are an integral part of life trajectories, then medical anthropology should examine the cultural construction of the "good death" as an indicator of human health, consider the relationships between its ideals and realities, and attend to the inequalities of dying as we should for the other periods of the human lifespan. If we are to achieve even a small measure of resonance with the dying process, then we must reflect on own emotions and experiences of loss as we attempt to understand those of other people. Becker (1973) suggests that the repression of death is necessary and healthy for daily living, that it inspires the heroic deeds of human individuals and the great works of human societies. I suggest the opposite: that through a greater consciousness of our mortality, we can better understand and improve upon the human condition.

NOTES

1   It should be noted that Aries first presents these arguments in rudimentary form in his *Western Attitudes Toward Death* (1974). This text is superceded by *The Hour of Our Death* (1981), in which he further expands and develops the same arguments.
2   It should be noted that the UK Department of Health has since increased support for hospice care and community-based services (Department of Health 2006).

REFERENCES

Annas, George, 2004 The Rights of Patients: The Authoritative ACLU Guide to Patient Rights. Carbondale IL: Southern Illinois University Press.

Aries, Phillippe, 1981 The Hour of Our Death. New York: Alfred A, Knopf.

Barrett, Ron, 2008 Aghor Medicine: Pollution, Death, and Healing in Northern India. Berkeley: University of California Press.

Becker, Ernest, 1973 The Denial of Death. New York: Free Press.

Broeckaert, Bert, and Rien Janssens, 2002 Palliative Care and Euthanasia: Belgian and Dutch Perspectives. Ethical Perspectives 9(2–3):156–175.

Burrs, Fay A., 1995 The African American Experience: Breaking the Barriers to Hospice. *In* Hospice Care and Cultural Diversity. Donna Lindenfeld, with Audrey K. Gordon and Bernice C. Harper, eds. New York: Haworth Press.

Byock, Ira, 1997 Dying Well: The Prospect for Growth at the End of Life. New York: Riverhead Books.

Clark, David, with Henk ten Have and Rien Janssens, 2000 Common threads? Palliative care service developments in seven European countries. Palliative Medicine. 14:479–490.

Clark, David, with Neil Small, Michael Wright, Michelle Winslow, and Nic Hughes, 2005 A Bit of Heaven for the Few: An Oral History of the Modern Hospice Movement in the United Kingdom. Lancester UK: Observatory Publications.

Cohen, Lawrence, 1992 No Aging in India: The Uses of Gerontology. Culture 16:123–161.

Counts, Dorothy and David Counts, 2004 The Good, the Bad, and the Unresolved Death in Kaliai. Social Science and Medicine 58(5):887–897.

Eck, Dianna, 1983 Banaras: City of Light. London: Routledge & Keegan Paul.

Erickson, Pamela I. 2008 Ethnomedicine. Long Grove IL: Waveland Press.

Fabrega, Horacio, 1975 The Need for an Ethnomedical Science. Science 189:969–975.

Farmer, Paul, 2004 Pathologies of Power: Health, Human Rights, and the New War on the Poor. Berkeley: University of California Press.

Glaser, Barney, and Anselm Strauss, 1965 Awareness of Dying. Chicago: Aldine.

Gongal, Rajesh, with Pradeep Vaidya, Rajshree Jha, Om Rajbhandary, and Max Watson, 2006 Informing Patients about Cancer in Nepal: What Do People Prefer? Palliative Medicine 20:471–476.

Good, Mary-Jo Delvechio, with Nina Gadmer, Patricia Ruopp, Matthew Lakoma, Amy Sullivan, Ellen Redinbaugh, Robert Arnold, and Susan Block, 2004 Narrative Nuances on Good and Bad Death: Internists' Tales from High-technology Work Places. Social Science and Medicine 58:939–953.

Green, James, 2008 Beyond the Good Death: The Anthropology of Modern Dying. Philadelphia: University of Pennsylvania Press.

Greiner, K. Allen, Subashan Perera, and Jasjit Ahluwalia, 2003 Hospice Usage by Minorities in the Last Year of Life: Results from the National Mortality Followback Survey. Journal of the American Geriatrics Society S1(7):970–978.

Hahn, Robert A., 1995 Sickness and Healing: An Anthropological Perspective. New Haven CT: Yale University Press.

Hallenbeck, James, 2003 Palliative Care Perspectives. Oxford: Oxford University Press.

Ham, Christopher, 2009 Health Policy in Britain. London: Palgrave Macmillan.

Harding, Richard, and Irene Higginson, 2005 Palliative Care in sub-Saharan Africa. The Lancet 365(9475):1971–1977.

Janzen, John M., 1978 The Quest for Therapy: Medical Pluralism in Lower Zaire. Berkeley: University of California Press.

Johnson, James W., 1992 Go Down Death. In Trials, Tribulations, and Celebrations: African American Perspectives on Health, Illness, Aging, and Loss. Marian G. Secundy and Louis Nixon, eds. Yarmouth: Intercultural Press.

Justice, Christopher, 1997 Dying the Good Death: The Pilgrimmage to India's Holy City. Albany NY: SUNY Press.

Kastenbaum, Robert, 1993 Reconstructing Death in Postmodern Society. Omega – Journal of Death and Dying 27(1):75–89.

Kastenbaum, Robert, 2001 Death, Society, and Human Experience. Boston: Allyn and Bacon.

Kaufman, Sharon, 2005 ...And a Time to Die: How Hospitals Shape the End of Life. New York: Scribner.

Kaufman, Sharon, and Lynn Morgan, 2005 The Anthropology of the Beginnings and Ends of Life. Annual Review of Anthropology 34:317–341.

Kleinman, Arthur, 1978 Concepts and a model for the comparison of medical systems as cultural systems. Social Science and Medicine 12:85–93.

Kleinman, Arthur, 1988 The Illness Narratives: Suffering, Healing, and the Human Condition. New York: Basic Books.

Kleinman, Arthur, and Peter Benson, 2006 The Problem of Cultural Competency and How to Fix It. PLoS Medicine 3(10):e294.

Kumasaka, Lydia, and Al Miles, 1996 My Pain is God's Will. American Journal of Nursing 96:45–47.

Lawton, Julia, 2000 The Dying Process: Patients' Experiences of Palliative Care. London: Routledge.

Long, Sharon, 2005 Final Days: Japanese Culture and Choice at the End of Life. Honolulu: University of Hawaii Press.

Matsuyama, Robin K., with Christina Grange, Laurie Lyckholm, Shawn Utsey, and Thomas Smith, 2007 Cultural Perceptions in Cancer Care among African–American and Caucasian Patients. Journal of the American Medical Association. 99(10):1113–1121.

Moskowitz, Ellen, and James Nelson, 1995 The Best Laid Plans. Hastings Center Report 25(6):S3–S5.

Murphy, Robert F., 1990 The Body Silent. New York: W W Norton.

Myerhoff, Barbara, 1978 Number Our Days. New York: Touchstone.

Nuland, Sherwin, 1993 How We Die: Reflections on Life's Final Chapter. New York: Vintage.

Onwuteaka-Phillipsen, Bregie, with Aagnes van der Heide, Ingeborg Keij-Deerenberg, Judith Rietjens, Mette Rurup, Astrid Vrakking, Jean Georges, Martien Muller, Gerrit van der Wal, and Paul van der Maas, 2003 Euthanasia and Other End-of-life Decisions in the Netherlands in 1990, 1995, and 2001. The Lancet 362(9381):395–399.

Panourgia, Neni, 1996 Fragments of Death, Fables, and Identity: An Athenian Anthropography. Madison WI: University of Wisconsin Press.

Payer, Lynn, 1988 Medicine and Culture. New York: Penguin Books.

Rosaldo, Michelle, 1980 Knowledge and Passion: Ilongit Notions of Self and Social Life. Cambridge UK: Cambridge University Press.

Rosaldo, Renato, 2004 Grief and a Headhunter's Rage. In Death, Mourning, and Burial: A Cross-Cultural Reader. A. Robben, ed. Oxford: Blackwell.

Rothman, David, 1997 Beginnings Count: The Technological Imperitive in American Health Care. Oxford: Oxford University Press.

Schopenhauer, Arthur, 1969[1844] World as Will and Representation. Volume II. Gloucester: Peter Smith.

Seale, Clive, 1998 Constructing Death: The Sociology of Dying and Bereavement. Cambridge UK: Cambridge University Press.

Seale, Clive, 2004 Good and bad death: Introduction. Social Science and Medicine 58(5):883–885.

Shostak, Marjorie, 2000 Return to Nisa. Cambridge MA: Harvard University Press.

Spiecker, Ben and Jan Steutel, 2001 Multiculturalism, pillarization, and liberal civic education in The Netherlands. International Journal of Education Research 35(3):295–304.

Starr, Paul, 1982 The Social Transformation of American Medicine. New York: Basic Books.

Stoddard, Sandol, 1992 The Hospice Movement: A Better Way of Caring for the Dying. New York: Vintage.

van der Geest, Sjaak, 2004 Dying Peacefully: Considering Good Death and Bad Death in Kwahu-Tafo, Ghana. Social Science and Medicine 58(5):899–911.

Wikan, Unni, 1990 Managing Turbulent Hearts: A Balanese Formula for Living. Chicago: University of Chicago Press.

Winston, Carole A., with Paula Leshner, Jennifer Kramer, and Gillian Allen, 2005 Overcoming Barriers to Access and Utilization of Hospice and Palliative Care Services in African-American Communities. Omega 50(2):151–163.

World Health Organization, 1948 Preamble to the Constitution of the World Health Organization. Official Records of the World Health Organization 2:100.

PART **V** **The Road Ahead**

CHAPTER 25

Operationalizing a Right to Health: Theorizing a National Health System as a "Commons"

Sandy Smith-Nonini
and Beverly Bell

INTRODUCTION

Recently advocates for equity in health care have reasserted the importance of health as a human right. The notion of health rights is usually traced to the Universal Declaration of Human Rights (UDHR) by the United Nations General Assembly in 1948, which asserted that all people were entitled to security, dignity, and wellbeing (JAMA 1998). The UDHR, which evolved as a response to the widespread abuses of World War II, set out language that became adopted in dozens of constitutions and treaties worldwide.

Although political rights such as bans on torture or freedom of expression have been more widely taken up by Western nations, the UDHR also spoke to social and economic rights such as access to health care, fair labor practices, access to food, as well as asserted that health policies of governments may violate rights (JAMA 1998).

The advent of the journal *Health and Human Rights*, published by the Francois-Xavier Bagnoud Center for Health and Human Rights at Harvard University, and other scholarly writings (Farmer 2003; MacDonald 2007; Smith-Nonini 2010) have helped establish health rights as a new arena of ethical, legal, and social science debate.

A Companion to Medical Anthropology, First Edition. Edited by Merrill Singer and Pamela I. Erickson.

However, volatile debates over health reform in the United States and widespread adoption of neoliberal policies, including privatization of health services and the cuts in social services in many poor nations, suggest that health rights are a concept more often evoked in the breach, than universally honored.

Health rights differ from human rights, a concept in the West evoked most often in cases of coercive violations against individual bodies, since economic rights have gone unrecognized in the capitalist world (Donnelly 1989). While a climate of respect for human rights can be cultivated through education, in contrast, health rights, which in impoverished settings require proactive intervention by trained workers, raise a different set of concerns, such as which parties are responsible for delivering and financing services. In cases of access to medicines for AIDS patients in developing countries, health rights activists have effectively challenged both government and multilateral development policies (Akukwe and Foote 2001). But health rights movements, focused on access to a wider range of health services, have had more limited impacts to date on politics. After two decades of neoliberal economic policies, there remains much debate about the role of states in social services. There has been movement toward state support of health services for the poor by political leaders elected in response to public rejection of ineffective neoliberal policies (e.g., Venezuela, Thailand, Bolivia). But with the notable exceptions of Nepal (Adams 1998) and El Salvador (Smith-Nonini 2010), health rights movements have not usually gained sufficient public support to reshape national policies or leadership.

Since health rights movements are often led by health workers and other development advocates, intellectual debates over rights to medical care carry special import. For example, the Latin American social medicine movement was influential in shaping health workers' support for universal care in Chile, Venezuela, Brazil and El Salvador (Tajer 2003), and the recent Obama Administration push for health reform has reframed debates over access and costs of care in the United States.

Social analysis of health systems and institutions is more common in medical sociology than anthropology. Budrys (2001) distinguished two sociological schools of thought on health systems: functionalists versus conflict theorists. While members of both schools are critical of the biomedical model, they break down in her distinction between positivist reformist accounts, which assume that health systems are mostly effective and argue for incremental change (functionalists), contrasted with critics who emphasize the failings of systems and inherent conflicts of interests in a class-based and divided society (conflict theorists). She further divides conflict theorists into those favoring micro-level versus macro-level scales of analysis.

Issues of scale and methodology help explain why medical anthropology has had relatively little to say about national health systems. Medical anthropologists are often committed to giving voice to marginalized groups, and most interpretivist scholars, focused on systems of meaning, use qualitative approaches and tend to favor micro-level analyses (e.g., patient – provider relations; folk models of disease, etc.). In contrast, political economists or critical theorists emphasize conflict and power, and many work at larger scales, combining qualitative and quantitative material. In the last 15 years, medical ecologists have often combined critical analysis with biology and systems analysis (Baer et al. 2003; McElroy and Townsend 2004). Yet, most medical ethnographies today continue to emphasize forms of difference (over commonalities) at micro- or mid-level scales, and would fall in the conflict-theory camp by Budrys' (2001) criteria.

In this chapter we adopt an unconventional approach combining the conflict theory orientation of critical medical anthropology with comparative systems analysis of national health systems. Budrys (2001) correctly evinces concern about applying the term socialized medicine to existing national systems, noting that outside of Eastern Europe this descriptor hold little purchase. Most modern national health systems were pieced together in a period dominated by capitalist economics, and represent more of a patchwork of state and private services, than a coherent system (Walt 1994; Budrys 2001).

Adopting a systems approach to analyzing health policy offers some useful insights. By systems thinking, we refer to widening the gaze of the researcher to a set of actors and relations that become interconnected in such a way that they produce a pattern of goal-oriented behavior that persists (Meadows 2008). When enhanced by understandings of ecology and power relations, a systems perspective helps illuminate aspects of public health as a demographic phenomenon (e.g., relationships of infectious disease to poverty and migration, or of obesity to corporate food regimes) that have commonalities across borders, and which labor and capital flows under globalization have enhanced. While it is true that forms of inequality often result from privileged actors interacting with institutions to create policies that favor profit-making and extractive practices, an overemphasis on political conduct to the exclusion of systems design can lead researchers to underestimate the degree to which existing bureaucracies, forms of productivity, and capital flows, as well as medical practices, professional privilege, and scientific paradigms, become perpetuated and persist over time.

Yet, while health rights is a relatively new concept, clearly in the neoliberal period and the age of AIDS, social movements are increasingly bringing issues of health rights to the forefront of public debates in many countries, and even some economists now characterize the public's health as a necessary prerequisite for development and capitalist growth (Sachs 2005). Concepts of health and human rights presuppose a humanitarian body politic in which global citizens share goals of creating an inclusive moral order, similar to Rousseau's description of a state's commitment to the well being of its citizens as a social contract. Such an imagined community is not unlike a "commons" or common property regime – a set of social relationships that indigenous societies built to manage shared access to collective property rights or resources (Gowdy 1998). This interdisciplinary concept, which has seen a recent revival in work on political ecology and systems theory, offers a productive approach to operationalizing universal health rights. It provides an example of the fruitfulness of anthropologists bringing their insights to comparative studies of health policy.

Scholars define such "commons" in non-capitalist settings as social relationships built around rights of access to property or goods or services viewed as both valuable and scarce. Rights to common resources or services are shared by members of a group, each of which has a claim to a benefits stream (Bromley and Feeny 1992). Successful commons regimes require some boundaries or participation rules for a pool of members, and management is most successful when all users participate in the commons and help set enforceable rules. Other characteristics of successful regimes include a high degree of trust among users, a means for monitoring compliance with rules, and systems for accountability by administrators/service providers to users (Nonini 2007).

In a perusal of the academic literature, it is striking how rarely medicine and health services are mentioned as potential "commons." Generally, scholars in public health and medical anthropology have ignored the concept of the commons as relevant to health or medical systems. Searches of medical and health databases turn up only the odd article using the term in a title or abstract. This chapter seeks to explore why this is so and what benefit for a medical anthropology approach might be gained from discussing health and medical services as a commons.

In Europe a consensus favoring universal access to health is long established, and while there are active debates on improving national health systems, most health systems in Europe and Canada would seem to fit the above definition of a commons. In contrast, there is an ongoing debate in the United States about the ethics and economic wisdom of funding universal access to health services. Given the pervasive neoliberal climate of recent decades, it is not surprising that health planning journals in both the United States and Europe tend to be dominated by operational issues related to efficiency and cost-savings.

As Bromley and Feeny (1992) noted, cooperative strategies evolve over great periods of time. The notion of collective rights to health services is not new. Both real and perceived health of populations has been a key aspect of state formation in the industrialized world. One of the earliest forms of collective insurance in Europe, for example, was government regulated "sickness funds" in 1883 Germany under Bismarck's rule (Light 2005). The German system evolved into an insurance system tied to employers, but tightly regulated by the state, while the British and French health systems, in contrast, are examples of strong state intervention in management of medical care (Moran 1999). In a massive two-volume study of world health systems between the years of 1960 and 1987, Milton Roemer found steady rises in shares of GDP devoted to health in every industrialized country (1993). Total health expenditures by the late 1980s ranged from a low of 5.3% of GDP in Greece to a high of 11.2% in the United States.

In most countries, two-thirds or more of this spending came from the public sector, the exception being the United States, where voluntary insurance and private funding prevailed. However, even in the United States, with its strong private sector dominance, recent decades have seen increasing penetration of government regulatory and funding mechanisms in medical practice (Light 2001) in the name of managing medical inflation.

Universal access to health is an ideal stated in constitutions of many developing countries, but resources are lacking to realize the goal in many such settings. Roemer's review of national datasets showed that until around 1980 trends of health expenditures were rising in most countries for which data were available (1993). The United Nations Development Program (1997) documented sizeable gains in life expectancy and in infant and child mortality in most developing countries, yet many of the poorest countries saw worsening health indicators since the 1980s according to UNICEF reports (Black 1999). The setbacks are likely linked to the AIDS epidemic, as well as to cutbacks of 25–50% in health and education budgets required in neoliberal structural adjustment policies that became the prerequisites for governments to restructure foreign debt (Kim et al. 2000; Smith-Nonini 2000). So it is ironic that while a "right" to health has gained force in the industrialized world in recent decades, access to essential medical care has become even more of a luxury in the developing world.

Just as the notion of a health commons is lacking in the United States, so also is the concept of community health absent in most debates, compared with the Global South. In international development discourse, community participation is considered a key criterion for health care promotion in developing countries (Morgan 1993). Yet, during research on national health systems for this project, we were struck by the relative absence of community as a concept in most comparative studies of national health systems. Measurements of efficacy became reduced to cost-effectiveness or to macro-level measures of mortality and morbidity, while questions of quality of care and public acceptance of services were marginalized, and this absence of attention to community-level feedback and acceptance is reflected in design of national systems.

This is related, of course, to the professional dominance and specialization that prevails in medical practice, reinforced in teaching hospitals and health service institutions. The disconnect speaks volumes about the chasms that exist in the public sphere in areas of institutional transparency, health care efficacy, and channels for public feedback between consumers and suppliers of health services worldwide. It also speaks to the widening inequality gap that characterizes societies in the industrialized and developing worlds (e.g., see Kim et al. 2000). In both the North and the South, there seems to be merit in developing a language and common knowledge base for discussion of a health commons.

This chapter will first explore the relevance of "the commons" to healthcare, with an argument that this concept can help us overcome the well known problems of applying capitalist market theory to health and medicine. We then examine a specific highly regarded national health care system – that of France – in detail, interposing qualitative material with statistics, and paying attention to equity of access, patient acceptance, politics of health reform in the neoliberal period, and persisting forms of exclusion. In concluding sections the French case is put back into a comparative context with brief descriptions of other relatively successful national health systems, with attention to both commonalities and variability. We conclude with some remarks on the challenges presented by consideration of health as a commons.[1]

WHAT IS GAINED BY DISCUSSING "A HEALTHCARE COMMONS?"

There are several arguments for thinking of health as a commons. Firstly, this debate would strengthen the concept that governments and economies have an obligation to collective social welfare, and that the health of populations should be maximized and thought of as a public good (e.g., as opposed to health care as a private luxury available only to the privileged); this is a much-needed corrective to the dominant neoliberal model which treats generation of economic profit as the primary social good, and tallies services connected with human welfare as a social cost that must be justified on economic grounds. Realization of the above goal necessitates debates over public access to services, and in the context of democratic governance, is likely to lead to state-level planning and either a method of global financing (e.g., under a single budget) or some other system of shared costs in which equity is guaranteed by the state.

While social justice goals would call for expanding services to the underserved, financing such an expansion requires acknowledgement that some medical goods and services constitute a limited good – and some services must be rationed. In reality, as the recent US health reform debate has helped to clarify, rationing has been with us all along, but in the United States it has most often been carried out on the basis of ability to pay, and to the degree it is done subtly by physicians, remains "under the radar" of public discourse (Relman 2005). The importance of expert knowledge notwithstanding, in a society which makes health services part of a public commons, this debate cannot be "swept under the rug."

Related to the above question, while service to the public has long been at the center of medical and health ideology and rhetoric, in democratic societies this notion has only rarely been developed to include democratic management of such services and goods. But in an educated society and in one with a developing notion of public ethics, there is no reason why community oversight and feedback should remain an unrealized goal.

Why is Health Care so Seldom Thought of as a "Commons?"

Unlike common property regimes, such as those for land, water, or fishing rights, for which use-rights have evolved over centuries, the notion of public access to a commonly managed set of health services has a more recent history. Scientific medicine is a relatively new tradition, even in the industrialized world. Collective policies to guarantee access to medical services only date back 100–150 years in Europe. As Moran (1999) noted, it was not until after the 1920s when the average person seeking a doctor's care in the United States was likely to actually benefit from that care.

Medical anthropologists have found family-based remedies for routine complaints, as well as specialized healers for serious illness, in nearly every human culture studied (Erickson 2008). Medical pluralism dominated in most places – with afflicted people often seeking care from multiple sources. Gift-giving and barter were/are common methods of paying healers in indigenous and village-level economies (Singer and Baer 2007). Perhaps the earliest historical precedent for state involvement in access to care was a system of taxation tied to health care in Greece (Roemer 1993). Likewise, early Islamic, Greek, and Roman empires provided opportunities for compilations of medical knowledge. In medieval Europe care for the sick initially fell under auspices of Catholic charity. The origins of public health authority can be traced to municipal responses to plagues in Italy (Hays 2000). Not until the Enlightenment was there a revival of study of Greek medical texts, combined with the turn toward secularism and experimentation associated with scientific medicine.

Another caveat in thinking of health as a commons is that successful common property regimes tend to operate around scarce resources that populations value highly (Bromley and Feeny 1992: 4). While medical care fits this definition, most public health scholars today agree that curative medical services are not the basis for a population's health. Rather public health is a complex and often invisible phenomena – the product of a collection of basic resources like clean water and nutrition, sanitation, emotional wellbeing, education and occupational health (McKeown 1991). Since complex and indirect systems of cause and effect are difficult for the public to perceive, and the medical–industrial complex has gained such prestige and dominance in the West, many in the public think of good health as simply an absence of disease.

Private biomedical markets greatly reward curative medicine, while public health remains medicine's underappreciated "little sister." The growth of the medical technology and pharmaceutical industries has exacerbated this trend (Baer et al. 2003).

Given this history, state management of medical and health services always entails the risk that essential, yet unprestigious, aspects of public health services will become a neglected commons. Plus conversely, since many health services, such as clean water, sanitation, and disease control are not divisible, there are likely to always be "free riders" – in that some individuals are likely to benefit from these systems even though they do not invest in them (e.g., by paying taxes) (Bollier 2002a)

Tied to this dilemma is the heavy degree of professional dominance that characterizes medicine, in which expert providers tend to dominate decision making about management of health services. Medicine is often cited as the classic example of politically successful professional dominance (Freidson 1970). Even in health systems with a large degree of state intervention, the public interest is often in tension with, or subservient to, cultures of professional dominance and policies that may favor providers' interests, or the interests of suppliers of pharmaceuticals and medical technology (Petryna et al. 2006).

But there is no reason to regard expert knowledge as an insurmountable hurdle. In the literature on the commons, there are other examples of commons (e.g., fisheries) in which management is heavily reliant on technical experts, and certainly, as Light (2001) has noted, even in the age of privatization, the growth of state regulation of medicine has proceeded apace.

WHY A HEALTH CARE COMMONS IS SUPERIOR TO A MARKET

If the goal is to maximize the condition of health for a population, multiple problems emerge from organizing health services using market mechanisms – a fact that is now recognized by most health administrators, although perhaps poorly understood by many in the public, given the market-centered rhetoric of recent decades. The best example is the US medical system, which, despite its strong dependence on private funding, is the least cost-effective system in the industrialized world – the country spends a higher percentage of its GDP on health than any other country (now over 14%), yet consistently ranks poorly (e.g., recently 17th) among OECD nations on public health indicies (WHO 2000). Despite this spending, over 44 million Americans remain uninsured. Robert Kuttner, in his classic study of markets (1997) described the American approach to buying health services as a "dysfunctional" model yielding "perverse results."

Unlike the case for many commodities we need to live, a competitive marketplace doesn't work with medicine. Often, a sick person is not in a position to shop for care, with the exception of routine ailments, he/she is likely to be dependent on the expert knowledge of a doctor to know what is wrong Even when there is competition between insurance plans, the market functions poorly, since health plans are oligopolies (at best) and limit patient choice (Kuttner 1997:115). Interestingly, the period since the early 1980s, when the US government began intervening to create a more market-driven system has also been the period in which bureaucracy and regulations have intervened most heavily into MD–patient relationships and professional autonomy (Moran 1999; Light 2001).

A fundamental factor in medical inflation is the fact that health care is labor intensive (not unlike other services that involve personal care) – so productivity stays relatively constant, while inflationary pressures (e.g., for increased salaries) rise (Kuttner 1997:117). This is exacerbated in medicine by the high degree of specialization (and the advanced training it requires), and by the power that the medical profession has acquired in modern society (Conrad and Schneider 1992; Weiss 1997; Baer et al. 2003).

In addition, a central and unavoidable dilemma of cost-control in health services is the supply-driven nature of the system. Due to the central role of medical expertise in both diagnosis and therapy, the doctor or healthcare provider is effectively both consumer and purchaser, creating inflationary tendencies. Comparative studies of variations in medical practice have demonstrated the perverse aspects of such a system – e.g., the more beds in a medical center, the more likely administrators will exert pressures on the medical staff to keep them filled, while the more surgeons in an urban medical center, the more surgeries are likely to get done (Wennberg 2004).

Finally, there is the well known "moral hazard" long recognized by health insurers, which is the more coverage provided to an individual, the more care they are likely to receive. Desiring to provide the best quality of care available, and cognizant of high patient expectations (and the risks in a litigious society for lawsuits for missing a critical diagnosis), physicians are more likely to recommend expensive diagnostic procedures when they know a patients' insurance will cover the costs (Kuttner 1997) and the problem of over-prescribing medicines has become more acute with the rise of direct marketing of pharmaceuticals on television (Angell 2005; Petryna et al. 2006).

In general, studies show that preventive health pays off for a society due to higher productivity in the workplace and fewer tertiary care costs for chronic disease (Kiefer 2000). However, in many areas of medicine, there is a lack of feedback between services delivered and demand. With end-of-life care, for example, medical technology such as respirators are often used for ethical reasons, and the high costs incurred have no direct connection to producing a healthier population. Likewise, while some forms of medical technology save money, more often new technology inflates costs for care when coverage for it becomes a standard benefit in insurance plans (Kuttner 1997).

The above problem is complicated by the profit-motives and research agendas of biotech firms and corporations producing health related products. Despite extensive federal subsidies to pharmaceutical companies for drug research, drug prices spiraled out of control, tripling in the decade leading up to the new millennium (Bollier 2002b). New Medicare drug benefits put in effect by the Bush Administration were a debacle for cost-control, because the White House and Republican legislators rejected price controls on federal drug purchases. The political favoritism was likely linked to Big Pharma's generous campaign contributions (Angell 2005; Public Citizen 2001).

ANATOMY OF A WORLD CLASS HEALTH SYSTEM: A CASE STUDY OF FRANCE

The fact that scholars rarely discuss a health and medical commons as such, may be a fluke of nomenclature. Perhaps, as Bollier notes, it is a matter of "learning to see the commons" (2002a:1). If we consider existing national health systems as evolving cultural systems – each embedded in the distinctive historical trajectory and political and economic relations of its respective state – then a comparative analysis of the more comprehensive health systems in industrialized states provides a set of templates for discussing key elements and best practices for a health and medical commons.

In 2007, Michael Moore's new film "Sicko" had enlivened the debate over health reform in the United States just as the Peoples Health Movement began to gain traction abroad as a transnational social advocacy. Many viewers of "Sicko" likely remember the nighttime scene in Paris when Moore accompanied a doctor on a house call to treat a man sick in bed with a stomach ache and fever. For Americans old enough to remember the 1960s, the scene evoked nostalgia for the bygone days of the 1950s and 1960s when doctors made house calls and enjoyed hero status in the public psyche (Light and Levine 1988).

The authors of this chapter met as part of a non-profit collaborative[2] to document a foreign country that offered universal access to health care. We reviewed reports on a variety of European systems and that of Canada before "narrowing down," and we found ourselves intrigued by the French system, which the World Health Organization had ranked at the top of the chart in a 2000 comparative analysis of national health systems. The WHO gave France high marks for government spending on health, population satisfaction and for indices such as infant mortality and life expectancy.

We crossed the Atlantic in December 2007 to take a closer look at the French system and see what lessons it might offer for creating a world-class health system. In two weeks of meetings with dozens of health workers and patients we encountered a system which was outstanding globally in terms of its coverage, but which was the center of an ongoing debate over the role of the welfare state in an increasingly neoliberal Europe (Smith-Nonini et al. 2009). Progressive health activists we spoke with were alarmed at indicators of creeping privatization that passed costs for care to patients and threatened the social security system. Yet in terms of health care delivery, even the more alarmed critics agreed that the system they were dedicated to saving deserved its stellar reputation.

All legal residents of France have access to universal health coverage, and undocumented residents get coverage after three months. There are gaps in access, mostly tied to immigration status combined with stigma and real socio-economic constraints (Didier 2004). But those served by the system – including the very poor and chronically ill – likely receive better care than anywhere in the world (WHO 2000).

The philosophy of egalitarianism underlying the system dates back to the French Revolution. But France's current health system grew out of a series of reforms pushed through the legislature between 1958 and 1960 by President Charles DeGaulle. His interventions were popular, in part because in the aftermath of the Nazi occupation, the French people shared a strong sense of unity and common moral responsibility for the welfare of the nation (Immergut 1992). Didier Menard, a general practitioner and advocate for universal health who we spoke with explained: "In France, one has always tried to protect the weakest, not by a system of charity as you have in the US, but by the system itself. For the people who don't have money, there is a system where the poor can receive care. They have access, theoretically, to everything in the system."

French medical student Julie Castro, put it this way: "Universal access is not working completely but the basic value, equity, is still a cornerstone. If you arrive in a bad state at a public hospital in France, you will be cured …whatever your language, whatever your status. In case of a major emergency, you have access. Even though the structure is overwhelmed ... and is being reorganized in a more economically efficient direction, still the quality of care is good."

No charges but the taxi fare: the French system at work

Unlike systems that might be described as socialized care, like that of the UK, in which medical institutions are state-run, most French hospitals and clinics are privately run. Also unlike the UK, in France, whether the facility is public or private, most patients pay "up front" for care, and are reimbursed afterwards for around 75% of the costs (Interview data, Brunner 2009). The French system also offers quite a contrast to the American system, where immigrants and low-income people are generally left out altogether. In France, 100% of low-income workers' health costs are paid through the social security system. Another program, State Medical Assistance, covers all costs for the unemployed and those who fall below a certain income level. Whereas in the United States, Democrats' proposals to extend health coverage to immigrants drew vehement Republic opposition, in France, immigrants gain the right to access after three months of residence. Unlike the US system where insured patients with a serious or chronic condition often find themselves bankrupted by "co-pays" and other uncovered costs, in France, the sicker you are, the less you pay. Serious illnesses like tuberculosis or cancer, chronic conditions like diabetes, and major operations like open-heart surgery are covered by the state at 100% (Interview data, Capell 2007; Fassin 2004).

We gained a first-hand account of why this matters from Lili Beaulieu and Maurice Leblanc (not their real names), a pair of newlyweds we met in Paris. We initially met the effervescent, stylish Lili for tea in a "swanky bar" on a frigid grey December afternoon. This led to dinner plans so Lili could introduce us to Maurice, her husband, a math professor who had recently completed a round of chemotherapy for a malignant tumor. Later, when I (SS) visited their polished wood-floored, bookcase-lined flat in a once-elegant neighborhood, the two of them told the story of their ordeal:

> Only shortly after their marriage, following a routine doctor's visit, Maurice had been diagnosed with a malignant tumor in the breast, a cancer rarely found in men. It was actually the second time he had faced cancer. The first had been 30 years ago, and he had dutifully gone for check-ups every two years since. As with his first bout with cancer, Maurice had surgery to remove the tumor, then went for a year of chemotherapy treatments at a cancer center in the city's southern suburbs. When I asked what he had had to pay out-of-pocket for his care, Maurice at first looked puzzled, then grinned, and said, "Nothing at all."

> Had he been an American who survived cancer surgery and a year of chemo – even one of the lucky Americans who had insurance that covered such things – Maurice's co-payments might have run into tens of thousands of dollars. If uninsured, his fees could have easily have run over a hundred thousand, with a large chunk required up front. Yet despite scores of doctor visits, the surgery and scans, in all this time Maurice reported that he had paid not one dime out of pocket – not even up front to be reimbursed later. Even physical therapy was covered 100%.

> Maurice's voice trailed off as he recounted the chemo; talking about the illness, he acknowledged, was depressing. Lili jumped up and gave him a comforting hug, as she confirmed his account, noting: "The only thing we had to pay for was the taxi!"

This level of coverage requires some trade-offs and different priorities, compared with US health care. The French government reimburses doctors far less per service than insurance companies in the United States. But unlike their US counterparts, young French doctors are not repaying loans for their training since French medical schools are run by the state and are free. Also, the state covers two-thirds of most doctors' social security taxes (a tax which typically amounts to about 40% of income). Furthermore, doctors pay only a small percentage of their US counterparts' malpractice insurance costs.

But all is not rosy. The national insurance system has run constant deficits since 1985 and the debt has ballooned to $13.5 billion. During the 1990s the portion of French medical costs coming from general revenues quadrupled to 40%. The Sarkozy Administration pledged to drastically reduce the health deficit, and many health workers we interviewed expressed concerns that France would resort to profit-driven managed care of the sort that has so frustrated and enraged US patients. But despite French cost overruns, the country makes more efficient use of health funding than does the United States which lays out 16% of its gross domestic product on health care (more than any other nation), compared with just 10.7% in France.

The French health budget relies on social security taxes paid by the working population. For a worker, 20% of gross salary goes for social security, a large portion of which pays for health care. However, the scope of what social security covers is shrinking, so today most people carry one or two private insurance plans that cover most or all of the remainder.

The café owner's perspective: middle-class resentments

Opinions on the French health system vary depending on the status of who is speaking. Many small business owners and others in the French working class and *petit bourgeoisie* who helped elect conservative president Nicolas Sarkozy, believe that universal access to health care is a cause of the ballooning deficit and out-of-control taxes. Pascal Rochard, owner of a "dollhouse-sized" café which serves up crepes, wine, and lots of second-hand smoke, is one such citizen. As the lanky restauranteur whipped up our vegetarian omelettes on our first evening in Paris, we mentioned to him our mission. He launched into lecture mode with the passion of a seasoned political observer. Pascal argued that he, his wife, and three kids were paying too dearly for their health coverage.

> For the average person the French system doesn't work well. I have two supplemental health insurance policies, and my costs have tripled in the last two or three years. Ten years ago there was no need for people to carry all this private insurance. The system worked better then. Now it serves poor people the best. I earn 1600 Euros out of which they take 300 for my social security. Five years ago I got reimbursed 100% for my cholesterol medicine. Now I only get 15% reimbursed, with another 30 or 40% reimbursed from my private insurance. Some medicines they call 'comfort medicines' and don't reimburse anything.

> He went on to declare: "There's a 54 billion Euro deficit in social security, and still immigrants come from all over Europe to use the system. Gypsies come from Yugoslavia and Romania and knock on the door of clinics, and doctors must treat them. And social security has to pay for it! We can't take care of everyone in the world!"

Social security: linchpin of the system and neoliberal target

With a medical degree almost in hand (pending completion of a thesis on the role of the World Bank in Malian AIDS care), Julie Castro is a self-described product of the humanitarian generation, having completed medical internships in Africa, India, and a refugee camp in Thailand. But she finds herself alienated by the neoliberal values that have crept into the system at home: "In medical school, if you say 'I am in this because I care about the common good,' it's like you're a green alien.... The drug multinationals enter every day more into the university, and it's accepted. I didn't want to meet with the drug companies who were offering breakfast and coffee, and my colleagues couldn't understand that. The more patients a doctor sees, the more money you get. This has ruined the system."

She pointed out that in addition to health care, social security's benefits include retirement, care for infants and children, and coverage for work-related accidents. Guaranteeing these fundamentals was key to France's egalitarian social contract. But these days, Castro said, "everyone talks about the 'hole of social security,'" and the public has accepted the notion that "we have to cut the (health) budget and make people take more responsibility" – which she considers code for shifting the burden of care to the individuals. Advocates like Castro maintain that balancing the budget by slashing social security will be "penny-wise" and "pound-foolish," since it will provoke breakdowns in public health.

Some physicians have responded to cutbacks by raising their fees much higher than the state-recommended fee. They take advantage of a tradition called "tact and measure" in which, for purposes of tact – to maintain a gracious interchange – the patient pays what is requested of him/her at the time, with the understanding that if he/she feels that he/she was overcharged, he/she can later take measures to retrieve the surplus funds. "But no one does," one doctor told us. The "fee hikes" coupled with tact and measure have de facto turned some services into luxuries. The house calls depicted in "Sicko" are one example: while the tradition still exists, doctors have added such a steep surplus to the state-sanctioned charge that today only the wealthy request the physician treat them at home.

In spite of the cutbacks, however, French health achievements remain impressive. The country has far more hospital beds and doctors per capita than the USA, and far lower rates of death from diabetes and heart disease. Deaths from respiratory disease, which is often preventable, are only 31.2 per 100,000 people in France, or half of the rate in the United States. France's infant death rate at 3.9 per 1,000 live births, looks stellar compared with 7 deaths per 1000 in the US, and French people enjoy an average life expectancy that is two years higher than that of Americans (Capell 2007).

Universal care as "band-aid": the open wound of immigrant inequality

Medical anthropologists Didier Fassin (2004) and Carolyn Sargent (2008) have observed, however, that while the French set world records on health indicies such as life expectancies – 75 years for men and 82 for women – there are deep inequities that are often overlooked such as widely disparate mortality rates for men that are tied to socio-economic class (Didier 2003; Sargent 2008). Those worst hit are people living just above the poverty line, who are neither eligible for the free State Medical Assistance program nor have the funds to pay extra fees that the system has recently been shifting to patients. In addition, quality of life for African immigrants slips further and further behind that of citizens, affecting health status in indirect ways.

> One day as we trotted down the Paris Metro steps, late for an appointment, we encountered a middle-aged woman in a long bright African print dress and headscarf standing "stock still" as "bundled-up" subway riders streamed around her. She stared uncomprehendingly at the Rue de Aqueduc exit sign. Clearly what had her flummoxed was not the orientation of streets, but the unfamiliar art of reading.

> We offered to help. The tension drained from her thin, drawn face as she pulled out a dog-eared shred of paper with directions to a health clinic. As we talked, she revealed that she was from Mali and had only been in France a month. She told us she was "sick from the cold" – understandable, given the below-freezing weather and her open-toes sandals and thin cotton wrap that failed to cover her arms. We pulled out our map and guided her to the nearest public clinic a few blocks away, then hurried on to our own appointment. Afterwards, we wondered aloud: what happens to new immigrants like this woman when clinics refuse to serve the *sans papiers*?

The USA and France are host to two of the largest immigrant populations in the world. Plus like the United States, anti-immigrant sentiment in France has turned ugly. The separate reality of Africans in France became clear to one of us (BB) while accompanying an HIV-positive patient to the Chateau Rouge district, unofficially called "Chateau Africain." When a disturbance broke out in the back of the bus, a man yelled, "Go back to where you came from, savage."

In a speech during his former post as mayor of Paris, Jacques Chiraq famously sympathized with French working-class families' resentment at immigrants, referring to "… a French worker who works with his wife, who earn together about 15,000 francs and who sees next to his (Council house), a piled-up family with a father, three or four spouses, and twenty children earning 50,000 francs via (social security), naturally without working…If you add to that the noise and the smell, well the French worker, he goes crazy. And it is not racist to say this."[3]

Recently, channels to citizenship for the foreign-born have eroded, and immigrants to France face increasing restrictions on qualifying for public aid. Deportations have increased dramatically. It is a stark contrast with years past when immigrants were seen as essential to the national economy (Fassin 2004). Franc Moisson City, an outlying suburb once famous for its wheat crop, is today known for the worst poverty in Paris. Its urban landscape is marked by endless rows of nine-story cement buildings much like those in 2005 news reports on immigrant riots in response to police violence. The "city" contains 12,000 people, dominated by poor, single working women and children.

To reach Dr. Didier Menard's medical practice, you cross the small lobby of one of the ugly high-rises, take a mini-elevator to the eighth floor, then walk up to the ninth on a "chewing gum-studded" staircase. The converted two-bedroom apartment housing his clinic is dingy and run-down – there is no telling how many ill people have dried their hands on the one grayed hand towel in the bathroom.

This man with thinning hair and beaming eyes behind gray glasses is something of a legend for his practice that offers free health care even to those excluded from the system, and for his fierce public advocacy. He has long helped publish the magazine

Pratique "the journal of utopic medicine," and proudly shows us stacks of issues going back thirty years. We gathered in his little consultation room, after a day of seeing patients, surrounded by art and handicrafts from Africa and the Middle East. Didier passed around a bottle of Port, and reflected on his work: "Here, even with the precarious population that I treat, anyone with a serious illness can have the same care as everyone else. I can call over and get my patients access to a scanner, an MRI, lab tests. No one will ask, 'Can they pay?' That is still possible."

"But we are scared that tomorrow will not exist anymore. From the beginning, the capitalists have not ceased trying to destroy it. I think they are in the process of succeeding."

Didier and Castro are part of a movement – The National Coalition against Medical Franchises and for Access to Care for All, whose slogan is "Health Care Is Not a Commodity," which has sixty branches throughout France, and includes political parties, unions of doctors and nurses, social service agencies, and associations of sick people. Its goals are to keep the state committed to accessible health care for all, and to defend the principle of public health within the social security system. Grassroots organizing, however, is no easy task in France, where an extremely centralized system of government has encouraged a mindset in which citizens tend to look to the state to set policy, and frown on citizen advocacy. One result has been an extremely weak record of community participation or civil society activism in health policy, compared with other countries. (Nathanson 2007). This legacy, together with the historically influential role of physicians in France, helps explain why the movement advocating for health equity tends to be doctor-led. The movement is small, but members we spoke with felt optimistic about its growth because, as one put it, "people are so attached to their health care."

Are National Health Systems Examples of Evolving "Commons?"

European health systems that offer universal coverage vary from more hierarchical and centralized models like France and Britain, to models better described as "corporatist," or state-regulated competition between private provider networks, such as in Germany. In the UK, for example, which has arguably had the most success governing medical cost inflation, the National Health System (NHS), which dates back to 1948, gives citizens access to care, but maintains control over demand through the gatekeeping role of general practitioners in primary care clinics, who work directly for the NHS and govern access to specialty and hospital care. After a period of state budget cutbacks under Margaret Thatcher, the system became famous for long waits and poor quality care. Complaints by patient organizations, combined with pressures from organized medical professionals, led to reforms allowing expanded "internal market" mechanisms within the NHS in the 1980s (Moran 1999) which some have described as a second tier of care for those able to afford these services.

In Germany, in contrast, access to health care has a longer and more democratic tradition, dating to over 1,300 municipal "sickness funds" which in the 1880s, a time of rapid industrialization, became governed by health reforms of the "Bismarkian state" requiring employers to carry compulsory medical insurance. However, the rise of the Nazi state led to organized medical doctors gaining control over the health

system, which they maintained after World War II, creating a network of strong, vertically integrated private provider associations that, while crosscut by state and regional
regulation, lack the strong federal control associated with the UK system. The organizational strength of medical professionals, combined with market pressures, have led
to high national spending on health in Germany (10.4% of GNP in 1997), and created strong inflationary pressures. Another weakness is the tight linkage of coverage
to employers which creates a system in which workplace inequalities are replicated in
access to medical care. Unemployed or marginally employed workers may lack full
access or coverage for their dependents (Light 2005).

Canada's system is similar to the British NHS in having a tax-supported system,
access by virtue of citizenship and a global budget at the federal level, but unlike Britain, its health facilities are private and each Canadian provincial government enjoys a
great deal of autonomy in administering the system. Despite spending more than the
British (e.g., 9.3% versus 6.7% of GDP in 1997) rationing has also become an issue in
Canada, where there are waiting lists for some technical procedures such as MRI scans
and coronary bypass surgery (Moran 1999). High physician salaries have been an
inflationary issue in Canada, and the country has chronic shortages of doctors in
many remote areas, similar to the United States (Fuchs and Sokolovsky 1993).

Japan, which maintains a level of health spending midway between the British and
Canadian systems (7.3% of GDP in 1997) has similarities with the Canadian system in
that health services are privately owned, and with Germany, in that most health insurance plans are tied to employment. Each plan is required to offer a minimum set of
benefits. Similar to the British, in Japan hospital physicians work on salary with fixed
wages, while clinic physicians are paid on a "fee-for-service" basis. Patient share a co-
payment for most services. While Japan has had some success in controlling medical
inflation, it has faced difficulty controlling drug prices, and prescribing drugs has
become a popular way for physicians to supplement their incomes (Sokolovsky 1993).

While these systems differ in important ways, they all have achieved a level of success in covering the medical needs of their populations and all of them score higher
on indicies of population health than industrialized countries that lack universal coverage such as South Africa and the United States. The bulk of funds for these systems
is public in origin, although this may take the form of compulsory social insurance
(e.g., Germany) rather than taxation. In a comparative survey of systems in industrialized nations, Navarro concluded that, regardless of whether health services themselves were public or private, a single government source of funding provided the
most ideal combination of cost-control and extension of basic services to historically
vulnerable populations such as poor women and children (1985).

In his study of world health systems, Roemer concurred that tax-based systems have
great merit in responsiveness on the basis of health needs, but he cautioned against
the hazards of wasteful management and corruption in totally state-managed systems.
He noted however, that the evolution of systems in industrialized countries has been
from voluntary funds to mandatory social insurance, most likely because they offer
advantages in overcoming "adverse risk selection," in which sicker or chronically ill
patients are excluded from full coverage – a phenomenon that has come to characterize many US health plans in the last decade (1993).

Although cost-control has been a universal theme in health reform since the 1980s,
Freeman (1998) observed some convergences in how systems respond to pressures,

with command and control systems like that of the UK finding savings through micro-efficiencies, while corporatist systems like that of Germany reform in the direction of more macro-controls such as global budgeting. Another convergence that Moran noted is the trend in multiple countries towards defining a minimal package of benefits that all plans, public or private, will offer (1999).

Challenges That a Health Care Commons must Overcome

A common objection to universal coverage is the assumption that there will be a "free-rider" problem – that if care is free, people who are not truly sick will take advantage of services and tie up the system. In a 2004 article, Roger Lewis, M.D., made the case that emergency medicine in the United States is an example of a "tragedy of the commons" – referring to Garrett Hardin's (1968) argument that common property regimes inevitably fail – because there is a subset of users who overuse the services, causing degradation of quality and "burn-out" of ER staff (Lewis 2004). However, there is an important distinction between the "open access" regime that exists now with emergency services and a managed commons, which usually involves a defined group with some form of restricted membership and a process for allocating benefits.

Lewis asserts that emergency services are "available without restriction," yet are "limited resources" due to budgetary constraints and competing county, state, and municipal priorities. Yet the haphazard coverage that results could hardly be called a product of community management, as there is no global logic to the distribution of services. As Bromley and Feeny (1992) point out, often when there are chronic problems of resource shortages with a commons, the main problem is the absence of effective group management for sustained use (Bromley and Feeney 1992:11).

Lewis acknowledges that the well known lack of primary care access for poor patients is a big part of the explanation for overuse of ER services, but he does not consider the question of whether emergency services might function much more successfully, while maintaining open access to the public, if the uninsured had another place to go for routine care. Ironically, care of the uninsured is exactly what universal access is aimed at fixing. Of course, access to care is not the "magic bullet" for poverty-related health problems, but in this population especially, it is a huge step towards resolving the US health care crisis, especially in urban centers. "Free-rider" concerns, which also emerged in the debates over President Obama's health reform, are not the stumbling block that many conservatives in the United States fear. As has already been noted, health services are already successfully managed by the public sector in Canada, Europe, and Japan.

A health care commons would also help to remedy the historically fragmented relationship between public health and medicine, and the long-recognized need to integrate health planning and delivery of care (Garrett 1995; Budrys 2001). At present there is duplication of services – for example many public health clinics offer similar services to those of emergency rooms – providing care for the uninsured. Yet this coverage is "spotty," poorly financed, and often of questionable quality due to the chronic under-financing of health at the state and municipal levels. Many experts agree that a network of primary care clinics, offering both comprehensive care and routine emergency services would be far more cost-effective.

The lack of integration complicates management of infectious disease and epidemics. Often a familiar cycle is repeated – underfunded public health authorities miss initial signals of a problem or fail to gain the attention of political authorities – e.g., the TB epidemic in New York City in the early 1990s (see Smith-Nonini 2004) – then once the problem is recognized, an awkward "dance" ensues as the CDC, backed by a disconnected and fragmented public health system, tries to coordinate and prioritize care with medical institutions governed by physician specialists. The poorly understood model of public health (based on risks in populations) comes up against the dominant ethic of curative care, which resonates more strongly with a media and public raised on heroic doctor stories. Reliance on the private sector to bridge gaps often falls short, as was illustrated by the 2004 shortages of flu vaccine in the United States, and the global shortage of affordable drugs for treating diseases that affect mainly poor populations such as drug-resistant tuberculosis or AIDS (Gandy and Zumla 2003).

Heller and Eisenberg (2002) have called this the tragedy of the "anti-commons" – when scarce resources (such as biomedical expertise or lifesaving drugs) are underused because the owners sequester it rather than making it available to those who have need (Heller and Eisenberg 2002:141). With emerging diseases such as drug-resistant TB or AIDS, in which a few untreated cases in a poor population can lead to widespread contagion, the links between access to quality medical care and public health consequences become apparent. This is why universal coverage, combined with global planning and integration of services, leads to better health outcomes (Gandy and Zumla 2003; Garrett 1995; Smith-Nonini 2004).

Scholars have observed the classic vulnerability of most commons to population growth or "in-migration" (Bromley and Feeny 1992). Such weaknesses seem at odds with the goal of universal access to health care. But this is really a matter of how "cost-benefit" is defined. Firstly, bringing the underserved public into a health and medical commons would, over time, improves the general health of the population, reducing costly outlays for tertiary care services and untreated infectious or chronic conditions. A healthy population would be more productive, resulting in positive economic repercussions.

In addition, as a more inclusive body politic becomes the norm, a likely outcome would be more public pressure to integrate foreign policy with domestic goals, which would mitigate against "beggar thy neighbor" trade agreements such as NAFTA, which has impoverished Mexican small holders and contributed to the immigration that now challenges the US health system (Audley et al. 2004).

Second, given that much medical inflation is linked to the supply-driven nature of health care, clearly the key to managing costs is to publicly regulate providers through a democratically governed global (centralized) budgeting for resources, which would likely involve strategies such as capitation fees rather than a "fee-for-service" approach. Much experience in Canadian and European systems and the better-run HMOs show that management at the level of providers and services is increasingly acceptable to publics. In reality, medical care has always been rationed at the level of providers, but because this decision-making was cloaked by the esoteric nature of medical practice and the levels of trust and prestige bestowed on physicians, it was not recognized as such by patients (Budrys 2001). Collective approaches to practice and managed care are also increasingly accepted by professionals. In the last decade solitary practices and reliance on "fee-for-service" has diminished in favor of group practices and health centers or plans based on teams of providers.

In thinking about the question of feasibility it helps to look at comparable systems already organized as a commons. Perhaps the classic case is that of scientific research. Without the public accountability of peer review and the collegial exchange that takes place in a scientific "community," basic science cannot advance (Jordan 1993; Bollier 2002b). We've seen evidence of the failing of private science in the fraud scandals of recent years over corporate "scientists" failing to reveal their conflicts of interest in scientific journals, and the shrinking of basic science research in many universities which have become over-reliant on corporate funding and have scrapped many basic science divisions on the altar of promises of future profits from patentable products (Nonini 2007).

Another classic example, is the experience of blood donations, in which "gift economies" have proven superior to private systems by several criteria, including the quality of the blood, safety for donors, and costs (Bollier 2002b:33). The safety and ethics of organ donation systems, likewise, become skewed by corruption and the powerful market created by a few desperately ill wealthy individuals who will go to great lengths to secure access to a life-saving organ for transplant. Markets for donor organs almost always cross a steep trajectory of class from the wealthy sick in First World urban medical centers to the most impoverished individuals in nations like India and the Sudan.

Faced with an absence of leadership from Washington prior to the Obama presidency, states such as Maine, Vermont, and Massachusetts moved ahead to enact universal health reforms. Similar proposals are under review in Oregon and California. Even some hospitals are finding that it is cheaper to offer free preventive care to poor patients with chronic conditions than to cover the tertiary care costs of treating uninsured patients once they become seriously ill (Eckholm 2006). Businesses have been passing more costs for health premiums to employees, but it is becoming clear now even to Wall Street that high medical costs threaten the global competitiveness of US businesses. In an ironic twist, some of the same capitalist lobbies that stymied cost controls in the early 1990s have become the new "cheerleaders" for some form of national health insurance.

The new People's Health Movement (PHM), founded by representatives from 92 countries, is another sign that health rights are gaining international acceptance. The PHM, which emerged from a 2000 meeting in Bangladesh to mark the failure of the United Nations' "Health for All by 2000" campaign, has been seeking a million signatures on a charter calling for health and equity to become the highest priorities in international development.

"YOU HAVE BEEN WELL-TREATED:" A GOOD DOCTOR DESERVES A GOOD SYSTEM

In the cramped apartment–clinic in Franc Moisson, a row of African, Asian, Middle Eastern, and French patients sat quietly in chairs lining the wall. Kids played inside a large hollow red plastic boot and locomoted wooden train cars across the floor.

Dr Didier Menard had been at work just shy of eight hours, but still had seven adults and four kids waiting to be seen. I (BB) had come with a woman patient that Didier had helped me contact. She had thought carefully before giving me the name "Djessa." Passionately private about her HIV-positive status, she did not want her true name and the virus mentioned in the same sentence. She would not go to the center for undocumented women with HIV/AIDS lest she see someone she knew. She refused to go to a café for an interview, afraid that someone might overhear us. So Djessa took me in tow to her pending appointment in one of the few places she felt safe to talk of her illness: Didier's clinic. After a short wait in the treatment room with Djessa, the good doctor knocked on the door and came in. He showed her a paper, and explained that her most recent tests show that she'd been cured of a serious infection he was treating her for. The jovial doctor laid a hand on her back and smiled big. "You've been well-treated. You have a good doctor."

Not only that. Thanks to the French state, the doctor was able to provide excellent care to this impoverished, legally unrecognized, African single mother with HIV, free of charge, thereby reducing the chance the infection would spread and allowing her to once again become a productive worker and responsible mother. Such connectedness between individual and societal health is recognized as a basic premise by those who see health care as a right that must be defended in a global commons.

Clearly, there is a shift underway from the notion that access to health care is a *privilege* to the idea that health care is a *right*. The above examples of systems with universal coverage offer multiple models for how rights to health can be operationalized. The ethos of the commons evokes a pragmatic international humanitarianism which fosters comparative analyses of systems and pushes health reform debates beyond the overworked "state versus private market" dichotomy. To conceive of health as a commons helps cut through ideological rhetoric and move toward the democratic goal of involving patients/citizens as stakeholders at the table alongside medical providers in the construction of an equitable health system.

NOTES

1   Portions of this article were previously published in Smith-Nonini (2008).
2   Other 'Worlds are Possible": http://www.otherworldsarepossible.org/.
3   This speech became famous when it was "sampled" in 1995 by the French band "Zebda", on their hit "Le bruit et l'odeur" from the album by the same name. English translation: http://en.wikipedia.org/wiki/Le_bruit_et_1%27odeur/.

REFERENCES

Adams, Vincanne, 1998 Doctors for Democracy: Health Professionals in the Nepal Revolution. Cambridge/UK; New York: Cambridge University Press.
Akukwe, Chinua and Melvin Foote, 2001 HIV/AIDS Global Trust Fund: Need for an Equitable and Efficient Governance Structure, Washington, DC. Foreign Policy In Focus, June 1.
Angell, Marcia, 2005 The Truth About the Drug Companies: How They Deceive Us and What To Do About It. New York: Random House.
Audley, John, Demetrios G. Papademetriou, Sandra Polaski, and Scott Vaughn, 2004 NAFTA's Promise and Reality: Lessons from Mexico for the Hemisphere. Carnegie Endowment for International Peace. Electronic document. www.ceip.org/pubs

Baer, Hans. A., Merrill Singer, and Ida Susser, eds, 2003 Medical Anthropology and the World System. 2nd edition. Westport CN: Praeger.

Black, Jan Knippers, 1999 Inequality in the Global Village. West Hartford CN: Kumarian Press.

Bollier, David, 2002a Ruled by the Market: Reclaiming the Commons. Boston Review 27(3–4).

Bollier, David, 2002b Silent Theft: The Private Plunder of our Common Wealth. New York: Routledge.

Bromley, D. W., and D. Feeny, 1992 Making the Commons Work: Theory, Practice, and Policy. San Francisco: ICS Press.

Brunner, Stephanie, 2009 The French Health Care System. Medical News Today, June 8. Electronic document. http://www.medicalnewstoday.com/articles/9994.php/.

Budrys, Grace, 2001 Our Unsystematic Health Care System. New York: Rowman & Littlefield.

Capell, Kerry, 2007 The French Lesson in Health Care. Business Week, July 9.

Conrad, Peter, and Joseph Schneider, 1992 Deviance and Medicalization. Philadelphia: Temple University Press.

Donnelly, Jack, 1989 Universal Human Rights in Theory and Practice. Ithaca NY: Cornell University Press.

Eckholm, Erik, 2006 To Lower Costs, Hospitals Try Donating Care to Uninsured. New York Times, October 25: A1, 13.

Erickson, Pamela I., 2008 Ethnomedicine. Long Grove IL: Waveland Press.

Farmer, Paul, 2003 Pathologies of Power: Health, Human Rights, and the New War on the Poor. Berkeley: University of California Press.

Fassin, Didier, 2004 Social Illegitimacy as a Foundation of Health Inequality: How the Political Treatment of Immigrants Illuminates a French Paradox. *In* Unhealthy Health Policy. Arachu Castro and Merrill Singer, eds. Walnut Creek CA: AltaMira Press.

Freeman, R., 1998 Competition in Context: The Politics of Health Care Reform in Europe. International Journal for Quality in Health Care. 10(5):395–401.

Freidson, Eliot, 1970 Profession of Medicine. New York: Dodd, Mead.

Fuchs, Beth C., and Joan Sokolovsky, 1993 The Canadian Health Care System. *In* National Health Care. C. J. Spreding, eds., pp. 195–205. Hauppauge NY: Nova Science Publishers, Inc.

Gandy, Matthew, and Alimuddin Zumla, eds., 2003 The Return of the White Plague: Global Poverty and the 'New" Tuberculosis. London and New York: Verso.

Garrett, Laurie, 1995 The Coming Plague: Newly Emerging Diseases in a World out of Balance. New York: Penguin Books.

Gowdy, John, 1998 Limited Wants, Unlimited Means: A Reader on Hunter-Gatherer Economics and the Environment. Washington DC: Island Press.

Hardin, Garrett, 1968 The Tragedy of the Commons. Science 162:1243–1248.

Hays, J. N., 2000 The Burdens of Disease: Epidemics and Human Response in Western History. New Brunswick NJ: Rutgers University Press.

Heller, Michael A., and Rebecca S. Eisenberg, 1998 Can Patents Deter Innovation? The Anticommons in Biomedical Research. Science 280 5364:698–701.

Immergut, Ellen, 1992 The French Case: Parliament vs. Executive. Health Politics. Cambridge MA: Cambridge Press.

JAMA, 1998 Health and Human Rights: A Call to Action on the 50th Anniversary of the Universal Declaration of Human Rights, Commentary. Journal of the American Medical Association 280(5):462–464.

Jordan, Brigitte, 1993 Birth in Four Cultures: A Crosscultural Investigation of Childbirth in Yucatan, Holland, Sweden, and the United States. Prospect Heights IL: Waveland Press.

Kiefer, Christie, W., 2000 Health Work with the Poor: a Practical Guide. New Brunswick NJ: Rutgers University Press.

Kim, Jim Yong, ed., 2000 Dying for Growth: Global Inequality and the Health of the Poor. Monroe ME: Common Courage Press.

Kuttner, Robert, 1997 Everything for Sale: The Virtues and Limits of Markets. New York: Alfred A. Knopf.

Lewis, Roger J., 2004 Academic Emergency Medicine and the 'Tragedy of the Commons'. Academic Emergency Medicine 11(5):423–427.

Light, Donald, 2001 Countervailing Power: The Changing Character of the Medical Profession in the United States. *In* The Sociology of Health and Illness. 6th edition. Peter Conrad, ed. New York: Worth Publishers.

Light, Donald, 2005 Comparative Models of 'Health Care' Systems. *In* The Sociology of Health and Illness. 7th edition. Peter Conrad, ed. New York: Worth Publishers.

Light, Donald, and S. Levine, 1988 The Changing Character of the Medical Profession: A Theoretical Overview. Milbank Quarterly 66(Supplement 2):10–32.

Meadows, Donella H., 2008 Thinking in Systems: A Primer. White River Junction VT: Chelsea Green Publishing.

McElroy, Ann, and Patricia. K. Townsend, 2004 Medical Anthropology in Ecological Perspective. 4th edition. Boulder CO: Westview Press.

MacDonald, Théodore H., 2007 The Global Human Right To Health: Dream or Possibility? Oxford UK: Radcliffe Publishing.

McKeown, Thomas, 1991 The Origins of Human Disease. La Vergne TN: Lightning Source, Inc.

Moran, Michael 1999 *Governing the Health Care State: A Comparative Study of the United Kingdom, the United States and Germany.* New York: Manchester University Press.

Morgan, Lynn, 1993 Community Participation in Health: The Politics of Primary Care in Costa Rica. New York: Cambridge University Press.

Nathanson, Constance, 2007 Disease Prevention as Social Change: The State, Society, and Public Health in the United States, France, Great Britain, and Canada. New York: Russell Sage Foundation.

Nonini, Donald M., 2007 The Global Idea of "the Commons" New York: Berghann Books.

Petryna, Adriana, Andrew Lakoff and Arthur Kleinman, 2006 Global Pharmaceuticals: Ethics, Markets, Practices. Durham NC: Duke University Press.

Public Citizen, 2001 The Other Drug War: Big Pharma's 625 Washington Lobbyists. Report produced by Public Citizen's Congress Watch. Electronic document. http://www.citizen.org/congress/article_redirect.cfm?ID=6537/.

Relman, Arnold S., 2005 The Trouble with Rationing. *In* The Sociology of Health and Illness. 7th edition. Peter Conrad, ed. New York: Worth Publishers.

Roemer, Milton I., 1993 National Health Systems of the World, Volume Two: The Issues. New York: Oxford University Press.

Sachs, Jeffrey D., 2005 Macroeconomics of Health: No Health Available at $7.50 per Person per Year. *In* Beyond Borders: Thinking Critically About Global Issues. Paula S. Rothenberg, eds., pp. 364–367. New York: Worth Publishers.

Sargent, Carolyn, 2008 Maternité, Liberté, Egalité: Burning Cars and Health Costs in the Immigrant Suburbs of Paris. Paper presented at the Annual Meeting of the Society for Applied Anthropology, Memphis TN, April 3.

Singer, Merrill, and Hans Baer, 2007 Introducing Medical Anthropology: A Discipline in Action. Lanham MD: AltaMira Press.

Sokolovsky, Joan, 1993 The Japanese Health Care System. *In* National Health Care. C. J. Spreding, ed., pp. 168–190. Hauppauge NY: Nova Science Publishers.

Smith-Nonini, Sandy, 2000 The Smoke and Mirrors of Health Reform in El Salvador: Community Health NGOs and the Not-So-Neoliberal State. Dying for Growth: Global Inequality and the Health of the Poor. Jim Yong Kim, ed. Monroe Me: Common Courage Press.

Smith-Nonini, Sandy, 2004 The Cultural Politics of Institutional Responses to Resurgent Tuberculosis Epidemics/New York City and Lima, Peru. *In* Emerging Diseases and Society:

Negotiating the Public Health Agenda. Randall M. Packard, Peter J. Brown, Ruth L. Berkelman and Howard Frumkin, eds., pp. 253–290. Baltimore MD: Johns Hopkins University Press.

Smith-Nonini, Sandy, 2008 Conceiving the Health Commons: Operationalizing a "Right" to Health. In The Global Idea of 'the Commons'. Donald M. Nonini, ed., pp. 115–135. New York: Berghahn Books

Smith-Nonini, Sandy, Beverly Bell, and Patrick Bond, 2009 When You've Got Your Health ... Guaranteed Access to Health Care. In Who Says You Can't Change the World?: Just Economies on an Unjust Planet. Report by Beverly Bell and the Other World's Collaborative. Electronic document. http://www.otherworldsarepossible.org/.

Smith-Nonini, Sandy, 2010 Healing the Body Politic: El Salvador's Popular Struggle for Health Rights from Civil War to Neoliberal Peace. New Brunswick NJ: Rutgers University Press.

Tajer, Débora, 2003 Latin American Social Medicine: Roots, Development During the 1990s, and Current Challenges. American Journal of Public Health 93(12):2023–2027.

Weiss, Lawrence D., 1997 Private Medicine and Public Health: Profit, Politics and Prejudice in the American Health Care Empire. Boulder CO: Westview Press.

Wennberg, John, 2004 Practice Variations and Health Care Reform: Connecting the Dots. Health Affairs "Web Exclusive," 7 October. Electronic document. http://content.healthaffairs.org/.

WHO, 2000 World Health Report. Health Systems: Improving Performance. Geneva: World Health Organization.

FURTHER READING

Castro, Arachu, and Merrill Singer, eds., 2004 Unhealthy Health Policy. Walnut Creek CA: AltaMira Press.

Freudenheim, Milt, 2006 Health Care Costs Rise Twice as Much as Inflation. New York Times, September 27: C1, 7.

Urbina, Ian, 2006 "Trusty Druggist Has New Role: Diabetes Coach." New York Times. 30 December, A1-A15.

Walt, Gill, 1994 Health Policy: An Introduction to Process and Power. Johannesburg: Witwatersrand University Press.

Washburn, J., 2005 University, Inc.: The Corporate Corruption of American Higher Education. New York: Basic Books.

Wells, Alan, 2004 Framing Health Care as a Right: Is That the Best Way to Foster Reform? Virtual Mentor 6(9). Electronic document. http://www.ama-ssn.org/ama/pub/category/3523.html/.

WHO, 2006 The Current State of World Health. In Beyond Borders: Thinking Critically About Global Issues. Paula S. Rothenberg, ed., pp. 356–363. New York: Worth Publishers.

Yamin, Alicia E., 2000 Protecting and Promoting the Right to Health in Latin America: Selected Experiences from the Field. Health and Human Rights 5(1):116–148.

CHAPTER 26

As the Future Explodes into the Present: Emergent Issues and the Tomorrow of Medical Anthropology

*Merrill Singer
and Pamela I. Erickson*

ANTICIPATING THE FUTURE

The Society for Medical Anthropology of the American Anthropological Association launched its flagship journal, *Medical Anthropology Quarterly*, in 1997 with what has become a well known "lead-off" paper by Nancy Scheper-Hughes and Margaret Lock (1997:6–41) entitled "The Mindful Body: A Prolegomenon to Future Work in Medical Anthropology." The goal of these authors was to position a problematized body at that center of future theoretical conception within medical anthropology. It is fair to say that this objective has been achieved. In 21st century medical anthropology discourse it is broadly accepted that the body is "simultaneously a physical and symbolic artifact, [that is] both naturally and culturally produced, and [as such is] securely anchored in a particular historical moment" (Scheper-Hughes and Lock 1997:7). But, what of the future of the medical anthropological body? As we progress deeper into the new century, what will be the tomorrow of work and focus in the subdiscipline in our rapidly changing world?

A Companion to Medical Anthropology, First Edition. Edited by Merrill Singer and Pamela I. Erickson.

The title for this chapter is adapted from an account offered in the book *The Futurists* compiled by Alan Toffler (1972), a renowned thinker, author, and founder of the world futurist movement. In this edited volume, Toffler celebrates, among many others, anthropologist Margaret Mead and her contributions to our effort to predict and prepare for what lies ahead for human societies. In her lifetime, Mead observed vast and often rapid changes in the human world and, while never a member of organized groups like the World Futurist Society or active in what we now call the Futures Studies movement, she nonetheless commonly wrote in an anticipatory mode (Mead and Textor 2005). Based on her experiences over several decades in Manus, Mead knew well that sweeping change can come very quickly, that people can change old lives for new ones, but always within frames of cultural understanding and rarely with a full awareness of "the big picture."

As many writers in the futurist vogue stress, including those who have participated in what has come to be called "Anticipatory Anthropology," imagining the future is always a challenging and to a degree fanciful task because we never have enough of the pieces in sight to fully envision the whole puzzle; or, as more jocosely summarized by Danish physicist Niels Bohr: "Prediction is very difficult, especially if it's about the future." The reason, as futurists emphasize, is because there are always unanticipated "wildcards" that arise and help to create a world different from the one we expected. A now classic case in point in health was the 1981 emergence of HIV/AIDS, which exploded into a world that was anticipating the demise of infectious diseases as primary factors in the health (at least) of developed nations. Now, just shy of 30 years since the discovery of HIV/AIDS, it is hard to ever again imagine a world that will be free of infection.

Despite challenges of this sort for accurately anticipating the future, it remains a critical task in planning efforts, at both the individual (e.g., choosing to major in medical anthropology or to focus on particular health issues) and collective levels (e.g., Panflu preparedness, graduate program curriculum design). We know the future, including the future of medical anthropology, will not be quite as we imagine it, and that wildcards aplenty will emerge to tilt the world in new and unforeseen directions. Still, it is possible to scan our present world and suggest a set of factors, established and emergent, that would appear to be of likely importance in sculpting the future of our subdiscipline as we move ever deeper into the 21st century.

It is necessary, first, however, to raise a question at the heart of any discussion of this sort: does medical anthropology have a future, or, will it and its parent discipline join fields like phrenology (the tactual assessment of personality based on the array of bumps and valleys on the skull) or spiritism (which once defined itself as a science of the spiritual realm) as defunct approaches in human research. As a named field of study, of course, medical anthropology is not really very old, having only coalesced into a distinct field in the shadow of the Second World War. Assuming that the bleakest forecasts of the human future – such as demise of our planet, or our species, or at least technologically advanced society based on non-renewable fuel sources – do not come to pass (and this is no small assumption), then there are some very good reasons to believe that not only is medical anthropology a field with a future, but one that can make significant contributions to understanding and improving human health.

Central to this future is our ability to, as Scheper-Hughes and Lock maintained, make clear to all concerned the fallacy of a biotechnological salvation that ignores or at least minimizes the importance of the social and the cultural nature of the human predicament now and ever more so in the future. Here again, our experience with HIV/AIDS is instructive. While new biomedical treatments certainly have improved the quantity and quality of life for people living with the disease, the expected vaccine has not been achieved despite considerable investment of resources in its research and development. However, the fundamental importance of human culturally constructed and socially mediated attitudes, knowledge, perceptions, emotions, networks, imaginings, and behaviors in the pandemic has been repeatedly affirmed. This recognition opened the door for anthropological work on HIV/AIDS (e.g., institutes within the NIH began to include medical anthropologists at the table), and hundreds of anthropologists passed through the opened door into the world of HIV/AIDS research and applied work around the globe. The body of work that resulted is now quite extensive, including many recent book-length publications (Biehl 2007; Bourgois and Schonberg 2009; Butt and Eves; 2008, Fasin 2007; Feldman 2008; Padilla 2007; Singer 2009a; Susser 2009; Thornton 2008; Whelehan 2009; Whelehan and Bolin 2009).

This discussion suggests that predictions about the future of medical anthropology must begin with understanding aspects of its past. As various histories of the field (including the chapter by Elisa Sobo in this volume) stress, medical anthropology became a distinct and named arena of scholarship and application because of a confluence of historic circumstances and agentive initiative by would-be medical anthropologists. Historically, the external demand for an ethnographically oriented behavioral health field emerged after the Second World War with the political push for the economic and social development of postcolonial nations (Frank 1991), an ongoing task that entails direct confrontation with critical health issues in diverse cultural and geographic settings. Also of importance was the recognized need within the domains of public health and health care for experts on culture and health in light of the growing recognition of the importance of cultural diversity and health inequalities in community health and health care competence (Foster and Anderson 1978). A number of anthropologists who found work in the health arena (e.g., with agencies of the federal government, as did Margaret Mead during the war) began to recognize the personal and professional benefits of organization, leading to the creation and internal promotion of the field that came to be called medical anthropology. In short, a particular and historic array of health and political economic factors created a social environment that fostered the creation of medical anthropology by a small group of highly motivated founders.

In this light, as seen from the vista of the ethnotemporal present, there appear to be a number of key *ecobiosocial* factors – to which the medical anthropologists of tomorrow will creatively respond – that seem likely to play a key role in shaping the field, its methods (see Gravelee Chapter 4, this volume) and frames of understanding (see Sobo, Chapter 1, this volume). We use the term "ecobiosocial" to refer to economic, ecological, biological, and social relational forces that impact human health. In describing the changing ecobiosocial face of our world, the International Social Science Council (2009) stressed that: (1) the planet is becoming more crowded with the world population expected to increase by 50% by 2050; (2) populations are sharing physical if not always social space, as a result of migration, local disruptions caused by extreme weather events, the ever intensifying toll of wars on civilians, and other pressures; (3) humans are increasingly an urban species (by 2020, two thirds of the world's population will be living in cities); (4) the planet is becoming more polluted, with growth outpacing the supply of resources and the waste products of manufacture and consumption building up in the environment; (5) social relations are become more unequal, but, because of modern communication technologies, the poor can see (and hence emotionally feel the effects of recognizing) what they do not have and may never have, an important source of health-damaging stress as Dressler notes in Chapter 5 of this volume; (6) there is increasing cultural juxtaposition, with burkas and blue jeans sharing the same social spaces, pre-scientific ideas and advanced technologies comingling in emergent lifeways, and, as Baer observes in Chapter 17 of this volume, plural health care settings bringing together diverse therapies.

This listing of changes suggests a number of key factors that will significantly impact medical anthropology in the future. In the discussion below, these factors are grouped heuristically (in that the processes involved are often intertwined and elements of one grouping could easily be listed with another) below and then examined individually. While traditional topics in medical anthropology, as reviewed so effectively by the contributors to this volume, will certainly remain key issues within the purview of medical anthropology, we anticipate increasing attention being devoted to the following issues:

- Health Effects of Globalism Intensified
- Anthropogenesis and the Growing Crisis of Environmental Health
- Pathogens Gone Wild
- The Profitable Body
- Modern War and Daily Violence
- Human Rights and Inhuman Wrongs
- The Demand for Relevance and the Application of Medical Anthropology.

HEALTH EFFECTS OF GLOBALISM INTENSIFIED

The nature and social impacts of globalism have been discussed at length, within and beyond anthropology, seen for example in the discussion of nutrition and globalism by Himmelgreen and Romero-Daza in Chapter 12 of this volume. What of its health implications and what do they mean for the work of medial anthropology in the future? Part of the answer is offered by the International Social Science Council (2009) which notes: "Although globalization brings people closer together technologically, economically, politically, and culturally, it also leads to increasing economic and social differences. Child mortality, education and life expectancy are a few of the areas where the gap remains huge."

In introducing the journal *Globalization and Health*, Martin (2005) reminds us that the process of globalization is reshaping the social geography of humans on the planet and its health effects have both universal and context-specific features. On the one hand, globalism, with its characteristic enhanced speed of transportation, technological diffusion, and within and cross-border flows of people, products, and pathogens, facilitated the spread of diseases like SARS in 2003 (which diffused from

Guangdong province of China over 35 countries around the world within a few weeks) and the Influenza A H1N1 pandemic of 2009 (which rapidly moved from Mexico to over 30 other countries). This scenario is likely to recur in the future, repeatedly so, perhaps with drastic consequences that will come sooner rather than later than we expect (Davis 2005). On the other hand, as seen in the quite different profile of Influenza A HINI in Mexico and the United States, the impact of epidemics is never uniform across geographic space; local health status, social relations, living conditions, medical facilities, access to care, and a host of other factors help to create a mosaic of differing local epidemics within the framework of the broader pandemic. Moreover, Martin points out that change can move in the opposite direction: disease can impact patterns of globalization, as seen, for example, in the implementation of quarantine laws and the major economic effects of the AIDS pandemic. Woodward and co-workers (2001) have developed a conceptual framework for identifying various pathways by which globalization can directly or indirectly impact health outcomes and health equity in interaction with local conditions. Exploring the utility of this framework and the varied on-the-ground actualization of global effects is a task well-suited to medical anthropologists.

A common theme in the globalism discourse is the rising role of the market and the shrinking role of governments in determining local events, including health events. However, many analyses employ a de-socialized view of the processes involved in globalism, presenting them as a mechanical progression driven by market forces that transcend human decision-making, indigenous worldviews, and the existing structures of social relationship. Navarro (2002:82) challenges this perspective noting that: "governments appear as prisoners of international economic forces that determine what they can do. This economic determinism is imposed on the world's western, eastern, northern, and southern populations."

In fact, as Navarro (2002:90) points out, even global corporations "rely heavily on the government of the country in which they are based for creating the national and international conditions favorable to their reproduction and expansion." An example of this pattern is described by Lee et al. (2009) with regard to the cigarette market in South Korea. In 1988, South Korean bowed to neoliberal pressure (in the form of threats of US trade sanctions) to open its market to foreign tobacco companies. Seeing South Korean women with their low rates of smoking as a desirable market, transnational tobacco companies used market research to fashion a marketing campaign tailored specifically to the consumer preferences, cultural characteristics, and changing social roles of women in South Korean. The advertising campaign targeted women with specific cigarette brands, made use of women-centered venues, and women-oriented advertising messages aimed specifically at younger women entering the labor force. Between 1988 and 1998, rates of smoking among young women in South Korea jumped from 1.6% to 13% (Lee et al. 2009). These researchers conclude that a tobacco control strategy based on "a gender perspective… is urgently needed to protect and promote the health of Korean women." Again, this kind of research would benefit from the immersion strategies and examination of the emic perspective characteristic of much research by medical anthropologists.

As the South Korean tobacco case suggests, a central component of globalism is the movement of products around the world, sometimes with significant adverse health impact on the consumer. Singer and Baer (2009:2) have introduced the term "killer commodities" to label "goods that are sold for a profit that result, either directly during use, indirectly through their impact on the environment, or during manufacture on workers, in a notable burden of injuries and death." As in the case of tobacco, which involves a product long known by producers to be linked to cancers and other adverse outcomes, the dangers of killer commodities are often recognized by their producers and sellers or little effort has gone into assessing their inherent risks before they are produced and sold on the open market. In other cases, the harmfulness of a product may not be known until the (sometime delayed) consequences begin to be felt. In either case, killer commodities, as exemplified by the distribution of Chinese baby formula laced with the industrial chemical melamine in 2008 or the sales of salmonella-tainted peanuts from Georgia that has killed eight people and sickened 500 more across the United States around the same time, are already an important global health threat that is likely to get worse as globalism advances. Woodhouse and Howard (2009:35), for example, note that there has been "a steady stream of news stories documenting that industrial chemicals emitted during the manufacture, use, and disposal of consumer products cause cancer and birth defects; impair respiratory, nervous, and immune systems; disrupt the body's hormonal balance and reproductive capacities." Further, they point out that more than a million different consumer products, containing various combinations of 100,000 different commercial chemicals, most of which have not been assessed for their toxic qualities, are on the market today. Barring effective regulation, these numbers are likely to continue to increase significantly in the future, as is the "killer commodity body count, in terms actual deaths, but also [in terms of] all injuries and inflicted human suffering..." (Baer and Singer 2009:399).

Linked to this phenomenon, and of growing importance in the health of developing nations, is the local dumping of damaged, used up, and otherwise discarded consumer products and byproducts of commodity manufacture by the developed world. In economics, the term "externalities" or external costs is used to refer to the consequences of a corporation's actions that may have a detrimental effect on others. To the degree that costs can be kept external they do not diminish the bottom line. For example, in 2005 the United Nations Environmental Program (UNEP) released a report on the dumping of nuclear and hazardous waste off the coast of Somalia, which has Africa's longest coastline and no governmental capacity for coastal patrol. According to Nick Nuttal (quoted in Majtenyi 2005), a UNEP spokesman: "There's uranium radioactive waste, there's leads, there's heavy metals like cadmium and mercury, there's industrial wastes, and there's hospital wastes, chemical wastes, you name it... It's not rocket science to know why they're doing it because of the instability there."

Nuttall reported that European companies paid subcontractors $2.50 per ton to dump waste into the ocean as compared with $250 a ton for disposal of such waste in Europe. Notably, one of the effects of the Asian tsunami of 2004 was the spread of smashed barrels of hazardous waste along Somalia's shores and up to 10 kilometers inland. The health impact was extensive. According to Nuttall (quoted in Majtenyi 2005): "[The] problems range from acute respiratory infections to dry, heavy coughing, mouth bleedings, abdominal hemorrhages, what they described as unusual skin chemical reactions... So there's a whole variety of ailments that people are reporting from these villages ..."

Another form of dumping with significant health effects that also is likely to increase in the future is the "recycling" (or more appropriately, scavenging) of consumer products, as happens currently with items like lead–acid automobile batteries. Increasingly, industrialized countries have responded to popular demand for a safer local environment by shipping obsolete consumer items to developing nations for reprocessing. In the first six months of 1993, for example, waste product traders from Australia, the United Kingdom, Japan, and the United States shipped over 16,000 tons of battery scrap to the Philippines (Cobbing and Divecha 1994). Used batteries commonly are processed in small "cottage factories" located in residential neighborhoods. A study by Suplido and Ong (2000) in Manila, for example, investigated 11 shops that recycle automobile batteries. Workers in these shops recharged used car batteries, changed their casings, and replaced battery terminals. They also recycled batteries by breaking them down into their component parts, sending some of these to other shops for further processing. During battery disassembly, workers were exposed to dried oxide paste. Smelting was only done in a few of the shops, but workers hand-delivered recycled metal components to larger-scale smelting operations. Most of the workers in these shops and their families lived either on the second floor above the shop or in ground level rooms adjacent to the shop.

Blood testing found that 94% of battery workers had blood lead levels (BLLs) above the World Health Organization's permissible occupational exposure limit ($40\,\mu g/dL$ for adult males and $30\,mg/dL$ for adult females). The mean BLLs ($49.88+14.95\,\mu g/dL$) of all of the children of battery shop workers was significantly higher than the established CDC level ($10\,\mu g/dL$) that is used to define lead poisoning.

Findings like this are not unique to the Philippines or to battery recycling. The harvesting of components from discarded First World production by the poor in the Third World is now a global phenomenon. Similar patterns are found with computer recycling of "e-waste" and other electronic products. A long list of potentially harmful substances, including chlorinated solvents, brominated flame retardants, PVC, heavy metals, plastics, and various gases are used in the manufacture of electronic products and their components. A CRT monitor can contain as much as eight pounds of lead, while a flat-panel TV contains mercury in the lamps used to light the screen. These toxins are released at all points throughout the operating life of electronic commodities, but especially at end-of-life in landfills or unregulated recycling sites. Exemplary of the scale of the problem, the Basel Action Network (2002), a non-government organization focused on preventing the export of toxic waste from industrialized to developing nations, coordinated a study of e-waste processing in China, India, and Pakistan. The report of the study, entitled *Exporting Harm: The High-Tech Trashing of Asia,* describes a site in Guangdong Province in the south of China called Guiyu (including the town and surrounding villages), which has been referred to as the e-waste capital of the globe. As many as 150,000 people in Guiyu are employed in the unregulated processing of obsolete computers and other electronic products shipped primarily from the United States. Water samples taken in Guiyu contained extremely high levels of various toxins, including barium, cadium, chromium, and lead. Similar sites and similar exposure to consumer product toxins have become a growing world health problem.

Anthropogenesis and the Growing Crisis of Environmental Health

The types of environmental health problems discussed by Townsend in Chapter 8 and Whiteford and Padros in Chapter 9 (of this volume), involving direct human involvement in the creation of ecological crises that, in turn, result in health consequences for communities, regions, or even the whole species will undoubtedly be of central importance in defining the work and utility of medical anthropology in coming decades. As Baer (2008:3) stresses, global warming swiftly advances changes in climate patterns that "will have severe economic, political, social, and health consequences as the 21st century unfolds." Medical anthropologists are only now beginning to work on what is likely to become one of the foremost health issues in the new century, but this pattern of limited involvement will certainly change over the next few years as the health burden of climate alteration becomes more evident.

Moreover, at the same time that climate change is disrupting the geophysical feedback mechanisms that sustain our planet's habitable environments, Earth is also beset by multiple forms of air pollution, plastic pollution of the oceans, depletion of edible sea-life forms, nuclear dumping, acid rain, disappearance of wetlands, pesticide and other chemical pollution, soil contamination and salinization, ocean acidification, deforestation, and loss of biodiversity through extinctions. As a result of these growing degradations and disruptions of natural systems, Pimentel et al. (1998) estimate that "40% of human deaths each year result from exposure to environmental pollutants and malnutrition." It is likely that over time a growing portion of this severe toll will be due to *ecocrises interaction,* a type of adverse synergy that has been labeled a *pluralea* ("multiple threat") process (Singer 2009b). It is becoming increasingly clear that the various environmental calamities we face should not be seen as stand-alone threats to human health. Adverse human impacts on the environment intersect and the resulting interaction significantly exacerbates the overall human (and plant and animal) health consequences, creating the potential for catastrophic outcomes (Rees 2003).

For example, the threat of one of these intersections stems from our fundamental and constant need to inhale oxygen from the air around us. While at ground level the layer of air that we inhabit seems far-reaching, it is evident from astronauts' observations that it is but a fragile bluish mist that narrowly parallels the contours of Earth's surface. An at-rest, average-sized adult in cool weather must breathe in approximately six pounds of oxygen from this layer every day. Breathing is so critical to human survival – because of its fundamental role in the production of the energy needed to sustain life – that it is not a voluntary act. Yet access to "clean air" is becoming an issue of considerable global health concern. The human footprint on the environment and the shadow it casts on the air we breathe, asserts Nadakavukaren (2006:2), "has expanded exponentially during the past two centuries, particularly in the years since World War II." As a result, the air we breathe today contains multiple pollutants of diverse origin. Each of these sources alone poses grave health risks, but even more so because of the interaction among the substances they produce and release into the atmosphere.

One growing source of global air pollution is the positive feedback loop linking wildfires and global warming. The dry conditions brought on by global warming "favor fire, and more fires release more carbon dioxide from burning vegetation, which in turn favors more warming" (US Climate Change Science Program 2009:3). Human activity (in contributing to both global warming and wildfires) may play a critical role in promoting this mutually enhancing and ultimately very dangerous pluralea process. As Chris Field (quoted in Shwartz 2009), a member of the Nobel Prize-winning Intergovernmental Panel on Climate Change and the founding director of the Carnegie Institution's Department of Global Ecology at Stanford University, warns: "Essentially we could see a forest-carbon feedback that acts like a foot on the accelerator pedal for atmospheric CO_2." Similar kinds of interactions are developing between global warming and the elimination of wetlands (leading to more and more intense flooding), between rising temperatures and water pollution (leading to increasing numbers of environmental refugees), and numerous other environmental intersections.

PATHOGENS GONE WILD

The level of threat from infectious disease in the 21st century suggests that our world is very different than health experts in the not very distant past imagined it would be. As Binder et al. (1999:1311) indicate: "After World War II, there was widespread optimism in the United States that good sanitation, vaccines, and antimicrobial agents would conquer infectious diseases. However, public health successes of the 1960s and 1970s were followed in the 1980s and early 1990s by ominous developments, such as the recognition of the extent of the HIV/AIDS epidemic and the resurgence of diseases such as tuberculosis."

As a result, globally, infectious diseases today are the leading cause of death, and even in highly developed nations like the United States infections constitute the third leading cause of mortality. Moreover, the threat posed by infectious agents has been rising. Beginning during the closing years of the 20th century there has been a growing concern among public health officials, health care providers, and the general public about what have been termed *emerging diseases*. Notably, in response, the Springer Publishing Company has launched a book series entitled *Emerging Infectious Diseases of the 21st Century* that already has ten titles. The discovery of new pathogens, some of which are widespread in human populations by the time they are recognized, has been occurring at a particularly rapid pace in recent years. On average, three new human infectious diseases are identified every two years, with a new pathogen being described in the health literature every week. Four kinds of emerging infectious diseases have been described: (1) conditions caused by newly discovered pathogens (e.g., SARS), often involving a zoonotic species that has moved from an animal reservoir to humans, or the discovery of a pathogenic cause of an already know disease, as has occurred in recent years with several different types of cancer (see Manderson, Chapter 13 of this volume); (2) expansion of a familiar disease into a new region or habitat (West Nile viral disease in the USA); (3) marked increase in the local incidence of a known disease (e.g., the sudden jump during the 1990s of Coccidioidomycosis infections in Kern County, California); (4) *re-emerging diseases* characterized by increased severity or duration of an older disease or its heightened resistance to previously effective treatments (e.g., TB). The appearance and spread of emerging diseases appears to be a consequence of several factors , including major environmental changes like deforestation and reforestation, intensification of agriculture, dam construction and irrigation, mining, housing and road construction, increased concentration of people in overcrowded and densely packed cities (particularly in the developing world), the global movement of people, and the development of pathogen resistance to overused and misused antibiotics. Because all of these changes are expected to continue, and even to accelerate in coming years, the threat of new and renewed pathogens is significant, especially in developing nations, where potential syndemic interactions between old and new infectious diseases is great, immunocapacity may be compromised by dietary deficiencies, prior infections, and stress, and health prevention and intervention infrastructures are weakest.

As has frequently been seen with infectious diseases like HIV/AIDS or with influenza epidemics, as indicated by Erickson in Chapter 10 and Singer and colleagues in Chapter 7 (of this volume), the health issues involved include far more than biological processes (Dunn 2008; Lindenbaum 2001; Paxson 2008). Human social behavior is a fundamental component shaping the course and impact of an epidemic. Thus, so-called "risk behaviors," a common target of epidemiological response to infectious disease, are shaped by social environments and structures of social relationship as much or more than being simply a product of individual level acts, attitudes, and understandings. Moreover, as seen in the HIV/AIDS epidemic, social and biomedical responses from stigmatization to the allocation of resources reflect underlying social patterns. Consequently, in a world in which pathogens seemingly have gone wild (i.e., are proving to persistently act in ways that frustrate human initiative), a field like medical anthropology that both brings an ecobiosocial perspective to on-the-ground examination of social and contextual factors in health related behaviors and seeks to assess the emic perspective and social experience in health crises is a valuable asset (Orzech and Nichter 2008). Further, notes Lindenbaum (2001:380), the anthropological study of epidemics "provides a unique point of entry for examining the relationships among cultural assumptions, particular institutional forms, and states of mind."

THE PROFITABLE BODY

While medical anthropologists long ago realized that the body offers multiple natural symbols for thinking about the world and constructing health and illness, increasingly they have come to recognize that this arena of their work involves investigating the way the body is seen and used as a source of profit. One product of this insight is a significant expansion in the amount of work being done on the pharmaceutical industry and manufactured medicines. Medical anthropologists, for example, now recognize that the global distribution of commodified pharmaceutical drugs has led to the use of these commercial laboratory remedies in ways that go far beyond their intended purposes and patterns of use, such as crushing antibiotic capsules and applying them to wounds, the emergence of folk injectors who administer individual antibiotic injections, and the diversion of psychotropic pharmaceuticals for illicit street drug consumption. Even without the indigenization of pharmaceutical products, the global pharmaceutical industry, in all of its activities from "bioprospecting" and the commercialization of traditional medicines, to clinical trials, the operation in local environments of manufacturing plants, worldwide marketing of its products (to physicians and directly to the public), lobbying of policy makers, and direct and side-effects on patients is having global health impacts, both beneficial (for some) and adverse (for many others). Documenting and assessing patterns of pharmaceuticalization has become an emergent role for medical anthropologists, as noted by Quintero and Nichter in Chapter 14 of this volume.

Beyond pharmaceuticals, biotechnology is beginning to capture the attention of medical anthropologists, including as Parker and Fertzgerald (see Chapter 18 of this volume) emphasize, technologies of care. Some researchers have conducted ethnographic studies of new reproductive technologies, organ transplant systems, the growth of the body tissue and body fluids industries, and the new genetics arising from the mapping of the human genome. With regard to transplants, new technologies like the ventilator and other life-support mechanisms have facilitated the procurement of solid organs from "brain-dead patients," such as those killed in motor vehicle accidents. Although the notion of "brain-death" is universally recognized, its significance is mediated by culture and hence of subdisciplinary concern (Lock 2002). Researchers have noted that the primary beneficiaries of biotechnological developments are people in developed nations, while people in developing countries may be forced by impoverishment to provide the seemingly disposable body parts that make many organ transplants possible. As Nancy Scheper-Hughes aptly observes: "Organ transplantation now takes place in a trans-national space with both donors and recipients following the paths of capital and technology in the global economy. In general, the movement of donor organs follow modern routes of capital: *from South to North, from third world to first world, from poor to rich bodies, from black and brown to white bodies, productive to less productive, and female to males bodies*" (Scheper-Hughes 1998:5)

As a result, the intersection of biotechnologies, cultures, and structures of inequality in diverse spaces is becoming an essential focus of medical anthropological work and looms as topic of even greater importance in the future.

Modern War and Daily Violence

As Carol Nordstrom (1997:114–115) aptly comments, "militaries operate on one single truth: the strategic employment of violence." This fact is of note because there are mounting global tensions arising from conflict over growing demand and dwindling availability of natural resources (e.g., peak oil extraction will occur during this century and then begin to decline) as well as emergent climate changes that are expected to intensify resource conflict (e.g., over productive land and potable water). During 2008, for example, the United States officially spent almost $700 billion on "defense." (Sweetman 2000). This amounts to more than double the combined cost of the next five largest military budgets in the world. At the same time, the US economy was falling deeply into recession, its infrastructure was increasingly in tatters, and almost 50 million of its residents lacked health insurance coverage. This pattern is not limited to the largest countries in the world. Sudan is spending $25 per capita on the military and only $1 per capita on health care (Foege 2000). Similarly, the money used to purchase 28 missiles by South Korea in 2005 could have purchased immunizations for 120,000 people against common diseases or it could have provided safe drinking water to as many as 3.5 million people for three years.

Consequently, the level of carnage that can be produced by future wars – including, in addition to the number of battlefield injuries and death produced by ever enhanced armaments, added levels of suffering inflicted through war-associated sexual crimes, mass displacements, and malnutrition, as well as the broader tendency of war to both promote the spread of infectious diseases and leave behind enduring emotional and physical scars on combatants and non-combatants alike – is likely to set new historic records. Currently, the 20th century is known to be "the bloodiest in human history" (Garfield 2008:25). World Wars I and II together caused at least 80 million deaths. Since the end of World War II, and stretching into the 21st century, there have been over 150 wars around the world (10 of which, thus far, began since the turn of the new century), with as many as 25 million (and probably many more) deaths, most of them civilians (Levy and Sidel 2008). Barring an unexpected slowdown in the frequency, ferocity, and wide distribution of 21st century war, the casualties and social consequences of armed conflict will unavoidably be high on the agenda of medical anthropology in the future, a turn that has already begun within the subdiscipline. Adding to this trend is the growing appearance of inter-ethnic and other internal wars and the type of rampaging violence unleashed by the collapse of political and social order in failed state systems.

Of course, war is not the only context in which violence and health intersect. There is as well the issue of what increasingly is referred to as "everyday violence." This concept became central to the purview of anthropology with Nancy Scheper-Hughes' (1992) wrenching account in *Death Without Weeping: The Violence of Everyday Life in Brazil*. It was only after returning from her research in Brazil that Scheper-Hughes (1992:16) reported that: "I recovered my sensibilities and moral outrage at 'the horror, the horror' of what I had experienced. The horror was the routinization of human suffering in so much of impoverished Northeast Brazil and the 'normal' violence of everyday life."

As the tensions of population increase and overcrowding, inequality and lack of access, and stigma and discrimination grow, the toll of this form of violence will grow and further help to define the world encountered by medical anthropologists in the future.

The noteworthy feature of everyday violence is that it does not erupt suddenly and unexpectedly and break the normal routine of peaceable interactions. Rather, it becomes or at least defines the routine of daily life for many vulnerable populations, especially the poor and marginalized residents of inner-city slums and shanty towns in the world's "megacities" and smaller towns, prison inmates, the homeless, street drug users, and commercial sex workers. Women and children are the most common targets of everyday violence and the most likely to suffer the cascade of health problems that it triggers.

In urban environments, the location of an ever greater share of the world's population, everyday violence is often referred to as "street violence." As Cintron (1997:151), observes, the cultural logic of violence on the street rests on the acceptance of "a kind of brute cause and effect relationship in which the humiliation of someone call[s] for an equivalent humiliation of the offender. Its ethos [i]s 'an eye for an eye, a tooth for a tooth,'" a life orientation that carries "a mythic, destructive clarity" that quickly sweeps away ambiguity and allows a rapid, clear and often intentionally devastating response. Underlying this ethic and the logic of street violence are four assumptions: "life is tough; most people are not to be trusted; always be wary; and defend yourself or get beaten up" (Cintron 1997:154). In his life history account of a US street drug user referred to as Tony, Singer (2006:72) states: "The threat of violence – emotional and physical – daily preparation for violence on the street, and enduring the agony of violence-inflicted pain were all commonplace to [Tony] as an integral part of the world of street drug use and sales. He had come to accept violence as he had bad weather, harsh but unavoidable."

A critically important subtype of everyday violence has been called "private violence" because it takes place out of public sight behind the closed doors of an individual dwelling or equivalent concealed spaces. Included here are domestic violence, intimate partner violence, and child abuse. Increasingly, anthropologists have been paying attention to the impact of violence on health (Merry 2008; Rylko-Bauer et al. 2009; Scheper-Hughes and Bourgois 2003; Singer and Hodge 2009), a focus that will prepare the subdiscipline, as has been suggested by Hermann et al. (1999), for a 21st century that will be even bloodier than its predecessor.

Human Rights and Inhuman Wrongs

The issue of suffering, especially when imposed by the action of others, conjoined with the problem of access to quality health care, are entry points of medical anthropology into issues of human rights, including its stance toward the notion of health as a human right. Since World War II, anthropology has struggled with this issue and was initially at least hesitant to insist on the existence of universal rights in light of the prevailing culture diversity of values around the globe. The first "Statement on Human Rights," written just after the war by Melville Herskovits and thereafter adopted by the American Anthropological Association's (AAA) Executive Board, responded to an international effort led by the United Nations to craft what would eventually become the Universal Declaration of Human Rights. In the grisly shadow cast by Nazi atrocities during the war, the Declaration was intended to serve as a statement of unity among nations affirming global respect for human dignity and inalienable liberties. As reflected in its statement, the AAA rejected the idea of the existence of universal human rights and refused to participate in activities that would lead to making normative judgments about particular cultural practices deemed by some to be inhumane.

This response was contested by many anthropologist at the time and ever since these events first occurred. As Micaela di Leonardo (1998) and others (Rylko-Bauer et al. 2006) affirm, anthropologists long before World War II were involved in various social justice and human rights initiatives, and continued to do so after the war, including the fight against McCarthyism, promotion of the civil rights movement, the debunking of racism, support of the environmental justice and women's rights movements, and the struggle to gain acceptance of health as a human right. These efforts successfully challenged the finality of the initial AAA stance, while not ignoring the importance of being alert to Herskovits' cautions. The foundation of the growing involvement of medical and other anthropologists in Human Rights issues is that (rigorous scientific) anthropology can make important contributions to lessening human suffering and that moral detachment in the face of suffering is not neutral, it helps sustain suffering in the world. Silence, from this perspective, speaks louder than words.

In recent years, the moral compass of anthropology has swung away from Herskovits's position. At the turn of the 21st century, the AAA (1999), in accepting that anthropology in use involves the application of scientific skills and knowledge to the solution of immediate human problems, adopted a Declaration on Anthropology and Human Rights that is an unambiguous rejection of Herskovits' position. According to this document: "Anthropology as a profession is committed to the promotion and protection of the right of people and peoples everywhere to the full realization of their humanity, which is to say their capacity for culture." This statement, which has helped to advance the growing focus on human rights issues in anthropology, reflects the view that is it possible to "create knowledge that is at once empirically grounded, theoretically valuable, and contributes to the ongoing struggle for greater justice" (Speed 2006:75). On this basis, the involvement of medical anthropologists in human rights issues and in opposition to violations of human rights has continued to grow.

Among the "human wrongs" for which the 20th century will forever be marked is that of *genocide* (and its companion term *ethnocide*), a 20th century term coined by Polish jurist Raphaël Lemkin to label efforts (the necessary intentionality of which have been much debated) to wipe out a people and cultural way of life. Hinton (2007:432), in assessing the link between globalism and genocide, raises a critical human rights issue for the 21st century: "Globalization ... potentially intensifies the crisis of meaning and existential despair that modernity tends to generate... Perhaps, this suggests, the world will continue to be plagued by genocides in the twenty-first century, as anomic individuals are drawn to visions of 'progress' that are predicated on the need to annihilate abstract categories of beings who serve as icons of their feelings of existential dread and nothingness."

That the crisis in Dafur, Sudan already has been labeled the first genocide of the 21st century, likely affirms Hinton's apprehension, while suggesting the criticality of this issue for medical anthropology in the coming years.

As this discussion suggests, medical anthropologists are skilled and positioned to carry out important work that contributes to the establishment of universal health care, safe environments, freedom from poverty, access to adequate diets and clear water, and protection from violence as inalienable human rights.

THE DEMAND FOR RELEVANCE AND THE APPLICATION OF MEDICAL ANTHROPOLOGY

From its inception, medical anthropology has defined itself as an arena of applied research and scholarship, as indicated by Trotter in Chapter 3 of this volume. The relevance (and closely tied to it, the funding) of medical anthropology will in no small part be measured in the tighter economic environment of future decades by the ability of medical anthropology practitioners to participate in (and provide leadership for) the design, development, implementation, management, evaluation, improvement, and up-scaling of interventions intended to prevent or limit the effects of the threats to health and human wellbeing described in this volume. As Peacock (1997:9) has noted with reference to anthropology generally, "Whether it survives, flourishes, or becomes extinct depends on anthropology's ability to contribute: to become integral and significant to our culture and society without becoming subservient." Consequently, there is likely to be increasing pressure for policy-relevance research and language in anthropology, and the active involvement of anthropologists in the translation of their findings for policy makers, as Page suggests in Chapter 15 of this volume with reference to drug policy.

Medical anthropology's contribution in the future, even more so than today, often will take place in multidisciplinary multi-sited team efforts designed to address pressing human health challenges around the globe, as highlighted by Janes and Corbett in Chapter 6 of this volume. The chapters in this book, by addressing many (although certainly not all) key topics in medical anthropology, help to chart the path from the past of the subdiscipline, through contemporary work in the field, into the future of medical anthropology.

REFERENCES

Baer, Hans, 2008 Toward a Critical Anthropology on the Impact of Global Warming on Health and Human Societies. Medical Anthropology 27(1):2–8.

Baer, Hans, and Merrill Singer, 2009 Killer Commodities and Society: Fighting for Change. *In* Killer Commodities: Public Health and the Corporate Production of Harm. Merrill Singer and Hans Baer, eds., pp. 399 – 415. Lanham MD: AltaMira Press.

Basel Action Network, 2002 Exporting Harm: The High-Tech Trashing of Asia. Electronic document. http://www.ban.org/E-waste/technotrashfinalcomp.pdf/.

Biehl, João, 2007 Will to Live: AIDS Therapies and the Politics of Survival. Princeton NJ: Princeton University Press.

Binder, Sue, Alexandra Levitt, Jeffrey Sacks, and James Hughes, 1999 Emerging Infectious Diseases: Public Health Issues for the 21st Century. Science 284:1311–1212.

Bourgois, Philippe, and Jeffrey Schonberg, 2009 Righteous Dopefiend. Berkeley: University of California Press.

Butt, Leslie, and Richard Eves, eds., 2008 Making Sense of AIDS: Culture, Sexuality, and Power in Melanesia. Honolulu HI: University of Hawaii Press

Cintron, Ralph, 1997 Angel's Town: Chero Ways, Gang Life, and Rhetorics of Everyday. Boston: Beacon Press.

Cobbing, Madeleine and Simon Divecha, 2005 The Myth of Automobile Battery Recycling. Greenpeace. Electronic document. http://www.things.org/~jym/greenpeace/myth-of-battery-recycling.html/.

Davis, Mike, 2005 The Monster at Our Door: The Global Threat of Avian Flu. New York: The New Press.

di Leonardo, Micaela, 1998 Exotics at Home: Anthropologists, Others, and American Modernity. Chicago: University of Chicago Press.

Dunn, Elizabeth, 2008 Postsocialist spores: Disease, bodies, and the state in the Republic of Georgia. American Ethnologist 35(2):243–258.

Fasin, Didier, 2007 When Bodies Remember. Experience and Politics of AIDS in South Africa, Berkeley: University of California Press.

Feldman, Douglas, Ed. 2008 AIDS, Culture, and Africa. Gainesville, FL: University Press of Florida.

Foster, George, and Barbara Gallatin Anderson, 1978 Medical Anthropology. New York: Alfred A. Knopf.

Frank, Andre Gunder, 1991 The Underdevelopment of Development: From a Personal Preface to the Author's Intentions. Electronic document. http://www.druckversion.studien-von-zeitfragen.net/The%20Underdevelopment%20of%20Development.htm/.

Garfield, Richard, 2008 The Epidemiology of War. In War and Public Health. Barry Levy and Victor Sidel, eds., pp. 23–36. Washington DC: American Public Health Association.

Hermann, Charles, Harold Jacobson, and Anne Moffat, 1999 Violent Conflict in the 21st Century: Causes, Instruments, and Mitigation. Chicago: American Association for the Advancement of Science.

Hinton, Alexander, 2007 Genocide and Modernity. In A Companion to Psychological Anthropology. Conerly Casey and Robert Edgerton, eds., pp. 419–435. Carlton Vic., Australia: Blackwell.

International Social Science Council, 2009 World Social Science Forum 2009: One Planet – Worlds Apart? Electronic document. http://www.forskningsradet.no/en/Event/World+Social+Science+Forum+2009+One+planet++worlds+apart/1240290464299/.

Lee, Kelley, Carrie Carpenter, Chaitanya Challa, Sungkyu Lee, Gregory Connolly, and Howard Koh, 2009 The strategic targeting of females by transnational tobaccocompanies in South Korea following trade liberalization. Globalism and Health 5(2). Electronic document. http://www.globalizationandhealth.com/content/5/1/2/.

Levy, Barry and Victor Sidel, eds., 2008 War and Public Health. 2nd edition. New York: Oxford University Press.

Lindenbaum, Shirley,2001 Kuru, Prions, and Human Affairs: Thinking About Epidemics. Annual Review in Anthropology 30:363–385.

Lock, Margaret, 2002 Twice Dead: Organ Transplants and the Reinvention of Death. Berkeley: University of California Press.

Majtenyi, Cathy, 2005 UN: Nuclear Waste Being Releases on Somalia's Shores After Tsunami. Voice of America, February 25. Electronic document. http://www.voanews.com/english/archive/2005-02/2005-02-23-voa23.cfm/.

Martin, Greg, 2005 Globalization and Health. Globalization and Health 1(1):1–2.

Mead, Margaret, and Robert Textor, 2005 Margaret Mead And The World Ahead: An Anthropologist Anticipates the Future. New York: Berghahn Books.

Merry, Sally, 2008 Gender Violence: A Cultural Perspective. Malden MA: Wiley-Blackwell.

Nadakavukaren, Ann, 2006 Our Global Environment: A Health Perspective. Long Grove IL: Waveland Press.

Navarro, Vicente, 2002 Neoliberalism, "Globalization," Unemployment, Inequalities, and the Welfare State. In The Political Economy of Social Inequalities: Consequences for Health and Quality of Life. Vicente Navarro, ed., pp. 33–108. Amityville NY; Baywood Publishing Company.

Nordstrom, Carolyn,1997 A Different Kind of War Story. Philadelphia: University of Pennsylvania Press.

Orzech, Kathryn and Mark Nichter, 2008 From Resilience to Resistance: Political Ecological Lessons from Antibiotic and Pesticide Resistance. Annual Review in Anthropology 37: 267–282.

Padilla, Mark, 2007 Caribbean Pleasure Industry: Tourism, Sexuality, and AIDS in the Dominican Republic. Chicago: University Of Chicago Press.

Paxson, Heather, 2008 Post-Pasteurian Cultures: The Microbiopolitics of Raw-Milk Cheese in the United States. Cultural Anthropology 23(1):15–47.

Peacock, James, 1997 The Future of Anthropology. American Anthropologist 99(1):9–17.

Pimentel, David, Maria Tort, Linda D'Anna, Anne Krawic, Joshua Berger, Jessica Rossman, Fridah Mugo, Nancy Doon, Michael Shriberg, Erica Howard, Susan Lee, and Jonathan Talbot, 1998 Ecology of Increasing Disease: Population growth and environmental degradation, Bioscience 48(10). Electronic document. http://dieoff.org/page165.htm/.

Rees, Martin, 2003 Our Final Hour: A Scientist's Warning: How Terror, Error, and Environmental Disaster Threaten Humankind's Future in This Century – On Earth and Beyond. New York: Basic Books.

Rylko-Bauer, Barbara, Merrill Singer, and John van Willigin, 2006 Reclaiming Applied Anthropology: Its Past, Present, and Future. American Anthropologist 108(1): 178–190.

Rylko-Bauer, Barbara, Linda Whiteford, and Paul Farmer, eds., 2009 Global Health in a Time of Violence. Sante Fe NM: SAR Press.

Scheper-Hughes, Nancy,1992 Death Without Weeping: The Violence of Everyday Life in Brazil. Berkeley CA: University of California Press.

Scheper-Hughes, Nancy, 1998 The End of the Body: The Global Traffic in Organs for Transplant Surgery. Electronic document. http://sunsite.berkeley.edu/.

Scheper-Hughes, Nancy, and Philippe Bourgois, eds., 2003 Violence in War and Peace: An Anthology (Blackwell Readers in Anthropology. Malden MA: Wiley-Blackwell.

Scheper-Hughes, Nancy, and Margaret Lock, 1997 The Mindful Body: A Prolegomenon to Future Work in Medical Anthropology. Medical Anthropology Quarterly 1(1):6–41.

Schwartz, Mark, 2009 Global warming damage could be worse than predicted. Stanford University News Service, February 18. Electronic document. http://news-service.stanford.edu/news/2009/february18/aaas-field-global-warming-ipcc-021809.html/.

Singer, Merrill, 2006 The Face of Social Suffering: Life History of a Street Drug Addict. Prospect Heights IL: Waveland Press.

Singer, Merrill, 2009a Introduction to Syndemics: A Systems Approach to Public and Community Health. San Francisco CA: Jossey-Bass.

Singer, Merrill, 2009b, In press Beyond Global Warming: Interacting Ecocrises and the Critical Anthropology of Health. Anthropological Quarterly.

Singer, Merrill, and Hans Baer, eds., 2009 Killer Commodities: Public Health and the Corporate Production of Harm. Lanham MD: AltaMira Press.

Singer, Merrill and G. Derrick Hodge, eds., 2009 The War Machine and Global Health. Malden MA: AltaMira Press/Roman Littlefield Publishers, Inc.

Speed, Shannon, 2006 At the Crossroads of Human Rights and Anthropology: Toward a Critically Engaged Activist Research. American Anthropologist 108(1):66–76.

Suplido, Maria, and Choon Nam Ong, 2000 Lead Exposure among Small-Scale Battery Recyclers, Automobile Radiator Mechanics, and Their Children in Manila, the Philippines. Environmental Research 82(3):231–238.

Susser, Ida, 2009 AIDS, Sex, and Culture: Global Politics and Survival in Southern Africa. Malden MA: Wiley-Blackwell.

Sweetman, Bill, 2000 In Search of the Pentagon's Billion Dollar Hidden Budgets – How the US keeps its R&D spending under wraps. Jane's International Defence Review. Electronic document. http://www.janes.com/defence/news/jidr/jidr000105_01_n.shtml/.

Thornton, Robert, 2008 Unimagined Community: Sex, Networks, and AIDS in Uganda and South Africa. Berkeley: University of California Press.

Toffler, Alan, 1972 Futurists. New York: Random House.

US Climate Change Science Program, 2009 Thresholds of Climate Change in Ecosystems: Final Report, Synthesis and Assessment Product 4.2. Washington DC: National Science and Technology Council, US Geological Survey.

Whelehan, Patricia, 2009 The Anthropology of AIDS: A Global Perspective. Gainesville FL: University Press of Florida.

Whelehan, Patricia, and Ann Bolin, 2009 Human Sexuality: Biological, Psychological, and Cultural Perspectives. London: Routledge.

Woodhouse, Edward, and Jeff Howard, 2009 Stealthy Killers and Governing Mentalities: Chemicals in Consumer Products. In Killer Commodities: Public Health and the Corporate Production of Harm. Merrill Singer and Hans Baer, eds., pp. 35–66. Lanham MD: AltaMira Press.

Woodward, David, Nick Drager, Robert Beaglehole, and Debra Lipson, 2001 Globalization and health: A framework for analysis and action. Bulletin of the World Health Organization. 79(9):875–881.

FURTHER READING

Singer, Merril and Pamela I. Erickson, 2009 Nothing to Play Around With: Dangerous Toys for Girls and Boys. *In* Killer Commodities: Public Health and the Corporate Production of Harm. Merrill Singer and Hans Baer, eds., pp. 67–93. Lanham MD: AltaMira Press.

Index

A Companion to Medical Anthropology, First Edition. Edited by Merrill Singer
and Pamela I. Erickson.
© 2011 Blackwell Publishing Ltd. Published 2011 by Blackwell Publishing Ltd.